Fourth Edition

Teaching the Gifted Child

James J. Gallagher
University of North Carolina at Chapel Hill

Shelagh A. Gallagher
Chicago Academy of Sciences

Allyn and Bacon
Boston • London • Toronto • Sydney • Tokyo • Singapore

Series Editor: Ray Short
Editorial Assistant: Christine M. Shaw
Production Administrator: Annette Joseph
Production Coordinator: Holly Crawford
Editorial-Production Service: Lynda Griffiths/TKM Productions
Composition Buyer: Linda Cox
Photo Researcher: Susan Duane
Manufacturing Buyer: Megan Cochran
Cover Administrator: Linda K. Dickinson

Copyright © 1994, 1985, 1975, 1964 by Allyn and Bacon
A Division of Paramount Publishing
160 Gould Street
Needham Heights, MA 02194

Library of Congress Cataloging-in-Publication Data

Gallagher, James John
    Teaching the gifted child / James J. Gallagher, Shelagh A.
Gallagher. -- 4th ed.
      p.   cm.
    Includes bibliographical references (p.   ) and index.
    ISBN 0-205-14828-X
    1. Gifted Children--Education--United States.   I. Gallagher,
Shelagh A.   II. Title.
LC3993.9.G35   1994
371.95--dc20
                93-36642
                CIP

Printed in the United States of America

10 9 8 7 6 5 4 3 2 1   99 98 97 96 95 94

Photo Credits: Stephen Marks: pages 35, 68, 103, 184, 220, 251, 350; Brian Smith: pages 145, 283, 317, 392; Jim Pickerell: page 3.
Text Credits: Pages 120–121: Excerpts from *Discovering Meaning in Elementary School Mathematics,* Sixth Edition by Foster E. Grossnickle and John Reckzeh, copyright © 1973 by Holt, Rinehart and Winston, Inc., reprinted by permission of the publisher.

Dedication

The authors would like to celebrate the patience and forbearance of the rest of the Gallagher family during the three decades that this book has been in creation or revision in one form or another. Rani Gallagher, wife of the senior author and mother of the junior author, has lived with this project from the beginning. Three sons and brothers—Kevin, Sean, and Brian—have grown up with it. As other authors are well aware, these family members have been neglected in some ways so that this project could be completed. We are grateful to them.

We would like to dedicate this book to those students who have special gifts and talents. Too often they have waited expectantly for exciting and challenging ideas to be presented in the educational programs that would feed their insatiable curiosity, and too often they have been disappointed by the thin gruel of a standard curriculum. If this book can improve their chances for a better educational experience, then we have achieved our purpose.

Contents

PART III   *Information-Processing Strategies   279*

Preface

This fourth edition of *Teaching the Gifted Child* has emerged during an era of turbulence and change in U.S. education. There is a remarkable national consensus that the educational system in the United States is not serving its students well. A few years ago, the governors of the 50 states—with the maximum range of political persuasions—all agreed to a set of national goals. These goals were then endorsed by President George Bush.

In many ways, these national goals were a criticism of the current products of this nation's education. We are told in one of the goals that we should be first in the world in mathematics and science by the year 2000. Since we were embarrassingly far from that goal when it was written, this is clearly a call for reform and change. The goals also call for the schools to provide a challenging curriculum in math, science, language arts, social studies, and geography—implying that this was not the case when the goals were written.

This call for reform and restructuring sounds as if the reformers have discovered education of gifted students; what they propose (e.g., more emphasis on complex curriculum and greater emphasis on the instruction of thinking processes) is what has been stressed in these special programs for gifted students for a very long time.

New Additions

We have substantially updated the text from the previous edition, adding material for the new discussions on intelligence—what it is and how it can be stimulated. We have also included some new thoughts on a problem-based curriculum and its implications, as well as new methods of student evaluation through performance-based and authentic assessments. However, we have kept those organizing concepts that have, we have been told, added much to the clarity of the book in the past. Some old friends are still here: The gifted students Cranshaw, Zelda, Joe, and Sam have been brought up to date and a new, thoroughly modern, young girl—Stephanie—has been added to enrich our case studies that illustrate much about gifted students and gifted education.

We have kept the structure for the curriculum differentiation discussions—content acceleration, content enrichment, content sophistication, and content novelty—but the examples within the various content fields have been changed and supplemented. Finally, we have stressed the special issues related to groups of gifted children which previously have not been studied separately—students from cultural minorities, students with disabilities who have outstanding intellectual gifts, and gifted girls.

Organization of the Text

The book is organized into three major parts.

Part I: The Gifted Child and the Changing School Program
The beginning of the text focuses on the description of gifted children. The changes in our views of intelligence play a major role in these discussions. It also influences our opinions about the distinctive characteristics of this population of children. Five gifted children are introduced and reappear throughout the text to bring a degree of reality and practicality to the discussions. The concluding chapter of Part I is devoted to the changing school program. It describes how the schools have attempted to adapt their practices to the special needs of gifted students.

Part II: Content Modifications for the Gifted
Part II contains five chapters that cover the traditional curriculum subjects: mathematics, science, language arts, and social studies. In addition, there is a special chapter on the visual and performing arts. In each of these chapters, an attempt is made to categorize various curriculum adaptations made by schools in trying to meet the extended knowledge needs of gifted students. To aid the reader in organizing this vast set of knowledge, the material has been organized in each chapter in terms of content acceleration, content enrichment, content sophistication, and content novelty.

Part III: Information-Processing Strategies
The next two chapters focus on key intellectual processes that programs for gifted students attempt to enhance. The first of these chapters focuses on problem solving and problem finding. It deals with the various models that have been developed to instruct gifted students to use these thinking processes more efficiently. Particular attention is paid to problem finding as one of the key educational emphases for gifted students, since it is crucial to quality performance in the sciences and the arts. The second chapter in Part III reviews what we know about creativity—a major objective in many programs for gifted students. An analysis of both the creative person and the creative process is included, along with methods for enhancing the process.

We next focus on the educational setting in which special programs are to be delivered. Some form of reorganization of the traditional programs seems necessary to be able to carry out the goals of differentiated content and skills mastery. The array of learning environment adjustments, plus the evidence for their effectiveness, are presented.

Considerable attention is given to the topics of program evaluation and individual assessment, since these seem to be at the heart of the new educational reforms. The topic of student acceleration is also highlighted as one means of trying to reduce the time commitment to school that many gifted students must make to prepare for their careers—a commitment that can easily extend to over a quarter of a century of schooling. Finally, some thoughts are provided on issues of special teacher preparation.

Increasing interest and concern is being expressed for youngsters who have come to be known as *nontraditional gifted* students. They have unusual intellectual talents, and their abilities may be hidden by differing values and attitudes that do not fit well within the mainstream educational efforts. These would include gifted students from culturally different families, gifted underachievers (those with great potential but mediocre performance), gifted students who have a disability, extremely young gifted students, and gifted girls, who have had to overcome a variety of societal attitudes and values that tend to downgrade their potential abilities. For each of these groups, some attempts have been made to discover their talents and to make special educational adaptations to meet their special needs. These attempts are reported here.

Appendices
The Appendices include additional information on how to obtain more knowledge on the subject of gifted children. They describe organizations and journals that are available to continue the reader's interests that have, hopefully, been piqued by this book.

The Gifted Child and the Changing School Program

Part I contains the first three chapters of the book and is designed to set the stage for the remainder of the text. In order to discuss intelligently what should be done for gifted children in the educational setting, one must (1) describe who gifted children are, (2) understand the special needs and characteristics of these youngsters, and (3) note the specific and distinctive program changes that are made necessary in the school by these special needs.

Chapter 1 reviews current definitions and methods of identification. The definition of gifted children has become more complex in recent years. Thirty years ago, an intelligence quotient (IQ) score on an individually administered intelligence test would have been considered all that was necessary to identity a gifted child. By implication, if not by actual statement, genetics was considered to control the presence or absence of giftedness in the individual. At the present time, there is a strong tendency to view giftedness as multidimensional. Its development is clearly influenced by environmental forces or at least by the interaction of environment and genetics. This changes one's views on identification and, to some extent, the definition as well.

Chapter 2 focuses on the distinctive characteristics of gifted children. In that chapter, the rather extensive literature on characteristics is reviewed. Recent studies are examined that chart the characteristics of specific subgroups—gifted women, gifted leaders, and so forth. Some of the subgroups that have received considerable attention, such as gifted children with special needs or special individual talents, will be discussed within later chapters devoted to those subgroups.

Finally, Chapter 3 discusses briefly the nature of the program changes that schools are now considering for meeting the needs of gifted children. In that chapter, as well as in subsequent chapters, an attempt is made to distinguish three major components of adaptation in the school: changes in curriculum content, changed emphases in teaching certain skills and strategies, and modifications of the learning environment.

It is the diversity of ability and performance noted among school children of the same age that forces attention to the needs of gifted students and requires special educational modifications that challenge such students. In the United States, the principle of universal education guarantees that such student diversity will continue through the upper grades and into the secondary schools. In some cultures, such diversity is often handled by allowing children of low performance to leave school early and by focusing resources on a very small percentage of children of high performance who are encouraged to seek higher education. It is increasingly recognized that in order to participate effectively in our complex technological society, the United States has a great need for large numbers of highly competent students. The design of programs for gifted and talented students reflects both those technological needs and the desire to produce individuals with an understanding of their cultural heritage, greater insight into themselves, and a keen awareness of the society in which they live.

Chapter 1

Definition and Identification of the Gifted Child

Key Questions

- What is *high intelligence*? How is it defined and measured?
- How have viewpoints on intelligence changed recently?
- How are gifted students identified for special educational programs?
- Can teachers identify gifted students accurately?
- Do different identification strategies yield different groups of children as gifted?
- Who are Cranshaw, Zelda, Joe, Sam, and Stephanie?

Who are the gifted children and youth in our society? Are they the creators, the thinkers, and the leaders of the next generation? As we shall see, it is likely that many of the children discussed in this book will be key members of the next generation of leaders and producers of our society. How they fare in the U.S. educational system and in U.S. society in general will influence strongly the character and future of that society.

In the United States, we are justly proud of our egalitarianism and our demand for equal opportunity for education for all, but we are equally proud of our goal of individualization, to fit the program to each child's needs. We have moved far toward providing access to education for all, but we are less effective in meeting the differing needs and abilities of individual children. For those children at the extremes—children with disabilities and children with special gifts—the commitment to individualization has been halting and incomplete. Failure to help children with disabilities to reach their potential is a personal tragedy for them and their families; failure to help gifted children reach their potential is a societal tragedy, the extent of which is difficult to measure but which is surely great. How can we measure the loss of the sonata unwritten, the curative drug undiscovered, or the absence of political insight? These gifted students are a substantial part of the difference between what we are and what we could be as a society.

In *On the Origin of Species,* published in 1859, Charles Darwin propounded his notion of the survival of the fittest. But who are the fittest in our modern culture—the heavyweight champion of the world, the president of the United States, a genetic scientist, an artist, a physician? The athlete thinks of fitness as physical prowess and skill; the teacher considers fitness as the ability to pass on important ideas from one generation to another; and to the clergy it is the moral leadership that distinguishes humanity from the animal. Each of us defines *fittest* to suit our own needs.

The teacher, faced with overwhelming daily pressures, is hard pressed to gain perspective on the problems of gifted children and is eagerly seeking specific guidance. Often justifiably impatient with esoteric discussions about definition, teachers and others in our society sometimes fail to recognize that the definition of *giftedness* is bound to the culture. Our definition is as much a part of the end of the twentieth century as television, gene splicing, nuclear reactors, and space shots.

This chapter will review the various issues that define gifted students and the variety of approaches to identification that are in current use.

Definition of the Gifted Child

Each culture appears to feature the type of giftedness that it rewards or values. The ancient Greeks produced great orators; the Romans, who followed them, produced excellent engineers. The Renaissance artists of sixteenth-century Italy, the German composers of the seventeenth century, and the English writers of the nineteenth century illustrate the emergence of talent that is specially rewarded in a particular culture at a particular time. As we view the differing talents that emerge from cultures with differing values, we may in fact be observing the remarkable adaptability of the human intellect. In our society, there are many versions of a definition of *gifted children*. The two definitions presented in Figure 1–1 are indicative of current thinking and policy. Each has been generated at the federal level and many states have followed the essence of these federal definitions with their own statements.

Although the Marland definition is now over 20 years old, the majority of states still pattern their definitions of gifted students on this model. There are some interesting phrases in Marland's definition that reveal much about our current attitudes about gifted children in our schools. These children "require differentiated educational programs." In other words, it does no good to find gifted children if we do not intend to do something distinctive about their education. They have outstanding abilities and "are capable of high performance." That is, their ability may not be showing itself well at this time and needs to be discovered and stimulated. Finally, gifted children are expected to "realize their contribution to self and society." In other words, it is not just these individual students who are our concern, it is the hope that they may improve the society as a whole. But in the definition, "outstanding abilities" implies ability to do what?—to hopscotch, to knit, to play table tennis, to program a VCR? Obviously we have something more significant in

FIGURE 1–1   Definition of the Gifted Child

Marland (1972) Definition

Gifted and talented children are those identified by professionally qualified persons who by virtue of outstanding abilities are capable of high performance. These are children who require differentiated educational programs and services beyond those normally provided by the regular school program in order to realize their contribution to self and society.

Children capable of high performance include those with demonstrated achievement and/or potential ability in any of the following areas:

1. General intellectual aptitude
2. Specific academic aptitude
3. Creative or productive thinking
4. Leadership ability
5. Visual and performing arts

Javits (1988) Definition

The term gifted and talented student means children and youths who:

1. Give evidence of higher performance capability in such areas as intellectual, creative, artistic, or leadership capacity or in specific academic fields; and who
2. Require services or activities not ordinarily provided by the schools in order to develop such capabilities fully.

Sources: From *Education of the Gifted and Talented* (Report to the Congress of the United States by the U.S. Commissioner of Education) by S. Marland, 1972, Washington, DC: U.S. Government Printing Office. From Jacob K. Javits Gifted and Talented Students Education Act (Title IV, Part B of P.L. 100-297).

mind: the ability to master and use those symbol systems that lie at the heart of the operation of our modern society.

The Javits definition has simplified the language somewhat from the earlier Marland definition, but both discuss capabilities rather than achievement, and both state the necessity for these students to receive special educational services.

Different Concepts of Giftedness

Should a good definition of gifted students be the first thing that we consider or the last? On one hand, a good definition helps to draw boundary lines around the concept that one wishes to discuss or pursue. On the other hand, one has to know a considerable amount about the phenomenon *before* one can write a good definition. For example, if you are not a physicist, try to write a good definition for a *quark*. That is part of the reason why we continually write and rewrite the definition of gifted children as we learn more and more about these different youngsters.

There are two very different concepts of giftedness abroad in the educational field today. Many of the arguments between educators and psychologists about the definition of gifted students have these different concepts at their base. One concept views giftedness as *potential*. A child is observed to possess the qualities that make it more likely that he or she will achieve outstanding school and life performance. It says little or nothing about whether the child is actually performing in a productive manner at this moment.

The opposite concept is one that giftedness represents the actual *production* of outstanding work. These distinctions are not merely abstract arguments or a basis for philosophical discussion. Depending on whether one chooses the first or the second of these concepts, what is at stake is eligibility for special classes or services. For example, if our criteria for membership in a program for gifted students requires that the student show outstanding performance as well as outstanding aptitude, then many students with potential, but not showing current superior performance, will be left out of the program. In fact, this is exactly what happens in states and communities that require outstanding *performance* as part of the criteria for admittance to the program. However, if one takes the view that giftedness is potential, then some of the students who are so identified may likely not achieve very much and, consequently, disappoint both themselves and their families.

The age of the child who is being discussed also has a considerable influence on which of these two key dimensions is applied. The younger the child, the more difficult it is to use the achievement or production criterion. Apart from one or two remarkable prodigies, few youngsters can demonstrate such outstanding performance or attainment to justify using past performance as one of the indicators of giftedness. The older the child, the more likely that we must include *both* original potential and the past experience of the individual as key factors in identifying program eligibility.

Mixing these two concepts, potential and production, can lead to glorious and indecisive arguments about who is gifted. For example, are there more mathematically gifted boys than girls? If one takes the production criterion, the answer is most certainly yes. If one takes the potential criterion, then the answer is probably not. Are there differences in intellectual ability between various races and ethnic groups? If one takes the production criterion, the answer is certainly there are major differences. If one takes the potential criterion, the answer is probably not.

A story often attributed to Mark Twain can illustrate this point. It seems that there was a man who lived an exemplary life and then went on to his final reward, appearing before the Pearly Gates and St. Peter. St. Peter informed the man that he had lived such an exemplary life that he could request anything he wanted as a special reward.

The man considered for a moment and then suggested that one of the things he had always wanted to do in life was to meet the most intelligent person who had ever lived on the face of the earth. St. Peter thought that this was a reasonable request, so he took him over to a group of people standing off to one side of the gates and said, "That man over there is the most intelligent man who ever lived." The new arrival was shocked. He said, "There must be some mistake. I know that man. He ran a corner grocery store in my town. He was never anything special." St. Peter replied, "Ah, but what he might have been!" Obviously, St. Peter (in this story) used the concept of potential, rather than production, to define giftedness.

Renzulli has presented a definition that focuses, although not exclusively, on production.

> *Giftedness consists of an interaction among three basic clusters of human traits—these clusters being above average general abilities, high levels of task commitment, and high levels of creativity [see Figure 1–2].*
>
> *Gifted and talented children are those possessing, or capable of development, this composite set of traits and applying them to any potentially valuable area of human performance. Children who manifest, or are capable of developing, an interaction among the three clusters require a wide variety of educa-*

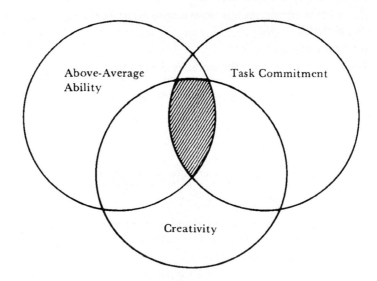

FIGURE 1–2 Renzulli's Three-Ring Conception of Giftedness

Source: From *What Makes Giftedness?* (Brief #6, p. 10) by J. Renzulli, 1979, Los Angeles: National/State Leadership Training Institute. Reprinted by permission.

tional opportunities and services that are not ordinarily provided through regular instructional programs. (1978, p. 261)

Another shift in the concept of intelligence from the standard reliance on verbal ability so important to schooling is the work by Howard Gardner (1985) and his theory of multiple intelligences. He believed that it would be useful to consider seven distinctive types of intellectual behavior: linguistic, logical-mathematical, spatial, bodily-kinesthetic, musical, sense of others (interpersonal), and sense of self (intrapersonal) (see Figure 1–3). In this sense, we would have to assess children on several different dimensions and declare them gifted in one or more of them. These distinctions between intellectual domains become even greater as the children mature and their interests crystalize (become more of personal interest) around some of these domains. Currently there is no set of measurements or protocols available to assess students on these separate domains, although Gardner does address tasks that illustrate the seven domains (Ramos-Ford & Gardner, 1991).

FIGURE 1–3   Gardner's Multiple Intelligences

Linguistic Intelligence

The ability to use language in written and oral expression to aid in remembering, solving problems, and seeking new answers to old problems (novelist, lecturer, lawyer, lyricist)

Logical-Mathematical Intelligence

The ability to use notation and calculation to aid deductive and inductive reasoning (mathematician, physicist)

Spatial Intelligence

The ability to use spatial configurations; important in pattern recognition (architect, sculptor, mechanic)

Bodily-Kinesthetic Intelligence

The ability to use all or part of one's body to perform a task or fashion a product (dancer, surgeon, athlete, etc.)

Musical Intelligence

The ability to discriminate pitch, hear themes, and produce sensitive music through performance or composition; sensitive to rhythm, texture, and timbre (musician)

Interpersonal Intelligence

The ability to understand the actions and motivations of others and to act productively on that knowledge (teacher, therapist, politician, salesperson)

Intrapersonal Intelligence

The ability to understand one's own feelings, motivations, cognitive strengths, and styles (just about anything)

Source: Ramos-Ford, V., & Gardner, H. (1991). Giftedness from a multiple intelligences perspective. In N. Colangelo & Gary Davis (Eds.), *Handbook of Gifted Education*. Boston: Allyn and Bacon. Adapted by permission.

New Views of Intelligence

A central feature of any definition of gifted is the concept of intelligence. But what precisely is intelligence? One of the most active areas of investigation in the past decade has focused on this question. Several new models of intelligence have been developed, many of them based on information-processing models. A few such models will be presented briefly here and will appear again throughout the text.

Sternberg (Sternberg & Davidson, 1986) and his triarchic theory of intellectual giftedness focused on three major dimensions of intelligence (see Figure 1–4). The three dimensions include (1) how we process information through an internal representation of the world, (2) how we use past information to deal with current situations, and (3) how we adapt to real-life environments.

Sternberg's emphasis on metacomponents (or how we plan and make decisions) represents a particularly new venture not often considered in earlier models or intelligence tests. Another relatively new notion in that model includes the ability to adapt to real-world environments, sometimes by modifying the environment or seeking a more friendly environment. It means not merely "fitting in" to school or college but trying to change the institution or, if necessary, finding a more friendly one as the most intelligent course of action. Intelligence can mean the ability to interact constructively to the extent of asser-tively changing the environment (e.g., changing jobs or residences) if one does not like it or if one feels that the current interactions are not positive. As yet, Sternberg's model has had little impact on the identification of gifted students besides alerting educators to the limitations of current models and instruments.

Kaufman and Harrison pointed out the limitations to the new models of intelligence for the practical educator.

Neither theories or research investigations meet the practical needs of practitio-ners who must identify gifted children: intelligence tests do meet these needs. Until those who frown on intelligence tests come up with new measures from their theories that are well standardized...and until they have shown empirically that their measures are demonstrably better than existing intelligence tests for gifted assessment, then we can see no logic for abandoning contemporary intelli-gence tests. (1986, p. 155)

Guilford's (1967) earlier model of the structure of intellect contained four dimen-sions—semantic, symbolic, figural, and behavioral—that correspond fairly well with Gardner's multiple intelligences. These dimensions contain language, by which we com-municate thoughts and feelings; mathematics, by which we build and construct with accuracy; music, by which our spirits soar; and art, which gives us a sense of pleasure from proportions and colors, and sometimes provides us with a symbolic portrait of our world and of our own feelings. It is an excess of one or more of these abilities occurring early in the developmental process that enables us to define, for our time and place, giftedness.

The fourth dimension—behavior—represents children who are sensitive to or em-pathic with regard to the interpretation of self and other behavior. This dimension, similar to Gardner's dimensions of knowledge of others and knowledge of self, has never received the same attention as the other domains because of the difficulty of providing good paper-and-pencil tests to measure that dimension.

FIGURE 1–4   Sternberg's Triarchic Theory of Intellectual Giftedness

SUBTHEORY: Information Processing on Internal Representation of Objects or Symbols

Knowledge Acquisition Components (Processes used in learning new things)

Selective Encoding	Sifting out relevant from irrelevant information
Selective Combination	Combining selectively encoded information to form an integrated, plausible, whole
Selective Comparison	Relating newly acquired information to information acquired in the past

Metacomponents (Processes used in planning, monitoring, and decision making in task performance)

Recognizing the Problem	Identifying a problem for solving from a mass of available information
Defining the Problem	Sharpening the parameters of the problem so that it can be addressed
Generating Steps to Solve Problems	Listing the services of tasks that have to be addressed to solve the problems
Selecting a Strategy	Choosing a method of attack that will lead to problem solution
Representing Information about the Problem	Aiding the problem solution through various displays of information
Monitoring Problem Solution	Applying judgment on the satisfactory nature of the solution

Performance Components (Processes of inductive and deductive reasoning)

Inference	Discovering one or more relationships between objects and events
Mapping	Recognizing a relationship between relationships
Application	Using a previously inferred relationship to cope with a particular problem or relationship

SUBTHEORY: Information Processing Based on the Past Experience of the Individual

Ability to Deal with Novel Tasks	Ability to appropriately apply *available* knowledge to new situations
Ability to Automatize Information Processing	Ability to make the application of some knowledge automatically, requiring no new thinking (i.e., walking, speaking, reading)

SUBTHEORY: Processes of Adapting to Real-World Environments Relevant to One's Life

Adaptation	Process of achieving a good fit between self and environment
Shaping	Process of modifying the available environment to create a better fit
Selection	Process of moving from one environment to another to find a better fit

Source: Adapted from R. Sternberg & J. Davidson (Eds.). (1986). *Conceptions of giftedness.* New York: Cambridge University Press. Reprinted by permission of Cambridge University Press.

Five Gifted Children

The one factor that youngsters who are labeled *gifted* have in common is the ability to absorb abstract concepts, to organize them more effectively, and to apply them more appropriately than does the average youngster. Apart from that, however, the range of other variables, such as social abilities and personality, is almost as great as one would find in a random selection of youngsters of a given age. Therefore, it is not meaningful from the standpoint of the teacher to talk about the social abilities of gifted children or the emotional adjustment of gifted children, because gifted children vary so widely in these characteristics.

To aid in the discussions of past research and programming, as well as to generate a range of variations into this discussion, five children, aged 10, are introduced here. All five of these children meet some criteria of giftedness, but they differ quite markedly in their other characteristics. The reader is advised to study carefully these personal descriptions and refer to them from time to time, as the children are looked at in light of different research findings and educational programming. These children will appear throughout the book to illustrate various aspects of giftedness.

Cranshaw is a big, athletic, happy-go-lucky youngster who impresses the casual observer as an "all-American boy." He seems to be a natural leader and to be enthusiastic over a wide range of interests. These interests have not yet solidified, however. One week he can be fascinated with astronomy, the next week with football formations, and the following week with the study of Africa.

His past history in school has suggested that teachers have two very distinct reactions to Cranshaw. One is that he is a joy to have in the classroom. He is a cooperative and responsible boy who not only performs his own tasks well but can be a good influence in helping the other youngsters to perform effectively. On the other hand, Cranshaw's mere presence in the class also stimulates in teachers some hints of personal inferiority and frustration, since he always seems to be exceeding the bounds of the teachers' knowledge and abilities. The teachers secretly wonder how much they really are teaching Cranshaw and how much he is learning on his own.

Cranshaw's family is a well-knit, reasonably happy one. His father is a businessman, his mother has had some college education, and the family is moderately active in the community. Their attitude toward Cranshaw is that he is a fine boy, and they hope that he does well. They anticipate his going on to higher education but, in effect, say that it is pretty much up to him what he is going to do when the time comes. They do not seem to be future oriented and are perfectly happy to have Cranshaw as the enthusiastic and well-adjusted youngster that he appears to be today.

Zelda shares similar high scores on intelligence tests to those manifested by Cranshaw. Zelda is a rather unattractive girl who is chubby and wears rather thick glasses that give her a "bookish" appearance. Her clothes, while reasonably neat and clean, are not stylish and give the impression that neither her mother nor Zelda has given a great deal of thought to how they look on this particular child. Socially, she has one or two relatively close girlfriends, but she is not a member of the wider social circle in the classroom and, indeed, seems to reject it.

Teachers respond to Zelda with two generally different feelings. They are pleased with the enthusiasm with which Zelda attacks her schoolwork and the good grades that she gets. At the same time, they are vaguely annoyed or irritated with Zelda's undisguised feeling of superiority toward youngsters who are not as bright as she; they tend to repel Zelda when she tries to act like an assistant teacher or to gain favors that are more reserved for the teacher.

Zelda and her family seem to get along very well with each other. The main source of conflict is that the family has values that Zelda has accepted wholeheartedly but that are getting her into difficulty with her classmates. Her father is a college professor and her mother has an advanced degree in English literature. They seem to value achievement and intellectual performance almost to the exclusion of all other things.

Their social evenings are made up of intellectual discussions of politics, religion, or the current burning issue on the campus. These discussions are definitely adult oriented, and Zelda is intelligent enough to enter occasionally into such conversations. This type of behavior is rewarded much more by the parents than is the behavior that would seem more appropriate to her age level.

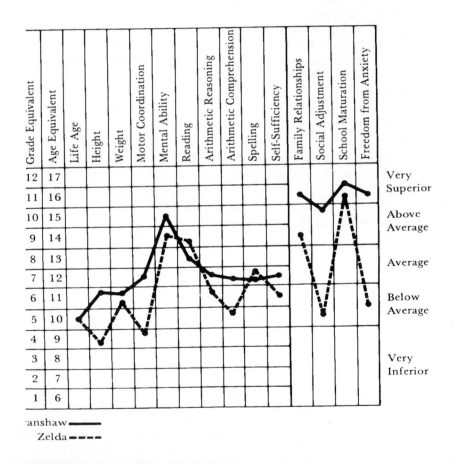

FIGURE 1–5   Profiles of Gifted High Producers

Figure 1–5 shows the range of abilities in different developmental areas for Cranshaw and Zelda. If all the points on the scale were at the same height as their mental ability, there would be little trouble placing them, educationally. Cranshaw shows a wide variation from the physical development of an average 11-year-old to the mental abilities of an average 15-year-old. This means that any standard placement at any level will displace Cranshaw either physically, academically, or socially.

Zelda has an intellectual and academic profile similar to Cranshaw's. Both are doing as well as might be expected on the basis of these measurements. Zelda is slightly inferior to Cranshaw in arithmetic. However, it is in the personal-social area where real differences are apparent. Whereas Cranshaw's adjustment here has the same superior rating as his academic record, Zelda has social difficulties. She is not accepted by her peers and worries about it. Figure 1–6 shows some sentence-completion results from Zelda. In this task, Zelda was supposed to finish some incomplete sentences. The italicized words are the sentence stems and the rest of the sentences shown in Figure 1–6 indicate how Zelda finished each one. Intellectual striving and social yearning are both quite apparent. Her inability to understand how her own behavior causes antagonism is also apparent—and quite important.

Whereas the two preceding children have in common a high academic performance, the following cases are low-producing, high-ability children.

Joe is a tall, lanky youngster who seems to have in common with Cranshaw only his score on an intelligence test. Joe has a certain amount of charm and has a good many friends in his peer group; however, he is anything but a leader. Whenever any task requiring responsibility comes up, he is likely to default. Moreover, in a group he tends to be a complainer and operates against the effective operation of the group itself. Joe is described by his teachers as a "foot dragger," a "work dodger," and a monument of passive resistance. As such, he has been a source of pain and frustration to teachers

FIGURE 1–6   Sentence Completion—Items from Zelda

There are times when I am mad at the world.

My mind is underdeveloped as yet.

My greatest trouble is friends.

Many of my dreams are nightmares.

Secretly I wish to be like Marie Curie.

I cannot understand what makes me tick—Why I am so unlikable to certain people.

My worst trait is that I argue.

My chief worry is getting along with people.

My teachers don't like me.

It is fun to solve what has been unsolved.

If I could have three wishes, I would wish for:
  1. Universal peace.
  2. Goodness to all.
  3. As many other wishes as I wanted.

throughout his years in school. Teachers report considerable difficulty in getting Joe to do any more than the bare minimum that is requested of him. This is doubly frustrating because they all know, by his scores on intelligence tests, that these assignments should be easy tasks for him. They have all tried, in their various ways, to get him to do something extra: to read another book, to do a report, or to become interested in something more than the direct assignments given to the average youngsters.

Joe has a complete battery of excuses and reasons why he should not do these things. He seems to feel that he is being unjustly pushed and that the demands on him are entirely unreasonable. He tends to reject the notion that he is smart, saying, "Who says so?" and generally does not seem to be happy in school except when in the company of his friends.

His family wants Joe to do well and is more than a little irritated with him about his attitude. His father, who is an attorney, worries that if his son maintains his present attitude, the boy will hurt himself and his future. There does not seem to be a great deal of understanding between father and Joe. The father reacts to his son's resistance by increasing the pressure on him. This, in turn, increases Joe's resistance.

Of the children discussed in this book, Sam probably is the least likely, from the standpoint of background and family situation, to be found in a program for gifted students. But unlikely things happen all the time in school, and this is one of them. Sam is a physically mature boy whose family immigrated from the Southeast to a northern urban community three years ago. The family consists of the mother, grandmother, and two younger siblings. Sam remembers his father as a big, burly laughing man with terrifying bursts of temper, who has not been around for almost two years. Sam himself is puzzled about his father's whereabouts, and his mother will not share with him any of her own thoughts on this matter. As the oldest boy, he somehow feels both the responsibility of trying to be the "man in the family" and his own lack of competence for that task.

His mother now works part-time, and the grandmother takes care of the household. Sam spent his first two years in school in the rural South and does not remember much about his school except that it was easy and pleasant. When he moved, his third-grade teacher perceived his alertness and responsiveness through his rough exterior. A year later, he was given tests to determine his ability; he scored high for students from environmental disadvantaged circumstances, but not as high as Cranshaw and Zelda. Most psychologists would suggest that, given different circumstances—perhaps the same environmental background that Cranshaw and Zelda had—Sam would score 10 to 15 IQ points higher than he scores today.

Despite these abilities, Sam is not doing particularly well in school, and there are hints that he will be troublesome from a behavioral standpoint, because he has formed friendships with peers who seek excitement and adventure. Sam is already aware firsthand of drug traffic and crime, even though the neighborhood in which he lives is not one of the worst in the city. The challenge for the school, and for society as well, is to provide a future goal of importance and practicality for Sam so that he will be motivated to use his intellectual talents to the maximum.

For Sam, who was raised in a family much more interested in country-western music and rock and roll than in the clever turn of phrase honored in Cranshaw's and Zelda's homes, it was natural that some of the expression of talent came through this medium. Two of Sam's recreational joys are to play drums for the local drum-and-bugle corps and to accompany TV rock-and-roll stars when his mother can stand it. When he is "beating the skins," Sam has a kind of sense of order and rightness of things that seems akin to the joy of the mathematician who solves a formula or the poet who finds just the right alliteration for a stanza.

Should we support the development and encouragement of diverse talents or the single dimension of verbal excellence? Students who are gifted and talented have a rare flair for confronting us with questions about our basic educational values. Figure 1–7 shows the profiles of Joe and Sam. It is easy to see that Joe's high performance on a mental-ability test represents his only really high point on the scale. His achievement test scores are only little advanced for his grade level, and his teacher claims that his classwork is below average for his grade level. In the personal-social area, he shows poor family relationships and school motivation, which probably relate to his ineffective performance.

Sam's profile shows less academic performance—only average for his age group. This is somewhat understandable, in view of his uneven language development. His

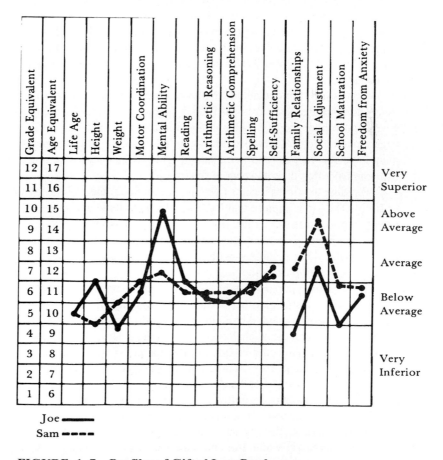

Joe ━━━
Sam ▬ ▬ ▬

FIGURE 1–7   Profiles of Gifted Low Producers

mental-ability score seems to be quite an achievement, considering his past experiences. His problems do not seem to be in the personal-social area but in his limited educational background. In school programs it is somewhat natural to assume that problems lie within the child rather than in his or her surroundings. With Sam, that is clearly a wrong assumption. The problems in defining the gifted, as represented by Joe and Sam, are serious enough that Chapter 13 is devoted to this topic.

Our final student is Stephanie, a tall slender girl with a penchant for creative work. Her test scores would barely get her into a gifted program on the basis of traditional criteria and, for reasons that will become apparent, she might not get recommendations from some of her teachers either. She has some special abilities in mathematics and art but her dominant characteristic is her strong desire for independence in decision making. Stephanie believes in herself wholeheartedly and is not often swayed from her chosen path by persuasion or occasional threats.

Often, teachers think that simply placing two gifted students together will create a wonderful bond of friendship, but that is not always the case. Considering the differences between Zelda and Stephanie, one can begin to see why (see Figure 1–8).

Stephanie has a flair for art and, given her choice, she would spend all day building, molding, sculpting, and developing—anything that would feed her desire for expression. Although Stephanie dabbles in all art forms, from photography to computer graphics, her special love is for jewelry. Her self-made jewelry frequently adorns her very modern wardrobe.

What is truly unique about Stephanie's creative talent is that it recognizes applications and relationships across disciplines. She seems to readily recognize the elements of chemistry in photography. The composition of metals is a current fascination, since she began making her own jewelry. Stephanie's long work with design, shape, and measurement have also helped reinforce a natural grasp of mathematics—especially geometry—that teachers often do not expect to find in girls.

"Pressing the limits" seems to be the predominant theme in Stephanie's life, for good or for ill. The same impulse that leads Stephanie to bend and shape metal into new forms drives her to press her limits in other areas. She seems to be virtually incapable of following simple directions; she always approaches assignments with her own added creative twist. This, combined with her avant-garde dress, causes some teachers to think of her as distracting and annoying.

For a certain other group of teachers, who enjoy creativity, Stephanie is a dream come true. "I can't wait to give her something new, and then stand back to see what will happen," one teacher said. Although many admire Stephanie's creative talents, there's no doubt that she can be a challenge in the classroom. When those times arise when Stephanie is not allowed a creative outlet for her work, she can become stubborn and recalcitrant. Mundane, rote, or drill-type tasks drive her crazy, and she openly defies her teachers with accusations of "useless busywork."

Stephanie's parents are quite befuddled by their daughter. Her father works at a mid-level corporate job, and her mother is a small business owner. Neither would claim a creative bent, nor do they possess extraordinary intellectual skills. As a result, they find Stephanie amazingly wonderful and unmanageable. From day to day, they do not know whether to praise her inventions or to warn her against extreme risk taking. Already, Stephanie shows signs of recognizing her intellectual edge over her parents and uses her

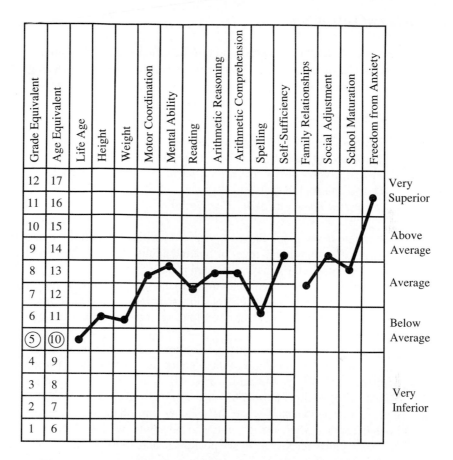

FIGURE 1–8   Profile of Stephanie

powers to help win her way during arguments. Both of Stephanie's parents are concerned that her adventurous inclinations will lead to early and dangerous experimentation with drugs and sexuality, but they feel somewhat powerless to stop her.

Opinion about Stephanie among her classmates is divided. She has a clique of admirers and followers who try to emulate her style of dress and artistic attitudes. Other students, however (among them Zelda), think of her as too show-offish, even frighteningly free spirited.

A summary of Stephanie's test scores shows a marked discrepancy in her skills. She has extremely advanced general reasoning ability, which is reflected primarily in mathematics skills. In comparison, her verbal skills are not as advanced, although still above average. This is probably due to Stephanie's abhorrence of rote assignments associated with spelling drills and reading comprehension questions. Stephanie's family relationships are only fair, since she recognizes that she can control her parents even though she genuinely loves them. Most pronounced is Stephanie's freedom from anxiety as she presents her uniqueness to the world with complete assurance and conviction.

Identification of Gifted Students

Many people think that identification of the gifted is a simple matter—that, in fact, these students identify themselves. Many do, of course. Consider a passage written by John Stuart Mill at the age of 6:

History of Rome

The Rutuli, a people living near the sea, and extending along the Numicius up to Lavinium, opposed him. However, Turnus their king was defeated and killed by Aeneas. Aeneas was killed soon after this. The war continued to be carried on chiefly against the Rutuli, to the time of Romulus, the first king of Rome. By him it was that Rome was built. (Cox, 1926)

It is safe to say if one finds a 6-year-old writing in this fashion or composing sonatas or reading at a sixth-grade level or beating adults at chess, then one has found a gifted child, even without the benefit of formal measurements.

Unfortunately for the conscientious teacher and educator, many children who appear to be gifted by our definitions do not show such remarkable performance, and so we must pursue other methods to search them out, so that the students can receive appropriate educational services.

In those children we call gifted, there are no unique characteristics not found in other children. It is the combination of these elements and their early (by age) appearance that sets them apart. We do not find it particularly unusual to see a 10-year-old playing chess. It is worthy of comment, though, when a 4-year-old does it. It is the early appearance of talent in a developmental sense that catches our attention. Hagan stated, "It should be remembered that giftedness is relative, not absolute. We identify an individual as gifted or potentially gifted because he or she possesses more of a certain characteristic or characteristics than others" (1980, p. 5).

Intelligence Testing

It is difficult to venture into the identification of giftedness without raising the topic of intelligence testing. In an era where our lives seem to be controlled and regulated by numbers—social security, telephone, or credit card—a special place is reserved for the IQ score. It has been said that once a person has received information about his or her IQ score, that number becomes indelibly etched in his or her cortex as if it had been burned there with hydrogen fluoride: He may forget his address, his telephone number, his spouse's name, but he will never forget that number—his IQ! If it seems to be high enough, it can suddenly be divulged uninvited in casual conversation at parties or in chats with neighbors. However, there is very little real appreciation of what such a score actually means. Few laypersons realize that their IQ score is a function of a particular test, thus interpretation is impossible without reference to the tool used to obtain it. The same person can quite legitimately obtain IQ scores varying as much as 25 or 30 points, depending on the test used.

Since the intelligence test remains one of the strongest measures of intellectual giftedness, it is worth a brief review of just what we are talking about when we refer to an IQ score. The usual way of obtaining an IQ score is to give a child a series of items that have previously been given to a representative sample of children of the same age. The score of that child, when compared with that of all children of that age, can give a comparative measure called a *deviation IQ* (how far the child deviates from the average performance of his or her age group). These deviation scores can then be translated into IQ scores. A brief description of the subtests on the Wechsler Intelligence Scale is given in Table 1–1.

Carefully review the subtests of the WISC-R in Table 1–1 and ask yourself these questions: Are there important aspects of giftedness that are not being measured by these

TABLE 1–1   Subtests of the Wechsler Intelligence Scale for Children (WISC)

The WISC-R has 12 subtests: 6 comprise the *Verbal Section* and 6 comprise the *Performance Section*. To avoid the administration of unnecessary items, the subtests have guidelines for discontinuing the testing after the child makes a certain number of consecutive errors. Also, the subtests on the Performance Section are timed.

Verbal Section	*Performance Section*
Information *(30 items)*—Measures the student's knowledge of general information and facts. Examples include "What do we call a baby cow?" and "What are hieroglyphics?"	**Picture Completion** *(26 items)*—The student is shown a picture in which an important element is missing. The student must either verbalize or point to the missing element.
Similarities *(17 items)*—Measures the student's ability to perceive the common element of two terms. Examples include "In what ways are an apple and a banana alike? Anger and joy? Mountain and lake?"	**Picture Arrangement** *(13 items)*—The student is given a series of pictures that represent a story but are in the incorrect order. The task is to sequence the pictures in the correct order.
Arithmetic *(18 items)*—Measures the student's ability to solve problems requiring arithmetic computation and reasoning. This is primarily an oral subtest requiring concentration.	**Block Design** *(11 items)*—The student must look at pictures of certain designs and reproduce these using red and white blocks. Basically measures visual analysis and synthesis.
Vocabulary *(32 items)*—The student is told a word and must orally define it. Items range in difficulty from *knife, umbrella*, and *clock* to *obliterate, imminent*, and *dilatory*.	**Object Assembly** *(4 items)*—This subtest for visual organization and synthesis requires the student to put together four jigsaw puzzles.
Comprehension *(17 items)*—Measures the social, moral, and ethical judgment of the student, who must answer questions such as "What are you supposed to do if you find someone's wallet or pocketbook in a store?" and "Why are criminals locked up?"	**Coding** *(45 items)*—Requires the student to copy paired or coded geometric symbols within a certain time limit. There are two parts: A for children under age 8, and B for individuals of age 8 and over. The coding subtest measures visual-motor speed, coordination, and, to a certain extent, memory.
Digit Span *(14 items)*—Includes two parts: Digits Forward and Digits Backward. The student is given a series of digits at a rate of one digit per second.	**Mazes** *(supplementary, 4 items)*—Requires the student to use skills in visual planning to complete a number of progressively more difficult mazes.

tests? Does past experience have anything to do with how well one will perform on some or all of these tests? We can see why Cranshaw and Sam, with similar native abilities, might be performing differently on these tests.

The fourth edition of the Stanford-Binet Scales (Thorndike, Hagen, & Sattler, 1986) represented a major change in the approach to measurement of intelligence by this well-known instrument. The scores on the new test seem to measure ability and predict achievement as well as the previous versions, but the style of the test has been substantially changed. The new authors have established subtests measuring specific abilities and memory instead of presenting items by age level. It is essentially no longer an *age scale*, but a *deviation IQ scale*, such as the Wechsler scales. The subtests are clustered under Crystalized Abilities, meaning those that have been influenced by opportunity (e.g., Vocabulary, Quantitative); Fluid-Analytic Abilities, representing more basic perceptual abilities (e.g., Pattern Analysis, Copying); and Short-Term Memory (e.g., Copying Bead Patterns, Memory for Digits).

One knows intuitively that an IQ score of 140 is "good." It is clearly better to be advanced in development than it is to be retarded or slow in development. But how much better is it, and how does the child rate with other children of the same age? Extensive experience with the distribution of IQ scores has yielded consistent curves such as that shown in Figure 1–9. The Wechsler Adult Intelligence Scale (WAIS) and the Wechsler

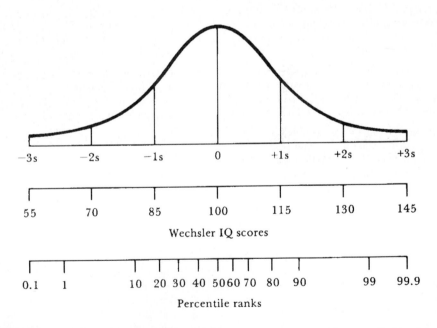

FIGURE 1–9   Relationships Between Wechsler Scores and Percentile Ranks

Source: Biehler/Snowman: *Psychology Applied to Teaching,* Seventh Edition. Copyright © 1993 by Houghton Mifflin Company. Used with permission.

Intelligence Scale for Children (WISC) both have a mean of 100 and a standard deviation of 15. The 1960 and 1972 revisions of the Stanford-Binet use standard scores that have a mean of 100 and a standard deviation of 16. For all practical purposes, this one-point difference in standard deviation is of no significance; thus, one can also interpret Stanford-Binet IQs by referring to the WISC and WAIS scales in the figure.

Figure 1–9 shows us that an IQ score of 140 falls above the 99th percentile, meaning that the person who obtained such a score performed better than 99 people of his or her age level and less well than only 1 person out of a theoretical 100. The typical IQ curve also shows that as one approaches the upper and lower limits, there are fewer and fewer people, so that an IQ score of 130 or above on this type of measure would identify about the top 3 percent of a particular group.

Although IQ tests clearly do not measure all of what one considers to be important in a discussion of intelligence, they do measure much of what is necessary to current academic success. Thus, the predictive power of an IQ score for future academic attainment remains impressive and has been the reason for its enormous influence in educational circles.

What Kind of Intelligence Is Measured?

Table 1–2 shows several types of mental functions. A large number of preliminary tryouts of the prospective test item will establish an age level at which one would expect the average child to succeed and by which one can discover if the children's performances follow expected practices (i.e., older children should find the item easier than younger children).

The list itself is interesting because not all of these mental functions are sampled equally on intelligence tests. Which ones are not? And why? The memory items are familiar to all students, particularly the vocabulary or long-term memory items. As noted, this type of item stresses the importance of rich language and conceptual understanding. A youngster from a culture that does not stress language—even if he or she is a talented student—is likely to do *relatively* more poorly on such items than on reasoning items or on short-term memory, which are less dependent on past experience.

The two domains in intelligence that are least frequently observed on intelligence tests, although they are undoubtedly important in charting the talents of gifted children, are *divergent reasoning* (seeking many answers to the same question, e.g., "How many uses can you find for a newspaper?") and *evaluation*. Since both these characteristics are deemed important for imaginative and creative work, why are such items so infrequently seen on standard tests compared to the prevalence of memory, association, and convergent reasoning items? There would seem to be both logical and practical reasons. First, the primary purpose of the intelligence test is to predict school achievement. If school achievement consists primarily of memorizing facts and doing simple kinds of problem solving, test items that measure memory and convergent reasoning will be sufficient to predict which students will do well. Even in classes for gifted students, it is often rare to find much emphasis in class discussions on divergent or evaluative thinking (Gallagher, Aschner, & Jenné, 1967).

TABLE 1–2   Sample of Intelligence Test Items and Mental Functions Measured

Mental Function	Sample Item	Supposed Cultural Influence
Short-Term Memory	Repeat exactly as I say it: cow–zebra–giraffe–mongoose	Very little influence of experience except for the set of attending to an adult
Long-Term Memory	What is an ocelot? What do we do with a wrench?	Substantial influence of culture; experience, particularly reading experience, can build substantial vocabulary
Association	*Ball* is to *bat* as *puck* is to ____ ? Name the one that doesn't belong: blue sweet red orange	The richness of language depends partly on experience and partly on the ability to store and retrieve associations and concepts; environment in part and constitutional influences in part
Reasoning—Convergent	If Jerry is taller than Pete and Pete is taller than Moe, then____ is taller than ____.	Relatively small influence of culture; basically an internal intellectual process
Reasoning—Divergent	What would happen if all the water were shut off from your city?	Depends on self-confidence, freedom from criticism, and knowledge of subject area
Evaluation	Compare and judge Capote and Mailer for their portrayal of the male figure in the novel. Which would you rather have—$5 to spend now or $25 at the end of the week?	The criterion used to choose a proper answer has to be culturally learned

The second reason is less kind to the test constructors. It is simply that such items are painfully difficult to score. If we include such divergent items as "Tell me all the words you can think of when I say *round*," or "Tell me what would happen if everybody in the world went deaf," how could a person score the answers? One could not simply count all the responses; some of them may be silly or redundant. The placement of such an item on a group intelligence test would cause havoc and could not be keyed properly for scoring.

Similarly, evaluation test items are difficult to score. If we ask a question such as "What is best..." or "What is most appropriate..." there would be legitimate differences of opinion on what the right answer ought to be. One of the standard evaluative questions we ask ourselves as a society is Which candidate is better for a particular political office? and it is easy to see what violent differences of opinion can be obtained from such a simple item. The ability to use good judgment is a crucial element in our intelligence, but it is abominably hard to measure. So, as long as the easily scored items seem to do the predicting job (school performance), there is a tendency to go along with the existing measures.

One of the questions that emerges from a consideration of the diverse multicultural society of the United States in the 1990s is Are there core items of intelligence that can be considered, regardless of the cultural background of the individual student? Frasier (1991) has identified several characteristics that she believes represent the core elements of intelligence:

- The ability to meaningfully manipulate some symbol system held valuable in the subculture
- The ability to think logically, given appropriate information
- The ability to use stored knowledge to solve problems
- The ability to reason by analogy
- The ability to extend or extrapolate knowledge to new situations or unique applications

Although the traditional way to determine unusual ability in young children has been to give items on tests that reflect the linguistic and verbal symbol system that is the core of U.S. school programs, there are other ways to measure these core elements.

Sam shows a remarkable ability to problem solve in the community, to find alternative ways to repair household appliances, and to apply what he has learned in interpersonal and intrapersonal situations in the social settings of his neighborhood as well as in the classroom. Consequently, he is able to get along with many different people and is seen as being "street smart." Sam's ability to reason from analogy and to use stored knowledge to solve problems is quite observable, even if it is not done in the style of the traditional verbal symbol system required by his school.

Other measures have been used to measure reasoning and the ability to think logically—measures that do not require the use of the verbal symbol system. One example of this approach can be seen in the Raven Progressive Matrices tests. The growing popularity of the concept of crystalized abilities to describe those skills that have emerged through a sequential mix of native ability and experience (e.g., vocabulary) raises an important question in student assessment of abilities. What should be done with students who did not have the opportunity to build vocabulary either because English is a second language or because they lack linguistic models or attention?

Other instruments that would seem less dependent on particular experiences have been sought in order to determine the more fundamental abilities of the student. The Raven Progressive Matrices tests (Raven, 1956) have been used for this purpose. An example of an item on the Raven Matrices test is given in Figure 1–10. The sample item requires little verbalization or past linguistic skills, and has been used to discover high-ability students from cultural minorities or economically disadvantaged home settings as an alternative to more conventional methods. It is not yet clear how helpful such alternative measures are in accurately assessing the abilities of gifted students from culturally different environments.

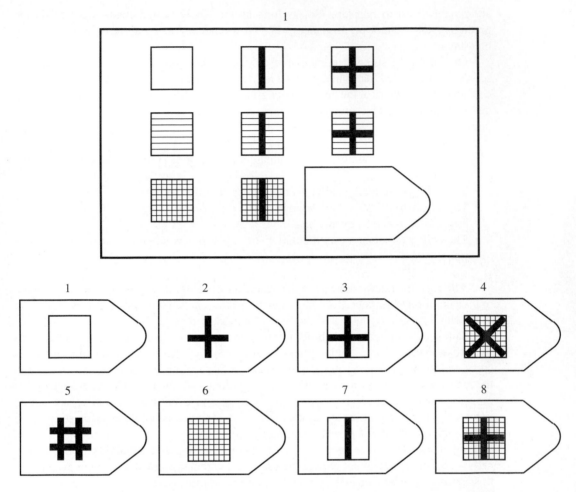

FIGURE 1–10   Sample Item from Raven Matrices Test

Source: From *Advanced Progressive Matrices* (Set 1, p. 7) by J. C. Raven, 1958, London: H. K. Lewis & Co., Ltd. Copyright 1958 by J. C. Raven, Ltd. Reprinted by permission.

The Hidden Gifted

Teacher Identification

The most common means of identification of gifted children in the first half of this century was teacher nomination. In this situation, the actual definition of gifted children becomes those children who are doing very well in school—much better than their companions. What is wrong with this particular definition? Many children who have a high aptitude for reasoning and conceptualization may not be performing well in school.

Such a definition would rule out Albert Einstein, Thomas Edison, and Winston Churchill, who constitute three students who might not be labeled "gifted" by teacher nomination.

With the extension of current identification techniques to once again include teacher judgment, and sometimes parental judgment, the question arises as to how effective or efficient these observers can be of giftedness. Earlier studies were quite pessimistic about the ability of teachers to find children of high ability or potential without missing many gifted students or wrongly identifying conforming students as gifted.

Although there is abundant evidence that teachers *without* special instruction have serious difficulty in nominating gifted students, there is a remaining question as to how much improvement might be shown if teachers were given systematic training on the topic. Gear (1978) conducted a study involving 48 teachers, 24 randomly selected to be in a training group and 24 in a control sample. The experimental teachers were given a five-session training package that dealt with terminology of gifted education, definition of gifted and talented, selection criteria, the role of intelligence tests in the selection process, and the characteristics of gifted children.

Gear found that the teachers who received special training were able to be *twice* as effective in identifying gifted students as were the teachers without special instruction. This increased effectiveness was achieved without increasing overreferrals (students named as "gifted" who are not). The important message from this study is that it appears possible to provide systematic training that will bring teachers to an improved level of effectiveness.

One of the more common devices to aid teachers in identification is the Renzulli Scales for Rating Behavioral Characteristics of Superior Students (Renzulli, Smith, White, Callahan, & Hartman, 1976). These scales have 10 items each in areas such as learning, motivation, creativity, leadership, and visual and performing arts. Using a one-to four-point scale, the teacher is to rate items such as those listed in Table 1–3. The total scores are then often used as part of a multiple set of instruments and procedures for identification.

Since all of the various methods currently in use have some negative features, the predominant strategies employed by many school systems today is to use a collection of instruments or procedures and use committee judgment to resolve cases with ambiguous information. Figure 1–11 indicates the range of identification practices now in use in attempting to identify the economically disadvantaged gifted and talented student (Baldwin, 1989). The figure includes cognitive, psychosocial, creative products, psycho-motor, motivation, and creative problem-solving areas.

This type of approach appeals to many educators who feel that if enough indicators are taken, children with high ability will show up in the total portrait, if not on a single index. This approach is often used when there is special interest in finding minority-group gifted students who may not score sufficiently high on verbal tests but will reveal other dimensions of talent or ability when all the measures are considered.

The degree to which there is diversity in current identification practices may be judged by a survey of 200 teachers, administrators, and psychologists (Alvino, McDonnel, & Richert). The answers to the survey revealed that over 120 different tests, rating scales, and other techniques were employed. In the areas of art, music, or leader-ship, when highly talented youth are sought, techniques such as auditions, rating scales,

TABLE 1–3   Sample Scale Items: Teacher Ratings of Behavioral Characteristics of Superior Students

Scales	Sample Items
Learning Characteristics	1. Has unusually advanced vocabulary for age or grade level; uses terms in a meaningful way; has verbal behavior characterized by "richness" of expression, elaboration, and fluency 2. Is a keen and alert observer: usually "sees more" or "gets more out of" a story, film, poem, etc., than others
Motivational Characteristics	1. Strives toward perfection; is self-critical; is not easily satisfied with own speed or products 2. Is quite concerned with right and wrong, good and bad; often evaluates and passes judgment on events, people, and things
Creativity Characteristics	1. Displays a great deal of curiosity about many things; is constantly asking questions about anything and everything 2. Displays a keen sense of humor and sees humor in situations that may not appear to be humorous to others
Leadership Characteristics	1. Is self-confident with children his own age as well as adults; seems comfortable when asked to show work to the class 2. Tends to dominate others when they are around; generally directs the activity in which he is involved
Visual and Performing Arts Characteristics	1. Incorporates a large number of elements into artwork; varies the subject and content of artwork (art) 2. Is adept at role playing, improvising acting out situations, "on the spot" (dramatics) 3. Perceives fine differences in musical tone (pitch, loudness, timbre, duration)

Source: Renzulli, J., Smith, L., White, A., Callahan, C., & Hartman, R. (1976). *Scales for rating the behaviorial characteristics of superior students*. Wethersfield, CT: Creative Learning Press. Reprinted by permission. Original work published by Creative Learning Press, Inc., Mansfield Center, CT.

and personal judgment were the methods most often used. The investigators concluded that "beyond the intellectual and academic categories there is a relative paucity of formal, not to mention validated, measures being used to identify gifted students" (1981, p. 131).

Despite numerous warnings that standard instruments might not be appropriate for certain cultural groups, Alvino, McDonnel, and Richert (1981) found they were being used anyway, perhaps out of frustration by the lack of other, better instruments or procedures. One of the ways that has been suggested to counteract the negative influences of culture on the identification of gifted students has been proposed by Richert (1991). She suggested that relevant ethnic, racial, or sexual groups be identified and then scores on appropriate instruments be aggregated. The top percentage from each group would then be chosen as participants in the program for gifted students. Thus, if the figure were 10 percent of the total student population would be involved in the special program, 10 percent would be Hispanics, 10 percent would be African Americans, 10 percent would be Asians, and 50 percent would be boys.

STUDENT_____ BIRTHDATE_____ AGE____ SEX____ GRADE____ DATE_____

Area	Assessment Items	Mode of Score	Data Card Info	Ratings					B-NA	No. of Items	Raw Score	Area Score (RS ÷ N)
				5	4	3	2	1				
	1.1 General IQ											
1. COGNITIVE	1.2											
	1.3											
	1.4											
	1.5											
	TOTAL COGNITIVE											
2. PSYCHOSOCIAL	2.1											
	2.2											
	2.3											
	2.4											
	2.5											
	TOTAL PSYCHOSOCIAL											
3. CREATIVE PRODUCTS	3.1											
	3.2											
	3.3											
	3.4											
	3.5											
	TOTAL CREATIVE PRODUCTS											
4. PSYCHOMOTOR	4.1											
	4.2											
	4.3											
	4.4											
	4.5											
	TOTAL PSYCHOMOTOR											
5. MOTIVATION	5.1											
	5.2											
	5.3											
	5.4											
	5.5											
	TOTAL MOTIVATION											
6. CREATIVE PROBLEM-SOLVING	6.1											
	6.2											
	6.3											
	6.4											
	6.5											
	TOTAL CREATIVE PROBLEM-SOLVING											
MATRIX TOTALS	Maximum Points for This Matrix											
	STUDENT TOTALS											

FIGURE 1–11   Baldwin Identification Matrix 2

Source: Baldwin Identification Matrix 2 in *Baldwin Identification Matrix 2 for the Identification of Gifted and Talented,* by Alexinia Y. Baldwin, Published by Trillium Press, New York, 1984. Reprinted by permission of the author.

Modified versions of this approach to identification have been used in special schools in math and science, as well as in summer programs such as Governor's Schools, which provide special learning experiences for talented youth at the secondary school level in many states. No reported ill effects have been noted on the overall programs by the use of such an adaptation of traditional practice (Kolloff, 1991).

Identifying the "Right" Children

The practical question that these new conceptualizations of intelligence raise is Are we identifying the wrong group of children as gifted with our standard procedures? Is there another group of children with unidentified potential that is waiting for a new set of tests or protocols to be developed so that they can be identified and their talents nurtured? It is a provoking thought. Since there is little direct evidence one way or another, it is hard to become too dogmatic about it. The most that could be said at this time is that the group of "gifted" children now found in our schools would likely change, but little, with the introduction of new search techniques or procedures. The reason for that is the general superiority of gifted students across the spectrum of intellectual activities.

Those whose performances are superior to that of their agemates in memory and reasoning test items will likely be superior in executive function (decision making) and creativity as well. As will be seen in more detail in Chapter 2, there tends to be a generalized set of skills rather than isolated talents that mark the gifted individual, although there are outstanding individual exceptions to this general rule.

The choice of identification instruments depends largely on which of the two major concepts are accepted for definition: *achievement* or *potential*. As Goldberg (1986) pointed out, when achievement is the criteria, then rating a student's performance in academic subject areas, or judging musical performance on an instrument, or reviewing a portfolio or graphic work, or examining examples of creative writing, or evaluating actual performance in leadership roles would be the key to identification. On the other hand, if potential is used, rather than aptitude test scores, performance on specially designated drama or dance exercises or observations of everyday behavior may be used. The attempt to measure potential assumes that we can examine behaviors that are correlated with a high level of achievement, or with those characteristics that mark high achievers in talent areas, so that we can make valid predictions of the probability of future achievement. The accumulated evidence of the results of such predictions suggests that these standard measures of aptitude or intelligence predict very well, though not perfectly, later school performance.

The procedures noted above were used mainly for elementary school students. Changes in the identification process for secondary-level gifted students are provided by Hoover and Feldhusen (1987).

1. There is a greater reliance on the student's self-nomination based on interest and personal needs.
2. There is less reliance on global measures of aptitude, such as IQ tests, which provide little help in making programming decisions for a particular student.
3. Students may enter under one option—for example, extra school programming—experience great success, and subsequently move into additional areas.

4. Identification is tailored to the special characteristics of the program service, as well as to students' unique talents and needs.

Finding Nontraditional Gifted Children

The desire to find nontraditional gifted children hidden to us by our standard practices, regardless of their economic or ethnic differences from the mainstream, has led to a variety of changes in local and state identification policies. All 50 states encourage local school systems to take certain steps designed to find underrepresented students and to give those students the opportunity to participate in special programs for gifted students (Coleman & Gallagher, 1992).

Some of the policies suggested by states to find hidden gifted are discussed next.

Encouraging Greater Public Awareness of Giftedness.   The importance of recognizing intellectual gifts is not often appreciated by the general public. Special strategies have to be invoked to make certain that talented youth do not "fall through the cracks"—especially youth from nonstandard families or environments.

- Alert persons in these special populations of the availability of programs for gifted students.
- Conduct a formal community awareness campaign to recruit support and resources for talent development.
- Conduct an annual "child find" in cooperation with community and other state agencies to locate gifted students who were overlooked.

Screening Procedures.   Typically, schools will establish a screening procedure that identifies a large pool of potentially eligible students for a more thorough examination. Some suggested screening policies are:

- Require a plan for staff development of general education staff to increase their ability to identify students with hidden talents.
- Encourage the use of checklists to help teachers recognize underachieving students who may be gifted.
- Encourage the use of autobiographies to assist in the identification of gifted students from special populations.

Formal Identification Procedures.   States have focused on the use of multiple criteria to make formal identification, such as:

- Encourage the establishment of child study teams to make the placement decision.
- Use multiple identification criteria with the clause "No single criterion should prevent identification."
- Use portfolios of student work samples to document giftedness together with rating scales to assess the work in the portfolios.
- Reevaluate or retest students who show compelling reasons why their existing scores underestimate their true abilities.

With the help of such guidelines, a larger number of students with special potential from economically disadvantaged circumstances are being identified. A recent study (Scott, Perou, Urbano, Hogan, & Gold, 1992) confirmed that minority parents are much less likely to ask that their children be examined for eligibility to programs for gifted students *even when* their children are clearly eligible. A major talent search seems to be warranted.

Does the Identification Strategy Make a Difference?

There have been only a few attempts at comparing the effects of adopting differing strategies for identification. Does it really make any difference? Will the same children show up anyway, regardless of the method of identification?

One answer to these questions was provided in a study by Shore and Tsiamis (1986), who compared two groups of children. The first group was selected on the basis of traditional measures of intelligence and achievement and the second group was selected on the basis of teacher and parent identification. The researchers found that the second group (which had been identified by offering a suitable program and opening the doors to those interested) was not distinguishable from the group selected by the school on the basis of formal tests! They concluded that formal selection by testing was not necessary for a substantial number of gifted pupils and that the resources previously used for such identification processes could be redirected to program development and services and to the search for hard-to-find special populations of gifted students such as minority gifted and underachieving gifted students (p. 100).

In another attempt to see if different strategies of identification would yield the same children, Dirks and Quarforth (1981) approached a small-town population of 159 fourth-graders with two different identification strategies: *breadth* (students who scored in the top 10 percent in three of five areas—grade, creativity test, behavior traits, achievement tests, and group intelligence test) and *depth* (students who scored in the top 2 to 3 percent on at least one of the same five areas). Using either of the two methods, 50 percent of the students would have been identified as gifted. Of the remainder, the *breadth* method tended to get high classroom achievers who had moderately high IQ scores and who were well thought of by their teachers; the *depth* model included more of the children with extremely high IQ scores but who might be underachievers. Dirks and Quarfoth believed that the *depth* model was superior in that it was less likely to overlook students of outstanding intellectual potential.

High IQ by Mistake?

There can always be some doubt about an IQ score that is too low, in terms of program eligibility, but the same cannot be said of IQ scores that are very high. As Silverman has pointed out, "Though low scores on IQ tests may be of questionable accuracy, this does not mean that high scores are also inaccurate. Children with exceptionally high IQ scores usually profit from advanced course work taught at an accelerated pace" (1986, p. 139).

Obviously, if a student is performing in a remarkable fashion in producing creative work, or performing in an outstanding way in class in a similar fashion to other identified gifted students, then one should be suspicious of a low IQ score or teacher rating obtained by that student. Some form of careful committee review should be used in such instances.

Identification for State Approval

Much of the identification efforts currently being conducted by schools are being done to certify to state authorities that the students in their special programs do meet the qualifications for a gifted program. Without such requirements it would be likely that the schools would take a much more informal approach to identification.

Gallagher and Courtright (1986) identified two different types of definitions of gifted students that seem to continually get intertwined in identification discussions. The first concept of gifted encompasses students who are outstanding in any area of individual differences. This would include mental abilities beyond those of immediate use to the schools. The second concept includes children who could be referred to as academically advanced and whose performances would predict excellent academic success. Renzulli (1986) has identified a similar dichotomy in discussing "schoolhouse gifted" versus creative-productive giftedness. The second of these groups is much harder to identify and measure than the first. A survey of professionals in the field of education for the gifted revealed that identification of gifted students remains in third place in topics of research importance—*curriculum* and *social adjustment* were ranked first and second (Renzulli, Reid, & Gubbins, 1992).

As our understanding of high intelligence increases, we can continue to expect changes in our definition of gifted students and in the instruments and procedures we use for identification. Two of the five children described in this chapter (Sam and Joe) might not have been referred to as gifted 20 years ago. Perhaps 20 years from now, some of the five students may have lost the cultural value necessary to deserve the term *gifted*, if, in fact, the term itself remains and is not changed to something more appropriate (Gallagher, 1991).

Unresolved Issues

No book that addresses a major educational topic should imply that all the issues are settled. In the field of the education of gifted students, as in other major topics in education, there is much to be learned and much that needs to be discarded from what we think we know today. What follows are, in the authors' opinion, the most important questions remaining in each of the major topics covered by this book. A few of these unresolved issues will be included at the end of each chapter.

1. If the environment is partially responsible for the development or the suppression of giftedness, is it possible to create special environments to increase the total number of children that we could call gifted?
2. If the IQ test is not totally satisfactory as an identification tool, where are the other tests or scales (that measure such characteristics as aesthetic sensitivity, creativity,

metathinking, and imagination) that we can use to support the broadened definition that we want?

3. If our definition of gifted changes as the values of our society change, what will the definition be in 2000? What values will be downgraded and what values will be more highly regarded?

Chapter Review

1. Giftedness is currently viewed as a multidimensional set of characteristics that may include academic aptitude, spatial perception, creativity, executive function, leadership, and superior perception in interpersonal and intrapersonal relationships.

2. Each culture tends to define giftedness to meet its own needs and values.

3. Intellectual ability is no longer considered to be determined exclusively by genetics but by some mix or interaction between genetics and progressive experiences.

4. One definition of gifted children now in use is based on superior performance rather than on measures of potential or aptitude.

5. Many gifted children may not identify themselves through outstanding performance, however, and need to be sought through a variety of teacher ratings, tests, self-surveys, and performance indexes.

6. Intelligence testing that asks children to respond to questions requiring memory, association, and logical thinking remains the prime tool for identification of intellectually superior children.

7. New views of intelligence include metathinking skills such as executive function, planning, decision making, and the like.

8. Tests of intelligence traditionally do not include items that measure divergent thinking, evaluative thinking, or metathinking and thus are limited in their full display of intellectual capabilities.

9. Teacher identification of gifted children traditionally has been faulty, overlooking large numbers of intellectually superior children while identifying others as gifted who do not show that degree of intellectual superiority.

10. Teacher efficiency for finding gifted children can be improved with specific training but still needs to be supplemented with other measures.

11. Current practice for identification most often employs multiple criteria using tests, ratings, and performance-relevant evidence (e.g., math performance) tailored to the specific educational program that is to be instituted.

12. Case studies of gifted children reveal many individual differences in personality, motivation, and performance in children who all meet the criteria of giftedness.

Readings of Special Interest

Gardner, H. (1985). *Frames of mind: The theory of multiple intelligences.* New York: Basic Books. *Gardner is one of the most persuasive of the new psychologists studying intelligence. He presents his views of the seven types of intelligence (linguistic, musical, logical-mathematical, spatial, bodily kinesthetic, social, and self) that he believes form the base of human potential and presents some implications and applications that flow from his theory.*

Sternberg, R., & Davidson, J. (Eds.). (1986). *Conceptions of giftedness.* New York: Cambridge University Press. *This book contains a collection of chapters written by distinguished social scientists or educa-* tors who discuss their views of what giftedness means from their perspectives. It is probably the best source for understanding the newer approaches to intelligence.

Weinberg, R. (1989). Intelligence and IQ: Landmark issues and great debates. *American Psychologist, 44* (2), 98–104. *This is a brief but cogent review of the long-standing discussion about intelligence and the measures that we use to try to assess it. It reviews and brings up to date the nature-nurture controversy and presents some views of what the future of this issue is likely to be.*

References

Alvino, J., McDonnel, R., & Richert, S. (1981). National survey of identification practices in gifted and talented education. *Exceptional Children, 48,* 124–132.

Baldwin, A. Y. (1989). The purpose of education for gifted black students. In C. J. Maker & S. W. Schiever (Eds.), *Critical issues in gifted education: Defensible programs for cultural and ethnic minorities* (Vol. 2, pp. 237–245). Austin, TX: Pro-Ed.

Coleman, M., & Gallagher, J. (1992). *State policies for identification of non-traditional gifted students.* Chapel Hill: University of North Carolina at Chapel Hill, Gifted Education Policy Studies Program.

Cox, C. (1926). *Genetic studies of genius. Vol. 2. The early mental traits of three hundred geniuses.* Standford, CA: Stanford University Press.

Dirks, J., & Quarforth, J. (1981). Selecting children for gifted classes: Choosing for breadth vs. choosing for depth. *Psychology in the Schools, 18,* 437–449.

Frasier, M. (1991). Response to Kitano: The sharing of giftedness between culturally diverse and non-diverse gifted students. *Journal for the Education of the Gifted, 15* (1), 20–30.

Gallagher, J. J. (1991). Educational reform, values, and gifted students. *Gifted Child Quarterly, 35* (1), 12–19.

Gallagher, J., Aschner, M., & Jenné, W. (1967). *Productive thinking of gifted children in classroom interaction* (CEC Research Monograph Series B5). Arlington, VA: Council for Exceptional Children.

Gallagher, J. J., & Courtright, R. (1986). The educational definition of giftedness and its policy implications. In R. J. Sternberg & J. E. Davidson (Eds.), *Conceptions of giftedness* (pp. 93–111). Cambridge: Cambridge University Press.

Gear, G. (1978). Effects of training on teachers' accuracy in the identification of gifted children. *Gifted Child Quarterly, 22,* 90–97.

Goldberg, M. (1986). Issues in the education of gifted and talented children: Part III. *Roeper Review, 9,* 43–50.

Guilford, J. (1967). *The nature of human intelligence.* New York: Fund for the Advancement of Education.

Hagen, E. (1980). *Identification of the gifted.* New York: Teachers College Press.

Hoover, S., & Feldhusen, J. (1987). Integrating identification, school services, and student needs in secondary gifted programs. *Arkansas Gifted Education Magazine, 1*, 8–16.

Kaufman, A., & Harrison, P. (1986). Intelligence tests and gifted assessment: What are the positives? *Roeper Review, 3*, 154–159.

Kolloff, P. (1991). Special residential high schools. In N. Colangelo & G. Davis (Eds.), *Handbook of gifted education* (pp. 209–215). Boston: Allyn and Bacon.

Ramos-Ford, V., & Gardner, H. (1991). Giftedness from a multiple intelligences perspective. In N. Colangelo & G. Davis (Eds.), *Handbook of gifted education*. Boston: Allyn and Bacon.

Raven, J. (1956). *Progressive matrices*. London: H. K. Lewis & Co.

Renzulli, J. (1978, November). What makes giftedness? Reexamining a definition. *Phi Delta Kappan, 60*.

Renzulli, J. (1986). *Systems and models for developing programs for the gifted and talented*. Mansfield Center, CN: Creative Learning Press.

Renzulli, J., Reid, B., & Gubbins, E. (1992). *Setting an agenda: Research priorities for the gifted and talented through the year 2000*. Storrs, CT: The National Research Center on the Gifted and Talented.

Renzulli, J., Smith, L., White, A., Callahan, C., & Hartman, R. (1976). *Scales for rating the behavioral characteristics of superior students*. Wethersfield, CT: Creative Learning Press.

Richert, E. (1991). Rampant problems and promising practices in identification. In N. Colangelo & G. Davis (Eds.), *Handbook on gifted education* (pp. 81–96). Boston: Allyn and Bacon.

Scott, M., Perou, R., Urbano, R., Hogan, A., & Gold, S. (1992). The identification of giftedness: A comparison of white, Hispanic, and black families. *Gifted Child Quarterly, 36* (3), 131–139.

Shore, B., & Tsiamis, A. (1986). Identification by provision: Limited field test of a radical alternative for identifying gifted students. In K. Heller & J. Feldhusen (Eds.), *Identifying and nurturing the gifted* (pp. 93–102). Toronto: Hans Huber.

Silverman, L. (1986). The IQ controversy conceptions and misconceptions. *Roeper Review, 8*, 136–139.

Thorndike, R., Hagen, E., & Sattler, J. (1986). *Stanford Binet-Intelligence Scale*. Chicago: Riverside.

Wechsler, D. (1974). *Manual for the Wechsler Intelligence Scale for Children-Revised*. New York: Psychological Corporation.

Chapter 2

<hr>

Characteristics of
Gifted Students

Key Questions

- Why should the characteristics of gifted students be of educational significance?
- What happens to gifted students after they grow into adulthood?
- Are gifted students more emotionally unstable than the average student?
- Are boys more gifted in math and science than girls? Are girls more gifted in the arts than boys?
- In what way do families influence the development and crystalization of gifted abilities?
- Are racial and ethnic differences prevalent in giftedness? What might be the cause of such findings?

What are gifted children really like? There is a great curiosity about such children. Are they remarkably different from other children in social and personality characteristics? The question could be subdivided and posed: Are children with high creativity or great talent in the visual and performing arts different in personality characteristics? The expansion of the definition to include other abilities (see Chapter 1) makes it even more difficult to draw generalizations, but there have been a number of attempts to seek answers to these questions. In this chapter, as well as subsequent ones, the authors will try to cluster by subcategories what is known about these students.

As seen in the brief descriptions of Cranshaw, Zelda, Sam, Joe, and Stephanie, a superior performance in measures of intelligence does not guarantee homogeneity in family, social, or academic characteristics. Therefore, whatever general statements are made about characteristics of gifted students, there always will be many individual exceptions.

A common experience in the schools can illustrate the importance of exceptions to the rule. A psychologist may be invited to give a talk on the characteristics of gifted children. She states that research indicates gifted children are more emotionally stable than average children. This statement stimulates an experienced teacher to ask, "If what you say is true, how is it that I had a very emotionally unstable gifted child in my class last year?" The teacher then proceeds to document his statement with examples of the behavior and problems of this particular child. The psychologist responds by saying that she is talking about the "typical gifted child."

The teacher then remembers another child who contradicts the generalization the psychologist has made. In all too many instances, adequate communication is never reached. The teacher goes away mumbling that if only psychologists would get down to the teachers' level and experience the classroom situation, what they say could be of more use to the teacher. The psychologist goes away muttering to herself that teachers can't seem to go beyond their own experiences in such discussions.

The major difficulty in using an individual case to try to establish a general rule is this very problem of "typicalness." If the approximately three million children of 12 years of age were lined up on the interstate highway in New York, they could form a line extending all the way to Chicago. If a teacher then drove from New York to Chicago, he or she could get a reasonably good picture of the physical characteristics of the children. Suppose that the youngsters who have been called academically gifted children tied red bandanas around their necks; one could then get some general impression of whether, *on the average*, they tended to be larger or heavier than the other children without bandanas.

If someone came to the teacher after this interesting drive and asked what he or she thought about the physical characteristics of gifted children, the teacher might very well say, "Well, I thought they were a little bit heavier than the other children." At the same time, however, the teacher would remember the very thin, scrawny boy east of Toledo who, although he had a red bandana around his neck, did not fit the general statement that the teacher had just made.

The facts about characteristics of giftedness do not imply causation. For example, a discovery that gifted students are more popular should not cause one to jump to the conclusion that a high IQ score will cause one to have greater social popularity; it very well may be that a third factor, such as "high family status" in the community, is related and responsible for both.

If there is always this range of scores on any characteristic, what good does it do to talk about averages? Actually, such research plays an important role; it demonstrates that we should not expect that two characteristics such as giftedness and emotional maladjustment to appear together in a child. When they do, it is a sign that there is something very wrong and that there should be a careful assessment of what factors are causing this gifted child to become maladjusted instead of assuming that the giftedness would lead to maladjustment.

Life-Span Studies

The group of children who have high academic aptitude as measured by IQ test scores and academic attainment have been studied more thoroughly than any other group—probably because they are the easiest to discover. Cranshaw is a fine example of this type of child. He has been considered special by his teachers since he entered school. His manifest ability and leadership qualities have endeared him to teachers. Despite his favorable status, however, some interesting and important questions have been raised concerning Cranshaw and other children like him. Some of these are:

Is their intellectual aptitude equally distributed across various subject fields?
Do their high-ability scores predict high adult adjustment and achievement?
Does high mental ability hinder or facilitate social and emotional adjustment?
Does the very high IQ child have special adjustment problems?

There have been a few studies that have tried to look at gifted students over time to determine what happens to them at various educational levels or what happens to them after they leave school. Some studies begin with creative or gifted adults and retrospectively try to discover what they were like in school.

The Terman Longitudinal Study

Much of what we know about what happens to children with high academic aptitude when they become adults is the result of the remarkable contributions of Lewis Terman and his associates. They organized a longitudinal study of approximately 1,500 children, which has now been in progress for over 70 years. This sample of children was drawn from California schools in the 1920s. Field studies were conducted again on this sample in 1927–1928, 1939–1940, and 1951–1952, with mail followups periodically interspersed, the last of which was conducted in the late 1970s.

It is no coincidence that Terman is noted for his development of the Stanford-Binet Intelligence Test, as well as for his work with the gifted, since the test itself was the instrument by which he identified the superior children in his study. His findings of their overall superior school adjustment were influential in exploding the then-popular notion that gifted children were weak, puny, unpopular, and disturbed. A summary of the findings on the general characteristics of this group follows:

1. *The average member of our group is a slightly better physical specimen than the average….*
2. *For the fields of subject matter covered in our tests, the superiority of gifted over unselected children was greater in reading, language usage, arithmetical reasoning, science, literature and the arts. In arithmetical computation, spelling and factual information about history and civics, the superiority of the gifted was somewhat less marked….*
3. *The interests of gifted children are many-sided and spontaneous; they learn to read easily and read more and better books than the average child. At the same time, they make numerous collections, cultivate many kinds of hobbies, and acquire far more knowledge of play and games than the average child….*
4. *As compared with unselected children, they are less inclined to boast or to overstate their knowledge; they are more trustworthy when under temptation to cheat; their character preferences and social attitudes are more wholesome, and they score higher in a test of emotional stability….*
5. *The deviation of the gifted subjects from the generality is in the upward direction for nearly all traits. There is no law of compensation whereby the intellectual superiority of the gifted tends to be offset by inferiorities along non-intellectual lines. (Terman & Oden, 1951, pp. 23–24)*

Even if it can be shown that there is one group of children in the school system superior to the rest in ability to learn and who are above average in other characteristics, is it possible to demonstrate that such superiority will last? The great contribution of longitudinal studies is that children can be followed into adulthood to see how they adjust in later life.

Terman summarized the followup career performance of 800 men in his sample as follows:

The achievement of the group at mid-life is best illustrated by the case history of the 800 men, since only a minority of the women have gone out for professional careers. By 1950, when the men had an average age of 40 years, they had published 67 books (46 in the field of science, arts, and the humanities, and 21 books of fiction). They had published more than 1400 scientific, technical, and professional articles; over 200 short stories, novelettes, and plays and 236 miscellaneous articles on a great variety of subjects. They had also authored more than 150 patents. The figures on publications do not include the hundreds of publications by journalists that classify as news stories, editorials, or newspaper columns, nor do they include the hundreds, if not thousands, of radio and television scripts.... The level of education attained by this group was over ten times that expected of the general population. (1954, p. 224)

On the evidence of both the life-history followup and the test-retest information, it is fair to say that this group gave little evidence of declining from its lofty position attained on the tests in middle childhood. On the contrary, they showed a tendency to *increase* their advantage over the average individual. In this fashion it seems that the intellectually rich get richer. However, all was not milk and honey for every member of this gifted group. A later chapter will focus on the information available on the "underachievers" in the sample.

Oden noted, "All the evidence indicates that with few exceptions the superior child becomes the superior adult.... Two thirds of the men and almost as large a proportion of the women consider that they have lived up to their intellectual abilities fully or reasonably well" (1968, pp. 50–51). It also must be noted that no one of the singular brilliance of an Einstein or Edison or Lincoln has yet emerged from this group. It is likely that great fame relies on so many imponderables and is so statistically unlikely that even a sample as large as Terman's with its distinguished membership would not be expected to yield the genius that appears once or twice in a generation.

Women in Terman's Study

The consciousness-raising movement for women in past years has encouraged a reevaluation of some of Terman's data with particular attention to the women in the study. Sears and Barbee (1977) attempted to track the 671 women in the original sample and were able to locate 430 of them, about 65 percent. The researchers wished to know what the women were doing, their level of life satisfaction, and how they compared with other, more representative, women.

Sears and Barbee found the sample evenly split between homemakers and working women. The satisfaction that the women felt with their lives seemed to be linked with other well-recognized variables. For example, those women with happy family lives as children reported themselves to be more satisfied with their lives than women from unhappy families, regardless of the career choice.

In order to draw some comparison, Sears and Barbee found a representative sample of women drawn by the Institute for Social Research at the University of Michigan without regard to their intellectual ability. The times of interviews were relatively close: 1971 and 1972. Some of the findings are reported in Figure 2–1.

Contrary to what might be expected, these gifted women had experienced somewhat less divorce than the typical sample and were found less often in the "housewife" category. The most striking difference between the groups was found in college gradua-tion, with two-thirds of the Terman women graduating, whereas only 8 percent of the representative sample graduated from college. In terms of reported "life satisfaction," both sets of women were positive and roughly equivalent, whether or not they were employed or working as housewives. Sears and Barbee pointed out a truth worth remem-bering:

> *The life-style which brings happiness to one woman with one kind of life experi-ence does not necessarily bring it to another woman with a different experiential background.… Our gifted sample identified circumstances which would allow for the possibility of a happy life on their own without a husband, took advantage of these, and were asked to cope comfortably with their lives thereafter. (1977, p. 60)*

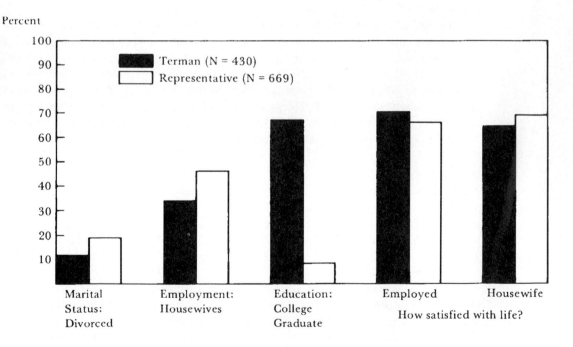

FIGURE 2–1   Terman Gifted Women versus Representative Women on Marital Status, Employment, Lifestyle

Source: Stanley, Julian C., et al. *The Gifted and the Creative: A Fifty-Year Perspective.* The Johns Hopkins University Press, Baltimore/London, 1978. Reprinted by permission.

Recently, there has been a growing recognition that however monumental this Terman study has been (over 60 years, so far), it has certain limitations worth remembering. We should remember that the children were chosen for the study on the basis of verbal skills, with little attention paid to abilities in the visual or performing arts, and that no adjustment was made for multicultural differences. Further, they generally came from large or medium-sized public schools, rather than rural areas. Since they were originally screened by teacher referral and then tested, it might well be that youngsters such as Joe and Sam would not even make it to the testing phase of the selection of the sample. Therefore, the Terman students are predominantly white, upper middle-class, and high achieving, and all of the Terman data presented here should be viewed with that fact in mind.

The Subotnik Studies

No matter how extensive or comprehensive the Terman longitudinal study was, one can wonder whether some of the findings were due, in part, to the particular time (1920s through 1940s) or place (California) of the study.

A recent followup of the graduates of the Hunter College Elementary School—a school especially designed for high-ability children—is instructive in this regard (Subotnik, Kassan, Summers, & Wasser, 1993). Subotnik and colleagues were able to track down 210 of the 600 persons who attended the school from 1948 to 1960 and interviewed 74 of them. Similar to the Terman study findings, the graduates shared certain general characteristics. For the most part, the Hunter College Elementary School graduates achieved at a high societal level, were predominantly professionals, and led comfortable and satisfying lives. Also in line with the Terman findings, none of them achieved a startling level of eminence because of a major accomplishment or creative breakthrough.

One major difference in the two studies, however, was in the role played by women. Only two of the women respondents identified themselves as predominantly homemakers, with the vast majority being career women with master's and doctoral degrees. In the Terman study, only about half of the women were career oriented. This difference seems to be clearly related to the changing role of women in the society during these different decades.

The authors of the Hunter College Elementary School study have raised an interesting question: Were these gifted students too comfortable to be creative? Most of these gifted students found it relatively easy to achieve at a comfortable level in society. Rather than the well-rounded person with many social interests that many of them turned out to be, the authors wonder if these students would have accomplished more if they had retained some sharp, ragged edges. Was the school actually *too* successful in encouraging them to experience widely? One of the women stated it this way:

> *I'm very admired and respected where I work.... I don't want to be a senior vice president; I don't want to be president of the bank. That doesn't interest me. I don't want to devote that much of my energy and time to my job. I want to have time to spend with my family, to garden, to play tennis, and see my friends and read.... I'm very happy with my life. (p. 78)*

Well, what is wrong with that? There seems to be a potential conflict between personal interests and societal interests. The authors felt that a certain amount of unhappiness or discord might be necessary to drive the person to commit enough energy to becoming more productive and successful. The case of Norbert Wiener, reported in his *Autobiography of an Ex-Prodigy*, is instructive. Growing up with a domineering father who drove him unmercifully to accomplish, he spent part of his adult life in mental hospitals—clearly an unhappy man. He also discovered and created the field of cybernetics, which has been at the heart of much of the electronic age in which we now live. Does this mean that we, as educators, should initiate trouble for the student in order to create an imbalance, so that the student is dissatisfied—and driven—to accomplish more? We always seem to come back to individual values and societal values when we deal with gifted individuals. We will revisit this issue in our chapter on creativity.

Bloom Retrospective Studies

Another classic retrospective investigation of how gifted performers became who they are was conducted by Benjamin Bloom and his colleagues. They posed the interesting question of what the early life and schooling was like for 120 world-class performers in tennis, sculpture, swimming, piano, mathematics, and science.

Through interviews with the performers and those close to them, Bloom (1985) found some general patterns in the life history for most of these persons regardless of their particular fields. Among the patterns was an early identification and encouragement of the talents of the children by the parents or other members of the family. The parents of these children often went to great lengths to ensure that they obtained competent instruction in their special area of talent, and modeled a pattern of strong commitment to particular interests in their own lives.

The enthusiasm of the parents for their children's talent provided a strong reinforcement for the child. One of the pianists reported, "There was an awful lot of praise and an awful lot of attention. Play for the family, play for this one, play for that one. There was so much reward for performing that I've always loved it" (Bloom, 1985, p. 37). The parents of the sculptors were avid collectors of the child's early art work: "I have everything he ever made...it was out on display in the house all the time" (p. 106). The parents of the research neurologists put a strong emphasis on professional work as an educational goal for their children: "I think from the time I was born, my mother and especially my father wanted me to become a professional person" (p. 355).

Despite these favorable early factors, however, Bloom and his colleagues felt that the great accomplishments of these individuals could *not* have been predicted from age 11 or 12. Being good as a young student is one thing, substantial adult accomplishment is quite another: "In between academic success and adult achievement is a long process of development requiring enormous motivation, much support from family, the best teachers and role models possible, much time, and a singleness of purpose and dedication that is relatively rare in the United States at present" (1985).

The special irony in this situation is that so many people feel that gifted students have it easy because of those special talents that they were born with, when, in reality, the gifted achievers probably are among the hardest working of all students!

Different Cognitive Processes

One educationally relevant question is whether gifted students show a different pattern of cognitive processes than do average students. For example, suppose that gifted students are significantly more able to carry out executive planning and decision making (the metathinking stressed by Sternberg in Chapter 1) than average students. If that is true—and it appears to be—then the teacher can give special assignments to such students that stress problem finding, problem solving, and decision making and can help them build more effective strategies for carrying out such tasks.

In an extensive review of available literature, Rogers found that gifted students are superior to average students in the following characteristics:

1. *Recognizing the problem to be solved,*
2. *Readily and spontaneously generating series of solution steps,*
3. *Setting priorities for the directions to take in solving a problem,*
4. *Selecting representation of information more like an expert would,*
5. *Deciding which resources to allocate to a problem-solving task,*
6. *Monitoring solutions systematically,*
7. *Taking longer preconceptual time in solving a problem—longer "front end" analysis. (1986, pp. 29–30)*

The presence of such skills challenges the teacher to put them to use in the assignments that they provide in the classroom. These students will be able to do problem solving and planning activities more extensively than average students, although that does not imply that such thinking processes should not also be stressed with average students to the level possible.

Another characteristic that Rogers found that differentiated the gifted from the average learners was the greater autonomy of gifted learners—that is, they are less influenced by the opinions of others (or the surroundings) and more able to make judgments based on the situation itself. This characteristic leads to a greater interest in independent study on the part of gifted students—a willingness to take responsibility for their own ideas.

The question as to whether giftedness represents a difference in degree or a major qualitative difference has very important educational implications. If the difference is merely one of degree, then the educational adaptations need be only ones of degree— assignment of more work or assignment of work on a more sophisticated developmental level. If there is a difference "in kind" or a qualitative difference, then a very different approach has to be taken to the educational adaptations for the students.

Berliner (1986) presented a convincing argument on whether giftedness is "more" or "different." He drew on the *catastrophe theory* of René Thom. In these terms, a "catastrophe" occurs when gradually changing phenomena suddenly evolve into something else. For example, when one lowers the temperature of water, it will at some point change its state into ice, or when one raises the temperature of water, it can change its liquid state into steam. In this case, a gradually changing phenomenon—the temperature—transforms water in a sudden and discontinuous result.

Berliner raised the analogy with giftedness, in that the gradual increase in cognitive abilities and skills reaches a point when it suddenly becomes different, as well. In this way, gradual increments in mathematical knowledge may at some point allow the individual to be able to master calculus and its many applications. That transforms a *quantitative difference* into a very *qualitative difference* when one compares a student who is ignorant of calculus and another student who is knowledgeable of it.

A student may gradually increase his or her vocabulary to the point where he or she is now able to produce an outstanding poem with impressive symbolism far beyond what would be possible for the average student. In this way, a quantitative difference produces a qualitatively different result.

As noted in the previous chapter, the essence of intellectual giftedness is the early mastery and comprehension of many concepts and clusters of concepts. This early development is apparently accomplished both through a genetically determined receptive nervous system and the progressive experience with symbol systems such as language, music, mathematics, and art. It is these associative networks and linkages that are mainly tapped by intelligence tests, which is why they predict academic achievement so well. The term *working memory* has been used to refer to the ability of the individual to access these stored associative networks.

Carr and Borkowski (1986) have pointed out the link between *divergent thinking* (the ability to give many different and unique responses) and *memory skills*. The researchers gave tests of *metamemory* (students'ability to plan how to memorize material efficiently) and divergent thinking to a group of 98 fifth- and sixth-grade children participating in programs for gifted students in the Midwest. They found a modest, but significant, correlation between scores on memory and scores on creativity.

To understand why there would be such a relationship, imagine for a moment what the response of the highly gifted students would be to the divergent thinking task of "How many ways can we solve the wombat problem in Australia?" or "the plight of reindeer in Alaska?" It is doubtful that even the brightest students in the United States could produce many useful responses to these questions. It is clear, then, that the ability to respond effectively to divergent thinking questions is based on the presence, *within the working memory of the gifted child*, of a large number of these associative networks that the child can call on for diverse and original responses to such questions. It also reflects the important goal of educators to help the gifted student develop and master as many of these associative networks as possible. This means teaching content as well as thinking strategies.

Carr and Borkowski stated that "explicit training of metacognitive skills may enhance academic achievement, intelligence and creative problem solving" (1986, p. 43). This study and many others combine to suggest strongly that the blending together of instruction in student strategies with significant content is the direction that we should be following in gifted education.

Performance of Academically Gifted Students

Once the basic skills of reading have been learned, there are almost no additional cognitive barriers that need to be surmounted before youngsters can proceed, often on their own, to rapidly improve their breadth of knowledge and skills. However, in the area of arithmetic, achievement is measured by a student's ability to progress through a series of a well-defined hierarchy of skills. Thus, in order to attain a score in arithmetic computation at the sixth-grade level, a third-grade child would not necessarily have to have great depth of mathematical knowledge but merely knowledge of such arithmetic operations as subtraction of fractions or long division.

If it is true that the results of arithmetic competence are dependent on the way achievement tests were constructed, then perhaps results in other content areas also are dependent on the nature of the tests. A gifted child may score four grades above his or her own grade level in social studies, but that may merely mean that he or she has absorbed an extensive collection of isolated facts and does not necessarily have a comprehensive knowledge of the basic concepts or ideas of social studies or how to apply these ideas in other situations. Until we can become more effective constructors of achievement tests that measure depth of understanding as well as breadth, such as the new emphasis on outcome-based assessment, these skyrocketing achievement scores obtained by gifted students may mean much less than we would hope.

The individual profiles of Cranshaw and Zelda that show them three or four years in advance of their agemates are by no means uncommon. Unless some special programming is provided for them, they will be condemned to review material in their school that they mastered two or three years ago.

It is always interesting to compare results in such studies with children from different cultures. Lovell and Shields (1967) reported on the first 50 youngsters they examined who scored an IQ of 140 or more in two large cities in the north of England. They used similar rating scales to that used by Terman and found that the mean rating given by British teachers for this sample was very close to that given by American teachers to Terman's sample 40 years before. The children who scored in this high IQ range were rated outstanding in desire to know, originality, truthfulness, willpower, perseverance, and sense of humor, among other characteristics. The poorest rating, which was still rated "above average," was freedom from vanity and egotism—which seemed to be a problem particularly with boys.

A similar finding was noted by Landau (1981), who analyzed responses of 537 gifted children in Israel chosen by intelligence tests, compared with 180 children of average ability. These gifted students accepted the adjectives *dominant, conscientious, self-sufficient, self-disciplined,* and *bright* as applying to them. They showed many interests and engaged in many activities, and Landau concluded that "the gifted child is a multifaceted, multivaried human being" (p. 31).

With results from three differing cultures and a half century in time showing essential agreement, there is some confidence that Terman's results are representative of the high-academic-aptitude group, even given the limitations already noted on the possible bias of the selection process in both samples.

Self-Images

It has become increasingly popular to study the self-image of gifted students and to compare such self-concepts with those of students with average ability. For example, a large study of the self-image of mentally gifted high school students was conducted by Tidwell (1980). She collected data on 1,593 school-identified, mentally gifted secondary school students from a large metropolitan school district in California; girls and minority groups were well represented. All of these students (mean IQ score of 137) were administered measures of self-concept, self-esteem, locus of control ("Do I feel I can control my life?"), and attitudes toward school and fellow students.

The findings were similar to the findings from the Terman studies. This group showed a high self-concept, viewed themselves as good learners, liked school, and felt that they could control their lives through their own actions. One interesting finding was that they viewed themselves as happy, even though many felt unpopular with their peers. Their feelings of happiness apparently did not depend on peer approval.

Hoge and McSheffrey (1991) attempted to answer this question by giving the Harter Self Perception Profile to a group of 280 academically gifted pupils, in grades 5 through 8, who were in self-contained enrichment classes. The Harter scale has five subscales: *scholastic, social, athletic, appearance,* and *conduct,* in addition to a global self-concept. The findings from this study indicated that the self-images of these students were relatively independent from one another. For example, a student can have a high opinion of self in the scholastic area and a low opinion in the athletic area. Zelda would surely fit into that pattern.

Hoge and McSheffrey concluded that social acceptance was the major factor of general self-esteem. Perceived scholastic competence was also a significant contributor to global self-worth, particularly with girls. The gifted student can feel good about himself or herself in some dimensions but not necessarily in others, and, in fact, can have a rather poor opinion of self in certain domains such as social acceptance or physical appearance.

Some studies show gifted students have higher self-concepts, some show lower self-concepts, and still others show equal levels of self-concept with average students. One clue we can use to help solve this puzzle is the particular tests that are used help to determine the results. If a self-concept test is measuring general self-image ("Do you feel good about yourself?"), we can obtain limited differentiated results through such comparisons of average and gifted samples. On the other hand, if the test asks specific questions about specific domains in self-concept (social, academic, physical, etc.), then gifted students consistently show a higher self-image in the *academic* area—and why shouldn't they? (Kelly & Jordan, 1991).

When answering one of these self-concept scales, Zelda correctly perceives her superior academic performance compared to that of her classmates. On that subscale of the self-concept test, she scores quite high. However, she also correctly sees that her social acceptance and her physical abilities are not outstanding and scores herself as average or below on these subtests.

If we use only the global overall self-concept score, then Zelda may not look very different from her peers. But if we ignore the intraindividual differences in Zelda's responses across various self-concept domains, we will have an inaccurate portrait of her complex and multiple self-images.

Incidentally, since self-concept is often based on individuals measuring themselves against their available peers, the academic self-image of gifted students often goes down when they enter a special class or a school with other gifted students. They correctly see that they are no longer so superior to the members of their group; they become more modest in their self-assessment on the self-concept scales (Jenkins-Friedman & Murphy, 1990; Olszewski, Kulieke, & Willis, 1987).

Social Status of High-Aptitude Students

Cranshaw is one of the most popular students in his class. His good humor, willingness to help others, and lack of negative personality characteristics lead him to be well accepted and an often-chosen friend and workmate in his classroom. The results of a multitude of studies, most of them using sociometric techniques that ask students to identify friends or potential workmates or seatmates in class, show that children with high academic aptitude are generally more popular and better accepted than the average student in the classroom, contrary to one of the most persistent misconceptions about such children.

Although Cranshaw was revealed popular by sociometric techniques, Zelda was not. She irritated other youngsters with her superior, know-it-all attitude and did not seek out a large number of friends. (It is likely that her parents would obtain a similar rating of limited social acceptance if such were taken in their neighborhood.)

Therefore, the generalization that high-academic-aptitude children are popular does not fit Zelda's case. The teacher soon realizes that intellectually gifted children are usually popular or unpopular for the same reasons that other children are popular or unpopular. To the degree to which these children have desirable characteristics such as openness, willingness to help, and good humor, they are popular. To the degree to which they show opposite tendencies, they will not be popular regardless of their ability level.

Joe is quite a different matter from either Zelda or Cranshaw. He probably would get a number of peer choices, but this is not likely to bring much comfort to his teacher. It is likely that an examination of the children who choose Joe would reveal that *they* are also difficult children to cope with in the school situation, and the grouping together of such students could cause difficulty in handling the class. Sam, with his good humor and bubbling energy, is also likely to show up positively on many of the social choices of the other youngsters in the classroom.

Figure 2–2 shows two examples of how gifted students cope with the special problems of being called gifted.

FIGURE 2–2   Gifted Children on Being "Gifted"

My sister is very jealous of me. She gets mad at me when I bring home an award for something. But I try to make her feel better by taking her to the show, buying her a gift, or something to make her feel better. I love her and don't want her to be mad at me. I have lost lots of friends because they have gotten mad at me for receiving awards and for being called on to watch the class, or help the teacher pass out papers, or something like that.

But I have nice friends in my class my own age, and they are gifted students! I enjoy that because they understand what I mean. I enjoy doing book reports and commercials. And we also got to do an interview with a person who we admire such as a news reporter, governor, or someone like that. So I interviewed Don Woods: it was fun. I got to go into his office and on their set. I enjoyed it a lot. I enjoy going to school and learning new things and meeting new people. I enjoy acting, singing, reading, and swimming.[*]

Being gifted can be one of the greatest advantages in school and other places. It can mean things come easier, we catch on faster, get done faster, and have a lot of time to do things we like. Gifted kids usually use these advantages and are very thankful for them, but there is also a price to pay for being gifted that I think parents never realize.

To begin with, I want to draw your attention to what being referred to as "gifted" can do to a gifted kid. If a kid is called "gifted" in front of a class, friends, or anybody, they think the Kid is a real nerd who spends all of his time doing extra projects, homework, reading, and helping the teacher. I think you're smart enough to understand what that can do to someone.[†]

[*]*Source*: Patricia Dobbs, Life as a gifted student, *Roeper Review*, 1988, 8 (1). Reprinted with permission of Roeper Review, P.O. Box 329, Bloomfield Hills, MI 48303.

[†]*Source:* Rolf Hains, Dear Mom and Dad, *Roeper Review,* 1988, 10 (4). Reprinted with permission of *Roeper Review*, P.O. Box 329, Bloomfield Hills, MI 48303.

Personality Characteristics of High-Aptitude Students

Whether a gifted individual is well adjusted or disturbed is a matter of considerable interest to all of us because of the potential impact such a person may have on our lives. If a truck driver of average ability becomes mentally disturbed, he is likely to be a serious problem for his family, friends, and those unfortunate drivers he may meet on the highway. If a gifted secretary of state or the foreign minister of another nation becomes deranged, the potential for international mischief is enormous. It is more than casual curiosity, then, that prompts us to ask whether there is a link between genius and insanity. Fortunately, the available evidence suggests that this link does not occur, except in unusual sets of circumstances.

Although the Terman studies performed a major service for gifted students in abolishing the image of gifted students as physically weak and sickly, it ironically created something of a new myth that also is troubling to those who work with gifted students. This new myth is that gifted students are inevitably well adjusted and have fewer problems or troubles than average students and, by extension, require less care and attention in the counseling area.

An interesting study by Derevensky and Coleman (1989) asked 70 gifted youngsters (ages 8 to 13) in a Toronto school for the gifted, "What are the things to be afraid of?" The answers of these gifted students involved fears generally expressed by youngsters who were chronologically older. The gifted students were less involved with fears of ghosts or animals than in such topics as death and nuclear war. The most common fears mentioned were nuclear war, death (to themselves and to loved ones), and violence (the fear of being molested, sexually abused, etc.), a media focus at the time of the study.

The tendency of gifted students to focus on larger societal fears such as war, famine, or climatic changes is confirmed in other studies by George and Gallagher (1968) and Clark and Hankins (1985). It appears that gifted students' increased ability to imagine and conceptualize allows them to paint their fears on a larger conceptual canvas than youngsters of more limited abilities.

One night Zelda's parents came into her bedroom to find her shivering under her blankets and obviously in some anxiety. When they asked her what was wrong, she said that she had had a bad dream about a "nuclear winter," which frightened her with the prospect that all humankind would be destroyed. The surface appearance of easy adjustment of these youngsters to their academic setting can often mask or disguise underlying fears that need to be recognized and expressed. Gifted children, like all students, should have the opportunity to work through their fears through discussion and expression.

The evidence remains strong that the earlier findings of good general emotional adjustment holds true for these students. A large sample of over 5,500 children between the ages of 6 and 19 were tested with the Revised Children's Manifest Anxiety Scale. The 584 children in the sample who were attending classes for the gifted were extracted from the sample and their responses compared with the rest of the students (Scholwinski & Reynolds, 1985). To questions such as "I have trouble making up my mind," "It is hard for me to get to sleep at night," "I have bad dreams," "I worry a lot of the time," "My feelings get hurt easily," and so on, the gifted students scored significantly lower as a group on all of the anxiety scales.

The number of investigations carried out on the personalities of gifted individuals has now become quite impressive. A recent review of the available studies on the personality dimensions of gifted adolescents (Olszewski-Kubilius, Kulieke, & Krasney, 1988) provides a good summary of those findings: "When differences are found between gifted students and their non-gifted, same-age peers, they tend to be favorable to gifted students. Gifted individuals have been found to exhibit lower levels of anxiety and tend to be well adjusted with fewer indications of psychological problems" (p. 351).

It is always worth reminding ourselves that these are averages that are being reported and there are always exceptions to these general statements. Joe, for example, proves that such statements do not include all gifted students, as does the growing literature on suicides and delinquency of some gifted students.

Another distinction between averages and individuals is provided by a study of loneliness and depression in 175 junior and senior high school students who attended the Governor's School of South Carolina (Kaiser & Berndt, 1985). The researchers found that the majority of gifted adolescents are exceptionally well adjusted and that their success goes hand in hand with a healthy self-confidence and self-esteem, but Kaiser and Berndt also found that "nearly one in eight of the gifted students in our research reported not only significant loneliness but also depression and anger. A pattern of depressive symptoms (helplessness, introversion, guilt, and low self esteem) together with high stress, should be considered indicators of a possible success depression" (p. 76).

A "success depression" can come from being unjustly rewarded for results that did not come from one's own efforts or initiatives. Zelda occasionally faces a type of "success depression" when her uncle and aunt come to visit and rave over Zelda's high grades, when Zelda privately believes that she obtained those grades with little effort and feels a little guilty about accepting such praise.

Suicide

The issue of suicides in gifted individuals has been addressed in an interesting study by Shneidman (1971). He chose a sample of 30 individuals from the Terman longitudinal study, 5 of whom had committed suicide as adults. Using measures of *perturbation* (a degree of upset over interpersonal relationships or perceived failure), indicators of suicide and *lethality* (a retrospective view of one's life with thoughts on death), the role of the "significant other" in one's life, and the view of a "burned-out life," judges were able to predict with great accuracy which 5 of the 30 individuals committed suicide. Basically, this finding demonstrated that the forces influencing suicides for any person are also operating when a gifted adult takes his or her own life.

Delinquency

Even though the majority of identified gifted students turn out to be law-abiding and moral citizens, there are interesting exceptions. What leads some highly intelligent children to become delinquents or criminals, and do they differ in some significant way from delinquents of average ability?

There are few research studies, and limited anecdotal evidence, to help answer these questions. Anolik (1979) compared 30 institutionalized male juvenile offenders with IQ scores of 115 or above with 30 who were of average ability on tests of personality and opinion. These comparisons indicated that both groups had had maladaptive family experiences, had been underachievers in school, and were mildly psychologically disturbed. The offenses committed by both bright and average groups did not differ.

If the bright delinquents differed from the average delinquents in any way, it was in a tendency to be less neurotic and psychopathic. Anolik concluded that bright delinquents might be more responsive to such interventions as group psychotherapy. However, these results reinforce the general pattern that differences between bright or gifted samples and average groups are shades of degree, not kind.

One of the standard ways of studying the relationship between giftedness and delinquency has been to find out how many adjudicated delinquents score high on tests of intellectual ability. Such an approach will inevitably underestimate the number of students in this dual category of giftedness-delinquency. The reason for the underestimate would be that many of these students turn out to be substantial underachievers who would not be nominated for programs for gifted or recognized as gifted by teachers or other educational personnel (Seeley, 1984).

After an entire school career of poor performance, it is likely that adjudicated delinquents will not do well on an IQ test. An interesting question is: Why should they *want* to do well on an IQ test? To please the teacher? The principal? Not likely!

Mahoney (1980) pointed out that gifted youths become delinquents only when environmental conditions are exceptionally unfavorable. Still, we will not be totally comfortable with that answer until we have studied in more depth the population of delinquents to see how many potentially gifted youngsters might be hiding undiscovered there. As Seeley said, "These youths have none of the usual markings" (1984, p. 69).

One further observed characteristic is worth noting. Many teachers have testified that one of the most troublesome personal characteristics of gifted children is their all-consuming interest on one topic (e.g., dinosaurs, computers, astronauts, etc.) to the exclusion of everything else. But there is another trend, as well, recognized in many high-achieving gifted adolescents, and that is the desire to "eat the whole world," to master all subjects, and to be so interested in everything that they cannot bear to make a decision, to seek one career direction that would, in effect, cause them to abandon all the others to which they have been attracted.

Once we recognize this problem, we can understand how many multitalented gifted students delay and refuse to bring closure to a career choice. They cannot bear to leave all those "might-have-beens" behind. An inability to resolve this issue causes some gifted individuals to take an assortment of doctorates and law and medical degrees as they continue to pursue a somewhat adolescent desire to master all knowledge.

Gender, Racial, and Ethnic Differences

One of the most disturbing results of many of the early studies on the characteristics of high-aptitude children was the consistency with which these studies yielded ratios of gender, race, and ethnic backgrounds in gifted populations that were different from those that occurred in the general population. For example, Terman (1925) noted in his initial studies a gender ratio in his gifted sample of 138 males to 100 females compared with 106 males to 100 females in live births (children who survived birth).

Terman also noted major ethnic and racial disparities: "Data on racial origin indicate that, in comparison with the general population of the cities concerned, our gifted show a 100 percent excess of Jewish blood; a 25 percent excess of parents who are of native parentage; a probable excess of Scotch ancestry; and a very great deficiency of Latin and Negro ancestry" (1925, p. 82).

If the IQ score represented genetic potential exclusively, then we would have on our hands the possibility of a socially explosive piece of information—that some ethnic or racial groups might be superior to others in intellectual development, to say nothing of the conclusion that men appear to be smarter than women.

Now that environmental factors are accepted as playing an important role in the full development of crystalized abilities, we no longer have to puzzle over such strange "genetic" findings, since those groups doing less well on IQ scores are clearly those who have had less opportunity for full intellectual development through the maximum use of environmental opportunities.

Gender Differences

Most studies of early intellectual development (before the age of 8) fail to yield differences between the sexes on measures of general intelligence (fluid abilities). However, the measurement of specific aptitudes (crystalized abilities) within specific intellectual domains changes that portrait. Fox summarized the available information on gender differences in the field of mathematical aptitude as follows:

> *By the end of secondary school years, young men are quite superior to young women with respect to mathematical reasoning ability. Among very gifted seventh and eighth graders, the gap at the higher levels of mathematical reasoning ability is quite large. In three years of testing mathematically gifted students, the Study of Mathematically Precocious Youth (SMPY) found 167 boys, and only 19 girls, who as seventh and eighth graders scored 640 or above on the Scholastic Aptitude Test in Mathematics. (1977, p. 115)*

The effects that the overall school climate has on producing such results can be seen in an investigation by Casserly (1979), who studied 12 U.S. high schools that enrolled over twice the proportion of girls in their Advanced Placement mathematics and science courses than the national average. These high-incidence schools, as far as girls' participation is concerned, had the following characteristics: Teachers of such courses actively recruited girls for the classes. These teachers exhibited few signs of sex-role sterotyping in their thinking or in their classroom behavior. They expected high-level performance from the girls as well as the boys, and they demanded it from both. Such high-incidence schools demonstrate the importance of creating a comfortable and encouraging environment for learning, particularly when there are other social and cultural barriers that can be thrown in the way of children like Zelda and Sam.

For these purposes, Zelda and Stephanie are members of a minority group—a group that has nothing to do with religion or skin color or ethnic characteristics. They are girls—gifted girls. Zelda and Stephanie's strong desires to do well in school have come up against stereotypes of women's roles and biases that, while apparently lessening, are still present. Zelda has heard an aunt say, "She is so bright, it is too bad she wasn't born a boy." Stephanie has been told by teachers, her peers, and the media that girls "don't like science and mathematics."

Like other minority groups, gifted girls are in danger of behaving according to the stereotype constructed for them by the culture. After all, if people are told often enough that they are lazy, greedy, drug prone, or any of the other stereotypes circulated for minority groups, many of the members of that group will start to act that way. If a girl has learned that girls do not argue with the opinions of others and are somewhat unimaginative, she may begin to believe it and act accordingly.

Boys and girls apparently grow up in markedly different worlds in the United States, where different social roles and different life patterns are imposed from without, by both family and culture (Morse & Bruch, 1970). Some girls appear to avoid competition, especially when it is competition with boys, and even to avoid success—which they believe can bring negative social consequences (Lavach & Lanier, 1975).

This idea is seemingly borne out in other studies (Wolleat, 1979). Generally, girls have been found to do as well as, or better than, boys in the area of school achievement. Yet in adulthood, women seem rarely to reach the top level of creative scientist, writer, or musician, for example. This limited production does not seem to be explained entirely by their often having to play the complex combination of roles of wife, mother, and career person. A lifelong set of lower intellectual expectations for women by the society, and sometimes by their family, can also have the effect of diminishing ambition and eroding self-confidence. Khatena (1982) summarized the situation by pointing out that gifted women may interrupt their career during childbearing years, may take less desirable jobs in order to be with their husbands, and in many of the ways noted above show a conflict between career and family not found in males. The special influence of gender role on performance will be touched on further in Chapter 4.

Racial and Ethnic Differences

The growing number of minority students in U.S. schools causes us to raise the issue of crystalized abilities and aptitudes in these groups. How much of a rarity is Sam? Does the fact that he is from a racial minority and gifted make him an extraordinary, unusual person? Is the discovery of Sam and his talents a rare find? According to the research available in this area, the answer is that finding a gifted student who is a member of a minority group is not unusual, but it is less likely, using standard measures. Although students with high academic aptitude can be found in all walks of life and in all racial and ethnic groups, they are more likely to be found in some groups than in others. The groups with a higher than average prevalence seem to place a greater emphasis on intellectual and academic values and have more extensive opportunities to develop talents and skills already present in the child.

Another finding, reproduced a number of times, is that although generally more boys than girls are found in searches for gifted and talented youngsters, in African-American populations high-ability girls outnumber the boys more than two to one. The lack of opportunities for African-American boys compared to those available to African-American girls in the culture leads one to speculate that part of the full realization of intellectual potential lies in perceived opportunities in the adult society by the youngster involved. The same reasoning can lead to a possible explanation as to why more gifted boys than gifted girls are found in the general population. It is one more piece of evidence that the schools cannot be viewed apart from the society and the culture in which they exist. The failure of schools to develop African-American, or Hispanic, or Native-American potential can be seen as part of a general failure of the culture to provide opportunities and academic incentives.

Very High-Ability Children

If a child attains a remarkably high IQ score—say, a Binet IQ of 170 or 180 (achieved by 1 child in about 100,000)—does this set him or her too far apart from other students, socially and intellectually? Many people feel that it does. Tim is an example of a child who scored at the top level of the Wechsler Intelligence Scale for Children. At the age of 8, in the middle of the second grade, Tim was capable of giving definitions like this:

Diamond: a hard rock mined in Africa that sparkles and is of high value
Gamble: to risk something, to take chances
Shilling: a dollar in some other country
Microscope: like a short-range telescope to see something very small
Belfry: a bell tower

His fund of information was truly remarkable. Even when he was missing some quite advanced questions, he was revealing his superiority, as in the following examples:

What does the stomach do? *Takes your food and throws it all over your body.*
What is the capital of Greece? *Rome.*
Where does turpentine come from? *Maple trees.*
What does C.O.D mean? *Careful on Delivery.*

Can Tim, and other children like him, ever communicate effectively with their agemates? In this instance, Tim was having trouble socially, but it had to do only indirectly with his ability. In reality, his trouble was a sense of inferiority—not intellectual inferiority, of course, but physical inferiority. In order to hide his feelings about his poor ability in sports, he tried to impress other children with his mental ability; this was not a striking success. However, his father found some time to help him with his physical coordination and sports skills. Tim's obnoxious mannerisms were reduced coincident with his better performance in the physical area.

Norbert Wiener is a remarkable example of early extreme giftedness combined with parental ambition. At the age of 7, he entered school and was placed in the third grade. By 9 years of age, he was admitted to high school; by age 11, he entered Harvard College; and by age 18, he had a Ph.D. in mathematics. He had to spend several years in relatively low-level occupations because people were wary of hiring an 18-year-old Ph.D. But was formal schooling the major contributor to Wiener's performance? Wiener himself reported that his father tutored him at home and that other specialists tutored him as well. His father was a perfectionist and severe taskmaster who accepted only high-level performance and accuracy.

Wiener's early expertise in mathematics finally became translated into his origination of a new field—that of cybernetics. In many ways, our computer-based society owes much of its origins to the genius of Norbert Wiener. Wiener paid a high personal price in terms of periodic mental illness and general personal unhappiness. Was all of that early family pressure and drive to achieve worth it? Of whom shall we ask the question—of Wiener himself, or of the generation of people who live better lives for his excellent, if personally tormented, work? We might get different answers.

One of the earlier investigators deeply concerned about the problems of extremely high-ability children was Leta Hollingworth. One of her projects was an intensive analysis of 12 children who scored above 180 Binet IQ. According to test-standardization data, such children should appear about once in one million cases. She felt that these youngsters were so far beyond the abilities of their age group that they would have difficulties in making both educational and social adjustments. Hollingworth suggested that there were five general conduct problems with which they must learn to deal:

1. *To find enough hard and interesting work at school.*
2. *To suffer fools gladly.*
3. *To keep from becoming negativistic toward authority.*
4. *To keep from becoming hermits.*
5. *To avoid the formation of habits of extreme chicanery. (1942, p. 299)*

Naturally, a child who appears only once in a million times is of such an unusual nature and character that the school program cannot possibly be drastically revised or changed in order to fit his or her particular needs. What is needed may be special tutoring sessions on an individual basis, with a skilled person who realizes the particular pitfalls awaiting this type of youngster.

Even with children of extraordinary ability, it appears to take a favorable set of educational circumstances to bring them to full bloom. Feldman studied three prodigies who at a preadolescent age were already performing remarkable feats in chess playing and music. Feldman listed what he believed to be the common circumstances in their young lives.

1. *The children are taught by remarkable teachers, each a master of his field and a master teacher.*
2. *Each teacher has a distinctive style; the styles are different, but there is a coherence to how each teacher carries out his plan of instruction.*
3. *All curricula (in chess, music, and I believe in mathematics as well, al-though I have had less experience in the latter field) recapitulate in some sense the history of the field. For example, in chess, both masters guide their students through the games of all the world champions of chess, often going back 150 years.*
4. *The teachers are at least as passionate and committed to the field in which they work as are their pupils; they are also enormously dedicated teachers, reflective and vigilant about their instruction.*
5. *None of the teachers was a child prodigy himself. (1979, p. 343)*

Albert and Runco (1986) have been following a group of 40 boys who all scored above 150 IQ, in a longitudinal study, together with a sample of 26 boys who achieved in the top 40 of participants in the Study of Mathematically Precocious Youth. The families of these boys with high IQ scores appeared to have different personalities from those boys high in mathematics, stressing achievement through independence, whereas the parents of the high IQ boys were more sociable, socially confident, and self-controlled and accepting. Albert and Runco presented an interesting hypothesis that *differences in parental personality*, rather than similarities, may foster child creativity by creating an early experience of family complexity necessary to the development of the creative potential.

Most of the published descriptions of child prodigies are of boys who have achieved outstanding early fame in fields such as mathematics, chess playing, music, and science. The impression that is left is that there are few girls that would qualify for the term *prodigy*. Goldsmith (1987) has corrected that view by describing collections of girl prodigies in art, music, chess playing, science, and mathematics. She has also pointed out that historically, there have been examples of outstanding women prodigies despite the societal bias and prejudice against them: "The existence of girl prodigies—even in times and cultures which attach relatively little value to the feminine pursuit of excellence—provides evidence for the power of individual determination to achieve self-expression. But it is still sobering to contemplate how many gifts have gone unheeded over the centuries" (p. 82).

Origins of Academic Giftedness

The search for the origins of academic giftedness is a fascinating one. Is heredity foremost or is environment? Or are they equally important? If the environment is influential, which environment? At what age level? (Similar issues on students superior in the visual and performing arts will be discussed in Chapter 8.)

Genetic Influences in High Academic Aptitude

There is no question that academic aptitude is inherited, at least to some extent. Educators are so involved in environmental changes that they often overlook or underestimate the influence of heredity. Our general observation that most gifted families resemble those of Zelda and Cranshaw, whereas many fewer are like Sam's, does not help us answer the question. If a child has both highly intelligent parents *and* a rich environment, we still do not know to which characteristic, or in which combination, we can assign the favorable results.

The emergence of young prodigies such as those referred to by Feldman in the previous section is one indication of genetic potential, since it is hard to conceive of any combination of environmental circumstances that would result in a 7-year-old master chess player or pianist without extraordinary native ability to begin with. Also, Sam's presence in the gifted group would be another indicator of genetic origin, because his environment, if anything, is aggressively anti-intellectual in character and not supportive of intellectual growth.

Another phenomenon not entirely explained is the tendency for firstborn children to be more talented than their subsequent siblings. Among National Merit finalists from two-child families, there are about twice as many firstborn as second-born. In three-child families there are as many firstborn as second- and third-born children combined. The same result was obtained on a group of 600 talented African-American students (Altus, 1966).

Zajonc (1976) reported on the relationship of ability to family size and spacing of children. He found that, over a 20-year period of time, students who were the born first in the family traditionally scored higher in Scholastic Aptitude Tests than did students who came later in the birth order. Zajonc accounted for this consistent difference by a confluence model, which states that firstborn children have more opportunity to exclusive attention and communication with parents, are likely to be more dominant, and have more opportunities to be rewarded for intellectual performance.

Scarr and Arnett summarized decades of research on the developmental patterns of adoptive children. The purpose of such research was to determine if these children's intellectual abilities more closely conformed to that of their biological parents (heredity) or to their adoptive parents (environment). They concluded:

> *The adoption studies support the notion that adopted children benefit...from their better-than-average home environments (including schools, neighborhoods, and other correlated environments). In this sense intelligence is malleable.... At the same time, the similarity to the IQ correlations of biological mothers with their children given up for adoption indicates the likelihood of a genetic constraint on the degree to which individual differences in intelligence may be influenced. (1986, p. 79)*

All of these evidences lead to the prevailing view that in the relationship between genetics and environment, genetics sets boundary lines of intellectual performance—an upper limit and a lower limit—that the individual will be able to achieve. Whether the individual is near the top of that boundary line or near the bottom is dependent on his or her environmental circumstances.

This point rarely has been made better than in comments made over 100 years ago by Frances Galton, reported in Dennis and Dennis:

> *Everybody who has trained himself to physical exercises discovers the extent of his muscular powers to a nicety. When he begins to walk, to row, to use the dumbbells, or to run, he finds to his great delight that his thews strengthen, and his endurance of fatigue increases day after day.... But the daily gain is soon discovered to diminish, and at last it vanishes altogether. His maximum performance becomes a rigidly determinate quantity.... There is a definite limit to the muscular powers of every man, which he cannot by education or exertion overpass.*
>
> *This is precisely analogous to the experience that every student has had, the working of his mental powers.... He glories in his newly developed mental grip and growing capacity for application and, it may be, fondly believes it to be within his reach to become one of the heroes who have left their mark upon the history of the world. The years go by; he competes in examinations of school and college, over and over again with his fellows, and soon finds his place among them. He knows he can beat such and such of his competitors; that there are some with whom he runs on equal terms, and others whose intellectual feats he cannot even approach. (1976, p. 2)*

Families of Gifted Children

A number of attempts have been made to bring together a variety of information related to gifted children and their families (Olszewski, Kulieke, & Buescher, 1987). There are some interesting structural differences in families of gifted children that encourage a variety of speculations. As noted earlier, one of these is the clear indication that many gifted students are *firstborn* children in their families. Another structural factor of interest is the high incidence of parental loss, particularly the loss of father, among eminent individuals. One explanation for this relationship is that "father loss" frees the gifted child from adult dominance and allows him or her to develop early intellectual maturity and the freedom to do creative work (Albert, 1980).

If such structural features as birth order and parental loss seem to influence the full development of intellectual ability, then surely the family interrelationships would also be expected to determine the shape and form of the expression of giftedness of the student. The accumulation of evidence is quite compelling on this point. Families in which there are high expectations for academic achievement, and in which the family environments are both cohesive and child centered, result in high-performing gifted students who may not, however, be the most creative of individuals. In contrast, creative children and adults seem to "have family environments that stress independence rather than interdependence, are less child centered, have tense family relationships, and more expression of negative affect which results in both a cognitive freeing and motivation to attain power and leadership" (Olszewski, Kulieke, & Willis, 1987, p. 25).

Cornell and Grossberg (1987) compared the results of the Family Environment Scale—given to the parents of 83 children (ages 7 to 11) who were attending special programs for gifted students—with teacher ratings and measures of personality adjustment given to the students. They found a positive link between mutually supportive and open family relationships and the child's rating on self-esteem and overall adjustment. The families of gifted students scored high on cohesion and expressiveness, which indicate that the families place great value on mutually supportive relationships and open expression of thoughts and feelings in the family, but do *not* stress achievement orientation.

In Zelda's family, for example, Zelda is highly prized by her parents, who are particularly demonstrative over her academic performance and success. Having a good relationship with her parents, Zelda is anxious to please her parents and understands that what will please them most is her obtaining good grades and distinction in school. These represent powerful motivators for her and may very well shape not only her later childhood but much of her adult life as well.

In contrast, Cranshaw's parents seem much more relaxed and open to whatever channel Cranshaw's talents seem to take. His parents have their own interests that they are pursuing and the life of his family does not necessarily revolve around him or the other children. When disagreements occur, they are expressed, but within the context of overall secure and supportive relationships. It is out of such a climate that more creative individual expression is likely to emerge.

Although a certain amount of family stress and even some alienation seems to be a pattern for some creative people, this does not necessarily mean that the school should attempt to reproduce tension in the hope of creating more imaginative and original students. What it seems to imply is that a more relaxed and open environment, which rewards a wide diversity of student performance, is likely to be more desirable than a single-dimension emphasis on achieving direct academic goals of the school.

An innovative study was carried out on twins involved in programs for the gifted (Renzulli & McGreevy, 1986). The purpose of this study was to identify twin pairs, one who was placed in an educational program for gifted students and one who was not. A total of 33 pairs of twins were found in the northeast region of the United States.

The experience of the twins seems to be merely a variation on the problems of siblings with a outstanding brother or sister. The problem in a family when one of the children makes the basketball team and the other does not, or one becomes a soloist in the school band or plays the lead in the school play and the other does not, always requires some sensitive handling within the school and within the family. The negative feelings that were encountered here did not seem to be serious or permanent but did disrupt the relationships. Sufficient steps need to be taken to repair the damage. This is particularly true in the identical twins bonding situation.

Interestingly enough, some of the parents felt that the twin who was not selected was, in many cases, more creative than the one who achieved straightforward academic high performance and they reported that the "wrong twin" was selected for the gifted program. This type of situation has caused teachers to wonder if we are identifying the wrong children and that we should be finding "creative" children if we only know where and how to look for them.

Children of High Creative Potential

Perhaps the most exciting characteristic of the human mind is its ability to process and reorganize information and produce a unique and original product. Some children, often referred to as "creative children," seem to do this much more often than their classmates. What combination of circumstances or forces tend to enhance the likelihood of such creative behavior being produced?

There has been a general assumption that the child who is creative has a different pattern of personality traits that distinguish him or her from students who may be academically efficient, but without this ability to produce new and valued ideas. Table 2–1 gives examples of different stories told to the same stimulus by a high academic student and a high creativity student.

Three major factors have been named most often as closely linked to creativity: self-confidence, full access to personal association networks, and resistance to social pressures.

Self-Confidence

It takes an abundance of self-confidence, if not courage, to stand against the majority of one's peer group, to say nothing of possibly being seen as challenging the authority of the teacher with idiosyncratic productions. Bandura (1989) has pointed out the enormous

TABLE 2–1   Different Stories Told to Same Picture Stimulus

High IQ Student	*High Creativity Student*
(Stimulus: Man sitting, staring out a small window.)	
Mr. Smith is on his way home from a successful business trip. He is very happy and he is thinking about his wonderful family and how glad he will be to see them again. He can picture it, about an hour from now his plane landing at the airport and Mrs. Smith and their three children all there welcoming him home again.	This man is flying from Reno where he has just won a divorce from his wife. He couldn't stand to live with her anymore, he told the judge, because she wore so much cold cream on her face at night that her head would skid across the pillow and hit him in the head. He is now contemplating a new skid-proof face cream.
(Stimulus: Man working alone in an office setting.)	
There's ambitious Bob, down at the office at 6:30 in the morning. Every morning it's the same. He's trying to show his boss how energetic he is. Now, thinks Bob, maybe the boss will give me a raise for all my extra work. The trouble is that Bob has been doing this for the last three years, and the boss still hasn't given him a raise. He'll come in at 9:00, not even noticing that Bob had been there so long, and poor Bob won't get his raise.	This man has just broken into this office of a new cereal company. He is a private-eye employed by a competitor firm to find out the formula that makes the cereal bend, sag, and sway. After a thorough search of the office, he comes upon what he thinks is the correct formula. He is now copying it. It turns out that it is the wrong formula and the competitor's factory blows up. Poetic justice!

Source: Getzels, J., & Jackson, P. (1962). *Creativity and intelligence.* New York: John Wiley and Sons. Reprinted by permission.

feelings of self-efficacy (perceived ability in a given domain such as writing or music) that creative persons have, and must have, to survive negative comments.

James Joyce's novel, *The Dubliners*, was rejected 22 times, and Gertrude Stein was writing poetry for 20 years before publishing a poem. The characteristics of creative persons are that such rejection only means that all of the people doing the negative reviews are wrong, whereas for the majority of people, such experiences would shake our own confidence in ourselves and our abilities.

Cranshaw showed some of this characteristic when he persisted in his design of a Martian landing module (he was interested in space exploration at the time) despite hoots from his classmates and some doubting statements from his teacher. He persisted and came out with a product that was admired by all.

Full Access to Personal Association Networks

Self-confidence also aids the student in being able to explore the full range of associations that he or she has stored, which means more associations available to recombine into a creative product. Stephanie would not be worried, as Zelda would, as to whether some of her cognitive associations are "proper" or not. The student who shows creative behavior seems less concerned with taboos, whether they are parental or teacher or peer related. So, unacceptable aggression can be displayed in their stories, as can attacks on revered figures—all become potential grist for their creative mill. Who would write a satiric portrait of Abraham Lincoln, for instance?—not Zelda, certainly; Joe, perhaps, to be deliberately outrageous; Cranshaw might do it as a reaction to the way Lincoln was glorified in other books; and Stephanie might write about Lincoln's wife.

Resistance to Social Pressures

Students who lean to creative work seem to be relatively immune to the normal social or peer pressures, or even the normal pressures that the teacher applies to attempt an efficient working environment so that "things get done." It was pointed out to Cranshaw once in the middle of a dispute that all 10 of the other people present were on one side and he, Cranshaw, was on the other. Never daunted, Cranshaw merely pointed out, "I am right and all the rest are wrong." From where does such immunity from social pressures spring?

Surely a lifetime of, in fact, being "right" is a help. It gives strong self-confidence that your view is the right one. Also, with a strong background of success, and the academic status that such success brings, there is strength to resist others. The self-confidence that comes from family acceptance of individualism must also play a role.

The ability to resist such pressures is one key to creativity, since any new idea, in any field, must run afoul of many disbelievers who will point out that if an idea is novel, it is surely wrong. Unless such independence of view is modified by social sensitivity, though, it can lead the child, who is concerned above all about the rightness of something, into substantial peer conflict or special problems with the teacher.

The reader who wonders why creative youngsters, with their sense of humor and independence, should be less preferred by teachers than the high-IQ students, should grasp the point through the following classroom excerpt.

The teacher, by judicious planning and organization, has tried to get across the concept of *revolution* to his social studies class. For two weeks, various types of revolutions have been studied and reports made. Now, 15 minutes away from the weekend, the teacher is ready to try to bring forth the larger generalization of *revolution* as a concept.

Teacher: Now we have learned a little bit about the French, Russian, and American revolutions, and we have seen that, although they each had their own local characteristics, perhaps they had some things in common too—what do you see as some of the common elements?

Sharon: Well, they each had a rebel and a loyalist faction.

Teacher: All right; that is one thing in common.

Bob: Yeah—If the English had won, Benedict Arnold would have been a hero—

Mike: Nuts—he was a traitor to his country.

Mary: No one who deserts his own side is a hero.

Pete: Aw, he [Bob] is just trying to start an argument again.

John: Wait a minute, maybe he has a point there.

Jean: (incredulously) You mean you think that Benedict Arnold was a hero, too?

The teacher stands frozen as the last five rapid-fire comments occur in the space of about 10 seconds. What is he to do? Bob had done it again—derailed the class discussion and started the class off in a different direction. As the teacher surveys the rapidly deteriorating scene, five or six students wave their hands frantically, wanting to get their opinions heard on Benedict Arnold. As the precious sands of time drain away, the teacher realizes that there is no time to get the class back on the track again; they will have to start all over again on Monday. How can the teacher help but feel some resentment toward Bob, whose fertile, but undisciplined, mind had thrown a monkey wrench into many such discussions during the year, sometimes with relevant diversions and sometimes just to hear himself talk?

If there is a single purpose or goal to the activities of a class, the divergent thinker is bound to be an abrasive irritant, guaranteed to win few bouquets from the teacher. It should be clear that the creative youngster would not be as docile or as pliable as other students. Since this student does not seem to be particularly dependent on teacher approval, it is no surprise to find that teachers generally prefer the high achiever to the highly creative child when questioned as to the desirability of having either in the classroom.

There is another strategy used in discovering the true nature of creative children and adults, and that is to identify them by their excellent and distinctive *products*. The creative musician describes herself with a unique composition; the writer by a short story, and so forth. This approach has been used often with adults (MacKinnon, 1978; Barron, 1969). When this approach is taken, there appears to be greater emphasis on the personality characteristics of the creative individual.

Would Cranshaw be just as creative if he had been raised with different, less enthusiastic, less permissive parents, or in a less enlightened school? Most social scientists who have studied creativity would say that the answer is no. Although personal characteristics of intelligence, risk taking, and strong motivation obviously are important ingredients in the total recipe, there also needs to be a societal approval of the domain or field in which creative production is acceptable, and in the group of teachers, critics, and peers who evaluate the contributions of the individuals in those domains. Such creativity does not develop in an environmental vacuum. It interacts with the content field and the relevant people who make judgments about creative performance.

Traditionally, creativity has been seen as an internal process operating solely within the artist, writer, or scientist. Recently, creativity has been viewed as an interaction between a particular environment and internal thought (Greeno, 1989). These interactions with the environment cause the individual to reorganize existing concepts and produce unique results. Thus, a community of writers, an institute for scientists, or a cluster of impressionist painters all create an environment that makes creativity by the individuals in the group more likely. Students of high ability who are grouped together often comment on the stimulation obtained by interacting with other students of similar abilities.

It is no surprise that tests of creativity that measure only the individual and his or her capabilities do not predict actual creative performance very well. In order to be truly good at predicting who will be creative, one would also have to know in what field the creative behavior is going to be exhibited and who the critics and judges of the work will be (Csikszentmihalyi, 1988).

Unresolved Issues

1. Despite the intense interest in creativity and the nature of the creative child, there is a doubtful link between creativity tests in childhood and creative performance in young and later adulthood. Creative performance seems to require a strong portion of personal characteristics such as intense interest and persistence in the face of difficulty, as well as specific cognitive skills. How can we identify true creative potential early?

2. The special issue of gifted girls and women highlights the role that the cultural milieu has on our attitudes, motivation, and performance. How can we encourage more creative productivity from gifted girls without, at the same time, losing the feminine characteristics of nurturance and sensitivity that the male population might well aspire to?

3. Is giftedness, at some point, a discontinuous characteristic? As in the catastrophe theory where small increments can result in huge consequences, should we treat giftedness in our schools as merely more of the same abilities that all students have, or some special combination of factors that require special attention?

Chapter Review

1. Knowledge of the special characteristics of gifted students should encourage educators to plan programs that can take these characteristics into account.

2. The broadened definition of *giftedness* requires different sets of characteristics for different subcategories. By far the most information available is on children of high-academic ability.

3. Terman's 60-year longitudinal study of children of high academic aptitude finds them to be better adjusted, have broader interests, make more friends, and end up in more successful careers than average students. Such findings are confirmed by studies in the United States, England, and Israel.

4. Although the majority of children with high academic aptitude appear to have made good emotional adjustments, there is a small, but meaningful, percentage who are anxious or depressed to a serious level.

5. When occasional emotional disturbance or suicidal impulses do appear in gifted children and adults, they appear for the same reasons of family conflict and self-deprecation that are found in people of average ability.

6. Major differences have been found favoring boys in high performance in mathematics and science. Such differences appear to be the consequence of differential encouragement and rewards for boys in those fields.

7. The origins of measured academic ability seem clearly linked to both hereditary and environmental factors.

8. Even extraordinarily gifted students, measured by IQ scores, appear to need a favorable environment and good instruction in order for their talents to flourish.

9. Families appear to play a highly significant role in determining whether the child with high aptitudes will achieve at a significant level or not. World-class scientists and artistic performers report that their parents encouraged them, saw to it they had good instruction to develop their talents, and provided much praise and reward for their productions.

10. Some students who are gifted seem to have a "success depression," or a reaction to exaggerated praise for work that the students know is not their best effort.

11. Although high ability may be found in individuals in every ethnic and racial group, there do appear to be gender, racial, and ethnic differences in the prevalence of high-aptitude children. These differences are widely interpreted to be due to different environmental opportunities.

Readings of Special Interest

Bloom, B. (Ed.). (1985). *Developing talent in young people*. New York: Ballantine.
   This classic retrospective reports on world-class achievers in a variety of endeavors such as tennis, neurology, music, sculpture, and so on. One theme of the book is the importance of the families in encouraging the full development of the children's talents. The families did this through obtaining special instruction for the children at an early age in each child's area of talent and by encouraging and supporting the child in his or her early work.

Horowitz, F., & O'Brien, M. (Eds.). (1985). *The gifted and talented: Developmental perspectives*. Washington, DC: American Psychological Association.
   This book contains numerous contributions by psychologists assessing the current state of knowledge about gifted individuals. The selection of chapters includes topics on the nature of intelligence and thinking, identification, minority gifted students, and the social development of gifted students.

Oden, M. (1968). *The fulfillment of promise: 40 year follow-up of Terman's gifted group*. Stanford, CA: Stanford University Press.
   This is the last of five major volumes describing the life history of a major sample of gifted youth first identified in California at the age of 10 or thereabouts in the 1920s. This volume provides a portrait of the sample as they move into advanced middle age. It is an important text for showing clearly that gifted children turn out to be significant contributors in adulthood.

Subotnik, R., Kassan, L., Summers, E., & Wasser, A. (1993). *Genius revisited: High IQ children grown up*. Norwood, NJ: Ablex.
   This is a followup study on the graduates of Hunter College Elementary School in New York City. This school was especially designed to create a highly favorable educational environment for high-ability students. One clear difference from the Terman studies was the almost universal pattern of gifted women in the workforce. This was generally attributed to the changing role of women in U.S. culture. The graduates were largely successful professionals, but were not extraordinary creative producers in adulthood.

References

Albert, R. (1980). Family positions and the attainment of eminance: A study of special family positions and special family experiences. *Gifted Child Quarterly, 24*, 87–95.

Albert, R., & Runco, M. (1986). The achievement of eminence: A model based on a longitudinal study of exceptionally gifted boys and their families. In R. Sternberg & J. Davidson (Eds.), *Conceptions of giftedness*. New York: Cambridge University Press.

Altus, W. D. (1966). Birth order and its sequelae. *Science, 151*, 44–49.

Anolik, S. (1979). Personality, family, educational, and criminological characteristics of bright delinquents. *Psychological Reports, 44*, 727–734.

Baldwin, A. (1991). Ethnic and cultural issues. In N. Colangelo & G. Davis (Eds.), *Handbook of gifted education* (pp. 416–427). Boston: Allyn and Bacon.

Bandura, A. (1989). Human agency in social cognitive theory. *American Psychologist, 44* (9), 1175–1184.

Barron, F. (1969). *Creative person and creative process*. New York: Holt, Rinehart and Winston.

Belmont, J. (1989). Cognitive strategies and strategic learning: The socio-instructional approach. *American Psychologist, 44*, 142–147.

Berliner, D. (1986). Catastrophies and interactions: Comments on 'the mistaken metaphor.' In C. Maker (Ed.), *Critical issues in gifted education: Defensible programs for the gifted* (pp. 31–38). Rockville, MD: Aspen.

Bloom, B. (1985). *Developing talent in young people*. New York: Ballantine Books.

Brody, L., & Benbow, C. (1987). Accelerative strategies: How effective are they for the gifted? *Gifted Child Quarterly, 31*, 105–110.

Carr, M., & Borkowski, J. (1986). Metamemory in gifted children. *Gifted Child Quarterly, 31* (3), 40–44.

Casserly, P. (1979). Helping able young women take math and science seriously in school. In N. Colangelo & R. Zaffrann (Eds.), *New voices in counseling the gifted*. Dubuque, IA: Kendall/Hunt.

Clark, W., & Hankins, N. (1985). Giftedness and conflict. *Roeper Review, 8*, 50–53.

Cornell, D., Callahan, C., & Lloyd, B. (1991). Socioemotional adjustment of adolescent girls enrolled in a residential acceleration program. *Gifted Child Quarterly 35* (2), 58–66.

Cornell, D., & Grossberg, I. (1987). Family environment and personality adjustment in gifted program children. *Gifted Child Quarterly, 31*, 59–64.

Csikszentmihalyi, M. (1988). Society, culture, and person: A systems view of creativity. In R. J. Sternberg (Ed.), *The nature of creativity* (pp. 43–75). New York: University Press.

Derevensky, J., & Coleman, E. (1989). Gifted children's fears. *Gifted Child Quarterly, 33*, 65–68.

Eilber, C. (1987, June). The North Carolina School of Science and Mathematics. *Phi Delta Kappa*, 773–777.

Feldhusen, J., Sayler, M., Nielsen, M., & Kolloff, P. (1990). Self concepts of gifted students in enrichment programs. *Journal for the Education of the Gifted, 13* (4), 380–387.

Feldman, D. (1979). The mysterious case of extreme giftedness. In A. Passow (Ed.), *The gifted and the talented: Their education and development (Seventy-eighth Yearbook of the National Society for the Study of Education. Part 1)*. Chicago: The University of Chicago Press.

Fox, L. (1977). *Changing times in the education of gifted girls*. Address given at Second World Conference on Gifted and Talented Children, San Francisco.

Galton, F. (1976). The classification of men according to their natural gifts. In W. Dennis & M. Dennis (Eds.), *The intellectually gifted*. New York: Grune & Stratton.

Gallagher, J. J. (1988). A national agenda for educating gifted students: A statement of priorities. *Exceptional Children, 55* (2), 107–114.

Gardner, H. (1985). *Frames of mind* (2nd ed.). New York: Basic.

George, P. G., & Gallagher, J. J. (1978). Children's thoughts about the future: A comparison of gifted and non-gifted students. *Journal for the Education of the Gifted, 2*, 33–42.

Goldring, E. (1991). Assessing the status of information on classroom organizational frameworks for gifted students. *Journal of Educational Research, 83* (6), 313–326.

Goldsmith, L. (1987). Girl prodigies. *Roeper Review, 10,* 74–82.

Greeno, J. (1989). A perspective on thinking. *American Psychologist, 44,* 105–111.

Hoge, R. D., & McSheffrey, R. (1991). An investigation of self-concept in gifted children. *Exceptional Children, 57,* 238–245.

Hollingworth, L. (1942). *Children above 180 IQ.* New York: World Book.

Janos, P., & Robinson, N. (1985). Psychosocial development in intellectually gifted children. In F. Horowitz & M. O'Brien (Eds.), *The gifted and talented developmental perspectives* (pp. 149–195). Washington, DC: American Psychological Association.

Jenkins-Friedman, R., & Murphy, D. (1990). Advice from a caterpillar: Ameliorating diminished self-concept among newly placed gifted students through systematic teaching about abilities. *Perspectives on Talent.* World Council on Gifted and Talented Students. Monroe, NY: Trillium Press.

Kaiser, C., & Berndt, D. (1985). Predictors of loneliness in the gifted adolescent. *Gifted Child Quarterly, 29* (2), 74–77.

Kelly, K., & Jordan, L. (1991). Effects of academic achievement and gender on academic and social self-concept: A replication study. *Journal of Counseling and Development, 69,* 173–177.

Khatena, J. (1978). Some advances in thought on the gifted. *Gifted Child Quarterly, 22,* 55–61.

Khatena, J. (1982). *Educational psychology of the gifted.* New York: John Wiley & Sons.

Landau, E. (1981). The profile of the gifted child. *Gifted children: Challenging their potential.* New York: Trillium.

Lavach, J., & Lanier, H. (1975). The motive to avoid success in 7th, 8th, 9th, and 10th grade high-achieving girls. *Journal of Educational Research, 68,* 216–218.

Lovell, K., & Shields, J. S. (1967). Some aspects of a study of the gifted child. *British Journal of Educational Psychology, 37,* 201–208.

MacKinnon, D. (1978). *In search of human effectiveness.* Buffalo, NY: Creative Education Foundation.

Mahoney, A. (1980). Gifted delinquents: What do we know about them? *Children and Youth Services Review, 2,* 315–329.

Maker, C. J. (1989). Programs for gifted minority students: A synthesis of perspectives. In C. J. Maker & S. Schiever (Eds.), *Critical issues in gifted education: Defensible programs for cultural and ethnic minorities* (Vol. 2, pp. 322–328). Austin, TX: Pro-Ed.

Martinson, R. (1972). *An analysis of problems and priorities: Advocate survey and statistics sources. Education of the gifted and talented.* Report to the Congress of the United States by the U.S. Commissioner of Education and background papers submitted to the U.S. Office of Education. Washington, DC: GPO.

Morelock, M., & Feldman, D. (1991). Extreme precocity. In N. Colangelo & G. Davis (Eds.), *Handbook of gifted education* (pp. 347–364). Boston: Allyn and Bacon.

Morse, J., & Bruch, C. (1970). Gifted women: More issues than answers. *Educational Horizons, 49,* 25–32.

Oden, M. (1968). The fulfillment of promise: Forty-year follow-up of the Terman gifted group. *Genetic Psychology Monographs, 77,* 3–93.

Olszewski, P., Kulieke, M., & Buescher, T. (1987). The influence of the family environment on the development of talent: A literature review. *Journal for the Education of the Gifted, 11,* 6–28.

Olszewski, P., Kulieke, M., & Willis, G. (1987). Changes in self-perceptions of gifted students who participate in rigorous academic programs. *Journal for the Education of the Gifted, 10,* (4), 287–303.

Olszewski-Kubilius, P., Kulieke, M., & Krasney, N. (1988). Personality dimensions of gifted adolescents: A review of the empirical literature. *Gifted Child Quarterly, 32* (4), 347–352.

Perkins, D., & Simmons, R. (1988). The cognitive roots of scientific and mathematical ability. In J. Dreyden, G. Stanley, S. Gallagher, & R. Sawyer (Eds.), *The Proceedings of the Talent Identification Programs/ National Science Foundation Conference on Academic Talent.* Durham, NC: Duke University Talent Identification Program.

Rabinowitz, M., & Glaser, R. (1985). Cognitive structure and process in highly competent performance. In F. Horowitz & M. O'Brien (Eds.), *The gifted and talented developmental perspectives* (pp. 75–98). Washington, DC: American Psychological Association.

Rand, D., & Gibb, L. (1989). A model program for gifted girls in science. *Journal for the Education of the Gifted, 12* (2), 142–155.

Reis, S. (1989). Reflections on policy affecting the education of gifted and talented students: Past and future perspectives. *American Psychologist, 44*, 399–408.

Renzulli, J. S. (1987). The positive side of pull-out programs. *Journal for the Education of the Gifted, 10* (4), 245–254.

Renzulli, J., Hartman, R., & Callahan, C. (1971). Teacher identification of superior students. *Exceptional Children, 38*, 211–214.

Renzulli, J. S., & McGreevy, A. M. (1986). Twins included and not included in special programs for the gifted. *Roeper Review, 9*, 120–127.

Rogers, K. (1986). Do the gifted think and learn differently? A review of recent research and its implications. *Journal for the Education of the Gifted, 10*, 17–40.

Scarr, S., & Arnett, J. (1986). Malleability: Lessons from intervention and family studies. In J. Gallagher & C. Ramey (Eds.), *The malleability of children* (pp. 71–84). Baltimore, MD: Brookes.

Scholwinski, E., & Reynolds, C. (1985). Dimensions of anxiety among high IQ children. *Gifted Child Quarterly, 29* (3), 125–130.

Sears, P., & Barbee, A. (1977). Career and life satisfactions among Terman's gifted women. In J. Stanley, W. George, & C. Solano (Eds.), *The gifted and the creative: A fifty-year perspective*. Baltimore, MD: Johns Hopkins University Press.

Seeley, K. (1984). Perspectives on adolescent giftedness and delinquency. *Journal for the Education of the Gifted, 8*, 59–72.

Shneidman, E. (1971). Perturbation and lethality as precursors of suicide in a gifted group. *Life Threatening Behavior, 1*, 23–45.

Smith, J., LeRose, B., & Glasser, R. (1991). Underrepresentation of minority students in gifted programs: Yes! It matters! *Gifted Child Quarterly, 35* (2), 81–83.

Sparling, S. (1989). Gifted black students: Curriculum and teaching strategies. In C. J. Maker & S. Schiever (Eds.), *Critical issues in gifted education: Defensible programs for cultural and eth-*

nic minorities (Vol. 2, pp. 259–269). Austin, TX: Pro-Ed.

Stanley, J., & Benbow, C. (1986). Youths who reason exceptionally well mathematically. In R. Sternberg & J. Davidson (Eds.), *Conceptions of giftedness* (pp. 361–387). New York: Cambridge University Press.

Terman, L. (1925). *Genetic studies of genius. Vol. 1: Mental and physical traits of 1000 gifted children*. Stanford, CA: Stanford University Press.

Terman, L. (1954). The discovery and encouragement of exceptional talent. *American Psychologist, 9*, 221–230.

Terman, L. (Ed.). (1959). *Genetic studies of genius* (Vols. 1–4). Stanford, CA: Stanford University Press.

Terman, L., & Oden, M. (1951). The Stanford Studies of the gifted. In P. Witty (Ed.), *The gifted child*. Boston: Heath.

Tidwell, R. (1980). A psychoeducational profile of 1,593 gifted high school students. *Gifted Child Quarterly, 24*, 63–68.

VanTassel-Baska, J. (1987). The ineffectiveness of the pull-out program model in gifted education: A minority perspective. *Journal for the Education of the Gifted, 10* (4), 255–264.

VanTassel-Baska, J., Patton, J., & Prellman, D. (1989). Disadvantaged gifted learners: At risk for educational attention. *Focus on Exceptional Children, 22* (3), 1–15.

Vaughn, V., Feldhusen, J., & Asher, J. (1991). Meta-analysis and review of research on pull out programs in gifted education. *Gifted Child Quarterly, 35* (2), 92–98.

Wolleat, P. (1979). Guiding the career development of gifted females. In N. Colangelo & R. Zaffrann (Eds.), *New voices in counseling the gifted*. Dubuque, IA: Kendall/Hunt.

Zajonc, R. (1976). Family configuration and intelligence. *Science, 192*, 27–35.

Zappia, I. (1989). Identification of gifted Hispanic students. In C. J. Maker & S. Schiever (Eds.), *Critical issues in gifted education: Defensible programs for cultural and ethnic minorities* (Vol. 2, pp. 259–269). Austin, TX: Pro-Ed.

C h a p t e r 3

School Adaptations for the Gifted

Key Questions

- What are the major complaints that gifted students make about their school programs?
- What are the factors in the school situation that cause educators to establish special programs for gifted students?
- What are the major program objectives for special programs for gifted students?
- What is meant by the *love-hate relationship* of our society with gifted students?
- What does the term *continuum of services* refer to in the education of gifted students?
- What is a *magnet school* and how does such a school apply to the education of gifted students?
- What roles does *available time* play in the programs for gifted students?
- How does the educational reform movement affect gifted students?

The previous chapters have defined gifted children and provided some description of their special characteristics. This chapter will discuss briefly the variety of organizational and instructional strategies that schools have chosen in an attempt to adapt their programs to meet the special challenges of gifted students.

Consider for a moment what we expect from our public school systems. We expect the schools to educate an enormously diverse population of students from many different cultures in a fair and equitable way. They must provide, by law as well as intention, an appropriate education for children with disabilities as well as children from many different cultures, and they are also supposed to provide a stimulating and challenging educational experience for the brightest and most advanced students as well as the many children developing at an average rate.

We expect the schools to continue to educate all of these children, motivated or not, through the twelfth grade. A local school system that has many students dropping out before twelfth grade is not considered to be doing its job well. In addition, the schools, being a mirror of the society, reflect the social problems of the larger society. We expect schools to deal with societal crises such as drug problems, the sexual revolution and its related health issues, family restructing, and so on, and to do it with a dedicated force of teachers and administrators who often receive limited pay and limited respect from the rest of the community.

It is like being asked to carry a cup of coffee, answer the telephone, put on a pair of shoes, and whistle "The Star Spangled Banner" all at the same time. We could probably do any one of those tasks with little difficulty. It is the need to do them all at the same time that is the difficult part—and so it is with our schools. We become puzzled when we see the schools attempting to meet one of their goals such as stimulating gifted students, and not performing particularly well. It doesn't seem like such a demanding task. As Joe's father often complains, "Why can't the teachers give my boy more attention and then maybe he would straighten up and move ahead?"

Good question. If Joe were the only problem to deal with, most teachers could probably do a very respectable job in providing him with encouragement and stimulation. But teachers have many other tasks, sometimes conflicting with one another, and that is often where the problem lies. The challenges of educating gifted students is one that many teachers would gladly accept if they did not have 8 or 10 other challenges to face at the same time. That is one of the reasons why some form of special programming has been designed to aid teachers in meeting the multiplicity of tasks expected of them.

Love-Hate Relationship with the Gifted

There seems to be little doubt that we as a society hold ambivalent feelings about our gifted and talented youth. A strong love-hate relationship seems to exist between the society and the high-ability individuals (Gallagher, 1986). It is true that we are proud of our artists, scholars, and scientists who have achieved much with hard work, but we are also concerned about equity, and we are not sure about the justification for special programs for these gifted youngsters. The schools are caught in a tug-of-war between two legitimate educational goals: *excellence* and *equity*. This tug-of-war, or seesaw, between two legitimate goals has caused our interest in the education of gifted students to be up some years and down other years.

When circumstances turn unfavorable in the larger society, as, for example, in the *Sputnik* scare in the early 1960s or the economic challenges of recent years, then there is a hurried concern about whether we are giving sufficient emphasis to academic excellence. When we are having a national crisis of confidence in our ability to deal with our problems, when we worry about the economy or hunger or political unrest, our thoughts turn to one of our renewable natural resources—our gifted students.

One of a number of reports, *A Nation at Risk*, from the National Commission on Excellence in Education, expressed the concern in a dramatic fashion.

> *If an unfriendly foreign power had attempted to impose on America the mediocre educational performance that exists today, we might well have viewed it as an act of war. As it stands, we have allowed this to happen to ourselves. We have even squandered the gains in student achievement made in the wake of the Sputnik challenge. Moreover, we have dismantled essential support systems which helped make those gains possible. We have, in effect, been committing an act of unthinking, unilateral educational disarmament. (1983, p. 5)*

Another dimension of the struggle between excellence and equity is that the farther along in the educational system one proceeds, the more excellence comes to the fore as a priority. We establish, without apology, schools for gifted students at the professional level that would be severely criticized at the elementary-school level. What are our law schools, our medical schools, our advanced graduate-school programs, except programs for gifted students? These are well accepted by our society and we are enormously proud—justifiably proud—of the great contribution these institutions make to our nation. But if we suggest that a similar amount of special attention be paid to these same students when they are 8 or 9 years of age, we hear cries of special privilege and possible inequity.

One of the often unrecognized problems in U.S. education—which certainly has its share of recognizable problems—is the status of gifted students in both public and private education. A recent report on the state of educational excellence (Ross, 1993) describes some of the problems faced by these students within the framework of the general school program. *Lack of challenge* and *lack of student attention* are certainly high on the list of problems. Are U.S. students unique in this regard?

- Gifted and talented elementary school students have mastered from 35 to 50 percent of the curriculum to be offered in five basic subjects before they begin the school year.
- Most regular classroom teachers make few, it any, provisions for gifted and talented students. These youngsters spend most of their time working on grade-level assignments given to the entire class.
- The highest-achieving students in the nation reported to *Who's Who Among American High School Students* that most studied less than an hour a day. This suggests that they get top grades without having to work hard.
- Only 2 cents out of every $100 spent on K–12 education in the United States in 1990 supported special opportunities for talented students.

One way to compare the students of various countries is to examine the level of expectations of students who are going to enter higher education. Compare the questions that are asked of students from other countries with the multiple-choic Scholastic Aptitude Test in the United States:

- British and Welsh students are asked to write for three hours on questions about United States history such as, "Why did Virginians dominate the presidency from 1789 to 1825?" or "To what extent does the conduct of American foreign policy, 1954–1974, offer evidence for the existence and influence of a 'military-industrial complex'?"
- French students of philosophy and liberal arts, an area students may concentrate on in secondary school, are asked to write for four hours on such questions as, "How might one characterize rigorous thought?" or "What does one gain by losing one's illusions?"

It does not appear that we expect as much from our secondary students as other countries expect from theirs.

Educational Reform and Gifted Programs

One of the most popular pastimes in education is to discuss educational reform, since practically all educators can see educational areas that need improvement. In many instances, such discussions have remained at the talking level because the individuals involved do not possess the political power to make major changes in the system.

In 1990, however, President George Bush and the National Governor's Association made a serious effort at bringing such reform ideas into concrete form by agreeing on six national goals (see Figure 3–1) to be achieved by the year 2000. The U.S. Department of Education, for its part, embarked upon *America 2000*, a series of strategies designed to bring these national goals to reality. The goals indicate a mix of concerns reflecting both the need for *educational equity* and *educational excellence*. For those interested in gifted education, the desire to be first in the world in math and science is a goal that reflects a desire for excellence, as does the goal requiring the mastery of challenging curriculum, which will be assessed at grades 4, 8, and 12. The achievement of either of these goals would require some strong emphasis on programs for gifted and talented students.

One result of this apparent consensus across a broad political spectrum of opinion on needed changes is that major efforts were begun to restructure the U.S. public school system. Since programs for exceptional children have traditionally defined themselves in terms of the differences between themselves and the general education program, major changes in the regular program will inevitably spawn major shifts in the special programs, as well as bring their special educational operations into question. Figure 3–2 indicates some of the major reform devices in that era and what the projected impact would be on the education of gifted students.

Middle Schools

One of the major devices for reform has been the middle school, which is now in place in over half the school districts in the United States (George, 1988). The philosophy of the middle school stresses a strong emphasis on the affective life of the student; interdisciplinary content; a curriculum emphasizing inquiry, exploration, and discovery; team teaching; and flexible scheduling. Schools are often organized in groups of 100 students, to be taught by four teachers in a mixture of large-group and small-group settings.

FIGURE 3–1   National Education Goals

1. By the Year 2000, all children in America will start school ready to learn.
2. By the Year 2000, we will increase the percentage of students graduating from high school to at least 90%.
3. By the Year 2000, American students will leave grades four, eight, and twelve having demonstrated competency over challenging subject matter, including English, Mathematics, Science, History, and Geography.
4. By the Year 2000, U.S. students will be first in the world in Science and Mathematics achievement.
5. By the Year 2000, every adult American will be literate and possess the knowledges and skills necessary to compete in a global economy and exercise the rights and responsibilities of citizenship.
6. By the Year 2000, every school in America will be free of drugs and violence and offer a disciplined environment conducive to learning.

Source: America 2000 (1990). Washington, DC: U.S. Department of Education.

FIGURE 3–2   Educational Reform Devices and Impact on Gifted Students

Middle Schools

This strong movement to replace the junior high school stresses many similar goals to education of gifted students, such as stressing interdisciplinary curriculum, instruction in thinking strategies, emphasis on counseling, team teaching, and individualization. Many proponents also stress heterogeneous grouping, which threatens to exacerbate the lack of challenge that many of these students feel.

Site-Based Management

This drive to bring educational decision making back to the local school level is a reaction to excessive control of activities by a distant central administration or state department of education. How well gifted students will do will depend on who at the site knows about the special needs of gifted students. This is basis for some concern.

Cooperative Learning

This is an instructional strategy that has become quite popular. It stresses small-group activities around a central goal, with the team being evaluated by the performance of all of the members of the team. The stress on heterogeneous grouping in the small groups has caused some distress among teachers of the gifted, who admit to liking the approach if it is used with groups of gifted students.

Outcome-Based Learning

Outcome-based learning emphasizes products (demonstrated learning) as the basis for evaluating programs, as opposed to input measures (e.g., teachers employed) or process information (e.g., number of reports made). This movement could be of some stimulus for programs for gifted students if the expectations of performance are placed high enough to challenge this student group.

Accountability

All educators will be required to demonstrate how effective they have been in helping students to learn. Special programs, such as gifted education, would be required to demonstrate, with some tangible evidence, that the program achieves more than the regular program and justifies the additional expense and resources assigned to it.

Findings on the negative effects of ability grouping on low-performing students (Oakes, 1985; Slavin, 1988) have been used to stress the importance of heterogeneous grouping in the middle school student clusters and in the instruction itself.

Such policies, however, ignored strong evidence that grouping, when done with gifted and high-performing students for specific purposes, has produced major gains for gifted students (Kulik & Kulik, 1991). Many middle schools have maintained their honors programs and ability grouping for high-performing students in specific content fields such as math and language arts in an attempt to get the best of both worlds (middle school philosophy and gifted education).

Site-Based Management

This approach attempts to empower teachers and principals in a particular school building to make the key decisions of planning and organizing the school, to the maximum benefit of the students at that particular school. Site-based management is designed to reduce decision making on educational management that might be made by district office personnel or even by the State Department of Education.

It is not clear, at this writing, what the limits of the local decision making can be (e.g., they cannot decide not to teach children who have disabilities, since that would be against federal law; they will likely include math in the curriculum despite the dislike for the subject on the part of many teachers; if the state has a statewide testing program, can this school refuse to participate; etc.). On the other hand, it is likely that the local teachers and the principal will decide in what type of organizational setting gifted students will find themselves (e.g., regular class, resource room, special class, etc.).

Since there are over 14,000 school districts in the United States, and many schools within those districts, the range of what will happen under site-based management is likely to be extraordinarily diverse and, to a large degree, unpredictable.

Cooperative Learning

Although there are many variations on the basic theme (Slavin, 1988; Johnson & Johnson, 1990; Kagan, 1988), most cooperative learning programs stress small groups of four to six students working on a common task where the final grade depends on the performance of all students in the group, much as in an athletic contest.

Slavin commented on the broad uses of cooperative learning:

> *It is being promoted as an alternative to tracking and within-class grouping, as a means of mainstreaming academically handicapped students, as a means of improving race relations in desegregated schools, as a solution to the problems of children at risk, as a means of increasing prosocial behavior among children, as well as a method for simply increasing the achievement of all students. (1990, p. 3)*

Such a raft of expectations places a very heavy burden on any instructional strategy. As with the middle schools, there is an attempt in some cooperative learning settings to stress heterogeneous grouping (Slavin, 1990) so that the strong students can aid the weaker students and foster better social relationships between students from different family and cultural backgrounds.

Robinson (1990) criticized the method of heterogeneous grouping with cooperative learning, stating three major concerns:

1. The task presented would have to be at grade level to accommodate the slow-learning students, with a likely resulting loss of challenge to the gifted students.
2. The task will be presented at the pace of the grade-level students.
3. The performance of the group will likely be evaluated on basic or low-level skill measures.

A special concern for educators of gifted students was expressed by Renzulli and Reis:

You don't produce future Thomas Edisons or Marie Curies by forcing them to spend large amounts of their science and mathematics classes tutoring students who don't understand the material. A student who is tutoring others in a cooperative learning situation in mathematics may refine some of his or her basic skill processes, but this type of situation does not provide the level of challenge necessary for the most advanced types of involvements in the subject. (1991, p. 34)

Gallagher (1991) pointed out that cooperative learning can be a useful device to employ in more homogeneous groups of gifted students who, through this device, can learn the joys and frustrations of a group working toward a common goal.

Outcome-Based Learning

The interest of many private citizens in these discussions on educational reform has stirred an interest in outcome-based education. In other words, people are becoming increasingly concerned with what happens to a child after a specific educational program has been applied to him or her.

One of the popular devices in gifted education, *portfolio assessment*, would seem to be in order here. In this approach, the student collects all of his or her writings, artwork, or scientific papers over time, so that it is possible to see growth in the student over time through these sequentially produced products. The desire to employ outcome-based products can be helpful to gifted students, since it forces the instructors to determine what products will be acceptable. A teacher with high standards can demand more of such students with a carefully thought-out set of lessons, each requiring some form of product.

Accountability

The term *accountability* has become an increasingly popular word used by the public to express its general suspicions about the public schools and their performance. Consequently, it is not a favorite term of teachers because it implies a simple link between teaching and student performance. In reality, however, many powerful factors that influence student performance lie completely outside the schoolhouse. Some of these factors include (1) the student's own abilities and aptitudes, (2) the attitude of the family members to education and learning, and (3) the cultural milieu in which the student exists. Each of these can have as much to do with student performance as the classroom teacher's skills, and it is no wonder that the teacher may feel unjustly accused when criticized for the poor performance of students who are his or her responsibility.

This is not to say that education and the schools do not have a significant role to play in student performance. Indeed, teachers can inspire, content can intrigue, and the environmental setting of the school can be designed to enhance the opportunities for learning. Nevertheless, there is a major movement around the country to develop new performance-based, authentic measures that address more of the true goals of the school than do the familiar multiple-choice-type tests (Gallagher, 1991). Accountability procedures will also, of necessity, be applied to all the new reforms—the middle school, cooperative learning, site-based management, and so on—to determine the relative effectiveness of such new procedures. All of these issues will be revisited in the chapter on administration since they have played such a significant role in the efforts at restructuring of U.S. schools.

Problems of Student Diversity

As noted in an earlier chapter, one of the predominant reasons for directing special attention to gifted children is the diversity of ability and performance that one finds in many schools in this country. The extent of such diversity is incompletely realized by the general public and even by many teachers and administrators in the field of education.

In an unselected group of fifth- or sixth-graders, one is likely to find students performing at a second- or third-grade level in key areas such as reading, while other students are capable of performing at a secondary-school level. This presents the classroom teacher with some difficult problems. The strategy followed by most teachers in such circumstances is predictable. They first must deal with those students at grade level who are progressing as would be expected in the curriculum. Their second major task is to try to find some way to bring the youngsters who have fallen significantly below grade level up to par or at least close enough so that they can participate meaningfully in class activities. Finally, once these two major tasks are accomplished, the teachers can turn to those students who are significantly above average and plan extra activities or different experiences for these students. Unfortunately, the time, energy, and capabilities of many teachers are focused primarily on the first two groups—the average and below average— and time or energy runs out before the special problems of the above-average student can be addressed.

A Heterogeneous Classroom

One of the key questions posed by many educators is, To what degree does the regular classroom teacher provide a differentiated experience for gifted students as part of his or her regular instructional approach? It seems that if there is good evidence that the students are being adequately planned for within the regular program, there is less pressure to do something different or extraordinary for them outside that setting.

A major study involving classrooms and teachers across the United States has been conducted to answer that question. A sample of almost 2,000 third- and fourth-grade teachers responded to a survey of classroom practices that explored what types of changes teachers make to take into account individual differences (Archambault, Westberg, Brown, Hallmark, Zhang, & Emmons, 1993). The investigators found that only minor modifications in the regular classroom were made to meet the needs of gifted students. These results held for private as well as public school teachers.

A companion study focused on direct observations within the classroom in 46 third- and fourth-grade classrooms across the country, with classes divided between suburban, rural, and urban settings. In each class, an observer identified a gifted student and a student of average ability and noted the teacher interaction with each student over a two-day period (Westberg, Archambault, Dobyns, & Selvin, 1993). Again, the findings were that no differentiation took place in 84 percent of the classroom activities. The investigators concluded that "little differentiation in the instructional and curricular practices is provided to gifted and talented students in the regular classroom" (p. 139). The authors also noted that merely informing teachers about what they should be doing (e.g., using thinking skills) does not appear to be sufficient. Rather, teachers must be shown how to do those things.

These studies confirm more informal observations of many other educators. Therefore, if it is important that some additional, more challenging work be provided to gifted students, then some additional efforts must be designed to carry them out.

Imagine, for the moment, that Cranshaw, Zelda, Joe, Sam, and Stephanie by some coincidence have been placed in the same fifth-grade classroom. In addition to these bright youngsters, we have the entire range of ability and achievement that would occur if the class were chosen by such a chance method as assigning the children by alphabetical order. This would mean that the expected range in IQ scores might extend from about 70 to 150 on an individual intelligence test and that grade equivalent achievement scores would range from 2.0 to 10.0.

Sometimes curriculum plans for a fifth grade seem to be developed on the unjustified assumption that almost all 10-year-old children should be performing at a fifth-grade level. Instead, in such a heterogeneous class as described here, the range of reading achievement could be anywhere from nonreader to a high school level of proficiency.

In arithmetic, the range of achievement would not be as large because of the greater dependence of the student on the material presented by the teacher, but it still could extend from first- to eighth-grade performance. In such a situation, it would be rather foolish to plan around fifth-grade readers or arithmetic texts, as if handing the same books to all these diverse children represents good educational planning.

Since the subject matter dealt with in the fifth grade depends, to a substantial extent, on the reading skills that the students possess, it would be worthwhile to look at the problems caused by this range in reading. Mr. Jenkins, the teacher, is faced with the following problem: From a reading standpoint, eight students are not yet ready to cope with standard fifth-grade material. They have reading skills that range anywhere from first- to fourth-grade ability. This indicates that some amount of remedial work or developmental reading designed specifically to improve their reading skills (apart from the reading for content that should be done for social studies, science, and language arts) needs to be planned for these youngsters.

While 8 of the youngsters are not ready for fifth-grade material, Mr. Jenkins is faced with the problem that 8 of the other youngsters are very bored with it. They attained a fifth-grade reading level anywhere from two to four years ago. If Mr. Jenkins is going to begin to approach the aptitude and potential of these youngsters, the assignments for them must be predicated on a much higher level of reading and conceptual difficulty. This group includes Cranshaw, Zelda, Stephanie, and Joe—but not Sam, whose language problems have slowed his reading progress to an average level. In addition to this, however, Mr. Jenkins has 10 youngsters who fall within the general age and achievement level that is expected of 10- and 11-year-old youngsters. For these 10 children, the kind of curriculum and program that is followed in the ordinary fifth grade would seem to be reasonably appropriate.

Thus, Mr. Jenkins actually has three separate reading classes within the physical boundaries of his classroom. One is almost a remedial class, in which the emphasis is still on learning the skills that presumably should have been mastered in the primary grades. Another group represents the average, which is developing at a rate to be expected for normal fifth-graders. The third group, the one with which we are particularly concerned, is the group of bright youngsters who have far surpassed the level expected of fifth-graders and who are performing at an eighth- or ninth-grade level.

It is with this group that Mr. Jenkins's own limitations stand out. It is these youngsters who challenge the frontiers of Mr. Jenkins's own knowledge. He feels particularly insecure about his poor background in science. He does not know very much about such concepts as gravity or the time/space continuum. It is clear to him, and to the other students, that Cranshaw and two or three other youngsters in the class are much more proficient in certain special areas of science than he himself is. As any teacher recognizes, this is an extremely difficult situation, because if it becomes worse, it seriously endangers the concept of the teacher as a reliable informant in areas far beyond the boundaries of science. Every teacher has only so many "I don't knows" to expend before he or she loses the intellectual respect of the students.

Let us review for a moment Mr. Jenkins's three main problems. First, the wide range of abilities of the youngsters in his group makes planning very difficult and almost forces him to make many different lesson plans and programs for the different subgroups in his class. The second major problem lies in Mr. Jenkins's own limitations of content knowledge. It is quite obvious to a teacher that his or her own limitations in certain subject areas (such as arithmetic, social studies, or science) are going to limit severely the depth to which these areas can be investigated by the students. It is all well and good to direct the youngsters to other references where they can find out more about things the teachers does not know, but if the teacher does not know much about the content field, he or she is unlikely to know good references to it. The teacher is going to need considerable assistance before gifted youngsters can profit from such references.

The establishment of the middle school, with its group planning by teachers, is one attempt to cope with the problem of a lack of content expertise and other limitations of individual teachers. No one expects a college professor to teach biology and mathematics or history and chemistry, nor should one expect expertise in these varying areas in one elementary or middle school teacher. The middle school team, combining teachers of diverse backgrounds, can use the special strengths of the group to challenge gifted students in various subject matter areas as no one teacher could.

Mr. Jenkins's third problem area is his lack of knowledge of the appropriate methods of stimulating the high-level conceptualization and productive-thinking ability of the bright group. Naturally, he wants to stimulate productive thinking at all levels of his class group, but in the advanced group, which includes Cranshaw and his friends, it becomes particularly essential to their future development as scholars, professionals, and independent thinkers.

The range of existing adaptations of school programs for gifted children is quite remarkable and sometimes obscures the fact that they are all attempts to meet three specific problems: *wide range of ability, teachers' limitations in content areas,* and *teachers' lack of special methods.* By keeping in mind that practically all the modifications of educational programming and methods attempt to deal with these three fundamental problems, the reader will be able to avoid becoming too confused by the details of the programs themselves.

These issues are not the only ones that concern the schools, however. Sometimes even the undeniable virtues of a gifted student, well recognized by his or her parents, become a mixed blessing to both the student and the teacher in the context of the regular school. For example, Cranshaw's ability to think critically and to analyze situations may, in fact, threaten both peers and teachers. Zelda's large vocabulary and verbal facility can result in her projecting a dominant personality in the classroom that is not well received by the other students. Joe's ability and eagerness to question traditional conclusions can be a substantial irritant to the teacher.

Scholarly behavior may be a desirable characteristic in some quarters, but it would be hard to convince Sam of that. His peer group has values that are strongly antischool, and they look with suspicion on any student who would admit to enjoying school. Sam occasionally must use some of his high intelligence to disguise his intellectual interests. If he wants to read a book, he takes care to do it where others might not see him. He avoids the school library, although he sometimes gazes wistfully through the door at all of this accumulated knowledge. The danger is that his avoiding the appearance of learning can become a habitual routine that will prevent him from developing good study habits and achieving well in later school years. So, even the virtues that we see in individual gifted children can become special problems when they are placed in the framework of the social group in the classroom.

How Can the Schools Adapt?

No one special program that any school could devise could meet the individual educational needs of Joe, Cranshaw, Zelda, Sam, and Stephanie. It is obvious that diversity is still a major characteristic of any group of gifted youngsters. The number and type of school adaptations that have been attempted to meet these special needs are also impressive in their diversity. The variety of changes made in local school systems for the gifted student can actually obscure the more basic objectives of this special programming. There are probably three general educational objectives for special programs for gifted and talented students that would receive broad, general agreement and acceptance among educators.

1. Gifted children should master important conceptual systems that are at the level of their abilities in various content fields.
2. Gifted children should develop skills and strategies that enable them to become more independent, creative, and self-sufficient searchers of knowledge.

3. Gifted children should develop a joy and excitement about learning that will carry them through the drudgery and routine that is an inevitable part of learning.

The wide range of adaptations that various schools adopt for these students are actually an attempt, in one form or another, to help reach one or all of these objectives. There are other educational objectives that are more controversial, on which persons within the general field of education, as well as the special field of gifted education, might disagree. Nevertheless, these other goals become a part, sometimes implicit, of many program designs. Two of these appear frequently enough to add to the previous three objectives:

4. Gifted children should be helped to recognize the special responsibilities that accompany their gifts, and be sensitized to the needs that society has for the productive use of those gifts.
5. Gifted children should interact with other children of varying abilities and cultural backgrounds, and, through that interaction, appreciate the basic worth and value of each individual.

The first of these controversial objectives implies a type of "payback" responsibility for gifted students. Having been given extraordinary abilities, there is a feeling in some quarters that these individuals have a special obligation to put those abilities to productive social use. Those who disagree with this objective point out that this enlists the gifted child in the immediate purposes of the society, which may or may not be worthy. It also implies that someone is wise enough to know what the true needs of the society are. The art of Goya or Picasso has had profound effect on social thought and direction of their times, yet the immediate value of their paintings easily could have been questioned by teachers or principals when these artists were in their formative years. They might even been counseled to use their gifts for some more "practical" purpose in business or the sciences.

The second controversial objective is a concern to some educators, since it suggests that mere contact with others who are different from ourselves will result in mutual respect. We know that that is not necessarily the result of mixing people with different interests and motivations unless careful planning and clear social objectives are undertaken. Both of these objectives represent true value conflicts, on the part of educators and society, that have yet to be resolved. Since there is little disagreement on the first three objectives, we will concentrate in this chapter on how the schools are attempting to meet those.

School Adaptations

One of the challenges of planning for gifted students is to convince teachers and administrators that these students can have just as wide a variety of problems as any student. Galbraith (1985) summed up what he calls the "Eight Great Gripes of Gifted Kids" (see Figure 3–3). In those eight statements, one can see the overexpectations of teachers and parents of many gifted students plus the lack of challenge that they receive in school.

They do not feel rewarded for excellent products, since it is assumed that they did them with little effort. There is a tone of loneliness and of feeling different in several of those complaints—lonely because they feel that they are not understood by others and have interests different from their peers.

A lot of the "problems" that gifted students face would be gladly accepted by other students and their parents. For example, the decision that they have to make between a wide variety of alternatives in their choice of careers is hardly something that gains sympathy from those who would be happy with one viable career line. Nevertheless, the concerns that such students have about choosing a life career or channel can be just as anxiety producing as the problems of passing a course can be for other students (Delisle, 1984).

The public schools often organize themselves in certain ways in order to meet specific problems or issues, such as the presence of gifted students. So what are the special reasons for adaptation in this case? The previous chapter has presented some of these reasons.

1. *Rapid cognitive development.* This is the hallmark of giftedness and it means that these students will grasp new facts and concepts more rapidly than the other students and be able to understand more complex ideas than other students. The consequence of this fact is that these students will often be sitting with nothing to do, much of the time waiting for the other students to catch up—unless something special is done.
2. *More extensive knowledge base.* These students will also have stored away a greater variety of information from their past learning and this will make it progressively easier for them to incorporate new information into already existing understandings.

These two factors also explain why the most common complaint of gifted students about school is excruciating boredom unless something special or some program adapta-

---

FIGURE 3–3   The Eight Great Gripes of Gifted Kids

1. No one explains what being gifted is all about—it's kept a big secret.
2. The stuff we do in school is too easy and it's boring.
3. Parents, teachers, and friends expect us to be perfect, to "do our best" all the time.
4. Kids often tease us about being smart.
5. Friends who *really* understand us are few and far between.
6. We feel too differently and wish people would accept us for what we are.
7. We feel overwhelmed by the number of things we can do in life.
8. We worry a lot about world problems and feel helpless to do anything about them.

Source: Galbraith, J. (1985). The eight great gripes of gifted kids: Responding to special needs. *Roeper Review, 8* (1), 16. Reprinted with permission of *Roeper Review*, P.O. Box 329, Bloomfield Hills, MI 48303.

tion is not made for them. Imagine having to spend time learning the multiplication tables or the alphabet over and over again. Since the actual gap in knowledge base becomes larger between the average and gifted student as time goes on, the pressure to do something definably different increases as the children grow older.

3. *Heterogeneous culture.* The presence of a diversity of cultural backgrounds in the classroom in many U.S. schools is another factor that has played a major role in aggravating the issue of individual differences in schools. The greater the diversity of student abilities, attitudes, and values that exist in a given classroom, the more difficult it is for a lone teacher to meet the needs of each of the children, particularly those who deviate the most from the average.

These three factors are obviously interrelated and together force the schools to think about alternatives to the heterogeneous classroom. The adaptations that schools can make can be divided roughly into three major types. Schools can change the *content* of the lessons to be taught; they can change the *special skills* they wish the child to master; and they can change the *learning environment* designed to facilitate the learning of special knowledges and skills so the gifted students can be as creative, productive, and enthusiastic as possible.

There is an wide array of possible services to be provided to gifted students in the schools, as can be seen in Table 3–1. The variety of special provisions at every educational level can amaze and confuse people who do not realize that these are variations of a few major themes.

TABLE 3–1   Wide Array of Possible Services Provided to Gifted Students

Elementary Services	Junior High or Middle School Services	High School Services
1. Full-Time Classes	1. Counseling	1. Counseling
2. Pullout Classes	2. Accelerated Classes	2. Advance Placement Courses
3. Junior Great Books	3. Future Problem Solving	3. Accelerated Classes
4. Future Problem Solving	4. Junior Great Books	4. Foreign Language
5. Olympics of the Mind	5. Olympics of the Mind	5. Seminar
6. Careers Exploration	6. Career Education	6. Independent Study
7. Mentors	7. Mentors	7. Mentors
8. Saturday Classes	8. Individual Tutors or Mentors	8. College Courses
9. Summer Opportunities	9. AP or College Classes (Open to Some)	9. Career Education
10. Foreign Language— Exploratory Study	10. Higher Math Classes (open)	10. Correspondence Study
11. Grade Advancement	11. Foreign Language	11. Opportunities in Arts and Humanities
	12. Opportunities in Art, Music, Drama and Dance	

Source: S. Hoover & J. Feldhusen (1987). Integrating identification, school services, and student needs in secondary gifted programs. *Arkansas Gifted Education Magazine, 1,* 8–16. Reprinted by permission of John Feldhusen.

The Limitations of Time

One of the topics not sufficiently discussed in the development of special programs for the gifted is the fundamental issue of how much time is available for their instruction. Each school year is limited to 180 to 200 school days of about five hours a day. There may be a maximum of 1,000 hours of instruction a year. This seems like a generous amount of time in which an enormous amount of knowledge can be absorbed, and so it is, but the amount of knowledge that is available to be absorbed is increasing exponentially.

The so-called *knowledge explosion* has occurred in practically all fields, so that the amount of information available in a given subject may be doubling in a time frame of 10 years. Coupled with that knowledge explosion is another phenomenon that Molnar (1982) refers to as the *ignorance explosion*. In other words, knowledge has become available at such a rapid rate that the newest knowledge is known to only a very tiny segment of the population because we have not yet found a way to pass this new information along to many others. Molnar stated, "In science and technology alone, there are over one thousand computerized data bases which are searched at least two million times a year and five hundred and twenty-eight bibliographical bases with over seventy million citations" (p. 104).

The problem of the educator of gifted students is to determine what knowledge can be taught or should be taught within the limited time frame available. It is no longer sufficient merely to ask the question Would gifted students find a unit or topic such as the black holes in space interesting and intriguing? The answer to such a question is almost always yes. The second criterion that needs to be considered is What are the important and critical knowledge and skills that the student should master? and What are those relatively inconsequential sets of knowledge that should be put aside in their favor? Even with a remarkable information-processing individual such as the gifted child, these decisions have to be made.

Program Differentiation

One of the decisions that educators of the gifted find most difficult is precisely in which way the school curriculum should be differentiated for gifted and talented students. Many people outside (and some inside) the educational establishment expect some dramatically different educational procedure or content to be used that is not found in other parts of the educational program. They are often disappointed to find that the ingredients of the program for gifted students are recognizable to any observer of the educational scene.

Zelda's mother recently had that kind of disappointing experience. She had looked forward eagerly to visiting the resource room ever since she had been told that Zelda was enrolled in a special program for gifted students. The students in this somewhat smaller group were discussing economics, and the interchange between students in the class was vigorous, encompassing not only the role played by banks in the society but also a discussion as to the moral decisions that a banker makes regarding who receives loans and who is denied loans. Nevertheless, Zelda's mother was dissatisfied in that she somehow expected to see something dramatically different. She had seen and experienced such discussions before in schools, without it being labeled as "special program for gifted students." What Zelda's mother did not realize is that rarely do such discussions take place *at the age level* of these students.

The emphasis in the special programs for gifted students is on stimulation of the thinking processes of *creativity, originality, problem solving, and problem finding,* and increasing the *content depth and sophistication.* Observers are often heard to ask, "Are these not appropriate activities for the average learner and the slow learner as well?" The answer is of course. But in the programs for gifted students these occur in differing proportions. It is the proportions of these ingredients that often make for a different program rather than the nature of the ingredients themselves.

If one misreads a recipe and puts into a cake one cup instead of one teaspoon of baking powder, the overall results will be quite different, if not striking. One can still say the *ingredients* in the two cakes are all the same, but it is the *proportions* that change the character of the product itself. The bringing together of gifted students allows the teacher to spend a *proportionally greater* amount of time on developing inquiry skills and discussing abstract ideas and systems than would be possible in a group of slower learners.

A similar problem of adapting to a wide range of individual differences is found in the selection of textbooks from various grade levels. Renzulli, Smith, and Reis (1982) reported that a study by EPIE (Educational Products Information Exchange) revealed that over half of the fourth-graders in some school districts are able to achieve a score of 80 percent or higher on a test of the content of their math texts *before* they have opened their books in the fall. Similar results were found in science and social studies tests. Thus, the actual textbooks being used in the classroom contained much information already known to the majority of the students and certainly to the gifted students.

Why does this happen? One possible explanation is that teachers want to make sure that the majority of students in the class will be able to master the textbook and will not find it beyond their capabilities. In order to meet that criterion, teachers have to pay special attention to whether a textbook would be applicable for the average or slow-learning youngster, because no teacher wants to leave half of the students abandoned or unable fully to use the textbook. But the range of abilities and performance are so great in the classroom that selecting any one book is bound to place some students at a marked disadvantage.

Probably there is no solution to the task of choosing one textbook, and the problem may lie precisely in the concept of a *single* textbook. One of the advantages of the program for the gifted and talented is that it is possible to extend the concept of the textbook into a reference shelf of books where a wide variety of references can be used without concern about the reading level of the books.

Do social values make a difference in program design? A highly destructive and completely incorrect idea about instruction of gifted children has been satirically labeled the *cannonball theory.* This misguided notion is that the progress of gifted children is set at the moment of conception and that, like a cannonball once fired, it cannot be deflected from its inevitable path to superior performance. However, the surrounding environment and experiences do tend to shape and mold the gifted child, much as they do all children. Gifted children can be uplifted by a splendid teacher or depressed by an unimaginative one. They can be channeled into some lines of interest and away from others, and they can be negatively affected when the society as a whole gives signals that high ability is not valued.

Program Content

Breadth, Tempo, and Kind

Because the gifted child demonstrates a manifest ability to handle a complexity of ideas far beyond his or her life age, one of the natural school adaptations is a program providing content that stresses a greater complexity of ideas and higher levels of abstraction than can be mastered by the average student of that age. Passow (1979) pointed out that the curriculum can be changed in at least three ways: (1) in breadth or depth, (2) in tempo or pace, and (3) in kind.

An example of changing the curriculum in *breadth* would be to take a regular set of objectives on learning long-division processes and ask a gifted student to conduct these operations in a base other than base 10. Or while the students are discussing the American Revolution, ask the gifted students to discuss and relate the American Revolution to revolutions that have taken place in other countries.

Changes in *tempo or pace* generally represent an acceleration of the curriculum. Thus, gifted students can be taking algebra while still in the fifth grade or studying sciences and language arts that they would not encounter ordinarily for another one or two years in the school curriculum.

Finally, a change in *kind* would represent courses that do not ordinarily get offered at all. Examples of such courses would be the study of strategies for forecasting the future, or courses in symbolic logic, or examining the changing patterns of morality in our society. All represent a unique instructional program that gifted students might have particular use for as part of their total educational program.

It is hard to quarrel with the fact that a teacher who has had two three-hour courses in biology at the college level some 10 or 15 years ago is hardly equipped to present high-level concepts in the world of biology to gifted students; or that a teacher whose knowledge of history has been confined to a routine examination of military campaigns of the various wars in which the United States has fought is prepared to lead the gifted student into more sophisticated knowledge of historical trends through the ages. The schools have tried to handle such limitations in the past by suggesting that even though a teacher may not know the subject matter extensively, he or she could send the gifted students to references where they could find out for themselves. However, when a teacher does not know very much about a particular content area—and many elementary and middle school teachers fall into this category—then he or she often cannot send the student to appropriate reference sources. Therefore, one of the emphases in teacher training of the gifted has been an attempt to strengthen teachers' content knowledge in their own given areas of interest.

When teachers have not had the benefit of mastering the organization of ideas or concepts, then, in desperation, they may give gifted students like Cranshaw or Zelda longer and more extensive assignments of the same sort that are provided to the average student. Since the gifted students have the ability to absorb an almost unlimited supply of facts, they will often dutifully attack the new assignments and work hard at them. So they (and we) may never realize what they are missing—namely, the opportunity to explore larger and more important ideas.

Table 3–2 provides a brief description of how the focus of the same general topic areas might be modified in breadth or depth for differing levels of ability among students. In history, the slow students can profit best by discussing their own community and how it works, so that they can have hands-on experience based on personal perceptions. In the area of nutrition, a similar objective can be set by trying to provide as practical and direct an experience as possible for the slow learners so that they can use their perceptions to aid their mastery of the necessary ideas.

It would be unfortunate indeed if the same intellectual meal was presented to the gifted. In addition to understanding the basic ideas noted above, the gifted student can be thinking in terms of how all types of cultures need some type of government and can trace how these governmental patterns have changed from primitive to modern times. Similarly, the gifted student can be concerned about nutrition in the broader sense of how food becomes translated into bodily energy—a large step beyond just understanding the appropriate balance of carbohydrates, proteins, fats, and so forth. It is a major challenge of the educational system to provide for the diversity of abilities in a way that allows each student to perform at his or her appropriate level and rate.

Sawyer made a strong case for the inclusion of sophisticated and rigorous mastery of complex content:

> When I defended academic rigor, I meant to support the teaching of the basic knowledge required for our most promising youth to be productive in the real world of science, politics, religion, mathematics, literature, music. It is robbery of the gifted merely to teach them how to learn without teaching something worth learning.... The fact is that a gifted person needs even more knowledge than others before he can hope to make a significant contribution to his or her field. (1988)

TABLE 3–2   Curricular Levels of Abstraction by Ability Levels

Ability Level	*History*	*Nutrition*
Bright	Patterns of governing in cultures across time and national boundaries	The biochemistry of food and the translation of food into bodily energy
Average	The beginnings of U.S. government—our historical heritage	Understanding nutrition: classification of carbohydrates, proteins, fats, etc.
Slow	How local government works and influences me	Kinds of nutritious food to buy; samples of balanced meals

Curriculum Compacting

Another device found useful in content adaptation is a procedure known as *curriculum compacting*. Renzulli, Smith, and Reis (1982) stated that its purpose is to ensure that the basic knowledge a gifted student would be expected to know on any given topic area in fact has been mastered. Since we already are aware of the likelihood that much of the knowledge now presented to gifted students is already known to them, then the likelihood that they could move more rapidly through a set of standard content objectives is quite high.

Renzulli, Smith, and Reis (1982) suggested that three major steps should be taken in the compacting sequence. The first of these is to *provide a brief description of the basic material* to be covered. This means that if the knowledge to be compacted is, for instance, long-division facts, then these facts should be presented as such. The second major step is to *describe activities* that will be used to guarantee the proficiency of the student in these basic curricular areas. This might often take the form of a pretest to see if the student already knows the relevant material or to determine to what extent additional exercises are needed. Once the teacher has been satisfied that the basic systems of knowledge have been mastered, then it is possible to move forward into the third step, to *enrichment activities*, which will provide an advanced-level learning experience in that curriculum area.

For example, if certain students already know the basic story and purpose of the Mayflower Compact, then they perhaps can design a similar compact for explorers to a different planet or to Antarctica. This device tends to satisfy one of the major concerns of teachers—that gifted students may inadvertently leapfrog over some basic knowledge and skills in the process of accelerating through the material (Renzulli, Smith, & Reis, 1982). In this process, the teacher is first assured that the basic knowledge is mastered and is then free to go forward with enrichment activities.

Intellectual Skills Mastery

It has come as a shock to many of us that, if we keep our current traditions, children entering the first grade in 1994 will not emerge until the year 2010 if they go to college. If a child is gifted, then the possibility that he or she would be in some form of advanced schooling well into the first decade of the twenty-first century is very likely indeed. So the question we must ask ourselves is How well is our present educational effort preparing the gifted students for that new century? Will the information learned now be applicable then?

It is this concern that has caused those in gifted education to seek as a major educational objective the special mastery of various skills and strategies so that the student can be better prepared for the inevitable social and technological changes over the next two decades. When is a gifted child ready for the discovery of new ideas for independent searching and for inquiry? Sometimes it seems as if students must wait for professional or graduate school before they are allowed independent inquiry. When should the *idea gatherer* become the *idea producer*, and can this suddenly happen at the graduate level if the student rarely has been asked to be an idea producer in earlier educational experiences? Surely our educational system has more to offer the gifted student than the prospect of becoming an academic sponge sopping up facts that pour out when he or she is squeezed.

Much of the earlier efforts in the stimulation of thinking skills has been focused on various problem-solving techniques and devices. This approach is slowly being changed to take into account one of society's new developments. Since the premium problem solver may well be the computer, then it becomes more interesting to reflect on what a person needs to learn or do in order to become a problem finder.

Getzels (1982) has stressed the importance of *problem finding*. The emphasis on creativity and the stimulation of intellectual flexibility also lies behind these attempts to help the gifted child (and all children, for that matter) adapt to changing circumstances. In these lessons, we seek not the "correct" answer (i.e., the one the teacher has) so much as the unique answer with quality. We are not as interested in training a gifted student to execute the chemistry experiment correctly as we are that she or he tell us that the experiment itself is trivial and that a better one can be constructed. Part of this book will focus and elaborate on these concepts and ideas on the topic of the stimulating productive thinking abilities.

Learning Environment

A wide variety of modifications in learning environments from the standard school setting can be noted in the programs for the gifted and talented, and these changes are mostly designed to implement the desired adaptations in content and skills. The basic goals of these changes in learning environments are to bring gifted youngsters in contact with one another so that they can profit from each others' ideas, and to bring them in contact with an instructor who may have special skills that can help these students reach their appropriate abilities more effectively. Figure 3–4 indicates some of the usual learning-environment adaptations for gifted students. As can be noted, they extend in intensity from modest changes in the program within the regular classroom, to part-time experiences during the school day, to separation from the regular program in special classes or special schools.

The decision by local school authorities as to which of these strategies (or which combination of them) are most appropriate depends on the availability of specially trained staff, physical facilities, and general educational philosophy as represented in that school district. Many school systems of modest or larger size attempt to provide a continuum of services. Cranshaw, Zelda, Joe, Sam, and Stephanie might find a variety of programs in which they could fit. Whereas Cranshaw and Zelda might respond well to a special class, Sam and Stephanie might respond better to a mentor, and Joe might be at his best when he is helped by a consultant teacher in the regular program. There are no right or wrong answers as to which of these variations are most appropriate, and, as a matter of fact, there is little systematic research evidence regarding their relative effectiveness. Nevertheless, in an active program of gifted education in a school system, one can expect to find a number of examples of changes in all three of these major dimensions: *learning environments, content*, and *skills*.

FIGURE 3–4   Learning-Environment Adaptations for Gifted Students

Enrichment in the Regular Classroom

The classroom teacher provides special materials and lessons to help gifted and talented students. Students remain in the classroom for the school day.

Consultant Teacher

A specially trained teacher serves as a consultant to the classroom teacher in providing appropriate lessons and instruction for gifted students. The consultant teacher meets periodically with classroom teachers.

Resource Room

Gifted and talented students attend a resource room for a small part of the day and do special projects under the supervision of a teacher especially trained in working with gifted and talented students.

Mentor

People with special skills who work in the community and are not members of the school staff work individually, or in small groups, with gifted and talented students. Example: A scientist or musician tutors a student a few hours a week in his or her own specialty.

Independent Study

Gifted and talented students are trained in how to choose and carry out an independent study project under the supervision of appropriately trained personnel. Example: The study of traffic patterns in a local community as part of a transportation unit.

Special-Interest Classes

Special classes are established in specific content fields (e.g., symbols, logic, Egyptian history, creative writing, etc.) and are offered to students who have a special interest and would volunteer for the additional experience. Content is often attractive to gifted students.

Special Classes

Gifted and talented students receive basic instruction from a specially trained teacher in self-contained or special subject area classes (math or science). Students must demonstrate eligibility before participating.

Special Schools

The entire school may be devoted to special instructional methods and content for gifted and talented students. Students must demonstrate eligibility before participating. Example: Special schools in art or mathematics.

Gifted Students as Intellectual Volunteers

The traditional approach has been to identify gifted students and then plan a program to meet their needs. Another approach to the design of programs for gifted students is to create an attractive and unique opportunity and then invite any student to participate. If the program is sufficiently challenging, then gifted and talented students will want to participate and will volunteer. They then will be making a personal commitment instead of being told what they are supposed to do because they are gifted. There are a number of variations on this theme.

Enrichment Triad

One of the most frequently used strategies in the volunteer type of program is called the Enrichment Triad. Devised by Renzulli (1977), the Triad calls for a three-step process: First, the student explores a topic area; next, he or she is provided with various divergent and productive-thinking skills to stimulate the thinking processes through group training; and third, the student conducts individual or small-group projects that will be meaningful to him or her and to the society. The advantage to gifted students of this approach is that it allows them to be active learners, to do individual projects, and thus not be held back by the limited skills and knowledge of others.

Revolving Door

Another variation, at the elementary level, to provide special experiences for those gifted children who wish to participate is the revolving door procedure. In this procedure, students may volunteer for special projects and gain help from a resource teacher to frame the area of interest into a researchable problem and to obtain additional resources to address the problem. This procedure provides for critical feedback and finds outlets for the products of the students' work. The children may participate in this program for a while and then decide to stay in the regular class. As many as 20 to 25 percent of the students of above-average ability and high motivation may participate in such a program, which would include children traditionally referred to as gifted but also many other children of above-average ability who would not fit the usual criteria for giftedness.

Renzulli, Reis, and Smith stressed that the special advantages of the revolving door program consist not only in involving a large proportion of the student body but also "the revolving door approach means that a child 'earns' the opportunity to obtain special services by showing some or all of those traits research has associated with giftedness: Above average ability, task commitment, and creativity" (1981, p. 649).

Magnet Schools

The development of the concept of magnet schools is of special interest to those concerned with the education of gifted and talented students. Within a given school system, certain schools can be identified as having a particular emphasis or focus. One school might be identified as a *basic skills* school, where students would receive heavy emphasis on the mastery of the fundamentals of mathematics, reading, writing, and so forth. Another school might focus on *creativity and aesthetics*, teaching special courses in performing arts, creative writing, foreign languages, or exploration of alternative futures. Parents and students would be allowed to volunteer for the special school that they feel would be particularly responsive to the child's needs, or, alternatively, they can keep the child in the traditional elementary, junior high, or middle school.

In those schools emphasizing creativity, gifted students can move through basic minicourses into in-depth studies of their own choosing. Such individualization does provide the opportunity for gifted students to move at their own pace in a program area they can choose.

Center for the Advancement of Academically Talented Youth (CTY)

The current Center for Talented Youth at Johns Hopkins University emerged out of an earlier talent search program, the Study of Mathematically Precocious Youth (SMPY). The SMPY talent search program, which began at Johns Hopkins as an attempt to identify highly gifted students in mathematics, has evolved into special instructional programs for talented youth in their particular area of content specialty. More commonly offered at the secondary-school level, these special courses can stress excellence and content acceleration in mathematics or language arts. In this way, students who have shown, through the talent search, aptitude three or four years in advance of their agemates can have a stimulating experience by responding to advanced content that will challenge their abilities (Stanley, 1979).

Societal Values and Their Impact on Programming

Whether or not a local school system changes its curriculum, its methods of skills mastery, or its learning environment to meet the needs of gifted children and youth depends to a very large extent on the value systems held by the predominant groups who influence such school policy. Those who believe that such decisions are made solely, or even predominantly, on the basis of educational research or experience will continue to be confused or puzzled by what actually happens unless they recognize the impact of citizen values. A specific example that many have experienced will illustrate the point.

The Palcuzzi Ploy

Mr. Palcuzzi, principal of the Jefferson Elementary School, got tired of hearing objections to special provisions for gifted children, so he decided to spice an otherwise mild PTA meeting with *his* proposal for gifted children. The elements of the Palcuzzi program were as follows:

1. Children should be grouped by ability.
2. Part of the school day should be given over to special instruction.
3. Talented students should be allowed time to share their talents with children of other schools in the area or even of other schools throughout the state. (We will pay the transportation costs.)
4. Children should be advanced according to their talents, rather than their age.
5. These children should have specially trained and highly salaried teachers.

As might be expected, the "Palcuzzi program" was subjected to a barrage of criticism: "What about the youngsters who aren't able to fit into the special group; won't their egos be damaged?" "How about the special cost; how could you justify transportation costs that would have to be paid by moving a special group of students from one school to another?" "Won't we be endangering the children by having them interact with others who are much more mature?" "Wouldn't the other teachers complain if we gave more money to the instructors of this group?"

After listening for 10 or 15 minutes, Palcuzzi dropped his bomb. He said that he was not describing a *new* program for the intellectually gifted, but a program the school system had been enthusiastically supporting for a number of years—the program for *gifted basketball players!* Palcuzzi took advantage of the silence that followed to review his program again.

"Do we have ability grouping on our basketball team? Yes, we do. No doubt, the player who does not make the first team or the second team feels very bad about it and may even have some inferiority feelings. However, this will not likely cause the program to be changed.

"Do we allow part of the school day to be given over to special work? Generally speaking, the last hour of the day can be used, by tradition, for practice of basketball talents.

"Do we allow these children to share their talents with other students from other schools and other cities? Yes, we do, and, what is more, we pay the transportation costs involved without very many complaints being heard.

"Do we allow gifted basketball players to advance by their talents rather than by their age? Indeed, we do. Any sophomore who can make the team on the basis of talent gets the privilege of playing with seniors, and no one worries very much about it.

"Finally, do we have special teachers who are specially trained and more highly salaried than the ordinary teacher? Yes, we do, and although there is some grumbling about it from the regular teachers, this does not materially affect the program."

What does this tell us? The culture and the community will support the kinds of activities that they find necessary, valuable, and/or enjoyable. If they feel that a program is sufficiently necessary or sufficiently enjoyable, all sorts of objections are put aside as being relatively inconsequential. On the other hand, if the community is not fully interested or involved in supporting such a program, all kinds of objections can be raised as to why these things should not or cannot be done.

The student of human nature knows better than to think that, because Mr. Palcuzzi caught the PTA off balance, he therefore swept on to victory and the PTA unanimously resolved to support the institution of a special program for gifted children.

The opposition to such a program is often deep and emotional. To many people, there is something manifestly unfair about giving Cranshaw, a boy of superior opportunities and abilities, special help to do *more* with his superior abilities, when other children are still struggling to meet minimum requirements. To these people, it is disturbing that there is not a tidy balance sheet for life. The gifted person should somehow be morally or physically weak; the retarded child should have uncommon strength, so as to compensate for his or her limited mind. In this way, things would balance out. The fact that this is not so—indeed, it is often just the opposite—is disturbing, and attempts to swing the balance even more in favor of the favored (through special educational provisions) are objected to strenuously.

This is not to say that every person who has doubts about the value of special programs is reacting on this basis. It is a plea, however, for an understanding of human emotions, which, though often presented in disguised or rationalized argument, determine attitudes and decisions in this area of school policy. Another inhibitor of school action for the gifted is the frequently heard concern over the consequences we may spawn when we unleash the intellects of the bright students.

The gifted child's ability to use superior logic helps him or her to penetrate, among other things, current prejudices of the culture and society. Cranshaw is at his most troublesome in the class when he does exactly what we *say* we want him to do—think for himself. But if he thinks for himself, this means that he is going to want to make up his own mind about the virtues and sins of such controversial subjects as communism, religion, drugs, sex, economics, or politics. These topics are explosive and controversial, and many teachers and administrators try to avoid them. The movement to make our schools "antiseptic" by systematically ignoring every flesh-and-blood issue in our society has reached alarming proportions. To a large extent, this is a problem of administrative policy. If teachers are sure that they will receive backing from their superiors, they can explore controversial subjects with their students without looking over their shoulders to see which pressure group may descend on them.

Certainly, pressure groups in the community cannot get too aroused over a group of students memorizing the Bill of Rights. This can be done in safety and with a feeling of some patriotism. However, when gifted youngsters attempt to *apply* certain parts of the Bill of Rights to their society and suggest that maybe some of those articles are being actively violated in their own community, there may be some anguished second thoughts about the wisdom of allowing these youngsters to have free rein with their intellects.

In essence, the inquiring gifted child is the true challenge to educators and their own values, and to the society and its values. Do the school and the community really believe that the democratic process will triumph in a free exchange of ideas? Do they really believe that, given the free exchange of ideas, the values that we now cherish will survive and be strengthened by the test?

It is easy enough to say that we believe these things, but it is a little more difficult to practice them. If we do believe them, then we have the responsibility for allowing these youngsters the opportunity to explore answers other than only those we think are correct. If we are honestly committed to helping them think for themselves, then we cannot impress on them our own concepts of what is right or what is wrong. For one thing, they simply will not accept them; they will wonder, "If your values are so good, why are you so frantically trying to stop a fair investigation of them?" If we actively repress their tendencies to look at all aspects of an issue, all we will have done is delayed a more thorough, and perhaps a more destructive, reaction at a later date.

Finally, if we, as teachers, are to deal effectively with these youngsters, we must understand as thoroughly as possible our own emotional blocks that stand between us and full acceptance of these youngsters. One such block, whether verbalized or not, is that these youngsters are the most thorough threat to the status quo that one could possibly invent. These children are the innovators, the changers, the modifiers, the people who will remold and reshape our culture from the way it is today into the way it will be in the next generation. But this is *our* status quo. With all its faults and sins, we have become adjusted to it, and we may even like it.

The idea that we could contribute actively to its downfall by teaching these young-sters to use their intellectual abilities more effectively is a frightening one to many persons. Although this is an understandable reaction, it is not a very profitable one. The world and culture *are* going to change, whether we like it or not and despite all that we can do about it. Our only hope is that it will change in a direction favorable for us. This is not to say we should not be concerned about the potential for both benefit and harm that our interest in gifted students can create. But the more effectively we help these youngsters to perform, the more we can expect to see, as the fruits of our labor, these youngsters operating at their top capacity to shape their future, and ours, in ways that will be constructive.

Unresolved Issues

1. The amount of new knowledge that is becoming available to someone, somewhere each day is remarkable, yet the time we allot for schooling does not change very much. Obviously, under these circumstances, we will be teaching gifted children (and *all* children) a smaller and smaller portion of available knowledge. What are the rules for us to follow to determine which knowledge will be made available and which will be deemphasized?

2. The struggle to maintain a school program that stresses *excellence* and, at the same time, honors the principle of *equity* is a profoundly important one. Many people feel that interest in the individual differences of children, whether bright or dull, is the key characteristic to accepting both concepts. All too often, those advocating excellence are willing to forget those children of modest abilities, and those advocating equity seem more interested in a minimum performance standards than in allowing the bright child to advance.

3. How do we encourage the problem finders in our society without endangering them and ourselves? Galileo, Sir Thomas More, Henri Matisse, and Pablo Picasso all paid a price for seeing the world in a different perspective from the generally accepted one. Encouraging problem finding means encouraging a challenge to the status quo, with predictably negative consequences for the innovator. How do we train children to have sufficient diplomacy to enable them to challenge without infuriating?

4. A new burst of educational reform has moved into the American scene in the form of the middle schools movement, site-based management, cooperative learning, and so on. How should programs for gifted students fit into these new concepts and systems?

Chapter Review

1. Adaptations of the regular education program to the special needs of gifted students must overcome a complex love-hate relationship with giftedness in U.S. society. This societal uncertainty in response to giftedness leads to a widely fluctuating level of support for gifted programs.

2. One of the basic reasons for special programming for gifted and talented students is the diversity of student performance on academic and intellectual measures in a single class, which makes the classroom teacher's job difficult.

3. The heterogeneous classroom that would be composed of students of diverse performance would often yield three groups: average, below average, and above average. Most teachers find it important to deal with the average and below-average students first and consequently have little time to pay attention to the markedly above-average students.

4. The advent of the educational reform movement (middle schools, accountability, cooperative learning, site-based management, etc.) has implemented many changes to which programs for gifted students must adapt.

5. Special programs for gifted and talented students have three major program objectives: (a) the mastery of complex systems of knowledge in the content fields, (b) the mastery of skills leading to independence of inquiry, and (c) the encouragement of the joy of discovery and learning.

6. One of the major problems in curriculum decision making for the gifted is the limited time available for instruction. Curricula should be chosen by the criteria that they are important to the mastery of knowledge systems as well as interesting and entertaining.

7. Convincing evidence is available that the differential rewards in the social environment influence the shape and direction that giftedness will take in that society. A society that stresses music will produce gifted musicians; a society that stresses athletics will produce gifted athletes.

8. The difference in content between programs for gifted students and the average student lies in the proportion of time spent on certain concepts and activities. The more advanced the student, the more complex the content and the more emphasis on independent thinking processes.

9. There are several ways in which the program content can be changed for the gifted: in depth or breadth, in tempo or pace, and in kind.

10. If the program content is changed in depth or breadth, the basic concern is for the mastery of complex systems of knowledge within each content discipline.

11. Changes in skills mastery place the stress on efficiency in using techniques such as problem solving, creativity, and problem finding. The goals are to help gifted learners become autonomous in seeking knowledge.

12. An extensive continuum of learning environments exist for gifted and talented students, from enrichment exercises in the regular classroom at one extreme to special schools on the other.

13. Although many programs have been designed to begin with the special needs of the gifted students, some programs are now available that begin with a changed learning environment or program content. Special programs such as magnet schools and the revolving door procedure ask students to volunteer for these experiences rather than be tested for eligibility.

14. The extent to which special programs are made available for gifted students will depend largely on societal approval for such programs and on the values of the society as a whole.

Readings of Special Interest

Colangelo, N., & Davis, G. (Eds.). (1991) *Handbook of gifted education*. Boston: Allyn and Bacon.
   This multiple-author book brings together the specialized knowledge of over 40 authors dealing with such topics and identification, instructional models, creativity and thinking skills, psychological and counseling services, and special populations. Among the unique contributions are those by Kulik and Kulik reporting on ability grouping and gifted students, Tannenbaum on the social psychology of giftedness, and Morelock and Feldman on extreme precocity.

Ross, P. (1993). *A national report on gifted and talented education*. Washington, DC: U.S. Department of Education.
   This volume offers a comprehensive summary of the current status of programs for gifted and talented students in the United States. It focuses on the national interest in gifted education and has a variety of suggestions as to how education for high-ability students can be improved. It also includes interesting vignettes on individual students to highlight the general issues being discussed.

Shore, B., Cornell, D., Robinson, A., & Ward, V. (1991). *Recommended practices in gifted education*. New York: Teachers College Press.

This is a remarkable attempt to bring together the research underpinnings of major educational practices for gifted students such as acceleration, thinking skills, curricular differentiation, microcomputer use, and so on. The authors provide 100 such practices together with the background and support for each. It is a fine presentation of the state of the art in gifted education.

Special Issue: Gifted education and the school reform movement. (1991). *Gifted Child Quarterly, 35* (1).

Special Issue: Educational reform: Impact on gifted. (1990). *Journal for Education of the Gifted, 14* (1).
   These two major journals in the field of educating gifted students organized entire issues on the topic of educational reform and its influence on education of gifted students. Issues related to ability grouping, personnel preparation, and the role of technology and linkage with general education are discussed.

References

Archambault, F., Westberg, K., Brown, S., Hallmark, B., Zhang, W., & Emmons, C. (1993). Classroom practices used with gifted third- and fourth-grade students. *Journal for the Education of the Gifted, 16* (2), 103–119.

Delisle, J. (1984). *Gifted children speak out*. New York: Walker & Company.

Galbraith, J. (1985). The eight great gripes of gifted kids: Responding to special needs. *Roeper Review, 8* (1), 16.

Gallagher, J. J. (1991). Educational reform, values, and gifted students. *Gifted Child Quarterly, 35* (1), 12–19.

Gallagher, J. J. (1986). Our love-hate affair with gifted children. *Gifted Children Quarterly, 9* (42), 47–49.

George, P. (1988). Tracking and ability grouping: Which way for the middle school? *Middle School Journal, 20* (1), 21–28.

Getzels, J. (1982). The problem of the problem. In R. Hogarth (Ed.), *New directions for methodology of social and behavioral science: Question framing and response consistency*. San Francisco: Jossey-Bass.

Johnson, D., & Johnson, R. (1990). Social skills for successful group work. *Educational Leadership, 47* (4), 29–32.

Kagan, S. (1988). *Cooperative learning: Resources for teachers*. Riverside, CA: University of California.

Kulik, J. A., & Kulik, C. C. (1991). Ability grouping and gifted students. In N. Colangelo & G. A.

Davis (Eds.), *Handbook of gifted education* (pp. 178–196). Boston: Allyn and Bacon.

Molnar, A. (1982). The search for new intellectual technologies. *T.H.E. Journal.*

National Commission on Excellence in Education. (1983). *A nation at risk: The imperative for educational reform.* Washington, DC: U.S. Government Printing Office.

Oakes, J. (1985). *Keeping track: How schools structure inequality.* New Haven, CT: Yale University Press.

Passow, A. H. (Ed.). (1979). *The gifted and the creative: Their education and development. The Seventy-eighth Yearbook of the National Society for the Study of Education.* Chicago: University of Chicago Press.

Renzulli, J. (1977). *The enrichment triad model: A guide for developing defensible programs for the gifted and talented.* Mansfield Center, CT: Creative Learning Press.

Renzulli, J. S., & Reis, S. (1991). The reform movement and the quiet crisis in gifted education. *Gifted Child Quarterly, 35* (1), 26–35.

Renzulli, J., Reis, S., & Smith, L. (1981, May). The revolving door model: A new way of identifying the gifted. *Phi Delta Kappa,* 648–649.

Renzulli, J., Smith, L., & Reis, S. (1982). Curriculum compacting: An essential strategy for working with gifted students. *Elementary School Journal, 82,* 185–194.

Robinson, A. (1990). Cooperation or exploitation? The argument against cooperative learning for talented students. *Journal for the Education of the Gifted, 14* (1), 9–27, 31–36.

Ross, P. (1993). *National excellence: The case for developing America's talent.* Washington, DC: U.S. Department of Education.

Sawyer, R. (1988). In defense of academic rigor. *Journal for the Education of the Gifted, 11* (2), 31–34.

Slavin, R. (1988). Synthesis of research on grouping in elementary and secondary schools. *Educational Leadership, 46* (1), 67–77.

Slavin, R. (1990). Ability grouping, cooperative learning and the gifted. *Journal for the Education of the Gifted, 14* (1), 3–8, 28–30.

Slavin, R. (1990). *Cooperative learning: Theory, research and practice.* Englewood Cliffs, NJ: Prentice-Hall.

Stanley, J. (1979). The study and facilitation of talent for mathematics. In A. Passow (Ed.), *The gifted and the talented: Their education and development* (pp. 169–189). Chicago: University of Chicago Press.

Westberg, K. Archambault, F., Dobyns, S., & Selvin, T. (1993). The classroom practices observation study. *Journal for the Education of the Gifted, 16* (2), 120–146.

Part *II*

Content Modifications
for the Gifted

In Chapter 3, the possible variations of a school program for gifted students were listed in three major categories: *content, skills,* and *learning environment.* This section of the book will focus on possible changes in *content* to meet the needs of gifted children, the rationale for such changes, and some specific illustrative examples in five areas: mathematics, science, social studies, language arts, and the visual and performing arts.

As noted in Chapter 3, the rapid expansion of knowledge in recent years has led to an avalanche of new information in practically all content fields. The available time to teach this relevant information, however, has changed very little. There are still twelve grades to be completed before college. Despite the gradual lengthening of graduate and professional programs, this increase in instructional time is slight compared to the new information now available.

The serious question for the educator, then, is how to decide what competing sets of information to teach. The chase after total mastery of all available knowledge is clearly doomed, despite the seeming intent of some gifted individuals to chase after this goal by absorbing and seeking all information in sight. Each of the illustrative examples of differentiated curriculum content will fall into one or more of four major categories: *content acceleration, content enrichment, content sophistication,* and *content novelty.* An illustration of these content modifications can be seen in Figure 1.

1. *Content acceleration.* Perhaps the simplest of program modifications emerges from the recognition that gifted students are performing two, three, or more grades beyond their expected grade level on achievement tests. From this observation comes the conclusion

	Math	**Science**	**Language Arts**	**Social Studies**
Acceleration	Algebra in fifth grade	Early chemistry and physics	Learning grammatical structure early	Early introduction to world history
Enrichment	Changing bases in number systems	Experimentation and data collecing	Short story and poetry writing	Reading biographies of persons for historical insight
Sophistication	Mastering the laws of arithmetic	Learning the laws of physics	Mastering the structural properties of plays, sonnets, etc.	Learning and applying the principles of economics
Novelty	Probability and statistics	Science and its impact on society	Rewriting Shakespeare's plays with happy endings	Creating future societies and telling how they are governed

FIGURE 1   Illustrations of Content Modification for Gifted Students

that they should be given content that matches their level of attainment rather than their age. Some content fields are more adaptable to this strategy than others; mathematics is the prime example. Content acceleration means that the program provided to gifted fifth-graders will resemble the program given to average seventh- or eighth-graders, thus there might be an early introduction of algebra or geometry to the youngsters so favored.

The early introduction of topics such as grammatical structure or world history, as shown in Figure 1, also serves the purpose of allowing the student a knowledge base upon which other knowledge can be placed. The basic strategy behind this approach is that gifted students should be presented with advanced work as soon as possible so that they can learn to cope with complex systems of ideas.

2. *Content enrichment.* In this strategy, the teacher provides gifted students with a variety of materials or references that will elaborate on the basic concepts to be taught in the standard program. For example, if the students are involved in studying the westward movement in the United States, the gifted students could be assigned to read specific short stories, or asked to write a poem, or given films or filmstrips that provide more detailed and elaborated information about the western movement than time would allow the average student to master.

The basic strategy of this approach is that elaboration or enrichment of this type would establish more firmly the fundamental concepts to be taught, and that is considered more important than seeking new content or going on to the next level. Such a content choice is often desirable if the gifted students are assigned to regular classes and must, of necessity, be dealing with the standard curriculum.

3. *Content sophistication.* A somewhat different strategy is to provide material that will allow gifted students to see larger systems of ideas and concepts related to the basic content of the course. As indicated in Figure 1, such an approach would have the students learning the laws of economics, arithmetic, and physics. By mastering such abstract systems, the students would be able to apply such laws to daily phenomenon and build systems of abstractions that would greatly increase the gifted students' understanding of the world around them. Such an approach is more possible when gifted students are clustered together in special classes or resource rooms so that the teacher need not worry about overburdening the students of lesser abilities with ideas beyond their current intellectual maturity.

4. *Content novelty.* A fourth strategy is to introduce completely different material from the regular program that would not be provided to the average student, such as a minicourse on probability, an extended study of the impact of science on modern society, or the role of ethics in modern government (see Figure 1). Such topics represent a clear departure from the standard curriculum and would be introduced by the rationale that some important element in the gifted child's future may well be enhanced by these experiences, even though they may not be shared by other students. We accept content novelty much more easily at a later stage of the student's career—that is, not all children receive instruction in medical school curricula. Such content is restricted to a very few gifted students. The basic strategy of this approach is to provide experiences that the average student may never confront, on the rationale that some subjects will be useful to gifted students and their advanced career and academic goals (e.g., calculus or study of future societies) and that the gifted student has the available time to do it.

Not all curriculum adaptations will fit neatly into one or the other of these four categories. Some are both *novel* and *sophisticated* or *sophisticated accelerated.* These categories are designed to help you, the reader and/or teacher, think about variations in curriculum adaptations, not pigeonhole each possible curriculum variation into an artificial box. Each of these approaches has merit in certain education circumstances. The decision on which of these strategies, or which combination of them, is most appropriate for gifted students in a particular school in a particular community may be different from one place to another. Therefore, because the range of possible content offerings is almost unlimited, the choice of topics and materials becomes a critical issue in the education of gifted students.

Chapter 4

Mathematics
for Gifted Students

Key Questions

- What are some examples of curriculum diffentiation for students gifted in mathematics?
- How has the educational reform movement affected mathematics education?
- Why is acceleration one of the favorite strategies for students gifted in mathematics?
- What are some applications of mathematics to other fields such as art, social studies, literature, and so on?
- Why do gifted girls appear to have special problems in mastering mathematics?
- Is mathematics a *static* or *expanding* field today? Why?
- How can mathematics instruction help with the development of reasoning skills, problem solving, and problem finding?

There is probably no single subject so central to knowledge in all fields as mathematics. It has been called the Queen of the Sciences with justification. It plays a major role in art, music, architecture, engineering, and many other domains. Yet, the instruction of gifted students, and others as well, in mathematics often has been unimaginative or uninspired, particularly in the early grades. Why is this so? What can be done about it?

This chapter will discuss the nature of mathematics and some special characteristics of gifted mathematicians. Several examples of each type of curriculum adaptation—*acceleration*, *enrichment*, *sophistication*, and *novelty*—will be provided, along with some discussion of the special issue of women in mathematics and the teaching of the subject.

Cranshaw is very happy today. He has returned from school beaming proudly, brandishing a report card. He is particularly proud of the A he achieved in arithmetic, and his parents share his pride. After all, a grade of A is a mark of excellence and of considerable accomplishment. Of course, the A was not much of a surprise to his parents—Cranshaw had been getting 100s on his homework papers. His teacher had given him extra problems to solve in long division, which he completed very easily. When the teacher gave him more complex long-division problems, Cranshaw, never daunted, swept through them like a hungry grasshopper through a corn field.

Everyone is happy and all is right with Cranshaw's world of numbers—or is it? There are many people who have serious doubts that the reward for this homework is going to help Cranshaw become mathematically proficient in his later academic career. After all, the only thing anyone knows right now is that Cranshaw can do lots of long division as well as he can do a little bit of long division. Does he get those 100s because he understands the ideas behind doing division or because he is capable of robotically going through the drill that Mr. Jenkins showed him to do? Should he be allowed to move quickly to the next-higher level of concepts, such as beginning algebra or fractions? Or does he need something much more different and much more complex than this? Should he be studying the fundamental laws and principles in division and when they won't work? Or should he be investigating the role of mathematics in different fields? These are the questions that are being asked by educators and mathematicians.

For the other four gifted children, mathmatics poses special problems of quite different character. Zelda does not do especially well in arithmetic and seems to be influenced by a generally held attitude that math is a "boy's subject." Although this attitude is less strongly held than in previous decades, it would be a mistake to believe that such an attitude has evaporated in our culture entirely. Consequently, Zelda quietly gets her work done in a competent but not enthusiastic fashion as befits her role of a good academic student.

Stephanie, on the other hand, has no such qualms about math. In fact, next to art, math is her favorite subject. Stephanie has a special ability to understand what mathematics is all about and quickly grasps the concepts behind the drills she is assigned to do. Whether or not she realizes it, the connection between patterns in art and patterns in math help her "see" mathematical relationships better than Zelda does. Stephanie's problem is that she sometimes understands so well and so quickly that she sees no particular point in completing the many "worthless" exercises she is assigned. Stubbornly, she simply fails to do the homework because she knows she doesn't need to. Unfortunately, the homework is graded anyway, and Stephanie suffers because of incomplete assignments.

Joe, the gifted but troubled underachiever, has a different set of problems. Although he is a wizard at video games, which demand an extraordinary grasp of spatial relationships and eye-hand coordination, his classroom performance is less than scintillating. It is the preciseness of math that bothers Joe. For most problems he is asked to solve, there is inevitably a single right answer. How dull! His argumentative skills do not help him, and he finds few valid reasons to complain except to argue about dumb and boring assignments.

Sam has times when math is, to him, an exciting and interesting subject. He particularly likes the glimpses he has had into geometry and spatial and three-dimensional perspectives. He also likes the fact that much of mathematics is nonverbal and consequently allows him to perform without being called on (thus his own perceived limitations in this verbal dimension are not revealed). His grades in math are consistently better than his other subjects, but still not outstanding. This is partly due to the difference in his performance in classwork and homework, which is consistently good, and his performance under the pressure of end-of-unit tests, where he sometimes "clutches" under the strain of the time limits, resulting in lower grades than Mr. Jenkins would expect.

Mathematics as a Growing Subject Area

One of the first concerns of any serious presentation of mathematics is to change the image in the minds of students and teachers of what a mathematician is or does. Too often the common portrait of the mathematician is of a person who gains great pleasure from manipulating numbers and who delights in the knowledge that all the answers have already been discovered. The only tasks to be accomplished, then, would be to apply the proper formula and calculate the answer.

Such a portrait is unfair and almost totally misleading. Mathematics is not merely counting, measuring, or manipulating formulas, but, in its essence, is a way of thinking—of deductive and inductive reasoning. It is also an area of dynamic changes and exciting new discoveries, even as it was in the time of the Greeks when Pythagoras made many creative innovations in math that we take for granted today, just as though they had always existed. The concept of mathematics as a dynamic field should be presented to gifted children, since they will likely be using mathematics in some form in their careers.

Polya presented perhaps the best summary of the way in which mathematics incorporates invention and discovery:

Mathematics is regarded as a demonstrative science. Yet this is only one of its aspects. Finished mathematics presented in a finished form appears purely demonstrative, consisting of proofs only. Yet mathematics in the making resembles any other human knowledge in the making. You have to guess a mathematical theorem before you prove it; you have to guess the idea of the proof before you carry through the details. You have to combine observations and follow analogies; you have to try and try again. The result of the mathematician's creative work is demonstrative reasoning of a proof; but the proof is discovered by plausible reasoning, by guessing. If the learning of mathematics reflects to any degree the invention of mathematics, it must have a place for guessing, for plausible inference. (1954, p. vi)

Even gifted students are often unaware of the constantly changing nature of mathematics. Innovations in mathematical thought actually happen so frequently that mathematics is rarely considered the same discipline from one generation to the next. In our own lifetime, the introduction of Mandelbrot's formula describing fractals, identifying patterns in seemingly random events, is opening an entirely new avenue of mathematics to explore. Gleick described the role of invention and hypothesis in the formation of the concept of fractals:

Mandelbrot moved beyond dimensions 0, 1, 2, 3... to a seeming impossibility: fractional dimensions. The notion is a conceptual high-wire act. For non-mathematicians it requires a willing suspension of disbelief. Yet it is extraordinarily powerful.

Fractional dimension becomes a way of measuring qualities that otherwise have no clear definition: the degree of roughness or brokenness or irregularity in an object. A twisting coastline, for example, despite its immeasurability in terms of length, nevertheless has a certain characteristic degree of roughness. Mandelbrot specified ways of calculating the fractional dimension of real objects, given some technique of constructing a shape or given some data, and he allowed his geometry to make a claim about the irregular patterns he had studied in nature. The claim was that the degree of irregularity remains constant over different scales. Surprisingly often, the claim turns out to be true. Over and over again, the world displays a regular irregularity. (1988, p. 98)

The introduction of some mathematical ideas changes the very assumptions of mathematics and have a profound effect on the way we think about numbers. An example from ancient times is when the conversion from Roman numerals to Arabic numbers required the addition of the number 0. Before that time, there was no way to represent the concept of "nothing" or "zero" mathematically! With this in mind, it becomes increasingly clear why creativity and imagination are important skills to be used by gifted students interested in mathematics as a career field.

One of the most important inventions in mathematics occurred on the Greek island of Samos in the fifth century B.C. when Pythagoras made a number of astonishing creative discoveries linking mathematics to music, space, and the heavens. Pythagoras found a basic relationship between musical harmony and mathematics, noting that a vibrating string when divided into an exact number of equal parts will sound harmonious, when plucked, to the sound made by the vibrating string as a whole.

Having discovered that the world of sound is governed by the exact numbers, he did the same with space and devised the Pythagorean Theorem ($a^2 + b^2 = c^2$), providing the relationships that prevail in right-angle triangles. Bronowski stated

What Pythagoras established is a fundamental characterization of the space in which we move, and it is the first time that it translated into numbers.... The numbers that compose right angle triangles have been proposed as messages which we might send out to the planets in other star systems as a test for the existence of rational life there. (1973, p. 161)

As our knowledge of scientific fields expands and becomes more complex, there is a need for more complex mathematical models to help us understand and analyze the new phenomena under investigation. The emergence of statistics as a mathematical field was required by new social and biological scientific endeavors. If we can only communicate to these gifted students the idea that mathematics is a way of thinking whose full breadth and depth are still not known, we have accomplished a major instructional goal.

The Reform Movement in Mathematics Education

Similar to the reform movement in the field of science, mathematicians and math educators have been taking a serious look at the state of mathematics instruction in this country. Part of the concern about how mathematics is taught is the increasingly dismal results of international comparisons of the performance of students from different countries: U.S. students routinely fall behind the students of other industrialized countries in these studies. Recently the International Association for the Evaluation of Educational Achievement (1989) gave a mathematics test to students in 12 countries, including the United States. The test was scored much like the Scholastic Aptitude Test, with a possible high score of 800. As a part of the analysis, countries were compared to see which had the highest proportion of students receiving a score of 600 or above. The results showed that Quebec, Canada, had the highest percentage of students who excelled on the test, followed by British Columbia and Korea. Students in the United States were last in the proportion of students with high scores. Figure 4–1 shows the relative proportion of students' scores at exceptional levels from each country in mathematics and science.

U.S. educators are taking a hard look at the mathematics skills that their students should have. We need to produce more than "human calculators" to prepare our students for the future! Two reform reports, *Everybody Counts* (National Research Council, 1989) and the *Curriculum and Evaluation Standards for School Mathematics* (National Council of Teachers of Mathematics, 1989) summarized the changes that are supposed to take place in the mathematics classroom for all students. In a move that parallels the call for literacy in other disciplines, the mathematics community is calling for all students to acquire "numeracy," or the ability to easily use the mathematics necessary in adult life. According to the report *Everybody Counts*, numeracy extends beyond the ability to compute; it also includes understanding mathematical concepts, especially as they are represented in our everyday world through representation in the news media and in everyday events. All students are expected to learn to use the six mathematical modes of thought:

> *Modeling: Representing worldly phenomena by mental constructs, often visual or symbolic, that capture important and useful features.*
>
> *Optimization: Finding the best solution (least expensive or most efficient) by asking "what if" and exploring all possibilities.*
>
> *Symbolism: Extending natural language symbolic representation of abstract concepts in an economical form that makes possible both communication and computation.*
>
> *Inference: Reasoning from data, from premises, from graphs, from incomplete and inconsistent sources.*
>
> *Logical Analysis: Seeking implications of premises and searching for first principles to explain observed phenomena.*
>
> *Abstraction: Singling out for special study certain properties common to many different phenomena. (1989, p. 31)*

The mathematics classroom should be filled with the potential for discovery, and the opportunity for the exercise of curiosity should be infused into the classroom. Students should understand the role that mathematics plays in different disciplines and its relevance to everyday life. Mathematics understanding should be constructed by the students, with the help of a mathematics teacher who is a coach, mentor, and guide.

This change in the shape of mathematics education will cause educators of the gifted to take another look at how they differentiate programming for gifted students. Many people will ask, Why do anything different for the mathematically gifted? Are these skills that are complex, abstract, and inventive not those that have always been recommended for the gifted? The answer, of course, is yes, they are. However, there is room to allow gifted students to go farther, deeper, and faster than others. Part of the reason why adaptations are especially called for becomes more evident when one understands the special nature of mathematical talent.

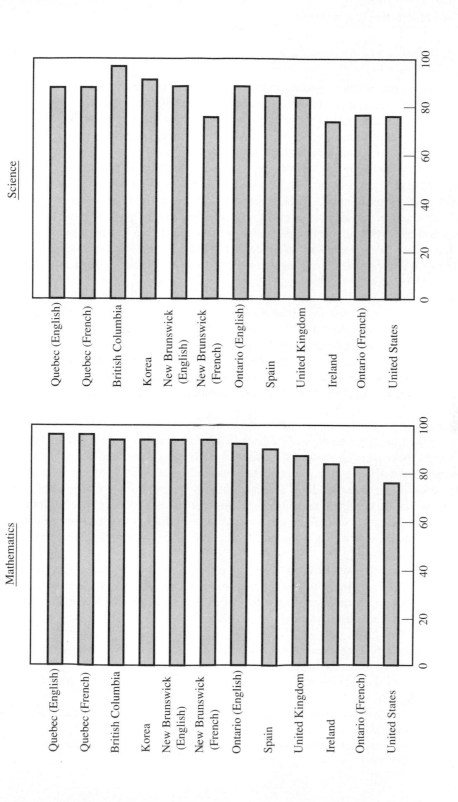

FIGURE 4–1 Percentage of 13-Year-Olds with a Score of 400 or More on an International Mathematics and Science Test, by Selected Countries and Provinces: 1988

Source: U.S. Department of Education, National Center for Education Statistics. *An International Assessment of Educational Progress, A World of Differences,* 1989, prepared by Educational Testing Service.

109

Characteristics of Gifted Mathematicians

The notion of mathematical reasoning as the marker of true mathematics achievement is, to a degree, reflected and paralleled in the description of the mathematically gifted. As discussed below, mathematical talent is often described as the raw talent necessary to acquire, quickly and intuitively, the very kinds of fundamental mathematical concepts and ideas that are discussed in the national reform reports.

Krutetskii, a distinguished Russian mathematician, suggested that there is a unique neurological organization in the mathematically gifted individual, which he refers to as the "mathematical cast of mind." He believes that this "cast of mind" shows up by age 7 or 8 and later acquires broad transfer effects. "It is expressed in a striving to make the phenomenon of the environment mathematical, in a constant urge to pay attention to the mathematical aspect of phenomena, to notice spatial and quantitative relationships, bonds, and functional dependencies everywhere—in short, to see the world 'through mathematical eyes'" (1976, p. 302).

As noted by Krutetskii, the origins of mathematical ability lie, in part, in the organization of the neurological system, Although he rejects the notion of innate presence of mathematical abilities, he does admit to the term *inclinations*. He advanced the hypothesis of the role of inborn characteristics of the brain in the case of mathematical giftedness: "And to the sacramental question, 'Can anyone become a mathematician or must one be born one?' we would hypothetically give the following answer: Anyone can become an ordinary mathematician; one must be born an outstanding talented mathematician" (1976, p. 361).

This response gives us part of the answer to the questions raised earlier in this chapter: If the role of the teacher of students in general is to make them good problem solvers and to have them understand fundamental mathematical concepts, then the role of the teacher of the gifted is to encourage the "outstanding talented mathematician" who uses these skills and understandings in a qualitatively different, more complicated, and creative way. To the argument that gifted students seem to already have the abilities and skills to do mathematics, one might respond that these abilities, even in gifted students, represent "diamonds in the rough" that need to be shaped and refined before they can be considered polished gems.

The result of this mathematical frame of reference is that mathematically gifted students can perform certain feats of mathematics with much more skill and dexterity than other students. Chang summarized the performance characteristics that Krutetskii identified as associated with a mathematical cast of mind:

1. *Swiftness in reasoning and tendency to maximally curtail reasoning associations in problem solving;*
2. *Ability to think abstractly, reason analytically, and to generalize broadly and rapidly;*
3. *Ability to perceive mathematical patterns, structures, relationships and interrelationships;*
4. *Flexibility to thinking and the need for searching alternative solutions;*

5. *A persistent task commitment directed to their work in mathematics; and*
6. *A tendency to view the world through a mathematical eye. (1985, p. 77)*

Another way to look at the characteristics of the mathematically gifted student is to look for common background characteristics or skills of a group of students who have performed at a level far superior to their peers at a very early age. That has been the purpose of the Study of Mathematically Precocious Youth (SMPY), conducted at the Johns Hopkins University by Julian Stanley. Stanley and his colleagues have made great strides in understanding the nature of students who perform well on standardized tests through their study of students who score 700 or above on the Scholastic Aptitude Test Mathematics subtest at the age of 12. In one study of 292 such students, Stanley found the following trends:

1. *The ratio of males to females in the group was 12:1 (269 males and 23 females).*
2. *Seventy percent of the females and 63% of the males were oldest children; 17% of females and 11% of males were only children in their families.*
3. *The children's parents were generally well educated.*
4. *The children's verbal skills (also measured by the SAT) were markedly lower than their mathematics skills, but were still superior to the average college-bound senior.*
5. *22% of the entire sample were Asian-American, only 2 of the students were black.*
6. *Most of the students also had very high general reasoning ability as measured by the Raven Progressive Matrices. (1988, p. 207)*

Although some of these characteristics, especially those describing gender, race, and family background, may be affected by current cultural barriers to girls, minorities, and economically disadvantaged to special programs, it is very useful to have a description of what the current pool of mathematically gifted students looks like. One additional interesting finding that Stanley noted was that the truly exceptional student of mathematics tended to have advanced skills in other areas as well:

Sheer high IQ alone is not sufficient. SMPY has observed repeatedly that non-verbal reasoning ability of the sort measured by the advanced (36-item) form of the Raven Progressive Matrices also seems important. (1988, p. 207)

This observation raises one of the more interesting quandaries in the education of the gifted—the identification of the mathematically gifted. Often, the identification measures used by school systems involve achievement tests, which measure mostly computational skills, and not the more complex and sophisticated skills described by Krutetskii and mentioned by Stanley. Greenes (1981) pointed out that one result is that sometimes students are "good exercise doers" but do not have the advanced mathematics reasoning ability to qualify for special mathematics programs. These students, who sound like Renzulli's "schoolhouse gifted" mentioned in Chapter 3, excel in a limited skill area but lack the sophistication of a mathematical thinker. If computation-based tests are used to identify students for a program that emphasizes mathematics sophistication, it is possible that these "good exercise doers" would find themselves in a program far beyond their reach and would experience damaging disillusionment and failure. Greenes recommended using the following kinds of skills to look for when identifying the mathematically gifted:

Spontaneous formulation of problems
Flexibility in handling data
Mental agility of fluency of ideas
Data organization ability
Originality of interpretation
Ability to transfer ideas
Ability to generalize

There also have been outstanding examples of the early development of the mathematical "cast of mind" (Krutetskii, 1976) in many prodigies from the United States. Two of these, William Sidis and Charles Fefferman, represent quite different outcomes. William Sidis was a mathematical prodigy who knew algebra, trigonometry, geometry, and calculus by the age of 10 and was admitted to Harvard University at age 11. He was graduated cum laude at the age of 16, but his emotional adjustment was always a problem and caused him to retreat into social isolation. He strenuously avoided all academic life and publicity until he died in his middle forties, penniless and alone. Many people feel that this is what happens to young prodigies, as if to say the faster the rocket goes up, the faster it comes down.

However, much more typical of early prodigies is the story of Charles Fefferman. At the age of 22, Fefferman is the youngest person in recent history to be appointed to be a full professor at a major university (the University of Chicago). Encouraged by his father, a Ph.D. in economics, he was taking courses in mathematics at the University of Maryland by the age of 12 and entered college as a full-time student at the age of 14. As a student, Fefferman combined his studies with a normal social life, socializing with his friends who were in junior high at the time. He has won a number of prizes for his work in mathematics, and at the age of 27 was the first recipient of the $150,000 Allan Waterman Award of the National Science Foundation (Montour, 1977).

Most of the prodigies that have come to the attention of educators have followed a similar pattern as Fefferman, but not as dramatic. Although some, like William Sidis, come to only a limited realization of their potential, most perform extremely well and make major productive contributions to the society.

Mathematically gifted students are in need of qualitatively different modes of instruction, even from an early age. Like other students, there is a great need to attract gifted students to mathematics. The *Everybody Counts* report cited evidence that the number of top high school students intending to major in mathematics or statistics has declined since 1976 (National Research Council, 1989, p. 17). Perhaps one reason why is that these students have become disenchanted because of inappropriate school programming. The next section explores ways to captivate the interest of mathematically gifted children.

Curriculum Adaptations

Four possible ways of modifying content were identified earlier in this book: *acceleration*, *enrichment*, *sophistication*, and *novelty*. Each of these approaches will be considered as they affect mathematics.

Content Acceleration

Because mathematics has historically been organized as a systematic and hierarchical curriculum, it is possible for gifted students to proceed through the regular curriculum requirements in a much more rapid fashion. This means that the school can accelerate the content by presenting topics such as algebra to fifth- and sixth-graders and calculus to gifted ninth-graders.

Occasionally, acceleration may mean physically moving a fine student such as Cranshaw or Stephanie into eighth-grade classes. Having mastered the fifth-grade material, the instructional objectives for the fifth-grade students, including long division or basic geometry, are replaced by what would ordinarily be eighth-grade objectives such as learning about polynomials or working with the Cartesian coordinate system.

One of the most well-known and popular programs that uses the acceleration approach was initiated by the Study of Mathematically Precocious Youth, originated by Julian Stanley (1979) at the Johns Hopkins University. Identification procedures used at SMPY and then later by its academic program component, the Center for the Advancement of Academically Talented Youth (CTY), are quite traditional and rely on existing information that is usually available or easily attained by most school systems (Fox, 1981). The first step in the talent search process is to identify youngsters with potential talent by asking the schools to identify all children who scored on the 97th percentile or higher on measures of standard achievement in the last grade in which they have been measured.

The second step is to invite this group of students to take the Scholastic Aptitude Test (SAT), which has been used traditionally to determine academic aptitude in mathematics and verbal skills for eleventh- and twelfth-grade students prior to college entrance. The SMPY program has found that by testing seventh-graders on eleventh- and twelfth-grade material, one can measure what outstanding and precocious youngsters are able to do.

The third step in the process is to place the identified students in a program that matches their capabilities. In most instances, this means providing accelerated content material through a special summer program, but in some cases it can include providing the youngsters with the opportunity to take college courses while still in high school or advanced courses while still in junior high school.

Stanley and Benbow (1982) used this diagnostic testing procedure, followed by prescribed instruction, in order to reduce the amount of time students spend on traditional content material. They eliminate what is already known by the students from the curriculum and provide opportunities to learn the rest in a much more rapid fashion. The basic principal used in the CTY math program is called *self-paced learning*: Students are provided with the materials and tools necessary to work at their own pace (usually much faster than in the regular classroom) with the assistance of a facilitator or mentor when it is necessary.

Stanley and Benbow claim that talented youth can master Algebra 1 in 15 hours or less if they are provided with skilled mentors and suitable materials. On the basis of their work of over a decade with talented students and longitudinal followups, these researchers cited the following benefits of their fast-paced program:

1. *Increased zest for learning and life, reduced boredom in school*
2. *Enhanced feelings of self-worth and accomplishment*
3. *Reduction of egotism and arrogance.... SMPY students who learn with their intellectual peers in rigorous settings...tend to develop more realistic understanding of their ability*
4. *Far better educational preparation than they would otherwise get*
5. *Better qualifications for the most selective colleges and improved chance of being admitted to them*
6. *Getting into college, graduate school, and a profession earlier, thus having more time and energy for creative pursuits*
7. *Increased opportunities to explore more specialties and hobbies*
8. *More time to explore various careers before marriage*
9. *Less cost.... Graduating from college in 3 years instead of 4 saves about one-fourth of total costs and can lead to paid full-time employment a year earlier than otherwise*
10. *Being an unusually well-prepared, advanced, entrant to college often brings the student to the attention of professors, who help him or her get started on important research early*
11. *It seems likely that accelerants will have considerably greater success in life, both professionally and personally (1986, pp. 378–379)*

The structure and ease of implementation of the SMPY/CTY model has made it a popular and much emulated program. Soon after the SMPY began, other programs were initiated that offered services to the regions not served by SMPY: the Talent Identification Program at Duke University serves the Southeast region; the Midwest Talent Search at Northwestern University serves the Midwest; and the Rocky Mountain Talent Search serves most of the nation's western states. Additionally, several states have adopted the talent search model for identification and programming on a statewide level.

The key to the widespread adoption of the SMPY program is that it deals with traditional and recognizable knowledge; the use of measuring instruments are well established in academic settings. There is an insistence on a full traditional academic program rather than isolated enrichment experiences for the gifted youngster, and earned credit for the student is given for the work that is done. Creativity, as such, is not taught in this program, although it may emerge as a natural part of many of the curriculum efforts.

However, ease of implementation and program planning should not be the only criterion for adopting or not adopting the program. Stanley and Benbow (1986) do not insist that such radical acceleration is appropriate for all students. Indeed, such acceleration should be carefully considered. Because the nature of mathematics instruction changes from very concrete in elementary school to very abstract in middle school and high school, some students who are very good at concrete or computation skills, or who have good intuitive sense for mathematics without substantial skills, could end up being pushed too far too fast into a very abstract subject matter. Stuart (1988) described this dilemma:

> *Acceleration is like so many things. It has worked well and it has been disas-*
> *trous.... [It] works well for some students as they take the next course at the*
> *university and do quite well, often going on to math or science careers. In fact,*
> *the students who have gone to [talent search] have, without exception, done very*
> *well in their accelerated program. However, in my opinion, the worst thing that*
> *can happen to a student in math is to be overplaced.... I find this is happening*
> *more and more, particularly with the students taking the AP calculus as juniors.*
> *Several of them in the last few years have struggled and then have not taken any*
> *math as seniors, and as little as possible in college.... I'm not sure how many*
> *students have struggled in math courses before I see them.... I believe that the*
> *trouble begins with identifying students to accelerate possibly as early as sixth*
> *grade. Often students who are well behaved and do well in arithmetic are*
> *identified as being mathematically gifted, which is often not the case.*

Content Enrichment

Content enrichment refers to the addition of different and extended examples and problems. Through this approach, gifted students should gain a much better understanding of the mathematical principles that are being taught. This is the rationale for enrichment—it means broadening the experience base of the student while keeping the same instructional objectives.

Creating Open-Ended Questions

One problem the teacher of the gifted is faced with is that mathematics textbooks generally provide problems that are very routine and flat; they leave little room for exploration. Answers to problems are often so apparent to gifted children that they give answers without even thinking about what they are doing. However, these closed and limited right-answer-based problems can be converted into open-ended problems, which are very appropriate for the gifted. Figure 4–2 gives an example of a word problem that was converted by Bartkovich from a very typical and predictable word problem to one that has many possibilities. Bartkovich then compared the two problems:

> *The [first] problem is easily solved by using the values given for T at times t = 0*
> *and t = 15 to find the values of b and c.... To solve this problem, a student merely*
> *uses simple algebraic manipulations, and the student is not required to possess*
> *any understanding of the meaning of the numbers or parameters. This presenta-*
> *tion never brings the cooling law to life or allows the students to experience the*
> *phenomenon.... The second presentation of the cooling problem brings the*
> *phenomenon to life and enables the student to learn by discovery, in contrast to*
> *being given a formula that is an accomplished fact. (1988, p. 268)*

FIGURE 4–2 **Conversion of a Traditional Mathematics Problem to an Open-Ended Format**

Problem 1

When a cup of hot tea is left in a room to cool, the temperature of the tea is an exponential function of time. As a matter of fact, the temperature T of the tea is given by $T = ae^{bt} + c$, where t represents the number of minutes from the first temperature measurement. The difference between the initial temperature and the temperature of the environment is represented by a, and b and c can be determined. You are given that the the tea is originally 120 degrees F and the temperature of the room is 70 degrees F. Also, at t = 15 the temperature of the tea is 98 degrees F. At what time will the tea be 77 degrees F?

Problem 2

Heat a cup of water to about 125 degrees F. Place the cup in a room and measure the temperature at regular intervals. Record and graph your data. Does the water cool at the same rate throughout the cooling process? Find a function that approximates the cooling phenomenon you have observed. Use your function to predict when the temperature will be 100 degrees F and when it will be within one degree of room temperature. How do your predictions compare with the observed data?

Source: Bartkovitch, K. G. (1988). Motivating the most capable youths in mathematics and science. In J. I. Dryden, S. A. Gallagher, G. E. Stanley, & R. N. Sawyer (Eds.), *Developing talent in mathematics, science and technology: Talent Identification Program/National Science Foundation conference on academic talent*. National Science Foundation Grant #MDR-8751410.

Several general characteristics can be identified that should be hallmarks of good creative problems for the gifted. Milauskas provided a good summary:

> *Try to find problems which are simple to state but have a twist of novel solution;*
> *Good problems sometimes contain insufficient or extraneous information, so that the student has to think in terms of necessary and sufficient conditions;*
> *Encourage alternative solutions and other extensions offered by students;*
> *Often the beauty of the problem lies in a novel or alternative solution rather than in the problem itself. (1987, pp. 72–73)*

The Property of Properties

If mastery of arithmetic is the objective for all students in a classroom, then one example of enrichment would be the use of these operations and deep understanding of the rules that drive the operations. Activities could be provided to students that either expand their use of properties or refine their understanding of why the properties work. Grossnickle and Reckzeh (1973) have referred to exercises such as these as developing mathematical power, or leading the student to deeper insight about how specific aspects of mathematics work. One example of expanding the use of a student's mathematical flexibility is by leading students to discover the many different ways one problem can be solved. For instance, one day Mr. Jenkins asked students to solve the simple multiplication problem:

$$\begin{array}{r} 34 \\ \times\ 15 \\ \hline \end{array}$$

The students began by working individually at their seats, but after a while Mr. Jenkins moved them into small groups. In the small groups the students were asked to compare not only their answers but their approaches to the solution. Imagine the surprise when the students discovered that there were many different ways to get to the same answer. The students were then asked to list the different approaches and to judge them on different criteria, including:

> Which resulted in the right answer?
> Which was shortest?
> Which applied mathematical rules? Which rules?
> Which included the most different kinds of operations?
> Which was most subject to simple errors?

By having the students rate their problem-solving techniques on these criteria, Mr. Jenkins subtly introduced to the students the idea that not only are problems open to many different kinds of solutions but also that mathematicians, when they solve problems, can compare different solution approaches and rate the worthiness of the solution on the merit of the approach as well as the solution.

Writing and Mathematics

The transition from closed right-answer questions to open-ended questions can serve another valuable purpose for providing enrichment experiences in mathematics. By having students explain their work as they solve a problem, much is revealed about their mathematical reasoning. As the teacher looks at the students' reasonings, he or she can make decisions about what kind of programming is appropriate for all students, including the gifted ones.

Figure 4–3 shows an example of how information can be gleaned from mathematics solutions that are explained verbally (California State Department of Education, 1989). In the first example, the student clearly understands the problem, the nature of the picture (not drawn to scale), and the solution. The next two examples reveal the misconceptions which led the students astray. By using writing in mathematics, teachers can discover not only whether or not students can get the right answer but also whether or not students are in sufficient control of mathematics laws and properties to apply them intelligently and consistently.

To Drill or Not to Drill

Writing and mathematics can also be used to help the teacher of the gifted resolve one of the stickiest questions in mathematics: whether or not to make gifted students do repeated drill or show their work. Often students with a "mathematical cast of mind" will automatically "see" an answer by using their unique mathematical intuition. In that case, it seems a waste to make a gifted child list out all of the steps necessary to solve a problem. In order to answer this question, it is necessary again to bring up the previous conversation about mathematical reasoning and mathematical power. To completely understand the com-

Look at these plane figures, some of which are not drawn to scale. Investigate what might be wrong (if anything) with the given information. Briefly write your findings and justify your ideas on the basis of geometric principles.

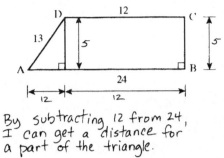

I cannot find anything wrong with this figure! When I draw a perpendicular line from point D, the triangle has suitable measurements, the rectangle has correct measurements also.

By subtracting 12 from 24, I can get a distance for a part of the triangle.

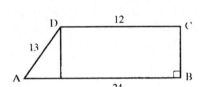

$$X + 24 + 12 + 13 = 90$$
$$X + 49 = 90$$
$$X = 41$$

Misconception:
Students bring in the "magic" number 90 when referring to angles, but they used it this time for a perimeter.

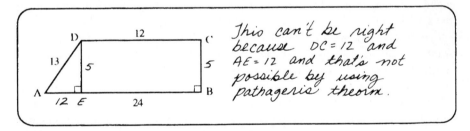

This can't be right because DC = 12 and AE = 12 and that's not possible by using pathageris theorm.

Misconception:
This student derived a correct relationship through the use of geometrical knowledge; but having made false assumptions based on the drawing, he failed to draw the correct conclusion.

FIGURE 4–3   Written Explanations of Mathematics Problem Solutions

Source: Adapted from California State Department of Education (1989). *A question of thinking: A first look at students' performance on open-ended questions in mathematics*. Sacramento, CA: California State Department of Education.

plexity of this issue, let's return to Mr. Jenkins's class and the problem he gave the students to solve earlier. The problem was:

34
× 15

Mr. Jenkins asked the students to show all of their work as they proceeded with a solution. Figure 4–4 shows the students' answers as they appeared on the paper. Notice that Stephanie, Sam, and Zelda have used three different approaches to the solution. Mr. Jenkins asked these students to form a group and discuss the different ways they got their answers. However, Joe and Cranshaw did not show their work, but instead simply wrote down the answer. Both answers were correct, and many teachers might be satisfied to know that their solutions were right. Mr. Jenkins, however, is just as interested in *how* the students got their answer as he is in the answer itself. So he asked the students to write out explanations of how they got their answers. Here are Cranshaw's and Joe's responses:

Cranshaw: The answer is obvious: 15 is really the same as 10 plus 5. So I multiplied 10 times 34 and got 340 and then divided that in half (because 5 is half of 10) and got 170. I added 340 and 170 and came up with 510. It was easy to do in my head.

The Problem:	34 ×15					
Stephanie	34 ×15	= 30 +4 ×15		30 ×15 450	4 ×15 60	450 +60 510
Sam	34 ×15	= 3(10 × 14.5)	+ 15 × 5	145 145 145 +75 510		
Zelda	34 ×15 170 340 510					
Cranshaw	34 ×15 510					
Joe	34 ×15 510					

FIGURE 4–4   Gifted Students' Problem Solutions

Joe: It was easy. Because 15 is half of 30, you can split the 34 up into two parts, 17 and 17. Then multiplying 17 twice by half of 30, 15, and adding them together, you get the answer, which is 510.

What a difference! Cranshaw's response reveals a very solid understanding of the laws, principles, and procedures that he used intuitively to arrive at a solution. Nothing to worry about there! Joe, on the other hand, even with the same intuitive power, has no idea of how he arrived at his solution. There can be no doubt that Joe did have an intuitive understanding of the problem, but without the support of mathematical reasoning skills, there is no way to know if Joe will be able to use his intuitive skills in a systematic or predictable way.

Mr. Jenkins, eager to respond to each student's needs, told Cranshaw that he can skip some of the drill and practice problems and proceed with an enrichment activity. Joe, however, was asked to do a few more problems than Cranshaw and to show his work so that Mr. Jenkins and Joe can both get a better handle on Joe's reasoning. From this example we can glean a valuable rule of thumb: If students can justify their intuitive reasoning, there is little reason to have them continue with practice exercises or show all of their work on every problem. However, if students cannot provide reasoning to support their intuitive leaps, then it is probably necessary to have them do some additional work.

Having students explain mathematics using words has emerged as a very powerful tool in the new assessment literature. Using writing as a part of mathematics not only helps the teacher "see" the students' reasoning as they work, it is also a very useful way to get gifted girls to be more expressive about mathematics. Verbal skills reputedly are, after all, "girl's territory."

Discovering Mathematical Principles

An excellent approach to enrichment for the gifted is to have them derive the mathematical principles and laws. These laws, generally handed to students unceremoniously, are the heart of mathematics and are considered laws and properties precisely because they can be applied in many situations. By providing gifted students with a series of similar exercises and then asking them to come up with a general statement that connects the exercises, these students can come to understand not only the law but the wide applicability and power of the law. Grossnickle and Reckzeh (1973) provided an example of such a set of problems:

> a) *Find the answers to the following:*
>
> | | |
> |---|---|
> | *4 1/2 ÷ 3 1/2* | *3/4 ÷ 1/2* |
> | *1/2 ÷ 2/3* | *6 ÷ 7 1/7* |
> | *5 1/2 ÷ 5 1/2* | *8 1/2 ÷ 4* |
>
> b) *In which of the examples is the quotient greater than 1? Less than 1? Equal to 1?*
>
> c) *See if you can discover the general rules that will tell when the quotient of an example is greater than 1. Less than 1. Equal to 1. Write a brief statement which describes the generalization.*

Grossnickle and Reckzeh also note that math puzzles, often provided to gifted students as "filler" to keep them occupied, can also be used to derive mathematical principles and laws. Puzzles are often tricky because they require an unexpected application of a mathematical rule. Having students state the rule as well as the puzzle solution will help solidify the importance of the rule in the students' minds. Again, Grossnickle and Reckzeh (1973) have provided an example of a puzzle that could be used for this purpose:

a) *Select any number*
b) *Now add the next higher number*
c) *To that sum add 9*
d) *Divide the sum in step c by 2*
e) *Subtract the original number*

What will always be true of this process and why?

Repeating the procedure several times, students will discover that the answer is always 5. To construct a general rule, a variable *n* is substituted and the puzzle solution becomes clear:

a) *Let* n = *number*
b) *Then let* n + 1 = *the next number*
c) *2*n + *1* = *the sum*
d) *2*n + *1* + *9* = *2*n + *10*
e) *(2*n + *10)/2* = n + *5*
f) n + *5* − n = *5*

As the students' explorations become more abstract, the application of the laws of addition, subtraction, and distribution all become clear, as does the inevitable answer. This is the difference between raw talent, "cast of mind," and developed skills!

Patterns and Number Relationships

Another way to introduce students to the characteristics of certain groups of numbers, and of the overlapping characteristics of certain numbers, is through the use of Venn diagrams. Gifted students, with their heightened potential for analytical thought and superior aptitude for visual reasoning (generally referred to a *visual-spatial ability*), can benefit greatly from working with numbers through identifying their patterns. Haag, Kaufman, Martin, and Rising (1987) have developed a series of such activities, including the one at the top of page 122.

In the first circle belong the set of numbers that are squares (1, 4, 9, 16, 25, and so on); the second circle is the home of positive prime numbers (including 2, 3, 5, 7, 11, 13, 17); and the third circle houses the positive dividers of 36 (1, 2, 3, 4, 6, 9, 12, 18, 36). Having established what some of these numbers are, Mr. Jenkins can proceed to give the gifted students some more advanced challenges.

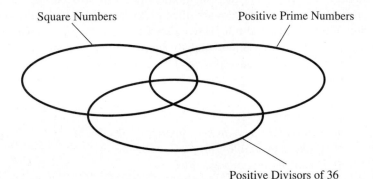

Square Numbers   Positive Prime Numbers

Positive Divisors of 36

Mr. Jenkins: Look at how the circles overlap. What kind of numbers would I put in the overlapping areas of the circles?

Stephanie: The numbers that belong to both groups. So it would be numbers that are both square numbers and a divisor of 36 or a positive prime number and a divisor of 36 or something like that.

Mr. Jenkins: Good! What would I put in the exact middle of the circle, where all three overlap?

Cranshaw: Only the numbers that belong to all three groups.

Mr. Jenkins: OK, then, where would you put the number 9 in the diagram?

Cranshaw: Well, it goes in the circle with the square numbers because its square root is 3.

Sam: It also goes in the group with the positive dividers of 36 because 36 divided by 6 is 6!

Mr. Jenkins: OK, if it belongs in both the squares category and the positive dividers of 36 category, where does it go on the chart?

Stephanie: In the overlap between those two circles.

[Mr. Jenkins places the number 9 in the overlap in the center of the diagram.]

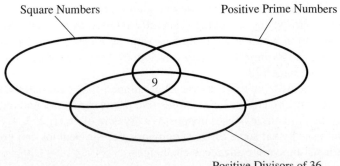

Square Numbers   Positive Prime Numbers

9

Positive Divisors of 36

Mr. Jenkins: Like this?

Zelda: Yes, because they both overlap there.

Mr. Jenkins: Are you sure? Look carefully.

Zelda: Well . . . oh! I guess not there because that has part of the other circle, too.

Mr. Jenkins: Good. Sam, come to the board and put the number 9 where it really belongs.

[Sam puts the 9 in the space created by the overlap in the circles.]

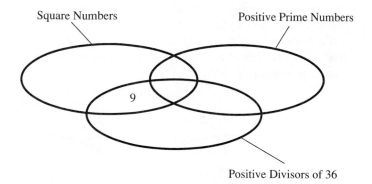

Mr. Jenkins: Great. By the way, where should we put the numbers that don't go in any of the circles?

Joe: You mean the wrong answers?

Mr. Jenkins: Well, that's an interesting question. Are the numbers that don't go in any of the circles the wrong answers?

Joe: Sometimes. Like 50 doesn't go anywhere in there.

Cranshaw: Yeah, but what about the number 1? It would be a wrong answer in some places in the chart but right in others. So it still belongs on the inside.

Stephanie: It sort of depends on the question you ask, because whether it's right or wrong depends on the question, not on the number.

Mr. Jenkins: Interesting point. Well, then, what do we call the numbers that go on the outside?

Stephanie (smiling): How about "numbers on the outside"?

Mr. Jenkins: Well, that would do for us, but I don't think that a stranger coming into the room would understand. How about something more specific?

Joe: How about "numbers that don't belong to any of the three sets"?

Mr. Jenkins: That's a good start, Joe. Think of a positive way to say that—without the "don't."

Joe: Er, well, I guess it would be "the numbers that do belong outside of the three sets."

Mr. Jenkins: I think that will do for now. (Later, of course, Mr. Jenkins will help the students convert this phrase into a statement about the set of numbers that does not meet necessary conditions.)

Having established the basic concept, Mr. Jenkins can proceed to give the students different kinds of challenges using the same diagram. For instance, he could place the letter *Y* in any area of the diagram and have students list all of the numbers that *Y* could stand for. At a really advanced level, he may ask the students to identify the area of the circle that is never used for these sets of numbers. Once established, he may ask them to rearrange the diagram so that there is no "wasted space" on the diagram. This develops both the students' number sense and their spatial ability. Very visual students like Stephanie are excellent at this kind of activity, and before long, she "sees" what the new arrangement should look like:

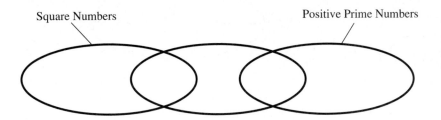

A Final Word: Acceleration versus Enrichment

Accelerate or enrich, move faster or delve deeper, cover more or cover thoroughly: This issue is of constant debate in many areas of gifted education, but perhaps nowhere so vehemently as in mathematics. With fast-paced programs as a very attractive alternative, but a new national emphasis on mathematical reasoning and problem solving, the issue has recently reemerged. Which way should a program go? Granted, any program for gifted should have some elements of both: Enrichment programs should also allow students to go further with their basic math and acceleration programs should lead students to deeper understanding of the nature of mathematics. But which of these alternatives should serve as the core of one's program? The answer depends largely on what one believes mathematics is and what its function should be. Wavrik (1980) outlined the philosophical beliefs that drive acceleration programs and enrichment programs, which are presented in Figure 4–5. Examining the philosophies and associated teaching approaches will help you, the teacher, decide which approach to take with your students.

Content Sophistication

Content sophistication, which is very important to gifted students, can help the students realize that mathematics is a very flexible and creative field. Often, children (and adults, too) think that mathematics is very rigid, constrained by problems that have a single right

FIGURE 4–5   Philosophy of Standard and Nonstandard Mathematics Instruction

Standard Instruction

A. Underlying Philosophical Basis

1. Mathematics is an essentially static collection of facts, methods, rules, etc.

2. These facts, methods, rules, etc., were created by geniuses. Mere mortals cannot or need not understand their genesis.

3. Mathematics instruction is a procedure for transferring a package of information from teacher to student.

4. Students learn mainly by drill and practice in the skills involved.

5. The main goal of mathematics instruction is to produce students who can solve problems. In the context of standard instruction this means that they:
   a. classify the problem
   b. recall the method appropriate for solving it
   c. correctly apply the method.

Pedagogical Consequences

1. Mathematics is broken into a succession of small pieces (units or skills).

2. The units are presented to a student in an order dictated primarily by difficulty and logical sequence. Instruction consists of cycles:
   a. introduction to the skill, fact or method
   b. practice or drill
   c. testing to determine mastery

Non-Standard Instruction

A. Underlying Philosophical Basis

1. Mathematics is more a subject of ideas than a subject of facts.

2. One can only understand an idea when one has, in some measure, thought of it oneself.

3. Understanding must be created. "Ideas must be formed in the student's mind and the teacher can only act as midwife." (Socrates)

4. People learn by being placed in an environment that stimulates, encourages, and supports their thinking.

5. The main goal of mathematics instruction is to produce students who can solve problems. In the context of non-standard instruction this means that they:
   a. analyze the problem
   b. use their understanding of mathematical ideas to devise a plan
   c. continue to work interactively with the problem until a method to solve is devised.

Pedagogical Consequences

1. A main role for the teacher is to structure the environment to support the development of student thinking.

2. The learner must assume responsibility for learning.

3. A teacher must attend to the development of successful attitudes.... A proper mental set is required,...which, among other things, includes an inquisitive spirit and high tolerance for frustration.

Source: From "Mathematics Education for the Gifted Elementary School Student" by J. J. Wavrik, 1980, *Gifted Child Quarterly, 24*, pp. 169–170. Reprinted by permission.

answer and a single approach to get to that right answer. Gifted students, with their love of the unknown and their penchant for creativity, can lose interest in mathematics if they perceive it to be a series of repetitive "plug-n-chug" problems where exercises are done simply to show, time and time again, that a given formula or process will do exactly what the teacher said it would do.

The question remains, How does one introduce the idea of uncertainty, originality, and creativity in mathematics? One of the most important writers and thinkers in the field of mathematics problem solving, George Polya, differentiates between demonstrative reasoning, which leads to proof and absolute answers, and plausible reasoning, which is based on inference, theories, supposition, and hunches. According to Polya, both of these kinds of reasoning are critical to mathematics:

> *Demonstrative reasoning is safe, beyond controversy, and final. Plausible reasoning is hazardous, controversial, and provisional. Demonstrative reasoning... is in itself (as mathematics is in itself) incapable of yielding essentially new knowledge about the world around us. Anything new that we learn about the world involves plausible reasoning, which is the only kind of reasoning for which we care in everyday affairs....*
>
> *Mathematics is regarded as a demonstrative science. Yet this is only one of its aspects. Finished mathematics presented in a finished form appears as purely demonstrative, consisting of proofs only. Yet mathematics in the making resembles any other human knowledge in the making. You have to guess a mathematical theorem before you prove it; you have to guess the idea of the proof before you carry through the details. You have to combine observations and follow analogies; you have to try and try again. The result of the mathematician's creative work is demonstrative reasoning, a proof; but the proof is discovered by plausible reasoning, by guessing. If the learning of mathematics reflects to any degree the invention of mathematics, it must have a place for guessing, for plausible inference. (1954, pp. v–vi)*

Polya developed a scheme for mathematics problem solving, along with a list of questions that should be asked at each stage. The steps and their associated questions are presented in Figure 4–6. Notice that the questions are varied in type and nature: While some questions ask about the problem, some are also questions that focus on the problem solver's metacognition ("Have I tried everything?" "Should I look at the problem another way?"). Similarly, some of the questions are very concrete and specific, whereas others are more abstract. A teacher of gifted students could use this list of questions to help differentiate levels of instruction in his or her class simply by differing the nature of the questions that are asked of different students.

One way that Mr. Jenkins can help his students is to teach them the problem-solving heuristics that lead to more flexible problem solving. Wheatley (1984) suggested five heuristics that are both valuable and easy for students to remember:

1. Look-for-a-pattern.
2. Make-a-list.
3. Guess-and-test.
4. Draw-a-diagram.
5. Break-into-parts.

FIGURE 4–6   Polya's Problem-Solving Questions

First

You have to understand the problem.

Understanding the Problem

What is the unknown? What are the data? What is the condition? Is it possible to satisfy the condition? Is the condition sufficient to determine the unknown? Or is it insufficient? Or redundant? Or contradictory? Draw a figure. Introduce a suitable notion. Separate the various parts of the condition. Can you write them down?

Second

Find the connection between the data and the unknown. You may be obliged to consider auxiliary problems if an immediate connection cannot be found. You should obtain eventually a plan of the solution.

Devising a Plan

Have you seen it before? Or have you seen the same problem in a slightly different form?
Do you know a related problem? Do you know a theorem which might be useful? Look at the unknown! And try to think of a familiar problem having the same or a similar unknown. Here is a problem related to yours and solved before. Could you use it? Could you use its result? Could you use its method? Should you introduce some auxiliary element in order to make its use possible?

If you cannot solve the proposed problem try to solve first some related problem. Could you imagine a more accessible related problem? A more general problem? A more special problem? An analogous problem? ... Could you think of other data appropriate to determine the unknown? Could you change the unknown or the data or both if necessary, so that the new unknown and the new data are nearer to each other? Did you use all the data? Did you use the whole condition? Have you taken into account all essential notions involved in the problem?

Third

Carry out your plan.

Carrying Out the Plan

Carrying out your plan of the solution, check each step. Can you see clearly that the step is correct? Can you prove that it is correct?

Fourth

Examine the solution obtained.

Looking Back

Can you check the result? Can you check the argument? Can you derive the result differently? Can you see it? Can you use the result, or the method, for some other problem?

Source: Polya, G. *How to solve it: A new aspect of mathematical method.* Copyright © 1985 by Princeton University Press. Reprinted by permission of Princeton University Press.

Solving word problems takes on a new twist when one of these heuristics (e.g., guess and test—estimation) is applied. Mr. Jenkins gives the class the following word problem:

A farmer had chickens and rabbits. One day he saw 10 heads and 26 feet. How many rabbits did he see? (Wheatley, 1984)

Mr. Jenkins begins by asking the class if someone can find a way to set up the problem to be solved. Cranshaw and Stephanie shoot up their hands, and Stephanie is called on:

Stephanie: You need two formulas, one to show the feet part and one to show the head part. The feet part would be something times 2, for the chicken feet, added to something else times 4 for the rabbit feet, equals 26.

Mr. Jenkins: If I called the something for the chicken feet x and the something else for the rabbit feet y, how would it look? Cranshaw, come and write it on the board.

Cranshaw writes $2(x) + 4(y) = 26$.

Mr. Jenkins: That's right. Now what would the other formula look like?

Cranshaw again writes $x + y = 10$.

Mr. Jenkins: Hmm, Sam, is that answer OK?

Sam: Yeah, because one is for chickens and the other is for rabbits and altogether they have to be 10.

Mr. Jenkins: OK, great. But we're not going to solve it yet. First, we're going to get some idea of whether or not our answer is going to be reasonable when we're finished. Who can guess right now what the answer will be?

The students look a bit confused. How can they guess the answer without trying it out first?

Mr. Jenkins: Remember, we're not interested in the exact answer right now, but in an approximation. I wonder if there's a way we can figure out what the answer won't be. Let's say I have an animal pen with all the rabbits and chickens in it. Will there be 10 rabbits and 10 chickens in the pen?

Robert: No, because there can only be 10 heads total.

Mr. Jenkins: Right! Now, what else can someone tell me either about the number of rabbits or the number of chickens?

(Silence)

Mr. Jenkins: What if I told you that there had to be less than 8 rabbits?

Stephanie: Oh! There can't be 8 rabbits, because then there'd be more feet than we can have.

Mr. Jenkins: Why?

Stephanie: Because 8 rabbits times 4 feet is 32 feet and there can only be 26. But Mr. Jenkins, there can't be 7 rabbits, either.

Mr. Jenkins: You caught me! Very good. Now, if we can say that there are less than 7 rabbits, is there something similar we can say about the chickens?

Stephanie: You know, Mr. Jenkins, we can't really solve this at all.

Mr. Jenkins: Why not?

Stephanie: Because one of the rabbits or chickens might be missing a foot.

Mr. Jenkins: Thank you for that observation. Let's assume for the moment that all of the animals are intact, and proceed. What can we say about the number of chickens?

Zelda: Nothing, because no matter how many chickens there are, there will always be less than 26 feet.

Mr. Jenkins: That's true, but if there are less than 7 rabbits and a total of 10 heads, what can we say about the chickens?

Amanda: I see. There have to be more than 3 chickens, because if there aren't the number won't add up to 10.

Mr. Jenkins: Right. We know that there are at least 3 chickens and less than 7 rabbits. Where do we look next for some clues? If there are 3 chickens, how many chicken feet will there be?

Everyone: 6.

Mr. Jenkins: What does that tell you about rabbits?

Joe (who has been writing furiously at his desk): That there can't be more than 20 rabbit feet, so there can't be more than 5 rabbits. And if there aren't more than 5 rabbits, there have to be at least 5 chickens, which means that there are at least 10 chicken feet, which means that there can't be more than 16 rabbit feet, which means that there can't be more than 4 rabbits.

Mr. Jenkins: Whoa!! Very good, Joe! Our guess is beginning to look pretty specific! We have to have less than 4 rabbits and at least 6 chickens. I think you've caught on to the idea now. Try solving the equations and see if the answer is less than 4 rabbits.

When the students finished the problem and came up with the answer (3 rabbits), Mr. Jenkins turned the discussion to the process, with a little help from Cranshaw:

Cranshaw: Mr. Jenkins, we could have finished this an hour ago!

Mr. Jenkins: Good point, Cranshaw. Why would we want to go through a process of estimation like we just did?

Sam: You spend less time messing around with answers that can't be true.

Zelda: You have an idea when you're done about whether or not you're right.

Joe: It uses up a lot of class time.

Mr. Jenkins (laughs): Well, all of that is true—thanks, Joe—but there are other reasons, too. When real mathematicians do their work, they don't have an answer waiting for them in the back of the book. It's very important that they have some ideas—that they can knock out some possibilities and include others before they begin their work with formulas. By practicing this process of estimation, you begin to get a "feel" for what is and what is not possible in solving lots of different kinds of math problems. Good estimation is as important to math as good addition or subtraction. OK, let's move on to something else....

A visitor to this class would have seen energetic laughing and students trying out various examples and having a good time. Some visitors get upset when they see students enjoying themselves in a game-like situation such as this. "Learning is a serious business," they often remark disapprovingly. So it is—much too serious to be solemn.

Content Novelty

Invention in Mathematics

One reason why mathematics so often appears to be a limiting field, bound by absolute answers and bereft of creativity, is that little time is spent in classrooms discussing the history of mathematics and the amazing mathematical inventions that have changed our concept of mathematical reasoning altogether. One very current example of a "mathematics invention" is Mandelbrot's discovery of a formula to predict fractals, associated with the chaos theory in science. The concept of fractals is that seemingly random patterns, such as the roll of waves on the seashore, actually can be predicted by using mathematical equations. Yet, before the year 1975, this form of mathematics did not even exist (Gleick, 1988). Younger children will be fascinated by more historical (and less abstract) changes in mathematics, such as the idea that the number 0 is a relative newcomer to the number system.

Studies of mathematical representation and classic mathematical patterns are fascinating to gifted children. Comparisons between the Roman, Arabic, and Egyptian number systems can provide a source of interesting conversations about the impact of the way numbers are represented on the ideas behind different mathematical systems. Studies in different mathematical bases can have the same result.

To engender a sense of playfulness and mathematical fun for students, they can be introduced to some of the classic mathematics patterns. Pascal's triangle, Ulam's conjecture, Fibonacci numbers, and arithmetic and geometric sequences are all valuable resources for introducing students to the beauty and elegance of mathematical patterns. Figure 4–7 presents some of these patterns and the so-called secrets behind them. Once students understand a pattern, such as Fibonacci's sequence, they can research the amazing connection between that pattern and natural phenomena such as the growth pattern of leaves on trees, the chromatic scale, and patterns of genetic transference.

The Fibonacci sequence—in fact, any mathematical pattern—can help students discern number relationships. Some gifted students, like Sam, have a good "feel" for these

FIGURE 4–7 Mathematics Patterns

Ulam's Conjecture

1. Take any positive integer.
2. If the integer is even, divide by two; if it is odd, multiply by three and add one.
3. Do the same thing with the new number, and so on.
4. Ultimately, you will reach 1.

Example:
12----6----3----10----5----16----8----4----2----1

Fibonacci Sequence

Find the pattern in the following sequence of numbers:
1, 1, 2, 3, 5, 8, 13, 21, 34, 55, 89, 144, 233, ...

Solution:
1 + 1 = 2
1 + 2 = 3
2 + 3 = 5
3 + 5 = 8
5 + 8 = 13
8 + 13 = 21

Pascal's Triangle

This is a triangular arrangement of numbers that contains a number of different pattern sequences.

Example:

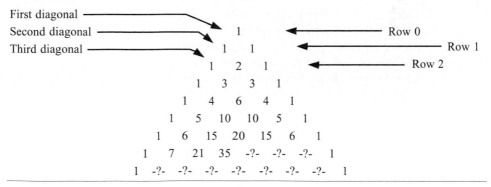

relationships. For Sam, this deep understanding emanates from his love of music, which is filled with complicated numerical patterns and relationships. Although Sam is most accustomed to hearing the relationships as they pervade the music he loves so much, he is also able to grasp them in his math class.

For students like Sam, advanced understanding of mathematical relationships can be cultivated through a comparison of these patterns. Figure 4–8 shows an activity that Mr. Jenkins found to try to push Sam's understanding a little further. The idea behind the exercise is to have Sam understand the relative additive power of the Fibonacci sequence

FIGURE 4–8 **Exercise Using the Fibonacci Sequence**

Steps	*Fibonacci*	*Sequence A*	*Sequence B*	*Sequence C*
1	1	1	1	1
2	1	2	8	4
3	2	4	12	9
4	3	8	16	16
5	5	16	20	25
6				
7				
8				
9				
10				
11				
12				
13				
14				
15				

in relation to other number sequences. First, Mr. Jenkins asks Sam to identify the kinds of patterns in each column (sequence A doubles each previous number, B adds 4 to each previous number, and C is a sequence of squared numbers). Mr. Jenkins then asks Sam to predict which number sequence will result in the highest numbers. Sam, who thinks he already sees the relationship between the patterns, chooses sequence C because he thinks that square numbers will become largest fastest. Upon completion of the exercise, however, Sam is surprised to find that the sequence that ended up being largest was one that seemed slowest at the beginning! When asked to rank the sequences in terms or relative power, Sam creates the following hierarchy:

Most Powerful:

Sequence A
Fibonacci sequence
Sequence C
Sequence B

Sam discovers that mathematical patterns may vary in terms of their additive power over short or long sequences.

Mathematic Applications and Other Disciplines

Math, like science, can take on the appearance of being something strange and foreign and removed from the dealings of everyday life—especially math such as algebra or geometry. Even with the use of word problems, math often seems like a completely useless subject because it is so hard to apply! One of the most useful adaptations a teacher can do to make a math curriculum novel and pertinent is to reveal to students the ways that it is applied in different disciplines.

Mathematics and Art.   The applications of mathematics in art are numerous, but the most accessible are in geometry. Students can learn to apply geometric principles to create their own artwork, based on classic examples in art history. Optical art, studies in dimension, and historical use of patterns in pottery and engravings can be duplicated by students as they systematically use different shapes and forms in geometry. As they do so, the students also learn to integrate the fundamental nature of these shapes and patterns into their minds. Figure 4–9 shows how the concept of dimension can be explained through geometry and the relationship between lines.

Mathematics and Social Science.   Applications of numbers to the social sciences are numerous; some of the most interesting to gifted children will involve the representation and interpretation of statistics. Lively discussions can spring out of a comparison of two graphs depicting the same information but using different scales. The different interpretations of the two graphs will show students how numbers can be "twisted" to misrepresent findings. Other interesting discussions can evolve out of trying to determine the exact meaning of some advertisements, such as those that claim "9 out of 10 dentists recommend Britey-Brite toothpaste." Analyses of statistics given in TV commercials are interesting and enlightening to many students. The use and abuse of numbers will introduce important notions of the ethics of using numbers responsibly.

Mathematics and Literature.   Although the connection between mathematics and some disciplines like science or social science is relatively clear and easy to make, using math in other disciplines is more difficult. In literature, for example, the fundamental similarities between mathematics and language are very abstract (both are systems of communication based on symbolic representation and both operate within the confines of specific rules of grammar or operations) and may be too difficult for young children to grasp. However, a clever teacher can embed mathematics into reading activities so that students can see that math can be applied to almost every human endeavor. Keese provided one example of how he used the classic Edgar Allan Poe story "The Pit and the Pendulum" to give his students some mathematics challenges. At certain points in the story, Keese stopped the tale and asked students to work out the math that is described:

> 2. *"My outstretched hands at length encountered some solid obstruction. It was a wall, seemingly of stone masonry—very smooth, slimy, and cold. I followed it up, stopping with all the careful distrust with which certain antique narratives had inspired me. This process, however, afforded me no means of ascertaining the dimensions of my dungeon...."*
>
> 2a. *Why does this process not determine the dimensions of the cell?*
>
> 2b. *Devise and describe procedures for determining the dimensions of the cell. (1981, p. 208)*

Step 1

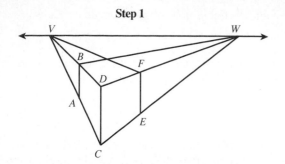

Draw a box in two-point perspective. Label the points as shown. Make height *CD* and width *CE* of your box about the same. For example, *CD* = *CE* = 6 cm. Do not erase the vanishing lines. Your first letter will fill the front face of this box. Select a distance between the first and second letters by drawing a vertical line *GH*. If you used 6 cm for the width *CE*, then use about 1 cm for *EG*.

Step 2

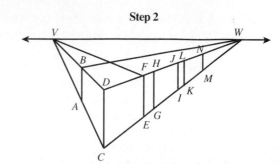

Select a width for your second box by drawing a vertical segment *IJ*. This box will eventually house your second letter. If you used 6 cm for *CE*, then use about 3 cm for *GI*. Next, select a width for the space between the second and third boxes by drawing in a vertical segment *KL*. If you used 1 cm for *EG* then use .5 cm for *IK*. Repeat this procedure for the third box.

Step 3

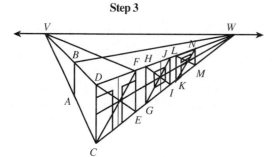

Now design a letter on the front face of each box. Draw in diagonal lines *CF*, *DE*, *HI*, *GJ*, *LM*, and *KN*. The points where these diagonals intersect are the perspective centers for each front face. Draw vertical lines through these centers. Label the center in the first box *P*. Draw line *PW*. Use this line to center each block letter on its front face.

Step 4

Draw all the top vanishing lines from the top front corners to the back edges of the solid letters. Draw all the vertical edges at the back of the solid letters. Draw all the remaining vanishing lines. With a pen or felt tip marker outline all the edges of the solid letters. Erase all other lines. Decorate.

Draw a two-point perspective view of your name or initials in solid letters.

FIGURE 4–9   Examples of Dimension in Art Through Geometry: Drawing Block Letters in Two-Point Perspective

Source: Discovering geometry: An inductive approach, Michael Serra, 1992. Key Curriculum Press, P.O. Box 2304, Berkeley, CA 94702. Reprinted by permission.

These questions serve several purposes. They give the children a chance to use their creativity to devise a (realistic) means of finding the dimensions of the cell. They are also required to spontaneously recall and apply their skills in geometry in the process. An added benefit is that the students must read the story very carefully in order to gather as much information as they can, resulting in a much more complete understanding of the story!

Although not as common, stories based on mathematics and mathematical theme can capture the imagination. The classic novel *Flatland: A Romance of Many Dimensions* (Abbott, 1963) about a two-dimensional land inhabited by squares, triangles, and polyhedrons will captivate students while showing them a novel application of the principles of geometry. After reading the story, students can be assigned the task of creating their own mathematics tale, using mathematical formulas or principles as their guides.

Mathematics and Technology.   With the publication of the *Professional Standards* by the National Council of Teachers of Mathematics, we can finally put to rest the question of whether or not to use calculators in the classroom. Surely we want students to be able to do basic addition, subtraction, multiplication, and division on their own. Certainly we want them to understand the principles behind other more advanced calculations of sine and cosine. But the calculator can and should be used to enable students to move swiftly through these functions once they are understood.

For gifted students the calculator can be used to provide concrete examples of the relationship between algebraic and spatial representations of different mathematical formulas. For example, graphing calculators can help gifted students convert a formula for a parabola from the algebraic equation to its graph. Another way of looking at this task would be to ask students to find the equation that fits the points provided on a Cartesian coordinate system. As students experiment with different formulas while trying to "connect the dots," they will discover what changes they have to make to create a curve that is higher or wider. From these explorations can evolve generalized statements about the roles of the different parts of this formula.

An increasing number of interesting and discovery-based computer software programs are being introduced on the market. Computers can be used in a number of ways to help differentiate instruction for gifted students in the regular classroom. Software packages can be purchased to provide these children with the chance to move more quickly through the regular curriculum.

Dover described the following needed areas of development in the microcomputer field:

1. *The development of sophisticated software for use with gifted students.*
2. *Agencies working toward the betterment of gifted education should commit themselves to developing enrichment programs involving computers.*
3. *A training program to meet the need for teachers of the gifted to become computer literate! (1983, p. 84)*

Computers can help good teachers do their jobs better, but they cannot bypass or provide an alternative to poor teaching. It is important that as we continue to consider the possible role of the computer in the classroom, we do not mistake it for a panacea in education or as an alternative to providing excellent training from a human teacher, guide, or mentor.

Mathematics and Gifted Girls

The idea that there would be discovered a fundamental difference between the sexes in some areas of intellectual performance strikes many people as almost un-American. Yet the findings in the area of mathematics are quite clear: Girls of all ability levels consistently perform less well on measures of mathematics achievement or aptitude than do boys. This is no less true of gifted girls than of girls of average ability. What remains unclear is the reason why.

The research in the area of mathematics and gender has still not provided a definitive answer to the "why" question of girls and mathematics. Part of the reason is that the question of nature versus nurture is virtually impossible to unravel by the time children are old enough to study. The other reason is that the issue is so politically heated that everyone who has a stake in the matter tends to see only one side of the issue. The two major arguments in the research debate is that the achievement difference is due to some genetic or biological difference or that the difference is due to environmental factors supported by a cultural belief that mathematics is a part of the world of men.

The issue of biological differences received its broadest publicity after the publication of an article by Stanley and Benbow (1982). They reported the results of almost 40,000 seventh-grade students from the mid-Atlantic region of the United States who took the Scholastic Aptitude Test as part of the SMPY talent search in 1980, 1981, and 1982. With a relatively equal number of boys and girls sitting for the test, the average scores on mathematics clearly favored the boys by an average of 30 points.

Even more decisive were the results at the highest levels of the test. When the students who scored 700 or higher on the test (an extraordinary performance for a 13-year-old) were studied, it was found that 260 boys made this high score, yet only 20 girls reached that level of performance. This results in a startling 13:1 ratio of boys to girls. In this subject area, boys produce more outstanding performances than girls, a result that Benbow and Stanley (1982) hypothesized may be related to differences in the ability of boys and girls to perceive spatial relationship—to see shapes and patterns.

Although no one can deny the possibility that there may be some biological or genetic differences that account for part of the infamous "math gap" (however, the research shows that the impact of this difference looks smaller and smaller all the time [Linn & Peterson, 1986]), it is also hard to deny the cultural hypothesis. This hypothesis basically claims that the deck is stacked against girls, where mathematics is concerned. Mathematics has long had the label of being a "masculine" activity, and not the proper venue for girls. And the difference looks particularly bad when one considers the fact that verbal skills of boys and girls, which once tended to favor girls, have pretty much equalized. Part of the reason for the continued mathematics discrepancy is access to information about mathematics. As Colangelo pointed out:

If you don't learn mathematics in a formal mathematic course, you are not going to learn it because it's not the kind of thing that kids down the street talk about.... Whereas in English, and especially in Social Studies, there are things you can learn by watching television, by chatting with others, or by reading Time *magazine. (1988, p. 236)*

Zelda's ambivalence about high performance in mathematics being tied to masculinity is not at all unusual, even in these days of greater freedom for girls to seek broader career choices. A study by Leroux (reported in Reis & Callahan, 1989) demonstrated that the perception of math as a male domain is still prevalent in our society. When asked, females in the study still reported that males were more capable than females in math; males reported that females were more capable in literature. Reis and Callahan summarized the nature of the bias: "Math and science achievement are often linked to innate abilities, more than achievement in any other discipline. Further, our culture subscribes to an assumption that males have more of those innate abilities" (1989, p. 106).

Such beliefs invariably filter into the classroom, where girls are still treated differently from boys. In a study of over 100 fourth- to sixth-grade classes, Sadker and Sadker (1985) found that boys still dominate in the classroom and are still encouraged to dominate, whereas girls are encouraged to sit still and behave. In fact, one of the most surprising—and distressing—of their findings was that of all of the groups studied, high-achieving girls received the least attention—hardly the kind of finding one expects in this so-called liberated age.

One natural question that emerges from this difference is Can we find classrooms where girls are encouraged to perform? Eccles (reported in Reis & Callahan, 1989) did find classrooms where girls had relatively higher levels of achievements and she studied the characteristics of those classrooms. What she found was a set of classroom qualities that positively affected girls' confidence and positive attitudes toward math, leading to their equivalent achievement. The characteristics of these classrooms included:

Frequent use of cooperative learning opportunities

Frequent individualized learning opportunities

Use of practical problems in assignments

Frequent use of hands-on opportunities

Active career and educational guidance

Infrequent use of competitive motivational strategies

Frequent activities oriented toward broadening views of mathematics and physical sciences—presenting mathematics as a tool in solving problems

Frequent use of strategies to ensure full class participation

Other ideas that have proved successful is to group girls together so that boys do not have an opportunity to dominate and the girls cannot rely on the boys for help. In studies of gender-segregated classrooms, it has been found that females make greater gains than females in traditional settings (Fox, 1977; Lee & Byrk, 1986).

Studying the lives and accomplishments of female mathematicians also helps provide role models of achieving females. Table 4–1 gives a brief list of some eminent female mathematicians, who, although they have made substantive contributions to the field, are very rarely mentioned in mathematics textbooks. By infusing the works of these women into the curriculum, talented females can learn that they are just as entitled to join the world of mathematicians as are males.

Another area of concern is females and the use of computers. Like mathematics, computers are perceived as a male realm, and females are less likely than males to take advantage of the learning opportunities that computers provide. In an interesting book

TABLE 4–1   Noted Women Mathematicians

Name	Year of Birth	Contribution
Maria Agnesi	1781	Agnesi wrote a calculus textbook, which was later used by students of mathematics. She was recognized by the Queen of Italy and the Pope for her excellence in mathematics.
Mary Fairfax Somerville	1780	Somerville studied mathematics on her own; she had to have her brother's teacher buy a geometry textbook to use to study. As an adult, she studied mathematics and astronomy and wrote several books on mathematics and science.
Sophie Germain	1776	Fascinated by patterns, she studied the shapes made by sand on a drum when the drum was hit. She converted this pattern into mathematical formulas.
Roswitha	?	Educated because she was a nun, she was fascinated by the movement of the earth, sun, moon, and stars. She learned mathematics to help explain this movement.
Emmy Noether	1882	She taught mathematics at home by a private tutor, and became one of the first women to teach mathematics at a university. Forced to leave Germany during World War II, she later became a college professor in the United States.
Hypatia	370 A.D.	Daughter of a mathematician, Hypatia was a popular mathematics instructor of her time. Her special interests were in conic sections, astronomy, and algebra.
Ada Byron Lovelace	1816	Daughter of the poet Lord Byron, Lovelace's talent in mathematics was noticed early by family friends, including Mary Somerville (see above). She spent most of her time in mathematics studying the technique of finite differences.
Emilie du Chalet	1706	Like others, she disguised herself as a man to gain entrance into the intellectual world. Her studies were in calculus and she was best known for her famous translation of Newton's masterpiece, *The Principia*.

entitled *The Neuter Computer*, Sanders and Stone (cited in Callahan, 1988) summarized some of the reasons why males continue to dominate. A summary of their findings include:

Girls see males operating computers more often than females.

Computers are related to mathematics, hence, to masculinity.

Computers are perceived as machinery (not as a tool), hence masculine.

Computer software is male oriented, with emphasis on competition, war, death, and sports.

The assertiveness of males in the classroom doubles where the computer is concerned—boys leap at the chance to use them; girls patiently wait their turn (which often never comes) or will actually give up time on the computer for boys.

This last point brings up another important issue in mathematics programming for gifted girls. Stephanie has no problem in mathematics, but she does have a problem with Sam, who consistently competes with her for time on the computer. According to Sam, Stephanie has less right to the computer than he does because she is a girl. Unless programming for gifted girls includes teaching gifted *boys* that girls can do math, then only half of the problem will be solved—and the easier half at that.

The Teacher of Mathematics

If we can teach only as much as we ourselves know, then we have a special problem in the teaching of mathematics to gifted students, particularly at the elementary school level. By far the majority of elementary school teachers are women who have faced the same cultural stereotypes as Zelda. Many have avoided mathematics at every turn and may have only a standard elementary textbook and one three-credit college course to prepare them for students like Cranshaw and Stephanie, who may easily surpass the teacher's mastery of mathematics.

Computer programs that allow talented students to proceed at their own pace can help, but computers cannot compensate for inadequately prepared teachers. A stronger emphasis on majors and minors in university teacher-training programs can also provide an antidote to the mathematics anxiety symptoms, which can lead to mathematics avoidance, and, in some measure, cheat gifted students from some exciting intellectual adventures. Certainly if the national reforms recommended in the *Everybody Counts* and *Professional Standards* reports are to be realized, substantially more training will be necessary for many, many elementary school teachers.

The idea that there should be special mathematics content for the gifted is based not only on their unique mathematical understanding but on the different educational purposes served by achievement for different children. There is a genuine question as to whether students whose education will terminate at the secondary level should be subjected to Boolian algebra or set theory, as opposed to the mastery of interest rates and family budgeting. The gifted students, bound for further advancement in the educational system, should be preparing to master those higher mathematical levels, and need a strong early foundation to do so. Such content fields as set theory and calculus seem to more adequately prepare those students for that goal.

One optimistic sign is found in the content of the national reports. With increasing attention to problem solving and conceptualization in mathematics, both teacher training and curriculum should become more aligned to the gifted students' needs. As these curricula are implemented, teachers should also be able to identify more easily those activities and skills that are uniquely suited for the gifted. The future looks quite bright for a stronger mathematics program that will challenge gifted children.

Unresolved Issues

1. Where will teachers of gifted mathematicians come from? Currently there is a type of Russian roulette being played in which gifted youngsters are issued one of a million available elementary teachers, based primarily on the community he or she is in and on the school she or he is attending. The odds are strong that the teacher knows little in depth about mathematics. New procedures need to be pursued by which gifted students can receive better mathematics preparation, such as team teaching or mentor approaches.

2. What are the fundamental concepts associated with complex mathematical reasoning? Contrary to the usual assumptions, we know very little about the relationship between the content of elementary school mathematics and the later mastery of more complex system of mathematics. As a result, unsolvable arguments arise as to whether teaching set theory or probability at early ages is useful for later mastery of college mathematics.

3. Given the time constraints of the current school year, what is more effective—teaching gifted applications of mathematics, which will teach students the relevance of knowing math and excite them with real-world applications, or teaching abstract mathematics, which will allow them quicker access to theoretical math? How will the need to attract more students into the fields related to science and mathematics affect this decision?

4. Will the new social and intellectual freedom for women release gifted girls from the rather clear hesitation that has been observable in their approach to mathematics? What can schools do to improve their approach to the mathematics anxiety issue?

Chapter Review

1. Mathematics is a key subject area for gifted students because it interrelates so intimately with other content fields, particularly the sciences.

2. Mathematics is a dynamic field in which innovation and creativity play a significant role, even in modern times.

3. Current national reform efforts in mathematics stress the need to teach problem-solving skills, real-life applications of mathematics, and number and figure "sense."

4. Students who are particularly gifted in mathematics may have a genetic characteristic that, combined with opportunity, predisposes them to a "mathematical cast of mind."

5. Content acceleration is one of the popular devices for curriculum modification in mathematics. Since it merely moves the curriculum forward, it does not have to be newly constructed or reconstructed.

6. Content enrichment includes activities that elaborate on the concepts to be learned at a given age level, and can be achieved through a variety of means, including creating open-ended mathematics questions, studying mathematical principles, and looking at mathematical patterns.

7. Content sophistication in mathematics can involve an emphasis on increasingly complex levels of questions about a given mathematics problem, as posed by Polya, or the use of rubrics.

8. Content novelty in mathematics can include material traditionally not incorporated in the standard curriculum sequence, including interdisciplinary connections and applications of mathematics.

9. Whether acceleration, enrichment, sophistication, or novelty is the method of curriculum adaptation depends on the philosophy of learning and education objectives supported by a particular program.

10. One significant concern in mathematics education is the special adjustment problems of women, for whom special barriers of enculturation cause them to be put off by the societal male orientation to mathematics.

11. National reports call for the increased use of calculators and computers in the mathematics classroom. A valuable tool for assisting students' mathematical understanding, it is critical that teachers receive the support necessary to use these tools well.

Readings of Special Interest

Benbow, C., & Stanley, J. (Eds.). (1983). *Adolescent precocity*. Baltimore, MD: Johns Hopkins Press. *Chapters are devoted to the description and outcome of rapid acceleration of students with high mathematical potential and aptitude, focusing on the Johns Hopkins program of the Study of Mathematically Precocious Youth. A positive report is made by many investigators who have followed these youths for a number of years.*

Connolly, P., & Vilardi, T. (1989). *Writing to learn mathematics and science*. New York: Teachers College Press. *This series of writings includes both studies and practical examples of how to integrate writing activities into the mathematics classroom. This book includes thoughtful pieces written by both theorists and practitioners who are dedicated to*

finding more probing ways of understanding what students learn in the math classroom.

Dreyden, J., Gallagher, S., Stanley, G., & Sawyer, R. (Eds.). (1988). *The proceeding of the Talent Identification Program/National Science Foundation conference on academic talent*. Durham, NC: Duke University. *This report on a major conference on academically talented students stresses the special issues related to women and minorities in mathematics programs and also draws together some of the work from the cognitive sciences and its implication for the teaching of mathematics.*

Greenes, C., Schulman, L., Spungin, R., Chapin, S., & Findell, C. (1990). *Mathletics: Gold medal problems*. Providence, RI: Janson Publications.

This collection of 100 mathematics problems require students to apply a variety of mathematics concepts and principles. In-depth discussion of the solutions are provided, along with a list of the skills that should be applied for each problem. Designed for grades 7–10, these problems could be used for upper elementary-aged gifted students as well.

Mitchell, M. (1985). *Mathematical history: Activities, puzzles, stories, and games.* Reston, VA: The National Council of Teachers of Mathematics.

An engaging set of activities are used to convey the history of mathematics to elementary-aged students. Stories, puzzles, and word games are all used to talk about the lives and contributions of such famous mathematicians as Euclid, Newton, Gauss, Agnesi, and Gemain. An especially nice treatment of women mathematicians is given.

National Council of Teachers of Mathematics. (1989). *Curriculum and evaluation standards for school mathematics.* Reston, VA: Author.

This major professional group makes a comprehensive statement about what mathematics instruction should be. The curriculum should focus on reasoning, problem solving, communication, and connections, and should involve serious exploration of geometry measurement, statistics, probability, algebra, and functions. A strong statement of an integrated and challenging curriculum is given.

Perl, T. (1978). *Math equals: Biographies of women mathematicians and related activities.* Menlo Park, CA: Addison-Wesley.

This book, entirely dedicated to women mathematicians, provides both a brief history of the lives of famous women mathematicians and describes the contributions they made to the field. Activities based on the mathematical work of each of the women are included along with the biographical sketches.

Polya, G. (1973). *How to solve it: A new aspect of mathematical method.* Princeton, NJ: Princeton University Press.

This seminal book describes the use of inductive reasoning in mathematics. It provides key problem-solving questions, examples of their application, and discusses in clear language why inductive reasoning is so important to math.

References

Abbott, E. A. (1963). *Flatland: A romance of many dimensions.* New York: Barnes and Noble.

Bartkovich, K. G. (1988). Motivating the most capable youths in mathematics and science. In J. I. Dreyden, S. A. Gallagher, G. E. Stanley, & R. N. Sawyer (Eds.), *Developing talent in mathematics, science and technology: Talent Identification Program/National Science Foundation conference on academic talent* (pp. 267–275). National Science Foundation Grant # MDR-875141 0.

Benbow, C., & Stanley, J. (1982, December). Sex differences in mathematical reasoning ability: More facts. *Science,* 1029–1031.

Bronowski, J. (1973). *The ascent of man.* Boston: Little, Brown.

California State Department of Education. (1989). *A question of thinking: A first look at students'* performance on open-ended questions in mathematics. Sacramento, CA: Author.

Callahan, C. (1988). Discussant reaction: Brilliant women for science, mathematics and engineering: Getting more than we deserve? In J. I. Dreyden, S. A. Gallagher, G. E. Stanley, & R. N. Sawyer (Eds.), *Developing talent in mathematics, science and technology: Talent Identification Program/National Science Foundation conference on academic talent* (pp. 230–234). National Science Foundation Grant # MDR-8751410.

Chang, L. L. (1985). Who are the mathematically gifted elementary school children? *Roeper Review, 8* (2), 76–79.

Colangelo, N. (1988). Discussant reaction: Bright girls in math and engineering. In J. I. Dreyden, S. A. Gallagher, G. E. Stanley, & R. N. Sawyer

(Eds)., *Developing talent in mathematics, science and technology: Talent Identification Program/National Science Foundation conference on academic talent.* National Science Foundation Grant # MDR-8751410.

Dover, A. (1983). Computers and the gifted: Past, present and future. *Gifted Child Quarterly, 27* (2), 81–85.

Eccles, J. (1987). *Understanding motivation: Achievement beliefs, gender roles and changing educational environment.* Paper presented at the annual meeting of the American Psychological Association, New York.

Fox, L. (1977). Sex differences: Implications for program planning for the academically gifted. In J. Stanley, W. George, & C. Solano (Eds.), *The gifted and the creative: A fifty-year perspective.* Baltimore: Johns Hopkins University Press.

Fox, L. (1981). Identification of the academically gifted. *American Psychology, 36,* 1103–1111.

Gleick, J. (1988). *Chaos: Making a new science.* New York: Penguin.

Greenes, C. (1981). Identifying the gifted student in mathematics. *Arithmetic Teacher,* 14–17

Grossnickle, F. E., & Reckzeh, J. (1973). *Discovering meanings in elementary school mathematics* (6th ed.). New York: Holt, Rinehart and Winston.

Haag, V., Kaufman, B., Martin, E., & Rising, G. (1987). *Challenge: A program for the mathematically talented.* Menlo Park, CA: Addison-Wesley.

International Association for the Evaluation of Educational Achievement. (1989). *Science achievement in seventeen countries: A preliminary report.* Oxford: Pergamon.

Jacobs, H. R. (1982). *Mathematics: A human endeavor* (2nd ed.). New York: Freeman.

Keese, E. E. (1981). "The Pit and the Pendulum": Source for a creative activity. In K. E. Easterday, L. L. Henry, & F. M. Simpson (Eds.), *Activities for junior high school and middle school mathematics: Readings from the Arithmetic Teacher & Mathematics Teacher.* Reston, VA: National Council of Teachers of Mathematics.

Krutetskii, V. (1976). *The psychology of mathematical abilities in school children* (J. Teller, Trans.). Chicago: University of Chicago Press.

Lee, V., & Byrk, A. (1986). Effects of single sex secondary schools on student achievement and attitudes. *Journal of Education Psychology, 78,* 381–395.

Linn, M., & Peterson, A. (1986). A meta-analysis of gender differences in spatial ability: Implications for mathematics and science achievement. In J. Hyde & M. Linn (Eds.), *The psychology of gender: Advances through meta-analysis.* Baltimore: Johns Hopkins University Press.

Milauskas, G. A. (1987). Creative problems lead to creative problem solvers. In M. M. Lindquist & A. P. Shulte (Eds.), *Learning and teaching geometry, K–12: 1987 Yearbook of the National Council of Teachers of Mathematics.* Reston, VA: The National Council of Teachers of Mathematics.

Montour, K. (1977). William James Sidis: The broken twig. *American Psychologist, 32* (4), 265–279.

National Council of Teachers of Mathematics. (1989). *Curriculum and evaluation standards for school mathematics.* Reston, VA: Author.

National Research Council. (1989). *Everybody counts: A report to the nation on the future of mathematics education.* Washington, DC: National Academy Press.

Polya, G. (1954). *Induction and analogy in mathematics* (vols. 1 and 2). Princeton, NJ: Princeton University Press.

Polya, G. (1985). *How to solve it: A new aspect of mathematical method* (2nd ed.). Princeton, NJ: Princeton University Press.

Reis, S. M., & Callahan, C. M. (1989). Gifted females: They've come a long way—Or have they? *Journal for the Education of the Gifted, 12* (2), 99–117.

Sadker, D., & Sadker, M. (1985). Sexism in the schoolroom of the '80's. *Psychology Today, 19* (3), 54–57.

Serra, M. (1989). *Discovering geometry: An inductive approach.* Berkeley, CA: Key Curriculum.

Stanley, J. (1979). The study and facilitation of talent for mathematics. In A. Passow (Ed.), *The gifted and talented: Their education and development.* Chicago: University of Chicago Press.

Stanley, J. C. (1988). Some characteristics of SMPY's "700–800 on the SAT-M before age 13 group":

Youths who reason extremely well mathematically. *Gifted Child Quarterly, 32* (1), 205–209.

Stanley, J. C., & Benbow, C. P. (1982). Educating mathematically precocious youth: Twelve policy recommendations. *Educational Researcher, 11* (5), 4–9.

Stanley, J. C., & Benbow, C. P. (1986). Youths who reason exceptionally well mathematically. In R. J. Sternberg & J. E. Davidson (Eds.), *Conceptions of giftedness*. New York: Cambridge University Press.

Stuart, B. (1988). Discussant reaction: Motivating the most capable youths in mathematics and science. In J. I. Dreyden, S. A. Gallagher, G. E. Stanley, & R. N. Sawyer, (Eds.), *Developing talent in mathematics, science and technology Talent Identification Program/National Science Foundation conference on academic talent*. National Science Foundation Grant # MDR-8751410.

Treffinger, D. (1990). *Encouraging creative learning for the gifted and talented*. Los Angeles: National/State Leadership Training Institute.

Wahl, M. (1988). *A mathematical mystery tour: Higher thinking math tasks*. Tucson, AZ: Zepher.

Wavrik, J. J. (1980). Mathematics education for the gifted elementary school student. *Gifted Child Quarterly, 24* (4), 169–173.

Wheatley, G. A. (1984, December–January). Problem solving makes math scores soar. *Educational Leadership*, 52–53.

Chapter 5

Science
for Gifted Students

Key Questions

- How does the practice of science in the real world compare with the instruction of science in the classroom?

- What societal changes have brought about a need for change in the science curriculum?

- How are science and problem solving related? How can teachers incorporate problem solving into science instruction for their gifted students?

- What does it mean to organize a curriculum around a scientific concept? Why is this approach advocated for gifted students?

- What are the special dilemmas facing gifted minorities and females in the science classroom?

- How should teachers adapt their own behaviors to model the scientific "habits of mind" they wish their gifted students to adopt?

Science has been leading the battle cry of "educational reform!" more fervently than any other discipline. The world is more and more dependent on science and its resulting technology, not only as sources of innovation but as a backbone of our daily lives. Although science is much more than the products it creates, it is hard to imagine a world without the telephone, the computer, or the pocket calculator. Even recent inventions, such as the facsimile machine (fax), seem to become a part of the fabric of our lives more and more quickly.

Scholars of social movements refer to a transition from the Industrial Age to the Information Age—where productivity will be measured by innovation and problem-solving skills instead of merchandise produced (Toffler, 1984). As we move into this era, the basic educational requirements for all people will change. In the past, part of the role of education was to create workers who were capable of succeeding in a *manufacturing society*. Now, however, we need to educate people to succeed in an *inventing society*.

Business leaders as well as scientists speak of problem solving and critical thinking as the basic skills for the twenty-first century. Even basic manufacturing jobs will require some fundamental knowledge of technology. For example, it is hard to imagine a job that will not require at least some knowledge of how to work a computer. If we are to control technology, instead of technology controlling us, people will have to understand the machines that they use, along with their benefits and dangers.

Scientists are joining with educators to call for two new goals in science education: first, to increase the number of individuals who become professionals in the fields of science and engineering, and second, to ensure that the entire U.S. citizenry is "scientifically literate"—that is, capable of understanding basic science concepts, of appreciating the role of science in society, and of surviving economically in a world that is dependent on technology.

The Sad Plight of Science Education in the United States

As was the case in students' performances in mathematics, recent comparisons of U.S. students with students from other countries in a variety of science areas has brought a collection of bad news. A major international study in 1988 (Jacobson & Daran, 1988) found that U.S. students ranked eighth out of fifteen countries in science achievement at the fifth-grade level, and fifteenth out of seventeen nations at the ninth-grade level. Even more distressing was the comparison of top-achieving high school students in biology. The U.S. students were last, and in advanced chemistry, they ranked eleventh out of thirteen. Clearly, science is a field in which the United States is lagging. The Science Report Card findings listed in Figure 5–1 provide documentation for a difficult situation and underlines the importance of reform and the need to provide opportunities for all students, with a special emphasis on gifted students.

This chapter will review the recommendations presented in reports for reform in science education and the way they affect science education for the gifted. The character-istics of scientists and the kinds of skills and attitudes that scientifically literate gifted children need will also be examined. The process of science will be explored, along with examples of curriculum and classroom practices that meet the requirements for the "new science." Finally, special issues and concerns regarding science education for gifted students will be explored.

Science Education Reform

Mr. Jenkins thoughtfully closed the book he was reading. He could see that he was going to have to change his science units! The book he was reading, *Project 2061: Science for All Americans* (see Figure 5–2), echoed the other reports that he had been reading. *Project 2061*, the standards of the National Teachers of Science Association, and the more generic *America 2000* all call for dramatic changes in the way science is being taught. "Hmm," he thought, "this could be interesting. I wonder how I could rework that plant experiment...."

National Science Reports: The Changing Face of Science Education

The need for science education to change is driven primarily by three elements:

1. The *information explosion* in science makes learning all science information impos-sible and impractical; there are more individual pieces of data to learn than we could ever hope to absorb and remember.
2. *Advances in technology* have changed the way science is conducted—refinements in measures and means of analysis make it possible for us to took at things closer up and farther away than ever before. This technology also gives us a means of storing the reams of new data, liberating our minds for more complex cognitive tasks.

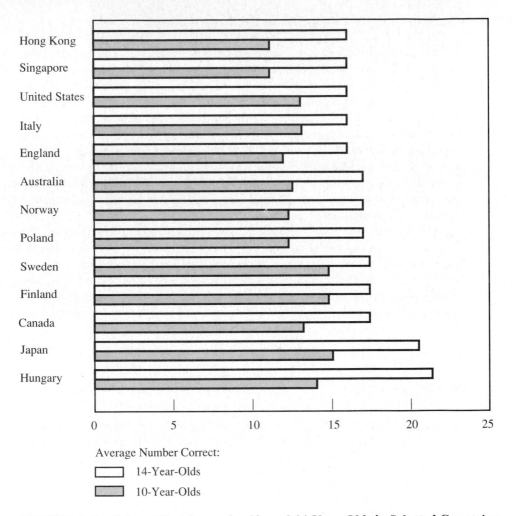

FIGURE 5–1   Science Test Scores for 10- and 14-Year-Olds in Selected Countries: Administered between 1983 and 1986

Source: International Association for the Evaluation of Educational Achievement, *Science Achievement in Seventeen Countries, A Preliminary Report*. The graph reported in this book is based on data collected in connection with a study conducted under the auspices of the International Association for the Evaluation of Educational Achievement (IEA). Responsibility for the analysis and conclusions rest with the authors, however, no endorsement by IEA should be inferred.

3. The *increasingly complex relationship between science and society* makes it necessary for students to develop higher-order thinking skills in science, as well as a perspective on science information that incorporates the viewpoints of several disciplines. The consequences of major advances in science and technology on individuals and society is one special area of interest.

- Only 7% of the nation's 17-year-olds have the prerequisite knowledge and skills thought to be needed to perform well in college-level science courses. Since high school science proficiency is a good predictor of whether or not a young person will elect to pursue postsecondary studies in science, the probability that many more students will embark on future careers is low.

- At grade 5, the U.S. ranked in the middle in science achievement, relative to 14 other participating countries.

- At grade 9, U.S. students ranked next to last.

- In the upper grades of secondary school, "Advanced Science Students" in the U.S. ranked last in biology and performed behind students from most countries in chemistry and physics.

- Only 35% of the seventh-graders and 53% of the eleventh-graders reported working with other students on science experiments on at least a weekly basis.

- 60% of the seventh-graders and 41% of the eleventh-graders said they never had to write up the results of science experiments.

- Only about 46% of the teachers of seventh- or eleventh-graders reported access to a general-purpose laboratory, and only 64% of the eleventh-grade teachers reported access to a specialized laboratory for use in teaching science.

FIGURE 5–2   Summary of the 1986 Science Report Card

Source: Mullis, I., & Jenkins, L. (1988). *The science report card: Elements of risk and recovery.* Princeton, NJ: Educational Testing Service.

Scientists, educators, and policymakers have all recognized that the combination of these three trends call for substantial revision of the science curriculum for all students. Several national reform reports have been generated from different agencies, most of which make parallel recommendations. Perhaps one of the most influential of these sets of recommendations is the *Project 2061* report generated from the American Association for the Advancement of Science (AAAS). In order to understand the direction that science education should take for gifted students, it is first necessary to understand the changing world of science education for all students.

The AAAS brought together a group of nationally renowned scientists to create a series of recommendations about what should be taught to students in science class-rooms. The group broke up into committees, gathered data from other scientists around the country, and compiled the results of their research. What emerged from this process was a report that describes the kinds of skills, attitudes, and information a functioning citizen should have in order to understand science and its relationship to the modern world. The following items are a summary of the core recommendations in the *Project 2061* report:

- Being familiar with the natural world and recognizing both its diversity and its unity
- Understanding key concepts and principles of science
- Being aware of some of the important ways in which science, mathematics, and technology depend on one another

- Knowing that science, mathematics, and technology are human enterprises and knowing what that implies about their strengths and limitations
- Having a capacity for scientific ways of thinking
- Using scientific knowledge and ways of thinking for individual as well as social purposes

The skills, attitudes, and information associated with these goals were further described in three broad areas: understanding the *scientific endeavor*, or how scientists work; understanding *scientific views of the world*, or the fundamental information that scientists know; and using *scientific habits of mind*, or the cognitive skills and affective attitudes that are critical to the practice of science.

Examples of the recommended topics or skills in each area are outlined in Figure 5–3. Just a quick glance at the list shows that these goals cannot be achieved by memorizing the periodic table! Instead, the science curriculum for all students will have to be restructured to adapt to this new approach to science.

In a similar effort, the National Science Teacher Association (NSTA) recently published a series of recommendations on how science curriculum and instruction need to

---

The Scientific Endeavor

The scientific endeavor stems from the union of science, mathematics, and technology.

Science, mathematics, and technology have roots going far back into history and into every part of the world.

Science, mathematics, and technology are expressions of both human ingenuity and human limitations with intellectual, practical, emotional, aesthetic, and ethical dimensions.

The various natural and social sciences differ from each other somewhat in subject matter and technique, yet they share certain values, philosophical views about knowledge, and ways of learning about the world.

Scientific Views of the World

The structure and evolution of the universe, with emphasis on the similarity of materials and forces found everywhere in it.

The general features of the planet Earth, including its location, motion, origin, and resources.

The basic concepts related to matter, energy, force, and motion.

The living environment, emphasizing the rich diversity of the earth's organisms and the surprising similarity in the structure and function of their cells.

Biological evolution as a concept based on extensive geological and molecular evidence.

The human organism as a biological, social, and technological species.

Scientific Habits of Mind

The internalization of some of the values inherent in the practice of science, mathematics, and technology.

Informed balanced beliefs about the social benefits of the scientific endeavor.

A positive attitude toward being able to understand science and mathematics.

Computational skills.

Manipulation and observation skills.

Communication skills.

Critical-response skills that prepare people to carefully judge the assertions made by advertisers, public figures, organizations, and the entertainment and news media.

FIGURE 5–3 Examples of Essential Learnings from Project 2061

Source: Adapted from Rutherford, F. J., & Ahlgren, A. (1990). *Science for all Americans*. New York: Oxford University Press.

change. Their recommendations included making the curriculum problem centered, flexible, and culturally as well as scientifically valid; including humankind as the central ingredient; being multifaceted with local or community relevance; using the natural environment, community resources, and current concerns; and sharing a perspective that scientific information can be used in a cultural/social environment. Instruction of this curriculum should be individualized and personalized, emphasize cooperative work on problems and issues, and be based on current research in developmental psychology (Harms & Yager, 1981).

The recommendations for new science curriculum and new approaches to teaching science pose interesting challenges for all teachers. A set of particularly interesting dilemmas will face the teacher of the gifted. The recommendations of reports such as *Project 2061* suggest that all students should be taught science in a way that had formerly been the sole territory of gifted students, with discovery-based activities and a conceptual organization of material. So, if what we used to call *content enrichment* or *content sophistication* for the gifted is now to be the core curriculum for all students, what are the new curriculum adaptations for the gifted going to look like? This will be the question we will explore as we look at examples of content acceleration, content enrichment, content sophistication, and content novelty in science for the gifted.

The Characteristics of Scientists

Despite the presence of science in almost every facet of our society, we are still surrounded by misconceptions and inaccurate stereotyping about scientists.

Brandwein (1986) spent many years in the company of scientists, studying their traits and observing their work habits. He identified three character-rooted habits that typified the scientist: (1) an understanding of the scope of knowledge and skills involved in the line of research, (2) a method of probing, and (3) a self-correcting method. Interestingly, these habits parallel the recommended "habits of mind" in *Project 2061*.

A study of the personality of creative male scientists conducted at the Institute for Personality Assessment Research (IPAR) by Gough (1976) found that the creative professional scientists in their sample shared in common an intuitive mode of thought that is generally characterized by a preference for theory over fact, possibilities over realities, and future orientation over thinking about the past. Most of the scientists also preferred using *analysis* rather than value positions to make decisions (although this may also be due to the fact that the sample was made up of all male scientists). Interestingly, in this sample of scientists, there were similar numbers of scientists who were extraverted or introverted—which runs contrary to the popular assumption that all scientists tend to be reclusive (Myers & McCaulley, 1987). Even more fascinating is the fact that these are the same general preferences that significant numbers of gifted adolescents show when given the same personality measure (Gallagher, 1990).

The many differences, in both personality and attitude, between scientists may disguise this common feature—the urge to learn how things and people work. Most scientists would feel attuned to the following statement by Loren Eiseley:

> *Down how many roads among the stars must man propel himself in search of the final secret? The journey is difficult, immense, at times impossible, yet that will not deter some of us from attempting it. We cannot know all that has happened in the past, or the reason for all of these events, any more than we can with surety discern what lies ahead. We have joined the caravan, you might say, at a certain point; we will travel as far as we can, but we cannot in one lifetime see all that we would like to see or learn all that we hunger to know. (1957, p. 12)*

At the heart of the scientists' motivation, then, is the fascination with finding things out—the "rage of the unknown" (Judson, 1980). The attitude is summed up in the fascinating series on science and scientists, *The Search for Solutions*, where, again and again, scientists say that the reason they became scientists was that they could not imagine doing anything else that was so much fun! Part of the role of the teacher of the gifted, then, would to be to create classroom situations that would encourage, support, and extend the curiosity and explorative nature that these students and professional scientists seem to share in common.

The Process of Science

The origins of modern science and the development of the scientific method have taken place within the last 400 years. They represent a way of trying to understand the world around us. To the young children learning about science, it must seem as though science has always been here, and it may be a surprise to them that it really began only a few hundred years ago. Professional scientists often balk at the idea that there is a single scientific method, but the process of exploration across science disciplines does have common elements. English scientist Francis Bacon offered a fourfold rule for scientific work: observe, measure, explain, and then verify.

A more recent and modern explanation was provided by Sher, a molecular biologist, while she was working with teachers writing science curriculum:

1. *Learn a great deal about your field.*
2. *Think of a good (interesting, important, tractable) problem.*
3. *Decide which experiments/observations/calculations would contribute to a solution of the problem.*
4. *Perform the experiments/observation/calculations.*
5. *Decide whether the results really do contribute to a better understanding of the problem. If they don't, return to step 2 (if you're very discouraged) or step 3. If they do, go to step 6.*
6. *Communicate your results to as many people as possible. Publish them in a scientific journal (and, if they're really neat, in the* New York Times*); go to conferences and talk about them; tell all of your friends. (1992, p. 3)*

The great addition of the methods of science to the already existing fields of philosophy has been that scientists not only reason and question as the early philosophers did but they also observe and measure. Since one of the primary characteristics of highly intelligent children is their reasoning ability and keen observation skills, it is no surprise that many gifted youngsters become interested in science and the systematic search for new ideas.

What Do Scientists Do?

Despite the many portraits in books, film, and on TV of scientists at work, the essential elements of science still seem to be a mystery to many students and adults. Gifted students need to be made conscious of science's essential activities:

Content expertise. The development of a thorough data base about a core area of interest and associated but ancillary topics.

Problem detection. The ability to discern key questions or gaps in understanding in a given area.

Observation. The perception of the environment to be studied, often through the use of specially designed instruments.

Classification. The sorting or ordering of objects of events according to key properties.

Measurement. The ability to order observations in magnitude with the help of a variety of instruments.

Hypothesizing. The formulation of a question to be tested through the use of observation and measurement.

Experimentation. The design of a set of procedures by which hypotheses are tested for the establishment of their credibility.

The basic idea that science is not so much a content field as it is a set of methods and a way of seeing and thinking used to discover new ideas or systems of ideas is a hard one for schools to project. It has been said that much of the problem in science education has been that too many teachers think science is a *noun* rather than a *verb*. With the new emphasis on realistic science instruction, the teaching of science as a verb is one of the primary goals teachers must achieve, especially for talented students who have the capacity and curiosity necessary to be new science innovators.

It is not merely the content and process of science that need to be encouraged but the sense of excitement in scientific discovery as well. As Coleman and Selby put it:

Whereas many students do not like school science—and form this opinion by the end of the third grade—many do like the science and technology that they see on television. They also like what they encounter at science and technology museums, planetariums, nature centers, and national parks. Many of these institutions facilitate science and technology education with their own after school, weekend, and vacation classes.... Because these programs are apparently more appealing than school science offerings, the innovative instructional approaches used in them should be examined and, where possible, applied to the classroom setting. (1982, p. 7)

Eylon and Linn (1988) reviewed the roles played by gifted students in science education. They found that in those studies that contrasted the performance of experts with those of novices, there were very different strategies adopted to cope with the problems presented by the teacher. The experts tended to plan out strategies, they took longer to respond to the problem itself, and used an established cognitive associative network to draw on for possible solutions.

In contrast, the novices tended to plunge into the problem and pay attention to the surface features of the problem itself. The novices lacked a repertoire of knowledge necessary to deal with the problem. Accordingly, Eylon and Linn suggested that rapid coverage of large numbers of topics was not the strategy of choice, but rather that "in-depth coverage of several science topics will benefit students far more than the fleeting coverage of numerous science topics" (1988, p. 251).

Curriculum Adaptations

One of the clear objectives of the curriculum for gifted students is to help them understand the experience of how the scientific way of thinking leads to an explanation of the world that is different from explanations provided by art, religion, logic, or magic. No matter what kind of differentiated curricular activities we discuss—acceleration, enrichment, sophistication, or novelty—the basic principles of expertise, problem detection, observation, classification, measurement, hypothesizing, and experimentation will play a central role in the curricula.

There seems to be wide general agreement as to the substance of new science curricula. One such list represents the general trend:

- *More authentic performance assessment of students and educators, and less emphasis on standardized testing;*
- *More critical and creative thinking and problem solving for students, and less emphasis on rote knowledge;*
- *More learning for understanding and less learning for grades and scores;*
- *More organization of time around student learning, and less organization of time around adult or bureaucratic needs;*
- *More diverse kinds of teaching and learning opportunities in order to accomplish the above goals. (Schmieder & Michael-Dyer, 1991)*

Such new requirements do not lessen the importance of essential facts and knowledge, but place the emphasis on new processes of learning and teaching.

Content Acceleration

The notion of content acceleration, or rapid movement through basic content, is somewhat at odds with the current movement toward teaching less content in more depth. Still, there is room for acceleration for gifted students within this new framework. In terms of the "new science," acceleration takes two forms: early exposure and intense focus.

The status of science teacher preparation and the infrequency of science instruction in the elementary school leads one to conclude that *any* systematic instruction of science provided to gifted students constitutes one form of content acceleration. A combination of three factors lead to a crisis in science instruction for the gifted at the elementary school level: lack of consistent instruction, inadequate teacher preparation, and textbooks not designed to meet the needs of the gifted.

A recent summary of the National Assessment of Educational Progress (NAEP) reported that 21 percent of classrooms assessed had one hour or less of science instruction per week, and 49 percent had only one to two hours per week (Mullis & Jenkins, 1988). These data support the findings of a second report (Weiss, 1987), which found that kindergarten through third-grade teachers spend an average of 18 minutes per day teaching science, although they spend twice that amount of time teaching math and four times that time teaching reading. Part of the problem was attributed to the poor preparation of teachers to conduct science instruction: Only 7 percent of the elementary school teachers questioned in the NAEP reported that they had general science certification.

Large numbers of intellectually average and below-average students in the secondary school, together with a steadfast insistence against ability grouping and the lack of scientifically sophisticated teachers, have led to some predictable trends. Among these was a lowering of the level of conceptualization at which the curriculum was presented. This reduced level of complexity was made necessary by the fact that slow learners would be quickly left behind by a curriculum placed at a high conceptual level that demanded a large amount of *prior knowledge* on the part of the students. A current review of several of the most popular basal science textbooks has shown that they do not contain substantial provisions for instructing or adapting materials for gifted students (VanTassel-Baska, Gallagher, Bailey, & Sher, 1992).

In addition, greater emphasis has been placed on functional and practical knowledge in the educational program. Introducing a topic such as "How a Car Operates" or "How to Balance a Checkbook" has dual virtues. In the first place, such functional knowledge is of interest and practical value to many students who will not be going into higher education. It also demands little prior knowledge on the part of the students, who can learn most of the essentials in the self-contained unit. No small influence in the choice of such self-contained topics is that the teacher can also become familiar with the topic without having an extensive background!

Although the "anything is better than nothing" philosophy has its points, the kind of early exposure that would be best for gifted children is one that introduces them to the behaviors and attitudes that are part of scientific thinking. Often this will involve the teacher of the gifted contacting someone who does have expertise to assist in some way— as a guest teacher or mentor, perhaps—or by providing opportunities for instruction off campus. One example of this kind of acceleration was tested at the State University of New York at Stony Brook.

In this program, a laboratory course in organic chemistry was incorporated into the regular school curriculum for sixth-grade gifted students. Once a week students participated in a two-hour laboratory session in which various chemical reactions were studied. Students were required to keep a laboratory notebook and to perform all experimental manipulations on their own. Once the students had been "deconditioned" of looking for "right" answers, they were capable of making accurate observations and drawing appropriate inferences from the data. Final assessment in the course took the form of both a written exam and a laboratory practical, thus measuring both scientific knowledge and science process skills (Kandel, 1983).

Acceleration as intense focus is perhaps best exemplified at the secondary level by the schools of the National Consortium for Secondary Schools Specializing in Mathematics, Science, and Technology (NCSSSMST). One group of schools in this consortium of particular interest is the 10 state-supported residential schools for gifted students (see Appendix D). These "public boarding schools" were formed to provide highly gifted students who have particular interests in math and science with an opportunity to pursue their interests in a more concentrated atmosphere. Most of these special schools require more courses in math and science for graduation than do regular high schools, and also offer more advanced and more complex science and math electives.

One example of the more intensified science instruction provided by these schools is the science core curriculum offered by the Illinois Mathematics and Science Academy (IMSA). Table 5–1 shows the change in sequence of courses. The change places instruction in physics and chemistry at the sophomore level, since they allow for a more fundamental preparation for biology later, and also leaves time for both physics and chemistry electives later in high school.

The IMSA sophomore physics course was written with two fundamental differences from a college-level physics course: (1) it incorporates discovery-based, hands-on laboratory experiences, so that students have to derive fundamental physical principles on their own; and (2) it starts with a nonmathematical treatment of physics in the first semester and moves to mathematical treatments involved in topics such as vectors the second semester. This latter adaptation was made to account for the disparity in mathematics training of the students who come from school systems across the state and also to make the course developmentally appropriate for the students, most of whom are extremely talented but not yet ready to comprehend the sophisticated abstractions of mathematics and physics.

TABLE 5–1   Course Models for Gifted Students

Grade	Course Sequence for Normal Students	Course Sequence for IMSA Students
10	Biology	Physics (nonmathematical progressing to mathematical) Chemistry
11	Chemistry	Biology (university level)
12	Physics	At least two more electives required for graduation
	Many students do not take a sequence in science. The majority do not take chemistry and physics.	All students required to take the basic physics, chemistry, and biology sequence plus additional electives; special adaptations are made to make courses developmentally appropriate

Source: Illinois Mathematics and Science Academy (1987). Reprinted by permission.

As it stands, the IMSA course sequence provides students with a grounding in physical and chemical concepts in their sophomore year, which prepares them for more complex science concepts such as biophysics or biochemistry. This curriculum sequence reverses the traditional order, which appears to be arranged with the expectation that all high school students would at least learn something about biology in tenth grade, even if they pass up the more complex and difficult chemistry and physics courses later.

Content Enrichment

The purpose of content enrichment is to provide an extensive range of additional experiences and examples so that the students' mastery of important ideas embedded in the standard curriculum is strengthened. For example, the systematic collection of observational data, of whatever sort—local traffic flow, temperature readings, height and weight changes in children, and so forth—would tend to reinforce the idea that measurements have to be taken precisely, often with special instruments, and that, when arrayed, they present an interesting portrait not often seen in casual notice.

Some of the activities included in basal science curricula can be adapted to provide stimulating and "real science" activities for all students in the classroom. These activities can be differentiated at various levels of difficulty or sophistication for gifted children. One example of this is to transform the "canned," predictable classroom experiments included in some texts into open-ended, student-generated laboratory experiments. One way of making this transition is by using the four-question approach developed by Cothron, Giese, and Rezba (1989). Once the class has established, with the teacher's help, the significance of the questions to be asked, they can use the following four questions to create student-generated laboratory experiences:

1. What materials are readily available for conducting experiments on (x)?
2. How do (x) act?
3. How can I change the set of (x) materials to affect the action?
4. How can I measure or describe the response of (x) to the change?*

Mr. Jenkins, who realized that his experiment on plants and fertilizers was far too planned and predictable, used this method to engage his students in their own research projects on plants. Here is how his students responded to the four questions:

1. What materials are readily available for conducting experiments on plants?
   Plants, soil, water or other liquids, light, fertilizer.

2. How do plants act?
   They grow, they get more leaves. Some get more flowers.

3. How can I change [plants, soil, water/liquid, light, fertilizer] to affect the action?

---

*This and the next listings are from Cothron et al., *Students and research: Practical strategies for science classrooms and competitions.* Copyright 1989 by Kendall/Hunt Publishing Company. Used by permission.

Liquid	*Soil*	*Fertilizer*
amount	*contents*	*brand*
type	*where it's from*	*how often used*
how applied		*natural or chemical*

4. How can I measure or describe the response of plants to the change?
   Measure the height of the plant, measure the circumference of the stalk, count the number of leaves or flowers.

With this technique, posing the hypothesis takes the simple form of: "If I change (something from the list in question 3—the independent variable), then the (something from the list in question 4—the dependent variable) will change." This structure of variable identification is simple and concrete enough that very young students can understand it, and yet it results in scientifically sound experimental procedures.

Another advantage of using this technique is that students can develop their own experiments using a similar set of materials, and the sophistication of the experiment can be placed at the students' abilities and interest levels. For example, when Mr. Jenkins used this approach to change his "canned" experiment on plants, these were the hypotheses the students developed:

Cranshaw: If I change the composition of the soil, then the height of the plant will change.

Robert: If I change the type of liquid, then the height of the plant will change.

Zelda: If I change the kind of fertilizer (natural or chemical), then the height of the plant will change.

Joe: If I change the force of application of water, then the height of the plant will change.

Sam: If I change the sound waves around the plant, then the height will change.

Stephanie: If I change the color of the water, then the height will change.

Amanda: If I change the quantity of fertilizer, then the height will change.

Notice from the list that even though Mr. Jenkins, for the sake of his own sanity, made the students use the same dependent variable (height), they all have very different projects, which are at different levels of ability. Robert and Amanda have very basic designs that will still provide critical basic information to the group when the results are compiled and discussed in class. Cranshaw and Zelda will both probably have to find something out about soil or fertilizer composition to understand their experiments, providing them with important and pertinent extension activities.

The projects planned by Sam and Stephanie are a little different, and were "special exceptions" made by Mr. Jenkins to capture their interest through the areas that already fascinate them (also, he knew that Sam will have to learn about sound waves and Stephanie may have to find out what components of food coloring might cause a plant to grow differently). And as for Joe, Mr. Jenkins is thrilled that he has opened his eyes and taken some interest—this is real stuff, not some boring, routine, predictable waste of time!

Reactions of some of the other gifted students are interesting, too. For example, Cranshaw, although a model student, is a little uncomfortable by the open-ended nature of the activity, because he cannot rely on an absolute "right answer" as he can in other areas. Zelda, always methodical, is very good at taking measurements and recording data precisely, but has some trouble using the divergent thinking skills necessary to come up with an initial hypothesis. In this way, these kinds of hands-on activities help Mr. Jenkins appreciate that even within a group of gifted students, remarkable differences can be observed.

The students will conduct their projects with lab partners or in small groups. When complete, all of the data will be compiled and analyzed to determine which of the variables affect the height of plants. This will serve as a perfect springboard for a discussion on photosynthesis. After their initial experience as scientists researching plant behavior, students at all levels should be more motivated to learn about the plant growth system; gifted students—like the ones in this book—will be able to return to the data again and again to extract more sophisticated interpretations from their work.

Many teachers fear that using inquiry-based approaches like this one takes too much time and that "real learning" (by which they mean learning facts) is sacrificed for the sake of discovery. Recent studies of the innovative science curricula developed in the 1960s suggest that this may not be the case. In an analysis of the studies conducted on Biological Sciences Curriculum Study and Physical Science Study Curriculum, it was found that students in courses using the inquiry-based techniques associated with those programs achieved at higher levels than other students in all achievement areas, including content acquisition and process skills. Achievement differences were highest in elementary school classes (Shymansky, Hedges, & Woodworth, 1990).

Instruction about important concepts can form the structure for an entire unit or it can be worked into a daily lesson. The concept of measurement is a process concept that most students experience at one time or another. The gifted students must concern themselves with such ideas earlier and in more depth.

Few laypeople realize that the character and limitations of measuring instruments often determine the amount and the direction of the growth of scientific information in a given area. This concept is rarely of concern if science is taught as functional applications or as a body of information to be memorized. It becomes important only when the teacher and students are attempting to act like scientists. The following excerpts from a class of sixth-graders show the teacher taking the students through (1) the relationship between rate, distance, and time; (2) the concept of direct measurement; and (3) the concept of indirect measurement.

Teacher: At first I want to begin with you—I want to be sure that you people can work some of these problems that involve figuring out how far it is to a certain place if we know how fast something is moving to a certain place and how long it takes. For example, if I'm riding in a car going 30 miles an hour and Kankakee is 60 miles away, how long will it take me to get to Kankakee? Margaret?

Margaret: Two hours.

Teacher: All right, now let's look at the other side of the problem. If I am going to Chicago at 30 miles an hour and it takes me four hours to get to Chicago, how far away is Chicago? You hold a steady speed and you don't stop for traffic lights (laughter from class). Jeanne?

Jeanne: One hundred twenty miles.

Teacher: One hundred twenty miles. If I tell you how long it takes to get there, you can tell me how far it is, if you know the rate of speed. If you know the rate of speed and I tell you how far away it is, you can tell me how long it takes to get there.

How about these figures of 186,000 miles per second—the speed of light—and we know that the moon is about 240,000 miles away, how long does it take light to get from the moon to me? I don't mean for you to work it out—just tell me what you would do to find out how long it takes light to get to the moon. Laura?

Laura: Well, you might divide the 186,000 into 240,000.

Teacher: Yes, and this will tell you how long it takes for light to travel from the moon to us.

Having been satisfied that this group of gifted children has these concepts in hand, the teacher proceeds to the next step—direct measurement.

Teacher: How do we measure relatively short distances between two places? I'm going to stop here. If I wanted to measure the distance between me and Charles, what's the easiest way to do it? Robert?

Robert: The yardstick.

Teacher: OK, you'd use a yardstick. Now when somebody figured out how long an inch is and how long a yard is, they put it out on a stick. We know this stick is pretty accurate because someone took it to Washington and compared it with the metal stick that measures one yard and they both turned out to be just about the same. So we know what one yard is and we can lay this out here and I can find out how far it is between me and Charles. Okay, now we've got the problem, and that is, of course, that you can't just take this yardstick and start measuring the distance to the moon—not yet anyway.

Note how the teacher brings in the concept of the standard measure in Washington, so as not to give the impression that we would accept any marked stick as a good measuring instrument. Now we see the logical development to indirect measurement.

Teacher: So here is the problem: You've got to measure the distance to an object we can't get to, can't pace it off, can't use a yardstick, and can't use a ruler. And yet there are ways of measuring these distances very, very accurately. Zelda, do you know something about this?

Zelda: Well, wouldn't you first try to estimate it? You'd estimate it if you could, and then after you estimate it—Oh, I don't know how you'd do it but first you'd have to estimate what you thought it should be.

Teacher: OK, Zelda, now how would you go about making an estimate, say, how far it is to the moon? What would you want to know about the moon first?

Zelda: Well, how big its orbit is…(trails off, obviously unable to answer).

Teacher: You can estimate how far away certain objects are from you. For example, I'll hold up this eraser. Now each of you make an estimate of how far away this eraser is from you. Now, try to think of the method you used to estimate how far away this eraser is. Robert, what method did you use?

Robert: Do you want to know the measurement?

Teacher: Did you make an estimate of this?

Robert: Yes.

Teacher: Well, how did you make it?

Robert: I thought about it in feet.

Teacher: Oh.

Robert: I estimated it at about 10 feet.

Teacher: Ten feet. Now, how did you get 10 feet? Why didn't you say 50 feet?

Robert: Because 50 feet is a lot farther.

Teacher: What did you do, Charles?

Charles: Well, I estimated it with a grown person of about 6 feet in height, and it was a little over that, so it was about 7 feet.

Teacher: You sort of mentally laid out a grown person here between you and this eraser and then estimated how many grown people you would have to put on the floor in order to get to the eraser. OK. This is one way. I guess a lot of people do it this way; they figure an adult man is somewhere near 6 feet, and how many men standing on each other's head will get up to the tip of that building…. Now, I'm going to ask you to imagine something else. Imagine that I hold up this eraser in a perfectly dark room. Well, let's say it's not this eraser but that it's the size of this eraser and that it shines. But the room is perfectly dark. Can you imagine this so that you cannot mentally lay out people on the floor to gauge the distance of that object? You don't see a thing in the room except that object. Ricky?

Ricky: You could see how bright or dim the light was.

Teacher: How bright or how dim. Is there any other thing that would give you a clue? Doug?

Doug: How large it was.

Teacher: How large. I think these are all the clues you could get. How bright it is and how large it is. You try to compare it to bright and large things you may have seen. Now, this gets difficult as we get out into space. If we try to see how large the moon is, we can do this: We can take a coin or a small object and hold it at arm's length and see what size object we need to completely hide the moon behind the object. Take a guess and what do you think I'd need? Ricky?

Ricky: A 50-cent piece.

Teacher: How many think a 50-cent piece would hide the moon? Well whatever size the object turns out to be, you'll find that exactly the same size object blocks out the sun. You are starting at a point where you know the sun is very much farther away than the moon, yet they both appear to be about the same size. Brightness isn't much of a clue because the sun is very much brighter than the moon and you were probably thinking of bright things being closer. Now, in order to understand something of the way that you measure these distances, it's necessary for us to know something about triangles. What's a triangle? John?

John: It is an object that has three sides connected at three corners. Straight lines.

Notice that the teacher patiently lets the students wander down false trails, much as they would in actual problem solving, before leading them in the fruitful direction. Next, the teacher develops the concept of angles, how they are measured and how to discover all the necessary facts about triangles. Once these facts are established, the students are ready to talk about measurements of distance in space.

The experienced teacher can realize what would happen here in an intellectually heterogeneous group. The teacher would soon have to slow the pace drastically in order to teach patiently each concept in order, thus irritating the bright students caught up in the excitement of ideas. Or the teacher might decide to cast adrift the slow learners and teach only the stars in the class. Neither choice is a happy one.

Despite the generally bad reputation of television as an intellectual wasteland, there are a number of series that challenge and portray important ideas. Programs like "Connections," "The Search for Solutions," "The Challenge of the Unknown," and "The Day the Universe Changed" all communicate the wonder, fascination, and interconnections in science. An excellent example of how these resources can be adapted to create a concept-oriented unit is provided by Kersh, Nielsen, and Subotnik (1987), who created a curriculum unit integrating biology, chemistry, psychology, and sociology. Using the film series *The Search for Solutions* (Judson, 1980) as a basis, this unit focuses on patterns as they appear across a variety of topics and experiences. Since the search for major ideas and understanding is part of the objectives of a curriculum for gifted students, the following generalizations were the foundation for the curriculum:

- Patterns are witnesses to the forces at work in the world.
- Patterns simplify information in ways that allow us to solve problems more readily.
- Patterns are nature's and humans' coded messages to one another.
- Patterns help us draw distinctions and make connections among facts, events, and ideas.
- One pattern found in the environment can be translated into other patterns.

Kersh, Nielsen, and Subotnik (1987) organized a six-week unit that stresses patterns across disciplines. Figure 5–4 reveals topics that include patterns within codes and cipher, language patterns in poems and limericks, geometric patterns in three-dimensional solids, and crystals and their patterning. In addition to these patterns, additional patterns to explore could be found in music or dance, or even in genetics. As these researchers pointed out, such integrative curriculum is not easy to produce but it can be done by a concentrated effort.

On a larger scale, science concepts can be explored across a series of units, as well as across grade levels. An example of a sequence of units focused on the concept of systems in the different science disciplines was reported by VanTassel-Baska, Gallagher, Bailey, and Sher (1992). Their project involved the work of scientists, science teachers, and educators collaborating in different groups to develop and write curriculum units around the concept of systems that would be appropriate for gifted students in grades 2 through 8. To meet the requirements called for in science education reform, each unit was required to meet certain criteria: use of technology; interdisciplinary connections; assessments using authentic activities; and student outcomes, including science content, science process, problem solving, and use of the experimental method.

Consistent with the desire to have students act like scientists, most of the units started with the presentation of an ill-structured problem—one where the initial situation does not

FIGURE 5–4   Pattern Unit at a Glance

Week One

Topic: Patterns within codes and ciphers
Sample Content: The history of codes and ciphers, number and alphabet ciphers, Morse code, breaking codes, etc.
Sample Objective: The student will apply knowledge of patterning in order to break an alphabet code.

Weeks Two and Three

Topic: Language patterns
Sample Content: Poetic stress/rhythm patterns, patterns within poetic forms such as limericks, etc.
Sample Objective: The student will demonstrate knowledge of the poetic patterning of limericks by creating an original limerick.

Weeks Four and Five

Topic: Geometric patterns
Sample Content: Tesselation patterns, polygons and their patterns, three-dimensional geometric solids, etc.
Sample Objective: The student will identify polygonal patterns by correctly labeling polygons found in the classroom.

Week Six

Topic: Crystals and their patterning
Sample Content: Identification of crystals, crystal growing, etc.
Sample Objective: The student will demonstrate knowledge of crystal patterns by predicting the kind of crystal, and its pattern, that a particular chemical solution will produce.

Source: Adapted from Kersh, M., Nielsen, E., & Subotnik, R. (1987). Techniques and sources for developing integrative curriculum for the gifted. *Journal for the Education of the Gifted, 11* (1), 56-68.

reveal the exact nature of the problem, nor is enough information provided within the problem to solve it. Students have to "mess around" in the problem and dig a little to get at the heart of the matter. This technique, known as *problem-based learning*, will be discussed in greater detail later in this chapter. Table 5–2 shows the sequence of the completed units. The units progress from simple systems to complex ones and from microsystems to macrosystems. They also incorporate all of the major science areas as the concept evolves from early elementary through middle school. Thus a student could receive systematic exposure to a single concept in science throughout his or her early schooling in a carefully laid out program sequence.

Content Sophistication

The purpose of content sophistication activities is to take advantage of the already superior knowledge and skills of the gifted students by allowing them to discover and explore more complex systems of ideas. One challenge of science education is to intrigue youngsters into searching for such conceptual systems and patterns in nature and then into

TABLE 5–2   Sample Systems Units

Grades	Unit Topic	Systems Studied
K–2	Small ecosystems	Plant growth system Effects of altering the system Effects of introducing new elements into a system
	Civilizations	Archeological digs: system of a dig system of a civilization interaction between dig and history
3–5	Acid spills	Chemical reaction system pH system
	Circuits	Circuit systems City wiring systems Electrical and social systems
6–8	Pollution of Chesapeake Bay	Chemical system Agricultural system Bay life system Regulatory system
	Nuclear power	Environmental system Regulatory system Human health system Power generation system Waste disposal system
	Disease and diagnosis	Human body system Social health system Governmental regulatory system

becoming curious about their origins. The geometric patterns of crystals, snowflakes, or honeycombs are fascinating once one starts to look for them. Judson stated:

> *We live by patterns. Intervals. Repetitions. Patterns set up expectations. Patterns in time. To perceive a pattern means that we have already formed an idea of what is next.... The spiral of a snail's shell, the spiral of the great nebula in Andromeda. The punch line of a joke tells us that a set of things we thought belonged to one pattern was really, all along, making a very different pattern.... Music is all pattern—too regular and the music is banal—but a great composer teases our sense of pattern, upsets expectations but then resolves the complexity by reimposing the pattern at a more encompassing level. (1980, p. 28)*

Another way to provide gifted students with increased sophistication in science is to expose them more to the so-called rules of scientific thinking and how scientists make judgments and decisions in different ways and for different reasons than other professionals.

Many challenges face teachers who take on the task of breaking down "rote and drill" learning and engage their students in critical thinking. Although this is true in all fields, it is especially true in science, where so many myths prevail over a realistic view of the actual practice of science. Myths of science include that all questions in science have certain answers, that the value of one theory over another is determined by personal preference, and that real science is simply a way of conducting experiments. To introduce students to a more realistic vision of science, several barriers of beliefs have to be broken.

These barriers have been studied in the context of learning in general and placed in developmental sequence by Perry (1970). In the first stage, referred to as *dualism*, students believe that all questions have right or wrong answers. In the second stage, *multiplicity*, students believe that some questions may exist that do not have answers (yet). Along with this new reality goes the belief that if no certain answer exists, then any answer is as good as any other. For example, if the Big Bang theory cannot be proved, it is no more valid than any other theory. In the third stage, *contextual relativism*, students come to understand that certain theories are preferred over others because they have met certain criteria. In science, the criteria would be agreement with data, logical consistency, or replicability. Students begin to realize that scientists live within a value system that drives the decisions they make and the way they think and work.

Gifted students tested on measures of Perry's scheme of intellectual development routinely score at one stage more advanced than average-ability students of the same age. Therefore, they are ready for more complex understandings of science. Table 5–3 outlines the stages, provides brief descriptions of student attitudes at each stage, and gives some ideas from Nelson (1989) that encourage progression from one stage to the next.

Another way to reveal to students the important elements of scientific reasoning and work is by revealing the criteria to them through self-assessment activities. Figure 5–5 shows an example of a self-assessment activity used by an astrophysics teacher working with gifted students (Moyer, 1992). Note that the rating sheet is separated into categories of critical thinking and scientific requirements. By making these criteria explicit to students and also making the students begin to think about judging themselves on these

TABLE 5–3   Developmental Sequence in Understanding: Science Applications

Stage	Attitude	Tasks	Science Applications
Dualism	Valid questions have certain answers; all answers are right or wrong.	Provide problems with multiple right answers or no right answers.	Introduce questions with no answer: What is the origin of the universe?
Multiplicity	Most questions have right answers, some don't. If right answers don't exist, any opinion is valid.	Introduce concept of differing perspectives.	Demonstrate how science perspective changes with new discoveries.
Contextual Relativism	Different disciplines interpret information differently because of their different ways of making judgments and decisions.	Introduce the field's applications and limitations. Show different interpretations in different fields.	Show how two science disciplines interpret phenomena differently.

Sources: Adapted from *Forms of Intellectual and Ethical Development in the College Years: A Scheme* by W. G. Perry, 1970, New York: Holt, Rinehart and Winston; and "Skewered on the Unicorn's Horn: The Illusion of Tragic Tradeoff between Content and Critical Thinking in the Teaching of Science," by C. Nelson, in L. W. Crow (Ed.), *Enhancing Critical Thinking in the Sciences*, 1989, Washington, DC: Society for College Science Teachers.

criteria, they begin to integrate and appreciate their contribution to the scientific endeavor. Although this example is for high school students, similar versions are easy to create for lower grade levels as well.

Teaching for content sophistication does not necessarily mean long discussions in abstract terms. It can be a sequence of activities with hands-on experiences and a group of students just "messing about."

Earlier in this chapter it was mentioned that one of the prevalent myths about science was that science consisted only of experimentation; in truth, however, experimentation is only a small part of a process of examination, questioning, observing, and speculating. From this more complete picture, one can see that specific, concrete data are useful to scientists only insofar as the data add fuel to the discussion of more abstract and theoretical explanations of phenomena. Because of this, the focus of curriculum experts of science who address themselves to the education of the gifted point out that data should be used as a prelude and a base for leading to larger ideas, and that data can supplement or elaborate on information related to the basic idea, system, or generalization.

In either respect, and similar to other areas of curricula, one would expect a major dimension in programs for gifted students to be topics utilizing the dimensions of explanation, evaluation, and expansion.

ASTROPHYSICS
Evaluation Criteria

Name:_____   Assignment: _____

Date Submitted: _____   Date Evaluated: _____

Specific Criteria	*Evaluation*		
STUDENT			
	H	M	L
• Level of Intellectual Frustration:	1 2	3	4 5
• Degree of Vagueness:	1 2	3	4 5
• Degree of Ambiguity:	1 2	3	4 5
INSTRUCTOR			
Scientific Skills	E	S	U
• Attention to Significant Figures:	1 2	3	4 5
• Correct Usuage of Mathematical Expressions:	1 2	3	4 5
• Correct Units shown through Process & Solution:	1 2	3	4 5
• Use of Appropriate Assumptions:	1 2	3	4 5
• Closure of Exercise:	1 2	3	4 5
• Thought-Provoking Conclusion to Experiment (i.a.):	1 2	3	4 5
Cognitive Skills	E	S	U
• Identification & Explanation of Assumptions:	1 2	3	4 5
• Identification of Relevant Mathematical Expression(s):	1 2	3	4 5
• Identification & Use of Relevant Data:	1 2	3	4 5
• Outline of Process used in Solution:	1 2	3	4 5
• Reasonableness of Incorrect Answers (i.a.):	1 2	3	4 5
• Persistance Shown in Finding Solution:	1 2	3	4 5
• Relevance of Solution to Problem:	1 2	3	4 5

Key:

H = High	M = Medium	L = Low	(i.a.) = If Appropriate
E = Excellent	S = Satisfactory	U = Unacceptable	

Concluding Remarks:

FIGURE 5–5   Self-Assessment Form for Astrophysics

Source: Moyer, E. (1992). *Self-assessment in astrophysics.* Report to the Director. Illinois Mathematics and Science Academy. Reprinted by permission.

Content Novelty

Another myth that seems to pervade the field of science is that because science is objective and removed, it has no impact on the real world. In fact, nothing could be further from the case. Science constantly affects the state of society and society also impacts on what issues are popular in science research. In a Report of the Commission of the Humanities, the vital importance of connecting science with other disciplines was made clear:

> *The need to interrelate the humanities, social science, science and technology has probably never been greater than today. They converge in areas such as biomedical research, the application of microprocessing and computer technologies, the conduct of government, arms control and the safe use of natural resources—subjects requiring interdisciplinary investigation because of their social and ethical implications. (Humanities in American Life, 1980, p. 6)*

An additional reason why interdisciplinary studies in science are important, and especially for the gifted, is that students who are science oriented do not leave school thinking that the other disciplines are not important or do not have their own valuable ways of interpreting experience. This century's most influential scientist, Albert Einstein, said:

> *It is not enough to teach man a specialty.... It is essential that the student acquire an understanding of, and a lively feeling for values. He must acquire a vivid sense of the beautiful and of the morally good.... He must learn to understand the motives of human beings, their illusions and their suffering in order to acquire a proper relationship to individual fellow men and to the community. This is what I have in mind when I recommend the "humanities" as important.... Overemphasis on . . . premature specialization on the ground of immediate usefulness kills the spirit on which all cultural life depends, specialized knowledge included. (cited in Seelig, 1959, pp. 66–67)*

One of the instructional goals for science instruction of gifted children is to help them see the relationships between various disciplines. This interdisciplinary approach of linking concepts across subject areas such as biology, chemistry, and physics has been difficult because each area is traditionally taught in isolation from one another. One approach to interdisciplinary study is to make the curriculum program problem oriented.

Slavkin and Slavkin (1988) proposed the use of macroscale problems, such as world hunger and famine. This is the type of macroproblem that is intriguing to many gifted students. It satisfies their interest in global affairs and contains elements of economics, transportation, political and human infrastructures, as well as the emphasis on the chemistry of the soil and plant biology. Some of the concepts that are naturally used in the process of studying such a macrounit in biology, chemistry, mathematics, and physics are noted in Figure 5–6.

The tasks necessary to make an impact on world hunger that Slavkin and Slavkin (1988) have identified are as follows:

1. Increase the crop yield per acre;
2. Breed new plants for resistance to predators and insults anticipated in the region;
3. Educate and train scientists and technicians focused upon agricultural opportunities;

FIGURE 5–6   Biotechnology and World Hunger

Clinical Manifestations of Hunger

1. Immune-deficiency diseases
2. Susceptibility to acute infectious diseases
3. Profound loss of energy
4. Central and peripheral nervous system deficiencies
5. Increased birth defects
6. Low-weight babies
7. Irritability
8. Generalized increased morbidity (diseases)
9. Generalized increased mortality

Priorities for Stabilized Agricultural Productivity

1. Economic development and political stability
2. Agricultural research
3. Enhanced alternative energy resources, farming technology, and farming expertise
4. National and local political infrastructure suitable to adjust to acute and/or chronic changes in food supply
5. Human infrastructure capable of scientific and technological contributions to food supply

Source: Adapted from Slavkin, H., & Slavkin, L. (1988). Science curriculum and teaching in the 21st century. *Journal of the Education of the Gifted, 11* (2), 35–51.

4. Develop modern farming practices, including the discovery of inexpensive fertilizers, herbicides, and pesticides compatible with human optimization;
5. Develop appropriate farm labor;
6. Develop appropriate transportation to facilitate the movement of foodstuffs through the region;
7. Develop suitable communication networks;
8. Develop suitable administrative services to optimize public utilization of limited resources; and
9. Develop suitable government policies to prepare the required infrastructure and policies to address crises as well as chronic food shortages.

Given such an agenda, the class of gifted students could break into teams to take different aspects of this list and attempt to discover what would be necessary to achieve these objectives. At the very least, they will come away with the early understanding that there are some problems that do not yield easily to bright ideas and that we have to live with for a long time.

Content novelty can be used for gifted students to explore topics that combine two fields of science, such as biology and chemistry, in particular ways or to explore the impacts of science on the larger society. The standard curriculum rarely has time for such cross-discipline adventures because it is too committed to students learning the basic facts within each scientific domain, such as biology.

Stepien, Gallagher, and Workman (1993) have presented a novel approach to the teaching of science as an interdisciplinary discipline in a course entitled *Science, Society and the Future (SSF)*, using an innovative curriculum and teaching technique known as *problem-based learning*.

Problem-based learning originated in medical schools (Barrows, 1988) to help medical students learn the metacognitive tasks associated with questioning and diagnosing patients. Central to this process is the presentation at the beginning of the semester of an ill-structured problem, which is the springboard for all of the learning that takes place. The ill-structured problem that the students face has many characteristics, including that there is not enough information in the initial problem statement for students to solve the problem. This single element serves to break students from the attitude cultivated in textbook problems that if they will read the problem statement enough, an answer will emerge.

Teachers in the problem-based technique act not as information purveyors but as metacognitive coaches, helping students analyze their reasoning processes and acting as a model for reflective thinking about thinking (Barrows, 1988). Students are allowed to pursue "blind alleys," regroup, and select different paths to follow with minimal redirection from the instructor—a process that parallels the behavior of professionals.

Stepien, Gallagher, and Workman (1993) translated this model to the high school level in the SSF course. Core to their use of the problem-based model with gifted students are that students work on a current science issue where information is incomplete and that the science issue has an impact on science, but also on ethics, government, economics, and has a human element as well. As a consequence, experts in problem-based learning refer to problem *resolution*, and not *solution*, as complicated issues of science and society can never be completely solved. Problem solving in this course is not treated as a heuristic but as the development of a problem-solving "toolbox" with skills that are used as needed in the problem-solving process. Very important to problem resolution is the use of cost/ benefit ratios and determination of long- and short-term consequences.

On the first day of class, students are presented with the ill-structured problem such as the one presented in Figure 5–7. From there, students are asked to answer the question What's going on? That simple question leads to a need for additional information, which then leads to research. Through a recycling of information gathering and What's going on? (problem finding or problem definition), students come to a decision about the core problem. As the students then work on the solution to the problem, interactions between science and society emerge. In the example presented in Figure 5–7 the interactions take the form of the conflict between the values of science and the policy of government. Some of the activities students complete in the class include not only science experiments but also work toward developing their own policy statement regarding the issue at hand. This way, students are forced to look at the same science issue from the perspective of the scientist and that of the policymaker.

Gifted students who have taken this course have responded enthusiastically to the interdisciplinary nature of their investigation. The following are two representative responses given by students when asked what they had learned in the course:

> *I learned how research works. There are no answers. There is no book you can go to look up the effect. Everything must be analyzed carefully. Overlooking the slightest detail can be disastrous.*

Problem Statement

You are the head of pediatrics at a large city hospital. Jane Barton is one of your patients. Doctor, what will you do in the case of Jane's baby?

Jane Barton is pregnant. She first came to you about two weeks ago after she and her husband received the results of tests ordered by her family doctor. The tests indicate that Jane and Ralph's baby is anencephalic. The couple is concerned about the fetus and wonder what to do if Jane cannot deliver a normal, healthy infant.

What Do We Know?	*What Do We Need to Know?*	*Examples of Learning Issues*
Jane is pregnant.	What is anencephally?	Anencephally: Cause, effects on
Ralph is her husband.	Is it genetic?	child, severity, morbidity,
The baby has anencephally.	Did Jane do something to make	quality and length of life.
Jane has been referred by	this happen?	Life support systems.
her regular doctor.	How long will the baby live?	Health care costs.
Jane and Ralph are	Will bearing the baby hurt Jane?	Emotional cost.
interested in options	Can the baby be cured?	Normal and abnormal fetal
available if the infant	If not, what are the options for	development.
is not normal.	Ralph and Jane (abortion)?	Pregnancy: potential risks to
	What positive use can the fetus	mother.
	possibly be used for?	Abortion: legal constraints,
	What are the laws about this?	ethics, health risk to mother.
	What is Jane's financial status?	Organ donation: government
	Can they afford hospital care for	regulation, uses of fetal
	Jane?	tissue.
	For the baby if it lives? (How	Doctor's personal ethics vs.
	long could it live?)	professional responsibilities.

FIGURE 5–7 Sample Ill-Structured Problem

Source: Adapted from Stepien, W. J., Gallagher, S. A., & Workman, D. (1993, Winter). Problem-based learning for traditional and interdisciplinary classrooms. *Journal for the Education of the Gifted, 16* (4), 338–357.

> *What may seem obviously wrong may possibly be right. Solutions are not 100% satisfactory most of the time. There is usually more than one best answer/ solution. The idea of what is mostly right differs from person to person. Life is full of grey areas. Sometimes we just have to live with the risks because the benefits are much greater. (Stepien, Gallagher, & Workman, 1993, p. 354)*

Research conducted in the class also revealed significant increases in the students' ability to spontaneously use problem finding as a part of their problem-solving process (Gallagher, Stepien, & Rosenthal, 1992).

Another program that has been designed around connections between the interaction of science and society is the Science/Technology/Society (S/T/S) program developed by Yager and his associates (Yager, 1988). S/T/S does not represent a particular curriculum organization or teaching technique, but instead is a framework for the development of materials that "redirect and redefine school science" (p. 181). The S/T/S program has three overall goals:

1. *Provide students opportunity to compare and contrast science and technology and to appreciate how science and technology contribute to new knowledge and power.*
2. *Give examples from the past and present of the profound changes science and technology have wrought on society, economic growth, and political process.*
3. *Offer global perspectives on the relation of science and technology to society, indicating the impact on developing nations and on the ecology of Spaceship Earth. (p. 186)*

S/T/S advocates using discovery and decision-making strategies in the classroom, practicing higher-level thinking strategies, using local resources and problems as a stimulus for science learning, engaging local experts as resources, and employing non-traditional methods of evaluating students. Because S/T/S acts as a broad set of general philosophy and guidelines, curricula that have developed under the program have many different faces. However, the general principles for S/T/S are consistent with the goals for teachers of the gifted, and some of these curricula may be worth seeking out as a part of a gifted student's science education.

Gifted students are often fascinated by the distant past and the far future. Their ability to use symbolic concepts enables them to project themselves into imaginary lands, and their curiosity drives them to think about where we, the human race, came from and where we are going. One clever device, intriguing to many youngsters, is the Cosmic Calendar devised by Carl Sagan (1977). He compressed the history of the universe into a single year, beginning the year on January 1 with the "big bang" that presumably began the universe. He demonstrated in this fashion how new upon the scene humans are, by pointing out that human beings do not even appear on the calendar until December 31. The first humans appeared on the earth at 10:30 P.M. on December 31 and all of our recorded history is in the last 10 seconds of December 31. From the Middle Ages to the present, in that cosmic timeframe, would occupy little more than 1 second. Several potential projects emerge from such a concept. How one could gather the information to make a reasonably accurate cosmic calendar would be one such question to pose to gifted students.

Another attempt at interrelating fields or disciplines can be done by asking the students to do historical time lines in various fields such as art, politics, science, and so on. Such a chart would allow the children to see the historical flow of great contributions in various areas—music, art, and literature—and link these trends to scientific advances. These pictorial interrelationships give the students a chance to integrate knowledge across content fields and historical times. One could discover that Bach is the contemporary of Peter the Great and Isaac Newton and that the scientific discoveries of Carl Gauss, Michael Faraday, and Georg Ohm are contemporaneous with the reign of Queen Victoria and the early life of Alfred Lord Tennyson and Charles Darwin. Karl Marx had made his contribution by the time Sigmund Freud had started on his discoveries of psychoanalysis, Claude Monet was painting, and Pyotr Tchaikovsky was composing music. The relationship of one major field of endeavor to another has never been an easy one to see. The construction of such historical time lines is an activity that is quite attractive to gifted students and from which they can gain insight into multiple relationships that otherwise might never be brought into conjunction with one another.

The Teacher of Science

This chapter has placed strong emphasis on science curriculum reform. Equally important as the new curriculum, however, will be the new science teacher. Below are listed some of the characteristics of the science teacher who emulates the behavior of real scientists.

1. Science teachers should be learning teachers, modeling the love of exploration and tolerance for uncertainty, which they are to encourage in their students.
2. To expose students to local resources and to interest them in the world around them, teachers must be willing to adapt, changing packaged curriculum materials to fit their local environments and resources.
3. Learning teachers are also researchers, continually gathering the latest information on whatever it is they choose to study.
4. *Mentor* is often the title ascribed to the new science teacher. To encourage higher-order thinking skills, teachers must adopt the attitude of a "cognitive coach" and allow for real discovery and problem solving.

Although perhaps a daunting list of traits, these characteristics have always been the hallmarks of an excellent teacher. If the "new science" is to succeed, these standards of excellence must become a new norm.

Earlier in this chapter several reasons were cited for the lack of systematic science instruction, especially at the elementary school level. These reasons include lack of resources, lack of instructional time devoted to science, and inadequate teacher preparation in science. To solve the problem of teacher preparation, new and intensive programs for teacher training will have to be developed, and teachers will have to be supported in their efforts to take advantage of those programs. The best and most innovative curriculum in the world will not work as well as it could when it is in the hands of a well-meaning and intelligent, but untrained, teacher.

Special Populations: Females and Minorities

Unfortunately, as our reliance on science and technology has grown, the number of professional scientists in the United States has declined. Already professional scientists project a shortage of 400,000 scientists and engineers by the year 2006—the year that most children born in 1984 would receive their undergraduate degrees from college (Massey, 1989). With the continuing shortage of scientists, and students' manifest lack of interest in the sciences, we are faced with a serious challenge to our current superiority in these fields. Science has not been seen as attractive, particularly to women and minority groups.

In 1990, African Americans comprised 12 percent of the nation's population and only 2 percent of its scientists and engineers; Hispanics comprised 9 percent of the nation's population and only 2 percent of its scientists and engineers; women comprised 51 percent of the nation's population, but only 11 percent of its scientists and engineers. Among the minorities, only Asian Americans appear in the sciences and engineering (4 percent) beyond their numbers in the society (2 percent) (Schmieder & Michael-Dyer, 1991). Schmieder and Michael-Dyer commented:

> *Unless programs are developed to attract and retain more women, minorities, and persons with disabilities into science, mathematics, and engineering (an estimated 85 percent will have to come from these groups), the nation will not be able to meet its technical personnel needs into the next century. (1991, p. 6)*

Compounding this problem is the fact that the proportion of women and minorities in the population is increasing: In the year 2020, 24 percent of the U.S. population will be Hispanic, as compared to 9 percent in 1984. However, only 53 percent of the population will be white, as compared to 74 percent in 1984. Thus, we will become more and more dependent on women and minorities to provide leadership in the field of science, even though they have traditionally not entered this field.

Mr. Jenkins realizes that when he presents science to his class, it must be in a way that not only gives Cranshaw an opportunity to explore an already well-established interest but will also capture the attention of Zelda, Stephanie, and Sam as well.

Gifted Girls in Science

Part of the problem of encouraging gifted girls to enter the field of science is that only recently have descriptions of scientists been created that are based on samples of professional women. Most early studies of the characteristics of scientists (including the ones cited at the beginning of this chapter) were conducted with samples of men. No wonder Zelda and Stephanie have trouble relating to the images with which they are presented!

When similar studies are conducted using females in careers that are supposedly atypical for females, the picture changes. Lemkau (1983) reported findings of a study that looked at the characteristics of females in "typical" and "atypical" careers. Her analysis revealed important differences as well as similarities between the two groups of women. Women in atypical careers reported more frequently that they were bright and assertive than the women with typical careers; women in typical careers reported being outgoing and tender-minded more often. However, no differences were found between the two groups in emotional stability, imagination, or experimentation. Evidently being in what was categorized as an atypical career did not cause undue emotional distress to the women in that group.

Although at first glance this makes females look similar to males in science careers, an interesting twist was added to the study. Lemkau had the women in her study fill out the personality inventory once for their workplace and then again to describe themselves in social situations. Analysis of the forms filled out for social situations revealed that the women in both groups perceived themselves to have more "masculine" traits in the workplace than in social situations. Perhaps one of the messages to send to gifted girls is that professional women make important distinctions between professional and social behavior in order to reconcile professional desires and the societal demands for particular gender-role behavior.

The desire to engage the interest of females in science has also prompted investigations as to the motivation and attitudes of gifted students toward scientific careers. Subotnik (1988) investigated the attitudes of 146 winners of the 1983 Westinghouse Science Talent Search, since these would most likely make up a group of potential future scientists. These students were given a choice regarding their motivation among curiosity, prestige, aesthetics, and "bettering the human condition." Both males and females overwhelmingly chose curiosity as their major motivation for doing research, although the girls, significantly more than the boys, chose "bettering the human condition" as a possible motivation.

Another gender difference was found in the response to the question as to what qualities the respondents most admire in their mathematical or scientific hero or heroine. Responses to this are presented in Figure 5–8. None of the 20 females identified creativity as an admired quality in a scientist; the majority of them responded that dedication to work was the most admired characteristic. In contrast, intelligence and creativity were the two characteristics most admired by the males in their scientific heroes.

It seems clear that girls entering science have a more humanistic concept and see devotion to work as the key characteristic of the scientist, whereas boys entering science seem much more intrigued by the task itself and the opportunity to do creative work. The humanistic interest of the girls in this study is consistent with other research that indicates that females, in general, tend to like to analyze data by making relationships; whereas males, in general, tend to like to analyze by making distinctions (Belenky, Clinchy, Goldberger, & Tarule, 1986). Nevertheless, 57 percent of these excellent science students reported a desire to investigate relationships between science and society—a topic that receives little attention in school science curriculum.

One common problem that faces even the science-prone gifted females is the traditional interactions that they have had in programs with gifted boys. Previous experience and observation have revealed that gifted girls often feel uncomfortable with the manipulation of tools and equipment and that the problem is compounded by gifted boys' tendency to commandeer equipment. The assertiveness of boys and the tacit social understanding that boys are entitled to the use of such equipment does not allow the girls to practice or to gain confidence in the use of materials and equipment.

Rand and Gibb (1989) reported a model program for gifted girls in science that attempted to counteract these issues. Their program, which is for girls only, has a female role model as a teacher, stresses family participation, provides an assortment of hands-on activities, and results in feelings of success.

In this Action Science program, for instance, the girls are encouraged to take part in the "squid dissection" and "rock collection and classification" as two examples of the use of dissection tools and equipment to gather rock specimens. Such a program appears to have success in the newfound enthusiasm of many girls for science and the feeling that they can do many things for themselves in terms of manipulating materials and equip-

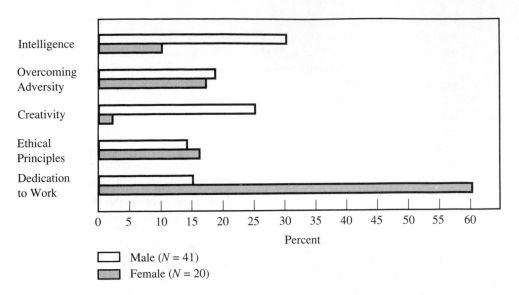

FIGURE 5–8   Qualities Admired in a Scientific Hero or Heroine (Westinghouse Talent Search Winners)

Source: From Subotnik, R. F. (1988). The motivation to experiment. *Journal for the Education of the Gifted, 11* (3), 19–35. Reprinted by permission.

ment. As a result of this and other programs focusing on gifted girls, Rand and Gibb have provided four suggestions that they believe would strengthen the interest of gifted girls in science:

1. Remember: Do not over-help young girls! *Let them gain valuable experience by thinking through a problem and trying various solutions. Encourage self-reliance or independence in girls.*
2. Encourage girls to trust their own judgment. *Discourage girls from seeking constant approval or verification from others before making decisions or moving to the next step. They need to develop confidence in their own abilities.*
3. Insist that girls use tools and equipment. *They should feel confident in their ability to identify and use equipment from basic hand tools to sophisticated computers and microscopes.*
4. Introduce female role models whenever possible. *This includes historical as well as females presently in science fields. Remember, also, that females such as mothers and teachers exert a very strong influence on a young girl's life; examine your own approaches to the areas listed above. (1989)*

One final caution: We can motivate, reinforce, and implement programs for gifted girls until they behave and think just as professional scientists do, but we will have solved only half the problem. Gifted boys also need to be taught to appreciate the contributions of their female classmates and women scientists. Only when boys and girls alike learn to share roles and responsibilities in the science classroom will we have created the proper environment to encourage all students to explore their interests and abilities in this fascinating field.

Minorities in Science

It is important to encourage all minorities to participate in math and science programs (see Figure 5–9). Much of the literature on minority participation in programs for the gifted continues to focus on the issue of equitable identification practices, as this is clearly the first step in encouraging participation. However, some work has emerged that helps shed some understanding on what factors are associated with minority students' continued interest in math or science.

Griffith (1988) reported a study of minority students who participated in A Better Chance (ABC) program that identifies gifted minority students and places them in boarding schools where they can receive rigorous academic training. Griffith sent ABC gradu-

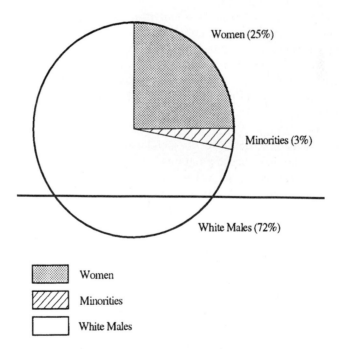

FIGURE 5–9   Scientists, Women, and Minorities: Proportions of Scientists

Source: Schmieder, A., & Michael-Dyer, G. (1991). *State of the Scene of Science Education in the Nation*. Washington, DC: U.S. Public Health Service.

ates a questionnaire that asked them about several aspects of their educational career, including high school and college characteristics, their experiences in high school and college, their family backgrounds, personal values, personality dynamics, and work orientations. These variables were then studied to see which ones were related to taking science and math courses in high school and to choosing a math or science career.

The results of the analysis showed that the best predictors of taking science and math courses were self-perception of ability in science and math, the perception of the math curriculum, identification of a high school math or science teacher as an important personal influence, and the academic atmosphere of the high school. Students who had taken advanced science and mathematics also were influenced by the challenge of the subject and their self-perceptions of ability. The major predictors of actually selecting a science or math career were many, but included especially the self-perceptions of high ability, enrollment in advanced math courses in high school, the influence of a science or mathematics teacher, and the perceptions of the high school math/science curriculum. Personal values, personality characteristics, and work orientation did not contribute directly to the students' selection of a math or science career, although parental values associated with education in math and science did contribute to such selection. From the results of this study, one can see that nurturing positive academic self-esteem and providing opportunities for advanced training would be important curricula adaptations for gifted minority students.

Within the science classroom itself, it seems that the changes advocated for all students are also those that are recommended for gifted minorities. After analyzing the characteristics of several successful programs for high-ability minority students, the COSMOS Corporation wrote a report titled *No Gift Wasted: Effective Strategies for Educating Highly Able Disadvantaged Students in Mathematics and Science.* The report made the following recommendations for adapting instruction for gifted minority students:

- Extension of time students spend learning
- Operation of special programs
- Provision of accelerated courses
- Use of hands-on learning techniques
- Provision of out-of-school activities

The Unfinished Agenda of Science

Finally, so that we do not let our advances in science blind us too much from what we do not know, Judson has proposed a set of eight problems that will take thousands of the best minds of the future to unravel:

1. What was the origin of the universe?
2. Needed: a unified theory in physics for four kinds of observable forces—weak, strong, electromagnetic, and gravitational.
3. What was the origin of the solar system?

4. What was the origin of life?
5. Establish the quantitative bases of natural selection and evolution.
6. What are the controlling processes that cause the fertilized egg to become the organism?
7. What are the mechanisms by which aging and death occur?
8. How does the human nervous system perceive, think, and process information? (1980, pp. 200–204)

Gifted students who are excited by the discovery of new ideas can also be encouraged to think about the ethical questions of science and its consequences. Past generations worried about the question Can we do it? The next generation of scientists may well worry about Should we do it? Should we keep elderly patients alive, even when their brains are dead or nonfunctional? Should we take extraordinary steps to help infants survive who are severely mentally handicapped and will likely remain so throughout their lives? Doctors who have been placed in the unenviable situation of having to make such decisions are, more and more, demanding that society as a whole arrive at some ethical guidelines. This topic will be further developed in Chapter 7.

Unresolved Issues

1. A new attempt at a "new science" may well change the structure of science instruction for everyone. When this happens, what will be the new educational adaptations that will stretch gifted students to develop to their fullest potential?
2. There has been a chronic shortage of science teachers in our public school programs. This is due, in part, to fewer students choosing this field but also to the fact that there are more job opportunities with better working conditions and higher financial rewards open to those who would qualify as science teachers. What are the conditions that will convince more of our youth to enter and stay with a career in science teaching?
3. Most of the teaching of science has been directed to the preparation of future scientists. Many gifted students will be entering other career fields, such as business, economics, or art, but will also need to understand science. Should they receive a different emphasis in secondary science programs from those students who see scientific fields as their career goals?
4. The emphasis to teach less information and more process-oriented goals in science will require that a substantial amount of "data" in the current curriculum be left out. Which information is most essential for students to have? Is the body of absolutely essential information in science different for average-ability and gifted students?
5. How can the interrelatedness of the various sciences be presented to gifted students? Subject areas of biology, chemistry, and physics have courses separated in space and time so the students do not see the linkage from one body of knowledge to another in these scientific fields. Even the most gifted students will not be able to make these conceptual connections without some carefully planned assistance.

Chapter Review

1. Science and technology have been, and will likely continue to be, an intimate part of the lives of all citizens, whether they are going to be future scientists or not.

2. There are many misconceptions that surround science and scientists. Evidence suggests that characteristics such as an insatiable curiosity and a strong desire to seek answers and to commit oneself to intensive and sustained work are distinguishing features of successful scientists.

3. National reports suggest that science instruction must change for all students. School science should require students to act like scientists, to engage in the exploration of scientific knowledge that will allow them to uncover fundamental scientific concepts.

4. Seven types of activities describe what scientists do: problem definition, information gathering, observation, classification, measurement, hypothesizing, and experimentation.

5. Intellectually heterogeneous classrooms, in addition to teachers with limited science knowledge, have inhibited the full growth of talented science students.

6. Gifted students should experience or reproduce in the science classroom the essential activities of the scientist. Curriculum structures such as problem-base learning provide an opportunity for students to see the scientific process from the moment of "sensing" the existence of a problem.

7. Novel concepts such as the historical time-line chart and the Cosmic Calendar can help students place past events and people in proper perspective and relationship to each other.

8. However sophisticated the curriculum, it is still filtered through the individual teacher, who determines the level and scope of classroom activities.

9. Gifted girls and minorities often need special encouragement and support in science, particularly in building confidence in their own judgments.

10. There are questions of enormous importance to humankind that still need answering and that provide a continuing challenge to the best minds of future generations.

Readings of Special Interest

Jackson, P. (1983). The reform of science education: A cautionary tale. *Daedalus, 112* (2), 143–166.
This is a comprehensive and thoughtful review of the fate of the federal government's initiative to improve science curricula in U.S. schools; this article serves as an excellent counterpoint to Science for All Americans. *Jackson believes that the movement of the 1960s was never as successful as it might have been because the material was too difficult for the average student. The scientists believed that the quality of the materials would overcome school politics in terms of*

marketing textbooks and the government's unease about its own responsibilities in supporting curriculum innovation. This is a fine development of the complexities of curriculum reform.

Judson, H. (1980). *The search for solutions.* New York: Holt, Rinehart & Winston.
This book is designed to accompany and provide background for teachers to a nine-film set by the same title. It covers different aspects of the scientific process: investigators, pattern, change, chance, feedback, modeling, prediction, evidence, and theory. It captures the key elements

of science in a readable but scholarly fashion. The film series is also highly recommended, although the book can stand on its own.

Medewar, P. B. (1979). *Advice to a young scientist.* New York: Basic Books.

Within this brief gem is a well-developed description of what it means to be a scientist. Medewar describes in very plain language how scientists think, what their day is like, and their particular joys and frustrations. This book would be a great basis for discussions about scientific "habits of mind."

Rutherford, F., & Ahlgren, A. (1990). *Science for all Americans.* New York: Oxford University Press. *This book is about scientific literacy and, sadly enough, it is desperately needed. Few students, gifted or not, seem to understand the basic nature of science. The international studies of science achievement consistently find U.S. students at or near the bottom, but the most distressing discovery is that many students view science as*

technology or as limited to the physical sciences. This book makes clear the importance of science to the human community. It is worth the attention of both students and teachers.

VanTassel-Baska, J., Boyce, L. N., Sher, B. T., Bailey, J., & Gallagher, S. A. (1992). *Consumer's guide to science curriculum.* Williamsburg, VA: Center for Gifted Education, College of William and Mary.

Developed under one of the Jacob K. Javits initiatives funded by the U.S. Department of Education, this compendium provides reviews of most of the major basal texts, special curricula, and ancillary materials. The criteria for the reviews were based on recommendations from educational reform reports as well as the commonly accepted criteria for sound curriculum. Each review contains a special section describing the curricula's appropriateness for gifted students. It is available through the Center for Gifted Education at the College of William and Mary.

References

Alamprese, J. A., & Erlanger, W. J. (1989). *No gift wasted: Effective strategies for educating highly able disadvantaged students in mathematics and science.* Washington, DC: COSMOS Corporation.

Barrows, H. S. (1985). *How to design a problem-based curriculum for the preclinical years.* New York: Springer.

Barrows, H. S. (1988). *The tutorial process.* Springfield, IL: Southern Illinois University School of Medicine.

Belenky, M. F., Clinchy, B. M., Goldberger, N. R., & Tarule, J. M. (1986). *Women's ways of knowing: The development of self, voice and mind.* New York: Basic Books.

Brandwein, P. (1986). A portrait of gifted young with science talent. *Roeper Review, 8* (4), 235–243.

Coleman, W., Jr., & Selby, C. (1982). *Educating Americans for the 21st century.* Washington, DC: National Science Board Commission on Precollege Education in Mathematics, Science, and Technology.

Cothron, J. H., Giese, R. N., & Rezba, R. J. (1989). *Students and research: Practical strategies for*

science classrooms and competitions. Dubuque, IA: Kendall/Hunt.

Eiseley, L. (1957). *The immense journey.* New York: Random House.

Eylon, B. S., & Linn, M. C. (1988). Learning and instruction: An examination of four research perspectives in science education. *Review of Educational Research, 58* (3), 251–301.

Gallagher, S. A. (1990). Personality patterns of the gifted. *Understanding Our Gifted, 3* (1) 1–13.

Gallagher, S. A. Stepien, W. J., & Rosenthal, H. (1992, Fall). The effect of problem-based learning on problem solving. *Gifted Child Quarterly, 36* (4), 195–201.

Gough, H. G. (1976). Studying creativity by means of word association tests. *Journal of Applied Psychology, 61,* 348–353.

Griffith, J. B. (1988, March 28–30). Better measures: Developing more minority mathematicians and scientists. In J. I. Dreyden, S. A. Gallagher, G. E. Stanley, & R. N. Sawyer (Eds.), *The proceedings of the talent identification program/National Science Foundation conference on academic talent.* Durham, NC.

Harms, N., & Yager, R. (1981). *What research says to the science teacher* (Vol. 3). Washington, DC: NSTA Monograph.

Humanities in American Life: Report of the Commission on the Humanities. (1980). Berkeley, CA: University of California Press.

Jacobson, W. J., & Daran, R. L. (1988). *Science achievement in seventeen countries: A preliminary report.* New York: Teachers College Press.

Judson, H. F. (1980). *The search for solutions.* Baltimore: Johns Hopkins University Press.

Kandel, M. (1983). An organic laboratory course for gifted elementary school students. *Journal of Chemical Education, 672.*

Kersh, M., Nielsen, E., & Subotnik, R. (1987). Techniques and sources for developing integrative curriculum for the gifted. *Journal for the Education of the Gifted, 11* (1), 56–68.

Lemkau, J. P. (1983). Women in male-dominated professions: Distinguishing personality and background characteristics. *Psychology of Women Quarterly, 8* (2), 144–165.

Massey, W. E. (1989, September). Science education in the United States: What the scientific community can do. *Association Affairs, 915–921.*

Medewar, P. B. (1979). *Advice to a young scientist.* New York: Basic Books.

Milgram, R. (1991). *Counseling gifted and talented children.* Norwood, NJ: Ablex.

Moyer, E. (1992). *Self-assessment in astrophysics: Report to the Director.* Illinois Mathematics and Science Academy.

Mullis, I. V., & Jenkins, L. B. (Eds.). (1988). *The science report card: Elements of risk and recovery. Trends and achievement based on the 1986 National Assessment.* Princeton, NJ: Educational Testing Service.

Myers, I. B., & McCaulley, M. H. (1987). *Manual: A guide to the development and use of the Myers-Briggs Type Indicator.* Palo Alto, CA: Consulting Psychologists Press.

Nelson, C. (1989). Skewered on the unicorn's horn: The illusion of tragic tradeoff between content and critical thinking in the teaching of science. In L. W. Crow (Ed.), *Enhancing critical thinking in the sciences.* Washington, DC: Society for College Science Teachers.

Perry, W. G. (1970). *Forms of intellectual and ethical development in the college years: A scheme.* New York: Holt, Rinehart and Winston.

Rand D., & Gibb, L. H. (1989). A model program for gifted girls in science. *Journal for the Education of the Gifted, 12* (2), 142–155.

Rutherford, F. J., & Ahlgren, A. (1990). *Science for all Americans: Scientific literacy: What is it, why America needs it, how we can achieve it.* New York: Oxford University Press.

Sagan, C. (1977). *The dragons of Eden.* New York: Ballentine.

Schmieder, A., & Michael-Dyer, G. (1991). *State of the scene of science education in the nation.* Washington, DC: Public Health Service.

Seelig, C. (Ed.). (1959). *Ideas and opinions.* Based on *Mein Weltbild* by Albert Einstein. New York: Crown Publishers.

Sher, B. T. (1992). *A guide to science concepts.* Williamsburg, VA: College of William and Mary, Center for Gifted Education.

Shymansky, J. A., Hedges, L. V., & Woodworth, G. (1990). A reassessment of the effects of inquiry-based science curricula of the 60's on students performance. *Journal of Research in Science Teaching, 27* (2), 127–144.

Slavkin, H., & Slavkin, L. (1988). Science curriculum and teaching in the 21st century. *Journal for the Education of the Gifted, 11* (2), 35–51.

Stepien, W. J., Gallagher, S. A., & Workman, D. (1993, Winter). Problem-based learning for traditional and interdisciplinary classrooms. *Journal for the Education of the Gifted, 16* (4), 338–357.

Subotnik, R. (1988). The motivation to experiment: A study of gifted adolescents' attitudes toward scientific research. *Journal for the Education of the Gifted, 11* (3), 19–35.

Tobias, S. (1990). *They're not dumb. They're different: A new "tier of talent" for science.* Tucson, AZ: Research Corporation.

Toffler, A. (1980). *The third wave.* New York: Bantam.

VanTassel-Baska, J., Gallagher, S. A., Bailey, J., & Sher, B. T. (1992). *Final paper: Developing science curriculum for high ability learners.* Center for Gifted Education, The College of William and Mary. Funded by USDOE Grant RFP# 90-048.

Weiss, I. (1987). *Report of the 1985–1986 National Survey of Science and Mathematics Education.* Research Triangle Park, NC: Research Triangle Institute.

Yager, R. E. (1988). A new focus for school science: S/T/S. *School Science and Mathematics, 88* (3), 181–190.

Chapter **6**

Social Studies
for Gifted Students

Key Questions

- Why do many gifted students consider social studies flat and uninteresting?
- What are some of the key assumptions in the teaching of history?
- What are some examples of differentiated curriculum for gifted students in the social studies?
- In the study of leadership, what are some of the major concerns facing leaders in any enterprise?
- What are some advantages and disadvantages of teachers of social studies as opposed to teachers of mathematics?
- Why does the study of the future seem to be a particularly appropriate area of study for gifted students?

Social studies should be one of the most exciting of content fields because it covers who we are individually (psychology), who we are collectively (sociology), where we have come from (anthropology and history), where we are (geography), how we govern ourselves (political science), and how we exchange desired goods to meet our needs (economics). Instead, for all too many students, this area of study turns out to be flat, stale, and useless. Why does this happen and what can we do to correct it? This will be the focal point of our discussions in this chapter.

The Textbook Problem

One thing that turns gifted students away from a subject such as history is that the textbooks often present an unconnected sequence of events. If the basic sources of information do not provide some clue as to the linkage or relationship of events to one another, then even the brightest students will not be able to discern the patterns that form the foundation for historical events.

Beck and McKeown (1988) studied standard history textbooks for young learners in terms of how these books handled the precursors of the American Revolution. There is probably no more significant question about U.S. history to bright young learners than "Why did we break away from England?" Beck and McKeown found that most of the textbooks presented many events preceding the American Revolution but did not link these events to the coming of the Revolution. For example, the textbooks provided information about the French and Indian War but not the two consequences about that war that made the American Revolution more likely: first, the broken promise by the British that they would give the land owned by the French to the Colonists; and second, the war left Britain in bad financial conditions, which it tried to deal with by taxing the Colonists. Both consequences angered the Colonists and made more likely a future split.

Similarly, although the textbooks tried to provide a portrait of colonial life, describing the various activities in the colonies during the period before the Revolution, many did not point out that the Colonists began to think of themselves as American rather than British, Dutch, or Swiss. They saw themselves as a separate people. The real meaning of the slogan "Taxation without Representation" meant that the Colonists already saw themselves as a separate people who were not being represented by British subjects in Parliament. Also, unless the issue of a struggle for power and control of one's own destiny are introduced, the Boston Tea Party may sound like an adult prank rather than one more event in a mosaic of a classic struggle for power by two opposing groups—the Colonists and the British government.

The responsibility of teachers in such a situation seems to be twofold. First, teachers can give students books and other resources that do make a legitimate effort to show the pattern of events or the reasons such events occurred. Second, the teachers should provide these connections themselves, to the degree that they are knowledgeable about the subject.

Problems of Elementary School Social Studies

The uncertain state of social studies for the regular students in elementary schools has been commented on by many observers, but perhaps none so critical as the social studies community itself (NCSS Task Force, 1989). Studies have pointed out that the average instructional time for social studies in the primary grades was 20 minutes per day, and at the upper elementary levels was 34 minutes per day (Lengel & Superka, 1982; Goodlad, 1984). The report of the Task Force was even more critical of the *content* of the lessons:

> *Student apathy—and even dislike—for a subject considered to be lifeless and useless is understandable in classrooms where strategies encouraging active involvement in grappling with human issues are absent; where forced marches through textbooks are frequent; and where the assumption prevails that memorization of names, places, and dates will somehow translate itself during adulthood into civic involvement. (p. 20)*

If this bill of fare is distressing to the average students, consider how much more irritating and boring it must be to gifted students who are searching for meaning and understanding of the social world around them. Fortunately, some of the specialists in the content field have taken things into their own hands and have begun to bring together some advanced conceptual frameworks that provide a better vision of the world and its people—past, present, and future.

Problems of Secondary School Social Studies

The secondary school programs in social studies face an even more difficult situation than the elementary school. Students, by this time, often have a choice of taking or not taking geography, economics, psychology, or anything else in the social studies area—with the possible exception of a mandatory American history course. Students' past experiences with this type of subject matter in elementary or middle school may well determine their choices. If that experience has been flat, stale, and unprofitable, then they may systematically avoid a whole area of study.

In 1986, the National Assessment of Educational Progress gave a representative nationwide sample of high school juniors a test covering such topics as the Constitution, civil rights, labor and industry, and international relations. The average score on basic knowledge multiple-choice items was a disappointing 55 percent correct—and many students lacked a fundamental understanding about the main ideas in the Bill of Rights, the Constitution, the Declaration of Independence, and other national documents. The results on tests of geography, economics, and civics were equally disappointing.

All of this depressing information galvanized an array of groups determined to do something about this sad story. As their colleagues in math and science decided, these groups (the National Council on Social Studies, the Bradley Commission on History in the Schools, the National Assessment of Educational Progress) wished to place their emphasis on meaning and on the application of ideas rather than memorization. All of this is good news for educators interested in the development of gifted students, since that is precisely what they have been recommending for these students all along.

The National Assessment of Education Progress (NAEP), well aware of the central role that assessment plays in driving the school curriculum, provided seven assumptions in the study of history around which it feels assessment should be based. The seven assumptions create a vision of what ought to be.

*Seven Assumptions in the Study of History**

First, historical study should connect people and events across time and include all kinds of human thought and activity: political, social, cultural, economic, technological, philosophical, and religious, as well as interactions among these activities....

Second, the study of U.S. history must analyze change and continuity over time, explore the range of choices that have been available to people, and examine the possibility that historical outcomes could have been different depending upon the options selected....

Third, to illuminate the range and depth of the human experience as well as differing perspectives, historical study should include famous people and ordinary individuals, events on the grand scale and in everyday life to convey the ideas and experiences that have shaped U.S. history....

Fourth, history should include the analytical study of the nation's political ideals of individual dignity, individual rights, civic virtue, democracy, the rule of law, equality of opportunity, liberty, popular sovereignty, justice, and the right to dissent....

Fifth, history has a spatial dimension—the places where human actions occur. For example, aspects of the natural environment, such as climate and terrain, influence human behavior; and people affect the places they inhabit....

*U.S. History Framework for the 1994 National Assessment of Educational Progress (Washington, DC: National Assessment Governing Board, U.S. Department of Education, 1993). Reprinted by permission.

Sixth, it is necessary to identify enduring themes that link people and events across time and space. People and events in history are not isolated and discrete. They are linked in many ways. The linkages are not static, either, but continuously evolving such that later generations will certainly perceive new relationships that are not evident to us. Among the many possible themes of U.S. history, the committees have selected four to emphasize in the assessment:

1. *Change and Continuity in American Democracy: Ideas, Institutions, Practices, and Controversies.*
2. *The Gathering and Interactions of Peoples, Cultures, and Ideas.*
3. *Economic and Technological Changes and Their Relation to Society, Ideas, and the Environment.*
4. *The Changing Role of America in the World.*

Seventh, using themes to relate particular facts requires the development of historical reasoning skills based upon the examination of evidence, the analysis of cause and effect, and appreciation of how complex and sometimes ambiguous the explanation of historical events can be....

The Bradley Commission (Gagnon, 1989), composed of a mix of teachers and scholars, made some key recommendations, as follows:

1. The knowledge and habits of mind to be gained from the study of history are indispensable to the education of citizens in a democracy. The study of history should, therefore, be required of all students.
2. The study must reach well beyond the acquisition of useful information. To develop judgment and perspective, historical study must often focus on broad, significant themes and questions rather than the short-lived memorization of facts without context. In so doing, historical study should provide context for facts and training in critical judgment based on evidence, including original sources, and should cultivate the perspective arising from a chronological view of the past down to the present day.

The "habits of mind" noted in the first recommendation included such characteristics as the following:

• Understand the significance of the past to their own lives, both private and public, and to their society.
• Distinguish between the important and the inconsequential, to develop the "discriminatory memory" needed for a discerning judgment in public and personal life.
• Understand how things happen and how things change, how human intentions matter, but also how their consequences are shaped by the means of carrying them out, in a tangle of purpose and process.
• Grasp the complexity of historical causation, respect particularity, and avoid excessively abstract generalizations.

The reader can note the similarity between the statements of what is needed given by these two groups. Other groups, representing some of the other fields such as geography, are making similar recommendations and statements. Given these proposed changes, where does that leave the education of gifted students in social studies?

Content Adaptations

Given all of these proposed curricular changes for the regular educational program, what will be the desired program for gifted students? Examples for content acceleration, enrichment, sophistication, and novelty will be provided, as well as a discussion of the basic characteristics needed by the teachers of social studies.

Zelda's parents have always been quite pleased with her work in social studies. She invariably comes home with high grades, and sometimes her parents are prompted to put her on exhibition because of the extent of her knowledge. Since her class is currently studying the South American continent, Zelda has an impressive array of facts regarding the imports and exports of each South American country and its major population centers, and she can reproduce from memory adequate maps of the topography of the various countries.

But what does Zelda know about the people of other cultures, their behavior, and how they interact with one another? She knows very little—and there is no reason why she should. Not only are such topics rarely discussed but sometimes they are systematically avoided in her classrooms. The notions that people act toward one another out of their fears, their hopes, and their prejudices, and that many of our social interactions today are based on such crass individual self-interests will remain a mystery to Zelda and to other bright and average children, until the social studies curricula focus attention on those dimensions, as well as on the geographical dimensions of social studies. Few children, no matter how gifted or talented, will be able to stumble on basic generalizations of human behavior across cultures or time without specific guidance or instruction.

Many educators of gifted children view social studies as a curriculum area of great potential but also of some threat. Gifted children, with their penchant for exploring beyond facts and seeking explanations and value judgments, are liable to be both a joy and an embarrassment to their mentors. Social studies, dealing as it does with people, may result in the gifted students drawing conclusions that the adult world is not all that it should be.

When Joe reads the Bill of Rights, for example, he may not stop at memorizing, but may begin to relate the concept of freedom of the press to events in his own town. He possibly may create an awkward situation for the teacher by asking for an explanation as to why we are not living up to the Constitution. For instance, letters to the editor never seem to publish critical comments about the real estate developer who contributes much advertising revenue to the local paper. Such a situation is unpleasant. We do not like to have pointed out to us that we adults are not models of virtue. We have ways of protecting ourselves from such embarrassments. One way to avoid such discussions is by keeping our talented students busy learning lots of nonembarrassing facts. Another way is try to impress on them our version of the truth. Neither of these subterfuges works entirely.

The social studies curriculum at the elementary level usually combines a large number of content fields into a single time space. Traditionally, subjects such as history, geography, economics, government, sociology, psychology, and anthropology are included in a complex mix of facts and ideas. Later, in the secondary schools, students may take specific courses in each of these subject areas.

The result of such a broad field of content is that there may be great diversity in the actual material covered, and some topics that should be of special interest to gifted students may not be covered at all. The basic theme of the content suggestions in this chapter is the emphasis on the development of the students' understanding of *self and society*. Young students need to have a growing sense of how they fit with the environment and with fellow citizens.

What is to be done? It is easy enough to tell teachers that the curriculum needs to be explored in depth or at a higher level of conceptualization. Teachers have been told that many times before. What teachers want and need to know before planning effectively for gifted children is *how* to explore at a higher level and what "depth" actually *means* in regard to a given problem or topic.

Instructional Principles

In a previous chapter, we discussed some of the major principles for instructing the gifted:

1. Teach to the highest cognitive level possible.
2. Teach gifted children to utilize all their thinking processes.
3. Teach important ideas about all aspects of their life and times.
4. Teach methods by which the gifted children can discover knowledge for themselves.

The difficulty of teaching higher-level concepts in this content field is similar to that found in the fields of mathematics and science. Unless students have a strong mastery of a core of knowledge, their ability to understand a generalization such as "the relationship of the mother country to the colony" will go unrecognized.

Kaplan provided three distinctively different dimensions of enrichment in the social studies, which she has recommended for a single structure for gifted students. These dimensions are *horizontal*, *vertical*, and *supplementary*, and bear a strong resemblance to the content-differentiation concepts (enrichment, sophistication, and novelty) used in this text.

> 1. *The horizontal dimension includes activities that provide further practice of learned skills, concepts, and generalizations. The focus is on application of acquired knowledge.... The gifted child studying the effects of news releases from various media sources on friends and family members, after studying a unit on "Man's Need to Communicate," is an example of this dimension within a particular social studies curriculum.*
> 2. *The vertical dimension includes activities that afford the gifted student with opportunities for learning beyond those considered to be basic or core of the curricular experience.... A gifted child who is assessing the effects of linguistic style within the black culture after participating in the unit on "Man's Need to Communicate" is an example of vertical enrichment.*

3. *The supplementary dimension is defined as the set of learning experiences that allows the child entry into areas usually omitted from the regular classroom.... The gifted child who is interested in electronics and pursues research on this subject after or while studying "Man's Need to Communicate" is acquiring supplementary experience. (1979, pp. 165–166)*

These conceptualizations match closely with this book's content differentiation categories: horizontal (enrichment), vertical (sophistication), and supplementary (novelty). Kaplan did not suggest that a major emphasis should be placed on the fourth area—acceleration (or speeding up the curriculum).

Content Acceleration

The structure of the social studies curriculum, including so many diverse domains of knowledge from history to psychology, makes it less likely that content acceleration will be a recommended strategy for differentiated programming. Nevertheless, many of the same reasons for considering content acceleration in mathematics and science applies as well in this area. World history can be presented in earlier grades so that gifted students can correlate the experiences across cultures with our own history. Such a topic as world history or world affairs can be distant and dry material, unless it is brought to life. One way to bring it to life is to engage the students as players in such a program as the Model United Nations.

Model United Nations
One of the problems with learning about governmental structures or political systems is that they seem so dry and unappealing when described in a textbook. A bland description of the different branches and functions of the Senate and the House of Representatives does not set a student on fire, nor does it adequately communicate the roles and relationships of our representative government. Gifted students, with their aversion to repetitive and rote kinds of learning, can quickly lose interest in history because of its emphasis on facts. Joe and Stephanie especially have become defensive about assignments like "name the capitals of all 50 states."

Simulations are an effective way to make some of the stultifyingly dull information presented in some social studies classes come to life. A particularly good example of a simulation that provides students with a meaningful context for learning content-specific information is the Model United Nations program. The Model UN is a nationwide simulation based on the issues and structure followed by the actual United Nations. Each year, a different issue is the focus of discussion and negotiation for participating schools. Students are selected for participation from within their own schools; usually a high grade point average and good speaking skills are included as criteria for participation.

Delegate teams from participating schools are assigned a country that they will later represent at a Model UN conference. The conferences are held at different locations throughout the United States. As many as 50,000 high school and college students participate in at least one of the 100 conferences annually. The function of the conference differs depending on the functions of the United Nations. Some conferences deal only with the functions of the UN Security Council, others deal with additional branches of the UN, in addition to the Security Council.

Preparation for the Model UN courses can be treated in different ways. Some schools treat the program as a cocurricular activity, others adapt courses in International Relations to parallel the issues selected by the Model UN each year. As students become engrossed in their roles as UN delegates, they learn about the philosophical and political positions of the country they represent. They additionally learn the procedures followed by the United Nations as it negotiates peaceful relationships and political stability between countries.

Hazleton and Mahroria, who have studied the effects of participation in Model UN programs, cite the following as the major advantages of having students participate in this kind of simulation:

> • *Having a format for practical application of political concepts and knowledge associated with international relations;*
> • *Learning first-hand the consequences of problems, solutions, and negotiations;*
> • *Active, not passive, learning of information; and*
> • *Motivation of intellectual curiosity which increases skills in cognitive strategies, reading and writing in the context of the issues under study. (1986, p. 151)*

In addition to these advantages of a change in educational context, these authors cite another report by Fletcher (1971), who offers several academic goals that students should achieve as a part of their experience in the Model UN. These goals include: "1) Knowledge of facts and principles... 2) Knowledge of the outcome of various strategies... 3) Knowledge of the structure of the underlying model of the game" (cited in Hazleton & Mahroria, 1986), as well as interpersonal skills in negotiation and persuasion and sophisticated manipulation of information associated with decision-making strategies. Surveys of Model UN student participants and faculty advisors indicate that both groups value most highly the enhanced knowledge and interest in International Relations and the firsthand experience in "practical politics" as the chief benefits of being a part of the Model UN.

Mr. Jenkins, in an effort to help students understand the real "ins and outs" of the governmental system, instituted his own simulation of a parliamentary procedure in his classroom as the students tried to develop a set of recommendations regarding the use of the school playground after school. The only rules that Mr. Jenkins required the students to use was that they followed the rules of parliamentary procedure to the letter—the students soon found that those were more than rules enough! Soon after they began their negotiations, students were coming up to Mr. Jenkins full of frustrations—Why did the government have to have so many restrictions as it developed laws and legislation? It made it so hard to get anything done! There were so many different points of view and compromises to be made! This, then, provided Mr. Jenkins with the perfect opportunity to teach the students about the purpose of the checks and balances that were built into our governmental structure—and the students were more than ready to learn!

The surprise that Mr. Jenkins got as he watched the gifted students in the class was that Sam emerged as the unexpected leader in the group. Soon after the class became engaged in the activity, Sam was "wheeling and dealing" with the other parties to try to work out special concessions and compromises. Although he had not really thought about it, Mr. Jenkins had created the perfect academic setting for Sam to apply some of the skills that he used on the streets as he negotiated the tricky territory of his neighborhood filled with disputed boundaries and power plays.

Other fields of study, such as economics, can be presented earlier—accelerated—so that these concepts can be used to enrich the gifted students' understanding of history and politics. Under ordinary circumstances, students will encounter economic concepts in some systematic fashion only in senior high school, if at all.

One such educational objective that the teacher of gifted elementary or junior high students could use in economics as a base for discussion and projects would be as follows: "The learner will know the historic development of economics and will compare and contrast contemporary economic systems in terms of their efficiency, the economic freedom of citizens, and the degree to which they are controlled by governments or small groups" (North Carolina Department of Public Instruction, 1979, p. 273). The ability to master such content is clearly within range of the upper elementary school gifted students and could be used as a springboard to higher-level conceptual understanding.

Content Enrichment

All students are expected to grasp ideas and concepts related to history and anthropology and think about how humanity has come to its present state. Gifted and talented students can explore more extensively into topic areas and gain additional understanding of the way in which various discoveries or developments have impacted our lives and culture. Because gifted students can more quickly master the traditional curriculum, there is a strong tendency to supplement that material with a rich mix of other available materials filled with facts and information so that the general principles are easier to perceive without the help of the teacher.

One specific example of many that could be chosen is presented by Burke (1978). He reviewed the early history of the British Isles to show how various developments modified and changed our ancestors. Burke pointed out that at the start of the thirteenth century there was a sudden change in climate in Europe, which has been referred to as the Little Ice Age; it caused great hardship to people who sought ways to survive severe weather. The first innovation to aid in that situation was the development of the *chimney*. Gifted students enjoy pursuing the various consequences that follow the introduction of such a novel addition to the social structure. They could, as Burke suggests, discover some of the following:

1. The chimney produced structural changes in the house. With the flue to conduct away sparks, the fire no longer had to be in the center of the room and the chimney could be used as a spine against which to support more than one room, and thus, could divide the structure into a variety of rooms, upstairs and downstairs.
2. There was a separation of social classes as a result, with those more privileged taking the better and warmer rooms upstairs, leaving the workers downstairs—perhaps the

beginning of the upstairs/downstairs separation of social classes in England. The Lord and Lady of the manor previously had eaten with the other nobles and workers; now they sought their own, warmer quarters.

3. The development of the chimney allowed more business to be conducted, by providing enough warmth to allow the paperwork to be continued in cold weather; this improved the commercial status of the farms and the workers.

4. The chimney and fireplace improved personal hygiene by providing for more comfort in bathing and encouraging the use of water for personal hygiene; it led to the development of lead conduits to begin to carry water to washbasins and privies.

5. Finally, the concept of romantic love was stimulated and encouraged by the fireplace. It introduced, for the first time, the concept of privacy by separating the large central room into different floors and separate rooms. Lovemaking became a personal, private, romantic activity. Nightdress also took the place of sleeping in one's clothes, which had been necessary in the earlier, chilly environment of the great hall. (pp. 158–161)

As Burke pointed out, and as the students can easily discern for themselves, not all of the changes that take place through the introduction of technology are necessarily positive. The separation into separate social classes here may be listed as one of the mixed benefits. Burke concluded, "The ties between the classes that had been expressed in the act of sleeping together before a common fire each night were broken. The tightly knit, agriculturally-based feudal world had gone up the chimney" (1978, p. 161).

Anthropology

Most social studies curricula are designed to introduce students, at one time or another, to the origins of humankind. For gifted students, this can be a topic of fascination that they may wish to pursue in some breadth. Situated in unwitting juxtaposition on the shelf in Cranshaw's bedroom there are carefully constructed models of a prehistoric brontosaurus and the *Enterprise*, from the "Star Trek" TV series. To dismiss this unlikely combination by saying that Cranshaw has broad interests does not do justice to the significance of these models. Cranshaw, through his intellectual talents, has the ability to transport himself to other times and other places. His ability to use verbal symbols as tools to create in his imagination past events, or future possibilities, or the land of fantasy enables him to be responsive to adventures that take him traveling from the present to the past, to the future, or to pure fantasy.

The more intelligent a student is, the more likely he or she will speculate on the origin of humans and what it is like to live in other places and times. Not surprisingly, such a student will be intrigued by subjects such as early history and anthropology and will be thrilled by the detective storylike assemblage of clues about our early origins.

Some teachers have found a device that brings home to the gifted students the strategies and approaches of the anthropologist: They suggest the students pretend to be future anthropologists, and ask them to deduce what they might know about our current culture from artifacts they recover from that culture. Suppose, for example, these future anthropologists encountered a soft-drink bottle, an old newspaper, and a tennis shoe. Students then would be asked to speculate on what could be learned from such objects.

Some of the common answers that one might expect from the soft-drink bottle would be that the culture had a high state of manufacturing efficiency in order to create glass bottles. If the label was still on the bottle, they could deduce by noting the ingredients listed on the label that we were concerned about the material we ingest. They could also discern, by the fact that we were ingesting liquid that does not seem strictly needed, that this culture was in a relative state of affluence. The old newspaper could be a gold mine, charting humanity's conflicts and follies. Students would discover in the newspaper our intense interest in sports, recreation, and amusement. The old tennis shoe could provide some indication of footwear in use at that time, and the sophisticated manufacturing process necessary to produce such an article. The possible physique and stature of human beings from that period could be estimated by the size and shape of the shoe.

Concurrent with these deductions, students could be introduced to some of the problems of the anthropologists. For example, if the old tennis shoe happened to belong to a professional basketball player, then the estimates of the stature of human beings in the era might be substantially incorrect. The assumption that the artifact may be typical of the era is one that can lead to incorrect generalization.

The students could then be asked to take on an individual project by looking in their own trash can to see what three or four artifacts they could find, and what they thought such objects would tell future anthropologists about who lived here, what their interests were, how they were organized in social groups, and what might have become of them. Such a task would teach the students how anthropologists reconstruct the distant, or the more immediate, past.

The students could then be led to a study of other people and settings, such as the natives of the Kalahari Desert. First, students would be introduced to a map of an archaeological digging that shows the position of the discovery of artifacts and the nature of the artifacts. The students then would be expected to speculate on their possible meaning. Students would be asked to think about what new data are needed to reach valid conclusions about climate, water supply, and so on. Slides that describe the physical environment surrounding the Kalahari Desert could provide additional information. Putting these bits of information together, students might make the following conclusions:

> The people of the Kalahari existed in small family groups that survived on hunting and mongongo nuts.
>
> They hunted with bows and arrows and spears.
>
> They made objects of the bones and shells.
>
> They ground meal of sorts with mortars and pestles.
>
> They had some religious ceremonies and dancing.

Further information could be provided with readings or visual aids of what is already known about the bushmen in the Kalahari. The additional data may force some revision of the earlier guesses or hypotheses—a useful antidote to bright students whose ability to spin off plausible answers to puzzles sometimes outruns their devotion to seeking data to prove or disprove their hunches.

Some of the basic ideas to be grasped by the students in their study of anthropology would be:

1. The environment as an important limiting factor in determining and controlling cultural characteristics, especially of huntering/gathering peoples
2. The beginning of the idea that cultures are adaptations to circumstances
3. An idea of the limits of archaeological interpretations reached in the consideration of artifacts, unless their symbolic meaning is understood and they are viewed in context with other data

The Study of Famous Documents

There are some key documents in American history that sum up much of what we stand for as a nation: the Constitution, the Bill of Rights, the Gettysburg Address, Roosevelt's Four Freedoms address, and so on. Most U.S. students come into casual contact with such documents. They know the documents exist, they may even be able to quote some passages from them, but they know very little about what is in them—what the context was that brought forth such elegant language.

One reason for such lack of knowledge seems to be the pressure of time on the teachers to cover all of the material for which they are responsible. For the average or below-average student, covering the language of these documents would require a good deal of time; for example, what is meant by "abridging the freedom of speech," "peaceable assembly," "redress of grievances," "forescore," or "self-evident truths"? Teachers could spend much of their allotted time just making sure that the students understood *what* the document actually said, without ever getting into a useful discussion about what the document really *meant*, then or now.

The same is not true of gifted students, however. They can quickly learn the words that they do not know, and are then ready to discuss the meaning of the documents. There is hardly anything more important for citizens to understand than the base of government upon which the United States stands. A resource room unit, a special class program, an honors program, or a special interest group in the middle school could, therefore, focus on the meaning of this nation's precious documents. Students would soon understand that documents are more than merely objects placed behind a hermetically sealed chamber in Washington, DC.

Table 6–1 indicates how the First Amendment of the Bill of Rights might be the key discussion point in a program for gifted students. In this instance, the discussion would revolve around the following question: Are there any limits to all of our freedoms or are they absolute and not to be abridged under any circumstances? Few of the students have thought about limitations to their freedoms.

Indeed, Joe is anxious to discuss why his parents have violated his rights of freedom from search and seizure by invading his bedroom and removing some compact discs that they felt were obnoxious and obscene. Joe thinks that his parents were attacking the Constitution with their invasion—another interesting discussion point.

TABLE 6-1   The Limits of Our Freedoms?

First Amendment	*Boundaries of Freedom?*
Congress shall make no law respecting an establishment of religion or prohibiting the free exercise thereof...	1. Suppose one of the beliefs of a particular religion is to crush all "false" religions? 2. Suppose a religion believes that only God cures one of illness, so no medicine or hospitalization is to be used?
or abridging the freedom of speech...	1. What does "no one has a right to yell 'FIRE' in a crowded theater" mean? 2. Should I be allowed to say that all Chinese people should be "sent back to China"?
or of the press...	1. Do I have a right to lie about someone else in a magazine article? 2. Can I publish military secrets?
or of the right of the people peaceably to assemble, and to petition the government for a redress of grievances.	1. Can I block traffic to protest higher taxes? 2. Can I sue the government for misusing public land?

Sampling Time Periods

The growing impossibility of covering the world's history, or even a nation's history, in a chronological style has become increasingly apparent. Such an approach can cover, only in a superficial form, the major events that happened within a given time period. One cannot go into depth on *why* such events happened, or what forces were at work to make them happen (World War II, for example), because of the time constraints and the need to cover so much other material.

For gifted students, another strategy has emerged that can make historical study more intriguing and valuable. This strategy consists of taking a narrow band of time in history, say from 1770 to 1790 in the United States, and studying that time period in depth. (See the problem-based learning, discussed in Chapter 5.) This would mean that the students would not only know the major events that occurred in that time period but would study the economy, culture, and social values of the times—in short, to gain an appreciation of the entire setting and the interacting forces at work to create the events.

This approach to curriculum is similar to sinking a shaft deep into a piece of land, and extracting a core of the earth, looking for geological information or hunting for oil. A detailed study of that narrow shaft of land will hopefully give the geologist a better understanding of the entire area of land. Similarly, by studying a narrow historical era with intensity, students will gain an understanding of the political and economic forces that may be at work in any era. The gifted students can then test out these ideas of the influence of major political or social forces by applying them to a different era in history.

For instance, by understanding that unrestricted power leads to excess in the treatment of others, such as King George III exemplified in revolutionary times, students can gain a better understanding of the importance of the Bill of Rights in constraining the unrestricted use of power by the government in the U.S. Constitution. The students can also realize why it is equally as important to restrict that power in 1999, or whatever, as it was during that earlier time period of 1860. One of the barriers to the use of time sampling turns out to be the knowledge base of the teacher.

Social Studies

With the many exhortations to teachers to stress thinking processes and higher-order thinking on the part of students, why are so many classrooms still lacking in stimulation and excitement? That was the question asked by Onosko (1991), who interviewed 56 social studies teachers nationwide from 16 separated secondary school departments. The department heads and principals of those schools were also interviewed.

What were the barriers to the promotion of higher-order thinking? The teachers identified (1) the need for content coverage and the consequent superficiality of the coverage, (2) large numbers of students to be taught, (3) lack of teacher planning time, and (4) culture of teacher isolation. Onosko found, in his interviews, that the teachers felt strongly that they needed to provide broad coverage for the subject matter despite the urging of scholars to take a narrow slice of history and use it to explore higher-order concepts. A hidden problem of many teachers is their concern that their own knowledge might not stretch to cover a topic in detail.

Geography

One of the school subjects that has tremendous, and generally unused, potential in encouraging interdisciplinary investigations is geography. In its proper study of the interaction of social and natural sciences, it can bring together biology, sociology, history, and so on. Instead, it has too often been seen as a dull and unimaginative recitation of state capitals and physical characteristics of countries. Students of advanced abilities, whether in regular classrooms or special class settings, can face such challenging problems as the effects of population increases or the impact of pollution on their own towns and states.

William Ward, a geographer for the U.S. State Department, has a list of four important "don'ts" in geography instruction. They also provide guidance as to what should be the real geography curriculum:

1. Don't confuse geography with location memorization. *Some of the questions geography students should be encouraged to think and write about would include how their parents or grandparents came to reside where they do, and how land uses in their neighborhood, city, and country have changed over the past several decades.*
2. Don't limit geography to map making. *Cartography, the art and science of map making, is undergoing mind-boggling leaps with the assistance of computer-generated graphics. But more important than plugging into the latest mapping program is proper guidance on how to use a map to tell a story or solve a problem.*
3. Don't get hung up on defining "geography." *One of geography's long-standing goals has been to bridge the schism between social and natural*

sciences. Long before ecology *became a household word, geographers were studying the dynamic relationship between people and their environments.*

4. Don't forget that geography is integrative. *We'll talk to anybody who can help us better understand the complex interplay of people and places, particularly now—when our world is faced with so many difficult challenges. More than any set of learned facts, this multidisciplinary perspective on issues that span from the local to the global is the most valuable geography lesson of all. (Ward, 1992, p. 28)*

Geography has been one of five areas singled out for special attention in the National Goals for Education (*America 2000*). The other areas are math, science, social studies, and language arts. The reason for such attention probably stems from some of the earlier results of the National Assessment of Educational Progress, which seemed to indicate a widespread ignorance of even the simplest geographic knowledge (e.g., being able to find France on the map of Europe or locating one's own state on an outline map of the United States). Such ignorance in the students of the nation that thinks of itself as the leader in the world in so many areas is a matter of considerable embarrassment for public policymakers, as well as the teachers and pupils. The mere presence of maps or jigsaw puzzles of the world apparently is not sufficient to get this knowledge across, even with our brightest of students.

It is unlikely and undesirable that we will retreat to teaching geography as an isolated subject, where students learn state capitals, major mountain ranges, and so on. Surely it will be integrated into lessons on history and economics. It is an enrichment topic that can easily be added in a resource room setting or in a cluster grouping within the regular classroom.

One example of how to teach the interaction of geography with human behavior is to present gifted students with a map of a country with which they are relatively unfamiliar (e.g., Rumania) that provides the major rivers, mountains, longitude and latitude, and other natural characteristics, and then to ask the students to place on that map the major cities and rail lines that they *expect* to be present. The students can then check their judgment against reality and find out more about how the natural characteristics of the country helped to form the communication lines and major centers of populations.

The field of social studies is so broad and diverse that there is a problem of selecting material from an almost unmanageable pool of knowledge that is constantly growing and changing. Whatever is chosen has to be selected for its generalizability, as well as its own interest and character. That is, the Age of Exploration may be chosen not just because it is an interesting period in the development of human potential but because we can learn about the merging of cultures, the clash between the status quo and the "explorers," and so forth. There are explorers today in the various fields of human knowledge, and these individuals have to cope with the status quo in their fields, just as the early explorers of the globe had to cope with the "flat earth" supporters.

This topic of exploration can lead to a dozen interesting avenues and can, thus, justify the time it takes to develop it. Time is the most precious of all teacher commodities, and it needs to be reserved for important educational goals as much as possible.

Global Awareness

The recent collapse of the former Soviet Union has eliminated one major purpose of our definition as a nation: "to oppose international Communism." Our preoccupation with the possible massive conflict with the Soviet Union blotted out our concern about what other goals we might have. If war is the failure to reach an accommodation between conflicting goals and values between two nations, then shouldn't our gifted students be studying social conflicts, their causes, and their solutions? Many people have suggested that global awareness should be a part of the curriculum (Roeper, 1988; Passow, 1988). Passow stated the following:

> *As an integral part of their education, we must sensitize gifted students and youth to the major problems our world societies face—among them poverty, famine, war and nuclear annihilation, racial/tribal conflict, depletion of resources, environmental pollution, cultural conflict, personal and communal health, genetic changes, population growth, employment, and quality of life. (1988, p. 13)*

In addition, we must teach them to use the many tools that we have within our means to combat these problems, lest the students dissolve into a pool of depression. We have advanced tools in conflict resolution techniques, in agricultural research, in democratic governmental structures, in institutions such as the Red Cross and the United Nations, and in advanced technologies that improve communications between different peoples.

The presence of weapons of mass destruction—rather than making war attractive to those who seek power, a name in history, or revenge against their neighbors—is actually forcing people to find alternative ways of dealing with conflict; the cost of failure to reach accommodation has become too high. To the paranoid leader who wishes his name to go down in history (consider that Adolf Hitler, for all his many faults, is remembered, whereas those who struggled for peace in his generation are forgotten), a nuclear war carries with it the threat that his name—along with his people, their history, and their land—will disappear in a mushroom cloud, which is hardly the way to erect a permanent monument to oneself.

Thornton Wilder's play, *The Skin of Our Teeth*, would make an interesting combination with such a unit of global concerns. The theme of the play is how we humans have narrowly escaped disaster at many times in our history—in fact, by the skin of our teeth—but we continue to persevere.

Content Sophistication

The search for larger ideas and complex systems is as clear a goal in social studies as in the sciences and mathematics. The problem lies in the complex interrelationship of forces at work to form the pattern or system.

Leadership

When the definition of giftedness was modified by the Marland report, the concept of *leadership* was included in the definition along with creativity and the visual and performing arts. But what is leadership? Is there only one kind or are there many?

Diversity in leadership styles from one setting or situation to another was raised in Chapter 2, but there do seem to be enough elements in common about leadership, in whatever context, to study it as a classroom topic. This is a topic that can well be of interest to gifted students. Just as we teach the mechanisms of how to be a scientist in order to educate gifted students in patterns of scientific behavior, so we can teach leadership in an effort to interest them in the essential elements of how to lead.

Gallagher, Oglesby, Stern, Caplow, Courtright, Fulton, Guiton, and Langenbach (1982) devised a leadership unit designed for the use of teachers in resource rooms or analogous settings. The goal of the team—composed of academicians and teachers of gifted students—that produced the unit was to present important concepts on leadership, determined by the academicians by a series of activities prepared for upper-elementary gifted students by their teachers. Common definitions of leadership and power were derived: "Leadership was defined as the exercise of power or influence in social collectivities, such as groups, organizations, communities or nations, to meet the needs of the group; and power was defined as getting someone or a group of people to do something that they would not ordinarily do" (p. 8).

The concepts that represented content sophistication in the instructional objectives of the teachers were the following:

1. *Leadership is the exercise of power to achieve the goals of the leader or the leader and followers.*
2. *Influence is the use of persuasion to achieve change; power is the use of force to achieve change.*
3. *There are many different types of leaders who play different roles (traditional, legal, charismatic, active/passive, positive/negative).*
4. *Different leaders are needed to meet different circumstances (establishing goals, creating structures to reach goals, maintaining or enhancing these structures).*
5. *There are many ways to become a leader. (Gallagher et al., 1982, p. 12)**

Another goal for the unit was to focus on the human feelings of the leader, to encourage students to place themselves in the leader's place with questions such as, "What do leaders worry about?" Other questions are noted here.

1. Will I make a serious mistake and ruin the entire enterprise? *The exercise of power, which is the essence of much leadership, is not without its negative consequences; for example, an incorrect decision may have disastrous consequences for which the leader will be held responsible (conscientious leaders will hold themselves responsible).*
2. Will I represent my group well in the inevitable conflict, crisis, or competition with which the group will meet? *Whatever the leadership position, the*

---

*This list and the next list are from *Leadership Unit: The Use of Teacher-Scholar Teams to Develop Units for the Gifted* (pages 8 and 12, respectively) by J. Gallagher et al., 1982, New York: Trillium Press. Copyright 1982 by Trillium Press. Adapted by permission.

time will inevitably come when the leader is forced to defend or put forth the interests of that group in conflict with others. It becomes important, then, for the leader to defend the interests of the group well. Most leaders have self-doubts, sometimes well hidden, about their own effectiveness and capabilities in this regard.

3. Do I have sufficient authority to carry out the responsibilities I have? *In a democratic government based on the principle of separation of powers, many political leaders concern themselves with whether they have the authority to carry out their tasks. While one naturally thinks of the President in this regard, such a concern could just as easily be felt by a principal of an elementary school, who feels a multitude of responsibilities but whose authority may be severely limited by the central administration and the school board.*

4. Do I have the time I need to get the job done? *When the leaders are elected officials, there is a natural time deadline, which causes those individuals to watch the calendar continually or look over their shoulders to see if the tasks they wish to accomplish during their term can be completed. Other leadership positions have real time limitations. The age of the leader and his or her personal health often become major concerns, whether discussed or not. As leaders grow older, they inevitably must worry about whether they will be given sufficient time by God or by fate to finish what they started. They often tend to cling tenaciously to the leadership position until they have done what they wanted to do.*

5. Who will follow me in this position? *Many leaders who have worked very hard to achieve certain objectives and goals are reluctant to turn over the reins of power to someone else whose commitment to those goals may be suspect. Thus, one can observe many leaders generating elaborate schemes that ensure some type of succession to guarantee the continuation of the same policy. Otherwise, the deposed leader may see all of his or her efforts undone by the new leadership.*

6. How will I be viewed now or in the future? *Whether we speak of the chairperson of the city council, the head of the League of Women Voters, or the president a local labor union, few leaders are ignorant of their place in history or indifferent as to how their stewardship will be viewed later on. Many of the decisions they make do not have the present in mind, but rather how their future image will be reflected. (Gallagher et al., 1982, pp. 60–61)*

If the students can gain, through illustration and discussion, a degree of empathy for the leaders, along with a sense of joy at the accomplishments that come when they are successful, then the students may even wish to emulate those leaders.

Another example of content sophistication might come from raising the typical discussion of our early American history to a larger and more sophisticated set of concepts. In this way, gifted students not only gain appreciation for their heritage but also gain an appreciation of larger elements of group and social behavior. For example, one can teach a detailed description about the Pilgrims and what happened to them, or one can

FIGURE 6-1   Student Ideas about Colonization[*]

1. Colonization is a time and place where a section of land is under the control of a larger country. This period is not usually more than 100 to 150 years long. It is usually a period in which the colony has very little or nothing to say and has few rights in governing itself. These people sometimes have to give a large section of their earnings to the country that rules them. There is no specific era to which colonization is confined. Colonies can be made at any time.

2. Colonization is an establishment in an undeveloped land brought about by help from a country toward finance and support. If people in the colony do not like its system of government or other things, they can rebel. The colony has many undiscovered natural resources and dangerous diseases or hostile natives. Sometimes it is inhabited by convicts or people seeking a land of free religion.

3. Colonization is when a country takes possession of unclaimed or claimed land and rules it. Where the colonial land is located does not matter as long as it is ruled by a country. A colony can be made any time. Most colonies were founded because of something that the mother country could get out of it—such as crops, mineral wealth, escaping religious persecution, etc. The colony usually was governed by the mother country or one man appointed by the mother country. The mother country usually got some of the benefits of the economy.

4. What makes a colony is that a group of people from a certain country go to a new, partially unsettled, country and build their homes and a community in a certain place. As they build their communities, they form ways of living, farming, mining, etc., and build a settlement. The government can be self-ruled, or ruled by the mother country. The economy depends on how it is ruled. If it is the mother country, the products are liable to be exported to her.

[*]Excerpts from a teacher assignment to present the broader meaning of colonization.

discuss those facets general to all colonization. It is the teacher who is the key to the level of complexity and thought considered in the classroom.

Following is a brief dialogue from a junior high social studies classroom. The teacher has presented the problem of what kinds of generalizations one can make about colonies, and, starting from the traditional discussion of the American colonies, has broadened it to help the students think at the higher or generalization level about the overall topic of *colony*, as illustrated by Figure 6–1.

Teacher: If you were to describe to someone what a colony was or what the term *colonialism* means, going back to our first day's discussion, what would you say about the time element? Mark?

Mark:[*] Countries were beginning to desire to have land in this area, now that it had been explored and they knew what it was like. There was no certain time limit, as the

[*] This student has already shown advanced conceptualization of the concept of colony in being able to divorce it from a specific time and place.

colonization period in Africa started as soon as it was partially explored. The same was true in North America and in South America.

Cranshaw: Well, I think what you meant was that to define a colony—a colony does not have to exist in any certain year or period of years to be a colony. But, it seems to me that colonies come in sort of waves. The Roman colonization, which is now Europe, colonized lots of these countries. And now the Soviet Union—it's a different type of colonization. They're satellites but it's definitely a type of colonization because they control them.

Teacher: I think this is a very interesting notion. This is sort of the Cranshaw Wave Theory of Colonization. This is worth investigating further, Cranshaw—see if you can pin down your theory down a little bit.

Leland: Well, I don't think that the place in *itself* is important, but I think indirectly it's important. It seems to me that the colonies that have the best natural resources and the best climate—closest to what it was in the mother country where the colonists came from— were the ones where the colonists achieved independence the soonest. For example, the United States was one of the first colonies in the hemisphere to get its independence and we have tremendous natural resources. And gradually, the colonies that don't have such good natural resources are now getting their independence. I think natural resources definitely help, because if they don't have natural resources, they have to depend on the mother countries, so they can't really revolt and be successful.

Curtis: I'll tell you another thing that is important in colonization: natural habitats. If there were a lot of jungle animals or maybe a lot of dangerous malaria or mosquitoes and things like that, it wouldn't be ideal for a colony, no matter what kind of geographical structure.

In addition to seeking a high level of generalization, the teacher would be interested in helping the gifted students generate a wide variety of thinking processes. As stated in the earlier chapters, it is fairly common in all classrooms to include the operations of description and explanation, but it is much rarer to find extensive use of the mental operations of evaluation or expansion (divergent thinking). The gifted need practice and guidance in making judgments on the relative importance, usefulness, and correctness of an event—in other words, in evaluation. Sometimes the evaluation takes the form of judging whether a particular idea fits a set of criteria. In the case of this particular classroom, once a generalization was reached, the issue would be whether the idea can be tested or matched by comparing a specific instance against the generalization—with a judgment made as to goodness of fit. The following is a dialogue along those particular lines:

Teacher: We agreed that today we ought to take up this business of the economic forces affecting a colonial area. I ran into this statement, and I would like you to consider it in light of the information that you have found. A statement of the record is: "The basic purpose of colonization is to increase the economic well-being of the homeland" (writes on board). Now, let's test this today by bringing together some data that you have. Who has a colonial situation that they've investigated that points to a contradiction of this statement? Sara?

Sara: Well, Massachusetts isn't—it was started in 1620?—and, well, for almost 50 years it had nothing or little to do with the homeland. And they backed it with mostly their own money. And then they finally took over. But, for a long time, it was almost like a separate country—and it's just a colony, more or less.

Teacher: All right. Now, why was the colony of Massachusetts established? Was it a commercial company or was it...

Sara: Yes, it was a commercial company. The people stressed that they wanted to worship in their own way. It was basically for economic reasons, and, of course, the thing that they wanted was to worship freely, although they didn't give that right to other people.

Teacher: If they did have an economic purpose, apparently it doesn't match this statement that the people of Massachusetts were not concerned about improving the well-being of the homeland?

Sara: No.

Teacher: Who else knows of a colony that you think presents an exception to this hypothesis? Bryan?

Bryan: Well, Greenland. Greenland does not help the homeland, but the homeland helps Greenland.

Leland: Well, with Greenland, we don't think there's anything there and there isn't anything much there that we can get to. But in a few years—with the way science is moving—we still don't know what's under that ice. The way science is moving now, we could probably make things that could get underneath the ice—well, heat making it melt, or something like that. So I think they probably colonized Greenland just because they thought that someday they might be able to get to use it.

Katie: (dubiously) In the 600s?

Mark: Well, I had New England—the Plymouth Colony. And the reason for settling there was purely for the freedom of religion. Well, they could have gotten freedom of religion over in Holland. But they wanted a place where they could keep their own customs, where other customs and other manners couldn't influence their children and such. And so they came to America for these reasons.[*]

Teacher: All right, let's accept that for the moment as a fact. Can we in any way stretch this, or *should* we try to stretch this to fall within the domain of this statement? Bill?

---

[*]In the process of trying to answer this basic question, the students have absorbed many facts—but it is not fact gathering for its own sake; rather, it is the use of facts to solve a problem.

Bill: If somebody is rich and they feed more people and they try to help a number of people leave England, so that there are less people to feed, then the government gets more.

Teacher: If we look at this from the standpoint of the homeland, as you have, then perhaps they were glad to reduce the number of dissatisfied or unemployed, or something of that sort.

Bill: And you could cut down on the number of soldiers you have, just to keep these Puritans from leaving.

Sara: Well, I have some conflicting evidence that people came over purely for freedom of religion. I read in this encyclopedia—I'm not saying that it's right or wrong—that the issue of freedom of religion was probably overstressed a great deal and that it was probably just as much, if not more, economic reasons. Because there was colonizing groups.

Leland: Well, I have something to say about the freedom of religion being the sole reason.

Teacher: All right. Go ahead.

Leland: Well, if this was the only reason—the freedom of religion—then why didn't Great Britain want to give the colonies their freedom when we asked for it? Why did they line up so many of their soldiers and try to put down the revolution when they could have just let us go anyway—unless they had some reason of their own?

Such discussions can then culminate in an assignment for the students to try to present the broader meaning of colonization, as shown in Figure 6–1.

One of the ways to intrigue gifted students is to present them with a large idea—some major law or generalization—and ask them to find information to confirm or reject that large idea. An example of a set of such large ideas that will drive much of the next few decades can be seen in Figure 6–2. These trends represent a consensus of ideas from teachers in one school system (a similar task could yield a similar list from any group of observant adults). What are the implications of the shift from an industrial to an information and service work force? What are the consequences for all of us if the work continues to become more globally interdependent? Students will be particularly interested in the different family models and their personal and social implications, especially since there may be many variations on the family in their own classroom.

Each of these questions could develop into a unit of four to six weeks, with students pursuing and reporting on the many different possible lines of consequences and implications. It is even more interesting to these students, since the immediate future is the one in which they will have to live and try to prosper. Each of the trends in Figure 6–2 has widespread impact on education and society and represents a curriculum of the future based on the trends of today.

Just as interesting to students are the considerations of what would happen if conditions were different, or what the future might be like if the ideas they have developed are applied. This stimulates use of the knowledge available to them and, as they exercise their own intellectual abilities, creates in them excitement and enthusiasm.

FIGURE 6–2   Curriculum for the New Millennium

- The world of work will be characterized by a continued shift from an industrial work force to an information and service work force.
- Technology will play a major role in almost all segments of the work force. Tomorrow's workers will need skills and attitudes different from those of today's workers.
- The population that the educational system will serve will be quite different from today's population. It will be more ethnic and paradoxically both younger and older.
- The world will continue to become more globally interdependent.
- The American family will continue to be diverse. No single family type will represent the majority of Americans.
- Our society will demand an even more convenient lifestyle, expecting all institutions to deliver their services with ease and speed.
- The locus of control in education will continue to shift from the federal to the state level and from the central office to the building level. Decision making within school districts will be shared more with teachers.
- A shortage of qualified teachers and administrators will necessitate alternative approaches to training, recruiting, and certifying professional educators.
- Alternatives to public education will continue to grow in popularity and to gain public support.
- The number, frequency, and complexity of values questions confronting educators will increase dramatically.

Source: Hay, L., & Roberts, A. (1988). *Curriculum for the new millenium.* Fairfield, CT: CASCD. Reprinted by permission.

The discovery of major generalizations about economics or history are rarely aided by an indiscriminate flood of information. The mass of information regarding human history often tends to disguise, rather than reveal, major patterns or themes to which we want our gifted students to attend.

The Waves of Human Progress, presented by Toffler (see Table 6–2) in his *The Third Wave* (1980) presents major movements that have shaped human progress. Although any of these broad and sweeping conceptualizations can be contested, they allow for reflection on the interrelationship of factors in human progress. The shift from agricultural to industrial development can be focused on by examining the change in the family from a nuclear unit to one where the breadwinner(s) had to leave the home and often travel long distances to get to work.

The inability of parents to provide immediate supervision of their children, as they did in the Agricultural Era, is only one of the various consequences of such changes. The students can chart such changes, as well as the new transportation and communication systems that evolved because they were made necessary by the need to move goods from producer to consumer.

The new Information Age is one in which the gifted students themselves sit on the threshold. Will Toffler's view of the " electronic cottage," where the essential work will be done in one's own home by means of easy access to ultra-sophisticated electronic

TABLE 6–2   Developing Waves of Human Progress

	Major Activity	*Consequences*
Wave I (4000 BC–1700 AD)	Agriculture	• Blending of production and consumption • Large nuclear families • Human and animal power • Decentralized economy • Self-sufficient communities
Wave II (1700s–2000s AD)	Industrial Development	• Separation of production site from consumption site • Pools of capital—corporations • Majority rule—representative government • Workers—repetitive work, punctuality, obedience • Enormous use of energy sources • Systems of distribution and communication • Smaller families
Wave III (2000 AD)	Information Age	• Minority power—reduction of majority rule • Semi-direct democracy—Electronic voting • Reallocation of decision-making—local, state, national • Workplace—Electronic cottage, decentralized production • Worldwide Electronic communication system • Prosumer—balance between work and productive leisure

Source: From *The Third Wave* by Alvin Toffler. Copyright © 1980 by Alvin Toffler. Used by permission of Bantam Books, a division of Bantam Doubleday Dell Publishing Group, Inc.

computers, come to be? Will we once again center family life around the home and all be part of a massive communication system linking us to libraries, decision makers, and so on? How will the job market change? What new jobs will appear? What old ones will vanish?

These are topics of grand concern with enormous consequences—topics right down the alley of most gifted students eager to think about the unfolding world of their tomorrow. A variety of units can be developed around the effects of advancing technology, the changing workplace, the new communication systems, and the like, which make for very attractive natural small group projects.

Content Novelty

There are innumerable possibilities for content novelty in the broad field of social studies. Such choices should be made not merely on the basis of student interest but should meet standards of importance and continuity as well.

Conflict Resolution

One of the newly developing areas of interest in social science is conflict resolution. The idea behind such a study is that we can profit from a careful analysis of how we choose to resolve conflicts. It is in the nature of human beings to be in conflict with their families, friends, perceived enemies, and others, through larger organizations and political units. Our history books document our various failures to resolve conflicts without the use of violence. In great detail many of these volumes follow military campaigns, the ebb and flow of battles, and so forth. There is rarely such documentation of the development of peace treaties, labor arbitrations, or political compromises.

Above all, there is little attempt to teach the ability to resolve issues so that both parties in the conflict feel somewhat satisfied with the resolution. The seeds of further conflicts are often sown by the resolution of a present clash. For example, it is widely thought that World War II owed some of its origins to the Versailles Treaty, which resolved World War I but humiliated the losers and raised a generation that harbored, and finally acted on, feelings of revenge.

When Cranshaw was 6 or 7 years old, he went through a period when he and some of his friends would play with toy soldiers. They would construct and act out battles. The noise of such encounters sometimes became overwhelming, and Cranshaw's mother on one occasion lost her temper with the din and intruded on one of the battles. "You are always playing war," she exclaimed. "Why must you always fight, fight, fight, and kill each other all the time?" The boys were startled by this unaccustomed outburst. Soberly, Cranshaw said, "How do you play peace, mother?" There was a long thoughtful pause, and Cranshaw's mother retreated to the living room to mull this one over.

This incident later became one of the staples of family conversation, when parents get together to exchange the clever sayings of their children, but Cranshaw's question is still a good one—one that is deserving of attention by the educational community.

Interdisciplinary Study

Another area of novelty that has become increasingly popular deals with topics or units that are interdisciplinary in nature. Such topics show the students how various subject areas can interweave with one another.

The call for curriculum units that cut across disciplines stems from the recognition that it is important that gifted students can see the conceptual linkage and association across fields such as biology, chemistry, psychology, and sociology. If one great talent of gifted students is to be able to see relationships, then this talent should be taken advantage of in the special and differentiated curriculum that they would experience.

The Study of the Future

Another area gaining popularity as a content novelty is *futurism*. Recently, Joe came home and told his father that he was beginning to study a new topic in school—the future. Joe's father became visibly upset. He often became upset at the school, which he considered to be filled with incompetents. He became particularly angry at what he considered another example of fuzzy-headed thinking, of trying to study something that hasn't yet happened when the students don't even know about the Revolutionary War and the Civil War. He said, "How can you study something where you can't even grade the student on correctness?" What Joe's father does not understand is that the future contains the opportunity to teach interaction of forces, consequences, and sequential relationships.

Joe's father asked the question that is asked in more temperate terms by others: Why, indeed, study the future? The purpose of the study of the future is to anticipate the consequences of current trends. Many current trends in dimensions such as world population and erosion of natural resources seem to possess the potential for a large number of future problems, and the understanding of these trends can be the first step in trying to prevent undesirable consequences. As was discussed in Joe's class, our world is certain to run out of oil sometime in the not-too-distant future. We have the potential for space travel and for a major expansion in robotics. These probable changes will have a deep impact on the lives of children now growing up. Those children capable of thinking about these complex ideas should have the opportunity to explore them systematically.

An additional interesting concept from the futurist approach is the *wild card*. When we are making our future projections, we are basing them on current knowledge and trends. We do not often anticipate a totally different and unexpected event—the wild card—that would completely revamp our ideas about ourselves. Past and present wild cards would include the discovery of penicillin, the atomic bomb, AIDS, or jet engines. Each of these discoveries changed much of the world in which they were introduced, and probably made grossly inaccurate those predictions and forecasts in health, politics, and transportation that were constructed prior to their entry upon the scene.

But there are always wild cards in our future—some more foreseeable than others—and gifted students might well speculate on some likely wild cards that could be coming up and their potential effect. Examples are a reliable and universally available and acceptable birth-control method, and a new strain of grain that could grow in the desert regions. Such exercises should not be seen as a relaxing game, but as a serious attempt to try to anticipate the type of future world in which the students will live.

Another example of content novelty is presented by Whaley (1984). Many of the insights or understandings we would hope gifted students to reach involve issues and situations where the degree of complexity is such that it is difficult to master the central ideas or concepts. The example shown in Figure 6–3 accomplishes the task of simplifying an extraordinarily complex situation into a cognitively manageable one in which the students can apply their own understandings and perspective. By proportionately reducing the world population to a village of 1,000 people, Whaley has helped to bring into sharp perspective some of the issues facing the United States in its relationship with its world neighbors and has provided a base for some important discussion. The students can now gain some insight into why the United States as a nation is not universally loved or admired, but is envied by other countries that are less fortunate.

Whaley identified four goals for using future studies:

1. *Developing the skills and concepts necessary to understand complex systems*
2. *Developing more sophisticated and positive ways of thinking about possibilities for the future*
3. *Understanding the nature of change in developing a means for coping with rapid change*

4. *Developing abilities which help students identify and understand major issues which will shape the future (1984, pp. 5–6)*

One of the favorite devices for presenting alternative futures is through the medium of *science fiction*—a favorite reading topic for many gifted students. By creating an imaginary future, one can explore the possible effects on human beings and their societies through some major change or shift (e.g., the development of extrasensory perception, or the discovery of an alien race, or the ability to travel through time). These can be extraordinarily rich sources for discussion when propelled by authors such as Isaac Asimov, Poul Anderson, Arthur C. Clarke, Ursula LeGuin, and many others who use the future to call our attention to changing environments and their effects on people.

FIGURE 6–3　The Kettering Exercise

Objective:　To illustrate to students the imbalances of the current world order.
Process:　Present students with the following information and point of view from the Findlay-Kettering Committee on International Awareness Fact Sheet.

Food for Thought

If all the world were a village of 1,000 people:

- Imagine that we could compress the world's present population of over three billion persons into one town of 1,000 people, in exactly the same proportions.
- In such a town, there would be only 70 U.S. citizens.
- These 70 Americans—a mere 7% of the town's population—would receive 50% of the town's income.
- This would be the direct result of their controlling over half of the town's available material resources.
- These 70 Americans would have an average life expectancy of 70 years.
- The other 930 would have an average life expectancy of less than 40 years.
- The lowest income group among the Americans, even though it included a number of people who were hungry much of the time, would be better off by far than the average of the other townspeople.

Questions:

- Could such a town, in which the 930 non-Americans were quite aware of both the fact and means of the Americans' advantages, survive?
- Could the 70 Americans continue to extract the majority of raw materials essential to their own standard of living from the property of the other 930 townspeople?
- While the 70 Americans were using over half the resources to maintain their own comfort, could they at the same time convince the other 930 to limit their population growth by saying that resources of the town were limited?
- Would some of the 70 Americans have to become soldiers and would some of their material and human resources have to be devoted to military efforts in order to keep the rest of the town at its present disadvantage?
- Shouldn't all of us try to learn more about the have-not nations of this world and become more aware of their importance to our own well-being?

Source: From *Future Studies: Personal and Global Possibilities* by C. Whaley, 1984, New York: Trillium Press. Copyright 1984 by Trillium Press. Reprinted by permission.

Unfortunately, there is a good deal of pseudo-science fiction available; it provides little more than an old adventure tale dressed up in futuristic garb. Figure 6–4 gives an example that shows that the story of Rock Wesley, space jockey, is really just an old western in disguise.

Mr. Jenkins had just started his resource-room class on a unit on futuristics and had asked each of the students to think about what the future world of the year 2020 might be like. A few of the students responded with more or less traditional comments, describing more sophisticated transportation and communication. Then Joe raised his hand. When called on, Joe said, "I think in the year 2020 the world will be populated by little green men and women with three eyes and three arms, all running around without their clothes on."

Half of the class collapsed into guffaws at the mental picture, while the other half was angry at Joe for being outrageous again. Mr. Jenkins made a mental note to stick another pin in his Joe doll that he keeps in a convenient place at home, but regained his composure and said, "Now, Joe, what we need to do with this and all the other forecasts that we are making, is to see if they fit the standards that we have talked about. Let's review them."

1. A forecast should be clearly articulated, stated with a minimum of ambiguity, and given a specified time frame.
2. A forecast should be plausible and self-consistent. If it contradicts current knowledge or beliefs about reality, the basis for doing so should be carefully laid out.
3. A good forecast is imaginative. It should demonstrate insight into the selection of its component parts and the judgments about their interaction.
4. A good forecast should reveal clearly its justification or the basis on which it rests.

"Joe, I think you are going to have some work to do, particularly to meet the standards of plausibility and justification, but you might try it this evening and see if you can come back with your forecast tomorrow."

Mr. Jenkins had used Joe's statement as a vehicle for getting across to the students that standards must be applied for *forecasting* and that conjecturing about the future is not just a simple matter of suggesting any random thought that might occur to someone. In short, there is mental discipline required in looking at the future, and it is a serious topic, not just amusing byplay.

FIGURE 6–4   The Space Western—A Pseudofuturistic Tale

Western

Rock Wesley, cowhand and deputy marshal, swung down from the saddle of Old Paint in the dusty cattle town of Nowhere, Nevada. As he turned the corner and entered the Last Chance Saloon, Dirty Dog Dawson, his deadly enemy, stepped from behind the door, jammed a six-shooter in Rock's back, and said, "Stick'em up."

Space Western

Rock Wesley, ace space jockey, jetted into the Spaceport Galinda on the sixth planet in the Star System Aldebaran. He used his portable jet pack to jet into the local multicolored pleasure palace. As he passed through the electronic curtain, Dirty Domingo, his alligator-headed enemy from the planet Mephisto, materialized from the fourth dimension, stuck a laser blaster in Rock's back, and said, "Stick'em up."

Mr. Jenkins also had a funny feeling that Joe may very well be back the next day with a complex and detailed explanation of why it is both plausible and justifiable to think that in the year 2020 the world will be populated by unclothed little green men and women. At least Joe's talent for being imaginative was stirred, even if his suggestion was a thinly disguised attempt at challenging the authority of the teacher.

Books discussing the near future hold much fascination for us, even as the fortune-teller held for past generations. Many of the current books use a myriad of statistics, not crystal balls, tracing trends and projecting what those trends might signify in the future. A possible task of such an independent study might be to conduct a *cross-impact analysis*—trying to discover the effect of megatrends on other important elements in our lives (see Table 6–3). If we are moving in the direction of an information-based society and away from heavy industry, then what does that mean will happen to major industrial centers like Pittsburgh or Detroit? Gifted students need to understand that posing such questions is the first step to preparing for major shifts in emphasis in the society.

Gifted students look forward eagerly to the future. We can capitalize on that interest and provide them with tools to cope more effectively with that rapidly approaching time.

TABLE 6–3   A Model of Cross-Impact Analysis

If This Event Occurs:	*What Will Be the Impact on These Variables?*			
	Population	*Food Production*	*Natural Resources*	*Pollution*
Population • Increases • Decreases • Levels Off	/////////////			
Food Production • Increases • Decreases • Levels Off		/////////////		
Natural Resources • Increased Use • Decreased Use			/////////////	
Pollution • Increases • Decreases				/////////////

The topic of the future is a fertile ground in which the imagination and divergent thinking can operate. In history, there is only one event to be considered and we can only have a reaction to "what might have been," but the future allows for many different possibilities still to be played out.

The Teacher of Social Studies

The question of who shall teach social studies to gifted students has not received nearly the attention that a similar question would in the areas of mathematics or science. It is clear that in mathematics one of the requirements of the students is an intensive content mastery of the hierarchical math system. It is hard to draw a youngster through that system without some degree of mastery by the teacher. If the teacher can apply this mathematical system to practical situations, this is fine—but it is not absolutely required because these systems themselves have an internal logic and consistency about them. Similarly, in science we would hope the teacher will engage in some type of scientific activity and so could communicate, if not model, the behavior and the philosophy of the scientist.

One of the ways to channel the desire of gifted students to be active with our desire to have them reproduce the approach of the professionals to a subject area is to ask them to be a historian of their own community. We are always interested in questions such as, Where did we come from? Who are our ancestors? What kind of life did they lead in earlier times?

Reis and Hebert (1985) presented a set of questions that could be asked if someone were interested in doing such a project—a Type III project in the Renzulli Triad model— where the student actively collects data or information for a particular purpose. A group project on the history of one's community can be organized, with various students fanning out across the community in search of people and/or documents that would answer questions such as those listed in Figure 6–5.

This could provide the class with a fascinating project—one that might even have local merit and receive local recognition. Using documents from the county courthouse, or conducting oral histories from long-time members of the community, as well as collecting information from genealogies, family bibles, diaries, and so on, can give students a sense of discovering history. They will likely have to face the problems of contradictory memories or facts and of testimony that does not match "facts." Is the history written by a member of a cultural majority the same history as that written by a member of the cultural minority? Why not?

One thing is sure: After the experience of trying to *be* historians, the students will never again read an account in a history book without wondering, Who collected this information? What were their sources? How reliable is the information that I am reading? The realization of the subjectivity of history might be the most profitable discovery of all—that history is rarely written by "disinterested" people and often has a less-than-outstanding factual base to back up the statements that are made. Students would also have a better understanding of the phrase, "History is written by the winners."

FIGURE 6–5   Student Questions to Investigate Local History

1. What was here before the city?
2. Who was the first settler of our town? Is there a written biography of him/her?
3. Were there any natural disasters that changed our town? In what way?
4. Which was the first church in our city? Who built it and when?
5. Is there any folklore associated with our city? Our region? Our county?
6. How did certain historical events affect the people in our area (e.g., Civil War)?
7. Did anyone famous come from our area? How has that person's contributions affected our city?
8. Who was the town's first elected official?
9. What was life like for employees of our town's early factories or industry?
10. How did clothing styles change over the years?
11. What is the oldest building in this area? What is its history?
12. What would it have been like to be your age in the seventeenth century?
13. When were written documents or records of our town first kept?
14. Is there a written history of our city, region, county, or state?

Source: Reis, S., & Hebert, T. (1985). Creating practicing professionals in gifted programs: Encouraging students to become young historians. *Roeper Review, 16,* 78–82. Reprinted with permission of the *Roeper Review,* P.O. Box 329, Bloomfield Hills, MI 48303.

In social studies, the teacher is free to explore the breadth as well as the depth of subject matter. The extraordinary range of topics, from anthropology to history to psychology, allows the teacher great latitude in selection of content, and there is less of an obvious requirement for content sophistication or depth. Nevertheless, it is important for the teacher to master, at some level, important ideas or concepts from one of the fields in this broad area so as to communicate effectively with gifted students.

To encourage this content mastery, teachers in some training programs for gifted education are asked to take a series of courses in some content field, such as history or economics or psychology, in order that they add a depth of understanding of important ideas and concepts. When they have mastered these ideas, they can help gifted students explore them. It is in this arena that personal experience—travel and similar activities— can be brought to bear to enrich the content. For example, a teacher who has been to Greece or Rome can talk about ancient civilizations with a personal touch that is interesting to students, and a teacher who has been on an anthropological dig can transmit some of the excitement of that experience. As always, enthusiasm for the subject and willingness to explore new avenues with the students are key teacher attributes.

Program Evaluation

In the end, there will be little progress toward a more complex curriculum unless the evaluation of such a curriculum matches in complexity the desired goals. Figure 6–6 gives an outcome-based type of item. In this item, students are asked to use the knowledge they have learned to solve a practical problem. Such questions such as those posed in

FIGURE 6–6   A Unit-Ending Simulation in High School Economics

You are the president of a large company which is facing a major surplus of products that you are unable to sell. Will a cutback in production solve the problem? Your major task is to get your company into a good financial position. If you are successful, you will be given a large bonus. If you are unsuccessful, you will be fired. Prepare a presentation to your Board of Directors.

1. Market research shows that for every $1 rise in price, 500 less of the product will be demanded. You want to supply 700 units for every dollar rise in price.
   • Develop formulae for demand, supply, and equilibrium.
   • Graph the company's position.

2. If you are a monopoly, will this change the way you would solve this problem?

3. If you have a surplus:
   • What will happen to your workers?
   • What will happen to companies that produce complementary products?
   • If you are forced out of the business, what will happen to companies that produce substitute products?
   • What could this do to the entire economy?
   • How could the government help in this situation?

Source: From *Horace's Compromise* by Theodore Sizer. Copyright © 1984 by Theodore R. Sizer. Reprinted by permission of Houghton Mifflin Co. All rights reserved.

Figure 6–6 would be enough to convince any student that he or she had better abandon the old style of memorization and get into a problem-solving mode. Even gifted students will have their work cut out for them with such questions, which really combine aspects of sociology, ethics, and economics.

The field of social studies is so broad and diverse that there is a problem of selecting material from an almost unmanageable pool of knowledge that is constantly growing and changing. Whatever is chosen has to be selected for its generalizability, as well as its own interest and character. That is, the Age of Exploration may be chosen not just because it is an interesting period in the development of human potential but because we can learn about the merging of cultures, the clash between the status quo and the "explorers," and so on. There are explorers today in the various fields of human knowledge, and these explorers have to cope with the status quo in their fields, just as the early explorers of the globe had to deal with the "flat earth" supporters.

This topic of "exploration" can lead us into a dozen interesting avenues and can thus justify the time it takes to develop it. Time is the most precious of all teacher commodities, and it needs to be reserved for important educational goals as much as possible.

Unresolved Issues

1. Can preadolescent gifted children understand complex human emotions and motivations sufficiently to pursue these dimensions in the curriculum? Can 10-year-old gifted children, even with advanced mentality, grasp the passions and drives of

adults, or the role that the perception of approaching death has on an aging leader? Must such topics be postponed until the children are older?

2. One of the least understood topics in social studies, yet one of the most important for modern times, is the field of economics. Most elementary school teachers and many secondary school teachers have had little more than a passing contact with this rapidly expanding field. How can gifted children be introduced to this topic effectively?

3. Much of the information in current textbooks that deals with psychology or sociology is years out of date in covering the current status of these fields. How can the schools keep up with these rapidly advancing and changing fields so that a focus could be kept on human beings and their society?

Chapter Review

1. Social studies includes a diversity of subject areas, such as history, psychology, sociology, anthropology, economics, and geography, creating many problems of curriculum selection and choice.

2. Too many times, gifted students at the elementary level are provided with a low conceptual level of activities or a menu of facts, such as a routine review of another country's resources or geographic characteristics.

3. The differential curriculum for gifted students should teach to high conceptual levels and help the students gain the skills to search for and discover knowledge for themselves.

4. Content acceleration can focus on conflict resolution or on economics, which, when learned, can be applied effectively to other content areas, such as history or anthropology.

5. Gifted students can learn the connectedness of human culture through such illustrations as the multiple impacts of an invention like the chimney.

6. Content enrichment can further investigate the applications of famous documents, such as the Bill of Rights, instead of just learning what they are.

7. Students can be taught to be their own historians or anthropologists and to discover the problems faced by these scholarly fields in collecting valid data.

8. Content sophistication may be represented by the study of significant major trends in our society to explore their possible consequences.

9. Leadership, an area often included in the definition of giftedness, is a potential area of curriculum differentiation. It is a topic many teachers wish to present to these future leaders.

10. Gifted students appear to view the future with some pessimism and alarm, and need to learn how other persons have learned to cope with future problems.

11. The study of the future is another popular curriculum adaptation for gifted students, since it teaches them skills for forecasting, projecting current trends, and exploring alternative paths.

Readings of Special Interest

Burke, J. (1985). *The day the universe changed.* Boston: Little, Brown.

This book of astonishing scope identifies particular ideas throughout history that have changed people's viewpoints of the world and themselves. The link between certain inventions and their impact on our social world and how we govern ourselves becomes particularly interesting to students of high ability. This book was first seen as a popular TV series following in the footsteps of Civilization, The Ascent of Man, *and so on, drawing on a broad scope of human experience to present certain key generalizations about the human condition.*

Ogbu, J. (1992, November). Understanding cultural diversity and learning. *Educational Researcher,* 5–14.

The interest in multicultural issues has dramatically increased in social studies curriculum over the past decade. This article, written by an noted anthropologist, discusses cultural diversity and differential school success and describes the ef-

fects of minority status on achievement—something of relevance for educators working with minority gifted students—as well as presents a lesson in cultural anthropology.

Richardson, W., & Feldhusen, J. (1984). *Leadership education: Developing skills for youth.* West Lafayette, IN: William Richardson Enterprise.

This is an excellent guide for teachers who wish to pursue the development of a curriculum unit that will emphasize leadership. Three aspects of leadership education are stressed: information on the nature of leadership education, leadership from the perspective of leader and group member, and leadership from an organizational perspective. Each chapter provides specific objectives and topics such as committee organization, parliamentary procedures, and communication skills. Group activities are covered with enough detail to be useful in a program for gifted students in secondary school.

References

Beck, I., & McKeown, M. (1988). Toward meaningful accounts in history texts for young learners. *Educational Researcher, 17,* 31–39.

Bradley Commission on History in Schools. (1989). Building a history curriculum: Guidelines for teaching history in schools. In P. Gagnon (Ed.), *Historical literacy.* New York: Macmillan.

Burke, J. (1978). *Connections.* Boston: Little, Brown.

Burns, J. (1978). *Leadership.* New York: Harper & Row.

Competency Goals and Performance Indicators, K–12. (1979). Raleigh, NC: North Carolina Department of Public Instruction.

Gallagher, J., Oglesby, K., Stern, A., Caplow, D., Courtright, R., Fulton, L., Guiton, G., & Langenbach, J. (1982). *Leadership unit: The use of teacher scholar teams to develop units for the gifted.* New York: Trillium.

George, P., & Gallagher, J. (1978). Children's thoughts about the future: A comparison of

gifted and nongifted students. *Journal for the Education of the Gifted, 2* (1), 33–42.

Goodlad, J. I. (1984). *A place called school.* New York: McGraw-Hill.

Hay, L., & Roberts, A. (1988). *Curriculum for the new millenium.* Fairfield CT: Fairfield Public Schools.

Hazelton, W., & Mahroria, W. (1986). External simulation as teaching devices: The model United Nations. *Simulation and Games, 17* (2), 149–171.

Hoffman, L. (1989). Effects of maternal employment in the parent family. *American Psychologist, 44* (2), 283–292.

Kaplan, S. (1979). Language arts and social studies curricula in the elementary school, in A. Passow (Ed.), *The gifted and talented: Their education and development* (pp. 155–168). 78th Yearbook of the National Society for the Study of Education. Chicago: University of Chicago Press.

Landau, E. (1979). The young persons' institute for the promotion of science, in J. Gallagher (Ed.), *Gifted children: Reaching their potential* (pp. 105–109). Jerusalem: Kollek & Sons.

Lengel, J. G., & Superka, D. P. (1982). Curriculum patterns, in I. Morrissett (Ed.), *Social studies in the 1980s. A report of project SPAN*. Alexandria, VA: Association for Supervision and Curriculum Development.

Marland, S. (1972). *Education of the gifted and talented*. Report to the Congress of the United States by the U.S. Commissioner of Education. Washington, DC: U.S. Government Printing Office.

Muessig, R. (1987). An analysis of developments in geographic education. *The Elementary School Journal, 87* (5), 571–589.

NCSS Task Force on Early Childhood/Elementary Social Studies. (1989). Social studies for early childhood and elementary school children preparing for the 21st century. *Social Education, 53*, 14–23.

National Council on Social Studies. (1988). Social studies for early childhood and elementary school children preparing for the 21st Century. *Social Education, 53*, 14–23.

National Council on Studies. (1988). Standards for the preparation of social studies teachers. *Social Education, 52*, 10–12.

National Assessment of Educational Progress. (1992). *Framework for the 1994 NAEP U.S. History Assessment*. Washington, DC: Council of Chief State School Officers.

North Carolina Department of Public Instruction. (1979). *Competency goals and performance indicators, K–12*. Raleigh, NC: Author.

Onosko, J. (1991). Barriers to the promotion of higher order thinking in social studies. *Theory and Research in Social Education, 19* (4), 341–366.

Passow, A. (1988). Educating gifted students who are caring and concerned. *Roeper Review, 11* (1), 13–15.

Reis, S., & Hebert, T. (1985). Creating practicing professionals in gifted programs: Encouraging students to become young historians. *Roeper Review, 16*, 78–82.

Reis, S., & Hebert, T. (1985). *North Carolina Standard Course of Study (1985)*. Raleigh, NC: North Carolina Department of Public Instruction, p. 273.

Reis, S., & Hebert, T. (1990). *Geography learning of high school seniors*. Princeton, NJ: Educational Testing Service.

Renzulli, J. (1983). Guiding the gifted in the pursuit of real problems: The transformed role of the teacher. *Journal of Creative Behavior, 17* (1), 49–59.

Roeper, A. (1988). Should educators of the gifted and talented be more concerned with world issues? *Roeper Review, 11* (1), 12–13.

Stanley, W. B. (1985). *Review of research in social studies education: 1976–1983*. Washington, DC: National Council on Social Studies.

Toffler, A. (1980). *The third wave*. New York: Bantam.

Torrance, E., Bruch, C., & Goolsby, T. (1976). Gifted children study the future, in J. Gibson & P. Channels (Eds.), *Gifted children looking to their future*. London: Latimer.

Ward, W. (1992). Remapping geographic education. *Education Week, 12* (12), 28.

Whaley, C. (1984). *Future studies: Personal and global possibilities*. New York: Trillium Press.

Chapter 7

Language Arts for Gifted Students

Key Questions

- What are the major subdivisions of language arts?
- What are some of the major dimensions of language that are important to modern society?
- What does cultural literacy mean?
- What are some of the limitations on teachers of language arts in effective programming for gifted students?
- How are portfolios used in the assessment of student progress in the language arts?
- What are some of the differentiated curricular suggestions for gifted students in language arts?

The area of language arts includes major areas of skills development as well as specific content in the field of language and literature. In both mathematics and language arts, gifted students are expected to problem solve and create—displaying evidence of skills mastery and content knowledge. Consider the four important subdivisions of language arts: *writing, reading, speaking,* and *listening*— all complex skills to be developed. Since these skills enhance the use of language, and since language is the key to content mastery, it is no surprise that gifted children who are generally very good in language development, and those subjects that rely on language, enjoy the language arts activities.

This chapter will present a series of program objectives for gifted students in the language arts. In addition, it will illustrate curriculum differentiation in the dimensions of content *acceleration, enrichment, sophistication,* and *novelty.*

Of the gifted students discussed in this book, Zelda and Cranshaw are very fond of language arts and look forward to that part of their school day. Even Joe expresses a liking for the subject, as compared with mathematics and science. But Sam and Stephanie find the area uninteresting and would much rather study mathematics and art than engage in language arts activities. Although Zelda and Cranshaw express highly positive attitudes toward language arts, their reasons are very different, which underscores the impression that this broad and comprehensive field has something to offer everyone.

Zelda likes the structured nature of grammar and linguistics and is intrigued by the revelations of hidden systems and order in literature and in poetry. She feels at home in most structured situations and, because her vocabulary and linguistic skills are very high, she is able to perform excellently with little effort. On the other hand, Cranshaw likes language arts because it gives him the opportunity to use his imagination and his creative bent. He particularly likes to write short stories and poems and feels that this is one field where he can cease being a passive learner and become an active expresser of ideas.

Joe likes language arts for quite a different reason. In this area, there is not the same pressure for daily output and sustained academic work that one finds in science and mathematics classes. It is true that there can be long-range assignments for book reports or themes, but these are in the future, and Joe is an expert at postponing such tasks beyond their deadlines. Even so, he likes the class discussions and genuinely likes to read some literature.

Stephanie tends to display a type of passive resistance, doing only the minimum necessary assignments. On the other hand, Sam finds other students' fascination with words a puzzling thing. He does not get joy out of manipulating words or constructing complicated puns.

Whether the skill to be learned is designing a plot for a short story, arithmetic computation, or dribbling a basketball, the principles of skills instruction remain the same. Teachers hope to bring the student to:

1. An awareness of the rules governing the skill
2. The chance to practice the skill under supervision and instructor feedback
3. The ability to generate products of their own—a speech, a poem, a literary critique, and so on

Language Arts Objectives for All

The objectives in language arts fall into the broad categories of receptive abilities, expressive abilities, and integrative abilities. Many of the objectives require students to apply judgment to the information being received. Students are expected not merely to accept information at face value but to be concerned about the intention of the sender and to recognize that a person who is communicating may have more than one intention. It is often surprising to observers in education that gifted students, who can be extremely sophisticated in their knowledge of the laws of the physical world and of mathematics, can be unbelievably naive when it comes to interpreting the motivations of other individuals. A strong language arts program should help those students to become more sophisticated regarding the purposes and directions of others, as well as more aware of their own feelings.

In addition, gifted students should be encouraged to express themselves with imagination, to develop original and unusual ideas, and to learn the skills that will provide them with the mechanisms for clearer and more effective expression. In the areas of both communication reception and communication expression, gifted youngsters can be expected to learn early to relay their own needs and ideas to others, and also to interpret carefully the information they are receiving.

Table 7–1 (VanTassel-Baska, 1992) presents some major language arts goal for gifted students and contrasts them with the goals for a basic educational program. Teachers in general education would, naturally, aspire to all of these goals listed for gifted students, but time is the enemy of many teachers who must cut short the more advanced thinking processes in favor of assuring that basic goals have been sufficiently met.

The distinction between programs for gifted students and the standard program is often due to the limited time available. The program for gifted students can assume that the basic information has already been mastered, or can be mastered in a very short time,

TABLE 7–1 **Major Language Arts Goals and Outcomes in Gifted and Basic Educational Programs**

Gifted Program Goal in Language Arts and Underlying Outcomes	*Basic Education Goal in Language Arts and Underlying Outcomes*
To develop critical reading behaviors*	To develop reading skills
The gifted learner will be able to:	The typical learner will be able to:
a. analyze material read from high quality children's literature and selected classical and contemporary adult literature b. interpret reading material in various genres c. evaluate authors' perspective and point of view d. draw inferences based on selected readings e. use deductive reasoning to understand arguments in written form f. develop analogical reasoning skills based on reading	a. read with fluency selected material b. develop vocabulary at appropriate levels c. read with comprehension d. appropriately use various genres of reading material e. develop library reference skills f. develop analytical and interpretive skills in reading

Source: From *Planning effective curriculum for gifted learners* (pp. 37–45) by J. VanTassel-Baska, 1992, Denver: Love Publishing Company. Reprinted with permission.

* Basic reading goal and underlying outcomes will be tested at each appropriate level in the gifted program to ensure mastery. The *emphasis* of the program, however, is best reflected in the outcomes given here.

by gifted students. This gives the teacher working with these students time to pursue analysis, synthesis, and evaluation topics, as noted in Table 7–1.

Although these objectives can be challenging, the lack of emphasis on high quality has led some to suggest that these objectives can be met with marginal performances in all of these areas. Educational reform and restructuring is touching all of the disciplines, and language arts is no exception. Just as the nation's students are found to be ill-prepared in science, mathematics, and social studies, so are they ill-prepared in English and language arts. Colleges and businesses alike report that students are entering their professional lives unprepared to read and communicate with sufficient skill or technical expertise.

For many years, there have been concerns about the writing ability of this country's youth. This would be particularly true of gifted students, since they would generally be expected to be in positions, as adults, where they would have to communicate effectively with others. Some gifted students might have writing as the major part of their job responsibilities (e.g., scientists, reporters, novelists, etc.).

Figure 7–1 shows some sample language arts goals for gifted sixth-graders. Here, the emphasis is on analysis and evaluation rather than simple comprehension. The assumption is that such students have already learned the basics of reading and communication and now need to involve themselves in interpretation.

Again, the difference between the regular program and the program for gifted students is one of degree. The figure is not meant to imply that such goals should not be one piece of a set of goals for all students, but that these goals should form the predominant part of a program for gifted students.

FIGURE 7–1 Special Language Arts Goals for Gifted Sixth-Graders

Goal #1: Develop Critical Reading Behaviors
- Understand the literary structures of motivation, theme, climax, and story development
- Write essays based on original ideas

Goal #2: Develop Critical Listening Skills
- Identify relevant information, bias, and details from oral messages
- Take accurate notes on underlying ideas presented orally

Goal #3: Develop Proficiency in Grammar and Usage
- Recognize and use all basic sentence patterns
- Write a coherent theme free of mechanical errors

Goal #4: Develop Proficiency in Oral Communication
- Use multiple media in an effective manner
- Organize an effective presentation of 10 minutes in length

Goal #5: Analyze and Evaluate Various Literary Forms (Genres) and Ideas (Themes) in World Literature
- Create a piece of literature in any form or style, based on a given idea
- Compare and contrast literary forms at appropriate levels

Goal #6: Develop Expository and Technical Writing Skills
- Develop a content outline for a report
- Use multiple sources in preparing research reports

Goal #7: Develop Cross-Cultural Understanding Through Studying the Literature, Art, and Music of Selected African, Oriental, Indian, and European Cultures
- Compare and contrast art forms from African, Indian, Oriental, and European traditions
- Conduct research that compares two cultures on key criteria

Source: From *Planning effective curriculum for gifted learners* (p. 35) by J. VanTassel-Baska, 1992, Denver: Love Publishing Company. Reprinted with permission.

The standard multiple-choice achievement tests give little clue as to how the students actually write. With the advent of authentic testing and portfolio assessment, it now has become easier to test the suppositions of teachers and other observers. The National Assessment of Educational Progress (NAEP) program invited 2,000 fourth-grade students and 2,000 eighth-grade students to participate in a special portfolio study. Slightly over half of the students at each grade level agreed (Gentile, 1992).

The English/language arts teachers of participating students were asked to help several of their students to choose a sample of their own best writing from the work the students had completed thus far in the 1989–1990 school year. Teachers were asked to select pieces that had involved the use of writing process strategies (such as revising successive drafts, using reference sources, consulting with others about writing, etc.). Although these were generally considered to be above-average students from above-average school systems, the results were termed universally dreadful (Gentile, 1992). Only 1 percent of the students at either grade level showed evidence of major revisions; less than half of the students showed any evidence of any type of writing process strategies.

In the narrative papers, only 8 percent of eighth-graders produced a "developed story" and 0 percent produced an "elaborated story." On persuasive papers, none of the papers were graded as "partially developed refutation" or "developed refutation." Considering that these were the best products from better students from better schools, the overall effect is to suggest strongly that the schools are not teaching writing very effectively, and that includes gifted students as well as others. In order to improve this state of unreadiness, Squire (1985) identified seven critical needs, which are presented in Figure 7–2.

Is there any real difference between language arts programs and objectives for the gifted and those for the average student, when this new push for excellence is considered? Isn't a description of a program for the gifted merely a description of a good program for an average classroom?

One of the educational objectives in the language arts that is specifically targeted to gifted youth is the encouragement of an *active* rather than a *passive* approach to the topic. That is, gifted students should be seen as producers of language products rather than as just receivers of useful information through the language arts.

Although one would expect gifted students to read many books, enjoy poetry, and listen to music (a passive mode), one would also hope to design experiences so that they can be active generators of ideas. This fits well into the observed characteristic of gifted students who play an active role in actually "doing things" rather than having things "done to them." It is also a recognition that the proper and effective use of the tools of the language arts will stand these students in good stead in the future, whether they become a member of the clergy, a physical scientist, or a politician. In all of these roles, the ability to communicate plays a central role in success and effectiveness. Many of the curriculum

FIGURE 7–2   Excellence in the Language Arts

1. Literacy must be redefined: High standards must be held for all students; effective communication will be more—not less—important in the age of technology; language arts must be considered part of the cultural heritage of our students.

2. All children must have access to the tools of learning and to the carriers of our culture. Libraries must be maintained and made accessible to all students, especially those from families in low socioeconomic backgrounds.

3. Stress must be placed on the higher thought processes essential to Reading and English. Students must be instructed beyond the level of word definition and sentence construction and to more complex ways of forming and analyzing language.

4. Technology must be used to strengthen reading, writing, and thinking. Word processing should be made an integral part of students' instruction in the practices of planning, drafting, editing, and publishing works. Use of computers for drill-and-practice is *not* recommended.

5. Both tests and textbooks must be strengthened. A move away from standardized tests, with their emphasis on sentence-level and word-level skills is essential. Essay and portfolio formats provide a more complex set of expectations on the student.

6. Our K–12 programs in literary education must be redefined. Quality literature must be reintegrated into language arts programs to create a common cultural vocabulary among students.

7. Teaching conditions and teacher education must be reconstituted to support achievement of excellence. Teacher preparation programs must respond to the above list and change their practices to develop teachers capable of a more complex form of teaching.

Source: Squire, J. (1985). *The labors of Sysiphys: Achieving excellence in schooling*. Address to International Reading Association. Reprinted by permission.

activities listed later in this chapter reflect the approach of creating an active role for gifted students.

The end product of work with gifted students is often a startling presentation, composition, or poem that makes the hard work and planning worthwhile. Figure 7–3 was written by a high school girl from North Carolina. She was nominated by her school and chosen as a Presidential Scholar, and was 1 of over 100 students honored at the White House during the bicentennial celebration. The task of the scholars was to write something of their forebears. This sensitive and perceptive piece was Deirdre Sumpter's response.

FIGURE 7–3   Sample of Student Writing

Blarney and Beethoven, Murphys and Hewitts
by Deirdre Sumpter

My father's birth certificate states that he was damed and sired by Mary Murphy and unknown.

His mother surrendered him up to the childless West Virginia couple who were caring for him, and she disappeared again into New York City.

In the harbor was a boat that several years before had carried an Irish girl to a country she dreamed would give her money and marriage. The boat returned her to Ireland; the country kept her out-of-wedlock son. That son once came back to New York City to try his hand at acting.

He fared no better than his mother. I never saw her, but there is more Irish mystic than West Virginia farmer in my face, mind, and father. Light shown crystalline in the court poetry of Eire when England's natives still ran naked in blue paint through the fog.

My mother's ancestors, the Hewitts, were German. If they came here for business, they found it. They intermarried with other respectable bourgeoisie and were assimilated a century ago.

Future generations kept Lutheran ledgers and know the inside of a bottle as well as any Irishman. My mother took voice lessons from her uncle and dreamed of singing opera. She married, and those dreams lie in a New York dump. The sunlight in red-carpeted dark-wooded Lutheran churches dances closer to God than any I've seen elsewhere.

My father teases my mother that the perfectionism of German train schedules keeps her overworked and guilt-ridden. Perhaps so.

Perhaps it is also the meter and passion of a Beethoven symphony that made an executive and a feminist of a Southern girl.

Perhaps it is the battle-glee of an Irish warrior that journalistically slays small-town corruption and cruelty.

A very American situation.

Mary Murphy lost her virtue. The Hewitts were never millionaires. My father never played Broadway. My mother never sang at the Met. I am better educated than an Irish peasant or a German shopkeeper.

I am free.

Before I die, I will give the future an Irish whiskey of Luther's taste distilled in my American present.

The task of the schools is to help nurture such talent early in the school years, so that it can reach fruition as children near maturity. One project that is often interesting to gifted students is to have them consider what life would be like if we had no language. Language usually comes so naturally to these students that rarely have they reflected on its universal importance to modern society. The proposition of eliminating language can help them quickly grasp its critical role in our society.

Another fascinating topic, worthy of a special project of study, is the special problems faced by children who are hearing-impaired, who cannot receive the linguistic input that forms the base for the development of speech and language. Perhaps some of the students know children who are hard of hearing or deaf, or perhaps there is a class or school for children who are hearing-impaired that would be able to display the development of alternative language systems, such as finger spelling and hand signs, or the ability to speech read (interpreting the facial movements of the speaker to comprehend the message).

One of the characteristics of U.S. schools is the cultural diversity of its students. The "tossed salad" of U.S. culture, with each of the cultural groups adding its own flavor and texture to the whole, has been applauded as superior to a single-dimension culture with a more narrow view of what is appropriate. This is because our diversity makes us more adaptable.

Although diversity does add spice to life, it also causes special problems for educators. Hirsch (1987) suggested that part of the way we communicate with others is to use a common base of knowledge that we have absorbed. It is this common storehouse of information that allows us to converse effectively with others. Hirsch produced a list of terms that literate Americans know, in the sense that they are able to recognize the term and say something about it, even if they lack full understanding.

Figure 7–4 gives a few of these terms. You, the reader or teacher, might check yourself, or your students from middle school and up, with regard to the ability to say something about each of these terms. It is interesting to note what a European bias is represented in Hirsch's list. It is the list most likely to be known to upper middle-class, white students. Even gifted Hispanic or African-American students may be unaware of many of these terms, but could probably produce another list—built on their own cultural experiences—that would baffle the children in the white majority groups.

Since the teaching of literature is one of those subjects that creates a common culture, few students of the authors' generations escaped *Tom Sawyer* or *Huckleberry Finn*. When someone complains about being talked into something against his or her will by saying, "You are getting me to paint the fence again," this allusion to the famous passage in *Tom Sawyer* is understood by most members of that generation, but would likely be a mystery to those from another cultural background.

One way to encourage greater understanding of other cultures is through content enrichment, to introduce representative literary pieces representing different cultures. The gifted students who learn and read rapidly could be given a diversity of reading lists so that they begin to understand the variety of backgrounds from which we Americans spring.

Once again, the obvious question is: Shouldn't all students be receiving a reading list that reflects our cultural diversity? The obvious answer is yes, constrained only by the

FIGURE 7–4   What Literate Americans Know (According to Hirsch)

- Hope springs eternal in the human breast
- Horace
- hormone
- hornet's nest, stir up a
- horns of a dilemma
- horse! a horse! my kingdom for a horse!
- horticulture
- Houdini
- house arrest
- House of Commons
- House of Lords
- House of Representatives
- Houston, Sam
- Houston, Texas
- Huckleberry Finn (title)
- Hudson Bay
- Hudson River

- hue and cry
- Hugo, Victor
- Huguenots
- humanist
- humanitarianism
- human rights
- Hume, David
- humidity (relative and absolute)
- Humpty Dumpty
- Hun
- Hunchback of Notre Dame, The (title)
- Hundred Years War
- Hungary
- hurricane
- Huxley, Aldous
- Huxley, Julian
- hybridization

Source: From *Cultural Literacy* by E. D. Hirsch. Copyright © 1987 by Houghton Mifflin Company. Reprinted by permission of Houghton Mifflin Co. All rights reserved.

time limits—which turn out to be more elastic for gifted students because of the rapidity with which they read and comprehend.

A fine example of potential cultural misunderstanding might come from the popular Australian song "Waltzing Matilda":

Once a jolly swagman camped by a billabong
Under the shade of a coolibah tree
And he sang as he watched and waited till his billy boiled,
*You'll come a-waltzing Matilda with me.**

It would be hard to guess how many Americans have happily sung this infectious tune believing it is a type of romantic ballad celebrating a man's attachment to his girlfriend, Matilda. Actually it is nothing of the kind. *Waltzing Matilda* means carrying one's bundle ("swag"), or going on the tramp. A *swagman* is a man or tramp carrying his swag, which means a bundle wrapped up in a blanket. A *billabong* is a water hole in a dried-up bed of a river. A *coolibah* is a eucalyptus tree. A *billy* is a tin can used as a kettle. The final part of the song reveals that the hobo is caught stealing sheep, leaps into the pond, and drowns—so much for romanticism. It does indicate, however, how a degree of cultural understanding proceeds the correct interpretation of what one reads or hears (Hirsch, 1987, p. 17).

*From *Waltzing Matilda*. Music by Marie Cowan. Words by A. B. Paterson. Copyright © 1936 by Allan & Co. Prop. Pty, Melbourne. Copyright © 1941 by Carl Fischer, Inc., New York. Copyrights Renewed. All Rights Reserved. Used by Permission.

Curriculum Adaptations

Since gifted students have often been able to achieve three or four grades in advance of their classmates in language-related subjects, it is likely that they will be bored and frustrated by the age-grade curriculum if such is presented to them. If they lack some elements of that age-grade program, they can quickly master it and go on to many different options.

Content Acceleration

The basic reason for content acceleration in language arts is the same as for acceleration in mathematics. The early mastery of certain skill areas (e.g., calculus, grammatical structure, the models of poetic construction, etc.) allows gifted students to use these skills in their own creative products and in understanding the complexities of other subject areas.

Khatena (1982, pp. 124–125) suggested the advancement of analogous thinking by distinguishing the following in the use of language:

Simile	*A comparison between two things different except in a single characteristic.*	*John is as fat as a pig.*
Metaphor	*Condensed simile, relating two things different in kind, as though they were similar or identical.*	*John is a pig.*
Personification	*Give lifeless objects attributes of life and feeling.*	*Time marches on.*
Allusion	*Comparison by use of familiar phenomena in mythology and literature legend.*	*She proved to be a good Samaritan.*

It does not take too much imagination to see what gifted children can do, once turned loose, to develop multiple examples of *similes, metaphors, personifications,* and *allusions.* Yet some type of direct instruction on their use would seem to be essential before they can be fully utilized. Just because a gifted child uses *personification* (e.g., the building creaked and groaned as if in pain) does not mean that he or she fully understands it.

One way to extend the young gifted students' already well-developed sense of language is to introduce them to the simile, the metaphor, personification, and so on and to encourage them to use these techniques in exercises like the well-known poems from *Hailstones and Halibut Bones* (see Figure 7–5). Students can be asked to do their own versions of the colors, or shapes (what is square?), or numbers (what is 5?—fingers, basketball team, cents, etc.).

Poems such as *What Is Orange?* can be used to help the teacher assess whether or not the students have mastered the concepts of simile or metaphor by asking students to find as many as they can within the poem itself.

FIGURE 7–5   Sample Exercise in Poetry

What Is Orange?
Orange is a tiger lily,
A carrot,
A feather from
A parrot,
A flame,
The wildest color
You can name.
Orange is a happy day
Saying good-by
In a sunset that
Shocks the sky.
Orange is brave
Orange is bold
It's bittersweet
And marigold.

Orange is zip
Orange is dash
The brightest stripe
In a Roman sash.
Orange is an orange
Also a mango
Orange is music
Of the tango.
Orange is the fur
Of the fiery fox,
The brightest crayon
In the box.
And in the fall
When the leaves are turning
Orange is the smell
Of a bonfire burning...

Sources: "What Is Orange?", copyright © 1961 by Mary LeDuc O'Neill. From *Hailstones and Halibut Bones* by Mary O'Neill and Leonard Weisgard, III. Used by permission of Doubleday, a division of Bantam Doubleday Dell Publishing Group, Inc.

The important goal here is to turn outstanding students into producers of ideas and images instead of just receivers (readers or viewers) of such images as posed by someone else. Once they have experienced the thrill of producing words that are found to be valuable or entertaining by others, the motivation to continue writing is substantially increased.

Gifted children are often so clever and facile with language that it is easy for the teacher to assume that they have mastered skills in the language arts field when, in fact, they have not. Cranshaw can weave a clever plot but still knows little about the use of adverbial clauses or the uses of language to create moods. In their reading, most of these bright students will gallop through a short story or a book, only catching the major plot line and enjoying the interaction of characters.

Until they are asked to pursue some of these stories in depth, students will never understand the underlying structure or be able to use such structure in their own creations. For example, Mindell and Stracher posed the following questions dealing with character development, plot, and point of view; these items force the student to reflect on the author's use of language skills. Such analyses usually occur at the secondary-school level, but they can be taught to gifted children at an earlier age.

Character Development

Think about a favorite book character and tell:
   How did he act?
   How did he talk?
   How did he react to what happened to him?
   How did others act toward him?
   In what way was he like or unlike other characters you've read about?
   How did the character change in the course of the story?

Plot

Sequence?
Conflict (between characters, man and environment, values within the person)?
Relationships between characters and events?
Climax of story (how built, suspense, use of cliffhangers)?
Any subplots?
Flashbacks in this or another story you've read?

Point of View

Can you think of any books in which the story is told by:
   An outside person?
   The main character of the story?
   Or an author who is omniscient (knows the thoughts and feelings of all the characters)?
   In what way might a story be different depending on whose point of view is expressed? (1980, p. 75)

Gifted students who are encouraged to pursue this type of analysis will begin to see the literary structure emerge and become visible. Once understood, these structural elements—character development, plot, and point of view—can be used to generate new and more complex products of their own.

Foreign Languages

One of the potential forms of content acceleration in language arts is the learning of a second or third language in elementary or middle school. U.S. visitors to Europe are always astonished to see young European children speaking and understanding two or three languages by the time they are 10 or 11 years old. Of course, they are immersed in a multilingual environment, which aids that development immensely. However, if curriculum compacting has assured that gifted students have already mastered the regular curriculum, then we should feel free to give a second language in a special group setting in middle school, or junior high school, or in a resource room or special class in the elementary school.

The principle of *immersion* also seems relevant to the instruction of the second language here. In this case, immersion means the total use of the second language for all communication during the school day, rather than in one 50-minute class session. Obviously, this is more possible in a special class or resource room setting than it is as part of the regular class, where most of the students would be involved in other types of study. There is probably no more useful set of learning for those students who are part of the next generation—if what we hope to be international leadership and cooperation for the United States—than to have them conversant in the native tongues of others with whom they will be dealing.

Content Enrichment

The purpose of content enrichment in language arts is to allow gifted children additional time to practice skills of expression and communication and to extend the students' boundaries of space and time and be receptive to the great and sensitive minds of the past. Literature can be viewed as a time machine, transporting students into the past ages and into the future, as well as expanding awareness of the present. From the early grades, where the students study characters and common cultural themes, to the secondary level, where universal themes of humankind such as the "search for immortality" are pursued, gifted students have a chance to learn about their present by pursuing their historical and cultural roots through poetry and literature.

In the language arts field, there are a number of examples of how to challenge gifted students who are in a heterogeneous class receiving the same basic information as average students. One such program is described by Moss (1980), using the topic of the fable as a focus of a variety of enrichment or elaboration activities. After reading a few fables in the classroom, the teacher leads the discussion about what a fable is. Moss reported the following definition that evolved from one group of third-graders: "A fable is a short tale which teaches a lesson or moral. The characters are usually animals, and they usually talk and act like human beings. Each character stands for something good (like being kind or wise) or something bad (like being greedy or vain)" (p. 24).

The children then tested their definition against some new fables that they analyzed. After creating and labeling their own fable characters, they became involved in the teacher-initiated question, Why were fables invented in the first place? Some of the students reached an awareness that the story is a natural vehicle for teaching important ideas or lessons through concrete images.

With this fundamental information in hand, the students were then encouraged to develop independent projects, and the gifted and talented students were allowed to design ones of their own special interest. One child wrote a book of riddles about fable characters; another made an illustrated dictionary of the interesting words he had found in the fables. One group printed and illustrated their own retelling of Aesop's tale *The Lion and the Mouse.* Several children created puppets, which they used to present an original production based on the fables of Aesop. Moss pointed out that this type of topic allows for education of gifted children within the heterogeneous classroom, but also gives them additional opportunities to engage in challenging and enriching activities through the use of independent and group projects stemming from the original unit.

As previously mentioned, literature can introduce the students to other cultures besides their own. What is "the culture" in a diverse and culturally pluralistic society such as the United States? Obviously, the culture of Cranshaw is not the same as the culture of Joe, nor is it the same as Sam's. Of all the youngsters being discussed, Sam probably had the least appropriate introduction to language arts and, as a consequence, did not really enjoy the time spent in this area. The content of the materials did not seem appropriate or interesting to Sam. In his earlier readers he read many stories about a farmhouse with a white picket fence, talking farm animals, the happy mother and father, and he knew that these had little to do with him, his background, or his cultural heritage. It was as different as if the books were talking about some Egyptian or Chinese culture.

Much more appropriate to Sam and his needs would be stories that not only deal with important issues like conflicts with authority or concepts of life and death but that also provide a setting and characters that are recognizable and real to Sam's experiences. Having Sam read a section of Wright's (1945) *Black Boy* can bring forth his interest and recognition of the problems. In one chapter, the story is told of the angry father, railing against a kitten that is meowing, demanding quiet so he could get some sleep. The boy in the story proceeds to draw a noose around the animal's neck and kill it, leading to the following exchange:

> *My mother hurried toward me, drying her hands upon her apron. She stopped and paled when she saw the kitten suspended from the rope.*
>
> > *"What in God's name have you done?" she asked.*
> > *"The kitten was making noise and Papa said to kill it," I explained.*
> > *"You little fool!" she said. "Your father's going to beat you for this!"*
> > *"But he told me to kill it," I said.*
> > *"You shut your mouth!"*
> > *She grabbed my hand and dragged me to my father's bedside and told him what I had done.*
> > *"You know better than that!" my father stormed.*
> > *"You told me to kill 'im," I said.*
> > *"I told you to drive him away," he said.*
> > *"You told me to kill 'im," I countered positively.*
> > *"You get out of my eyes before I smack you down!" my father bellowed in disgust, then turned over in bed.*
> > *I had had my first triumph over my father. I had made him believe that I had taken his words literally. I was happy because I had at last found a way to throw*

my criticism of him into his face. I would never give serious weight to his words again. I had made him know that I felt he was cruel and I had done it without his punishing me. (pp. 10–11)

This is a very different kind of story from that found in the usual readers, although stories from different cultural backgrounds are becoming more and more available. Youngsters like Sam can identify with the heroes of such stories because, for them, the predicaments are recognizable and important.

The basic message is that no single book or textbook can satisfy the rich literary talents or needs of the average student and certainly not of the gifted and talented student. There has to be a diversity of materials and program efforts to match in some regard the wide range of abilities, cultural backgrounds, and motivations in a heterogeneous neighborhood and school.

The introduction of poetry to young students occurs on a systematic and regular basis in public schools. Students even may be encouraged to try their own hand at rhyming and couplets. However, the specific skills involved in the development of a poem are rarely pursued or practiced, primarily due to the time it requires. With gifted students it is possible to proceed to this additional experience because they have mastered the other materials. Thaden (1984) has given some rules, listed in Figure 7–6, on how to put together a poem. This kind of instruction provides a structure that allows students to then use their own experiences and verbal facilities to produce unique results.

Well-developed skills in poetry can be used to extend the meaning and understanding of some common definitions, which can represent another dimension of concept enrichment. One popular topic could be exploring the range and scope of such a concept as

---

FIGURE 7–6   Getting Ready to Write Your First Poem

The Five-Step Poem

1. On the first line, write down a noun (a person, place, or thing).
2. On the second line, write down two adjectives (separate them with a comma).
3. On the third line, write three verbs that tell what the noun does (separate them with a comma).
4. On the fourth line, write a thought about your noun (a short phrase).
5. On the last (fifth) line, write the same noun as on the first line, *or preferably* a related noun (a synonym).

Examples

Trees	Commercials	Gail
Shady, bare,	Clever, stupid	Happy, gay
Branching, blooming, growing.	Amuse, inform, bare	Laughs, dances, sings
They eat your kites . . .	Icebox time	Not showing her inner thoughts
Trees	Advertisements	Woman

Source: The Five Steps from Barbara Zembachs Thaden, *A Poetry Unit for the Academically Gifted*. Adapted by permission.

heroes. Is a hero merely someone like Superman, who uses his special gifts to protect the helpless, or is it a soldier dying to save his comrades, or a mother denying her own wishes for the sake of her daughter?

There is always a debate as to what represents quality literature—literature that superior as well as average students should be expected to experience. In 1984, William Bennett, then chairman of the National Endowment for the Humanities, asked 325 journalists, teachers, business officials, and parents what literary works they thought students in the United States should be expected to study. Figure 7–7 shows the results of that inquiry. It would be interesting to pose the same question to populations of African-American or Hispanic citizens and see what *that* list would look like, and how many common volumes there might be. Nevertheless, this list represents the literature of the current mainstream culture, and gifted students should be familiar with many of these volumes.

The desire to use interdisciplinary materials has increased since this has become one of the major goals of middle schools. Two themes that are particularly amenable to such cross-disciplinary attention are the search for *patterns* and the concept of *change*.

Patterns can be found in chemistry (crystals), physics (space and time), genetics (generational similarities), as well as in language. Figure 7–8 shows a sample lesson plan for understanding language patterns (Kersch, Nielson, & Subotnik, 1987). Here, in only a couple of class sessions, the rhythms of language in limericks and poetry can be presented

FIGURE 7–7 Important Works in the Humanities

Literary Works American Students Should Study

1. **Shakespeare** (particularly *Macbeth* and *Hamlet*)
2. **American Historical Documents** (particularly the Declaration of Independence, the Constitution, and the Gettysburg Address)
3. **Twain** (*Huckleberry Finn*)
4. **The Bible**
5. **Homer** (*Odyssey, Illiad*)
6. **Dickens** (*Great Expectations, Tale of Two Cities*)
7. **Plato** (*The Republic*)
8. **Steinbeck** (*Grapes of Wrath*)
9. **Hawthorne** (*Scarlet Letter*)
10. **Sophocles** (*Oedipus*)
11. **Melville** (*Moby Dick*)
12. **Orwell** (*1984*)
13. **Thoreau** (*Walden*)
14. **Frost** (poems)
15. **Whitman** (*Leaves of Grass*)
16. **Fitzgerald** (*The Great Gatsby*)
17. **Chaucer** (*The Canterbury Tales*)
18. **Marx** (*Communist Manifesto*)
19. **Aristotle** (*Politics*)
20. **Dickinson** (poems)
21. **Dostoevsky** (*Crime and Punishment*)
22. **Faulkner** (various works)
23. **Salinger** (*Catcher in the Rye*)
24. **de Tocqueville** (*Democracy in America*)
25. **Austen** (*Pride and Prejudice*)
26. **Emerson** (essays and poems)
27. **Machiavelli** (*The Prince*)
28. **Milton** (*Paradise Lost*)
29. **Tolstoy** (*War and Peace*)
30. **Virgil** (*Aeneid*)

Source: W. Bennett (September 5, 1984), *Education Week, 4* (1), p. 129.

FIGURE 7–8   Sample Lesson Plan for Week Two—Language Patterns

Generalization to be Developed: Patterns are nature's and man's coded messages to one another.

Specific Objective: The student will identify the relationship between stress/rhythm patterns in poetry and the oral reading of such poetry.

Motivational Activity: Read several limericks to the class. Not only are they humorous, but they have an excellent rhythmic pattern. Their introduction here will set the stage for later activities involving the actual writing of limericks.

Primary Activity: Distribute information regarding poetic rhythm. Have students read and discuss how poetic stress patterns (rhythm) relate to the oral reading of poetry. Let students work in pairs with a textbook or a variety of poetry books and anthologies. The students will determine scansion and metric measurement of lines. Have all groups compare results. Note: Classics, such as Mother Goose, can be fun for this activity.

Materials: Handouts containing information regarding poetic rhythm, textbooks that contain poetry, and a wide variety of poetry books or anthologies.

Estimated Time Frame: One or two class periods.

Subsequent Activities: Using pre-determined stress patterns and metric lines, students, singly or in pairs, will write their own poems and read them to the class.

Source: Kersch, M., Nielson, E., & Subotnik, R. (1987). Techniques and sources for developing integrative curriculum for the gifted. *Journal for the Education of the Gifted, 11* (1), 64. Reprinted by permission.

and the students can be asked to create word rhythms of their own. This can satisfy the needs of the students to be producers rather than just receivers.

One of the devices by which students can become active participants in the learning process is through the development of a literature log. Each student keeps a running log representing their responses to reading assignments. The log entries are generally comprised of three parts. The first part answers the following question: What was the reaction about what you read? Verbalize your emotional response. The second part of the entry asks the student to link your reading with other experiences you have had or other writings that you have read. Write about these associations and explain how they fit the story. The third part of each entry asks the student to find a significant word, passage, feature, or phrase, and write it down along with an explanation of its beauty of significance. The teacher would periodically pick up the logs to read and comment on them. This approach puts into concrete form the student's reactions to a particular assignment and helps to clarify his or her reactions to a piece of literature.

Content Sophistication

What are some of the key values that need explanation—more explanation than can be given in the traditional language arts curriculum? Brandwein (1987) proposed a curriculum in the humanities that seems to fit the needs of gifted students at the elementary school level. One of the reasons why teachers avoid such topics is that they fear these ideas will be too abstract for many students of this age—a good reason for introducing topics of this kind in honors sections or resource rooms. Ideas might include the following:

TRUTH: *Individuals search for and express the reality of their experiences.* Students can be asked to portray a valid image of the environment through writing or art and to discuss how one validates "truth." Is there one truth or are there many truths? Such questions should stir the students to some additional complex issues and discussions.

BEAUTY: *Individuals perceive and express the beauty of their experiences.* Students can be asked to define objects and events in terms that satisfy their image of beauty. Can they gain agreement from their classmates on the nature of beauty in music, art, poetry, and the like? Why or why not?

JUSTICE: *Individuals seek and express the ideals of justice.* What is the code of justice? How does it fit with ideas of compassion and mercy? Are justice and fairness the same? Can the students find examples of injustice in their local newspapers? How would they create an environment in which justice prevails?

LOVE: *Individuals seek and express love.* How do love and kindness relate to one another? Can people love things (e.g., a painting) as well as individuals? Can people love an ideal (e.g., justice, democracy)? How would such love manifest itself?

FAITH: *Individuals seek and express their faith.* People are familiar with religious faith. Are there other kinds of faith that people have as well? Is faith an attempt to explain the unexplainable? How is faith presented through art, music, or the written word?

When one thinks about it, one realizes that very little in the school curriculum actually deals with many of the important questions in life. We even seem to go to some lengths to avoid them. How can we live with people different from ourselves without violent conflict? How can people be tolerant of others' views and still have a clear opinion of our own as to what is right and wrong? What is the "good life"?

These are questions that the world's greatest philosophers, artists, clergy, and scientists have spent their lifetimes struggling with. Should the brightest of our students, or any of our students, be kept from discussions that clarify, in their minds, who they are and what it is they stand for until they reach the university or advanced high school years? By that time, their confusion and internal contradictions may have become paralyzing.

How can we explore important ideas? Reading works of those who have thought deeply, listening to music that soars, and viewing art that has a code of its own to be broken are possible avenues to explore. Through discussions, roleplaying, and debates, the teacher can introduce ideas of importance with the goal not being group consensus but a greater clarity of what abstract ideas of justice, truth, and beauty actually mean to the students.

Joe is rapidly developing into an expert needler of adults. He is developing the skill of finding the contradictions between what adults say and what they do, and then asking, "How come?" The gap between adults' stated values and actions gives Joe and other perceptive youngsters plenty of room for this type of action. Values are topics that can blend many different disciplines in language arts and the social sciences.

Gardner has noted, "As a nation we managed to live for eighty-nine years with the phrase 'all men are created equal' before we freed the slaves. And we let another fifty-five years pass before we gave women the vote. We don't rush into these things" (1978, p. 38).

Such general values as "Love thy neighbor" and comparisons with how we behave are open to similar and obvious criticism. Paradoxically, Joe, in his criticism, has really begun to seek to define for himself what he will believe and what values he will live by. He "tries on" each value, like a suit of clothes, to see how it fits. However, the diversity, or lack, of values expressed in the typical U.S. community has made many leaders in the public schools extremely nervous about including any extended examination of values. Understandably, this avoidance tends to cause youngsters striving for idealism to believe they live in a valueless society dominated by self-interest and shadowy figures acting counter to the public interest. It is possible to help gifted students seek understanding of major moral principles. Gardner pointed out that we do have many fundamental values in common in our society, and these important, sophisticated ideas need to be pointed out and discussed. Some of these are:

1. *Justice and the rule of law.* The attempt to provide justice to all, although often falling short in practice, represents one of the most common themes of the U.S. society.
2. *Freedom of expression.* The right to speak one's mind, regardless of who it offends, is another proud tradition. Without it, it is likely that many of our other freedoms would vanish.
3. *The dignity and worth of each person.* Equality of opportunity for all—to give everyone a chance to reach their potential in a free society—is a consistent theme. The insistence on special education for all children who have disabilities is a clear reflection of that value.
4. *Individual moral responsibility.* We are each responsible for the consequences of our actions. Even when we make allowances for differences in backgrounds and opportunities, in the end, we are the captains of our fate and will be judged as such by our friends, neighbors, and communities.
5. *Our distaste for corruption.* In this case, the larger purposes of the society may be betrayed by hatred, fear, envy, the smell of power, or personal gain. Nevertheless, we agree that these things should not be, and we array our legal and social institutions to protect the larger society against personal frailty (1978, pp. 30–32).

If gifted children are helped to gain the perspective that the fight for human justice is a continuous one extending far into the past and, no doubt, far into the future, they need not despair about our being short of perfection now. Further, to understand that such a fight is a continuous quest and is not like a football game where there is a beginning and an end, where you win or lose and go home, is to bring gifted children to a point of wisdom that can carry over to many other situations.

Content Novelty

Some topics seem to have special appeal and value to gifted students, even if they may not seem appropriate or timely for the regular classroom. One of the common observations of gifted children has been their intense interest in moral and value issues. They seem more concerned and preoccupied with issues of right and wrong than do many of their agemates of more average abilities. Where does this interest come from? Why do these youngsters weep about poor or hungry children they have never seen? Does their advanced intelligence make them able to perceive these distant circumstances better than others? Certainly, however, such intelligence does not guarantee sympathy or empathy.

One day in class, Stephanie suddenly became upset during a discussion of the plight of starving African children. She broke into tears and for a period of time was inconsolable. It was clear that she felt very deeply about the injustice of innocents being hurt. The other children looked at her strangely and were, in turn, upset that a peer would show such intense emotion over something that was happening so far away.

It was then that the teacher realized the special burden felt by many talented and gifted students who had a more highly developed ability to empathize and to relate to faraway people, places, and times. Such ability can bring delight, when imagination carries one to adventures in distant places and distant times, but it can bring deep concerns about issues like justice and morality, which do not seem to be within the comprehension of children of average abilities at the preadolescent age to the same degree.

Stephanie's teacher has an additional concern: Who will instruct these talented youngsters in the areas of values, ethics, and morality? The churches in Stephanie's town, as in many others, have become decreasingly important in the lives of many of the citizens. The schools, nervous about offending members of the community by injecting themselves into controversial issues, have become jittery at the very thought of having a full-fledged discussion of the rights of citizens. There have been days and weeks where an open discussion of the Bill of Rights—to say nothing of population control or war and peace—could get the incautious teacher in a great deal of difficulty. Where, then, can Stephanie go for instruction—to her parents, whose own search for what is "right" is hardly more coherent than Stephanie's? Who will provide students such as Stephanie with the bedrock of evaluative concepts that will carry them through the difficult and important decisions that lie in front of them? There is perhaps no more important question that educational leaders must ask themselves.

It is a rare student who has heard a vigorous discussion in the public schools over rights of property versus civil rights, or the rights of employers versus the rights of employees—two of many issues about which many citizens are today seeking guidance. The reasons for this ethical vacuum are not hard to find. The schools, highly sensitive to partisan criticism, have tended to shun controversy as the easy way out. Another reason that keeps the public schools from more effective action is the philosophy that the school's primary mission is to pass on information and job skills, not values.

The focus of a typical unit or a discussion in the schools is: What is the right answer? However, suppose that there is no one set of correct answers, but only a large number of answers, depending on the values each person holds? How does a teacher finish a topic under those circumstances? Since many ethical issues are so open to debate characterized by highly charged emotions, many educators take the easy way out by ignoring the issues, saying that these are the problems of the church or the family, or by rationalizing them away on the basis of the supposed mental immaturity of the students.

We may be told that 10-year-olds have not had enough life experience to be able to make such decisions or to think clearly on such matters. Later on, perhaps much later on, they will be able to take up the discussion of these issues. And so they probably will—in the informal atmosphere of the college dormitory, where few discussion topics are avoided because of the fears of a nervous adult society that the younger generation will learn too much, too soon.

One drawback to the schools becoming involved in reading and discussing values and ethics may be the very real fear that such lessons on values could easily become indoctrination by teacher or school. This is a justifiable fear, but there is a way around the dilemma. The school can concentrate on *how* the children can make value decisions rather than the nature of the conclusion reached. By focusing on the *process* by which such decisions are made, the school does not need to take positions on such controversial issues as capital punishment, freedom and responsibility of the press, and the like.

One of the potential uses of language arts is to combine it with other subject areas in a multidisciplinary approach. The following examples link the social studies with language arts by stressing writing, communication, and value issues.

The Martian Expedition

The senior author once conducted a brief adventure into the ethical judgment of a group of gifted children, some of which is reproduced here (Gallagher, 1966). The purpose of the study was to determine whether a group of fifth-grade, intellectually superior youngsters from middle- and upper middle-class homes could meaningfully discuss ethical concepts and arrive at some resolution to problems presented to them. These children were seen for one hour a week in a group of 10 to 16 children.

For a period of seven weeks, these youngsters were taken on an imaginary trip as adult members of a first expedition to the planet of Mars. This theme allowed for the introduction of many problems that needed to be solved by the class; these were presented to the group for their discussion and resolution. The teacher maintained a neutral attitude and did not express his own opinions on the problems or eventual decisions.

The students were told that they were going to make an expedition to Mars. The teacher would be the captain of the voyage, and each of the students was given the opportunity to create the character that he or she would play in this expedition. The choice of characters in itself was most interesting. The majority of the children chose a scientific role, such as geologist, physicist, or biologist. Two of the youngsters chose to be doctors, and many others selected pilots or assistant pilots. Such free choices can tell one much about the children. One of the boys, who seemed the most insecure, chose to be a corporal in the security force. By implication, the lower the rank, the lower the duties or responsibilities expected of the individual. One of the girls in the class rejected the traditional feminine role by taking on a masculine character as her alter-ego during the trip.

The Food Shortage Problem.   The members of the expedition were informed that their spaceship had crashed on Mars and that it was likely to take about 11 months to repair the ship so that they could return to Earth.

The first problem presented to them was that they had only four months of food supplies and, thus, a serious difficulty in the distribution of this food. The students' approach to this problem followed a pattern repeated often in the weeks to follow. First, they tried to avoid making the difficult decision of how to divide the food supply. This represented the normal reaction of adults in such a situation—to solve the problem in a way so that the grinding and difficult ethical decision really does not have to be made. This could be done by finding edible plants on the planet, obtaining food from the natives, or even making artificial food; all these were suggested by the students.

In order to keep the problem as an ethical issue, the captain rejected all of these possibilities, at least for the immediate future, and forced the members into making some kind of a decision as to what should be done with the limited food. Eventually, after much discussing, the students agreed by majority vote that the food should be equally rationed among all members of the expedition. They rejected the notion that the captain should get more than his just share because he was the captain, or that the head scientist should get more because of his status or position. The concept of equality of treatment was clearly established. The alternative concept that special persons should obtain special rewards was rejected.

The Dying Crewman Problem.   Another rather difficult problem that was presented to the youngsters was that one of the members of the crew had been seriously injured and that both of the expedition doctors reported that he would surely die very soon. The ethical question presented to the students was whether the food, which was already in very short supply, should be given to this person or whether it should be withheld on the grounds that he was going to die anyway and those who were living would need all the food they could get.

This problem brought out more ingenuity in the group in their attempts to avoid the central issue. The majority had no trouble coming to a conclusion that the person should receive food, but the basis for the decision was that the doctors might not be right! Since doctors have been wrong before in their diagnoses, it would be wrong to withhold food and deliberately kill the person when he might have a chance to remain alive.

No one, in this instance, suggested that the person should receive food, even though he was going to die anyway, merely on the basis of his membership in the human community. The decision was not unanimous, and there were quite a few suggestions that the person should be allowed to starve to death on the basis that the other people needed the food more.

The Artistic Crewman Problem.   An interesting example of the rather finely developed sense of compromise of these gifted youngsters was revealed in another problem presented to them. One crew member was supposed to be working on the repair of the ship, but instead was so entranced by the beauties of the Martian countryside that all he wanted to do was to go off and paint Martian landscapes. He was neglecting his duty by doing this, even though his paintings were quite beautiful.

These students were loath to forbid completely this kind of activity and reached a compromise solution in which the artist would be allowed to continue his painting but would be encouraged to do it in his off-hours. He would be allowed, then, to work on the night shift—where his other skills would be demanded by the emergency situation. If he would agree to this, he would be encouraged to continue his painting, but if he did not agree and completely avoided his other responsibilities, he could be punished by having his painting materials confiscated.

The Natives' Rights.   Two additional problems presented to the children probably represented the most serious challenge to the youngsters' sense of right and wrong. They were told that they were in luck! One of their scientists had found some metallic deposits of the type necessary to repair the spaceship, but there was one problem. The only place that they could find this metal was in the holy ground of the natives. According to the natives, any outsiders coming into that ground would desecrate it. Thus, the crew would do serious insult to the religious feelings of the natives if they pursued the metal they needed. Should they do it?

For the first time, the students came face to face with the conflict between abstract standards and direct human needs. Although they all felt that the natives' religion should be respected, in the end the consensus was that they should take the metal. The guilt feelings of the students were manifest. They would take only so much metal as was absolutely needed. Furthermore, they would return that amount of metal plus payment for damages when they returned to Earth.

It should not be concluded from the lively discussion held over this question that these talented children now had insight into *why* some people transgress against standards that they hold in high regard. The most single striking observation of these students was that, although they had a well-developed sense of right and wrong, they had little or no understanding of the motivation of the transgressor. In most instances, he was "bad" or was dismissed casually as "nutty."

The conclusion drawn from these discussions was that intellectually superior children in the elementary grades were quite capable of conducting vigorous and spirited discussions of "right" or "wrong" behavior. Their own inexperience in dealing with such issues was also apparent, however. None had raised such questions before in school or in their families, and they were eager to discuss among themselves and with others what the resolutions might be to issues of deep and worrisome concern.

Although all of the content fields have the potential for eliciting value issues from students, the field of language arts is perhaps the most logical area. There, issues of good and evil, of literary works that reveal the conflict between the individual and the state, or the necessity for placing a quality dimension on a poem or short story all involve teachers and students in issues of values. However, many teachers try to steer clear of value discussions in their classroom, partly because such discussions may be controversial and partly because the teacher is not sure how such issues should be handled.

On the other hand, if value issues are never discussed in class, the students never get a chance to find out for themselves just where they stand on important issues, and never get a chance to play out their feelings and set of values against those of someone else. One of the substantial discoveries of the late elementary grades is that people of goodwill and friendship can differ in their judgment on important issues.

This is a puzzling discovery to students who have previously comforted themselves with the notion that anyone who opposed their particular position was either wrong or evil. Figure 7–9 provides a series of topics that could lead to value discussions in the classroom. In using these values, the teacher has to determine for himself or herself if the purpose of the discussion is to decide the issue on one side or another.

One of the topics from Figure 7–9 that will clearly get an instantaneous discussion is the positive and negative aspects of television. It is through such discussions that one may see some arguments that previously had gone unnoticed. For example, in the argument about television, Stephanie can mention the importance of being brought close to significant world events as a positive aspect, whereas Cranshaw might point out that the problem with television is not what is on television but that any television viewing takes up time that otherwise could be spent more usefully.

Some students with a desire for closure may wish for the discussion to end with a conclusion such as: Television is all right but there should be some limits to the viewing time or to what is viewed. However, such a conclusion is not necessary. It is enough that the students clearly understand the issue.

Another topic raised in Figure 7–9, the contributions of various immigrants to our nation, opens up the possibility of discussion of cultural differences and what the relative merits of cultural values are from one group to another. An extended discussion of this issue, together with some appropriate readings, could help the students see that cultural differences are an advantage to the "tossed salad" that is the United States, but that such diversity also results in more difficulty in reaching a common national position on some issues.

Finally, there is the issue in Figure 7–9 of determining, what was the most important event of all time. Someone is sure to bring up the birth of Jesus Christ as one option, whereas another student might argue vigorously for the discovery of electricity. Obviously this issue will continue to be argued by reasonable persons. The important thing to be learned from such discussions is what the underlying assumptions of the individuals are and how those assumptions fit into their own value structures.

In a discussion of conflicting values, what is to be learned is not necessarily which one is "correct" but rather to understand the basis of differences. For example, in Figure 7–9, one topic is whether the police have a right to monitor phone conversations. What is sought, through conversation, is to discover the underlying values behind the positions held by the students.

Those who answer no to the question are likely to hold that individual privacy should take precedence over other considerations and that police states use invasion of privacy to control the people. Those who answer yes are likely to hold to the value that the protection of the society against evils such as drug traffickers must take precedence over privacy in that instance, and that if a person is doing nothing wrong, why should he or she worry about who listens in? The important discovery that the students make is not necessarily who is right but the fact that we all have hierarchies of values and it is those values that are near the top of the hierarchy that will be activated in discussions about values.

By looking at the two hierarchies presented Figure 7–10, we can see a different values base for two different people. Which one is likely to be vigorously supporting programs for children with disabilities? Which one for reduction of taxes? Each can legitimately say they are for the other position.

The same self-awareness of values that one holds seems to be behind some of the efforts of Mortimer Adler and his Paidaia program (*Paidaia* means "the upbringing of the child," implying the general learning that should be the possession of all human beings) (Adler, 1982). Adler proposed three types of teaching strategies: *didactic instruction* through lectures, *coaching* through supervised practice, and *seminar teaching* through questioning and discussion.

FIGURE 7–9   Topics for Values Discussions

Politics: The suggestion has been made that we suspend all of our civil liberties (such as trial by jury, innocent until proven guilty, not having phone lines tapped, etc.) in the case of drug dealers, because they are so hard to catch and they are doing such damage to our society. What do you think?

History: The Statue of Liberty welcomes all to our shores, but U.S. immigration policy puts severe limits on who can come into the United States and remain here. What do you think our policy should be?

Sociology: The world's population is on course to double within 50 years, according to the latest projections of current trends. What should be our approach, as a world community, to the care and feeding of these new arrivals, given the problems we currently have with our existing population?

Politics: It has been said that a great president can only be made great through war. Surely many of our "great" presidents have been leaders during a time of national conflict and sacrifice. Can you think of how a president could be considered "great" *without* participating in a major war?

Family: The recent development of technologies (such as television, compact disc, air conditioning, etc.) all seem to have the effect of reducing our social and neighborhood contacts and commitments. Should we worry about how new inventions are affecting our families and friends?

Ethics: You have personal knowledge of other students who are taking computers from the school and selling them. What should you do about this?

It is the seminar method that allows for the exploration of values through a group discussion mode. In seminar learning, all students read a significant passage from literature (such as Sophocles' *Antigone*) or public documents (such as the Declaration of Independence). They are then led in discussion by the teacher, who raises questions and proposes issues for discussion (after first satisfying himself or herself that the students really understand what the passage shows).

For example, in using the Declaration of Independence, a portion of which is shown in Figure 7–11, the teacher might ask What is a " self-evident truth"? What does "all men are created equal" mean? Following that, he or she might wish to pursue the validity of the cause being discussed, or what might (or should) happen if a state wished to secede from

FIGURE 7–10   Hierarchy of Values

George	*Pete*
1. Industrial development	1. Help young children with handicaps
2. Reduce deficit	2. Health services for the elderly
3. Aid to private schools	3. More aid to public schools
4. Build more highways	4. Aid for environment
5. Help young children with handicaps	5. Industrial development
6. More aid to public schools	6. Reduce deficit

Source: From "The Role of Values and Facts in Policy Development for Infants and Toddlers with Disabilities and Their Families" by J. Gallagher, 1992, *Journal of Early Intervention*. Reprinted by permission.

FIGURE 7–11   A Segment of the Declaration of Independence

We hold these Truths to be self-evident, that all Men are created equal, that they are endowed by their Creator with certain unalienable Rights, that among these are Life, Liberty, and the pursuit of Happiness—That to secure these Rights, Governments are instituted among Men, deriving their just Powers from the Consent of the Governed, that whenever any Form of Government becomes destructive to these Ends, it is the Right of the People to alter or abolish it, and to institute new Government, laying its Foundation on such Principles, and organizing its Powers in such Form, as to them shall seem most likely to effect their Safety and Happiness....

the Union using a similar argument. Again, the purpose of the discussion is not so much to reach common agreement as to reach some common understanding of the values and issues that are at stake.

The Teacher of Language Arts

Besides supplying well-rounded content, the effective teacher of language arts must really have a love affair with the language. The joy seen at the students' initial clumsy efforts to express individuality will often parallel the gardener's excitement at seeing the first shoots appear above ground, and the teacher will nurture these early evidences of talent as tenderly as that gardener tends to young shoots.

Such joy may be tempered, however, by a class load of 75 children (in resource rooms) or, in secondary schools, of 150 or more students. Who would look forward to reading and correcting 150 themes, essays, or poems—many of them illegible and others of poor construction? In such a situation, despair is the likely human reaction.

With many teachers having a student load of 125 (or more), the assignment of a two-page essay (allowing 15 minutes for reading and commenting on each essay) would result in teachers spending an additional 31 hours of work per week. The one period of planning per day that each secondary teacher traditionally has hardly allows for the complex preparation necessary to stimulate higher-order thinking. In addition, teachers rarely work with other teachers—or even communicate with them—in the traditional secondary school program and therefore do not share innovative teaching strategies. All of these forces will have to be overcome if there is to be a serious effort to challenge students, especially gifted students, to the level of thinking to which they are capable in the traditional secondary school program.

Special classes, or sections focusing on gifted or high performing children, can help provide the teacher with somewhat smaller, if more challenging, groups and thus alleviate the more difficult of these tasks. Teaching teams in the middle school can also allow for flexibility of grouping students for this purpose.

There does seem to be help on the way from an unlikely source—technology. The growing use and availability of the word processor promises to provide students with more self-correcting capabilities. There will soon be no legitimate excuse for poor spelling or hard-to-read themes, nor can the students legitimately complain about the burden of rewriting. All persons engaged in writing know that it is only at least the third or fourth draft that they would want to display in public. Now, the computer provides a tool from which all students, gifted in particular, can profit.

Papert has pointed out that one of the major uses of the computer is as a writing instrument. Such a tool will allow teachers to avoid the painstaking job of teaching children to make corrections and to rewrite which often becomes such a messy business as to be discouraging to student and teacher alike. Papert stated,

> *My image of myself as a writer includes the expectation of an unacceptable first draft that will develop, with successive editing, into presentable form. But I would not be able to afford this image if I were a third grader. The physical act of writing would be slow and laborious. I would have no secretary. For most children, rewriting a text is so laborious that the first draft is the final copy, and the skill of rereading with a critical eye is never acquired. (1980, p. 30)*

With the computer as word processor, the end product is always neat and easily correctable. Thus, the teacher should have little hesitation in asking students to progressively refine and improve their ability to communicate through writing.

Another use of technology that may be utilized more in the future is the availability of videotape, which will extend the experiences of the students. The use of mentors—people with long experience and expertise in given areas—to supplement instruction for gifted students has been noted in a number of chapters in this text. One variation of this could be called a *distant mentor*. Shachter (1980) reported on a program called Profiles in Literature, a series of videotaped interviews distributed by Temple University that each include 30 minutes of discussion with authors and poets about how they work (p. 70).

In the Profiles in Literature series, author Judy Blume, reporting on her relationship with the characters in one of her books, says, "I get depressed when I finish a book, because it is like saying goodbye to old friends, so the best therapy is to start another book right away." In Profiles in Literature, Ann Petry talks about how she organizes a book: "Usually I begin with people who make the plot, and the plot should stem from the kind of people they are. I have to know how the story is going to end before I start, because the whole thing builds to this ending." John Ciardi describes the writing of poetry as "joyously difficult" and comments, "Some poor students get desperate before they have worked up a preliminary sweat. They have to give it a soul consuming effort…. A poem is never finished, it is abandoned in despair."

Prior to viewing the videotapes, the students are urged to read about the authors and some of their works, which helps them gain a greater understanding of the books themselves and, incidentally, increases their own reading. These distant mentors provide a way of bringing the students into contact with creative writers and artists. A variation on this theme could be to bring in local authors, artists, or poets to the classroom to be interviewed by the students themselves.

Program Evaluation

There are growing indications that attention to the development of specific skills, such as writing skills, can result in measurable student improvement. This is particularly true of students who are gifted, or at least above average in cognitive abilities. Stoddard and Renzulli (1983) reported on an experiment in the improvement of writing skills through the focus on basic sentence-combining techniques. Upper elementary school students received a special six-week program in how to change base sentences, such as those shown on the left, to a more integrated and complex sentence, on the right:

Battaglia glanced at first base. He went into his windup. Then he threw a hanging curve. Ryan knocked it out of the stadium.	Battaglia glanced at first base, went into his windup, and threw a hanging curve that Ryan knocked out of the stadium.

Students who received exercises in sentence combining, plus training in divergent thinking (creativity), showed the most improvement in writing skills, indicating that it is possible to combine creativity exercises (see Chapter 10) with standard curriculum in a productive fashion.

The evaluation of effective programming of language arts for students with outstanding gifts and talents has always been difficult. This is particularly true when the objectives are such things as "enhancing creative writing" or "encouraging imaginative thinking." Clearly, no simple pencil-and-paper test can be used to evaluate the quality of the work done.

The new reform movement stressing outcome-based education focuses on the products that the students have generated (Wiggins, 1992). More and more interest is being shown in the development of *portfolios*, or cumulative folders, that show a collection of the work of the students over time. Although this has been a process used in art education for some time, it is now being applied in other curriculum fields as well. Through this device, it is possible to see the developing maturity of successful students' works. For example, if an emphasis has been placed on the use of similes and metaphors, then the earlier products can be compared with later products in order to see the progression of skills utility.

Portfolios are also a useful device to indicate to the student how far he or she has progressed over a period of time. However, portfolios do not absolve the educator from a major task—the setting of criteria for excellence so that the work can be properly judged. Nor should portfolios be used as storehouses for all of the work of the student, resulting in a terrible cluttering of paper. Only significant work, representing serious student effort, should be included.

One more formal use of portfolios in program evaluation can be done via the "blind judges" test. In such a test, an early product and a later product from the same student are shown to a judge. The products are not identified as to when they were done (thus, the judge is blind in that sense). The judge is asked to identify which is the better product and why. If the program is successful, the accumulation of such judges' ratings should indicate that the students are progressing in certain definable ways.

There is perhaps no other dimension in the curriculum through which gifted children can operate more effectively than language arts. The ability of these students to understand how to use verbal skills in order to communicate is clearly observable. The study of literature represents the past speaking to the present, and can give students a portrait of their human heritage. It is also one of the few content fields where values can be discussed; those students who worry about the worth of an idea, the virtue of an approach, or the subtle presence of values in a supposedly value-free society should find language arts a challenging and exciting subject area. However, children cannot master these skills without instruction. This chapter has indicated some ways in which language arts might live up to its potential.

Unresolved Issues

1. How can we bring the creative and productive practitioners of language arts—the writers, poets, journalists, and so on—into more direct contact with students who wish to be proficient in these areas? Gifted students need models and mentors in these fields, as well as in the sciences.
2. Can we find ways for the public schools to feel freer to discuss controversial issues and to teach the nature of values held by social systems unlike our own as a means of increasing the sophistication of gifted students, who must eventually deal with such systems in their adult lives?
3. Can we devise microcomputer sequences or computer-assisted instruction programs to teach gifted students the mechanics of language arts so as to allow these students more time to be expressive and interpretive?
4. Can we develop more interdisciplinary curriculum units (e.g., language arts and social studies, as in values and politics) that demonstrate the application of language arts to other knowledge fields?

Chapter Review

1. Language arts is primarily a skills-development area focusing on *writing, reading, speaking*, and *listening*.
2. The principles of skills training are to convey awareness of the rules governing the skill, practice of the skill under supervision, and the generation of a product through the use of the skill.
3. Few students consider the pervasive importance of language to themselves or their culture until they are provided the opportunity to ponder about it and practice its use.
4. The structure of short stories can be brought to the attention of students by specific questions on character development, plot, and point of view of the short story.
5. Content acceleration can mean early introduction to foreign languages and to the technical tools of writing. Such programs report good success.

6. In content enrichment, gifted students can be taught that literature offers an economical way to learn of the achievement, failures, and aspirations of individuals or nations.

7. The fable represents one specific vehicle for teaching the skills of analysis and construction.

8. Gifted students should experience the works of writers and poets from many cultures other than their own in order to seek cultural universals as well as differences.

9. Many values are agreed upon in our supposedly value-free society. Among these common values are a concern for justice, freedom of expression, the worth of the individual, moral responsibility, and a distaste for corruption.

10. Values can be taught in the schools without the fear of indoctrination if we focus on the process of value development and application.

11. Existential guilt, which stems from having too much while others have too little, may account for some of the gifted child's concerns for troubled or downtrodden people.

12. Technology, in the form of the word processor and videotape, gives promise that more attention can be given to students' creative writing and understanding of the creative process.

13. The portfolio has become one device used for evaluation that fits well into the language arts objectives and activities.

Readings of Special Interest

Adler, M. (1982). *The paideia proposal.* New York: Macmillan.

One of the world's distinguished philosophers speaks for a group of educators, arguing for a return to high standards and a classical approach to education. Adler argues for three major goals: the acquisition of organized knowledge, the development of problem-solving skills, and the enlarged understanding of ideas and values. Such a proposal would fit well into a program for gifted students, and perhaps less well for those who have not had the advantage of a family committed to learning and education.

Hirsch, E. D., Jr. (1987). *Cultural literacy: What every American needs to know.* Boston: Houghton-Mifflin.

This book describes the common knowledges that allow us to communicate with one another. It is controversial, in the sense that it presents a Eurocentric view of culture, but the basic thesis appears sound.

VanTassel-Baska, J. (1992). *Planning effective curriculum for gifted learners.* Denver, CO: Love Publishing.

Although this book spans the full range of curriculum offerings, it is of special value in the field of language arts. It provides a clear differentiation of curriculum suggestions for gifted and average learners and also has curricular suggestions for special populations of gifted learners such as students with learning disabilities, students from disadvantaged circumstances, and six sample curricular units illustrating content from mathematics to language arts.

Moyers, B. (1990). *A world of ideas, II.* New York: Doubleday.

This is a collection of interviews between Bill Moyers and a series of noted artists, novelists, philosophers, and others. These are thought pieces in which Moyers explores with the individuals the responsibilities of the private citizen to the public social issues. It is a provocative and excellent device to stimulate the thinking of gifted students or the teacher of gifted students.

References

Brandwein, P. (1987). *The permanent agenda of man: The humanities*. New York: Harcourt Brace Jovanovich.

Gallagher, J. (1966). *Ethics and moral judgment in children: A pilot investigation*. Boston: Unitarian Universalist Association.

Gardner, J. (1978). *Morale*. New York: Norton.

Gentile, C. (1992). *Exploring new methods for collecting students' school-based writing: NAEP's 1990 portfolio study*. Washington, DC: National Center for Educational Statistics, U.S. Department of Education.

Hogan, E. (1981). *Hero poetry*. Chapel Hill, NC: Phillips Junior High School.

Kersch, M., Nielson, E., & Subotnik, R. (1987). Techniques and sources for developing integrative curriculum for the gifted. *Journal for the Education of the Gifted, 11* (1).

Khatena, J. (1982). *Educational psychology of the gifted*. New York: Wiley & Sons.

Mindell, P., & Stracher, D. (1980). Assessing reading and writing of the gifted: The warp and woof of the language program. *Gifted Child Quarterly, 24* (2), 72–79.

Moss, J. (1980). The fable and critical thinking. *Language Arts, 57*, 21–29.

Papert, S. (1980). *Mindstorms*. New York: Basic Books.

Shachter, J. (1980). Learning from authors in person and in mixed media. *Gifted Child Quarterly, 24* (2), 69–71.

Squire, J. (1985). *The labors of sysiphys: achieving excellence in schooling*. International Reading Association Address.

Stoddard, E., & Renzulli, J. (1983). Improving the writing skills of talented poor students. *Gifted Child Quarterly, 27* (1), 21–27.

Thaden, B. (1984, March). *A poetry unit for the academically gifted, grades 7–12*. Paper presented at the meeting of the North Carolina Association for Gifted and Talented, Asheville, NC.

Wiggins, G. (1992). Creative tests worth taking. *Educational Leadership, 49* (8), 26–33.

Wright, R. (1945). *Black boy*. New York: Harper & Row.

Chapter 8

Visual and
Performing Arts
for Gifted Students

Key Questions

- Why are the visual and performing arts considered supplementary, rather than critical, to the standard curriculum offerings of the public schools?
- What are some ways we can identify highly talented students in the arts?
- What are some common characteristics of creative artists?
- What are some ways that visual and performing arts can be integrated in cross-disciplinary study? With science? With social studies? With language arts?
- What are some curricular adaptations that can be made for gifted students in the arts? Acceleration? Enrichment? Sophistication? Novelty?
- What are the special characteristics and training that teachers of the visual and performing arts should have to cope with the very talented?
- How can programs for gifted students in the arts be adequately assessed to determine their effectiveness?

In 1972, when Commissioner of Education Sidney Marland presented a report to the Congress on the state of gifted children in schools in the United States, one of the major recommendations of that report was to expand the definition of gifted from solely academic and cognitive areas to include high aptitude in the visual and performing arts. This change in definition would result in identifying some youngsters as gifted who ordinarily would not be eligible for special programs under the more limited definition. One such youngster with a markedly different combination of talents is Stephanie.

Since Stephanie is the opposite of Zelda in so many ways, except for outstanding talent, it is not surprising that they have little regard for one another. Whereas Zelda is relatively well served by the traditional educational program, Stephanie is not. Some artists can be expressive and still live within the boundaries of a somewhat traditional framework. Johann Sebastian Bach was this kind of artist—a model citizen who lived a traditional life at home with his wife and many children. Stephanie, on the other hand, prefers the "outer fringe" of the artistic community. Not only does she not fit into the traditional culture but in many ways she positively avoids it. In her dress and attitudes, as well as in her art, Stephanie strives to represent an avant-garde philosophy—never doing anything the regular way when something unique or different could be tried. Because of her attitudes, Stephanie is always on the edge of being considered a behavior problem, since one of life's annoyances she finds particularly unnecessary are school rules. "Who cares whether or not I wear a stupid hat to school?" is a common complaint. "If I respect someone, it's not because I do or do not have something on my head!"

One of the problems that Stephanie has in school is that although she is relatively flexible within her artistic talent—she likes drawing, photography, jewelry design, and sculpture—she is remarkably inflexible outside of her art. In this case, inflexible may as well be interpreted as uninterested, because if Stephanie cannot connect what she is learning back to some area of art or expression, she simply cannot figure out why she needs to learn it. Some teachers try to dig their heels in and insist that Stephanie complete reports and assignments that are absent of references to art. They feel it is important because students have to realize that some things need to be learned simply because they need to be learned, and not because they apply to one specific interest. These are the assignments that generally find a comfortable and permanent home in the far back corner of Stephanie's desk. Relevance is of critical importance to Stephanie, unlike Zelda who would likely learn just about anything simply because she is told to.

Teachers who are successful with Stephanie allow her to continue to try to build connections, realizing that, in a way, Stephanie is creating a rich internal environment for her art to explore. Here are some ways that teachers try to help Stephanie learn basic facts through art:

Math: Computer graphing programs to help represent curves, lines, and angles; geometry and the development of perspective

Science: Analysis of paint composition; exploration of radiation in photography; the idea of creativity and discovery in science

History: Biography of artists; the role of culture in the development of art and art trends; attitudes of different social and cultural mileaus to artistic creation

Writing: Journal writing; biography of writers and the diaries of artists; analysis of articles written by artists for stylistic features

Mr. Jenkins is trying to find a mentor for Stephanie—an artist in the community who is sensitive to the need to be a well-educated person and who will help teach Stephanie, in her own language and on her own terms, that even artists need to have some mundane skills to survive in the highly competitive art world. Finding an artist in the community to work with Stephanie may be a sensible thing to do, but what about the schools and their commitment to the arts?

Schools and the Arts

The major questions, from the standpoint of the school administration, are To what extent do they have responsibility in providing an organized program for talented students in the visual and performing arts? and To what extent would they continue to see these kinds of activities as a supplementary or extracurricular experience but not as part of the regular curriculum? To these questions, the practicing artist might well respond, "Why do we have music, or dance, or poetry, or stories? Because it is only through these and other modes that particular kinds of human experiences can be communicated."

This chapter will address issues such as the problems of identification of talent in the visual and performing arts, the characteristics of creative artists, some of the curricular adaptations that schools have made for this group, and the nature of the teacher and teaching in these fields.

Identifying the Gifted in the Arts

There are few established standardized measures that can be used to identify the talented and gifted individual in the visual and performing arts. Zelda, strongly encouraged by her parents, has taken violin lessons for the past three years and has achieved a level of technical competence—although she would hardly be viewed as gifted in this area. In this sense, she duplicated a finding noted by many in the field: The opportunity to develop one's skill on an instrument often becomes a determining factor in further participation in school orchestras, bands, and the like. Zelda's past performance and lessons would lead her to the next level of experience and skills training and should allow her to express the talent she has. Other students, without Zelda's opportunities, will have a more difficult time expressing their full potential in these areas.

Tests

An example of the use of tests in the identification procedure for musically talented students is provided by Gordon (1980), who reported the results of his Primary Measures of Music Audition. These tests require no previous experience on the part of the student and consist of two musical phrases heard consecutively in a group-testing situation. The children are told to circle either identical or different faces, depending on whether or not the second musical phrase was the same or different from the first. Different sections of the test focus on tonal and rhythm functions.

Gordon reported that the tests have validity and test-retest reliability, and they allow for the early identification of children with special talent so that their instruction can be more complex and sophisticated than the music instruction for the general class. He also presented evidence to suggest that specific training in music can significantly increase performance of the students on the music aptitude test.

Expert Judgments

One of the stumbling blocks to the conduct of a special program for students talented in the visual arts has been the screening and identification task itself. Traditionally, judgments have been made by teachers or performers and have been extremely subjective in nature. The judgments in these cases have been heavily dependent on which judge was evaluating the work. Clark and Zimmerman (1987) have described a test that appears to bring a more carefully judged result. They present the students with four tasks: (1) draw an interesting house as if you were looking at it from across the street, (2) draw a person who is running very fast, (3) draw a picture of you and your friends playing in a schoolyard, and (4) make a fantasy drawing from your imagination.

Twelve separate dimensions are graded on a 1- to 5-point scale. These twelve dimensions include sensory properties, such as line and shape; formal properties, such as rhythm, balance, and composition; expressive properties, such as mood and originality; and technical properties, such as technique and correctness of solution. These total scores seem to correlate well with teacher ratings of talented art students and represent a device for screening large numbers of students.

By putting test booklets into categories such as poor, average, and excellent, one can develop a pool of possible candidates to be examined further. Figure 8–1 shows examples of the three categories. The results of the test seem to predict performance in classes, which may or may not require drawing skills (Clark believes that this is because drawing is an intellectual as well as physical task).

Below Average

Average

Above Average

FIGURE 8–1   Clark's Drawing Abilities Test: Running Person, Ninth Grade

Source: Gilbert A. Clark and Enid D. Zimmerman, *Resources for educating artistically talented students* (Syracuse University Press, 1987), page 162. By permission of the publisher.

Rating Scales

Renzulli, Smith, White, Callahan, and Hartman (1977) provide, in Figure 8–2, a teacher's rating scale for students who are skilled in music. In order to test the accuracy of the scale, 10 regular classroom teachers were asked to fill out the scales for each student in their class, while specialists in the art and music program for each school identified students who they considered to be most and least capable. When the teacher ratings were com-

FIGURE 8–2   Scales for the Rating of Behavioral Characteristics of Superior Students

Name: _____ Date: _____

School: _____ Grade: _____ Age: _____

Teacher or person completing this form: _____

How long have you known the child? _____ years, _____ months

Part V: Artistic Characteristics

 1. Likes to participate in art activities; is eager to visually express ideas.
 2. Incorporates a large number of elements into art work; varies the subject and content of art work.
 3. Arrives at unique, unconventional solutions to artistic problems as opposed to traditional, conventional ones.
 4. Concentrates for long periods of time on art projects.
 5. Willingly tries out different media; experiments with a variety of materials and techniques.
 6. Tends to select art media for free activity or classroom projects.
 7. Is particularly sensitive to the environment; is a keen observer; sees the unusual, what may be overlooked by others.
 8. Produces balance and order in art work.
 9. Is critical of own work; sets high standards of quality; often reworks creation in order to refine it.
10. Shows an interest in other students' work; spends time studying and discussing their work.
11. Elaborates on ideas from other people; uses them as a "jumping-off point" as opposed to copying them.

Add Column Total	
Multiply by Weight	
Add Weighted Column Totals	
Totals	

Source: Reprinted, by permission, from J. S. Renzulli, L. H. Smith, A. J. White, C. M. Callahan, & R. K. Hartman (1977). Copyright, 1977, by Creative Learning Products.

pared with the specialist ratings, those identified as gifted were generally rated higher by both groups than those who were considered least capable. The information gives some credibility that such a scale can identify some of the highly talented children. The limited amount of agreement between the scores given by general teachers and the specialists still calls for a multiple identification procedure.

Another approach to identification focuses on self-report. Biographical inventories allow students to express their feelings and interests. For example, the following statements, which the students are asked to apply to themselves, seem to be associated with artistic talent:

Enjoyed reading literary classics, not novels or mysteries

Preferred classical music

Felt career security less important than advancement potential, personal freedom, or self-expression

Preferred to work alone

Considered himself outstanding in speech and completion of artistic and academic work

Of course, if there are not any standardized scales available, one could merely ask the student, "Are you interested in the arts? Are you good at it? Would you be willing to work alone and without regard to material rewards?" Sometimes we overcomplicate identification and forget that to find out needed information, one may only have to ask the student for it.

Auditions

One of the most extensive of selection techniques was designed to identify high school students gifted in the arts for the Presidential Scholars program, which honors a handful of high school students from each state. The ARTS (Arts Recognition and Talent Search) program asked applicants to submit evidence of their outstanding work: a poem, a videotape of a dance performance, an audiotape of a pianist in performance, and so forth (Turnbull, 1981). In the fields of dance, music, and theater, live auditions are often a part of the selection process; those who will teach the performing artist often have more faith in their own judgment to perceive talent than in any aptitude tests or ratings. Students who showed outstanding talent in the ARTS program, as judged by experts in their fields of drama, music, or art, were recommended to the Presidential Scholars program and to other possible awards and scholarship sources.

Responses to Pilot Programs

A quite different approach to talent identification has been reported by Niro and Wolfe (1982). The first step in the Center for Theater Techniques in Education's program is to screen a large number of children. The screening results in a pool of youngsters who have high scores on the figural part of the Torrance Tests of Creative Thinking. This group is then provided with a theater-techniques program that stresses communications and the discovery of one's own capabilities.

One major focus of such a program has been on a theme of Communication: People and Places. This program leads the student to the general exploration of the questions Who am I? Who are the people in my world? and How do they interact? The content of the program is organized into four stages:

1. Introductory activities serve the purpose of strengthening individual and group resourcefulness and work on common tasks.
2. Students record the events of their own lives from birth to present, keeping in mind the use of these materials for joint dramatizations.
3. Students take surveys of their own neighborhood to provide historical, demographic, and geographic perspectives, which are then depicted.
4. Students examine literature for material that interprets urban and rural living, placing these in a larger worldwide context.

Any or all of these identification methods can be useful to identify talented students in the arts who have been previously active in a particular artistic field. However, these methods do not solve the problem of identifying talent in students without prior experience. We can judge a student's talent for dance or playing baseball simply by watching him or her play. To a student newly arrived in this country, who does not know the game, it would be unfair and inaccurate to make such judgments. That is why observations of the student under instruction become very useful.

Characteristics of Creative Artists

One of the traditional assumptions the general public makes of artists is that they are different in their attitudes, values, and personalities from the general public as well as from other academically superior students. Is there any objective evidence that one can bring to bear on that topic?

Getzels and Csikszentmihalyi (1976) studied 86 men and 93 women who were preparing for careers in fine art, advertising art, industrial art, and art education. When this group was studied on measures of values and personality, they *did* differ from the general population in having higher aesthetic interests and lower economic and social interests. They were more aloof, introspective, alienated, imaginative, self-sufficient, and experimental in outlook than the general population.

This study also tended to confirm the informal observations that female artists tend to be more dominant or "masculine" than other women, whereas male artists tend to be more sensitive or "feminine" than other men their age. One explanation of that finding is that by accepting both the masculine and feminine sides of their personalities instead of suppressing them, artists open up a wider range of experiences and feelings from which to draw in order to create their products.

Even among the artists sampled, the future fine artists were identified as less sociable, less conscientious, more imaginative, less worldly, and less conforming than other art students going into advertising and industrial arts. In other words, the fine arts students represented the far end of the continuum or distribution on those characteristics that seem to identify the patterns of attitudes and values of art students.

One of the common experiences of the creative scientist and the creative artist is that each must find his or her own problem on which to work. The student in the fine arts begins with a "blank canvas" and has to find or create the problem or the subject matter; similarly, the scientist must design a particular problem on which to work. That decision or selection often has more to do with the significance of the product than the technical qualities of carrying out the painting or the scientific experiment.

By providing 31 artists with a standard set of 27 still-life objects and asking them each to create a still-life production, Getzels and Csikszentmihalyi (1976) carefully studied how these artists created their products. The work of the artists during this process was rated for the number of still-life objects used, the depth of exploration of the objects, and the uniqueness of the combination of objects. When these rankings on "problem finding," on the development of a complex and unique product, were compared with ratings of originality and aesthetic value of the created product, by judges unaware of the students' previous work, there was a highly significant correlation between the two.

A followup study by Getzels and Csikszentmihalyi traced these 31 artists five to six years after their graduation. Of the 24 who were located, 8 had abandoned art as a career, 7 were marginal in their artistic production, and 9 had attained various levels of success.

Interestingly, several family characteristics seem related to success or failure. The successful artists tended to come from families of higher socioeconomic position, where the mother tended to work outside the home. Another difficult result to interpret was that 81 percent of the successful artists were eldest sons. Some 50 percent of the unsuccessful artists were middle sons, whereas none of the successful ones were. Success in studio courses was predictive of the more successful artist, but good grades in academic courses were not.

The "problem-finding" scores of the students in the experiment reported earlier still showed a small but significant relationship to success five or six years after graduation. Getzels concluded that the orientation toward problems may be the essential difference between the scientist and the technician, the artist and the copyist.

> *It seems that the one is content to apply his skill or talent in situations where the problem for solution is presented to him, and the other is impelled to apply his skill and talent in situations where he himself discovers or creates for solution; the latter's success depends not only on his craftsmanship but also on the quality of the problems he "finds." (1979, p. 387)*

One of the findings of Bloom (1985) and his colleagues in their retrospective analysis of world-class performers, which included concert pianists and sculptors, was that the schools did not seem to play a major role in the full development of the performers' talents. The only exception seemed to be that the children who revealed their talent for playing the piano early were often invited to give concerts or play the piano in school programs, concerts, and the like. The sculptors complained about their school experience, saying that art was treated as a craft rather than a supreme intellectual discipline and that the teachers did not seem to understand the potential depth of expression that could emerge through art.

However, there *have* been outstanding examples of public school innovation in this area of stimulating the talented in the arts. A report of the New Orleans Center for the Creative Arts (NOCCA) is one example (Kaufmann, Tews, & Milan, 1986). The center, which serves 250 students, offers professional arts training to the talented in dance, music, theater, visual arts, and writing. These students divide their time between their home school where they take their academic work and the NOCCA where they are taught in the arts by professionals in the various arts areas.

The State Board of Education waived regular certification guidelines to allow those in the professional world of arts who were skilled in instruction to become faculty at the center. In this instance, the students are made to understand that their choice, if they join the program of NOCCA, is not academics *or* art but rather a choice of art *and* academics. The presence of the center also increased general interest in the arts in the public schools. For example, a preparatory after-school program for the arts, providing dance experience to talented fourth- through eighth-grade students, was established.

It should be a matter of some discussion as to why art has never achieved a status equal to language in our public school programs. When the National Goals for Education were established in 1989 (*America 2000*), no mention was made of art—although mathematics, science, history, geography, and language arts were specifically noted. There has been an identification of art as a province of upper-class citizens, which has prevented it from being a property of the "common people" and, thus, an important aspect of learning for all.

In many ways, art has been considered an elitist topic, even as the education of gifted students has been considered elitist motivated. Few educators have thought of art as Murray Sidlin, former conductor for the New Haven Symphony, expressed it:

> *When words are no longer adequate, when our passion is greater than we are able to express in a usual manner, people turn to art. Some people go to the canvas and paint. Some people stand up and dance. But we all go beyond our normal means of communicating, and this is the common human experience for all people on this planet. (Day, Eisner, Stake, Wilson, & Wilson, 1984, p. vii)*

It is interesting that our yardstick for measuring success and good adjustment in the United States has been the engineer, the business executive, and the scientist—those persons who were represented in the early Terman study. But some observers, like Elliott Eisner, see such success is won at a price. He reports on a speech to successful business executives:

> *An ulcer...is an unkissed imagination taking its revenge for having been jilted. An ulcer is an unwritten poem; an undanced dance; an unpainted watercolor; it is a declaration from mankind that a thing of joy has not been tapped—and so it must break through muddily on its own. (cited in Buescher, 1986, p.15)*

Curriculum Adaptations

There is a greater tolerance for the separation of the student talented in the visual and performing arts from the rest of the students than in any other dimension of education. Special schools for dance, music, and drama are well accepted as appropriate placements for those who have extraordinary talent in these dimensions. The observer can hardly escape the conclusion that the visual and performing arts are essentially separated from the regular program in the public schools as well. There is a vaguely uncomfortable attitude toward the visual and performing arts that is shared by many educators. They view these topics as "extra" experiences, demonstrating the breadth of a school curriculum rather than being considered an integral part of the program. Consequently, they also can disappear quickly under conditions of budget restrictions.

Cranshaw once startled his principal, Ms. Brinkley, by expressing his interest in ballet dancing. Cranshaw's parents had taken him the evening before to the performance of the visiting ballet company. He had become fascinated with the extraordinary athletic ability and physical discipline that were displayed in the leaps and turns revealed by the male dancers. Nevertheless, Ms. Brinkley retreated to her office, reflecting on Cranshaw's psychosexual development and wondering if, in fact, his home life was everything it should be.

It has been said often that the public schools are a mirror of our society. The attitude of the public schools, in many communities, is that the visual and performing arts are an extra, a sideline, not truly a part of "basic" education, and this probably accurately reflects the view of the larger society as well. As a consequence, the arts rarely appear in the curriculum for the academically gifted or other students.

Eisner stated,

> I believe that we acquire minds. We are not born with minds, but with brains. The process of acculturation and education converts the brain into mind, expanding its power and range over a lifetime.... The school's curriculum should be regarded for what it is: a mind altering device. Curriculum is intended to be a device to change minds. It does that by either making available or by denying the availability of certain cultural tools and intellectual processes to young people. (cited in Buescher, 1986, pp. 10–12)

For the gifted student who is not proceeding to a career in arts, an understanding of art and what it can reveal about people, places, and things remains an important goal. As John Ruskin once said,

> Great nations write their autobiographies in three manuscripts: the book of their deeds, the book of their words, and the book of their art. Not one of these books can be fully understood unless we read the two others, but, of the three, the only trustworthy one is the last. (cited in Day et al., 1984, p. vii)

One interesting distinction between science (the culture of discovery) and art (the culture of creation) is that science builds on past discoveries and replaces them with new and better discoveries and instruments. The anatomy presentations of Leonardo da Vinci have been replaced by better and more accurate anatomical studies. The navigational instruments of the early Portuguese and Spanish explorers have likewise been replaced by other, more accurate, measuring tools. However, the art of the day still stands as a measure of creativity worthy in its own right—as interesting and valid today as it was then. The culture of creation is not a pyramiding field as is science, always building and replacing the past, but is instead a nonlinear event constrained only by the imagination of the creator and the means for expression available to him or her.

Those who are extraordinarily talented and gifted in these areas have a difficult road ahead of them in terms of not only their acceptance in school but, more important, their acceptance in the adult world afterward. The conditions for the acceptance of the artist, from an economic standpoint, in U.S. society are hardly less difficult these days than a few decades ago. The acceptance, within public schools, of the visual and performing arts as an important part of the curriculum is difficult for the faculty of that school, who often have had limited personal backgrounds and experiences in such activities themselves. Many teachers cannot identify with the students' needs in this area. This lack tends to isolate these programs more than any other ability area, to the detriment of everyone concerned.

Content Acceleration

This approach is designed to provide gifted students with opportunities for learning far in advance of the usual age. In the visual and performing arts an aspiring student can be moved rapidly through advanced material if he or she demonstrates competence in earlier lessons. This acceleration is often provided through separate or individual lessons in music, dance, or theater. Gifted students often find themselves to be quite young in comparison to those performers around them. They also find themselves faced with many demands for persistence and quality that are not usually a part of the rest of their academic program.

Advanced Placement

One form of content acceleration through the school curriculum is the Advanced Placement program. The nonverbal nature of artistic performance presents some unique problems in assessment, yet it is just as important that students who excel in the arts receive necessary recognition of superior performance as it is for those gifted students in standard academic curricula. The usual proof of academic performance involves a test of the acquisition of knowledge through standard achievement measures in subject-matter fields. However, in the arts, the key element is the synthesis of knowledge blended with creative ability to produce a product. The mere transmission of knowledge is not sufficient.

Dorn (1976) reported on a special nationwide project designed to provide Advanced Placement credit to secondary school students in a course on studio art. Each student produced an individual portfolio of his or her own products. These products were evaluated by over 500 professors and Advanced Placement teachers who, together, graded over 55,000 of these products along the dimensions of *quality*, *concentration*, and *breadth*. A team of five judges rated the three dimensions.

In quality, the judges looked for personal expressive content of the work and valued work that emphasized unique solutions. In concentration, the student was expected to submit several slides of artwork that reflected a long-range effort by the student to solve a particular problem in art. Finally, breadth was judged in four separate categories: use of space, drawing, color, and organization of three-dimensional materials. A composite score was then generated, which provided the basis for Advanced Placement credit. Over 80 percent of the students who were involved in the rating described by Dorn (1976) were judged as performing adequate college work and given advanced placement credit. Whether such an approach could be adapted to younger children who have had less time to develop these qualities remains to be seen.

Content Enrichment

The usual concept of enrichment assumes a standard curriculum that provides basic knowledge that then can be enlarged upon with additional enrichment experiences. This is often not the case in the field of performing arts. Stephanie has been to a modern-dance performance, an opera, an exhibition of modern painting, a symphony orchestra presentation, and several plays. But none of these experiences came to her in the public schools.

Bringing the arts to the schools means bringing the best, not second-rate or shoddy, presentations. As Sidlin pointed out,

> *A standard symphony orchestra is capable of dividing into eight string quartets, four woodwind quintets, two brass quintets, a percussion ensemble, and a chamber orchestra of about twenty musicians. These sixteen groups could be in as many locations, playing for and talking to small groups of students in their classroom or school auditorium. (1975, p. 31)*

Here is enrichment, or maybe even first-time experience, in the arts, which can be provided for the students.

Another example of enrichment is provided in Figure 8–3 by Krause (1979), who organized the enrichment activities into the three phases of Renzulli's Enrichment Triad: *exploration, group training*, and *individual and small-group investigations*. These three steps have the effect of first arousing the students' interest, then giving them some technical competence, and then allowing them to use their own talents and expressiveness in individual or group projects.

The arts have always had an uphill battle in their attempt to be more than an adjunct or add-on to the so-called real curricula of math, science, social studies, and so forth. Murray Sidlin, a distinguished symphony conductor, recalled his devious strategies for cutting physical education class in order to sneak into a music theory class that he desperately wanted to take. His experience has been repeated by many students eager to gain experience in the arts but frustrated by a school system that too often makes art students second-class citizens. Sidlin stated,

> *All through my public school life I was threatened, challenged, penalized and put in the middle all because of my great love for music. This was a lot of*

FIGURE 8–3　Goals and Objectives

Type I Enrichment—Exposure

1. Exposure to the arts using in-school and out-of-school experiences that include visiting artists, demonstrations, exhibits, and performances to broaden the children's cultural experiences.
2. Participation in directed activities at science centers, museums, libraries, and community resources to stimulate interest in investigations of specific topics.
3. Attendance at special student performances and displays of pottery, drawings, student-made books, filmstrips, slide presentations, bulletin boards.

Type II Enrichment—Group Training

1. On-going instruction in advanced techniques by experts and professionals in the arts to expand students' talents.
2. Experience in the use of a variety of media, materials, and methods to encourage creative problem solving.
3. Training and coaching in communication skills to enhance students' abilities in oral and written language.
4. Skill building in research techniques and reporting to develop self-direction and independence.

Type III Enrichment—Individual and Small Group Investigation

1. Exhibition of children's projects in special displays and shows in schools, libraries, and community centers.
2. Scheduling special performances in dance, music, and drama for school and community groups.
3. Composing original stories, poems, plays, and songs suitable for publication or performances.
4. Presentations of reports and projects in the regular classroom or library to demonstrate results of independent investigations and study.

Source: From *Enrichment through creative arts* by C. Krause, 1979, p. 23. Copyright 1979 by The Council for Exceptional Children. Reprinted with permission.

> *responsibility for a kid and this negative attitude discouraged several of my young talented colleagues along the way; either they or their parents gave in to the pressures that were brought to bear. A few of us* had *to go ahead, and we did. (1975, p. 32)*

Unfortunately, it is now true that much of the content enrichment in the visual and performing arts has to be searched for by the student, as Sidlin did, or by parents interested in broadening the cultural life of their child. The more opportunities the public schools provide for such experiences, the more we will likely see talents and interests emerge that may surprise and delight us.

Teachers can be significant forces for encouragement or discouragement. Figure 8–4 shows how a well-trained art teacher helped a student gain significant insights. On the other hand, there can be instances of discouragement that can make us wince with pain as we recognize the damage done to the student by a poorly prepared teacher. Figure 8–5 provides one of those experiences that all of us have had at one time or another.

FIGURE 8–4   The Evolution of an Artist

Although I have been creating artwork since I was very young, I consider my initiation into the role of an artist to have taken place during July of 1985. 1 was attending a summer program at Indiana University called "College Credit for High School Seniors." I was enrolled in an oil painting class with the wonderfully small number of eight students. We met three hours daily and had out-of-class assignments, as well.

My work was adequate, but I was not satisfied with what I was producing. I felt that I was on the edge of discovering something new about my art work; that I was groping for something that I knew was there. I discussed this topic with my instructor, who told me to persevere.

My "breakthrough" occurred exactly at the midpoint of the three-week program. I had started a painting of the model and was putting down big color shapes. My teacher came up to me and told me to stop. My proportions were off, she said; she wished to correct them before I really became involved in the painting, or else the finished product would turn out badly.

She asked me if she could scratch a few guidelines on the canvas with my palette knife, in order to show me what was wrong. I very begrudgingly said, "Yes," even though outsiders interfering with my work was one of my biggest hatreds at that time. She said, "The shoulders are wrong. Think of them as a plane, angled this way, see? Think of the hips as a box, with the legs extending out in this fashion. The head is on a neck, connected to a vertical line moving through the torso." Her arm flowed across my half-finished painting in a quick and graceful way. I was slowly becoming quite angry at her overindulgence, but held my tongue. "You see, Harold," she was saying, "sketch the chest as a structure, the human body first as a skeleton...." She finally ceased drawing and observed the results of her labors. The painting was a tangled web of chicken scratches, altered beyond comprehension by her enthusiastic hand.

My pulse hammered in my neck. I was really angry at this person who had intruded upon my work. Taking her suggestion, I tried to wipe the surface clean with some turpentine. The paint ran and smeared and now, full of rage, I threw the painting out. I set up and began a new piece. I painted now to spite her, to show her how angry I was. There, a box for the hips; there, a plane for the shoulders tilted in such a way. She was apologizing to me, but I was ignoring her, suddenly caught up in this new mode of painting. My brush seemed filled with an electric passion. Too soon, it was time to clean up. I stared at the amazing new work that I had just done; I saw my released anger, and what I knew was perhaps the biggest single step I might ever take in my art work. I had found what I had been groping for.

From that day on, my artistic abilities—particularly painting—have steadily increased. Perhaps the most important lesson that I learned from that experience was never to stagnate, never be afraid to be daring, to risk losing something to try out a new thought. I also learned never to shun what my instructors tell me and to take criticism well; one of the most important aspects of being a good artist. I still remember that sunny day in July. I remember telling my instructor that if I was ever to become an artist, it would be because of that day in her class.

Source: Clark, G., & Zimmerman, E. (1987). Tending the special spark: Accelerated and enriched curricula for highly talented art students. *Roeper Review, 10* (1), 10–17. Reprinted by permission, Roeper Review, P.O. Box 329, Bloomfield Hills, MI 48303.

Content Sophistication

How does content sophistication apply to the arts area? It is useful to have some type of organizing ideas or systems. One such system could be Bloom's well-known taxonomy of cognitive processes that can be applied to the arts. In this case, we will focus on the more complex categories: analysis, synthesis, and evaluation.

FIGURE 8–5   The Art Lesson—How to Draw a Rose

One day she gave us an art lesson where we were given a chance to color a picture the way we wanted to: We were going to be creative, she said, and color flowers for Easter. Miss Lucy handed each of us not one, but two, pieces of paper. On one was a black and white drawing of a long-stemmed rose with leaves. The second paper was blank.

"Now, today," she said, "we will color in the rose petals with red or pink, and make the leaves green. When you have finished your picture, then use the second piece of paper to make your own flower."

At last! I would be able to choose for myself and use all the beautiful colors in the basket that I so longed to use. I quickly colored my printed rose red and the leaves green. Then I set about to draw flowers on the blank paper. I must have made 20 trips to the color basket. I made flowers that were square, some that were triangular, some with petals, and some wavy and blending into and around and within each other. I colored in the entire piece of paper—not a speck was left uncolored—and I thought my flowers were beautiful: purple, lavender, orchid, yellow, green, blue, aqua, pink, rose, and peach. Then I realized I had forgotten about leaves.

"What on earth is that, Mary?"

"My flowers."

"There are no green flowers—and where are your stems and leaves?"

I sat dumbly. My flowers were much more beautiful than the rose. Couldn't she see that?

"Here," she said, handing me another sheet of paper, "now do it right."

I dutifully made a rose, colored it with an ugly orange-red crayon, and filled in the stem and leaves with green, pressing as hard as I could. I handed it to her, thinking I guess I'd better forget about illustrating my own books when I became a famous author.

I was 16 before I ever attempted to make another drawing or do a painting freehand. I still have both of those pictures and, when I look at them, I weep inside that my art teacher could not see the budding love for colors and textures, the creative weaving of forms and designs in my more-than-perfect flowers.

Source: M. Meeker, from the award-winning article, "On Trying to Be Creative," in the *Gifted Child Today*, November-December, 1990, pp. 2-5. Reprinted with permission from *The Gifted Child Today*, P. O. Box 6448, Mobile, AL 36660.

In *analysis* (the ability to break a whole into separate parts), the student may be asked to take some form of artistic production and divide it into its component parts. Subdividing a poem into couplets would be one example of analysis, as would be the study of the elements that create balance in an artistic portrait. The opportunities to use analysis to judge a creation critically is within the easy reach of upper elementary gifted students.

Synthesis, the bringing together of various elements to make a new product, can be obtained artistically by the linkage of separate elements of a painting into an artistic whole. Planning lessons for synthesis is somewhat more challenging. Two examples can be developing a mural to represent the food chain from fish to the dinner table, and depicting the key elements in the Civil War that led to Appamattox. These types of artistic syntheses could mark the culmination of a major unit demonstrating how art can represent emotions and feelings over a broad range of topics on one theme and, in one artistic depiction, express them all.

Finally, there is Bloom's domain of *evaluation*—making judgments about ideas, theories, solutions, and so on. The use of evaluation can allow students to develop their own criteria for judging TV shows, movies, or novels. Whether a student's criteria of goodness has to be related to artistic criteria generated by others is another topic of vigorous and continuing discussion in the classroom as well as in the art world. By using Bloom's taxonomy as an organizing concept, the teacher can challenge gifted students at the higher abstract levels of analysis, synthesis, and evaluation.

One device that can allow students to proceed on individual projects that pursue more content sophistication in arts is the use of special learning stations. Such stations can be established within a normal classroom setting or in a resource room, and are used to help the student explore concepts in an independent and accelerated manner.

Saunders (1977) suggested another organizing concept around which themes can be built and which teachers can follow in designing unit activities. He suggested that there are certain "core monuments" that are works of art, literature, and other products of creative human enterprise and natural phenomenon and that a study of these makes it possible to more readily grasp key humanistic themes. One example of such a production would be *Romeo and Juliet*, which deals with classic teenage problems of love/hate conflicts, parental conflicts, teenage marriage, generation gaps, and so forth. Another core monument is the legend of the Holy Grail; although it is not characterized by a single work of literature, it embodies humankind's search for truth and the struggle for purity against all temptation. This theme can be found in the modern musical *Camelot*.

Mary Shelley's *Frankenstein* is another core monument around which humankind's drive to be a creator and to replace God can be studied. The human imitation of God usually leads to disaster, which gives the tale a moral tone. Finally, another example of a core monument is the Bayeux Tapestry, which can be used because it records historical events and demonstrates people's drive for immortality by leaving their images and the record of their achievements in art as well as a thrust for superiority by warfare and invasion. Many other works of fiction can be used that represent the conflicts between good and evil, idealism and fears, and so on. Gifted students can grasp such concepts much more thoroughly and carry them farther into analysis, synthesis, and evaluation (to use the Bloom terminology). They can pursue such interests while students of average ability are pursuing the story line of various novels or plays.

Content Novelty

The entrenchment of the visual and performing arts in U.S. education is anything but secure. One has only to look at the National Educational Goals (*America 2000*) to see that while we are focusing on geography, language arts, and science, nowhere is there a specific goal for excellence in aesthetic performance or study. The arts have been seen traditionally as supplementary rather than the expression of the culture and history of the times in which they occur.

As a result, many of the innovative program efforts in this area have occurred during the summer months, when it is somewhat easier to develop a new initiative without interfering with the standard school curriculum. Such a program was begun at the South Carolina School of the Arts in 1984, in which gifted and talented students in the arts, selected by audition, came together to receive good experiences, direct instruction, and guidance from performing artists and practitioners in the various arts.

The presence of such a school, however, also provides the base for the development of curriculum materials for the public school systems. It also serves as a base for the training of graduate students in the arts and in education. The graduate interns who participated in this summer program were required to develop instructional activities around an interdisciplinary theme. Each of the units provided general exploratory activities as well as hands-on activities to allow students to emulate practicing artists, to follow up projects, and to encourage students to become producers.

The four components of South Carolina's Department of Education's overall framework for curriculum development in the arts are:

Aesthetic Perception: Awareness of the aesthetic qualities of works of art—manmade and in the environment—and involving the sensory and intellectual analysis of these perceptions.

Creative Expression: The making of art, either through production or performance; acquiring artistic knowledge and skills to express and communicate through the arts.

Cultural Heritage: Knowledge about the historical and cultural background in which works of art are created, including socio-economic, political, intellectual, ethnic, religious, or philosophical considerations.

Aesthetic Valuing: Involving the development of critical thinking skills and cultivating the ability to make intelligent and informed judgements regarding excellence in the arts (Uldrick & Cross, 1992).

It is hoped that the graduate interns of this program will return to the schools and successfully interweave what they have learned through their observations and their curriculum development activities to benefit the local school systems. In this type of outreach activity, a summer program can sometimes energize the regular public school programs.

Another activity that can be planned is a field trip to an art museum or gallery. How useful such trips are depends on the prior preparation of the teacher and students. Faced with a painting in a museum, many students can see only the two-dimensional content in front of them. It may be intuitively pleasing to the eye, but its essential meaning is locked in a "code of culture" that has never been explained to the students and so they are unable to unlock the full meaning of the painting itself. An analogy to this situation might be the foreigner who comes to the United States and is treated to a baseball game. The individual can describe what he or she is able to see on the surface, but all of the subtleties, strategies, and deeper meanings in the actions taking place will escape him or her.

Unless students are prepared for the experience with background information about the meaning of the painting and the composition, much of the experience will be meaningless. For example, Leonardo da Vinci's painting "Lady with an Ermine" portrays an elegantly dressed lady holding a small ermine in her delicate hands. Why an ermine? Why not a rabbit or a squirrel? These are the questions that curious students should be asking themselves. In this case, the ermine is a symbol of moderation and chastity. The lady in question was approaching her wedding after having been a mistress of another nobleman;

the painting was perhaps an attempt, among other things, to help her image. The exquisite rendering of the ermine is a tribute to the anatomical studies of da Vinci, but the selection of the ermine was determined by other cultural understandings of the times.

To encourage students to ask why the composition was made the way it was is the first step toward a larger understanding of the artistic style. Why does an artist have a window in the picture or place it in a certain space in the picture? Perhaps the artist wanted to show mastery of light and shadow, perhaps to reveal a landscape beyond that has particular significance. It is breaking the code of the artist that is often highly satisfying to the viewer, once the basic composition has been observed.

As in the other areas of study, students can learn much about the composition of a picture or a musical piece by attempting to do some creating of their own. This is a rare experience for many students, and unless they are given some technical lessons as to how to render a face or hands or three-dimensional perspective, it can be an embarrassing attempt for untutored artists.

The teacher can provide a variety of objects that students can choose to include, or not include, in a still-life drawing. The process of selection and the reasoning behind the selection and placement can be remembered by students as they view the product of another artist and share with the other artist the problem of placing objects in space in a composition and the particular solution that the artist has chosen.

Another standard element of content novelty is the *interdisciplinary curriculum.* In Chapter 6, a strategy to replace the chronological approach to human history was suggested. This strategy would take a narrow band of history (e.g., 1860 to 1870) and examine, within that band, the totality of human experience from science, geography, philosophy, cultural values of the times, and art. Art is, in fact, an almost unique contribution to our understanding of past times, since it represents the actual product of the times, not the verbal (or written) re-creation of the times that we get from history.

Since historians are not neutral in viewing the events that occur before them (the "discovery" of America was made from the perspective of the Europeans coming to this continent, but was not necessarily a view shared by those Native Americans already here), it is the art and writing of the times that must be relied on to illuminate portions of the times to us.

One such slice of history could well be the Age of Exploration, into which the Circa 1492 Exhibition gathered art from three different and separate cultures at the same time in history: European, Oriental, and Native American. These artistic endeavors were largely independent of the other, since each culture knew little of the other, independently developing, civilizations. The Age of Exploration spurred the process of cultural interaction, which has accelerated ever since. This slice in history, marked well by the artistic productions from these three separate cultures (Levenson, 1991) allows the students to study the evolution of cultures under different sets of circumstances, with the art helping to delineate the differing emphases and values of the cultures. Students should realize that art is a unique form of communication available to us.

Many activities that fit the term *content novelty* for gifted and talented children provide experiences for them to act out and gain experience in seeing different perspectives and other points of view. Many of these activities stress the combination of symbolic or three-dimensional perspectives, which force the child out of an exclusive dependence on verbal concepts and from a predictable but unexciting display of facts or passive viewing into an active learning experience.

Two examples of this type of activity are reported by Niro and Wolf (1982). The first, Airport, requires a controller to lead a fog-bound (blindfolded) pilot to a safe landing. This task forces the controller to take the perspective of the blindfolded pilot and guide him or her through a set of obstacles for a safe landing. If the controller tells the pilot to turn left from his or her own perspective, there may well be a crash, because the pilot will be going 180 degrees in the wrong direction. To get outside one's own perspective and into anothers is one of the goals of the drama.

The second example, Sculptures, also provides students with the task of planning together, as the sculptor moves the human body (clay) in ways that tell a story or express an emotion (see Figure 8–6). The range of activities that can flow from this basic situation are very large indeed, and the complexity can be increased to challenge the creative abilities of gifted children.

Extracurricular Programs

Although it is often difficult to integrate the visual and performing arts in the regular school curriculum, it sometimes is possible to include such activities in school-related extracurricular programs. The University of Denver reported just such a cooperative program, called University for Youth, organized collaboratively by the Jefferson County public schools and the University of Denver School of Education. This program provides special opportunities for unique experiences for talented and highly motivated students in the visual and performing arts (Seeley, Katz, & Linder, 1981). The following list describes a sample of short-term courses that are offered in the program, often taught by specialists outside the school system, university staff members, or graduate students:

Ceramics (Grades 1–3): Explore your own fantasy in the three-dimensional sculptural world. Learn the basic techniques used in creating ceramic works of art.

Exploring Art (Grades 2–4): Experiment with your creativity in a wide variety of materials. Create your own designs by painting, drawing, collage, and sculpture forms. All materials are provided.

Author and Author Illustrator Too! (Grades 4–6): Would you like to write and illustrate your own book, poem, short story, or even recipe? Students will develop and apply their own literary and artistic abilities.

Drawing Workshop (Grades 7–9): To draw expressively is to coordinate eye and hand. This workshop will focus on learning basic drawing skills while exploring a variety of materials, such as charcoal, oriental brush and sumi ink, pencil, and pastels. Master drawings of the past and present will be introduced to help students create their own beautiful and original drawings.

Just a Song and a Dance (Grades 7–9): Cruella Develle's "Two Dreadful Children" will be memorized, sung, choreographed, and staged for a final production. Students should have a cassette recorder.

FIGURE 8–6 Sculptures

Materials: None

Time: 15–30 minutes

Goals: 1. To experience the variety of ways in which the human body can be moved and shaped.
2. To learn to work together.

Description:

One staff person directs all of the action. Two people are chosen, or volunteer, and they stand before the group. One person is the Sculptor and the other is the Clay. The Clay does not move, but remains soft and pliable; the Clay cooperates with the Sculptor as the Sculptor shapes the Clay.

One at a time, each student changes one thing about the Clay (e.g., raising an arm, closing the eyes). This is done silently, with the Sculptor guiding and positioning the Clay. The Sculptor does not do anything to the Clay he or she would not want done to himself or herself.

From time to time, change the person who is the Clay. After a few rounds, add a second person to be Clay. This can continue until several people are Clay.

Variations:

1. Ask the Sculptors to sculpt the Clay into a scene of some sort (e.g., mother and child, two people hunting). The people not used in this vignette try to guess what has been created.
2. Have one Sculptor create one piece of Clay in a position that makes a strong statement. Other Sculptors add their creations until a whole theme or scene is portrayed.
3. After a group has created a sculpture, they freeze. The first person (the person who began as the first piece of clay) moves carefully out of the piece, goes to a large piece of paper, chooses a color, and paints a mark or shape to express how the body was while in that sculptured pose a moment before. The rest of the students follow one at a time, in the order in which they joined the piece, and add their line and color to the painting of the sculpture. These paintings can then be used as the form from which another group creates a sculpture.

Note: This exercise works best in a circle, so that all can see; staff persons can begin as Sculptor and Clay so that students get warmed up and comfortable. Once the activity is moving, the possibilities are limitless. When the class seems ready, move into improvizations, which should begin with material drawn from the group.

Source: Niro, L. D., & Wolf, M. H. (1982). *Talent search and development in the performing arts.* Center for Theatre Techniques in Education/Area Cooperative Educational Services. Reprinted with permission.

Theater in Motion (Grades 7–9): This exciting class emphasizes creative movement, dance, acting, theater choreography, and the poetry of Shel Silverstein. Students will give a presentation for the final session.

The cooperation of the school system and Denver University for the University for Youth program allows the school system to drastically extend its range of possible offerings in this special field.

The Teacher of Visual and Performing Arts

Where does one find the teachers who will operate in these fields? One of the distinguishing features of programs for the performing arts, as contrasted with the more typical curriculum area, is often the presence of a charismatic and dynamic figure at the center of the program. Durden (1983) described just such an instructional coordinator at the Northside High School of the Performing Arts in Atlanta, Georgia—Billy Dunsmore. He originally became interested in the performing arts through church activities and then turned to the public schools. His demand for total commitment, excellence, and effort from his students echoes the attitude of many music teachers, dance teachers, and drama teachers, all of whom recognize the absolute necessity of excellence in performance. Durden quoted Billy Dunsmore as follows:

> *Happiness comes from the development of a person's potential. The students of the arts are not in class because they are told they must be there, but because they wish to be there.... I instill in my students some simple rules to live and study by—don't try to be the best, do your best; you are getting better or you are busy getting worse; music is a holy activity. The same is true of teaching. It is not only an instruction, it also becomes a ministry of human need, a chance to serve. (1983, p. 96)*

Durden pointed out the close analogy between those objectives of the school of performing arts and those of athletic teams. The importance of rigor, enthusiasm, uncompromising standards to quality performance, and the demand for long hours of disciplined practice before, during, and after the season is shared by both areas.

The problem faced by the performing arts, and in fact by all of education, is how many Billy Dunsmores are there whose total commitment can inspire and raise students far beyond their expected performance to a level of achievement that inspires and draws continued commitment? We either must find more of such types of teachers or find a way to instill into existing teachers this kind of devotion to excellence and intolerance for the shoddy and mediocre.

Since the subject matter in this field has so often been presented to the gifted or interested students outside the normal school program, it is not unusual for their teachers in this subject matter to be performing artists themselves and for much of the instruction to be of the master/apprentice type—the "watch me and see how it's done" approach. One way to bring a stronger and more sophisticated program in the arts into the schools is to find ways to draw the artist into the public schools as a mentor or partner. In 1969 the Artist in the Schools Program was initiated, which gave financial support for artists who would be willing to work in the schools and provide missing expertise to the faculty. Despite considerable enthusiasm among school personnel for this approach, there has been little evidence of positive results from changes in student behavior or aspirations.

Yeatts (1980) presented a case study of one such artist-in-residence program. Some 150 high school students in a rural Virginia school system were given time released from regular assignments in English and social studies to work with community leaders or an artist-in-residence. The artist, Margaret Ritter, was a novelist and actress. She introduced the students to modern writers, prepared students for career investigations by teaching interviewing techniques, coached students in dramatic presentations, and helped them plan and make films and videotapes. Numerous field trips to plays, radio stations, concerts, and so forth were a part of the program. Students in the program showed significant gains in tests of English expression.

Although the students were wildly enthusiastic about the program, teachers in the regular high school program were reluctant to accept the artist-in-residence, and Virginia's Department of Education kept writing to Ritter about her certification deficiencies. The program was discontinued the next year by a financially unsupportive, albeit enthusiastic, school board. Yeatts concluded that better certification standards should be established that would allow performing artists to work in the public schools.

Szekely (1981) described an Art Partnership Network that brings into school systems college art majors who would "adopt" one or more gifted school children and work individually or in small groups with them. The children are chosen on the bases of teacher ratings and student display of a body of work or through audition. The goals of the program have been to develop the child's independence and risk taking, and to provide support and companionship in what is often a lonely task. Szekely stated, "Through example and through discussions of the work of the artists the art student introduces the child to the way that artists think, work, and live" (1981, p. 68).

The school's contribution to the Art Partnership Network is to provide flexible time schedules for the student, exhibition space, travel opportunities, and expanded library collection. Some of the characteristics of the college artists who would deserve participation in such a program were:

1. The ability to open their own work ideas and artistic selves to the child
2. The ability to inspire children to be dependable and faithful in their work, sharing both the joys and the problems and encouraging new ideas and ventures
3. Comfort in working with students in an individual program, rather than from a set curriculum or a predetermined set of problems.

Unfortunately, programs such as these often do not include the regular school staff, who could profit substantially by some in-service training experiences conducted by the artists. After all, it is this generation of teachers who often have been deprived in their own education of opportunity and experience in the arts and who can profit from some belated contact to broaden their own perspectives. By cooperating with programs like Artist in the Schools or the Art Partnership Network, the regular teachers may learn better how to bring art into their own teaching.

Program Evaluation

With a wide variety of special programs in the schools (e.g., summer programs, residential programs), we often wonder what happens to the youngsters who have participated. For those students who have had a special and intense experience with the arts, what happens to them over time, and how do they view the special experiences that they had?

Confessore (1991) followed a group of 27 adolescents who were judged talented in the visual and performing arts and had participated in the Johnson State Early College Summer Arts Program at Johnson State College in Vermont. He questioned them 10 years later to find out whether they were showing the same talents, attitudes, and perspective to the arts that they had as adolescents.

These students were selected to become involved in college-level studies in art, music, dance, theater, or creative writing. At the time of the followup survey, they were 23 to 27 years of age and were asked whether their art forms still play an important role in their lives, whether they still agree with the characteristics that were the selection criteria for the program, what their participation in the program might have had on their lives or subsequent involvement in the arts, and so on. The groups were roughly divided between male and female, although the vast majority of the males were in theater, whereas the females were divided among the five art forms.

Confessore (1991) found that art still played an important role in their lives; they still believed they had the same talented characteristics that were responsible for their being selected for the program; they were highly self-directed; and, by and large, they believed that the early college program had a positive effect on their lives and their involvement in art. One of the common responses was that the professional artists who participated as instructors in the program had a long-lasting and beneficial effect on their careers. The process of supplementing regular college faculty with professional artists seemed to have a very beneficial effect. Confessore concluded that this program, like other reported programs, indicates that talented adolescents benefit educationally and socially from well-designed acceleration and enrichment programs.

Unresolved Issues

1. The most substantial issue in this content field is how to convince educators who are in decision-making positions to regard the visual and performing arts as something other than an add-on or extracurricular activity, or even a source of relaxation from more sturdy academic fare.
2. A second issue is how to integrate professional personnel and performers in the visual and performing arts into the regular program. In the past, special training for the gifted in this area was accomplished in special schools, private lessons, or group activities representing an additional experience. In some schools, mentors or artists-in-residence programs have brought artists into daily contact with the schools, but these have been limited in number and scope.
3. Most gifted children will not choose a career in the visual and performing arts but could benefit and enrich their lives by being intelligent consumers and supporters of those who are in these fields. What kind of experiences and curricula should be prepared for the intelligent consumer of the arts?

Chapter Review

1. The identification of students gifted in the visual and performing arts is often done through audition or the presentation of individual products, rather than by testing.

2. Student response to introductory programs is another strategy for identification of talented students, particularly those who have had limited opportunities to perform or practice.

3. Creative artists seem to possess the ability to accept both the feminine and masculine sides of their personality and thus can draw on a wide range of experiences for their creative expression.

4. The most creative artists show a capacity to be good problem finders and to make unusual use of available stimuli for their productions.

5. A close analogy has been noted between the objectives for visual and performing arts and for athletics. The importance of vigor, enthusiasm, uncompromising standards, and long hours of disciplined practice is stressed in both domains.

6. The Advanced Placement program can offer a content acceleration opportunity in the arts for special experiences for gifted and talented students at the secondary level.

7. Programs in the visual and performing arts often are not recognized as important components of the education program within the school system, and are often viewed as a supplementary or elective activity.

8. Students can gain greater appreciation of artistic works by learning about the cultural symbolism that the works of art often represent.

9. Art can be used in programs for gifted students to illustrate other humanistic themes, as indicators or historical trends, and as markers for major cultural movements.

10. A number of extracurricular programs can be used to bring additional experience in visual and performing arts to all students. Specialists and performers in those artistic fields can participate in the instruction through this extra-school device or artist-in-residence programs.

Readings of Special Interest

Bechtel-Nash, A. (Ed.). (1984). *Viva las Arts: National directory of programs for K–12 artistically gifted and talented students.* Paramount, CA: Tom's Books.
This directory contains information on programs specially designed for the artistically gifted students in all 50 states. Organized on a state-by-state basis, it provides descriptions of special programs in these areas together with information regarding the age of students, financial requirements, and the person to contact for more information about specific programs. This is an especially useful book for educators who have been specialists in the visual and performing arts and who therefore have limited information as to where highly gifted students in this domain can receive special attention.

Day, M., Eisner, E., Stake, R., Wilson, B., & Wilson, M. (1984). *Art history, art criticism and art production: Vol. II. Case studies of seven selected sites.* Santa Monica, CA: Rand.
This is a major presentation of how seven school systems in the United States incorporated art into their educational curriculum. This study was supported by the J. Paul Getty Trust to illustrate that some school systems have been able to pay some meaningful attention to art within the framework of a public school system. Some fine introductory material discusses the special problems of art and its relationship with education. The case studies are detailed enough to give a picture of how art was supported at the local school system level.

Eisner, E. (1991). *The enlightened eye: Qualitative inquiry and the enhancement of educational practice.* New York: Macmillan.

This is a strong statement by an artist and educational psychologist on the benefits of using qualitative measurement (i.e., personal observation) in the assessment of educational programs. Using his experience in art to "see" the qualities that a work of art possesses, Eisner advocates the use of enhanced perceptivity on the part of the observer in evaluating the classroom and the complex interactions that are presented in the school program.

Getzels, J., & Csikszentmihalyi, M. (1976). *The creative vision: A longitudinal study of problem finding in art.* New York: Wiley & Sons.

This is a report of a unique longitudinal study of young artists at work, which then followed some of them several years later in their careers. The authors' interest in these studies focuses on "problem finding," the choice of the project by the artist. They find that young artists who are judged superior in problem finding in their work in school turn out to be superior in their artistic work years later.

Levenson, J. (Ed.). (1991). *Circa 1492: Art in the age of exploration.* New Haven, CT: Yale University Press.

This is the catalogue for one of the most elaborate exhibitions of art ever assembled to celebrate the five hundredth anniversary of the Discovery of America. The exhibit covers three major geographic areas of artistic expression at the time of Columbus: European, Asian, and Central and South American. There is much in the exhibition that reflects the history and culture of the times from these widely dispersed groups integrating art with the overall culture of the times. Worth many hours of reading.

Niro, L., & Wolf, M. (1982). *Talent search and development in the visual and performing arts.* Stratford, CT: Center for Theatre Techniques in Education.

This description of a unique program uses the visual and performing arts to identify talent and then to enhance these talents through systematic instruction. It seems especially, but not exclusively, relevant to inner-city student populations, where traditional instruments focus on verbal skills and may overlook latent verbal talents. This book effectively blends concepts of creativity into basic content in the arts.

References

Bloom, B. (Ed.) (1985). *Developing talent in young people.* New York: Ballantine.

Bloom, B., & Sosniak, L. (1981). Talent development vs. schooling. *Educational Leadership, 39,* 86–94.

Brigham, F., Bakkan, J., Scruggs, J., & Mastropieni, M. (1992). Cooperative behavior management: Strategies for promoting a positive classroom environment. *Education and Training in Mental Retardation, 27,* 3–12.

Buescher, T. (1986). Appreciating children's aesthetic ways of knowing: An interview with Elliott Eisner. *Journal for the Education of the Gifted, 10* (1), 7–15.

Chetelat, F. (1981). Visual arts education for the gifted elementary-level art student. *Gifted Child Quarterly, 25,* 154–158.

Clark, G., & Zimmerman, E. (1987). Finding the special spark: Accelerated and enriched curricula for highly talented art students. *Roeper Review, 10,* 10–17.

Cleveland, M. (1977). Creative music strategies based upon poetry and the language. *Journal for Education of the Gifted, 1,* 29–37.

Confessore, G. (1991). What became of the kids who participated in the 1981 Johnson early college summer arts program? *Journal for the Education of the Gifted, 15,* 64–82.

Dorn, C. (1976). The advanced placement program in studio art. *Gifted Child Quarterly, 30*, 560–568.

Durden, W. (1983). Northside High School of the Performing Arts: Lesson for excellence in education. *Daedalus, 112*, 95–111.

Ellison, R., Abe, C., Fox, D., Coray, K., & Taylor, C. (1976). Using bibliographical information in identifying artistic talent. *Gifted Child Quarterly, 20*, 402–413.

Getzels, J. (1979). From art student to fine artist: Potential, problem finding and performance. In A. Passow (Ed.), *The gifted and the talented* (pp. 372–388). Chicago: University of Chicago Press.

Gleick, J. (1988). *Chaos: Making a new science.* New York: Penguin Books.

Gordon, E. (1980). The assessment of music aptitudes of very young children. *Gifted Child Quarterly, 24*, 107–111.

Kaufmann, F., Tews, T., & Milan, C. (1986). New Orleans Center for the Creative Arts program descriptions and student perceptions. *Gifted Students Institute Quarterly, 11*, 5–14.

Krause, C. (1979). *Enrichment through creative arts.* Reston, VA: ERIC Clearinghouse on Handicapped and Gifted Children, Council for Exceptional Children.

Meeker, M. (1990, November/December). On trying to be creative. *G/C/T*, 2–5.

Renzulli, J., Smith, L., White, A., Callahan, C., & Hartman, R. (1976). *Scales for rating the behavioral characteristics of superior students.* Mansfield Center, CT: Creative Learning Press.

Saunders, R. (1977). *Relating art and humanities to the classroom.* Dubuque, IA: William C. Brown.

Seeley, K., Katz, E., & Linder, T. (1981). The university as a community resource for gifted: The university for youth. *Gifted Child Quarterly, 25*, 112–115.

Sidlin, M. (1975). Humanizing the humanizers. In R. Grove (Ed.), *The arts and the gifted.* Reston, VA: Council for Exceptional Children.

Szekely, G. (1981). The artist and the child: A model program for the artistically gifted. *Gifted Child Quarterly, 25*, 67–72.

Turnbull, W. (1981). National arts awards and recognition talent search. *Art Education, 34*, 32–34.

Uldrick, V., & Cross, J. (1992). The South Carolina Governor's School for the Arts—A legacy of artistic achievement and excellence. *Journal for the Education of the Gifted.*

Yeatts, E. (1980). The professional artist: A teacher for the gifted. *Gifted Child Quarterly, 24*, 133–137.

Information-Processing Strategies

The intellectual skills that identify gifted children were noted in Chapter 2 and now become the focus of attention in this section of the text. The great accomplishment of the brain and central nervous system is that they are able to add to acquired and stored information through the process of reasoning and information processing. The ability to generate *new information* through the internal processing of *available information* is one of the most impressive and valuable skills of humans.

Two pieces of information, such as (1) the world population is rapidly growing and (2) our difficulty with pollution, can be combined to reach a third piece of information: (3) unless we collectively try to cope with pollution, it will become a larger and larger problem. Gifted children can generate this type of new information much faster and at a greater level of complexity than average students of the same age. One major task for educators is to enhance these problem-solving, problem-finding, and creative thinking skills of gifted students through the educational program.

For 12 years, or more, students spend a great deal of time in school absorbing new information. As more and more information becomes available, there can be a frantic, and relatively nonproductive, scramble for teachers to keep pace—to try to teach all of the information that they have taught before and then to add the new information to the curriculum. There is another more favored approach in the teaching of gifted students. This approach is for teachers to instruct students in ways to process available information in order to solve a problem, or to sharpen the outline of a problem, or to help them learn how to seek relevant information from various sources, or how to create new or novel ideas from their existing base of information.

Many persons in the education of gifted students have realized the futility of chasing after more and more information, and have instead focused on teaching important and significant ideas, as noted in the previous chapters on curriculum, and on teaching gifted students the strategies for more effective information processing. We often use these information-processing skills without reflecting on them very much. If one wishes to find who was responsible for a particular crime, for example, and all of the available suspects except one can prove that they were elsewhere at the time the crime was committed, then the detective is likely to conclude that it is the person without an alibi who is the guilty party. The detective is a fine example of a problem solver—one who takes available information and draws conclusions from that data. A major task for educators is to enhance these skills that gifted students possess—problem-solving, problem-finding, and creative thinking skills—by means of an educational program or strategies.

The next two chapters will review what has been learned about the systematic instruction of these complex thinking abilities. Chapter 9 focuses on methods of stimulating problem solving and problem finding. Although all of these thinking processes often occur together while the student is seeking a solution, they are separated here for the purposes of making some necessary distinctions between the strategies used to enhance each dimension.

There is an important continuum of problems, from ill-defined to clearly defined. Where in that continuum a particular problem falls often determines the thinking strategy to be applied. In *problem solving*, there is typically a substantial amount of information already available to the student. It is the student's task, then, to try to organize that information in such a fashion that it can be processed in order to reach a conclusion or product. The simple solution of arithmetic reasoning problems is a good example of this skill.

In *problem finding*, there may be a good deal of information available on the topic but that information is often ill defined. It is the student's responsibility to organize it into an appropriate problem and then solve that problem. The ability to see the problem clearly is an extremely important talent, and one that often requires help from the teacher. The teacher must sometimes organize the experiences of the student to enable him or her to sort out significant problems from the mass of information available.

Creativity, on the other hand, refers to a mental process in which something new and original will be produced from the available information base. A new and unique combination of existing elements will produce a product that was not predictable in advance by either teacher or student. Creativity does not require the generation of a product unique to humankind. That is too much to ask of any student or adult. What *is* required is that the producer of the creative effort does not know that the product has ever been produced before. There is a certain exhilaration in producing a painting, a poem, or a scientific invention that is one's own. That feeling is quite different from the sensation of quiet satisfaction that the student gets by solving a puzzle or a problem that has been created by someone else.

Although gifted students may intuitively use all of these processes in an impressive fashion, it is the responsibility of educators to help them extend and advance these talents in order to make special use of their outstanding capabilities. It is a responsibility that has been increasingly accepted as a major goal for all students.

Chapter **9**

Problem Solving and Problem Finding for Gifted Students

Key Questions

- What are the essential differences between problem solving and problem finding?
- How are Guilford's intellectual operations linked to education of gifted students?
- How can analogous thinking be used to increase efficiency in problem solving and problem finding?
- How does the emergence of the computer affect education of thinking processes?
- What are some particular educational strategies used to enhance student problem solving and problem finding?
- What are the major steps in the creative problem-solving process?
- What is a thinking log?
- What evidence is available to demonstrate the effectiveness of special educational programs designed to enhance productive thinking?

The ability to solve problems is one of the most highly prized skills in education. A student who performs well in this area will be well rewarded. The schools traditionally have not focused as much on problem finding, which appears to be one of the most significant dimensions to creative art and science. The authors define the two processes in the following way:

> *Problem Solving*:   The ability to reach a previously determined answer by organizing and processing the available problem elements in a logical and systematic fashion. Usually there is only one or a very limited set of correct answers.
>
> *Problem Finding*:   The ability to review an area of study and to perceive those elements worthy of further analysis and study. Usually there are many possible answers in the problem-finding process.

Getzels (1982) addressed the "problem of the problem" (problem finding), pointing out that the distinguishing feature of creative artists is not their execution of the project but the *choice* of project to be executed in the first place. Similarly in science, Einstein was once quoted as saying, "The formulation of a problem is often more essential than its solution, which may be merely a matter of mathematical or experimental skill. To raise new questions, new possibilities, to regard old questions from a new angle, requires creative imagination and marks real advances in science" (Einstein & Infeld, 1938, p. 92).

One way to look at the processes of problem solving and problem finding is to consider them as two ends of a continuum that is made up of different kinds of problems. The ends of that continuum are marked by the terms *well-structured problems* and *ill-structured problems*.

Well-structured problems		Ill-structured problems

Well-structured
problems

Ill-structured
problems

In short, it is the nature of the problem itself that requires one to adopt different strategies in the process of solving them. Many of the well-structured problems can be found in school lessons because someone has carefully constructed a problem that illustrates a particular principle that the student is supposed to master. Many of the ill-structured problems (Simon, 1980) occur beyond the walls of the school—in the real world—where no one has been kind enough to simplify the often complex nature of the problem that must be dealt with in order to apply well-used problem-solving procedures to reach an answer. Figure 9–1 provides a summary of the distinctions between the well-structured problem and the ill-structured problem.

Well-Structured Problems

Educators tend to be much more familiar with using well-structured problems in the classroom. Well-structured problems often appear in the familiar form of questions that are posed at the end of a chapter in a textbook or in mathematics exercises. Certain characteristics identify well-structured problems.

FIGURE 9–1   Characteristics of Well-Structured and Ill-Structured Problems

Well-Structured Problem	*Ill-Structured Problem*
If I have two oranges and you have two apples and Charles has no apples or oranges, how many pieces of fruit do we have together?	*You are the owner of the local food co-op. Your favorite customers have all come in complaining about the insufficient supply of oranges. What should you do?*
• Problem definition is easily identified.	• Problem must be defined and possibly redefined.
• All information needed to solve the problem is provided.	• Additional information is needed to solve the problem.
• Focus on problem solution (cognitive psychology).	• Focus on the nature of the problem (epistemology).
• A single right answer can be identified.	• Many different solutions are possible.
• It is possible to work backwards to find the solution.	• With no clear problem definition and insufficient information, problem solving must work forward.
• Abstract context.	• Social context.
• Low motivation to solution ("cold cognition").	• High motivation to solution ("hot cognition").

First, *one right answer solves the problem*; no other answer exists. For example, consider the following problem:

> *If I have two oranges and you have two apples, how many pieces of fruit do we have together?*

The answer to this problem always has been and always will be 4.

Second, the well-structured problem has *all of the information necessary* to find a solution contained within the problem statement. Sometimes students have to hunt within the problem to identify the right information to use but it is always there. For instance, if the problem became:

> *If I have two oranges and you have two apples and Charles has no apples or oranges, how many pieces of fruit do we have together?*

students would then have to realize that the information about Charles is unnecessary to the solution of the problem.

Third, *well-structured problems can be worked backwards* to obtain the desired solution. If necessary, students could rephrase the original problem as:

$$? - 2 = 2$$

in order to reach the solution. In fact, the goal of the well-structured problem is generally *to find a solution*, not to deal with the nature of the problem itself!

Ill-Structured Problems

Ill-structured problems differ from well-structured problems in many respects, as seen in Figure 9–1. Whereas the well-structured problem starts with a well-articulated statement of the problem, the ill-structured problem has many possible problem definitions. A clear problem statement has to be formed from an undefined mess. Consider, for example, a problem such as this:

> *You are the owner of the local food co-op. Your favorite customers have all come in complaining about the insufficient supply of oranges. What should you do?*

This problem has no clear problem statement. A clear problem definition cannot be identified in the initial statement of an ill-structured problem. Thus, *problem finding* is the first task when working with an ill-structured problem.

Also, *additional information is needed* in order to create a problem definition and solution. In a well-structured problem, all of the information needed to solve the problem is contained within the problem; it is just a matter of digging it out. In the ill-structured problem above, it is easy to see that more information is needed. We know that there are some dissatisfied customers, but that's all. Why is the supply insufficient? Cost? Availability? Disease in the oranges? Lack of general demand? An outbreak of scurvy? Answers to these questions are critical both to problem definition and problem solution. In fact, additional information often creates the need for *problem redefinition*, as new data can change the shape of the problem.

The third characteristic is that the ill-structured problem *exists in a social context*, not in an abstract situation. In the preceding example, the social context is unclear (a part of the additional information that is needed). Part of the resolution has to do with the stake of the co-op owner in being a member of the community and a merchant. Part also has to do with the fact that those who are complaining are all favorite customers who generally get treated with additional care. All of these social roles will probably affect the way a resolution to the problem is reached.

Ill-structured problems also have *more than one possible solution*. Again, the solution is dependent on the new information that is brought into the problem situation and on the problem definition. The solution to the problem could go in many directions: It could have to do with locating a new supply of oranges, sending the customers to a different store, creating a rationing system for oranges, or distributing vitamin C to the community to help contain the scurvy. One of the goals of the student is to transform the ill-structured problem into a well-structured problem.

Superior Problem Finders and Problem Solvers

By the time that Zelda, Cranshaw, Joe, Stephanie, and Sam have reached their current age, they have become remarkably proficient at various forms of problem solving and problem finding without having been aware of what they were doing or how they were doing it. Imagine Cranshaw on the playground playing a game of touch football. An opposing player punts the ball, and Cranshaw immediately takes five steps forward, judging the arc of the punt as it leaves the punter's foot, integrating the sound of the foot meeting the ball and a dozen other variables, including a crosswind. As the ball nears the ground, Cranshaw moves two steps to the right to take account of the wind and cradles the ball in his arms successfully. This remarkable performance goes without comment from his friends because it is so commonplace. Most of them can do it just as well, and there was nothing unusual observed by them in the "simple" matter of catching a punt.

What is unusual, however, is the actual mental processes that the brain went through in order to accomplish this supposedly routine feat. The brain must have judged the arc of a parabola, must have made a number of complex mathematical and calculus-type computations almost instantaneously, and must have given incredibly rapid orders to a wide variety of muscle groups to move Cranshaw's body to the rapidly approaching ball. If we were to ask Cranshaw to explain how he caught the punt, he would be mystified and not be able to give detailed verbal descriptions of how he did it.

Somewhere in Sam's cumulative folder there is a note from a previous teacher about Sam not being strong in problem solving. That certainly would come as a surprise to Sam's family, neighbors, and friends. Sam is seen as a most effective young man in terms of troubleshooting electrical equipment, from toasters to radios and televisions—all types of household appliances. He seems to be able to identify clearly the nature of the problem and to understand the mechanisms or processes sufficiently so that he can come up with possible adaptations or solutions. In this very practical sense, Sam turns out to be a superb problem solver.

What the teacher probably meant was that in those mathematical or verbal tasks that pass for "problem solving" in an academic setting, Sam had not done well. We must be cautious in our judgments on such matters to make sure we do not overgeneralize from a specific and limited academic context. However, problem-solving skills are not an inevitable result of developing intellect, even when that intellect is advanced, and many events can occur in children's social environment and school that can make them less than proficient in these skills.

Students can become comfortable in the role of "fact absorber" and uncomfortable when asked to solve problems on their own. For example, Zelda has been rewarded so often for her encyclopedic knowledge that even when she is given the opportunity to do independent work or problem solving, she retreats into mastery of factual material, as in the following example:

Teacher: What might have happened if Lincoln had lived?

Zelda: I read where Lincoln was alive for several hours and some people had hopes that he might pull through. The plotters planned to assassinate the vice president, too....

Notice how Zelda sidestepped the adventurous question and slid back into her memory skills, where she is comfortable and secure. In contrast, Stephanie comes alive with questions like this, and gives a variety of ideas on how the country would be different if Lincoln had lived.

Education should ask more of gifted children than that they be walking memory banks. They also must be problem solvers and problem finders, and they will not reach that goal by passively soaking up more information. Intellectual independence is a hard-won prize, and it must be practiced diligently and with skill.

Joe has a quite different problem. He does not wish to try problems for fear that he will fail or look bad once again. He certainly does not want to problem find, where much work, effort, and risk of failure are involved. He would feel more comfortable calling the problems "dumb" and unworthy of serious effort or to play the critic and point out where others have made mistakes in their problem-solving efforts.

How can one capture the mental processes followed by these children when they themselves are unaware of them? Can we, as educators, improve on something (e.g., the operations of the brain) that we do not fully understand? The example of Cranshaw and the football was used for a particular purpose. Who would doubt that we can help Cranshaw improve his punt-catching ability? The coaches who can do it may know no more about the physics of bodies in motion than does Cranshaw. Nevertheless, they may have a number of practical suggestions that would aid in the catching of a football. Suffice it to say that we have developed many techniques designed to improve student performance, but it does help to have some models of mental operations available as a way to organize our own understanding of what is happening.

Productive Thinking and Gifted Students

One of the most accepted goals of educators of gifted students is that they should increase the productive thinking capacity of such students. It should not be thought that, just because such students are quite remarkable in their thinking abilities for their age, such skills cannot be substantially improved. As a matter of fact, some gifted students are so facile with their ideas that, as a consequence, they have little knowledge of how to approach a difficult problem that does not yield easily to the first attempted solution.

Raw Materials for Thinking

There are some necessary ingredients to the recipe for an effective problem solver or problem finder, and all of these ingredients would seem to be important to the effective learner. It should be no surprise that many of these elements show up prominently on intelligence tests.

Information Storage—Memory

The more information that a student has on a given topic, the more likely he or she will be able to be a productive thinker. It is important, however, that the information be accessible to the student. Whitehead (1929) coined the term *inert knowledge* to refer to information that has been learned but that cannot be easily applied. Learning about a law in physics or about logarithms that one cannot find any life applications for are examples of inert knowledge—knowledge that is clearly present in our memory but not usually of much practical use because it is rarely drawn forth to help in meeting a life situation or solving a problem. *Working memory* refers to information that *is* available to be used to solve a particular problem. Much more additional information on the topic may be available in one's long-term memory but it is not easily accessible for a particular problem.

Educational Implications of Memory
Students should be presented with a wide range of information in a given problem area so that they have such data available to apply to a particular problem. They should be encouraged to expand their working memories by seeking remote associations, as well as common associations, from their memories. For example, if Zelda is asked to think of some potential solutions for world hunger, she might focus on various crops that could be planted and grown. She would then be encouraged to think of other devices to increase food production, such as (1) using pesticides, (2) doing genetic research, and (3) limiting population growth. Zelda has all of that additional information in her long-term memory, but she needs encouragement to search it out and bring it to her working memory.

Association/Classification

One of the characteristics that gifted students seem to have in great supply is their ability to link pieces of information together. This skill enables them to bring many associations to the problem field and increases the likelihood of a positive result. The ability to cluster associations in larger groupings (e.g., furniture, carnivores, habitats, etc.) make for much learning economy, since the members of a class all become linked to the new item (e.g., sofa, as furniture, automatically gets linked to chair, table, bureau, etc.). A rich association network is one of the foundations of effective problem solving.

Educational Implications of Association/Classification

The teacher has many opportunities to encourage the establishment of associations and classifications by asking the students questions such as, How many things can you think of that are round? or by giving them tasks such as, Name all the machines that you can. Such questions that require the students to give multiple responses encourages them to seek out more associations and interesting clusters of ideas and things.

Reasoning

The ability to make the final statement to the following may be the most impressive of all human gifts:

> Susan is heavier than Jim.
> Jim is heavier than Mary.
> Therefore, _____.

This skill essentially allows a person to generate new information from information already available in his or her memory, and opens the door to greater understandings. Since gifted students are able to reason with more proficiency than their nongifted agemates, they will likely be using their reasoning processes when they are quite young. The ability to follow one logical path to its inevitable conclusion appears very different from the spinning out of many different responses to a question such as, What would happen if everyone in the world were born with three fingers and no thumb? Using logical reasoning processes, one might get answers such as no more baseball, gloves would become mittens, and cups would be redesigned. For example:

> If we have three fingers and no thumb,
> *And baseball requires a thumb for holding and throwing,*
> *Then we would have to give up the game of baseball.*

By convention, we don't give the full workings of the reasoning process in such situations but only share the final conclusion of the process with the questioner.

Educational Implications of Reasoning

Students with great intellectual power may be susceptible to the many problems that occur with the faulty use of logical reasoning and can use some exercises designed by the teacher that will demonstrate how false logic can be generated. The dissection of TV advertisements can be fertile ground for the analysis of faulty logic. Such lessons can help the children who are gifted to monitor their own thinking abilities and prevent many false conclusions.

Joe is using his own superior reasoning ability to answer the question about Lincoln surviving the assassination attempt. He states, "I think that Lincoln's first step would be to hang all of those who tried to kill him." The logical sequence that Joe appeared to be following was:

Lincoln, having survived, would be angry at his attackers;
His anger would cause him to seek revenge;
Therefore, he would want to hang them all.

However, the logical sequence depends on a number of assumptions, including one about Lincoln's character. Joe's teacher might well point out that Lincoln's character did not suggest that he was a vengeful man or that he would demand death instead of mercy. Since logical reasoning almost always requires the acceptance of some premises, gifted students, as well as all of us, can reach the wrong (or at least a disputed) answer and need to realize the basis for others' concerns about their conclusions.

Evaluation

The ability to make sound judgments is the essence of giftedness. Interestingly enough, this is one area of intelligence that is not often measured on standard intelligence tests, primarily because it is hard to score evaluation questions. Think about the question, Is *Rocky* a good movie? Some type of standard or criterion of what is "good" has to be established before the question can be answered, but few children or adults are aware of how this thinking process works. They just give an answer. One other major difference in evaluative thinking is that one can get very different answers to the same question, and be unable to tell which answer is right, unless everyone agrees on the same criterion.

Educational Implications of Evaluation
Teachers can give students extensive practice on the criteria used to generate evaluative statements. For example, how many criteria can one have to respond to the question, Are sugar cookies good for you? Classroom debates on evaluative issues are always interesting, as long as strict rules are followed on what information is to be used in the debates and the teacher encourages the students to make explicit what criteria are being used to reach judgments.

Metacognition

The ability to think about one's own thinking—*metacognition*—is a major self-correcting device. Metacognition also has the potential to expand one's problem-solving and problem-finding abilities. Much of the instruction of gifted students can, and should, take the form of educating the students in a variety of strategies such as brainstorming, creative problem solving, and future problem solving, which are really a set of approaches for the organization and processing of information. Some of the more commonly used metacognitive strategies will be presented later in this chapter as illustrations of how to help students think more effectively.

Educational Implications of Metacognition

Metacognitive skills not only result in better performance but they encourage the students to use these skills the next time they face a problem. Thus, these children progressively improve their use of cognitive strategies. In other words, it is a case of the "cognitively rich getting richer."

Not only are gifted students faster and more efficient in the use of elementary information processes (Jackson & Butterfield, 1986), but, more importantly, they increasingly use metathinking to solve difficult problems (Borkowski & Peck, 1986). It is clearly one of the responsibilities of educators of gifted students to take advantage of these already present capabilities to help students expand their repertoires of cognitive strategies.

For example, Stephanie talks to herself when she is faced with a difficult word problem in arithmetic. She asks herself which arithmetic operations—addition, subtraction, multiplication, or division—are required. Such reflection pays off in more accurate problem solving. Her teacher, knowing of Stephanie's love for math, may introduce her to the strategy of *estimation*, whereby she is able to make an initial judgment as to the ballpark in which the answer might be. Such estimation is a good protection against an errant answer that departs significantly from the estimation. By learning to apply such skills, Stephanie increases her distance between herself and the rest of the class in mathematics and is more likely to employ these successful strategies the next time, thus the intellectually rich get richer.

Guilford's Intellectual Operations

One of the most used thinking skills models in the education of gifted students is Guilford's structure of intellect (Guilford, 1967). This is partly due to the enormous efforts of many strong disciples such as Paul Torrance, Mary Meeker, Don Treffinger, and others who translated Guilford's ideas into educational applications.

Table 9–1 illustrates one of the three Guilford dimensions, that of *intellectual operations*. Whereas his content category provides the form in which the thinking will take place, and his product category indicates the result of the thinking, the category of operations concentrates on the means by which the product is reached. Guilford has proposed five general dimensions of intellectual operations in his model: cognition, memory, convergent thinking, divergent thinking, and evaluation.

Cognitive Memory

In the classroom, the distinction between cognition and memory is often blurred. In applying this classification system to the classroom, Gallagher (1968) combined the two into *cognitive-memory*. Cognitive memory represents the reception or reproduction of material. To use *Hamlet* as an example, cognitive memory skills would be activated first by having the students read the play and then by asking them questions that would have to

TABLE 9 1   Guilford System by Intellectual Operations

Operation	Example
Cognitive memory	Who did Hamlet kill by mistake?
Convergent thinking	Explain why Hamlet rejected Ophelia.
Divergent thinking	Name some other ways Hamlet might have accomplished his goals.
Evaluation	Was Hamlet justified in killing his uncle?

do with facts or ideas presented within the play itself. Any kind of interpretative statements or ideas would not fall under the cognitive memory category, which covers *what* happened, not *why* it happened.

Often, so much emphasis is placed on the stimulation of the higher thought processes that the impression sometimes is given that the collection and reproduction of facts is not very important. Such fact collection is, of course, the irreplaceable foundation for advanced thought. First, it is necessary to know what Hamlet did and said in order to make an evaluative judgment on his wisdom, or to produce alternative courses of action, or to reason out the impact of his behavior on his mother.

Convergent Thinking

Convergent thinking refers to the process whereby the student takes a large number of facts or associations and puts them together in certain predictable combinations to reach the one possible right answer. The clearest academic illustrations of convergent thinking can be found in arithmetic reasoning problems, where the student takes a variety of facts and operates to come out with the right answer. All instances of deductive reasoning involve convergent thinking.

Although convergent thinking has been identified most often with the sciences and mathematics, it is found quite regularly in other subject areas as well. Any problem that has a large amount of given information and requires close logical reasoning to reach a valid conclusion calls for convergent thinking. The suggestion in Table 9–1, "Explain why Hamlet rejected Ophelia," is of this type. The student must follow some type of deductive reasoning, such as:

> Hamlet was disillusioned with all women.
> Ophelia was a woman.
> Therefore, Hamlet, disillusioned with Ophelia, rejected her.

Of course, this is not the only possible interpretation, but it is typical of the logical process that the student must follow to arrive at a reasonable explanation.

Divergent Thinking

Divergent thinking represents a free and open type of intellectual operation in which the distinguishing characteristic is the large number of possible associations or problem solutions. The teacher who is interested in stimulating divergent thinking could pose the following problems: What other ways could Hamlet have used to trap the king? What other courses of action might have been open to Hamlet's mother? Suppose that Polonius had not been killed; how would that have modified or changed the eventual outcome of the play? All these questions attempt to make the student become more fully aware of alternative paths of action and of the development of the play itself. By considering such alternative lines of action, one gets a more thorough understanding of the particular sequence chosen by the author.

Evaluation

Almost any play or story will offer a rich field of discussion related to evaluative thinking. Evaluative responses require the student to establish some value continuum and then to weigh various alternative actions or persons against these values. For example, the question, Was Hamlet's plan to revenge himself moral or right? requires the student to draw a value dimension of rightness or morality and then to place this particular act or plan somewhere on this dimension. Although it might not be possible to prove directly which student's answer might be more correct, it is always possible to indicate the implications that could follow from certain decisions. For example, the teacher could point out that revenge breeds counterrevenge and that various feuds between families, clans, and nations are kept boiling through this mechanism.

The teacher could take a quote such as "There cracks a noble heart" and raise the issue as to how noble Hamlet really was. In a similar way, one could question the motives and approaches of each of the characters. More time could be allotted to such discussions with a gifted group, if the teacher is relatively certain that the necessary facts have been absorbed, since a lesser proportion of time would need to be spent on cognitive memory aspects.

Much of the stimulation of evaluative thinking can be tied to convergent thinking; for example, the teacher can ask the question, Was Hamlet morally right in his revenge plans? If we can imagine the student answering yes, we can further imagine that practically any teacher would follow this reply with the question, Why do you believe this? In this case, the student would be required to present a reasoned argument demanding convergent thinking, such as Hamlet was only doing to his uncle what his uncle had previously done to his father. In other words, the following logical sequence could be evoked:

People who do wrong should be punished;
Hamlet's uncle did wrong, and the only one in a position to punish him was Hamlet;
Hamlet, therefore, was justified in punishing his uncle through his plans for revenge.

No classroom can escape a certain amount of cognitive memory operations, since any thinking process must use certain facts and ideas that have been previously learned. It is a boring and uninteresting classroom, however, that confines itself mainly to this kind of activity, rather than using it as a prelude to other kinds of thinking performance.

In the instance of the class just described, the teacher used the facts that were established earlier to trigger some divergent thinking on the part of the students. The following sequences illustrate the teacher's approach and the students' responses.

Divergent Sequence. During the first 20 minutes of class, students deliver reports from their groups on facts and data they have found relating to problems agreed upon by the class, such as those that might be encountered if they stepped from a time machine and became the first settlers at the mouth of the Amazon River, Brazil, in A.D. 1500. After brief comments and discussions of the reports, the teacher makes a change to a new topic and a new approach to discussion.

Teacher: I am now going to be a combination Atlas, Hercules, Paul Bunyan, Popeye, and Pecos Bill! I'm going to pick up a continent and *move* it! (The teacher picks up a rubber-wire outline map of South America, which has been matched to the outline contours of South America as depicted on the large world wall map at front of room. The teacher "moves" South America south and westward, over toward the area of New Zealand.) Now, how would South America be different if it were moved over there? (The class shows rousing interest; a buzz of comments begins and many hands go up.) All right, Leslie, what do you think?

Leslie: Well, a lot of it would be cold that's hot now.

Kit: Part of it would still be in the tropics—it would still be hot.

Teacher: Would it change the Amazon Basin?

Class: Yes!

Jeannie: Maybe it wouldn't be discovered when it was. And maybe if it was, it'd be by different people.

Dan: There'd be some swell winter and summer resorts! (Some chuckles from class)

Leslie: The Indians would maybe come over from Australia instead of coming down from Greenland.

Sandra: Australia would probably be considered an island instead of a continent, compared with a big continent like South America next to it.

Katy: Australia would still be a continent!

Dan: Magellan's straits would be a lot different. They'd run right into the South Pole. He would have had a shortcut.

Cathy: Simon Bolivar and Pizarro they couldn't do much. They might not even have been there!

Katy: There wouldn't have been a Panama Canal—there'd be no need for one, really.

Leslie: Probably there would be a lot more oriental people on this (South America at New Zealand spot) continent, and there would be English settlers rather than Spanish— from Spain, which is so far away.

William: The Indians would probably come in down through the Philippines and some of those other Pacific islands.

Sandra: The theory of Africa and South America being connected earlier—that theory wouldn't exist.

One of the distinguishing features of divergent thinking in the classroom is the wide variety of ideas it stimulates, as can be seen by the previous exchange. The absence of a supposedly correct answer also seems to free the children from the inhibiting bonds produced by the fear of making a mistake; they become enthusiastic and excited by the ideas presented.

Most class sessions are a complex mixture of various kinds of thought processes. The teacher can plan to elicit certain combinations of thought processes, such as the evaluative and convergent operations in the sequence that follows. This is a common combination. The teacher will first ask the students to weigh or judge certain facts or ideas (evaluative) and will then ask them to justify their ratings (convergent).

Evaluative/Convergent Sequence.   The children have just returned from recess. Earlier in the morning, the class had been discussing some of the proposed solutions to problems they might encounter if they stepped out of a time machine and found themselves to be the first settlers at the mouth of the Amazon River in A.D. 1500. The class has been dealing with these problems for several days, both in small group work and in class discussion.

Teacher: The driver in our time machine told me that I could take three things back with me to Brazil in the time machine. So I decided to take (writes on the board) a tray of ice cubes, a car, and a rubber ball. What do you think of my choices? Jesse?

Jesse: (chuckling) Pretty bad!

Katy: Well, I think they're pretty poor choices. There are other things you could use more than a ball.

Henry: I don't see how a car would be useful. It would get rusted down there in the jungle, and the jungle's all full of weeds and heavy undergrowth. The car couldn't go through it, and so the weeds would just grow all over it. (Some laughter and other comments; general amusement over the teacher's obviously poor choices)

Teacher: Well, let's see what else I could take (writes on board)—How about a wallet full of money, a bicycle, and a jug of water?

Cathy: I don't think money would be any good—what are you going to buy?

Teacher: Jeannie, you seem to have an opinion on this. What do you think of my choices?

Jeannie: Well, I think I'd better start to go down the list. First of all, if we were the first settlers, what would we need money for? Number two—the bicycle—you couldn't ride it. There would be mountains and hills, and there would be too much undergrowth on the plains. And then, the jug of water—you could just as well take the ice cubes and let them melt.

William: Keep your jug!

Teacher: Why wouldn't water be good to take along in the time machine?

Sandra: It would get too hot.

Rhoda: Couldn't you put the jug into the Amazon River—tie it to a tree with a rope or a vine and let it down into the river—to keep it cold?

The teacher in this segment forced the students into an evaluation framework by providing some deliberately bad choices. The evaluative/convergent sequence is one of the most common in classroom dialogue. It consists of making a choice (evaluation) and then defending it (convergent reasoning). What is not nearly so common is the deliberate and explicit discussion of criteria by which the judgment is made—a direction in which this teacher is now headed.

The operations domain of the Guilford system—cognition, memory, convergent thinking, divergent thinking, and evaluation—has occupied much of the attention of educators, since the elicitation of these intellectual operations can be clearly triggered by teacher behavior (e.g., When was Washington born? for *memory*; What might have happened if Washington had drowned as a young boy? for *divergent thinking*; etc.). Guilford's intellectual operations can be easily tracked and charted in classroom interchange, and the ability to do this allows teacher trainers to help teachers to understand some of the possible consequences of different teacher questions.

The processes of thinking that lead to problem solving and problem finding can be located in the product and operations domains of the Guilford structure of intellect model. The goal of the problem-solving process would be to draw significant implications, or conclusions, from a body of available information around a given question. For instance, Why does water run downhill? may be such a problem. That question has to be solved through an understanding of the properties of water and the system of gravity. The intellectual operations predominantly used would be those of cognition, memory, and convergent thinking in a pattern of logical reasoning that would follow this sequence:

Water has weight and flows.
Gravity pulls things with weight toward the center of the earth.
It then follows that water should flow downhill.

Another task of problem solving might be to explain how television works (i.e., how a visual image gets sent thousands of miles and ends up in your television set, displayed with great accuracy on your screen). Again, a large amount of information needs to be assembled about cameras, transmission of electrical impulses, and so forth. Then, the transformation of visual impulses to electrical patterns has to be understood. The system within the TV set that receives the electronic impulses and amplifies them and spreads them across the screen has to be mastered. The student should also understand the implications of the controls on the TV set and the role that magnetism plays in shaping the vertical and horizontal dimensions of the picture.

Analogous Thinking and Problem Solving

The use of analogies has been one of the most frequently used measures in intelligence tests. Most people are all familiar with test items like: Bear is to Animal as Salmon is to _____. The ability to reason by analogy, to see associations between different things or events, has long served as a key to scientific discoveries. Gordon (1975) captured a remarkable diversity of these events to indicate how widespread and productive is this ability to draw analogies to link events together in order to solve problems. Table 9–2 gives an extended list of major discoveries that depended on analogous thinking, plus, of course, a powerful knowledge base.

Another example from Gordon comes from a familiar figure, Benjamin Franklin. Franklin's invention of the lightning rod resulted from an analogy drawn from witnessing

TABLE 9–2   Discovery Through Analogy

Discoverer	*The Analogy Experience*
Gutenberg (1460)	Developed the concept of movable type from observing the manufacture of coins.
Bissell (1859)	Saw a derrick pumping brine at a salt plant and used it to pump oil.
Harvey (1650)	Saw the analogy between heart action and a pump.
Arkwright (1780)	Saw red-hot iron formed between two pairs of rollers conceived of forming thread by pulling fibers through rollers at different speeds.
Franklin (1780)	"A great empire, like a great cake, is most easily diminished at the edges."
Brunel (1840)	Saw a shipworm tunneling through timber—used its formation of a tube as a basis for tunnel excavation.
Morse (1860)	Used stagecoach relay points as a basis for building relay stations for telegraph signals.
Whitney (1795)	Idea for the cotton gin came from watching a cat catching a chicken through the fence. The cat missed the chicken, but came away with feathers.
Dunlop (1887)	Had idea for air inflated tires from a garden hose.
Duryea (1891)	Spray injected carburetor came from observing his wife's perfume atomizer.
Bell (1910)	Bones of the human ear move by membrane—used that idea to move steel in the telephone.

From: Gordon, W. J. (1974). Some source material in discovery-by-analogy. *Journal of Creative Behavior*, 1974, Volume 8, #4. Reprinted with permission from the copyright holder, The Creative Education Foundation, Buffalo, NY.

the discharge of a Leyden jar emanating from what he called a pointed finger. Franklin speculated, "To know this power of points may possibly be of some use to mankind in preserving houses, churches, and ships from the stroke of lightning."

Samuel F. B. Morse, in inventing the telegraph, had to overcome a major problem: The signal sent over the wire became so faint that it was ineffective after a few miles. Gordon reported the Morse analogy that led to the solution:

> *No solution was forthcoming until one day when he was traveling on a stage-coach from New York to Baltimore. Then he saw the analogy between his problem and the relay post stations where horses were replaced just when they were beginning to tire... accordingly, Morse set up stations at appropriate distances along his telegraph line, where more power was added to his signal just as it was getting weak. (1975, p. 247)*

It is obvious that if ways could be found to enhance analogous reasoning through education, we would be doing ourselves and our students an enormous benefit. We can ask the students to think about space walks, for example, and to come forth with analogous situations. Underwater swimming is one plausible answer, with the necessity, in both environments, to get oxygen from some artificial source. The design of scuba-diving equipment would have some resemblance, then, to outer-space gear. As another analogy, one could apply the rapid growth and decay of bacteria due to an overcrowded environment to our own world population growth.

One of the most exciting and educationally relevant discoveries in developmental psychology was in the area of capabilities of even young children for analogous reasoning. Previously, it had been felt that such reasoning ability was not present until much later in the developmental process, at least until later school age.

Goswami (1991) assembled an impressive collection of research that demonstrated highly competent anological reasoning in children as young as 3 years old—as long as they have the knowledge base relevant to the relations used in the analogies. Even at this young age, when such relationships are shown as part of the study, students can use this thinking process. Whether they can spontaneously use their own memory stores to produce analogous reasoning has yet to be determined. What this implies is that we can design instructional programs and situations that will encourage analogous thinking at much earlier times in the school program than was previously considered possible. This discovery naturally fits gifted students even better than it does the average students.

Knowledge Network

The importance of a strong knowledge network of associations, to allow the student to effectively problem solve or problem find, has long been understood, if sometimes underestimated, in the education of gifted students. A person cannot solve the problem of growing plants in Antarctica if he or she doesn't know anything about the terrain, the climate, or the history of the area. However, what is required is not just a collection of facts but a network of associations and systems of ideas that can incorporate new knowledge easily into the system or network.

A recent series of studies compared the thinking processes of *experts* in a field with *novice* practitioners in physics (Chi, Feltovich, & Glaser, 1981), chess playing (de Groot, 1965; Chase & Simon, 1973), and medical diagnosis (Lesgold, Feltovich, Glaser, & Wang, 1981). The expert chess players apparently were able to see the significant configurations on the board more effectively than the novice players. They had a knowledge structure of the field of the chessboard stored away, which allowed them to see the significance of the patterns of chess pieces. Similarly, the expert physicists could make more out of new information by relating it to already stored concepts and systems of ideas, whereas the naive physicists depended on the information immediately available in the problem itself.

A very similar situation prevailed in medical diagnostics. Experts in medical diagnosis revealed how differently they approach a diagnostic problem to be solved than did the novice, but well-trained, physicians. The naive physicians depended almost entirely on the information gathered during the diagnostic examination; the experts called on broader sets of past knowledge through stored associative networks, which enabled them to place the new diagnostic information into a rich experiential context (Rabinowitz & Glaser, 1985).

All of these experts applied this rich associative network of past information and conceptualizations to a new problem with good effect. The educational implication of such findings is that teachers need to help students build these associative networks of knowledge as a base for problem solving and problem finding. The insight into a problem and the generation of a solution come not from some mysterious power from outer space but rather from the ability of the person to fit the new set of circumstances into an already existing personal web of associations. By recombining—or extending—this system of associations, he or she can reach a solution which, to the naive observer, seems almost miraculous.

One of the standard themes taught in upper elementary and middle school programs is that of *heroism*. By exposing students to literature, the teacher hopes to help the students realize that heroism is not just any courageous act but a deliberate sacrifice of self-interest (even of one's life) for a larger goal of the group. Cranshaw is more likely to hit on this generalization than Sam—not because his native ability is greater but because he has already read about the Greeks at Thermopolae, the Texans at the Alamo, and so on, and thus has a broader base of associations with which to integrate the new idea.

Problem Solving: Cognitive Flexibility Theory

One reason why it is so difficult for teachers to concentrate both on the students' factual knowledge base and on higher thinking skills is that the two seem to require two different kinds of teaching techniques. Spiro, Vispoel, Schmitz, Samarapungavan, and Boerger (1987) differentiated between the best ways to teach about facts and the best ways to approach higher-order skills in a theory that they call the "cognitive flexibility theory." The notion of *cognitive flexibility* comes from the need for students to be able to pull from a variety of already established knowledge bases and skill areas to apply to new and different problems or ideas. According to these researchers, optimal teaching techniques for these two goals are not only different but they are nearly diametrically opposed. Fact acquisition, they have claimed, is best done in well-structured domains. Some of the barriers to the flexible use of information and skills are the following:

> *First, because [factual] kinds of knowledge structures are frequently prepackaged, they tend to be overly rigid. As a result, they provide very little opportunity for adaptation to diverse contexts of use.*
>
> *Second, these modes of representation tend to isolate or compartmentalize aspects of knowledge that, in use, need to be interconnected. Again, the result is a limited potential for transfer.*
>
> *Third, they have frequently treated complex subject matter as if it were simpler than it really was; complexities upon which transfer depends have been artificially neatened.*
>
> *Fourth, they have often implicitly assumed that knowledge domains possess more regularity or consistency across cases of application than they actually do. (Spiro et al., 1989, p. 179)*

When combined, these four barriers create a curious argument about how problem solving should be structured for gifted students. Often, we assume that in order to make the application of complex and higher-order skills more accessible, we must place them in a context (a problem or an activity) that is purposefully constructed to be simple and leave out all of the messiness associated with a real problem. According to Spiro and colleagues, the process of simplifying problem solving may, in fact, make it more difficult for students to see how these skills can be used in other, more complex problems later on.

The New Problem Solver: The Computer

One of the latest tools in our search for better problem solving is the computer. Will the computer now do the problem solving, leaving us free to be more creative or at least to spend more productive time doing more effective problem finding? More likely, the computer will help us become better problem solvers.

When students learns to program the computer successfully, what they are really doing is learning to think in a sequential, step-by-step logical process. Everyone who has tried to program a computer, but leaves out a small step in the process, knows how unforgiving this tool is. One has to achieve 100 percent accuracy to use it effectively. Critics of the computer fear that it will cause students to think in a mechanical fashion, but this seems to be a groundless fear; instead, it will provide students with one more set of skills that can be used effectively at the right place and the right time. Papert pointed out, "Some children's difficulties in learning formal subjects such as grammar or mathematics derive from their inability to see the point of such a style [formal structure]" (1981, p. 5).

Since the same enthusiasms are being expressed for the current microcomputer as for the computer-assisted instruction movement in the 1960s, it is worth remembering what some of the limitations of that movement were. There were concerns that the highly structured material would inhibit diverse or original thought, that too little attention was paid to the unique characteristics of the learner, and that the tasks presented on the computer would be more simple than complex. Such reservations are a reminder that tools, however cleverly designed, can be effective only if they are integrated into the overall instructional program. The teacher using the computer still has to be sure that the curriculum content being addressed is significant and worthy of the students' time and has to have some clear educational objective in mind for the use of this tool.

The field of *artificial intelligence*—the development of computer programs that simulate human intelligence—is a fascinating one for many gifted students, and may even reveal a better understanding of how humans problem solve and problem find. One popular entertainment device is the computerized chess player that challenges and defeats most ordinary chess players and, at its most sophisticated level, will give even experts a difficult time. Few of us have stopped to think about the programmed instructions that had to be placed into that machine in order for it to perform in many ways like a complex thinking organism.

First of all, one would have to put in the parameters of the situation—that is, the rules of the game. For example, the player cannot move two pieces at once, cannot cross the boundaries of the board and then come back on the board again, and so on. With those parameters, plus the various characteristics of the pieces (how they move, their relative worth, etc.), one has the basis of a problem-solving situation. So, various rules can then be entered that guide the problem-solving activity of the computer chess player, such as try to exchange wherever possible when one's strength is greater than one's opponent, try to keep the queen out of danger except when the king is in imminent danger of checkmate, and so forth. In each successive play, there are various alternative moves that have to be weighed for their relative merit, and so these and other sets of rules have to be applied to each of the moves to see which move is the most favorable. In short, all of the strategies, or heuristics, going into a formal problem-solving situation are involved in the design of a program for a computer chess player.

How thoroughly the desktop computer will aid the educational process will depend on how imaginatively one can construct the tasks that will be performed on it. There is no difficulty in designing simple matching or basic calculations, which are easy to do on computers. It is much harder to develop a complex program that encourages decision making and will intrigue gifted students.

Several computer programs have been developed that allow students to conduct a business, such as running a bicycle shop (Minnesota Educational Computing Consortium, 1981). By providing the necessary parameters, just as the computer chess player is provided game rules, students are made aware of the available markets, the cost of doing business, and so on. In this fashion, the youngsters can get a full interactive experience of what it takes to run a business, what kinds of problems they will meet, and the decisions that have to be made in such an operation. As in all of the previous tools mentioned earlier, it is the actual design of the content by thinking human beings that eventually determines to what extent the tools can be used in the stimulation of complex thinking operations—one clear instructional goal for gifted students.

A welcome addition to the use of technology is provided by the Cognition and Technology Group at Vanderbilt (Bransford, Sherwood, Vye, & Rieser, 1986). This group has designed a series of videotapes that are presented to stimulate the higher thinking processes of students. The goal of the program is to help students become independent thinkers through the presentation of a problem. For example, while some young people are fishing, they find an eagle with a broken wing that has to be brought to treatment quickly or it will die. The problem presented to the students is how best to get the eagle to treatment.

Having been presented the problem through videotape, the students are divided into small groups in cooperative learning model and asked to devise a solution. The students have to identify and clarify the problem and present their version of the solution. The facts needed to solve the problem are embedded in the videotape, along with the information presented to the students. There is a follow-up videotape showing the answer to the students after they have done their work.

The use of such technology to increase the reality of the problem and motivate the students to define and solve the problem seems to be much more imaginative use of technology than the presentation of routine drills, which is the all-too-familiar use of advanced technology.

Stimulation of Problem Solving and Problem Finding

The instructional goal for teachers of gifted students is to enhance each student's natural bent toward all types of productive thinking. To do this, the teacher has to have in mind some skills or productive-thinking models he or she wishes the students to master, much as they would master rules of grammatical structure or mathematical operations.

One of the important issues in the education of gifted children is how best to present problem solving so that the students will master and retain the skills. Glaser (1984) maintained that there are at least two quite different strategies, as follows:

1. *Process oriented.* The students learn, through carefully designed problem exercises, the procedures for observing, monitoring, problem solving, and so forth. The problems have little to do with the curriculum content in the students' other lessons.
2. *Problem solving through content.* The students learn how to solve problems through working in established domains like mathematics and science. The same skills are taught as in the process-oriented strategy (observing, problem solving, etc.) but are executed by using concrete lessons in subject areas.

The reason given for supporting the first strategy, *process oriented*, is that it is unencumbered by specific content and thus the student has a better chance of learning the processes without being distracted by a specific content emphasis. The proponents of this method worry that a student who would learn problem-solving techniques in a particular content setting, such as mathematics, would be unlikely to see the application of these skills to English or social studies. The proponents of the second strategy, *problem solving through content*, maintain that it is hard to apply problem-solving strategies that have been learned in the abstract or in a game-like setting to specific content, and that linking the strategies with the content is the more effective way of assuming that the techniques will be used academically. Glaser believes that the second strategy is the one most supported by existing research, and this is the approach recommended in this text (i.e., combining the major ideas from content fields, as illustrated in Chapters 4 through 8, with the productive-thinking strategies discussed in Chapters 9 and 10).

An interesting illustration of the useful interaction between acquired knowledge and thinking performance is produced by Chi (1978). She compared the memory span performance of a group of 10-year-old chess players with a group of adults who did not know how to play chess. Using the typical digit span tests of immediate memory ("Repeat these digits: 4-7-3-8-2-9"), the adults were clearly superior. However, when asked to recall chess positions, the chess-playing children's memories were clearly superior to the adults' memories. Knowledge of the specific content field clearly helped to extend the memories of the children.

Parnes's Process of Creative Problem Solving

A familiar model designed to aid the learner was developed by Parnes, Noller, and Biondi (1977), as shown in Table 9–3. This five-step process is presented in such a way that the student understands the importance of each step. The first step is a careful observation period—*fact finding*—which enables the individual to have a base set of facts from which to act.

Parnes and his colleagues, like Getzels, focus on the importance of *problem finding*. The identification of an important problem to address is rarely discussed with students who are used to having predesigned problems presented to them by texts or teachers. It is in choosing which problems to solve, just as one chooses which curriculum events to include in a program, that we use the uniquely human capabilities. The challenge is: How do we develop curriculum that stresses problem finding? Many brilliant students with an otherwise excellent record through four years of college will stumble as they search for a good thesis or dissertation problem. It is difficult to avoid the conclusion that we have

Table 9–3 Steps in Parnes's Creative Problem-Solving Process

Steps	*Activities*
1. Fact-Finding	Collecting data about the problem; acting as a camara, observing carefully and objectively.
2. Problem-Finding	Looking at possible problems from several viewpoints; restating the problems into solvable form.
3. Idea-Finding	Generating many ideas and possible solutions.
4. Solution-Finding	Developing criteria for the evaluation of alternatives.
5. Acceptance-Finding	Considering all audiences who must accept the plan; brainstorming the concerns of all these audiences.

Source: Table appears in *Guide to Creative Action* by Sidney J. Parnes, Ruth B. Noller, and Angelo M. Biondi. Copyright 1977 Charles Scribner's Sons. Reprinted with permission of the copyright holder, The Creative Education Foundation, 1050 Union Rd., Buffalo, NY 14224.

been successful in teaching our best students to solve problems when they are presented but have paid relatively little attention to helping them find a problem worth solving.

Next in the creative problem-solving model comes the period of generating as many different ideas and solutions as possible—*idea finding*—and developing criteria to determine how to choose the best alternative—*solution finding* (e.g., the cheapest, the most acceptable, the most effective, etc.). Finally, Parnes emphasized convincing others— *acceptance finding*—about the value of the solution, which is an important step if one wants public cooperation for the plan.

Future Problem Solving

A popular adaptation of the creative problem-solving model was originated by Paul Torrance, who began the Future Problem Solving (FPS) program in 1974. This program involved teams of students who worked on a variety of problems of social importance that extended into the future. The FPS program has continued to evolve, and now has 175,000 students in local school teams working on three problems a year. Crabbe (1982) described the steps that the students take in future problem solving:

1. *Research and learn as much as possible about the general topic.*
2. *Brainstorm problems related to the specific situation presented.*
3. *Identify a major, underlying problem from the list of brainstormed problems.*
4. *Brainstorm solutions to the underlying problem.*
5. *Develop a list of criteria by which to evaluate the solutions.*
6. *Evaluate the solutions according to the criteria to select the best solution.*

The problem to be addressed might be that the world is in danger of running out of oil within the next century. However, the students are expected to probe further through discussion to find the underlying problem, which might be called The Increasing Energy Needs for the Future. With the problem identified, the students are then expected to propose some possible solutions. This is a particularly good task for students who have always believed that there is one right answer to every question. To see that there are a variety of possibilities, and that they will have to make a decision as to which of them seems most appropriate, is to give these students a task that is often quite novel to them.

The students can then develop a decision matrix, such as the one in Table 9–4 that will match the likely options against the criteria that the group decided were important in judging the merits of each option. In the end, the students may well conclude that it is some type of mix of strategies that may have to be adopted if the people of this planet are going to meet our rapidly increasing energy needs and accept the fact that all of the solutions involve costs.

Schools enrolled in this Future Problem Solving program also can participate in state competitions and ultimately in for a national competition, with its attendant publicity and excitement. In the end, the students will have had the experience of facing a difficult problem, thinking in some depth about it, and realizing that there are no quick or easy

Table 9–4   Decision-Making Model

Options	Cost	Environmental Impact	Public Safety	Other Changes Necessary (Cars, Houses, Etc.)	Long-Term Availability	Public Acceptance
Increase Oil Exploration						
Develop Nuclear Energy						
Develop Solar Energy						
Mine More Coal						
Develop Wind Power						
Utilize Steam Power						
Conservation						

solutions to many of the problems that they will face as adults. This is a valuable lesson to learn in days where many problems last only as long as a 30-minute television program.

Goal-Oriented Planning

Table 9–5 shows one type of planning model used in goal-oriented planning that can be applied by teachers and gifted students (Gallagher, 1986). The example in Table 9–5, planning for energy resources, represents a societal need and is a goal that is of concern to everyone in our society. The reader can note the similarity between the creative problem-solving model noted in Table 9–3 and the planning model presented in Table 9–5.

The first step in such a planning model would be to identify the size of the *need*: How much energy does the country need? To determine the answer to that question, we must first find out how much energy we have been using and see if there is any trend that shows consistent increases or decreases; we can then project future needs in some systematic way.

Once the needs are estimated and we are clear on our *goal* of energy self-sufficiency, then the next step would be to set an *objective* that would be quantitatively specific and time restricted. In this example, it is suggested that the objective should be that only 10 percent of our energy needs would be imported from other countries by the year 2000. This statement gives a quantitative objective and the date by which the objective is to be obtained. Once we know how much energy we must import, and have settled on our quantitative objective, we can then periodically chart our progress to that objective and see how well we are doing.

TABLE 9–5 **Planning for the Future (*Energy*)**

Step	Definition	Application
Needs	A quantitative statement of important lacks or deficits.	The U.S. will be dependent on other nations for 30 percent of energy needs by the year 2000.
Goals	A general statement of self-interest.	We should be energy self-sufficient.
Objectives	Specific quantitative desired result by a given time.	We should rely on others for only 10 percent of energy needs by the year 2000.
Alternative Strategies	Action alternatives designed to reach goals and objectives.	1. Increase nuclear energy. 2. Develop solar energy. 3. Find more oil. 4. Mine more coal.
Selection Criteria	Standards against which to weigh possible alternative strategies.	1. Safe to public. 2. Long-term source available. 3. Reasonably inexpensive. 4. Doesn't change many other things.
Implementation Needs	What institutional support needed to carry out desired strategies?	There may need to be legislation, more research and development; changes in public attitude needed. Determine how these will be accomplished through social institutions or strategies.
Evaluation	How do we know we are succeeding? Is the investment worth the cost?	Periodic reading on energy dependency and the degree to which the strategy appears to be reducing it.

The next step in the planning process is to generate *alternative strategies* (similar to Parnes's *idea finding*) that might be used to reach our objective. Some alternative strategies to cope with the energy problem could be the development of solar energy, an increase of nuclear energy, or the more effective or greater use of coal and oil. Systematic conservation of all our energy might be another strategy to be considered.

In order to make a rational choice between these strategies or combination of strategies, some *selection criteria* are established by which we can weigh the relative merits and demerits of each particular strategy against the others. In this case, we might identify safety, long-term sources of supply, low cost, and immediate usability as four major criteria that could be applied to the strategies. The choice is made more difficult, but more realistic, by the fact that one strategy may be the safest, another the most cost efficient, and so on.

The next step in the planning process is the *implementation needs* of a policy, which would determine how much money, personnel, and authority are needed in order to carry out the selected strategy or combination of strategies. *Evaluation*, in most instances, will consist of answering the questions, Have we reached our objectives? and Has anything also occurred as a result of our efforts that needs some attention?

This model, which goes from needs to evaluation, can be used to attack almost any problem. Examples of such problems include how to serve the large number of children with reading problems in a local school system, how to solve local traffic problems, and how to cope with the needs of mathematically talented children of school age in the United States.

Adler's Seminar Method

Mortimer Adler's *The Paidaea Proposal* (1984) describes a method of classroom discourse called the *seminar method*. In this method, Adler poses a major issue, often in readings that the students have been assigned. In the following excerpt, he has posed to a group of secondary school pupils the issue as to whether Machiavelli's principle, "Do anything, fair of foul, to maintain power" would work in today's world. The students must make an evaluative judgment and defend their judgment in group discussion.

> *Teacher:*   Who of you believe that Machiavelli's ideas would work today? Buffy, what do you think about it?
>
> *Buffy:*   I know, even as much as I try, I would never do everything I say, because I have done things where I have had to lead—and you have to lie. You can't keep all of the people happy all of the time—it's just impossible. And so you let people think you...
>
> *Teacher:*   Do you think if Stephanie tried to live in a world in which she agrees with… (Stephanie has said she would not be dishonest to get ahead)
>
> *Buffy:*   Most people would end up not liking her.
>
> *Teacher:*   You think Stephanie would not succeed.
>
> *Buffy:*   No, it depends on what she does.
>
> *Teacher:*   Who else is with Buffy? What do you think about Buffy's point?
>
> *John:*   I don't think she [Stephanie] would succeed at all. If you are perfectly honest, how could you lead a whole group of people because, like you said, every man isn't honest, so there would always be somebody out there trying to take her position.
>
> *Teacher:*   Who else?
>
> *Gertrude:*   I think that she has a view of the world that is kind of dreamy. It can't really happen that way, because there are people around you that are bad, so you have to deal with bad things.
>
> *Teacher:*   She is admitting that *most* people…
>
> *Gertrude:*   Right, but yet she thinks she's going to be honest and she can't be honest if somebody is not being honest with her.

Teacher: Now she can be if she doesn't want to succeed.

Gertrude: Right, if she doesn't want to succeed.

Teacher: And part of it is she doesn't want to get into the rat race, doesn't want to struggle in competition with others to succeed to get to the top, then she can get out. But she says she wants to succeed in the rat race—right?

Stephanie: Well, yes I'd like to succeed. I don't know that I necessarily—OK, I'll put it this way—I don't want to succeed to the point that I would do anything to get it.*

In this approach, the students are forced to take an evaluative position and defend it. The difficulties that this group of high-performing students had in evaluative thinking is evidence of their lack of practice in discussing such issues. Although these were secondary students, Adler believes that this method has proven its worth for students from the fourth grade and up with issues chosen for developmental appropriateness.

Group Problem Solving

Another strategy of increasing popularity is the design of group problem-solving methods, whereby the students, in small groups, join forces to solve a complex problem.

Sociodrama

A model by which feelings and thoughts can be displayed and analyzed in the classroom is the sociodrama—a group problem-solving process. The objective of sociodrama is to examine a group or social problem through dramatic methods. Torrance presented the steps to be followed, and the reader can note the similarity between this approach and the previously described models.

>   Step 1: Defining the problem. *The director, leader, or teacher should explain to the group that they are going to participate in an unrehearsed skit to try to find some ways of solving a problem of concern chosen by them.*

>   Step 2: Establishing a situation (conflict). *Culling from the responses, the teacher or director describes a conflict situation in objective and understandable terms. No indication is given as to the direction that the resolution should take. As in creative problem solving, judgment is deferred. (The conflict situation is analogous to problem definition in Parnes's creative problem-solving model.)*

>   Step 3: Casting characters (protagonists). *Participation in roles should be voluntary. The director, however, must be alert in observing the audience for the emergence of new roles and giving encouragement to the timid person who really wants to participate but is saying so only by means of body language.*

*Source: Adapted from Adler, M. (1989). *Great ideas: A seminar approach to teaching and learning* (videotaped series). Chicago, IL: Encyclopaedia Britannica. Reprinted by permission of Encyclopaedia Britannica Educational Corporation.

Step 4: Briefing and warming-up of actors and observers. *It is usually a good idea to give the actors a few minutes to plan the setting and to agree upon a direction. Members of the audience may be asked to try to identify with one or the other of the protagonists or to observe them from a particular point of view.*

Step 5: Acting out the situation. *Acting out the situation may be a matter of seconds, or it may last for ten or twenty minutes. As a teacher or leader gains experience as a sociodrama director, he or she will be able to use a variety of production techniques for digging deeper into the problem, increasing the number and originality of the alternatives, getting thinking out of a "rut," and getting group members to make bigger mental leaps in finding better solutions.*

Step 6: Cutting the action. *The action should be stopped or "cut" whenever the actors fall hopelessly out of role or are unable to continue; whenever the episode comes to a conclusion; or whenever the director sees the opportunity to stimulate thinking to a higher level of creativity by using a different episode.*

Step 7: Discussing and analyzing the situation, the behavior, and the ideas produced. *Applying the creative problem-solving model, it would seem desirable to formulate some criteria to use in discussing and evaluating alternatives produced by the actors and audience. In any case, this should be a rather controlled or guided type of discussion, wherein the director tries to help the group redefine the problem and/or see the various possible solutions indicated by the action.*

Step 8: Making plans for further testing and/or implementing ideas for new behavior. *There are a variety of practices concerning planning for further testing and/or implementation of ideas generated for new and improved behavior resulting from the sociodrama. If there is time, or if there are to be subsequent sessions, the new ideas can be tested in a new sociodrama. Or plans may be related to applications outside of the sociodrama sessions. (1975)*

Odyssey of the Mind

One national contest designed to stimulate students' creative thinking and problem-solving skills is the Odyssey of the Mind (OM). Founded in 1978 and now including international as well as national charter organizations, Odyssey of the Mind provides students from different schools the chance to work together and compete with each other as they come up with the most creative—but still feasible—solution to a problem. The OM program was designed to embody the following ideas, spirit, and philosophy:

Team effort

Divergent thinking is rewarded

Making new friends is encouraged

Encourages the development of individual creative skills

It's fun while learning

Youthful energies are channeled in positive directions

Academic achievement is not essential to participate
Creativity is fun (Micklus & Gourley, 1982, p. 14)

In teams of five to seven students, and with the aid of a teacher or coach, students take on two different kinds of problems as a part of the Odyssey of the Mind competition. A long-term problem is sent to teams in their home school sites for students to work on all year. A famous example of a long-term problem was the 1983 problem, Leonardo da Vinci Spring Car, where students were posed with the problem of designing and constructing a vehicle powered only by the use of springs. Student teams competing for awards at different levels (primary program intramural, local competitions, regional competitions, chartered association's final competitions, world finals, and/or college/university competition) are judged both for achieving a solution and for style, to encourage teams to think about aesthetics and elegance of solutions, as well as functional design.

A subset of five members of the team is also required to solve a spontaneous problem. Designed to help students develop skills of idea fluency and flexibility, the spontaneous problem is given to student teams who are then required to brainstorm ideas within a limited time frame. This practice makes students accustomed to trying to come up with original, yet feasible, ideas under pressure. The reader can note how similar these tasks are to the performance assessment tasks now being considered for comprehensive student assessment (Wiggins, 1992). Figure 9–2 is a sample of another OM problem.

National and international programs like OM help teachers of the gifted achieve several goals associated with higher-order thinking and collaborative work habits. The students generally have so much fun figuring out the solution to bizarre problems, they don't even realize how much they are learning!

Thinking Logs

A common challenge that faces the teacher of the gifted is to find a way to stimulate the kind of sustained thinking that results in problem solving and problem finding. One reason that the great inventors or philosophers of history made their unique contributions is, in part, due to the *habits of mind* that they developed. These habits of mind include making observations, looking for connections, employing active questioning, and staying open to new possibilities. How can a teacher help students adopt these kinds of skills and attitudes? One way is to have the students emulate the practices of the great thinkers. For example, many inventive thinkers like Darwin and da Vinci kept journals of their thoughts and observations. More than a diary, these journals acted as an intellectual record for these great men, helping them develop ideas and trace patterns of thought that might otherwise have escaped them.

Hollister (1992) adapted the idea of the journal in the creation of *thinking logs* for his students. The logs are the primary record of the students' thinking in their world studies classes. Like the journals of Darwin and da Vinci, they are designed to be a place where students can capture their ideas, new thoughts, and connections while they are still fresh. The journals also have structured exercises that stretch the students' thinking in new directions.

FIGURE 9–2   Sample Odyssey of the Mind Problem

Problem No. 5: "Cro-Magnon"

Divisions I & II

A. Introduction

The evolution of early human beings was a slow process. Customs, beliefs, and technology were slow to change. In today's world, where knowledge doubles each decade, it is hard to imagine simple tools not improving for hundreds, perhaps even thousands, of years.

Some ideas, although common knowledge today, were milestones in human progress. Imagine the first person to conceive the idea of planting seeds to produce crops. This concept, together with the invention of the plow, allowed humans to become food producers instead of food gatherers. The imagination of a few led us to the development of our present civilization. Let's recreate an episode from early life.

B. The Problem

Your team is to create a performance which takes place, at least in part, in a cave-like setting during our prehistoric past, such as the Paleolithic period. The team will show something that was discovered, invented, or made during our primitive past, and give its interpretation of this event. This may be done seriously or humorously.

Your team's tasks are to:

1. Make a cave painting/drawing during the competition. (See Limitation #11)
2. Make, prior to the competition, and include in the presentation, an early tool or utensil made from wood, stone, or a ceramic material.
3. Make, prior to the competition, and include in the presentation, an instrument or tool made, by the team, from a real bone.
4. Represent fire.
5. Make, and include in the presentation, a prehistoric real or fictional animal that moves.
6. Make, and include in the presentation, a prehistoric musical instrument. (This may not be the same instrument as in #3, above)

The spirit of the problem is to create and to perform a presentation which takes place, at least partially, in a cave during our prehistoric past. The team will make a painting/drawing, an early tool/utensil, an instrument/tool, a prehistoric animal, and a prehistoric musical instrument. It will also represent fire.

Source: Micklus, S. (1986). *Problem #5: Cro-Magnon*. Glassboro, NJ: Creative Competitions, Inc. Reprinted from *Make Learning Fun!* by C. Samuel Micklus, Ed. D. Creative Competitions, Inc., Glassboro, NJ 08028.

Short-Term Effects

An effort to judge the immediate effectiveness of special programming for gifted students in productive thinking was carried out in eight elementary schools in the Midwest. Some 420 students, judged to be gifted or superior in intellectual ability, were randomly divided into experimental and control groups. The experimental group received special instructions for two hours a week in the Program for Academic and Creative Enrichment (Kolloff & Feldhusen, 1984). The program focused on the teaching of thinking skills for a period of six months. The pull-out program had about 12 students in each group. Measures of cognitive ability showed gains in originality and verbal fluency but no changes in self-concept scores. The authors considered that these findings showed positive gains for the training of thinking processes.

Long-Term Effects

Little information is available on the long-term effects of various programs that are specifically designed to aid gifted students in improving their thinking abilities. One rare effort to evaluate the impact of a special program is reported by Moon and Feldhusen (1992) in a long-term followup of a pull-out program stressing thinking processes and independent learning. They were able to follow up a group of 23 seniors in high school who had been in the special program for three years and their families. In response to questionnaires and interviews, the students and their families generally reported specific benefits in improved thinking and problem-solving skills, with a lesser positive impact on independent study abilities.

Parents as well as students perceived self-concept development as the most important benefit of the program. The students reported that the program gave them self-confidence, self-understanding, and "the courage to be different"—the last characteristic being one of the important elements to adult creative performance. Results such as these must be tempered by the fact that they were only from one school and one program. Results need to be replicated across community and program lines before broad conclusions can be drawn.

Unresolved Issues

1. The design of an instructional program or set of strategies is needed by which teachers can systematically encourage problem finding in gifted and talented children. The great talent of either the gifted artist or scientist is to be able to pick a significant project worthy of his or her time. Educators should be able to devise methods by which this choice process can be done more effectively.
2. Many more documented instances are needed of student mastery or improvements following their experience with programs that stress productive thinking. It is important for educators to understand the classroom or instructional conditions under which such programs work.
3. Can problem-solving or problem-finding skills be taught by teacher surrogates (such as mentors), by specific computer programs, or by programmed learning systems, so that the teacher can focus on the application of these skills in specific content fields?

Chapter Review

1. *Problem solving*, the ability to process given information to a solution, and *problem finding*, the ability to perceive a field of events and identify elements worthy of further analysis, are key mental processes in gifted education.
2. Problems can be considered well structured or ill structured and the approach taken by the student must be quite different for either.
3. The formulation of a significant problem from an ill-structured situation is the most critical skill of the artist and scientist, but it has received relatively little attention in education.

4. Analogous thinking appears to be a key element in many inventions and creative solutions. It also is observable in young children under the right conditions.

5. Various models of thinking skills, such as Guilford's Structure of Intellect, can be used to understand the process of thinking and as a base for educators to translate the model into educational practice.

6. The computer represents a powerful model of problem solving. By learning to program computers, gifted students are learning to think in a logical and sequential fashion.

7. Parnes's creative problem-solving model can aid the student in finding important problems to address and then the process for solving them.

8. Adler's seminar thinking approach is designed to stimulate student judgment and evaluative thinking.

9. Models of long-range planning around significant social issues represent another kind of systematic device for helping students organize and attack problems.

10. Torrance's sociodrama and cooperative learning represent other systems that can be used to help students problem solve in groups.

11. When used for instruction, the evaluation of problem-solving and problem-finding systems noted in this chapter usually has rested on the personal testimony of those who use them, but there is some quantitative evidence suggesting that such programs can result in clear and definitive academic gains.

Readings of Special Interest

Borkowski, J., & Day, J. (Eds.). (1987). *Cognition in special children: Comparative approaches to retardation, learning disabilities, and giftedness.* Norwood, NJ: Ablex.

This is an interesting attempt to apply the general models of information processing to specific subgroups of exceptional children. Issues such as metacognition, executive control, working memory, processing speed and control, and so on are pursued experimentally and comparisons are made of the performance of the three groups of exceptional children.

Baron, J., & Sternberg, R. (Eds.). (1987). *Teaching thinking skills: Theory and practice.* New York: Freeman and Co.

Chapters are from a variety of experts in the study and stimulation of thinking skills. Some major programmatic approaches to the teaching of thinking skills and the evaluation of thinking skills in the classroom are included. Sternberg's triarchic theory of intelligence is featured in several chapters.

deBono, E. (1985). *Masterthinker's handbook.* New York: International Center for Creative Thinking.

This is one of the latest of products from the fertile mind of deBono, who has argued for 25 years for the validity of instructing students in the processes of thinking, often without the specific use of content. Although this content-free approach to the instruction of thinking skills has come under increasing criticism, his ideas are fresh and knowledgeable.

Perkins, D. (1992). *Smart schools: From training memories to educating minds.* New York: Fress Press.

This book suggests specific ways in which the new cognitive discoveries can be translated into classroom activities. Perkins introduces topics such as a pedagogy of understanding, a metacurriculum, and the cognitive economy of school (meaning that whatever else the school does, matters rotate around the cognitive achievement of students). It is an easy book to read, but one that is full of wisdom.

Siegler, R. (1986). *Children's thinking.* Englewood Cliffs, NJ: Prentice Hall.

This is a comprehensive and highly readable summary of some of the major theoretical approaches to the understanding of children's thinking processes. Major attention is paid to

Piaget's theory of development, as well as several information-processing theories. Separate chapters deal with perceptual development, language development, memory development, conceptual development, and the development of academic skills.

References

Adler, M. (1984). *The Paidaia program: An educational syllabus.* New York: Macmillan.

Baldwin, A. (1981). Effect of process-oriented instruction on thought processes in gifted students. *Exceptional Children, 47,* 326–330.

Bloom, B. S. (Ed.). (1956). *Taxonomy of educational objectives: The classification of educational goals.* New York: David McKay.

Borkowski, J., & Peck, V. (1986). Causes and consequences of metamemory in gifted children. In R. Sternberg & J. Davidson (Eds.), *Conceptions of giftedness.* Cambridge: Cambridge University Press.

Bransford, J., Sherwood, R., Vye, N., & Rieser, J. (1986). Teaching thinking and problem solving: Research foundations. *American Psychologist, 41* (10), 1078–1089.

Chase, W. G., & Simon, H. A. (1973). The mind's eye in chess. In W. Chase (Ed.), *Visual information processing* (pp. 215–281). New York: Academic Press.

Chi, M. (1978). Knowledge structures and memory development. In R. Siegler (Ed.), *Children thinking—What develops?* (pp. 73–96). Hillsdale, NJ: Erlbaum.

Chi, M. T. H., Feltovich, P. J., & Glasser, R. (1981). Categorization and representation of physics problems by experts and novices. *Cognitive Science, 5,* 121–152.

Crabbe, A. (1982). Creating a brighter future: An update on the future problem solving program. *Journal for the Education of the Gifted, 5,* 2–9.

de Groot, M. (1965). *Thought and choice in chess.* The Hague: Mouton.

Einstein, A., & Infeld, L. (1938). *The evolution of physics.* New York: Simon & Schuster.

Gallagher, J. (1968). *Analysis of teacher classroom strategies associated with students' cognitive* and affective performance. Final report #3325. Washington, DC: U.S. Office of Education.

Gallagher, J. (1979). Issues in education for the gifted. In A. H. Passow (Ed.), *The gifted and the talented: Their education and development.* 78th Yearbook of the National Society for the Study of Education, Part 1. Chicago: University of Chicago Press.

Gallagher, J. (1986). Our love-hate affair with gifted children. *Gifted Child Quarterly, 9* (42), 47–49.

Gallagher, J., Surles, R., & Hayes, A. (1973). *Program planning and evaluation.* Chapel Hill: TADS, Frank Porter Graham Child Development Center, University of North Carolina.

Gallagher, J., Weiss, P., Oglesby, K, & Thomas, T. (1984). *The status of gifted/talented education: United States survey of needs, practices, and policies.* Los Angeles: National/State Leadership Training Institute on the Gifted and Talented.

Getzels, J. (1975). Problem finding and the inventiveness of solutions. *Journal of Creative Behavior, 9,* 12–18.

Getzels, J. (1982). The problem of the problem. In R. Hogarth (Ed.), *New directions for methodology of social and behavioral science: Question framing and response consistency.* San Francisco: Jossey-Bass.

Glaser, R. (1984). Education and thinking: The role of knowledge. *American Psychologist, 39* (2), 93–104.

Gordon, W. (1975). Some source materials in discovery by analogy. *Journal of Creative Behavior, 8,* 239–257.

Goswami, U. (1991). Analogous reasoning: What develops? A review of research and theory. *Child Development, 62,* 1–22.

Guildford, J. P. (1950). Creativity. *American Psychologist, 5,* 444–454.

Guidford, J. (1967). *The nature of human intelligence.* New York: McGraw-Hill.

Guilford, J. (1968). *Intelligence, creativity, and their educational implications.* San Diego, CA: Robert R. Knapp.

Hollister, W. (1992). *Teaching logs.* Aurora, IL: Illinois Mathematics and Science Academy.

Jackson, N., & Butterfield, E. (1986). A conception of giftedness designed to promote research. In R. Steinberg & J. Davidson (Eds.), *Conceptions of giftedness* (pp. 151–161). Cambridge: Cambridge University Press.

Kolloff, M., & Feldhusen, J. (1987). The effects of enrichment on self concept and creative thinking. *Gifted Child Quarterly, 25,* 53–57.

Kurtz, B., & Borkowski, J. (1984). Development of strategic skills in impulsive and reflective children: A longitudinal study of metacognition. *Journal of Experimental Child Psychology, 43,* 129–148.

Kurtz, B., & Weinert, F. (1989). Metamemory, memory performance, and casual attributions in gifted and average children. *Journal of Experimental Child Psychology, 48,* 45–61.

Lesgold, A. M., Feltovich, P. J., Glaser, R., & Wang, Y. (1981). *The acquisition of perceptual diagnostic skill in radiology.* Pittsburgh, PA: Learning Research and Development Center, University of Pittsburgh.

Maker, C. (1983). Quality education for gifted minority students. *Journal for the Education of the Gifted, 6,* 140–153.

Micklus, C., & Gourley, T. (1982). *"Olympics of the Mind" coaches manual.* Glassboro, NJ: Creative Competitions.

Moon, S., & Feldhusen, J. (1992). The Program for Academic and Creative Enrichment (PACE): A follow-up study ten years later. In R. Subotnik & K. Arnold (Eds.), *Beyond Terman: Recent longitudinal studies in gifted education.* Norwood, NJ: Ablex.

Papert, S. (1981). Computers and computer cultures. In J. Nazzaro (Ed.), *Computer connections for gifted children and youth.* Reston, VA: Council for Exceptional Children.

Parnes, S., Noller, R., & Biondi, A. (1977). *Guide to creative action.* New York: Charles Scribner's Sons.

Rabinowitz, M. & Glaser, R. (1985). Cognitive structure and process in highly competent performance. In F. Horowitz & M. O'Brien (Eds.), *The gifted and talented developmental perspectives* (pp. 75–98). Washington, DC: American Psychological Association.

Schlesinger, B., Jr. (1982). An untapped resource of inventors: Gifted and talented children. *Elementary School Journal, 82,* 215–219.

Simon, H. (1980). Problem solving and education. In *Problem solving and education: Issues in teaching and research* (pp. 81–96). Hillsdale, NJ: Erlbaum.

Spiro, R., Vispoel, W., Schmitz, J., Samarapungavan, A., & Boerger. (1987). Knowledge acquisition for application: Cognitive application for transfer in complex content domains. In B. Britton (Ed.), *Executive control processes.* Hillsdale, NJ: Erlbaum.

Torrance, P. (1975). *Sociodrama in career education.* Athens: University of Georgia.

Whitehead, A. N. (1929). *The aims of education.* New York: Macmillan.

Wiggins, G. (1992). Creating tests worth taking. *Educational Leadership, 49* (8), 26–33.

Chapter *10*

Creativity: Its Identification and Stimulation

Key Questions

- What is the mental process referred to as creativity?
- To what extent is creativity a property of an individual, and to what extent is creativity an interaction between an individual and his or her environment?
- Do people who have been recognized as creative have distinctive personal characteristics?
- What are the best psychological conditions for the generation of creativity?
- What is brainstorming and what does it have to do with creativity?
- What is the PROP method for reviewing conflicting ideas?
- Can creativity be measured? How?
- Is there evidence that the deliberate stimulation of creative thinking is effective?

The ability to use the human mind to create a product—a poem, a sonata, a technological innovation—is one of the most impressive activities of the human species. Many scientists and artists are interested in precisely how such creativity takes place, and many more teachers would like to know what they could do to aid their students, particularly their gifted students, to develop this talent to a stronger degree. This chapter will explore the distinctive nature of the creative process and the creative person, and it will review the wide variety of program suggestions about how to enhance creativity within the framework of the educational system.

The reasons for an educational emphasis on productive or creative thinking are not hard to find. We are apparently in the midst of one of the major social transformations in our society. That transformation is a change in the major focus of the society itself, from being mainly a producer of goods and products to a producer and communicator of ideas. The rapid development of our complex computer capabilities has opened the door to what Alvin Toffler (1980) has referred to as the "postindustrial society." This poses a special challenge to educators, as they now must prepare students for a future society that no one can quite conceptualize. It is only natural to conclude that the best thing we can do for students would be to give them some intellectual thinking tools that can be useful in changing times.

One of the current issues is whether everyone can be creative, which suggests perhaps that excessive attention may have been paid to a few people who have had unusual opportunity to develop their personal talents. This position has an admirable democratic ring to it. We would all like to believe that we, too, could be fabulously creative if only the times and conditions were right. However, the review of creative individuals by Ochse (1990) causes him to conclude "however the favorable cultural climate, only a few people are likely to account for most of the creative products of the society" (1990, p. 56).

What this means is that cultures do not make greatness; they merely offer to those who have the requisite talents the opportunity to become great. This does not mean, of course, that all teachers should not encourage creativity in all students to the maximum. It does mean that some students will respond more dramatically to that encouragement than others.

Definition of Creativity

There is an impressive collection of definitions of creativity, each of which tries to capture the complexity in this mysterious process. The definition to be used in this chapter is *creativity* is a mental process by which an individual creates new ideas or products, or recombines existing ideas and products, in a fashion that is novel to him or her.

Boden (1990) makes a useful distinction by identifying two types of creativity. One type of creative effort is novel to the mind of the individual, although many others have also had the same idea in the past. A second type of creativity is an effort that is novel with respect to the whole of human history. It is expecting too much to ask young students that they have an idea novel to all of humankind, so when the authors discuss creativity, it is from the standpoint of an individual having an idea *novel to him or her*.

The exact internal mental process by which individuals create a new poem, an artistic production, or a new idea is not known. Therefore, educators have to focus on those external conditions that experience and experimentation have shown facilitate the generation of new ideas or products. There are a variety of attitudes, personality characteristics, and facilitating environments that can apparently increase the generation of new ideas or products. Likewise, a substantial collection of tasks designed to enhance individual cognitive processes associated with creativity have become available. Until the precise combination of mental operations by which creativity takes place is known, educators must concentrate on how to create a facilitating environment for creativity.

Foundations for Creativity

Educators have been asking themselves for some time what their proper role is in aiding students to enhance their creative potential. Surely we, as educators, can do something useful besides stand in the classroom and cheer student creativity. Since there are a set of definable cognitive skills and knowledges that seem to be linked to creativity, it would make sense to focus on those skills as an educational objective.

Adult creativity is composed of at least four major components:

1. Extensive knowledge about the topic at hand
2. Intense motivation to generate creative products as a vehicle for self-expression
3. A willingness to try different methods or consider ideas that may not be socially acceptable at this time
4. A facility with the necessary skills to generate new forms or products (MacKinnon, 1986; Bransford, Sherwood, Vye, & Rieser, 1986)

Given this complex recipe for creativity, we can ask ourselves how best to enhance the likelihood that students will use the maximum of their creative talent. Surely, just helping them manifest more divergent thinking is one small part of that total recipe; if the other components (e.g., high motivation) are not present, then such training, by itself, will probably not make a substantial difference. If all four of these elements must be present before a child or adult is fully utilizing his or her creative potential, then we must attend to the knowledge base, student motivation, the willingness to be different, and the mastery of specific cognitive skills if we wish this difficult recipe to work.

Knowledge Base for Creativity

The importance of teaching significant content can be seen as a way of building a knowledge base. Insight into a problem and the generation of a solution come not from some mysterious power from outer space but rather from the ability of a person to fit the new information into an already existing personal web of associations. By recombining or extending this system of associations, the individual can find a solution which, to the naive observer, seems almost miraculous.

The next two elements in the recipe for creativity are motivation and the willingness to be different. To understand these elements better, many investigators have focused upon the manifestly creative individual to discover how these elements came about in them.

Motivation and the Willingness to Be Different

The Creative Person

Who are the most healthy citizens in our society? Who are the citizens most able to use all their human potential, and what are their special traits or characteristics? These interesting questions have few answers because people tend to focus more attention on those children and adults who have special problems in adjusting to our society.

In trying to define *healthy*, one discovers that it is often considered the absence of something. That is, mental health is the absence of mental illness, physical health is the absence of physical illness, and so on. However, this is neither a satisfactory description of the state we seek nor a useful approach to its discovery. The psychologist Abraham Maslow (1970) took a different approach in studying the *self-actualizing* person—a person who appears to be using all of his or her talents and gifts. Maslow studied a group of the most outstanding "self-actualizers" through biographies or, in the case of contemporaries, through direct interview. Examples of people who fit Maslow's criteria of self-actualization would be Abraham Lincoln, Thomas Jefferson, Albert Schweitzer, Eleanor Roosevelt, Pablo Casals, Pierre Renoir, and Benjamin Franklin.

In his studies, Maslow tried to identify those characteristics that seemed to be possessed by all these people in greater or lesser degree. First, there was a lack of artificiality and a certain simplicity and naturalness about their approach. They appeared to have resolved the basic needs that plague other human beings and were thus free to use their abilities without straining for social prestige or placing a protective or defensive veneer over their real feelings. Maslow's subjects generally seemed to feel safe and unanxious, accepted, loved and loving, and to have basically worked out their philosophical and religious attitudes toward life.

Another definitive characteristic was the individuals' ability to focus on problems that lie outside themselves. They were concerned with larger issues, and their concern extended to humankind rather than to more self-centered or limited concerns. There was a quality of detachment in their ability to stand apart from the problems and the issues that concerned them, and they positively liked solitude and sought privacy for a time so that they could concentrate intensely on their work.

Above all, Maslow found one characteristic in particular to be common to all the people studied: a special kind of creativity, originality, or inventiveness. The level of psychic health reached by these individuals allowed them to overcome usual barriers and frustrations, and permitted them to produce with freshness and spontaneity. As Maslow well realized, such descriptions made these individuals seem almost unreal and unhuman.

He reminded the reader that these self-actualized citizens were not free from the failings of human beings. They were vain, they were prideful, they had temper outbursts, and so on. But sometimes their psychic strength enabled them to recover from crises such as family death or divorce with such dispatch as to be almost shocking. Whether or not one agrees with Maslow on all of these dimensions, most can certainly can agree that "the study of crippled, stunted, immature, and unhealthy specimens can yield only a cripple psychology and a cripple philosophy" (Maslow, 1970, p. 234). The careful and intensive study of self-actualizing people must be the basis for a more universal science of psychology and creativity.

One aspect of self-actualization is the development of a strong personal sense of morality. These feelings are relatively common in the writings of these self-actualized individuals, who often concentrated on the inhuman treatment or injustice received by some of humanity. Charles Darwin, noted more for his theories on natural selection than for being interested in moral behavior, revealed his moral revulsion at the treatment of natives in South America by Europeans on one of his trips to study plants and animals: "If this warfare is successful, that is, if all the Indians are butchered... the country will be in the hands of white Gaucho savages instead of copper colored Indians. The former being a little superior in civilization, as they are inferior in every moral value" (cited in Gruber, 1974, p. 432).

Although Maslow was certainly right in his assertion that many creative persons have shown outstanding maturity and mental health, this surely does not cover the full range of persons that are known to be creative. Many persons who are undeniably creative are less than perfect or even healthy human beings, sometimes revealing tremendous immaturity (e.g., Mozart), or a deep concern for one's own sexual identity (e.g., Hemingway), or periods of psychosis (e.g., Van Gogh).

The personal pain that these great writers and artists felt somehow is expressed in their creativity, and sometimes appeared to drive their creativity. The psychoanalytic explanation for creativity is that it may be a process by which individuals work out and express their personal problems, their anxieties, and their unresolved interpersonal problems. This position would seem to be true of some of our most creative persons in the past and is another facet of this fascinating question about what drives the creative person (see Ochse, 1990).

One of the burdens of those with multiple talents is how to decide which of their talents they wish to nurture and which they will allow to decay or go unused. Some young persons with talent are unable to make that choice and make themselves miserable trying to use all of their talents to maximum ability. The futility of that was foreseen by William James a century ago.

> *I am often confronted by the necessity of standing by one of my empirical selves and relinquishing the rest. Not that I would not, if I could, be handsome and fat and well dressed, and a great athlete, and make a million a year, be a wit, a bon vivant, and a lady-killer, as well as a philosopher, a philanthropist, statesman, warrior, and African explorer,...and saint. But the thing is simply impossible.*
>
> *The millionaire's work would run counter to the saint's; the bon vivant and the philanthropist would trip each other up; the philosopher and the lady-killer could not well keep house in the same tenement of clay. Such different characters may well conceivably at the outset of life be* possible *to a man. But to make any one of them actual the rest must more or less be suppressed. (1890, pp. 309–310)*

The Creative Person in Action

Based on the above description, three of the gifted students discussed in this book—Sam, Joe, and Zelda—would not seem to be likely candidates for highly creative performance. In each case the reason would be slightly different but the nonproductive results the same.

Parnes has given two general principles for the stimulation of creative potential. In analogous terms, he says that a person should "(1) feed his brain the fuel required for it to operate at full capacity and (2) remove the brakes that stop his associative mechanisms from functioning naturally" (1972, p. 21). What Parnes was referring to, naturally, is the richness of experience that the child has (the fuel) and the degree to which inhibition (the brakes) prevents him or her from fully exploring the problem space.

Sam, for example, has been fed limited "fuel" and needs to be made more fully aware of his own talents and his own perceptions. Sam's teacher could be working with him on an assignment to "see something unique on your way home from school, something beautiful or ugly you hadn't seen before." The ability to perceive one's own world is one of the prerequisites of creative performance.

With Joe and Zelda, the story is somewhat different. Zelda has a great desire to succeed, to please her parents, but that desire shows itself in the great need to look good to others, to be a "good student." What does a good student do? Zelda, in observing teachers and other students, has seen that the good student always has a hand up ready to answer the teacher's question and that the teacher seems pleased with such quick response.

Yet from Parnes's viewpoint, one of the essences of creative thought is the delayed response—the ability to inhibit the impulsive first reaction and let the associative thought flow without having to reach an immediate answer. One challenge to our educational program is how to convince Zelda that it is better to delay responses, to meditate or mull over a problem, than always to try to be first with the right answer.

Joe's problems are also different. His own sense of failure and his inability to take risks that would open his sensitive self-concept to possible criticism create brakes of a very personal sort. Even when the teacher encourages, pleads, and exhorts for unique ideas or the unusual association, Joe's self-censorship protects him from possible humiliation or failure. The price of such protection usually comes high. Joe has protected himself against derisive peer laughter, but he has shut himself off from the genuine excitement and self-expanding ego that comes from genuine production or creative thought. In Parnes's parlance, there is not much trouble keeping the engine running once it turns over, but sometimes very cold creative engines require a great effort to jump start.

Another dimension of personality that seems to characterize gifted performers is their intrinsic interest in the topic at hand. Amabile (1989) has stated that this *intrinsic motivation*, coming from within the individual, is a key to creative performance. The intense interest of children like Cranshaw or Stephanie, who get an idea of what they want to do and intensely seek to do it, regardless of classroom or social consequences—is a hallmark of those who create.

Mr. Brooks, the school counselor, received a rather unusual visit from Zelda's mother recently. She is an intense, serious woman who is extremely ambitious for her daughter. Perhaps it is not surprising that she holds a very low opinion of the school and its personnel, who never seem to do enough for Zelda. She recently had been reading in the popular magazines and books about creativity and now wanted to know what she could do at home to enhance Zelda's creativity.

Although Mr. Brooks had become used to thunderous attacks on the school curriculum as outdated, or even that the school was paying more attention to children with disabilities than to the talented, he was somewhat taken aback by this parental request for assistance. Unfortunately, he did not know what the accumulated research had to say on the creative individual, because the important literature that summarized the available data was in journals far from Mr. Brooks' ken. Such a literature largely shows the following:

1. Creative children are open to experiences of all kinds, taboo or not. There is an acceptance of traits often identified with the opposite sex, making the creative male appear more feminine and the creative female appear more masculine.
2. They are less likely to be swayed by the crowd or by social pressures. Their own sense of strong self-identity and independence allows them to trust themselves rather than rely on others.
3. They may be less close to parents and show an emotional detachment from them. The parents, themselves, may show strong intellectual interests and permissive child-rearing strategies (Stein, 1986).

Thus, there is no exercise that can be done for 15 minutes a day to improve the creativity of children. It is a lifestyle, a way of life, a habit of mind that must be adopted, and that means that no educational gimmicks will do the trick. In looking at the parental characteristics that seem to be associated with creativity, one sees that relative lack of emotional attachment and permissive child rearing allow children to have a certain lack of commitment to their families and social past, and to be free to strike out in new directions. The diverse intellectual interests of their parents allow the children to explore along new intellectual dimensions without fear of repression or parental disapproval.

At the same time that these characteristics provide part of the recipe of creative development, they may also cause difficulties for the teacher. Because creative people do not repress taboo subjects, they are likely to be embarrassingly frank. Because they are independent in attitude and social behavior, they are more difficult to control in a group. Because they have strong intrinsic motivation to pursue their own bent, they may resist attempts of the teacher or other persons to mold them in certain directions.

Even Cranshaw, with his favorable adjustment and acceptance, is sometimes seen by some teachers as being difficult. He is difficult because he will go his own way, regardless of the wishes of the teacher. Because he is Cranshaw, he does this with some diplomacy and thus keeps out of serious trouble, but not all creative persons are interested in keeping out of trouble. Indeed, some enjoy disorder and social complexity as well as cognitive complexity.

Stephanie is a fine example of a child who has had the type of family environment that creates a positive attitude and motivation for creativity. Stephanie's parents have allowed and encouraged her enormous energy to find multiple channels for expression. They have used praise judiciously to show their approval for her adventuresome nature. When she has "fallen on her face" in her attempts to try new things, which she did quite literally when she took up skating, they showed by their calm demeanor that failure was one of the expected consequences for innovators and that she should just get up and continue toward her goals.

The consequence of this approach is a young girl eager to grapple with life and its challenges, with a self-confidence built on past successes and parental support that makes future production more likely. Stephanie's parents probably did not sit down and agree on some master strategy for shaping their daughter's development. It likely came naturally to them. Some teachers and school personnel would seem to provide the same types of encouragement and support for student adventure in the same intuitive fashion. However, one should not depend on these favorable patterns to appear naturally. Specific in-service workshops and preservice teacher preparation programs need to include explicit instruction on methods of support and encouragement for the unique, unusual response with quality.

If Zelda's mother were to review carefully the general characteristics that seem common to creative persons, she might well conclude, "If that's the way a person has to be to be creative, maybe I don't want my daughter to be creative." And maybe she doesn't! For each personality characteristic that fits a pattern of creativity, there are pluses and minuses. The cost of being creative is sometimes being lonely, sometimes being out of step, and sometimes being surprised that others will deny or twist experiences that are perceived in embarrassing correctness by the creative individual. In each instance, one totes up the costs and decides whether it is really worth it.

Just as the child is embedded in the family, and owes much of his or her own development to that relationship, so the family is embedded in its own subculture, and the school embedded in the total society. The school can no more deviate sharply from that heritage than can the individual child, without causing great concern and disruption. So, if one tends to attack the schools for their unimaginative and lockstep programs, a sustained look at the society that spawned them might be in order.

Although it is useful to remember how important the social environment is to creative performance, the teacher still must try to encourage individual student performance. Klein summarized a variety of behaviors that seem linked to people who exhibit creative behavior:

1. Maximize options. *The process of choosing from alternatives is dependent on the perception of those alternatives. Creative individuals broaden their perceptions so that they can take in more stimulation.*
2. Defer judgment. *To defer judgment means that an individual will accept all ideas as plausible until further evaluations are made at a later date.*
3. Be inconsistent. *Consistency is counter to the notion of the dynamic interplay of what has happened in the past and what could happen in the future. A person should act because a behavior is growth producing rather than because it is consistent with previously stated values or patterns of behavior.*
4. Seek freedom. *Creative behavior means going beyond limits and not being confined by them in order to develop their uniqueness. Creative people must be free from conventions and habits.*
5. Action oriented. *Creativity is an active process. It demands reaching out beyond the safe known boundaries. It is not enough to say, "I could have done that." It means more than merely thinking good ideas. (1982, p. 259)*

A heartbreaking example of how things can go wrong in the search for creative opportunities is presented in Figure 10–1, which depicts a scene with which almost everyone can identify.

Creating a Psychological Environment for Creativity

It was noted earlier in this chapter that certain personality characteristics aid the individual in creative ventures: a strong sense of self, enjoyment of discovery and novelty, and so forth. But how can the psychological or physical environment or atmosphere in the classroom be designed to enhance novel ideas, independence, and high motivation?

Apparently, changing the physical environment can have a beneficial effect. Walberg, Schiller, and Haertel (1979) reviewed the variety of studies that have been done on the effects of open education versus traditional education. The presence of open space in the classroom and students' freedom to move around in that space, as seems necessary to finish their tasks, can contribute to some physical freedom and a sense of independence. Of particular interest are Walberg, Schiller, and Haertel's findings with regard to creativity dimensions. Reviewing a total of 41 studies, they discovered that there were strong indications of a positive linkage between open education and student expressions of creativity, curiosity, cooperation, independence, and self-concept. Apparently, how the

FIGURE 10–1   Trying to Be Creative

It was Christmas when I tried to be creative for the last time that year. In my letter to Santa, I asked for only one thing—an artist's box with those little squares filled with every watercolor there was. I had seen just what I wanted at the dime store. I wrote *please, please, please,* in my letter.

Christmas was one of those bleak, sleety, northern days that Texas calls Winter. We were all up at dawn and ran into the living room where the tree blinked its red and green and blue and yellow lights on the tinsel.

Mama loved Christmas, and she saved from one year to the next so she could fill the space under the tree with all kinds of presents for all of us. My brother was pulling his new red wagon in and out and knocking everyone over. My sister sat on the floor cuddling her baby doll.

"Where are my paints? I asked Santa for paints."

"Well, this present has your name on it," Mama said.

"This? This? That's not mine, that's Katy's. She wanted a doll in a buggy."

"But it's a beautiful buggy. It's white wicker, and look at the doll. It has a real silk dress, and beautiful blue eyes that close, and black eyelashes."

"Then you keep it. I asked for paints," I screamed.

She grabbed me and she was crying. "This is your big present. I made the dress myself. Whatever is wrong with you? Look at your sister; she loves dolls. Who can understand you? You're not a child, at all."

I grabbed the buggy with the doll in it. I wheeled it toward the front door, out into the drizzling sleet, down the steps, down the sidewalk to the ditch, and rolled it in—right into the muddy water.

"I wanted paints; I don't play dolls." I was crying. My heart was breaking.

Source: M. Meeker, from the award-winning article, "On Trying to Be Creative," in the *Gifted Child Today,* November-December, 1990, pp. 2–5. Reprinted with permission from *The Gifted Child Today,* P.O. Box 6448, Mobile, AL 36660.

learning environment is structured, from both a physical and psychological standpoint, does play an important role on the students' sense of freedom and the permission to use one's own intellectual resources in an atmosphere with less constraints. This release of intellectual inhibition seems to pay off, at least in more student expressions of creativity.

Self-Censorship

Many of the educational strategies utilized in attempts to encourage creative thought are based on an assumption that people have more novel ideas and associations available in our knowledge structure than we are, in fact, using. For a variety of reasons, we tend to censor ourselves and thus limit the number of ideas or associations that can be called on in any particular situation.

The larger the total number of ideas and associations available, all else being equal, the more likely there will be creative thought. This is why one can observe positive correlations between intelligence and creativity. One cannot have an innovative use of an idea or fact that is not available in one's memory bank! For example, how might the problem of reindeer in Alaska be solved? This problem may not yield many creative suggestions in most U.S. classrooms because the basic fund of information is not present in the first place. So, creativity depends, in part, on a large supply of ideas from the knowledge base mentioned earlier. One question is, Is the idea or association there to be accessed in the first place (the knowledge base) or is it being censored for some reason?

Censored areas might include ideas or associations that the youngster knows are not acceptable to important persons such as parents, peers, or teachers. Another forbidden area might be ideas or associations that would run counter to an important role that the child is playing in his or her peer group. If Sam wishes to be seen as strongly male in style and fashion, as he does, he might automatically reject any ideas or associations that could be interpreted as "feminine." One of the most frustrating experiences for teachers who are trying to encourage a student like Sam to develop to his full potential is that intellectual or academic activity, per se, is often seen as feminine and counter to the prevailing style of some male subgroups. Such teachers often feel that they are in powerful mental combat between the cultural subgroup and the traditions of the society over the soul of Sam and youngsters like him who have powerful native ability but who may be reluctant to make full use of it because to do so would contradict other values held by the student or by his peer group.

The goal of educators, therefore, is twofold. First, they need to provide the opportunities for youngsters to absorb a substantial supply of ideas and associations that are available to them for mental processing. Second, they must push back the boundaries of the forbidden territories. To this end, there are many educational strategies used to help the youngsters feel more relaxed, be less threatened, and enjoy more freedom, so that there is a climate created for a more accepting attitude for unique or unusual ideas.

It is an exhilarating experience for a youngster to generate an idea which, to his or her knowledge, no one else has thought of before. The pleased and excited expression on the face of the youngster who has produced a new idea (to him or her) that is valued by others is evidence of the self-enhancing value of creativity. However, although it is exhilarating, it also can be frightening or threatening to the child.

Zelda, whose self-confidence is low in spite of her strong abilities, can feel uneasy at generating an idea that no one else has suggested. Her first reaction to such a situation is that she must have made a mistake. The job of the teacher thus becomes to encourage youngsters like Zelda that a novel idea is not necessarily a bad or incorrect one, and that one's ability to produce such novel ideas is valued and important. Conveying the strong feeling that different ideas are important to produce is one of the significant contributions teachers can make to a youngster's full use of his or her talents.

The educational objective, then, is to focus on conditions that facilitate intellectual autonomy and a sense of personal competence that, presumably, will increase the motivation to employ creative thinking—a move that will ultimately benefit all of us.

Stimulation of Cognitive Skills

The fourth element in the recipe for creativity is a set of cognitive skills by which to process information. This ingredient, together with a knowledge base, motivation, and personal freedom, completes the desired combination.

The Creative Process

One approach to encouraging creativity is to try to understand and master the cognitive processes by which one creates. Those who create, as well as those who study creative persons, agree that there are processes or a sequence of stages through which a creative person passes in creating a product. Although many different terms are used to describe these stages, those suggested by Wallas almost seven decades ago (1926) have probably received the most widespread usage over the years. He proposed the following four main stages in the creative process:

1. *Preparation.* This is the stage in which information about the problem is gathered. It is primarily a problem-identification and fact-gathering period.
2. *Incubation.* In this stage, the person is not consciously thinking about the problem. There is some kind of internal mental process operating that associates new information with past information. A type of internal reorganization of the information seems to be going on without the individual being directly aware of it.
3. *Illumination.* This is the point at which the "happy idea" occurs. It has been referred to as the "Aha! phenomenon." In this stage, the creator suddenly sees the idea, concept, or solution to the problem.
4. *Verification.* This is the stage in which the idea that has been obtained through the first three stages is put to the test to see if it has validity. As some have said, this may be the "uh-oh" stage following the "Aha."

Although these stages are commonly observed, it does not mean that they must invariably occur in each instance or that they occur in a set time sequence. The reader is reminded of the models of problem solving and planning reported in the previous chapter and may note the similarity to this model of creative process. One stage in this process might represent months or years of planning or study, whereas, in other cases, it could occur in one day.

Educational programming has never been too successful in helping a student be more effective in the stages of *incubation* and *illumination*; it has concentrated most of its operation on the first and last stages, *preparation* and *verification*. Educators can present facts as the groundwork for the individual's learning about a particular problem or subject. Much of the school curriculum can be identified as stage-one activity. Then the student may be taught how to evaluate an idea once it is available—a stage-four type of operation.

Table 10–1 represents the authors' concept of different expectations that teachers need to consider for the different stages of the creative process. Most people are familiar with the teacher whose predominant evaluation of a composition seems to be in terms of neatness and well-organized form. On the other hand, there is also the teacher who feels that excessive emphasis on form might interfere with richness of content and innovative ideas.

As Table 10–1 indicates, it seems that neither teacher is entirely wrong nor entirely right. If the task is that of gathering or laying the groundwork for a problem (preparation), then one would want the material neat, well organized, and well stated. The individual has

TABLE 10–1   Expectations for Different Stages of the Creative Process

Stages of Creative Process	Expected Form	Predominant Thinking Operation	Personality Factor or Attitude Required
Preparation	Neat Well organized	Cognitive memory	Studiousness Sustained attention
Incubation	Sloppy		Intellectual freedom
Illumination	Often confused Incoherent	Divergent thinking	Risk taking Tolerance of failure and ambiguity
Verification	Neat Well organized Clearly stated	Convergent thinking Evaluative thinking	Intellectual discipline Following of a logical sequence

very little of a personal nature to add to the situation and has only to collect data that other people have organized for him or her. Similarly, whenever the person is trying to prove a point through verification, the material should be well organized, clearly stated, and reasonably neat. The very basis of verification is an orderly, step-by-step presentation of proof and disproof.

However, it is in the period when the creative act depends on incubation and illumination that the teacher should expect the material to be sloppy, confused, and incoherent. The individual not only has to collect the material but must produce new ideas or organization. Any new idea or organization of ideas can hardly be expected to be in perfect order or in clearly outlined form. So, in answer to the general question, Should a child be expected to have a neat, well-organized paper?, the answer would seem to lie in the purpose of the assignment itself.

Similarly, if the predominant thinking operation that is required at each stage of the creative process could be traced, one would see that, in the preparation stage, the predominant mental operation is that of memory and knowledge base. Persons who are studious, sincere, and highly motivated, like Zelda, can show their mettle by collecting large amounts of facts and information from such sources as reference books and encyclopedias.

In the incubation and illumination stages, the predominant thinking operation seems to be divergent thinking. Here, the individual is trying to get a new slant on the material that has been collected, a new way of organizing it, a uniqueness that has not been perceived before. This requires the individual to have multiple ideas, to be unafraid to make mistakes, and to live with the realization that every problem does not need to be solved before the end of the day. Stephanie tends to shine in these situations.

In the verification stage, on the other hand, a closely organized and well-reasoned approach to a problem is required. Here, persons with strong talents in the convergent-thinking area can show their abilities. Cranshaw should be able to do well at this task since he is very well organized.

Ideally, one would look for students who have strength in all these thinking processes, but there is reason to believe that excessive attention to any one of them is likely to inhibit the development of talents in the others. For example, high talent in convergent thinking is likely to lead the individual to hesitate to make statements unless there is solid proof for them or unless a closely knit and logical argument can be developed for a position. The student who habitually responds in this way certainly will not reveal the attitude necessary for the risk taking required of the divergent thinker.

Similarly, persons who specialize in divergent thinking may tolerate enough intellectual sloppiness that they are uninterested in or unable to follow through with any of their unique ideas to see if they have any real validity. What educators seem to need especially are methods by which we can strengthen the youngsters' understanding of the application of those processes that are needed at any given time and *when* to apply a particular intellectual operation.

In many ways, the personality factors and attitudes (shown in Table 10–1) required to perform well in stages one and four seem almost opposite to those needed in stages two and three. The strong intellectual discipline necessary for verification might seem to be at odds with the risk taking to be used in incubation. To be able to suspend one of these talents in favor of the other requires an unusual person with a sense of timing—one who knows the right time to use a particular strategy. Perhaps this is why the truly creative person is a rarity in our culture or in any other culture.

The important issue for educators is whether the various processes or stages of creativity can be enhanced through instruction. Can gifted children be taught rules or procedures to make their productive talents more efficient? Can they, in fact, learn this model of the creative process as part of their *metacognitive* repetoire?

As the number of investigations into the metacognitive processes (thinking about one's own thinking process) increase, there is a growing tendency to perceive them as one of the key reasons why gifted children perform intellectual tasks more efficiently than other children. In reviewing the rapidly increasing literature, Borkowski and Kurtz compared children with mental retardation, children with learning disabilities, and gifted children in terms of their use of metacognitive skills in solving various problems. They concluded that "gifted children used strategies more efficiently, learned new strategies with greater ease, transferred them to new tasks more readily, and were better able to verbalize their knowledge about cognitive processes than were average children" (1987, p. 135).

Despite these conclusions, Borkowski and Kurtz found that gifted children did not use *qualitatively* different strategies than average children; they merely used the existing strategies that both have available *more efficiently* and *more often*. Such students were able to transfer the strategies that they had mastered to novel problems much better than average children, although they almost certainly could do even better under a program of systematic metacognitive instruction.

Not only are gifted students faster and more efficient in the use of elementary information processes (Jackson & Butterfield, 1986) but, more importantly, they increasingly use metathinking to solve difficult problems. It is clearly one of the responsibilities of educators of gifted students to take advantage of these already present capabilities to help students expand their repetoire of cognitive strategies.

Question-Asking Strategies

One of the strongest and most persistent in-service topics for teachers of gifted children is the instruction in various questioning techniques that can be used in interchanges with students. Teachers are urged to use questions that will stimulate higher-level thought processes, as represented in Bloom's taxonomy and Guilford's structure of intellect (see Figure 10–2).

By learning the Guilford model, the teacher can learn to substitute divergent-thinking questions for memory ones. Instead of asking, Who was the winning general at Yorktown? a teacher may ask How would things be different today if the Americans had surrendered instead of the British? or an evaluative assignment such as: Compare the similarities and differences of the Russian and American revolutions.

Teachers can learn quickly the stems of questions or different structuring statements that precede different thinking operations.

Memory

Who...
What...
Where...
When...

Convergent Thinking

How...
Why...
Explain...

FIGURE 10–2   Question Asking à la Guilford and Bloom

Guilford's Structure of Intellect	Bloom's Taxonomy
Memory: Where did the battle take place?	*Knowledge:* List the major causes of World War I as stated in Jones's text.
Cognition: What did Bod mean when he said, "They'll rue the day"?	*Comprehension:* Explain the concept of detente and give an illustration of detente in action.
Divergent thinking: What if the battle had never started? What would have been the course of events in Russia?	*Application:* If the temperature rises and the amount of gas pressure increases, what would be the stress impact on the metal container?
Convergent thinking: In your opinion, was the Vietnam War justified?	*Synthesis:* Using the concept of gerontology, describe an ideal pattern of behavior in old age.
	Judgment: Using standards of literary criticism, critique Jones's essay on modern education.

Source: Adapted, by permission, from Feldhusen and Treffinger © 1980 by Kendall /Hunt Publishing Company.

Divergent Thinking

How many ways can you…
What would happen if…
Can I have a different idea…

Evaluative Thinking

Compare or contrast…
Which is the best…
Which is the most beautiful…
Which is the most sensible…

Teachers are justified in wondering whether all of these efforts to modify their questioning techniques will pay off in terms of student performance. Redfield and Rousseau (1981) reviewed 20 studies on the teachers' use of higher and lower levels of cognitive questions. They found that across these studies, gains in achievement can be expected when higher cognitive questions are used in the classroom. It appears that specific teacher instruction on cognitive processes and methods of inquiry can make a difference and are important components in teacher training and in-service training programs.

Figure 10–2 shows the question-asking strategies that can be linked to the Guilford Structure of Intellect or Bloom's taxonomy. Teachers can control the nature of classroom interaction by shaping their questions so that they deliberately seek certain types of thinking operations from the students.

Brainstorming

One common cognitive strategy applied in group situations, such as the classroom, to stimulate greater fluency of ideas is brainstorming. This technique has been used widely in management and industry, and many adaptations of it have been created to fit differing situations and purposes. One essential element involved in this method is having a group focus on a particular problem, such as how to bisect an angle, how to improve relations with Latin America, or how to avoid an unpleasant task in the proper way (as Tom Sawyer did in his fence-painting episode). The students are then invited to give as many ideas as they might have for possible solutions to the problem.

There are some important ground rules to be observed, however, if this technique is to work. The students should know in advance the rules of brainstorming, namely:

1. *No criticism is allowed.* Nothing smothers the free flow of ideas like a sharp critical remark or a guffaw of scorn from a peer or a teacher. The temptation to point out a faulty answer is very strong and needs to be checked quickly. Students need to know in advance that no critical comments will be entertained for the moment. Evaluation comes later.
2. *The more, the better.* Students can accept the proposition that the greater the number of ideas presented, the more likely the chance is that a good one will be among them. A premium could be placed on unusual or unique ideas.

3. *Integration and combinations of ideas are welcomed.* Students can be alerted to the possibility of combining or adding to previous ideas.
4. *Evaluation is done after all ideas have been presented.* The teacher can judge when the fluency or inventiveness of the class is lagging. At that point, he or she should encourage evaluative thinking on the part of the students.

Now, the classroom group can judge the relative merits of the ideas produced. The reader may well wonder if criticism, even at this point, might dampen the fluency of the group or the individual. But the time lapse between the original utterances and the criticism dulls its effect. In addition, the original thought may have been added to or changed by subsequent student statements and may no longer be identified as the production of any one individual. Let's see how this process could work. First, a problem is needed. We may presume that the teacher has already established the ground rules.

Teacher: Class, let's do some brainstorming on a very mysterious problem. What do you suppose happened to the lost colony of Roanoke?

Pete: I think they got on their ships, went out to sea, and a big storm came and sank it—everybody died.

Ruth: I think they got struck by a terrible epidemic and all died of some disease.

Henry: A band of Indians swooped down and massacred them.

Jim: If what Ruth and Henry said were true, why didn't…

Teacher: Remember, Jim, no criticism while we are "storming." (Class laughter at the reference to "storming")

Cathy: I think they got a disease, like Ruth said, and then they panicked and went on their boat to get help and all died and the ship eventually sank.

Note how Cathy combined previous responses to get a new one; also note how the teacher intervened to preserve the rule of "no criticism," and protected Jim from criticism by a humorous reference to the process.

Are there any disadvantages to this procedure? Yes! Most important is that something meaningful must be done with the results of the brainstorming. The final decisions on the "lost colony" must fit into the curriculum and the concept to be taught. Otherwise, this procedure can be considered merely an interesting game that has little or nothing to do with learning or with important school goals.

The stress on fluency can be emphasized by the teacher seeking multiple answers and rewarding children who can give them. Instead of asking, What category do kangeroos fall into?, replace it with, Name as many marsupials as you can. Instead of saying, Students, complete this unfinished poem, replace it with, Make up as many different endings as you can for this poem (give credit for as many different endings as can be given by one person). Instead of asking, What happened to Lincoln's killer?, replace it with, Make up as many different plausible stories as you can about Lincoln's killer's fate.

Figure 10–3 shows a picture of a buffalo (provided by Meeker, 1982) as a stimulus to encourage fluency, flexibility, and originality in students. Note, in particular, the carefully crafted directions that are given as a means of encouraging various types of thinking. It is interesting to imagine what the student output might be if the teacher simply asked the students to write something interesting about this animal. It is in the careful structuring of the activity that the teacher can get the desired type of thinking operations.

Attribute Listing

This technique is used to help students think about possible modifications or changes in an object, process, or system. Students are asked to list all the important characteristics of an item and then to suggest how changes in the various attributes would result in an improvement. For example, students might be posed with the problem of how to improve their playground. In order to generate useful ideas, they can first describe the item and its

FIGURE 10–3   Buffalo

This is a buffalo. Look at the picture. Describe the buffalo by thinking of as many words as you can. Put these words under the Buffalo Description List (on the left-hand page). This list is already started. The buffalo has a HIDE. The buffalo is SHAGGY. What else does the Buffalo have? Add your words to the list. Think of as many as you can.

   Now do something different. Think what the Buffalo reminds you of, not what you can see in the picture, but what you think about when you see a Buffalo. Maybe you think of NICKEL because the picture of a Buffalo is on the nickel. Maybe you think of WILD BILL because of Bill Cody, who was a buffalo hunter. Let your imagination go and think of as many ideas as you can when you see a Buffalo. Put your words in the Buffalo Imagination list.

   Now it's time to use your words to make a story about a Buffalo. As you make up your story, use as many of your words as you can from both lists—the Imagination list as well as the Description list. Be as creative as you can in writing your story. Be funny or scary, or serious, but be as original with your imagination as you can.

Source: Reprinted, by permission, *Divergent Production of Semantic Units* by M. Meeker, 1982, El Segundo, California, SOI Institute. Copyright 1982 by M. Meeker.

specific attributes. By describing the attributes of the baseball diamond on the playground as "a dirt area," one can think more easily of an alternative, such as planting grass. In a similar fashion, the water fountain, fence, swings, and so on can be examined as they are and what they could become.

Redefinition

Another dimension of thinking operations that are related to creativity, and to attribute listing for that matter, is the skill of redefinition, or the ability to find ways to improve existing products or processes. One of the approaches to such improvement is to analyze the nature of the object or process to be made better. If one is asked how to improve a screwdriver, for instance, it would be a useful first step to consider just what a screwdriver is and what its operation is. For example, an analysis of a screwdriver might look like the following:

> It has a round steel shank.
> It has a wooden handle riveted to the shank.
> It has a wedge-shaped end to enter a screw head.
> It is manually operated.
> Torque is applied to achieve a twisting movement.
> Pressure is exerted to keep the end in the slot.

Given this list of attributes, attempts to improve the design of the screwdriver could focus on changes of one or a combination of these factors. Similarly, more complicated types of analyses can be tried for improvement of such entities as public education, mass transit, modern marriage, or toys.

Although most of the exercises that have been used as illustrations have the element of play to them, or are game-like, one does not have to reach too far to find subject areas of deadly seriousness. Students respond well to topics that smack of the real world.

Originality

Gifted and creative students are often challenged and excited by the opportunity to produce unique responses, rather than just correct responses. Such requests can be made in any subject matter, from language arts to science. For example, consider the following:

1. The teacher can establish a game whereby words are presented for association to key words given by the teacher. Responses judged correct (or reasonable) and unusual receive two points; others receive one. For example, if the stimulus is *red*, responses such as *fire, pencil*, and *blood* will get only one point, whereas responses such as *spectrum, ultraviolet*, or *China* might receive two points. Such training exercises result in at least temporary improvement in student ability to think of the unusual response.
2. A more complex task would be to find a new way to communicate with one another by long distance if a "phone bug" chewed through all of the long-distance lines and made them unusable.
3. If one were suddenly faced with running out of petroleum, what variety of other sources of energy might be available?

The power of rewards to elicit novel behavior should not be lost on teachers who yearn for more originality or creativity in their students. It would be useful for teachers to think back over the last few days of their teaching and categorize all of the student behavior that they either praised or rewarded. They might be surprised and gain some sight into why certain behaviors persist in their classroom while others do not.

Consequences

Consequences tests provide not only an excellent measure of fluency and flexibility in the domain of divergent thinking but also a basis for seeking unique solutions to very real problems. In Figure 10–4, Barron (1969) reported the use of consequences to stimulate business leaders in Ireland to think about problems of potential happenings in advance of their arrival. The example posed in Figure 10–4 surely has much to do with the increasing intellectual freedom for girls and women in our society.

Similar problems can be posed with an emphasis on science, economics, or whatever the particular curriculum focus might be, such as What would happen if the dollar were devalued 100 percent? Such questions encourage intellectual stretching on the part of the students.

Treffinger (1990) has proposed some other typical tasks used to stimulate the dimensions of fluency, flexibility, and originality.

1. *Just suppose that... (any unreal or "contrary to fact" situation).* What would be the results? What if it were against the law to smile? What if the Loyalists had won the Revolutionary War? What if a child from Mars enrolled in your class?

FIGURE 10–4   The Stimulation of Divergent Thinking

Problem

Genetic changes produced by increased nuclear radiation prove to be sex-linked for intelligence alone, and it is specifically the intelligence of women that will undergo an increase in magnitude. In Ireland, what would be the consequences?

Solutions

The gradual elimination of male dominance in decision-making, in business, in government.
Emphasis on physical beauty by women, to cover their greater IQ.
Disillusion with intelligence as an indication of general ability.
Gradual female take-over of the initiative in partner selection for marriage.
Fall in population.
Homes would be better-planned and better-organized and equipped.
Children would get better home education.
Unlikely to affect traditional relationships, e.g., women not likely to become leaders in home with even a 15 percent increase in intelligence. Tradition and religion would discourage women as leaders.
Change in educational patterns as more women take graduate courses.
Increase in women in government.

Adapted from Frank Barron, *Consequences in political science* pp. 183–184, 1969, Holt, Rinehart and Winston. Used by permission from Frank Barron, Professor Emeritus, University of California, Santa Cruz.

2. *Product improvement*. There are plenty of things it might be fun to make better: the desks at school, the classroom, the playground, toys, books, tests, chalkboards, overhead projectors, and so on.
3. *Incomplete beginnings*. Create pictures, designs, or stories from incomplete beginnings. Here are some interesting shapes—what can you make from them? Here are some polygons—what can you do with them?
4. *New uses for common objects*. Usually, the ruler is used to measure things. What else might it be used for? How else might we use desks? Chairs? Calendars? Pencils? Books? Window shades? Bulletin boards?
5. *Alternate titles or endings*. For a story, a picture, or any situation, can we think of many possible titles? From a picture or the beginning of a story, think of (write down, act out, tell to others, etc.) many different endings. Can we all begin to make up a story, each person adding a line, or a character, or an event? (Each might finish it in his or her own way.)

Each of the devices described here can be used effectively with gifted students, who can be counted on to like the freedom and range of thinking they are asked to do. The procedures work best when applied to serious content objectives.

Synectics

Numerous cognitive strategies have been tried that would encourage children to take a different mental perspective. *Synectics* is an imaginative exercise designed by Gordon (1975) that utilizes analogy and metaphor to help the thinker analyze problems and form different viewpoints. Children are given a problem, such as how to cope with the bicycle traffic around the school. Synectics favors three types of analogy: (1) fantasy, (2) direct, and (3) personal.

The *fantasy* solution means anything goes; it is not subject to reality or logic. The students might suggest that a gas could be pumped into the tires to enable the bicycle to float over the traffic. *Direct* analogy means that the students will draw on a similar situation, such as the study of how rush-hour traffic is handled in the town or city. *Personal* analogy requires children to place themselves in the role of the problem itself. For instance, students might be asked to pretend they are bicycles and think like bicycles. A sample exercise of this type of synectics is shown in Figure 10–5. Such a device is designed to get the students outside their own skin and see a different perspective.

Study of Self-Instruction

We are all familiar with the way in which we try to modify our own behavior by talking to ourselves—by reminding ourselves that we should do this or not do that. By self-direction, or the use of executive control, we are taking control over our immediate environment. Don't eat that second piece of cake, Keep the left elbow straight when swinging the driver, Don't lose your temper with your boss, Never kick big dogs—all of these statements are designed to give us control over behavior that might otherwise get us into trouble.

FIGURE 10–5   Synectics Personal Analogy

One of the techniques described in the synectics approach for creativity is the use of personal analogy, or putting oneself in the role of some other person or object. The following is an outline of questions that might be used in this approach:

1. Imagine that you are a bicycle. What does it feel like to be a brand new bicycle? What color are you? Why? What kind of person is going to buy you? What will you have as extra equipment?
2. Where would you like to go on your first trip? How do you feel as you climb a long hill? What would make your trip easier? How does it feel to coast down the hill? Imagine your brakes are slammed on. How do you feel?
3. You are now 5 years old. What is the most exciting thing that happened to you as a bicycle? How have you changed? What does it feel like to be an old bicycle? What do you think will happen to you now? What can you do to make yourself more useful, to get back into shape?

This activity could be extended to involve direct analogies by asking questions such as: How is a bicycle like a television set? Or how are the gears like a book?

Source: From *Developing creativity in the gifted and talented* by C. Callahan, 1978. Copyright 1978 by The Council for Exceptional Children. Reprinted with permission.

Meichenbaum (1975) has developed a set of statements designed to create an attitude favorable to creative thinking, making students aware of their negative self-statements about their creative abilities and training them to make positive attitudinal statements. Figure 10–6 shows examples of self-reminders designed to set a fertile environment for creative thought and to provide an effective start on a specific problem. Students can be encouraged to make up their own such messages, appropriate to themselves, and then can be encouraged to use them when they have hit a dry spell.

Evaluating Sources

As educators become more and more impressed by the amount of things that need to be taught to students and the limited amount of time that there is for instruction, we begin to look for ways of helping students to become more effective and efficient in their learning. The mastery of a series of cognitive strategies that would allow for independent learning would seem to be one way to help the students become more efficient. The problem is not really to convince students to *think*—they were born with the capability to do that. The problem is to help them to *think effectively*. To do that, even the brightest of students need help.

For example, consider the skill of critical evaluation of material. Young children have been brought up to think of books, newspapers, TV news, and so on, as vehicles by which they can obtain necessary facts. It is not until rather late in the students' educational program that they begin to learn that such information is not devoid of error, and that often the presentation of the material is from a biased or self-interested perspective that tends to slant the information.

FIGURE 10–6   Examples of Self-Statements Used in Meichenbaum's Study of Self-Instructions

Self statements arising from an attitudinal conceptualization of creativity:

Set—inducing self-statements:

What **to do:**   Be creative, be unique.
Break away from the obvious, the commonplace.
Just be freewheeling.
If you push yourself, you can be creative.
Quantity helps breed quality.

What **not to do:** Get rid of internal blocks.
Defer judgments.
Do not worry about what others think.
Do not give the first answer you think of.
No negative self statements.

Self-statements arising from a mental abilities conceptualization:

Problem analysis—what you say to yourself before you start a problem:

Size up the problem; what is it you have to do?
You have to put the elements together differently.
Use different analogies.
Elaborate on ideas.
Make the strange familiar and the familiar strange.
You are in a rut—okay, try something new.
Take a rest now; who knows when the ideas will visit again. Good, you are getting it.
This is fun.
That was a pretty neat answer; wait till you tell the others!

Self-statements arising from psychoanalytic conceptualization:

Release controls; let your mind wander.
Free-associate, let ideas flow.
Relax—just let it happen.
Let your ideas play.
Let one answer lead to another.
Almost dreamlike, the ideas have a life of their own.

Source: Meichenbaum, D. Enhancing creativity by modifying what subjects say to themselves. *American Educational Research Journal,* 1975, pp. 129–145.

How can teachers help students sort out the truth from these less than neutral or accurate information sources? One way is to give students some rules by which such sources of information can be judged. For example, What really happened at Lexington when the English soldiers and American settlers confronted one another? Perhaps students can read a history book, but *which* history book? The story that is related depends on who is writing it and what perspective the author had. Figure 10–7 shows two versions of the same situation; one was written by an American historian and one was written by an English historian.

Swartz (1987) reported the work of a Massachusetts teacher, Kevin O'Reilly, in providing his students with the PROP method, a device for reviewing conflicting material. The PROP method consists of the following:

FIGURE 10–7   What Happened on the Lexington Green?

American Version

In April, 1775, General Gage, the military governor of Massachusetts, sent out a body of troops to take possession of military stores at Concord, a short distance from Boston. At Lexington, a handful of "embattled farmers," who had been tipped off by Paul Revere, barred the way. The "rebels" were ordered to disperse. They stood their ground. The English fired a volley of shots that killed eight patriots. It was not long before the swift riding Paul Revere spread the news of this new atrocity to the neighboring colonies. The patriots of all New England, although still a handful, were now ready to fight the English. Even in faraway North Carolina, patriots organized to resist them.

(Samuel Steinberg, *The United States: Story of Free People*)

British Version

At five o'clock in the morning the local militia of Lexington, seventy strong, formed up on the village green. As the sun rose the head of the British column, with three officers riding in front, came into view. The leading officer, brandishing his sword, shouted, "Disperse, you rebels, immediately!"

The militia commander ordered his men to disperse. The colonial committees were very anxious not to fire the first shot, and there were strict orders not to provoke open conflict with the British regulars. But in the confusion someone fired. A volley was returned. The ranks of the militia were thinned and there was a general melee. Brushing aside the survivors, the British column marched on to Concord.

(Winston Churchill, *A History of the English Speaking People*)

Source: From *Teaching Thinking Skills* edited by Joan Boykoff Baron and Robert J. Sternberg. Copyright © 1987 by W. H. Freeman and Company. Reprinted with permission.

P: Primary or Secondary?

Is the source giving an eyewitness account, having been present at the event or having firsthand knowledge of the event? Neither of the accounts in Figure 10–7 fits the *primary* criterion. Perhaps an eyewitness account by a British soldier, John Bateman, might be more definitive: "I testify and declare that I heard the word of command given to the troops to fire… and I testify that I never heard any of the inhabitants so much as fire one gun on said troops" (Swartz, 1987, p. 109).

R: Reason to Disort?

The testimony of the British soldier, John Bateman (who was actually present), that the British soldiers fired first seems quite convincing, until one learns that he made his statement while he was a prisoner of the American settlers! Under the circumstances, it is quite likely that he would have reason to distort his report. Few commentators on public affairs are totally neutral. The letters to the editor section in local newspapers are fine evidence for that. Students might also be asked to ponder the significance of the saying, "History is written by the winners."

O: Other Evidence Supporting the Statement?

Even the availability of an eyewitness with no visible bias may not be sufficient, given what is known about the reliability or limited perspective of a single witness.

The availability of many different eyewitnesses and their statements may help one piece together the likely sequence of events that might have taken place. The diaries of winning or losing generals may not be the ideal place to look for factual information.

P: Private or Public?

Finally, one must consider whether the information that is provided is made as part of a public statement or as a private communication. If it is a public statement, it needs to be viewed through the possible distortion of self-interest. What colonist would make a public statement that the colonists fired first, or what responsible British officer would state that his troops fired first? The public recriminations against either would likely be severe. However, a private letter written to one's wife about the events of the day, where there is less of a motive to look good or to look proper to the general public, might be considered more impressive evidence.

The essential feature of the PROP approach is that, with its use, students may grasp the essential point that all information that they receive may be slanted in one form or another, and that there are some techniques that can be applied to information that will enable a person seeking the truth to be more likely to find it. Such a technique of critically evaluating incoming information can be generalized to all manners events or learnings, and can be extraordinarily efficient as a result.

Cranshaw may recognize, for example, that the PROP procedure is similar to that of the scientific method, which is a set of techniques designed to control variables that might have a distorting effect on the results. The mastery of a series of methods to process information efficiently and effectively is one of the major objectives for all students and particularly gifted students. Evidence shows that it is the gifted students who will often be making decisions in adulthood—as business, professional, or political leaders—that may affect the lives of many persons.

Measuring Creative Thinking

One of the puzzles for educators interested in creativity is how to discover this capability in students. All students have this characteristic in varying degrees. But some students are much more able to perform consistently in this domain, and there is a felt need to find these especially gifted individuals so that teachers can aid their creative development.

Is there a test for creativity that can be given so that educators can help these students identify themselves? Callahan (1991) has reported three different approaches to this topic: (1) assess the students' performance on a variety of instruments that measure fluency, flexibility, and originality in verbal or nonverbal tasks, (2) obtain information about past creative work or tendencies through an autobiographical inventory, or (3) collect ratings on creative performance by teachers or others who observe the students at work.

Perhaps the most popular instrument for the measure of creativity is the Torrance Tests of Creative Thinking. It is also one of the few such tests that has evidence of reliability and validity. The test is made up of two parts: Thinking Creatively with Words and Thinking Creatively with Pictures. In the first part, the student answers questions such as, How many different ways can you think of to use a newspaper? In the second part of the test, the student is given a set of lines or curves and asked to complete the drawing and give it a title. These items are then scored for *fluency, flexibility,* and *originality* of response and, in the case of the drawing, on *elaboration.* Torrance (1984) reported significant correlations between performance on these tests and later accomplishments in life.

A second approach to the measurement of creativity is reflected in *biographical inventories* that ask individuals to reveal their lifestyles and past patterns of behavior. This is done under the quite reasonable assumption that the best prediction of an individual's future behavior is his or her past behavior. Such inventories, then, determine how the student has performed in the past. Has she engaged in creative work? Is her personality and lifestyle similar to that of creative people (e.g., a risk taker, willingness to be different, strong self-image, etc.)? On such a measure, Stephanie would stand out! Inventories of this type have proven to be somewhat successful, although they are of little value with students who have had few opportunities in the past to perform in a creative way.

The third method is to *gather information* from third parties who have been observers of the individual in question. Teacher rating scales, which ask if the student has many original ideas, or is self-confident enough to take a stand against the majority, or has produced work of uniqueness and quality can accomplish a similar result to the self-report in the biographical inventories, only this time the information is coming from outside observers.

Callahan concluded with a reasonable summary: "No *one* of the available instruments, by itself, seems to be a satisfactory measure of the elusive construct we call creativity, but individual instruments seem to measure some of the skills involved in creative thinking, a number of characteristics associated with creative behavior, or seem to be a reasonable means of assessing creative products" (1991, pp. 230–231). If creativity is a mix of environmental and social conditions married to the characteristics of certain individuals, then it would be expecting too much of an instrument that, at best, could measure only one part of the formula—the individual—to predict with great accuracy the creative act or the creative person.

Barriers to Creativity

Given the availability of all of these cognitive strategy suggestions, why doesn't such an environment appear more often in classrooms? Some of the more illuminating experiences of the authors have been to ask groups of teachers to pretend, for a moment, that creativity is a very bad quality for a child to show and that it has to be stamped out at any cost. These teachers are then asked for suggestions as to how this obliteration could be accomplished. No group of teachers has failed to arrive quickly at a large number of suggestions, among which they recognize easily some of their own teaching practices. Some of the major ways often mentioned by teachers to stamp out creativity are as follows:

1. *Establish a rigid curriculum, together with a limited time in which this curriculum is to be presented.* When there is a large amount of required material to cover, teachers are almost always less tolerant of unusual ideas or apparently off-the-track statements, no matter how interesting. Also, there has not been sufficient recognition of the tyranny of time and its limitations on teacher behavior. The end of the month or the end of the school year sometimes approaches with the speed of a jet plane, and conscientious teachers are filled with a desire to cover the necessary or required material. This, too, has the effect of less tolerance of error or diversions.

2. *Teach in content areas in which the teachers are not well versed.* Teachers recognize that ignorance or lack of knowledge on their part is a powerful inhibitor of student freedom. Many teachers are concerned about allowing too much freedom when they themselves lack the knowledge base to evaluate the unusual or different thoughts that occur.

3. *Accept only one source as valid.* Having a required textbook is one method that teachers consider as inhibiting creativity. No consideration need then be given to contradictions or conflicts among textbooks. Only facts, not ideas, should be considered.

4. *Do not allow discussion or evaluative statements on the part of the students.* The only act of student participation allowed should be the answering of factual statements or the regurgitating of the teacher's own ideas. Make it clear to the students that there is only one right way to do something. This will effectively discourage any imaginative approach by the students and should, if continued over a long period of time, effectively inhibit any creative impulses. Testing and grading for facts, rather than ideas, can also result in limited thought by the students.

Teachers generally show considerable awareness of these problems and often give strong expressions of guilt and exasperation when they find themselves trapped into behaving in a way that they know to be not conducive to productive student performance. This suppression of creativity, as recognized by teachers, calls for certain obvious modifications in administration and programming. Many times, the responsibilities for such changes lie in the hands of the administrator rather than in those of the teacher. Several desirable changes suggested by the teachers who have recognized these problems are as follows:

1. *Organize and base the curriculum primarily on the teaching of concepts rather than facts.* This would allow a large number of possible approaches to children who have a range of individual differences. Thus, a concept such as democracy can be presented in different ways and at different levels of abstraction for gifted and nongifted students. This recommendation implies that the teacher has a firm grasp of the basic concepts to be taught and of the necessary methods of pedagogy to implement them.

2. *Allow more individual assignments of projects under competent supervision.* The term *competent supervision* suggests that students be allowed to develop their own ideas without having to limit their performance to group activities and group designs. Considerable supervision time must be allotted to carry out the proposed individual

projects. These projects can be effective only if they are done under close supervision, wherein the students would be able to refine their ideas and thinking based on the feedback they obtain from the supervisor.

3. *Bring the students into contact with the maximum talent and knowledge available in the teaching staff.* Most school systems have at least one excellent teacher in each of the various subject areas. The task of the administration is to get that teacher and his or her ideas in contact with as many gifted children as possible. Whether this is done through closed-circuit TV, team teaching, or some other device, it should be a major goal of the creative administrator.

4. *Follow the general philosophy that truth is something to be sought rather than something that will be revealed.* One of the most presumptuous ideas that could be presented in any society is that its people have all the truth that needs to be passed on to succeeding generations. Teachers would be much better off to accept the position that much of the truth about people's affairs and their surrounding environment remains to be discovered. This means that a teacher's role would not be one of an authority but rather of a fellow seeker of truth, albeit a more sophisticated one.

5. *Provide more competence in content and pedagogy in teacher training.* Teacher training institutions must establish, first of all, a greater competence in content areas, as well as more knowledge of thought processes, how these develop in gifted children, and how they can be stimulated.

Is Creativity Training Effective?

Recently, Zelda's parents were informed by the teacher that her class was going to embark on a special training program to stimulate creativity in students. This encouraged and excited Zelda's parents, because they were aware that, although Zelda was extremely bright, she gave little evidence of originality or outstanding imagination. They felt that Zelda was relatively content to do extremely well on precisely what the teacher or her parents told her to do.

Some weeks later, the teacher again contacted Zelda's parents and announced that the school had evidence that their training program had been successful and that they had significantly improved Zelda's creative abilities. Since the parents did not see any manifest change or modification in Zelda, they were left wondering what it was that the teachers had done or why they were so sure that improvement had taken place.

Over the past few years, there have been numerous efforts to demonstrate that it is possible to provide training programs for increasing students' ability to think creatively. Most of these rely on a demonstration of effectiveness that follows a similar plan. First, a group of students is tested on a measure of creativity, such as the Torrance Tests of Creative Thinking. A specific training program is then provided to enhance characteristics linked to that dimension of creativity. Finally, the students are retested to see if they have improved. If students score considerably better after the training program is over than they did before the training program began, this is taken as proof of the effectiveness of the program.

However, a review of many of these effectiveness studies has raised a fundamental question about the value of such success "evidence" (Mansfield, Busse, & Krepelka, 1978). To understand one basic objection, consider the student who is asked in a pretest to name all the things he or she can think of that are round. Next, that student is given training in how to make multiple associations to given stimuli. After weeks of such practice, the same student is asked either the original question or some other question, such as Name all the things you can think of that are square.

Now that Zelda knows what is wanted (i.e., multiple answers and associations), can she give more answers of that type than before? Sure! Does this mean that she is more creative or will become a more creative adult? This isn't quite as easy to answer. The evidence that would really show if such training programs have permanent effects would demonstrate that the youngster can transfer the ability to think fluently or originally on a different academic problem. That is, given a problem situation in the classroom (e.g., how to improve student behavior in the cafeteria) and asked to think about possible solutions, the student should be able to generate more and better solutions to that problem if the cognitive strategies he or she learned are transferable or generalizable to another situation.

This is not to say that the teacher is wasting time in providing such training to the students, nor that Zelda will not get something emotionally useful out of such training. As rigid and as afraid of risk taking as Zelda is, any attempt to encourage her to loosen up and try new things, to realize that there are many acceptable answers to such questions, can be helpful to her *now*, even if it has a minimal effect on how well she can perform at age 25 or 30.

The point made by Mansfield, Busse, and Krepelka (1978), which seems legitimate, is that adult creativity is a mysterious blend of motivation, intelligence, personality, and opportunity. It is obvious that short-term training of simple cognitive skills probably will not dramatically change a person's eventual creativity. It can, however, change the youngster's responses or attitudes immediately, and that may be sufficient to justify it as a technique to be mastered.

Favorable influences of training on attitudes toward creative thinking are difficult to document, although testimonials abound. Perhaps the favorable testimonials occur because many divergent-thinking exercises are fun to do. It is not unreasonable to suggest that perhaps having fun is something Zelda needs to experience in a learning situation, and that realization may be worth the instruction, regardless of whether it has permanent long-term effect in other ways. It should be clear, however, that despite the great activity and proliferation of training materials to enhance creativity, the permanent effects of this type of instruction are still far from being proven.

If there is one conclusion to reach from this chapter, it probably would be that creativity is a complex mix of affective and cognitive factors that blend together in unique ways in all of us. If one wishes to strengthen the likelihood of occurrence of creativity, one can improve the cognitive strategies through exercises such as question asking (What would happen if...?) or one can create a more comfortable psychological environment so that the independence and desire for self-direction that stir in all children are not punished and that intellectual exploration and adventure someness are encouraged and rewarded. These two dimensions are not necessarily separate. Teachers who ask divergent-thinking questions that stress multiple answers are giving a signal that it is all right to produce "different" answers.

As in all educational strategies, there is a price to be paid for all of this exploration and intellectual freedom. Certainly, one price is *time*, since the number of false starts and blind alleys will increase in creative work. Another price is the loss of that deathly silent classroom clearly admired by some school administrators, where students know that absolute obedience to teacher requirements comes before diversity or any original thinking. The teachers who are willing to endure those losses and create the environment noted above can gain much satisfaction from the flowering abilities of their students.

Unresolved Issues

1. In training programs to enhance creativity—the generation of novel and valuable ideas—should as much emphasis be placed on the encouragement of personality and attitudinal characteristics linked to creativity (such as openness, willingness to contest current norms, and independence) as on the standard cognitive exercises that have received popular use?

2. How can educators release "creative thinking" from the limiting concept of a series of exercises done at a particular time of day or in a particular subject (such as art)? Creativity is not just a set of cognitive skills, like driving an automobile; rather, it is an attitude—a philosophy of life that imbues and affects the whole scope of the educational program and the life of the individual. There has been uncertain success in communicating that idea to teachers, however.

3. How can the sophistication in content fields be blended with additional adventures in the productive-thinking realm? Productive-thinking exercises, unless used in conjunction with important or significant content or important ideas, run the risk of being merely isolated "game playing" with no meaningful generalization to other instructional areas of the students' responsibilities.

Chapter Review

1. The stimulation of creative thought has been a major educational goal for gifted and talented students for a quarter of a century.

2. The focus of attention in education has been more on the creative person and creative process than on the creative products that are generated by these persons and methods.

3. Four specific components need to be present for adult creativity; an extensive knowledge base, intense motivation to create, a willingness to oppose the status quo, and mastery of cognitive skills.

4. Creative persons seem to value and seek personal freedom and self-actualization, even at the expense of social norms and social acceptance. They possess a high ability to tolerate uncertainty and they reveal impressive energy and self-confidence.

5. The creative process appears to be composed of many phases that require different thinking operations to be emphasized at different stages of the process.

6. Educational methods for the stimulation of creativity focus on a variety of procedures designed to improve cognitive skills related to creativity, and on creating an educational atmosphere that is conducive to intellectual adventure, risk taking, and originality.

7. Teachers can modify students' productive-thinking expressions by systematically structuring problems and questions in particular ways.

8. Some of the cognitive skills stressed in creativity training are question-asking strategies, brainstorming, attribute listing, originality, redefinition, and consequences.

9. The attitudinal and originality emphasis on creative thinking can be stressed through the use of synectics, self-instruction, and open education settings that encourage freedom and self-direction.

10. Teachers seem well aware of many instructional practices that may inhibit creativity, but they often have no alternative strategies to substitute for them.

11. A variety of cognitive measures assess cognitive processes that seem related to creativity: *fluency, flexibility, originality*, and *elaboration*. Caution is urged in using these instruments, since validity is not well established.

12. Support for the effectiveness of creativity training has generally been limited to evidence of increased performance on the same type of tasks that were involved in the training itself. The ability of students to generalize these learned skills to other tasks is not well documented at this time.

Readings of Special Interest

Alexander, P., Parsons, J., & Nash, W. (1991). *Toward a theory of creativity*. Lubbock, TX: Texas A&M University.
This is a review of the diverse theories that attempt to account for creativity. The authors build their own theory of creativity around a mix of biological, psychological, and sociological factors describing it as a process rather than a trait. Good as a review of various lines of thought.

Amabile, T. (1989). *Growing up creative: Nurturing a lifetime of creativity*. New York: Crown.
This volume presents the point of view of a social psychologist on the origins and development of creativity. The view is stressed that creativity rests on the intrinsic motivation of the individual which, in turn, depends on self-confidence, which depends on a variety of social and family factors.

Baer, J. (1993). *Creativity and divergent thinking*. Hillsdale, NJ: Erlbaum.
This important book reviews the relationship between divergent thinking and creativity. It re-
ports the conduct of several studies that tend to show that many of the tests of creativity are task specific and do not generalize to other situations. Referring to individuals as creative should be changed to refer to some specific domain. Various theories of creativity are discussed.

Gruber, H. (1976). *Darwin on man*. London: Wildwood House.
This is a remarkable biography on one of the greatest creative thinkers of them all. The origins of Darwin's thoughts on evolution are traced through an enormous collection of letters, diary entries, and other documents. It is a classic example of the progress made by a creative scientists through a complicated series of thoughts to a final conclusion.

Osche, R. (1990). *Before the gates of excellence: The determinants of creative genius*. New York: Cambridge University Press.

This is an extraordinary complete synthesis of current knowledge and theory about what factors influence the manifestation of creativity in people. The author pursues the search from psychoanalysis to the latest sociological data to draw a portrait of what makes the creative person create. In the end, he concludes, "They are likely to discover that before the Gates of Excellence the High Gods have placed sweat—the sweat of labour—often mingled with the sweat of pain."

Perkins, D. (1992) *Smart schools: From training memories to educating minds.* New York: Free Press.

This book suggests specific ways in which the new cognitive discoveries can be translated into classroom activities. Perkins introduces topics such as a pedagogy of understanding, a metacurriculum, and the cognitive economy of school (meaning that whatever else the school does, matters rotate around the cognitive achievement of students). It is an easy book to read, but one that is full of wisdom.

Treffinger, D., & Isaken, S. (1992). *Creative problem solving: An introduction.* Sarasota FL: Center for Creative Learning, Inc.

This book is a concise discussion of the importance of creative and critical thinking skills and a description of the six stages of the creative problem-solving process: Mess Finding, Data Finding, Problem Finding, Idea Finding, Solution Finding, and Acceptance Finding. The authors have now combined these stages into three components, which include getting the problem, generating ideas, and planning for action. Both convergent and divergent thinking have received attention in this new text and substantial attention has been provided to the first and last stages, Mess Finding and Acceptance Finding. This book is an easy introduction to the complex world of creative problem solving that has become such an important part of programming for gifted students.

References

Barron, F. (1969). *Creative person and creative process.* New York: Holt, Rinehart and Winston.

Boden, M. A. (1990). *The creative mind: Myths and mechanisms.* New York: Basic Books.

Borkowski, J., & Kurtz, B. (1987). Metacognition and executive control. In J. Borkowski & J. Day (Eds.), *Cognition in special children: Comparative approaches to retardation, learning disabilities, and giftedness.* Norwood, NJ: Ablex.

Bransford, J., Sherwood, R., Vye, N., & Rieser, J. (1986). Teaching thinking and problem solving: Research foundations. *American Psychologist, 41* (10), 1078–1089.

Callahan, C. (1991). The assessment of creativity. In N. Colangelo & G. Davis (Eds.), *Handbook of gifted education* (pp. 219–235). Boston: Allyn and Bacon.

Gallagher, J. J. (1979). Issues in education for the gifted. In A. H. Passow (Ed.), *The gifted and the talented: Their education and development.* 78th Yearbook of the National Society for the Study of Education, Part 1. Chicago: University of Chicago Press.

Gallagher, J., Surles, R., & Hayes, A. (1973). *Program planning and evaluation.* Chapel Hill: TADS, Frank Porter Graham Child Development Center, University of North Carolina.

Gordon, W. (1975). Some source materials in discovery by analogy. *Journal of Creative Behavior, 8,* 239–257.

Jackson, N., & Butterfield, E. (1986). A conception of giftedness designed to promote research. In R. Sternberg & J. Davidson (Eds.), *Conception of giftedness* (pp. 151–181). Cambridge: Cambridge University Press.

Klein, R. (1982). An inquiry into factors related to creativity. *Elementary School Journal, 82,* 256–265.

MacKinnon, D. (1986). *In search of human effectiveness.* Los Angeles: National/State Leadership Training for the Gifted.

Mansfield, R., Busse, T., & Krepelka, E. (1978). The effectiveness of creativity training. *Review of Educational Research, 48,* 517–536.

Maslow, A, (1970). *Motivation and personality* (2nd ed.). New York: Harper & Row.

Meeker, M. (1982). *Divergent production of semantic units*. El Segundo, CA: SOI Institute.

Meichenbaum, D. (1975). Enhancing creativity by modifying what subjects say to themselves. *American Educational Research Journal, 12*, 129–145.

Osborn, A. (1963). *Applied imagination* (2nd ed.). New York: Scribners.

Parnes, S. (1972). *Creativity: Unlocking human potential*. Buffalo, NY: DOK Publishers.

Redfield, D., & Rousseau, E. (1981). A metaanalysis of experimental research on teacher questioning behavior. *Review of Educational Research, 51*, 237–245.

Rutherford, F. & Ahlgren, A. (1990). *Science for all Americans*. New York: Oxford University Press.

Stein, M. (1986). *Gifted, talented, & creative young people*. New York: Garland.

Swartz, R. (1987). Teaching for thinking: A developmental model for the infusion of thinking skills into mainstream instruction. In J. Baron & R. Sternberg (Eds.), *Teaching thinking skills: Theory and practice*. New York: Freeman.

Toffler, A. (1980). *The third wave*. New York: Bantam.

Torrance, E. (1984). *Torrance Tests of Creative Thinking Norms—technical manual*. Los Angeles: Western Psychological Services.

Treffinger, D. (1990). *Encouraging creative learning for the gifted and talented*. Los Angeles: National/State Leadership Training Institute.

Treffinger, D., Isaksen, S., & Firestien, R. (1983). A preliminary model for creative learning. *Journal of Creative Behavior, 1*, 9–17.

Walberg, H., Schiller, D., & Haertel, G. (1979). The quiet revolution in educational research. *Phi Delta Kappan, 61*, 179–183.

Wallas, G. (1926). *The art of thought*. New York: Harcourt, Brace & World.

Chapter 11

Administration

Key Questions

- What are some administrative strategies (changes in learning environments) used for educating gifted students?
- What are some differences in educational strategies used by teachers in Asian countries?
- What is a mentor and how do mentors participate in programs for gifted students?
- What are some additional opportunities that have been made available through technology for gifted students?
- How can programs for gifted students prove themselves accountable?
- What is meant by portfolio assessment?
- What special skills and knowledges does the teacher of gifted students need?
- How do cooperative learning and other reform strategies intersect with gifted education?

This chapter will address the third component of program adaptation for gifted students: the structure of the *learning environment*. Although the two other components—content and skills adaptation—are important, either of these changes can sometimes be made exclusively within the classroom by the individual teacher. When one proposes changes in learning environments (special classes, resource rooms, and so forth), this can have an impact on the entire school organization and reverberate across schools, administrators, teachers, and students.

Perhaps that is why so much attention has been focused on these environmental adaptations. This chapter will review the various alternative settings and program options; discuss related issues such as program effectiveness, costs, and preferences; examine how state and federal education programs can provide additional assistance to local school systems; consider the influence of the educational reform movement; and discuss the preparation of personnel devoted to special educational opportunities for the gifted students.

There is no reason why all three of the possible adaptations—content, skills, and learning environment—cannot be included in a single program. There is good reason to believe that attempts to change the learning environment *without* taking advantage of the opportunity to change the content or the skills mastery will result in substantial missed opportunities and run the risk of creating the illusion of a special program when, in fact, very little has changed (Slavin, 1987).

Ask yourself how much difference would be created if a teacher took the eight or nine most intelligent and highly motivated students in each of three fifth-grade classes and put them all together in the same class. Suppose further that the teacher assigned to such a program has had no special preparation, and that there is no change in the curriculum to be covered, except that everything will move faster. Why should anyone be surprised if evaluations reveal little improvement in measurable student attainment for the "new" program as compared with students of similar ability in the more heterogeneous setting?

There are a number of pitfalls that await the enthusiastic administrator as he or she tries to develop special plans or programs for administrative adjustments for the gifted. One such pitfall is the assumption that the parents of gifted students, such as Cranshaw, Zelda, Sam, Stephanie, or Joe, will be wildly enthusiastic about any suggested change. Assistant Superintendent Campbell happened to meet Cranshaw's parents at a social gathering recently and talked to them enthusiastically about a new program for talented children that he is thinking of instituting. To his surprise, he got a very cool and reserved reception, with Cranshaw's parents raising all sorts of possible objections or problems. Will he be happy? Will he have too much work piled on him? Will it affect his grades? What will other students think of his being singled out this way?

The parents of high-achieving gifted children are in a different position than parents of children with disabilities, when consideration of a special program is requested of them. For the parents of the child with disabilities, any new effort is likely to be received with enthusiasm. Their child may not be doing too well in school at the time, and any change almost certainly is going to be for the good.

It is likely, however, that a gifted child is doing quite well in the existing program. A new program carries with it the risk of things going wrong, of unanticipated problems, and of possible losses. That is why some parents of gifted children are grateful, but cautious, about possible changes in existing programs for their children.

Teachers also should not be expected to cheer and throw their hats in the air at the prospect of a special program that would result in separating the gifted from the standard classroom. Some teachers assigned to the special program can picture themselves spending many more hours preparing for such a class. As an additional problem, the teachers who will have the remainder of the students may well feel they are being robbed of the only students that make teaching worthwhile to them. So there may be a respectful hearing of Dr. Campbell's proposal, but it is not likely that he will be carried off on the shoulders of a cheering throng at the next PTA meeting. Here, as everywhere else in this book, the issues of values, self-interest, and intent loom large, even when they are not immediately apparent.

Educational Reform in the United States

There has been a general movement toward educational reform that promises to restructure the entire educational system and, of course, gifted education along with it. Although educational reform has long been a popular topic within the education community, this particular reform movement appears to be led by political and educational leaders who feel that something is quite wrong about how the system is currently operating.

As was pointed out in Chapter 3, the reform movement—which includes middle schools, cooperative learning, site-based management, outcome-based learning, and accountability—can make major changes in the educational environment for the gifted student.

On one hand, our society wishes to keep all students from dropping out, and on the other hand, our society wishes to be first in the world in mathematics and science! The general movement toward restructuring the schools has the six goals in mind but is more

3

specifically concerned with elements of the educational enterprise. Some of the major elements of this movement are as follows:

- *Middle schools.* This is a strong movement to replace the junior high school and it emphasizes many similar goals to education of gifted students, such as stressing interdisciplinary curricula instruction in thinking strategies and emphasizing counseling, team teaching, and individualization.
- *Site-based management.* This concept is designed to bring educational decision making back to the local school level. It is a reaction to excessive control of activities by a distant central administration or state department of education. How well gifted students will do under site-based management will depend on who is at the site and who knows about the special needs of gifted students.
- *Cooperative learning.* This instructional strategy has become quite popular. It stresses small group activities (three or four students) around a central goal or task, with the team being evaluated sometimes individually and sometimes by the performance of all of the members of the team. The stress on heterogeneous grouping in the small groups has caused some distress among teachers of the gifted who admit to liking the approach if it is used with groups of gifted students.
- *Outcome-based learning.* This reform movement emphasizes products (demonstrated learning) as the basis for evaluating programs as opposed to input measures (e.g., teachers employed) or process information (e.g., number of reports made). This movement could encourage added stimulus for programs for gifted students.
- *Accountability.* All of education will be required to demonstrate how effective it has been in helping students to learn. One of those changes involves how students are grouped for instruction.

Heterogeneous Grouping

One of the concepts shared by some of the reform efforts such as the middle school and cooperative learning is a belief in the effectiveness of heterogeneous grouping. This approach seeks to equalize educational opportunity, and the feeling has been strong among advocates of these movements (George, 1988; Oakes, 1992; Slavin, 1990) that grouping or tracking students by ability gave certain students an unfair advantage. Grouping, in fact, appears to result in favorable results for gifted students (see Figure 11–1) but not for slow learning students (Slavin, 1987).

A concept such as heterogeneous grouping raises a potential conflict between educators of gifted students and the proponents of the reform movements, because one of the strong principles of gifted education is the advantage of grouping these students together for some of their instruction. A recent survey of randomly selected (from professional association membership lists) middle school educators and educators of gifted revealed major differences in attitude between the two groups around the issue of ability grouping, with the educators of the gifted favoring it and the middle school advocates against it. In most other areas besides ability grouping, there is general agreement between the middle school principles (such as interdisciplinary curriculum, focus on the affective life of the student, stress on thinking skills, flexible pacing, etc.) and the philosophy behind education of gifted students.

FIGURE 11–1   Ability Grouping: Guidelines

1. Although some schools programs that group children by ability have only small effects, other grouping programs help children a great deal. Schools should therefore resist calls for the wholesale elimination of ability grouping.
2. Highly talented youngsters profit greatly from work in accelerated classes. Schools should therefore try to maintain programs of accelerated work.
3. Highly talented youngsters also profit greatly from an enriched curriculum designed to broaden and deepen their learning. Schools should therefore try to maintain programs of enrichment.
4. Bright, average, and slow youngsters profit from grouping programs that adjust the curriculum to the aptitude levels of the groups. Schools should try to use ability grouping in this way.
5. Benefits are slight from programs that group children by ability but prescribe common curricular experiences for all ability groups. Schools should not expect student achievement to change dramatically with either establishment or elimination of such programs.

Source: Kulik, J. (1992). *An analysis of the research on ability grouping: Historical and contemporary perspectives.* The National Research Center on the Gifted and Talented. Research for this report was supported under the Javits Act Program (Grant No. R206R00001) as administered by the Office of Educational Research and Improvement, U.S. Department of Education. Grantees undertaking such projects are encouraged to express freely their professional judgment. This report, therefore, does not necessarily represent positions or policies of the Government, and no official endorsement should be inferred.

Do teachers in regular (heterogeneous) classrooms actually differentiate programs for gifted students, as Slavin would like the reader to believe? Two recent nationwide studies clearly indicate otherwise. A nationwide sample of nearly 2,000 private and public school teachers of third- and fourth-graders was collected. These teachers were asked how they differentiated their program for gifted students. Only minor modifications, at best, were reported (Archambault, Westberg, Brown, Hallmark, Zhang, & Emmons, 1993).

These results were confirmed by an observation study in 46 third- and fourth-grade classrooms in which two students, one gifted and one of average ability, were systematically observed (Westberg, Archambault, Dobyns, & Slavin, 1993). Very little differentiation was found in instructional and curricular practices. What Slavin *hopes* will happen certainly didn't seem to happen in this nationwide sample.

Cooperative learning, another major reform element, has many variations, but the basic principle is that students are placed in small groups and given specific tasks to accomplish together (see Slavin, 1988). Specific instruction is often given to the students on how they are to work together (e.g., praise, not criticism) and roles to play in the group (recorder, reporter, etc.).

In this cooperative learning approach, heterogeneous grouping has again been stressed. This is often done by forming a group of four students composed of one advanced student, two average students, and one below-average student. It is hoped that the team members would help each other get the task done and that the advanced student could assist the others in doing a quality task.

Some criticism of this approach from the standpoint of gifted education has focused on (1) the burden of the task falling on the shoulders of the above-average students who may be used as assistant teachers, (2) the tasks being geared to the lesser abilities of the other members of the group and being unchallenging to the bright student, and (3) the product may be judged as a group rather than through individual assessment (Robinson, 1992). See Figure 11–2 for a clear statement on cooperative learning.

FIGURE 11–2   Cooperative Learning: Recommendations

1. Cooperative learning in the heterogeneous classroom should not be substituted for specialized programs and services for academically talented students.
2. If a school is committed to cooperative learning, models which encourage access to materials beyond grade level are preferable for academically talented students.
3. If a school is committed to cooperative learning, models which permit flexible pacing are preferable for academically talented students.
4. If a school is committed to cooperative learning, student achievement disparities within the group should not be too severe.
5. Academically talented students should be provided with opportunities for autonomy and individual pursuits during the school day.

Source: Robinson, A., (1992). *Cooperative learning and the academically talented student.* The National Research Center on the Gifted and Talented. Research for this report was supported under the Javits Act Program (Grant No. R206R00001) as administered by the Office of Educational Research and Improvement, U.S. Department of Education. Grantees undertaking such projects are encouraged to express freely their professional judgment. This report, therefore, does not necessarily represent positions or policies of the Government, and no official endorsement should be inferred.

Few gifted educators complain about the basic thrust of cooperative learning, which contains many favorable features such as student involvement, getting away from teacher lectures, and learning good work habits. The major source of conflict is on the formation of the groups themselves (Gallagher, 1991).

Gifted learners will be influenced by all of these reform movements, even if these movements were not initiated with them in mind. As part of the overall fabric of public education, gifted students, as well as their teachers, must cope with change, just as all the other components of the educational enterprise must.

Figure 11–3 shows a list of the more common options now in use to modify programs for gifted education. These are organized roughly in order from limited to extensive adaptations and represent at least three major strategies.

One strategy would be to leave the gifted students within the regular class. The tactics of *enrichment* or *teacher consultant* fall under this general approach, emphasizing the importance of integrating gifted students with average students.

A second strategy tries to achieve two desirable goals at the same time. There is an attempt to give special instruction for a period of time in a special-ability or performance-grouped setting while still maintaining the students' basic identification with the regular program. *The resource room, interest classes, mentor,* and *independent study* approaches are examples of the partial special programs that are most popular.

The third major strategy stresses a more total separation of gifted students for special instruction. *Special classes* and *special schools* are examples of this separatist strategy.

It is easy to be confused by all of these variations and not see the underlying commonalities. In whatever way the interests and values of the local community may shape the particular approach, most of these administrative adaptations for gifted students have three basic goals in mind:

1. Provide gifted students with an opportunity to interact with one another so they can learn and be stimulated by their intellectual peers.

FIGURE 11–3   Program Options for Gifted Students

Enrichment in the classroom.   A differentiated program of study for the gifted is provided by the classroom teacher within the regular classroom without assistance from an outside resource or consultant teacher.

Consultant-teacher program.   Differentiated instruction is provided within the classroom by the classroom teacher with the assistance of a specially trained consultant teacher who will provide extra materials and teach small groups of students in the regular classroom.

Resource room/Pull-out program.   Gifted students leave the classroom on a regular basis for differentiated instruction provided by a specially trained teacher.

Interest classes.   Students volunteer for challenging classes on topics beyond or outside the regular curriculum (outer space, ethics, probability, etc.).

Community mentor program.   Gifted students interact on an individual basis with selected members of the community for an extended time period on a topic of special interest to the student.

Independent-study program.   Differentiated instruction consists of independent study projects supervised by a qualified teacher or mentor.

Special class.   Gifted students are grouped together for most of the day and receive instruction from a specially trained teacher.

Special school.   Gifted students receive differentiated instruction in a specialized school established for that purpose.

Magnet school.   A school is established that focuses on specific areas (e.g., foreign languages, creative writing, advanced mathematics, etc.). Students with special interests are encouraged to volunteer for such programs even if they are outside the students' own neighborhood school.

Summer program.   Many states have a variety of enrichment or fast-paced summer programs that can attract gifted students in art, mathematics, or general programs.

2. Reduce the variance within the group on instructionally relevant and challenging dimensions (e.g., past achievement) in order to make it easier for the teacher to provide instructionally relevant materials.
3. Place the gifted students with an instructor who has special expertise in working with gifted students or in a relevant content area.

With the exception of mentors and independent study, which focus on only the second and third of these objectives, all of the adaptations have these three goals in mind.

The notion of grouping students by performance makes a great deal of sense to a teacher such as Mr. Jenkins. He realizes that if the administrator does not group students by class, he will have to group them *within* the classroom. It is not likely that Mr. Jenkins, or many teachers, will be able to challenge students with a tenth-grade reading level and at the same time, in the same group, satisfy the needs of students reading third-grade material.

Nevertheless, the idea of ability or performance grouping is not an entirely popular one with the lay public. It raises images of favoritism, such as giving the best teachers to the fast group, or creating an intellectual elite. It must be said that such notions are not entirely without foundation. The public *should* be annoyed if grouping becomes merely a means of dispensing favors to influential citizens and their children, rather than being a part of an integrated and quality program concerned with the education of the slow and average learner as well as that of the high-aptitude child. Such objections from the lay public undoubtedly have played an influential role in limiting the number of school systems in the United States that use a separate grouping policy.

Administrative Adaptations Defined

A close examination has led many people to believe that an adequate education for children of all levels of intellectual ability requires dramatic changes in the existing structure of the education system itself (see *America 2000*). The problems that seem to weigh most heavily in the present situation are the lack of depth in content knowledge by the teacher; the impressive range of intellectual ability and achievement in the heterogeneous elementary class, with the consequent heavy demands for multiple planning by the teacher; and the teacher's limited amount of time to work at the high conceptual level for the brightest children in the group.

Enrichment in the Regular Classroom

This approach requires the least administrative adjustments by the schools and is based on the assumption that the classroom teacher, with some additional materials and a commitment to individual instruction, can provide an "enriched" experience for gifted students. This procedure has not been well received by parents, in particular, who feel it is not sufficiently intense and the situation requires the teacher to do things that she or he has little training to do or time in which to do it.

The clear superiority of students from other countries, particularly the Asian countries, over U.S. students in mathematics and science has caused a number of questions to be raised regarding the nature of the schooling that those children receive. Stigler, Lee, and Stevenson (1990) collected data from 120 classrooms in Taiwan, Japan, and Minneapolis and reported similar results as other larger international studies (International Association for the Evaluation of Educational Achievement, 1989). Stigler, Lee, and Stevenson stated, "Among the top one hundred first graders in mathematics, there were only fifteen American children. And only one American child appeared in the top one hundred fifth graders" (1990, p. 12).

Stigler, Lee, and Stevenson (1990) also noticed a number of interesting differences in classroom management on the part of the teacher that they felt might have some relevance for these results. They found that when they reviewed a category that stated, "No one is leading instruction in the class," this occurred 9 percent of the time in Taiwan, 26 percent of the time in Japan, and an astonishing 51 percent of the time in the United States. They attributed that high figure to result from the individual attention given to students by U.S. teachers, leaving the majority of students to fend for themselves. But they also felt that the Asian teachers often presented lessons in an interesting format that intrigued their students:

> *The teacher walks in carrying a large paper bag full of clinking glass.... By the*
> *time she has placed the bag on her desk, the students are regarding her with rapt*
> *attention.... She begins to pull items out of the bag, placing them, one by one, on*
> *her desk. She removes a pitcher and a vase. A beer bottle evokes laughter and*
> *surprise.... (Stigler, Lee, & Stevenson, 1990)*

The teacher goes on to conduct a lesson on how to discover which of the containers holds the most water and how such reports can be presented graphically. This is contrasted with the lessons in U.S. classrooms that often seemed disjointed and disrupted.

Of course, many of these differences reflect the entire culture; family interest in education and the view of education as a key to social status in adulthood is quite diverse in different countries. Still, it is distressing to find such dramatic dissimilarities in achievement when there are not similar differences in cognitive performance (Stevenson, Stigler, Lee, Lucker, Kitamura, & Hsu, 1985).

One of the arguments against educating gifted students within the regular classroom pertains to the reduction of difficulty of the regular program. It has been estimated that "dumbing down" of textbooks has resulted in textbook difficulty dropping two grade levels over the past 10 to 15 years (Kirst, 1982). Such simplification makes it even more difficult to provide challenging programs for gifted students who are already two or three grades beyond grade level before such "dumbing down" occurred. Kirst said that when Californians tried to reserve two slots on the statewide adoption list for textbooks that would challenge the top one-third of students, no publisher had a book to present. "They could only suggest re-issuing textbooks from the late 1960s, or writing new ones—a three- to five-year project" (p. 7). A recent trend to more complex content emphases in mathematics and history may reverse this "dumbing down" trend in textbooks and lessons.

Consultant-Teacher Model

This model also serves gifted and talented students within the regular classroom setting. A specially trained teacher works cooperatively with the students' classroom teacher to design and implement a differentiated curriculum. The classroom teacher maintains the primary responsibility for direct instruction of the gifted students. Although the consultant teacher may engage in some direct instruction for demonstration purposes, his or her main responsibility is to aid the classroom teacher. The use of consultant teachers is generally recognized as a strategy for the primary and elementary grades. It is a device that is popular as a *general* means of providing differentiated curriculum for the gifted without displacing the gifted students from their "home" classroom.

Resource-Room Model

In this model, gifted students are pulled out of the regular classroom for a specified amount of time (often one class period or an hour a day). These gifted students are grouped together and receive their instruction from a specially trained teacher. This approach differs from the consultant-teacher model in that the primary role of the re-source-room teacher is direct instruction of gifted students. The resource-room model is employed most often at the upper elementary grade levels. Its popularity as a means of providing differentiating programs rapidly declines past the elementary school level because of the different structure of the secondary school by content subjects, which makes the concept difficult to apply. Use of the resource-room model at the primary level is considerably greater than that of the consultant-teacher model.

Special Interest Classes

This program adaptation, sometimes referred to as the *revolving door program*, was pioneered by Renzulli, Reis, and Smith (1981) and is essentially a variation of the resource-room model. It places the emphasis on flexibility of grouping for special instruction. Students are allowed to move in and out of the special program as their particular interests dictate. These students come from a pool of the top students in ability who have demonstrated interest and productive performance. A student may opt for the special class on "outer space" but may not be interested when the special class stresses the history of Mediterranean culture. It allows the children to have the resource-room experience without committing to a semester or year-long responsibility. When the chosen interest area is completed (e.g., in six weeks), the students return to their regular classrooms (Delisle, Reis, & Gibbins, 1981).

Mentors

Another strategy growing in popularity, particularly at the secondary level, is called the *mentor* approach. This refers to a procedure by which a gifted student leaves school for a period of time, perhaps two or three afternoons a week, and comes under the supervision of some specialist in the community who is an expert in the gifted student's particular area of interest.

If the gifted student is particularly fascinated by computers, the school may arrange for the student to work part-time in one of the electronics laboratories in town. A pupil who looks forward to a career in medicine could spend some time working in the laboratory of the local hospital. A talented student in the performing arts could spend some time under the tutelage of a professional dancer in the local ballet company.

Such mentors provide content sophistication that would be impossible for a local school system to provide. After all, what school system could provide in-depth knowledge on early Egyptian architecture, the status of the white whale, black holes in space, or other exotic topics of possible interest to gifted students? Gold described the traditional view of the mentor:

> *Basically, the potential mentor in gifted child education possesses a high degree of competency in some particular endeavor (for example, genetics, Chinese history, French impressionists). An arrangement is made between the school and*

this individual to work on a one-to-one basis with some gifted and talented student interested in the same field. The contact leads ideally to a mutually satisfactory and fulfilling relationship for the mentor and his charge. (1979, p. 275)

Although a theoretically popular idea, mentors have turned out to be an administrative headache for many school systems. This is probably because of the degree of continued nurturance and leadership required from the school system to contact the mentors, make sure the relationship is proceeding appropriately, and provide some degree of tangible recognition and support for the mentors.

Many school systems have rules against students leaving the campus during school hours. Also, does insurance cover the student who might be injured when he or she is away from the campus? It is such mundane, but administratively important, issues that often limit the use of innovative approaches such as mentoring.

A variation on the mentor concept has been presented by Gray. In this version, Gray uses future elementary and secondary school teachers enrolled in an educational psychology course who received partial credit for volunteering services for gifted and talented pupils. These teachers and students follow a four-phase enrichment model for planning, conducting, completing, and presenting in a mentor-assisted enrichment project.

Phase 1: The mentor plans a proposed enrichment project. *In this phase, the mentor identifies a topic of personal expertise and organizes and develops some materials that would have the potential of motivating young students through active learning experiences and the promise of a rich informational background.*

Phase 2: The mentor and pupils agree on the actual project. *Interested pupils are provided the opportunity to explore a possible enrichment project and then jointly agree on the actual project to be done and a written schedule of learning activities and outcomes, with specific due dates for special assignments.*

Phase 3: Doing the project. *The responsibility of the mentor here is to provide novel materials and experiences, making sure, in particular, that the pupils understand and accept the purpose of each activity.*

Phase 4: Completing and presenting the project. *The end of the project is identified by a presentation of the project to the classmates. This gives a specific focus and direction for the project and allows the pupils to organize their ideas and experiences in an effective way that can be presented to the other students. (1982, pp. 17–18)*

This approach has a number of advantages over the community mentor program, primarily because it is part of a regular academic program. Expectations for performance are clear and not dependent on the intrinsic motivation of the mentor. The circumscribed time period that is involved also forces a necessary focus and limitation on the project, which enables a specific, if limited, set of activities around the key concept.

Independent Study

One of the most acceptable patterns for providing for gifted students, particularly at the secondary level, is *independent study*. In many ways, the term is unfortunate because it can imply a limited role for the teacher—send the students off on their own. Kaplan appropriately commented, "Independent study fails for the gifted when it is perceived as a process independent of teaching.... When the concept of independent study as an instructional mode is confused with the concept of independence, independent study is also likely to fail" (1979, p. 166).

There are many specific search skills and judgments that need to be learned by students often unaccustomed to being on their own and needing counsel and advice from the teacher. Even Cranshaw, as self-confident as he is, can be defeated by permission to do independent study that is not accompanied by careful preparation and supervision. He once expressed a burning desire to find out about knighthood, having recently seen some movies and television shows on the subject. His teacher allowed him free time to go to the library on an independent-study project. A few days later, he came back discouraged and frustrated, complaining that he could not find the material he wanted and was puzzled about what to do about the sparse material he did collect.

Without instruction in simple research techniques on how to use library indexes or how to use information from existing references to get more leads, the student will be like a child hungry in a field of canned goods because he does not have a can opener. The student also needs to know how to delimit the topic chosen to a manageable level. Perhaps Cranshaw could focus on (1) the value of chivalry in knighthood, (2) types of armor used by knights, or (3) the role of knights in a feudal society. Clearly, the general topic of knighthood can drown the student in its multidimensions.

A third skill that the student needs help in determining is whether there is sufficient material available on the proposed topic at hand. Perhaps the accessible sources do not have much material on knighthood—in which case the student should be shifted to a topic more easily developed within available resources. The librarian or media specialist should be a quick informant on this.

Some specific devices have been developed to aid the teacher and student in carrying out independent-study activities. One of these devices is noted in Figure 11–4, a specific learning contract, signed by the teacher and the student, that details the various steps to be taken in order that the project is completed.

Maker (1982) has presented such a contract for a younger child carrying out a science project that, when completed, would lead to a final report and presentation. It is a useful device for fixing the tasks to be done without forcing the student to carry out these tasks in any specific order. The student can use these contracts as a progress sheet, allowing him or her to see how much has been done and how much remains.

Special Classes

This model requires the grouping of gifted and talented students for instruction with a specially trained teacher in a self-contained class. That is, the teacher is responsible for the primary instruction of the gifted students in the major subject areas. This strategy

FIGURE 11–4 Student Contract

I, <u>   Amy L.   </u>, agree to do the following experiments or activities at the <u> science </u> learning center. I will work on my own as much as possible until I am finished. I will find my own materials and will work hard.

<u> × </u>	Look at an onion skin under the microscope. Draw a picture of how it looks.
<u> × </u>	Mix a solution of iodine and water and put it on an onion skin. Look at the onion skin under the microscope and draw a picture of how it looks.
<u> </u>	Do the taste test on all mystery powders and write what happened.
<u> </u>	Do the smell test on all mystery powders and write what happened.
<u> </u>	Make a clay boat that will float. Draw a picture of it and write how long it floated.
<u> × </u>	Make a clay boat that will float and carry at least five (5) marbles without sinking. Draw a picture of the boat and write how long it floated and how many marbles it held.

I will finish this contract on <u> Tuesday </u> and will talk about my experiments or activities with my teacher.

Signed,

_____

Student

_____

Teacher

Source: From *Teaching Models in Education of the Gifted* (p. 344) by C. J. Maker, 1982, Austin, TX: Aspen Systems. Copyright 1982 by PRO-ED, Inc. Reprinted by permission.

requires a specially trained teacher of broad experience and background to cover the wide range of content these students will require. It allows for the introduction of a substantially different curriculum on a systematic basis.

Advanced Placement Program

One of the most common curriculum modifications made at the secondary level is the implementation of one or several Advanced Placement (AP) courses. The AP program of courses was developed by the Educational Testing Service (ETS) to provide bright students with the opportunity to receive credit for college-level courses while still in high school. While originally offering a modest selection of courses in English, math, and history, the AP program has expanded to include virtually all subject areas, including mathematics, biology, chemistry, physics, computer science, English, several foreign languages, history, art, and music.

A common misunderstanding about the AP program is that it is a full college curriculum. In reality, the AP program is only a testing service provided by the ETS to students who pay the fee to take the test. Teachers who are interested in preparing students to take an Advanced Placement course receive guidelines and a general overview from the ETS of the kind of material that will be covered on the test at the end of the school year. The teacher is then free to construct the course around the necessary content. However, the ETS does not provide a specific curriculum structure.

In May, students who wish to take the AP test in English, for example, pay a fee to the ETS and take the test. However, enrolling in an Advanced Placement course does not automatically gain a student access to the AP test, nor does a student have to be enrolled in an AP class in order to take the test. Anyone who feels prepared in the subject matter—regardless of the mode of preparation—has the option of paying the fee for admission. It does not matter whether the student took a course called "Advanced Placement English" or if he or she simply read a lot of literature and knows a lot about grammar.

The test setting is very similar to other massive standardized test settings, such as the testing for the Scholastic Aptitude Test (SAT). The test is provided by the AP program and is scored by staff trained by ETS. Test results are reported on a scale of 1 to 5, with 5 being the highest possible score. Students who receive either a 4 or a 5 on the AP test generally stand a good chance of getting college credit for the course when they enter college.

However, AP classes should not be regarded as the panacea for programming for bright students at the secondary level. Because the information on many of the AP tests is based on facts (a portion of each of the tests consists of multiple-choice items), the courses tend to be designed to deliver a lot of content in a brief period of time. The standard approach that teachers use when faced with a lot of content and little time is to lecture. Although this may, in fact, parallel the college experience, it is not necessarily the kind of program that will stimulate higher levels of thinking in gifted students. Given the national reform emphasis on the use of higher-order thinking skills, interdisciplinary connections, and problem-solving strategies, it might be best for teachers to use more innovative instructional strategies geared toward, but not specifically following, the AP guidelines.

Students should be made aware that they have to receive a score of at least 4 or higher in most courses to place out of a class in college. They should also know that not all colleges accept AP tests as a college course in all subject areas. Students who want to take AP-level instruction for the purpose of placing out of college requirements should first know what courses his or her prospective college(s) will accept. Sometimes, it is not desirable for students to skip the first year of a specific subject area in college; many colleges have carefully constructed their course offerings so that the first year provides critical perspectives that a student might not get by taking the AP course in high school. Again, students, parents, and advisors, need to consider carefully whether or not placing out of college courses is a good idea if this is the reason for taking Advanced Placement classes.

Bartkovich, a mathematics teacher at the North Carolina School of Science and Mathematics, has expanded on the potential problems of a purely AP focus in the mathematics curriculum:

> *Teaching for tests, such as the Scholastic Aptitude Test or an Advanced Place-*
> *ment (AP) examination, can be a major culprit in a lack of motivational qualities*
> *in instruction. Teaching an AP course can be a positive motivator if the teacher*
> *uses the AP syllabus as a guide for developing course content. On the other*
> *hand, the test can become the exclusive focus of the teacher and the students,*
> *causing a course to deteriorate into memorization of acts solely for the sake of*
> *taking an exam. I often hear teachers complain about talented students who are*
> *"over-advanced" because they are great test-takers. The implication of the*
> *complaints is that these students are able to advance beyond their level of*
> *understanding and mastery by virtue of being excellent on standardized tests. I*
> *suggest that the problem is not a lack of knowledge, but of motivation. By*
> *focusing exclusively on tests and memorization of the required facts, talented*
> *students are able to advance beyond their level of motivation. As a result, when*
> *they do encounter difficult material, they may not have the motivation necessary*
> *to strive to overcome their particular hurdles. (1988)*

Even so, it would be a mistake to suggest that some students would not thrive in the AP-oriented classroom. Certainly, Cranshaw and Zelda would enjoy learning some material at a faster pace, and would probably benefit from the possibility of placing out of college courses. Hopefully, they would have teachers who would do more than reinforce Zelda's propensity for memorization, though. Stephanie would probably do best in an AP course that covers material not usually offered in high school, giving her a sneak preview of some of the interesting concepts and ideas she will find in college.

International Baccalaureate

The International Baccalaureate (IB) program has the same ultimate goal as the AP program—to provide college-level programming for bright and motivated high school students. However, the structure of the IB program is substantially different from the AP.

Originally developed in Geneva, Switzerland, during the 1960s, the IB program was formed as a standard international curriculum that would allow students from all over the world to meet the high school requirements in their own countries. As a result, the curriculum has a decidedly international bent. Students who enter the IB curriculum are prepared to take comprehensive examinations prepared in Geneva on a variety of school subjects. In order to earn the diploma, students must demonstrate mastery in two foreign languages, the study of man (including history, social science, and philosophy), science, mathematics, art, and computers. A cornerstone of the program is an additional course called "The Theory of Knowledge," which is an investigation into the philosophy of learning and the psychology of critical thinking (Freeman, 1987).

This bent toward self-as-learner and philosophical orientation to interdisciplinary connections makes the program perfect for students like Stephanie, whose inclination for creativity and divergent thinking would be served well by the broad, sweeping scope of the curriculum. In this context, she could learn some fundamental information that she otherwise might ignore out of boredom in a more traditional setting.

Schools who choose to implement the IB curriculum agree to offer an entire two-year course sequence. School board support is required before the program is made available for a school to phase in. Because it is a comprehensive program, and not a course-by-course smorgasbord like the Advanced Placement program, it costs more time and money to implement. However, it does provide an opportunity for schools without specialized emphasis to offer exemplary programing with a minimum of time devoted to planning scope and sequence, since they are already determined by the program. And it seems to be worth the effort—teachers, administrators, and students, as a rule, respond enthusiastically to the challenge of the program (Daniel & Cox, 1985).

Magnet Schools

One of the more unique educational variations available in the past few years has been designated the *magnet school*. This term defines specific educational programs offered in particular schools that can, by their unique nature, draw students or their parents into situations or environments in which they ordinarily would not appear through usual neighborhood school assignments. The gifted magnet school might offer special experiences in creative writing, futuristics, science experimentation, and so on, to entice and draw the student into an exciting program.

There is one substantial advantage to the use of magnet schools in designing a total program for gifted and talented students: It represents not a mandated change or student separation by school administrators but rather a particular program option that is chosen voluntarily by parents and students. If one designs a program that especially appeals to gifted students, then the magnet schools are going to be, in reality, a "school within a school" for gifted students, but it is not made so by the sorting of children by IQ scores.

Increasingly popular, magnet school programs do have several distinct advantages. Because they serve a single population selected for specific skills and/or characteristics, they are free to offer courses and develop instructional programs that are uniquely suited to those students. Having a "critical mass" of students with the same educational interests also has a social benefit, since the peer group can reinforce and bolster the academic interests they share—and sometimes more effectively than adults! Magnet schools provide an excellent opportunity to test out new kinds of pedagogy or curriculum approaches, making them an excellent laboratory to be accessed by the surrounding educational community and allowing them an unparalleled chance to model new educational ideas and assist with the translation of those ideas into more traditional educational settings.

Some of the disadvantages of the magnet school approach are predictable—the most obvious being the logistics of transporting children from their homes or regular schools to the magnet program, which can sometimes take quite a bit of time out of the students' day (and their parents' day, too). Working out collaborative group projects with students in this setting can be difficult since students cannot easily get together outside of school time.

Summer Programs

A number of different kinds of summer programs offer an alternative service for gifted students and their parents. One of the most widely recognized programs is the Talent Search (Stanley, 1989). Another summer program that reaches many students is the Governors' Schools conducted by more than 10 states. These programs are, for the most part, funded at the state level. Most are tuition free in order to maximize access to the program for students from families in low socioeconomic groups.

One key difference between the Governors' Schools and the Talent Search is the admission criteria used. The Talent Search is primarily dependent on achievement test scores and Scholastic Aptitude Test scores, whereas students attending the Governors' Schools qualify primarily through demonstration of skills in the subject area and overall ability as indicated through some standardized tests. Any student can be nominated for a Governor's School program by a teacher, parent, or school counselor. Subsequent auditions and reviews of test scores are used as the means of selecting students for the summer program.

The focus of the programs in the Governors' Schools varies from state to state. Some Governors' Schools have programs in the arts or humanities, some focus on mathematics and science, and still others use the summer as an opportunity for interdisciplinary studies. Across the nation, the various Governors' Schools have different content, length, and goals. However, they all have in common the philosophy that gifted students need to be brought together in a residential environment to study together and learn from each other as well as from their summer teachers.

Of the children discussed in this book, Sam and Stephanie would stand to benefit the most from the Governor's School setting. Sam will be able to take advantage of the fact that the program is without tuition, thus making the idea feasible. If the state he lives in has an arts program, then he would be able to pursue his love of music along with other, similarily inclined students. Sam might also learn about different kinds of music, about the discipline that musicians must adopt to become professionals, and, through philosophy and psychology class, that music does connect with other disciplines such as English and mathematics. Sam could be exposed to the "big ideas" behind the world of music, which might motivate him to become a better overall student as well as a better musician.

Stephanie, like Sam, could benefit from the specific training and interdisciplinary "big ideas" that are the focus of some Governor's School programs. But for Stephanie, the big impact would be in liberation from the constraints of the daily school program. Instead of being introduced to the concept of the "big idea" as Sam is, Stephanie would be delighted to find a place where she could study the things that she thought school should be about all along!

Special Schools

Until about two decades ago, special schools for high-ability students were limited to the private sector where various prep schools provided an advanced education for the students with sufficient money (or scholarships) who could afford to attend. The only exceptions to this were those schools specializing in the fine arts, such as the Julliard School of Music in New York City and the Boston Conservatory of Music, and day schools like the Bronx High School of Science.

Since that time, other specialized schools have developed that are supported by public funds focusing on high-ability students. Encouraged by the success of summer programs such as the Governor's Schools, some states began to plan a year-round residential school focusing on mathematics and science. The North Carolina School of Science and Mathematics and the Illinois Mathematics and Science Academy are two such schools. As of 1993, there were about 10 or 11 such state schools, with more being planned.

Such schools emphasize a strong math and science program but provide a comprehensive program across the typical academic secondary school curriculum. Students are chosen for such schools on the basis of aptitude tests, teacher recommendations, and sometimes the students' own statements of their personal goals in coming to the school. These schools, being publicly funded, also carry additional responsibilities and have become training centers to upgrade teacher skills in content fields and in the uses of technology in education from schools across the state. A recent evaluation of one of these schools (Gallagher, Coleman, & Staples, 1989) reported a high level of staff and student enthusiasm and satisfaction, with the alumni of the school enthusiastic about the education they had received. "The alumni spoke of the faculty with affection and respect. Excellent was the term used very frequently and they particularly admired the teachers who broke with established structure and worked with small groups and used unusual instructional strategies to capture their attention and interest" (p. 19).

Some of the advice of the alumni to the school administration included: "Do not make the school into a strict math and science program. Value the liberal arts side because it is one of the most important dimensions of the school" and "Be strong in outreach and help other schools learn what they have learned in this school." (Part of this recommendation may well have stemmed from feelings that the alumni had received a remarkable experience and felt guilty if only they, among all of the high school students in the state, could experience it.)

If there is a continuing concern about educational excellence, then we may well see a growing number of such schools that provide a demonstration of what is possible in public education when one combines a committed faculty with an outstanding group of students.

Extra-School Activities

One of the options available to administrators planning for programs for gifted students is to provide opportunities outside the standard school program. After-school or Saturday programs have become visible manifestations of such policy. These programs allow for diversity of content and also bring in some special instructors that ordinarily would not be available through the standard school program. For example, Feldhusen and Wyman (1980) reported that in addition to using volunteers from the regular school staff for a Super Saturday program, they were able to attract university professors for math education, an undergraduate computer science major, and an educational researcher to offer instruction in special computer courses. This program allows for small class sizes of 15 to 20 and no standard curriculum or grades to inhibit the adventuresome tone that such programs can take. There is a deliberate intent to separate this extra-school program from the standard program so that the students can experience more content novelty.

One of the potential negative elements to such programs is that their presence sometimes takes the pressure off school administrators to do something more constructive for the gifted *within* the framework of the regular program. The presence of extra-school activities, although desirable, in no way reduces the responsibility of the regular program to make appropriate adaptations as well.

Olson (1981) also reported on an intense three-week summer program in mathematics, writing, and science sponsored by Johns Hopkins University, which allows junior high school students to complete Algebra I and II in three weeks. Teachers for this program often come from university faculties. In past writing classes, the students were given the assignment of writing an anecdote on "poverty of the media," and the young students who focused on etymology studied Greek and Latin prefixes, stems, and suffixes. Small class size and a good instructional staff are some of the key factors of the program, which seems to be extremely well received by gifted seventh-graders.

Table 11–1 shows a variety of examples of gifted programs in terms of grouping, frequency of contact, site, teaching arrangements, and needed resources (VanTassel-Baska, 1981). These can fit reasonably well into the strategies noted above, and each adds relatively little cost to the educational process.

Technology: A Learning Tool for Independence

The potential of technology in education is still unfulfilled. Much of the current use of the advanced technology that has exploded over the last couple of decades has been limited to the design of exercises on basic skills learning or reproductions of workbook-type activities. It may be one of the advantages of programs for gifted students that they can explore some of the more adventuresome uses of modern technology in order to illustrate the full potential of these new tools. Barr (1990) presented some examples of how to integrate new technology into educational goals.

Making Learning More Independent

One of the fundamental goals of education for gifted students is the commitment to help the learners become more independent. A number of new technologies can help overcome the limits set by a particular teacher or library.

Electronic Data Bases
Electronic data bases store the content of books and periodicals, bibliographic data from libraries, pictures (including both art and photography), and numerical data from scientific experiments. Access to such data bases may be achieved by linking a computer to on-line data bases such as On-Line Public Access Catalog (OPAC). OPAC is available through many libraries, which may provide free public dial-up numbers to help students locate appropriate information with minimal time and effort.

There are also laser discs that can contain an optical storage technology by which dynamic visual data, such as motion pictures, can be kept stored. Since they are graphics oriented, they can provide another dimension beyond print for the student who is searching for needed information.

Making Learning More Individualized

The unique nature of the learning styles and the advanced knowledges that many gifted students possess make individualization an important goal of their education.

TABLE 11–1   Some Examples of Low-Cost Gifted Programs

	Example Program A	*Example Program B*	*Example Program C*	*Example Program D*	*Example Program E*
Grouping Procedures	Shared instruction periods coordinated through individual education plans made by regular teachers.	Cluster grouping of primary-level gifted students to a class. Other students are also assigned.	Part-time class of gifted children from a mixed grade grouping for grades 3–5.	Separate course/class for gifted middle school students or cluster in class with other students.	Individual mentorships or internships set up with community resource persons.
Frequency of Contact	150 minutes per week for shared instruction, ongoing differentiated education in regular classroom.	All day.	One hour per day or portion of one day per week (about 300 minutes total per week).	One class period or more per day, depending upon students' needs.	Two hours or more per week.
Site	Each school: Grades 4–6.	Each school: Grades 2–3.	Each school: Resource room, media center, etc.	Each school.	Home studio or work site of mentor.
Teaching Arrangement	All 4th–6th grade teachers plan together once a week for gifted students and arrange for a group contact time under leadership of teacher or other person.	One regular primary teacher works with cluster of gifted and with other assigned students.	Itinerant teacher or regular teachers freed for one hour per day work with students.	Junior high teacher conducts advanced instruction in subject as part of regular load.	Students are given release time to pursue independent research generated by mentor or internship. School coordinator meets regularly with students and mentors to discuss progress.
Resources Needed	Training of all teachers involved, plus materials.	Aide, resource teacher, and/or volunteers to assist, plus training for teacher, plus materials.	Training for teachers, plus a room or an area to conduct class, plus materials.	Training for teachers, plus some materials.	Volunteer mentors, plus transportation to off-school sites, plus a coordinator to find mentors, match students with mentors, and monitor progress.

Source: From Joyce VanTassel-Baska, *An administrative guide to education of gifted and talented children.* Washington, DC: National Association of State Boards of Education, 1981, p. 18. Reprinted by permission.

Computer-Aided Instruction

Although many such programs are basic-skills oriented, there are programs called Intelligent Computer-Aided Instruction that build up a model of what the student is thinking and provide new problems, questions, and information to foster the higher-level cognitive abilities in students (Resnick & Johnson, 1988).

There are also new programs of *hypertext* and *hypermedia*, which allow for a nontraditional search through existing material. One hypertext data base might consist of a series of texts such as a novel, reviews of the novel, a biography of the author, and historical events linked to the novel. The teacher could establish links between the passages in the text and the biography or historical documents that the student could explore.

Making Learning More Interactive

Learning that is accompanied by intelligent feedback is highly valued by most teachers, but how can educators accomplish this goal with the high teacher-to-pupil ratios common today?

Video Projection System

Collaborative learning can be attained by linking a projection system to video disk players, satellite down-links, and computers. The images on the screen can be manipulated by the students or teacher so that an interactive problem-solving approach can be pursued by an entire classroom.

Expert Systems

Specialized tutorial programs that can analyze student essays on grammar, syntax, and usage can free teachers from such drudgery and help them to concentrate on the conceptual message of the essay itself. Further, the criticism of the computer is more impersonal and neutral and does not involve the teachers in negative interchanges with the students. Instead, they can mediate any dispute between computer program and student.

Telecommunications Networks

Although tutoring by experts has been highly regarded as an excellent instructional strategy by educators in gifted education, it often fails because of the complicated logistics of getting the student to the tutor or vice versa. Computers linked to telecommunication networks can enhance and extend on-site visits with remote access to people, information, and services needed to maintain the continuity between on-site visits. Electronic bulletin boards also can allow students to ask questions, exchange information, and query data bases.

Making Learning More Interdisciplinary

One of the substantial advantages that gifted students possess is the ability to see linkages or associations between bodies of information. To add to this natural skill, other tools to enhance learning must be provided.

Generic Computer Problem-Solving Tools

Spreadsheets can be used to organize and analyze data from laboratory experiments in physics, chemistry, and biology. By manipulating the same data in different ways, the student can begin to see the similarities and differences in perspectives and problem-solving techniques between the various disciplines.

Simulations

The use of simulation software tools on the computer can simulate interdisciplinary problems that can help the student see the interconnections between disciplines, as well as see how important data can be obtained from a variety of disciplines in order to solve a problem. A problem on reducing environmental pollution, for example, may include information from chemistry, biology, and even social psychology that must be integrated to reach a solution.

Making Learning More Intuitive

Intuitive learning—that is, learning through nonrational or nonlogical means—is often prized by teachers, many of whom have little idea about how to enhance it.

Visualization Technology

High-resolution graphics programs allow students to explore the structure of complex molecules in three dimensions and to see microscopic activities, such as cell mitosis, as a dynamic process in real time. Such visual representations can add materially to the students' ability to understand such complex processes in ways that words alone cannot.

Graphing and Modeling

Programs that translate complex calculus equations into visual representation allow for some intuitive understanding not possible in two-dimensional, static print pages.

Despite these remarkable advances, such tools are rarely more effective than the people who use them. As Barr concluded, "Without a thorough understanding of the problems and a careful matching of the tools to the problems we propose to solve, technology will remain a solution in search of a problem" (1990, p. 93).

Acceleration

One of the most time-honored program adaptations has been to move gifted students through the system faster—a device called *student acceleration*. This technique is used primarily to shorten the long period of time that gifted students find themselves in an educational setting. This type of individual acceleration is to be distinguished from the *content acceleration* noted in earlier chapters, where the materials designed for older children were provided to these fast-developing youngsters. It is not uncommon for gifted students to spend close to a quarter of a century in school before beginning productive careers.

The basic purpose of acceleration, then, is to move these students more rapidly to the end of their apprenticeships and launch them into careers. The methods for doing this are widely varied, and the results that have been reported have almost always been favorable. One should not suppose, however, that because the evaluations have been positive the practice is either widely used or widely accepted. The need for such a move can best be illustrated with facts everyone knows about but still forgets from time to time.

As Table 11–2 shows, gifted students who anticipate being physicians are faced with the problem that they will be 18 years old by the time they finish high school, 22 years old by the time they finish college, 26 years old by the end of medical school, and, by the time they finish an internship or residency (to say nothing of other special training they might receive), they will be at least 29 or 30 years of age before starting productive work in their profession or career. Similar requirements can be found in many of the other professions and sciences.

Therefore, any educational adjustment that would reduce this extended period of time by at least two or three years could be of great benefit to the individual and to the culture, even in the absence of changes in the actual educational program that the youngster receives. It is important to remember that by the end of the sequence just noted, the student has been physiologically mature for as many as 15 years and many agemates may have been gainfully employed for 10 years. Yet many gifted students may remain intellectually and financially dependent through the most physically vigorous part of their adult lives.

Table 11–3 shows the various methods of acceleration for gifted children open to the teacher and the school administrator at practically all levels of the educational program. At the primary level, this includes admittance to kindergarten before the usual beginning age of 5 years. Another method has been the ungraded primary program. This provision enables a group of bright students to remain with one teacher, who will attempt to accomplish the goals of their primary year (grades K–3) in less than a four-year period. This technique also allows slow learners more than four years to complete the primary level, if that seems desirable.

The junior high years can be shortened by reducing the three-year program to two years, and the senior high program can be reduced either by early admittance to college or by inclusion of seminars in various subject areas that would qualify for college credit, as in the Advanced Placement program noted earlier. Even in college, the student may take

TABLE 11–2   Age of Completion of Educational Benchmarks for Medical Student

School Program Completion	Expected Age
Elementary school	12
Middle school	15
Senior high school	18
College	22
Medical school	26
Internship	27
Residency	29

TABLE 11–3   Most Common Methods of Acceleration of Gifted Students

Grade Level	*Type of Acceleration*
Primary (K–3)	1. Early admittance to school 2. Ungraded primary
Intermediate (4–5)	1. Ungraded classes 2. Grade skipping
Middle school	1. Three years in two 2. Senior high classes for credit
Senior high	1. Extra load—Early graduation 2. Advanced Placement

tests for course credit without having to sit through the course itself; this also represents a type of acceleration.

What is needed to make acceleration for gifted students work is a thorough knowledge of the needs and abilities of the individual person and of the administrative organization. This, together with genuine understanding for this type of action, will allow the goals to be accomplished with minimum personal dislocation of the students.

There is always the question as to whether *every* gifted child needs or benefits from acceleration. The answer is a resounding no. Consider, for a moment, Cranshaw, Zelda, Stephanie, Joe, and Sam. Sam, with his deficiencies in language development and his motivational problems, probably would not benefit and might even be harmed by any ill-advised attempt to accelerate him to a higher educational level. The same may be said for Joe. His inability or unwillingness to cooperate or to work even at his present level of ability makes it unlikely that putting him in an even more difficult competitive situation would stimulate him to more extensive action. Stephanie already has problems with content areas in which she has little interest. Acceleration, for her, may be useful at a later time.

Acceleration does seem to be reasonably feasible for Zelda and Cranshaw, as they are both doing well in their schoolwork. Zelda's personal problems, however, would remain, regardless of whether she is or is not accelerated. Some educational action would need to be taken on these problems, *in addition to* any possible acceleration. In this regard, it is worth noting that acceleration should never be considered as a substitute for other program differentiation; it should be considered merely a supplement to it. It probably will solve only the problem of the extended school program. Other problems will have to be dealt with in other ways. Since both Cranshaw and Zelda most likely are headed for professional work, the total time they spend in the educational system should be considered carefully.

There has been a rare consistency on the results of acceleration over the years. A few samples will suffice. As a result of their followup study, Terman and Oden suggested:

> *It is our opinion that nearly all children of 135 IQ or higher should be promoted sufficiently to permit college entrance by the age of 17 at least, and that the majority of this group would be better off entering at 16. Acceleration of this*

extent is especially desirable for those who plan to complete two or more years of graduate study in preparation for a professional career. (1947, p. 281)

A recent attempt has been made to synthesize all the available research results of the effects of acceleration on the performance of gifted children. Kulik and Kulik found 26 studies that compared students who had been accelerated for a year with comparison groups of equivalent ability. The studies came to the following conclusions: "Talented youngsters who were accelerated into higher grades performed as well as the talented older pupils already in those grades. In the subjects in which they were accelerated, talented accelerates showed almost a year's advancement over talented same-age nonaccelerates" (1984, p. 89). Such analysis is reassuring about the gifted students' ability to handle the academic challenge of the higher level, but it does not answer the question of socioemotional adjustment.

A more recent study of 65 early entrants into college found similar results (Brody, Assouline, & Stanley, 1990). On the basis of Scholastic Aptitude Test scores and previous academic performance, 65 students were selected to enter Johns Hopkins University two years earlier than the typical entrant. One-third of these students graduated in 3 1/2 years or less. Of them, 42 percent graduated with general honors, 35 percent with departmental honors, and 26 percent with Phi Beta Kappa status. Of the total 65 students, 8 withdrew before graduating, which is a smaller percentage than that of the entire class entering the same year, and 4 of these 8 students transferred to other universities where they all graduated—one with honors.

Despite these favorable results, there are still considerable negative attitudes found in educational circles toward this acceleration approach. These negative attitudes are apparently based on experiences with an individual child (Southern & Jones, 1991). The real reasons for the strong opposition to acceleration that one finds in school systems probably lie not in the actual research data, which are highly favorable, but in some hidden concerns or anxieties of both parents and teachers regarding this practice. One possible reason that has been suggested is the premature thrusting of the child out of the parental nest into the life of higher education.

After all, a child and a parent have only so many years together. Acceleration means that the child will leave home one or more years earlier than usual. However, this does not explain the concern of teachers for this procedure. Many teachers are worried about how such a procedure will affect the social and emotional life of the child and also about whether skipping ahead will not result in the child's missing some basic skills or knowledge.

Many educational administrators are concerned more with *operational feasibility*, or the ability to put a good idea into effective action, than with the research literature. As just noted, it is well established in the literature that early admittance to school—or admitting youngsters at the age of 4 or 4½ who have the requisite emotional, intellectual, and social development—does no lasting harm to children. It has the advantage of cutting a year off their total educational program, without their missing any of the curriculum. Nevertheless, very few school systems have adopted this procedure because of the problem of operational feasibility.

In order to put this provision of early admittance into effect in a school system, one must have some method of screening the 4-year-olds in the community to find out which of these children have the necessary characteristics to be accelerated. This procedure requires such expense in terms of professional time and diagnostic testing that it has been considered not feasible by most school systems.

One of the ritual statements made by educators is that each student should be allowed to progress at his or her own rate. When this philosophy is checked against actions in the case of acceleration of the gifted, one finds a puzzling contradiction. Despite the predominance of evidence in favor of it, very few systems implement this practice.

Program Accountability

Since 1965 and the War on Poverty, the U.S. public has been holding an increasingly wary and dubious view of the work of the public schools. During the 1960s, the schools were given an impossible task (reform the society, eliminate discrimination, and counteract the effects of poverty). When the schools did not accomplish these ambitious goals, alarm bells went off. Increasingly, the general public now wants to have some demonstrable proof that programs work (i.e., the programs do what their proponents say they will do). Programs for gifted students are not exempted from this requirement. They need to show benefits just as other programs do, especially since there is more money being expended for these programs.

Program Costs

The excess or additional costs of programs for the gifted have never been considered high, especially when compared with the costs of other special programs. Gallagher, Weiss, Oglesby, and Thomas (1983) attempted to obtain some cost ratio of how much extra is spent on programs that follow the popular strategies of teacher consultant, resource room, or special class. Local program directors, nominated by state directors of programs for gifted education as directors of exemplary programs, answered a survey on program costs. The biggest budget item in all programs was personnel.

The median cost for the resource-room strategy per pupil was 30 percent over the regular cost. The special class was somewhat less, at about 27 percent higher than average, and the teacher consultant was 16 percent higher. These were modest costs compared with special programs for children with retardation or learning disabilities that spend well over 100 percent in excess of the costs of the average student. The key to the viability of programs for children with disabilities is that much of these excess costs are assumed by the state and federal government and are not the responsibility of the local school system. The modest costs of programs for gifted students are not assumed at all by federal sources and rarely by state resources. Thus, the responsibility for bearing these excess costs—even though they are relatively small—usually falls on the local system, which all too often has financial difficulties.

Costs are only one side of the issue, however; *benefits* are the other. How can the benefits of these special programs be illustrated?

Program Evaluation

There are few terms in education that can strike fear in the hearts of educational administrators as much as *program evaluation*. This is partly because, in the process of initiating the program, the administrators most likely have made many claims for positive outcomes of the program in question. Therefore, it is likely that any comprehensive examination of the results of the program will be perceived as a disappointment or, even worse, a resounding failure. However, since *accountability* has become one of the watchwords of modern education, everyone must all participate in some form of program evaluation, whether we like it or not. Accountability, in practical terms, translates into the questions, Did you do what you promised to do? Did anything else of a negative or positive character occur? and Where is the evidence to support your claims?

Those who begin major innovations must now present specific goals and objectives, together with anticipated outcomes, if they expect to receive major financial support. The key question to be answered by the program developer is: In what way do I expect these gifted students to behave or perform as a result of this special program, which they would not have in its absence?

An example of a typical goal in gifted education would be as follows:

> Goal: *Creative thinking in gifted students will be improved following the initiation of the special in-service training program.*

Although this does give the flavor of what the educator had in mind for her or his program, it is quickly apparent that such a statement is of limited use. *How much* improvement will take place? Shouldn't students be gaining in these abilities anyway, with the passage of time and age? How long after the initiation of the program should the improvement take place?

The development of more precise quantifiable statements of expectations are made through program objectives, as follows:

> Objective: *Students will improve by 25 percent on the Torrance Tests of Creative Thinking within six months of the beginning of the program.*

This stated objective gives a clearer idea about how much is expected to happen, to whom, and by what specified time. It also gives the base for what instruments would be used in a program evaluation to measure outcomes.

Summative and Formative Evaluation

Two patterns of evaluation strategy, first made popular by Scriven (1973), can be used in programs for gifted students: summative evaluation and formative evaluation. *Summative evaluation* involves collecting information that would be provided to a decision maker who is faced with whether to give or deny support to a particular program. In contrast, *formative evaluation* is designed to collect information that would allow the program staff to improve the existing program. The basic purpose of the formative evaluation is to provide data for systematic improvement.

Naturally, summative evaluation substantially increases the anxiety level of people in education. An unfavorable result can lead to dismemberment of the program itself. It would be advisable for teachers and principals not to make any unusual requests of the school administration within a week of a forthcoming summative evaluation, because the school atmosphere is likely to be charged with doubt, anxiety, and naked fear.

The climate surrounding formative evaluation is remarkably different. In this setting the visitors come as aides and helpers. Callahan, Covert, Aylesworth, and Vanco (1981) described a formative evaluation of a local gifted program. That program focused on the stimulation of gifted students through the development of advanced thinking processes as described by Bloom's taxonomy. The evaluation team identified several serious problems with regard to the program as it then existed.

1. Activities were connected to goals in only the loosest sense; objectives listed for activities were rarely curricular objectives.
2. Activities selected were not sequenced to allow for skill development.
3. Activities were not of the type that would allow for multiple levels of inquiry, as made necessary by the choice to use the same unit content for all students in the program.
4. Activities were brief and well below the abilities of the majority of the students.

Instead of delivering this set of negative comments and then walking away, leaving the responsibility to cope with them with the local administration, Callahan and colleagues maintained their contact with the program and did the following:

1. Constructed and reviewed the results of a questionnaire assessing familiarity and attitude of the program staff toward certain basic curriculum concepts
2. Presented the program staff with some options available in planning for scope and sequence across the four grades of the program; from these options, the program staff elected to develop 24 content units and use 6 per year so that all four grades would be using the same unit with no repetition of units for students across the four years in the program
3. Presented an example of curriculum documentation format based on one of the previously developed units that would identify the major elements of the unit and activities
4. Discussed program rationale goals and general organization for instruction with the program staff
5. Discussed criteria for assessing objectives, resources, and activities with the program staff (1981, p. 160)

This type of formative evaluation tends to be extremely valuable to local school systems that may have very capable staff members but nevertheless may be unaware of the curriculum development and planning models that can be used to develop effective differentiated curriculum for the gifted. The school systems can well use the technical assistance that comes through this process.

Authentic Assessment and the Gifted

The call for educational reform presents classroom teachers with many challenges, including changing curriculum structure, altering instructional strategies, and teaching to different kinds of student outcomes. Perhaps the greatest challenge, however, comes in finding new ways to tell whether or not students are benefiting from all of these changes. Although traditional modes of testing have been successful at predicting later school achievement, they are not as successful in predicting a student's ability to perform well when solving open-ended activities involving inquiry or problem solving (Archbald, 1991).

If teachers think of their time with students as a conversation, then assessments are perhaps one of the most potent means of communication. Through assessment, teachers say to their students what they think is or is not important learning. After all, students know that information that is not assessed in the classroom does not have to be learned—that is why Joe endlessly asks Mr. Jenkins that time-honored question, "Will it be on the test?" Joe knows that if he is not going to be tested on the information at hand, he does not really have to remember it. Traditional assessments—with their emphasis on finding a single right answer to a question, time limits on completion, and working in isolation—send messages to students that are completely in opposition to the new goals and standards being suggested in educational reform documents. Filling tests with items that have a single right answer says to students, "There is only one way of doing things! All questions in the world have one right answer!" Time limits tell students, "It is more important to think quickly than it is to think carefully!" and having students complete tests on their own is just another way of saying, "If you don't know something, *don't* go find the answer from someone who does! You have to be the expert in all things by yourself!"

These are bad messages for all students, but they are particularly troublesome for the gifted. Gifted students, who often use their academic skill as a primary source of self-esteem, are particularly sensitive to the tacit messages, so that they can respond in such a way that they will continue to be successful in school. Either they do so willingly, believing in the above messages, or cynically. Cranshaw has bought the message sent through traditional tests hook, line, and sinker. He earnestly memorizes the vocabulary lists and formulas so that he can successfully give back to his teachers what he thinks they want to see. Stephanie sometimes gets so frustrated with bubble forms and questions that do not allow her to show off her abstract reasoning skills that she thinks of school as just a series of hoops to jump through. For her, "real learning" happens somewhere outside of school. In either case, the students adopt detrimental attitudes and behaviors. Authentic assessments are advocated as a means of bringing real meaning and activity to the classroom.

The components of authentic assessment point to the importance of emulating realistic and professional behaviors in the classroom. Several examples of authentic assessments are scattered throughout the book. Although they look very different, authentic assessments share common characteristics and common goals. Wiggins (1989), who has worked extensively on this subject, outlined the basic components of authentic measurements of student achievement:

- Measurements are essential, not needlessly intrusive, arbitrary, or contrived to "shake out" a grade.
- Measurements are enabling, constructed to point the student toward more sophisticated use of skills or knowledge.
- Measurements are contextualized, complex intellectual challenges, not atomized tasks corresponding to isolated outcomes.
- Measurements involve the student's own research or use of knowledge, for which content is a means.
- Measurements assess student habits and repertoires, not mere recall or plug-in skills.
- Measurements are representative challenges, designed to emphasize depth more than breadth.
- Measurements are engaging and educational.
- Measurements involve somewhat ambiguous (ill-structured) tasks or problems.

Self-assessment is a particularly important component of authentic assessment. When instructors take on the role of sole judge of student work, it is very hard for students to understand why good work is good and bad work is bad—it all seems very arbitrary. However, when students are made to take a critical look at their own work and evaluate it on their own, they begin to learn why they make the grades they do. At the same time, they gain control over improving their work, since they have a greater understanding of what is necessary to perform well. To make self-assessment really work requires some structuring on the teacher's part, though. An example of a well-structured self-assessment exercise is presented in Figure 11–5. To create an environment for successful self-assessment, the assignment has some key features incorporated. First, the instructor clearly states his or her *philosophy of assessment and grading*, making his or her own values known. Second, the instructor states equally clearly his or her *own expectations* for the students and acknowledges that the process may be awkward for them at first. Third, the instructor lets the students know that he or she will be *monitoring their ability to self-assess*, suggesting that the task is to be taken seriously. The instructor also allows students to assess his or her ideas and asks for their reaction to his or her approach in the first question. Finally, the instructor *asks the students to set a goal for the assignment* and for improving their performance the next time, sending the clear message that no matter how good their last assignment was, there is always something that can be improved.

By guiding gifted students through this process, they learn to become independent of other people's judgment. Many gifted students learn how to take small steps toward improvement rather than set their standards so high they are bound to fail. Others learn not to be overly critical of their own work as they see their instructors look at a paper as a work in progress instead of the ultimate product. All the while, they are learning what professionals value in good work and how to set and meet appropriate goals of their own making at their own pace.

FIGURE 11–5   Junior English Assessment

Self-Evaluation of Essay 1

My evaluation of your work is really a secondary device in service of a primary goal: Like a coach, I urge you on, push you to struggle more, guide you in developing techniques for a more elegant performance. Grades let you know where you are in that process and sometimes they motivate. But the primary goal is self-motivation. I do not want to grade in order to make you learn. Rather, I want to work with students who have their own learning goals. And if you have your own goals, you need then to assess your own progress. In working for yourself, you have made the critical step toward becoming an independent thinker.

Each time I make a major assignment, I will expect you to have set a goal for yourself. Perhaps, in writing this essay, you wanted mainly to understand better the three works, or perhaps you wanted a clearer understanding of the concept we have been studying. Perhaps you wanted to state a clear and workable thesis. Or maybe you wanted to concentrate on writing unified, coherent paragraphs. For a few of you, the main goal was simply to get the assignment over with. For some of you, setting a personal goal for an assignment will at first be extremely artificial, but at the outset, any new effort is uncomfortable and awkward. By rehearsing the effort, we begin to make it fit us, and in time our performance is nearly natural.

In completeing this form, you are beginning a rehearsal of self-evaluation. You will turn in these forms to me, but I will give them back to you. You will add them to your folder of written work.

1. What is your personal reaction to the philosophy of evaluation presented to you here?
2. Is the grade on this essay congruent with the expectations outlined in the assignment sheet? Explain why you believe you have received the grade assigned.
3. What goal did you set for yourself in writing this essay?
4. To what extent were you successful in meeting that goal?

Source: Barbara Allen Taylor, Illinois Mathematics and Science Academy. Reprinted by permission.

Portfolio Assessment

Portfolio has become a very popular word in educational jargon, but some people are confused as to what the word means. A portfolio is really just a folder of representative work, like the folder of work an artist keeps to demonstrate the range of his or her ability, or a stock portfolio, which would reflect the scope of someone's financial investment. Actually, a lot of elementary teachers already keep student portfolios—in folders of work use to keep their students' work organized! The difference is that in a portfolio, as it is currently discussed, the folder contains only representative work selected because is meets a certain criteria or purpose. Portfolios generally are structured to be either process based or product based. A process-based portfolio contains all of the work associated with a single assignment or unit, showing the development of a student's line of thinking from rough idea to finished work. A product-based portfolio would contain only end products—but a wide range of those products, with pieces selected by the teacher and the student to represent the student's best work. An especially effective culminating activity for students is to write an essay justifying why the work in their portfolio is best and what criteria they used to make their selections.

Implications of Authentic Assessment

All of the changes suggested by the educational reform movement in curriculum, instruction, and assessment provide exciting possibilities for altering approaches in the classroom in ways that have always been promoted for gifted students: real-life applications of information, advanced conceptual reasoning and problem solving, and self-directed learning, among others. At the same time, teachers of the gifted need to join into the conversation about the impact of these changes to the way we think about gifted students. Factual recall is no longer a benchmark for advanced achievement, but what will takes its place? What would a student advanced in "habits of mind" look like? What happens to "standard practices," such as curriculum compacting, in a curriculum that is based on essential understandings and significant concepts? What does "acceleration" mean in a concept-based curriculum? Can out-of-level testing using the SAT be justified when the National Standards Project, the National Assessment of Educational Progress, and many state assessments are quickly making the transition to more open-ended and authentic measures of skill and aptitude (Simmons & Resnick, 1993; Archbald, 1991)? Just as with the rest of the education community, educators of gifted students will have to reexamine old practices under this new educational paradigm, and recast or replace those practices in light of new national goals.

If this type of performance assessment is such a great idea, then why hasn't it been tried before? The shortcomings of this approach are that performance assessments are expensive and difficult to score. How does one evaluate, for example, the responses to the use of songs and poems of the Civil War to illustrate historical context? This requires some additional training of the judges or teachers who would be evaluating such exercises.

So, performance assessments are difficult to design, difficult to score, and expensive to administer. But they do seem to capture—much more fully—the true learning of the student, and they should certainly be a part of any program assessment of gifted students.

Federal Program Investment

The federal government has traditionally not invested large sums of money in the education of gifted students, but the Javits Act of 1988 did provide some resources, particularly for those who were focusing on the identification of economically disadvantaged gifted students or who had model projects or demonstration projects that illustrated special programs to find and educate such youngsters. Figure 11–6 briefly describes the purpose and kinds of projects supported under the act. A more complete listing of Javits projects in place in 1992 can be found in Appendix E.

Personnel Preparation

No matter how elaborate the program or how clever the exercises, the differential efforts for gifted students depend heavily on the preparation and motivations of the teachers with whom the students come into direct contact. Are there special characteristics that set the teacher of gifted students apart from other teachers? Are there special skills that these teachers should master and special knowledges that they need to possess?

FIGURE 11–6   Jacob J. Javits Gifted and Talented Students Education Program

What Is the Purpose of the Program?

The Jacob K. Javits Gifted and Talented Students Education Act of 1988 is designed to provide financial assistance to state and local educational agencies, institutions of higher education, and other public and private agencies and organizations that provide educational services to gifted and talented students. Special emphasis is on students from economically disadvantaged families and areas, and students of limited English proficiency. The purpose is to initiate a coordinated program of research, demonstration projects, personnel training, and similar activities to identify and meet the special educational needs of gifted and talented students.

Who Is Eligible to Apply?

State educational agencies, local educational agencies, institutions of higher education, and other public and private agencies and organizations (including Indian tribes and organizations as defined by the Indian Self Determination and Education Assistance Act and Hawaiian native organizations) are eligible.

What Types of Projects Are Funded?

The following kinds of projects are funded under this program:
- Preservice and in-service training for personnel involved in the education of gifted and talented students
- Model projects and exemplary programs for the identification and education of gifted and talented students
- Projects that strengthen the capability of state educational agencies and institutions of higher education to provide leadership and assistance to local educational agencies and nonprofit private schools in identifying and educating gifted talented students
- Programs for technical assistance and information dissemination

The answer to these questions is a qualified yes. Most of the authorities in the field expect that the teachers working directly with gifted students should have obtained a solid elementary, middle school, or secondary education preparation. In addition to that, they should have then learned some special skills and knowledge that would especially prepare them to work with these students. Sometimes such additional skills and knowledge are obtained through organized college courses, other times through extensive workshops or summer programs. There is currently much diversity in the methods by which teachers obtain the necessary skills to work most effectively with gifted students.

The Teacher: Desirable Characteristics

One of the favorite pastimes of some educators is to produce long lists of desirable characteristics of teachers of the gifted. These lists can have a rather paralyzing effect. A casual reading of them can give the impression that no human being can live up to such a set of characteristics. For example, consider the following:

Good health and physical superiority

Versatility of interests

Creativeness and originality

Unusual proficiency in teaching subjects

Active participating member of the community

Clear and consistent philosophy of education

Knowledge of theories of learning

Excellent sense of humor

Abundant physical energy

Anyone who could identify with that particular list has few self-doubts. One might add that the list omits one other important characteristic—a complete ignorance of practical economics. Anyone with an abundance of these qualities should be able to achieve a position at the highest executive or professional level of our society. There is probably more nonsense and less evidence dispensed about the needed characteristics of the teacher of the gifted than almost any other single issue in this field of gifted education. The preceding list of the all-encompassing virtues of teachers of the gifted is a good example of such nonsense.

One has to wonder about lists that include phrases such as *creativeness and original-ity*, or *participating member of the community*, or *excellent sense of humor*. Does this mean that teachers of children who are mentally retarded should not have an excellent sense of humor or be creative? Or teachers of art history? If the problem is how much of a given quality one should have, should the teacher of the gifted have 10 "zangs" of humor as opposed to 6 "zangs" for the classroom teacher? There is no experience or research to support such distinctions.

Does a teacher of the gifted have to be gifted himself or herself? There is probably no more frequently posed question, often by teachers who understand full well their own intellectual limitations. Certainly the teacher should be of superior intellectual ability, but, even more important, he or she should possess the enthusiasm to continue to seek new ideas and to be a model of inquiry in the search for new knowledge.

Ms. Parker, Cranshaw's teacher the year before, secretly suspected that Cranshaw had already outdistanced her in several areas of knowledge. But Ms. Parker's value to Cranshaw as a teacher did not rest in her storehouse of knowledge as much as it did in her enthusiasm for searching out answers to questions. Her excitement over finding the answers to problems and testing the results through experiments is infectious and encour-ages her students to do the same. While some people's passion is hunting, driving a sports car, or physical fitness, Ms. Parker's passion is finding out more about the world around her. Long after the details of any particular lessons will be forgotten, Cranshaw and the other students in his class will remember Ms. Parker's enthusiasm for the hunt for new knowledge.

Professional Standards

Most existing personnel preparation programs for teachers working with gifted students are designed to build on an already obtained degree in elementary or secondary education. The professional standards jointly agreed upon by The Association for the Gifted (TAG) and the National Association for Gifted Children (NAGC) state, "Degree programs with a major emphasis in gifted education should be offered only at the graduate level" (Seeley, Jenkins, & Hultgren, 1979).

The purpose of a special training program is to provide those special skills and sets of knowledge that will enhance the capabilities of the already qualified teacher to cope with these gifted youngsters. There would seem to be five major program areas that find their way into standard training programs. These are listed below with a brief rationale for each.

1. *Understanding the development of gifted students and the major school adaptations made for them.* There is fundamental knowledge about the differential rate of growth and development for gifted students that the teacher needs in order to place into perspective what instructional changes must be made. It is also helpful to know how the schools traditionally have coped with the special needs of gifted students. One or two introductory courses dealing with these topics are the usual method for providing for those understandings.

2. *Understanding how children generate new knowledge and appreciating the special capabilities of gifted students for such knowledge generation.* Traditionally, these requirements are met with a combination of coursework—that acquaints the teacher with many of the models of creative or productive thinking (see Chapters 9 and 10) and practicum experience, which will allow the teacher to practice, under supervision, the various methods that have been developed from these productive thinking models. This combination of theory and experience is designed to allow the teacher to enhance the creative and productive abilities of these youngsters.

3. *Acquiring an in-depth knowledge in a given content field—a content specialty.* The rationale behind this requirement is that the teacher of the gifted should have some expertise in some content field and should be especially enthusiastic about learning in that special-interest area. In the secondary schools, this would be typically the content field in which the teacher would teach—physics, mathematics, history, and so on. Even in the elementary schools, however, where many elementary school teachers have received a cafeteria of content information in their regular education curriculum, it is important that the teachers have confidence in their own sophistication in some content field and have some visible enthusiasm for seeking more information in that area. This requirement is usually met with some collection or subset of courses in a given field, such as a block of three courses in economics, mathematics, language arts, and so forth.

4. *Understanding other social, emotional, and educational needs of the gifted through special courses or experiences in measurement, counseling, curriculum development, and so on.* The teacher needs to be aware of the personal needs and special social problems of gifted students and to be able to participate in teams of professionals who can help in these areas. In a well-organized educational program for the gifted, there will be many different professional staff members who have capabilities to add to the students' programs (counselor, psychologist, librarian, curriculum coordinator, etc.). The teacher needs some basic understanding of the special issues in measurement, curriculum, and counseling for the gifted if he or she is to communicate and work productively with the specialists in these other fields.

5. *Appreciating the special set of experiences learned on site, under supervision, working directly with gifted students.* Even the experienced teacher who is used to the normal pace in the classroom is often startled and greatly surprised by the rapidity with which complicated ideas may be mastered by gifted students.

Recently, The Association for the Gifted (TAG) developed a set of professional development standards that reflects the current view of the field (Parke, 1989). These standards are presented in Figure 11–7.

FIGURE 11–7   Professional Development Standards of The Association for the Gifted (TAG)

1. Coursework for initial teacher preparation includes systematic instruction in the nature and needs of gifted and talented students. Because most teachers have gifted and talented students in their classes, it is important that they understand the needs of these students and methods for their instruction.

2. Educators providing direct service to gifted and talented students have completed the following:
   • An undergraduate emphasis in liberal arts or a content area
   • Professional coursework in general teacher education and/or content area
   • Teaching experience
   • Specialized training in gifted child education in accordance with CEC/NCATE guidelines for teacher education majors, or demonstrated knowledge of the nature and needs of gifted and talented students for content specialists

   Direct service is given by any person involved in policy development, program planning, or program implementation.

3. Noncertified individuals who offer specialized instruction or mentoring for gifted and talented students demonstrate understanding of the nature and needs of these students.

4. Educators specializing in content areas demonstrate mastery of the content area(s) in accordance with CEC/NCATE standards for personnel preparation and sufficient knowledge of the content areas they instruct to provide effective differentiated instruction to gifted and talented students.

5. Educators specializing in content areas demonstrate mastery of the content area(s) in accordance with professional standards and sufficient knowledge of the nature and needs of the gifted and talented to provide effective differentiated instruction to these students.

6. Educators with administrative or instructional responsibility for programs including gifted and talented students implement plans for their own continuing professional development. Plans include study in areas pertinent to the educational or personal needs of the professional such as educating the gifted and talented, content areas, technology, instructional strategies, decision making, school reform, etc. Master teachers, internships, graduate study, and cooperative learning are among the strategies that can be used for professional development.

7. Professional development opportunities in gifted children's education are available on a regular basis to all staff members. Workshops, lectures, professional libraries, newsletters, visitations, and demonstration teaching are among the professional development opportunities that can be available to staff members.

Source: From *Standards for programs involving the gifted and talented* by B. Parke, 1ᶜ by the Council for Exceptional Children. Reprinted with permission.

One of the keys to effective programs for gifted students clearly is the special preparation of teachers who work with such students. A recent review of requirements for certification or endorsement by Karnes and Wharton (1991) identified 21 states that report such requirements. These requirements represent additional experiences, on top of a standard certification in a content field or in elementary and middle school education. Although the requirements vary from one state to another, most include (1) an introductory course on the special needs of gifted students, (2) counseling and curriculum development courses for the gifted, (3) preparation in identification and working with special population or problems of gifted students, and (4) practicum involving some degree of supervised instruction.

Administrators

Most of the statements of goals of the teacher training for teachers of the gifted have come from the trainers themselves—professors who were preparing teachers. A different approach to this topic can be seen with administrators in a national survey by Cross and Dobbs (1987). They contacted all of the state directors for gifted and talented education and received an 80 percent reply to their request for rating various possible goals of a teacher training program.

These administrators rated practically all of the 20 items very high, with the highest being the ability to apply instructional models and educational strategies appropriate for use with the gifted and talented; to modify, adapt, and design special curricular units; to be aware of the educational and psychological needs of the gifted, and to identify procedures for culturally advantaged and culturally disadvantaged gifted. On the basis of these results, Cross and Dobbs believed that the course objectives in the special training program for teachers of the gifted should be as follows:

1. *The elements of curriculum design and instructional techniques, educational strategies, and appropriate delivery systems;*
2. *Educational and psychological needs and characteristics of the gifted and talented with specific attention to identification procedures for academic, creative, culturally disadvantaged, and the handicapped gifted;*
3. *Appropriate methods of program and student evaluation. (1987, p. 171)*

Unresolved Issues

1. One of the most conspicuous forms of intellectual waste involves keeping gifted students in the dependent role of student for as many as 25 years—a quarter of a century! In what ways can that time be shortened so that their talents can be used more productively to their benefit and to the benefit of society?
2. More effort is needed in helping the regular classroom teacher provide a better environment for gifted students. In elementary and middle school, most gifted children, even those in special part-day programs, will spend more time with their own teacher than with a specially trained resource teacher. The attitude and

skills of the classroom teacher are an often hidden source of potential strength in these programs.

3. Program evaluations of educational adaptations for gifted students often suffer from the lack of technical skills and understanding of the special evaluation problems posed by gifted students (e.g., the "ceiling effect" of many tests), so that the full abilities of the gifted students are not assessed. How can sophistication in program design be blended with sophistication in evaluation design so that the true measure of program value is captured?

Chapter Review

1. Most administrative variations for gifted education are designed to accomplish three things: (1) allow gifted students to interact with one another, (2) reduce intellectual and academic variance within the instructional group, and (3) place students with more knowledgeable teachers.

2. Current administrative options for program adaptation range from the most minimal change, *enrichment in the regular classroom*, to the most dramatic, *special schools*, with many variations in between.

3. Extra-school activities—after school, Saturday classes, summer programs—provide additional experiences in many communities. These extra-school activities often rely on outside personnel and resources beyond the school system.

4. The structure of the secondary school, by content subjects, dictates different types of educational adaptations, resulting principally in *Advanced Placement* and *independent study* programs.

5. Technology is advancing in many ways to make learning more independent, individualized, interactive, interdisciplinary, and intuitive. Two problems are that the hardware is expensive and the software is difficult and time consuming to produce.

6. An additional administrative adaptation to be considered is *acceleration*, or moving students through the educational system more rapidly in order that they complete the program and enter their careers at an earlier time.

7. The results of acceleration show few negative and many positive results when the acceleration is limited to one or two years.

8. Educational reform and restructuring are modifying general education and, consequently, education of gifted students. The middle schools, cooperative learning site-based management, and outcome-based learning are among the most popular of new structures and philosophies under trial.

9. Special programs such as *consultant teacher* or *resource rooms* appear to average 15 to 30 percent excess costs for each student. Such costs are modest when compared to the costs of programs for other exceptional children.

10. New requirements of program evaluation, performance assessment, and portfolio evaluation have resulted in special efforts to demonstrate, in some fashion, the impact of the special programs on gifted and talented students.

11. *Formative evaluation*, which yields information that can be used to improve the quality of an existing program, seems generally preferable to *summative evaluation*,

which yields only information that will decide whether to keep or abandon a program.

12. Reviews of the few program evaluation attempts have revealed generally positive results from programs in improving thinking processes and mastering high-level concepts.

13. The additional funds now provided by the states for gifted education are divided quite unequally across the country, with 27 states providing $1 million or less a year and 7 states providing $5 million or more a year to local schools.

14. The Javits program is a federal initiative in the education of gifted students offering school systems and universities resources to establish demonstration or exemplary programs, focusing on "hidden" gifted students. A national research center on gifted and talented was also established as a result of this legislation.

15. Special education preparation for teachers educating gifted students generally consists of a set of courses and experiences that are added to general elementary or secondary teacher preparation programs. Courses on the special needs of gifted students, differential curriculum and counseling, and assessment and evaluation, plus a practicum experience, are often included in such programs.

Readings of Special Interest

Buchanan, N., Feldhusen, J. (Eds.). (1991). *Conducting research and evaluation in gifted education.* New York: Teachers College Press.
This is a collection of chapters written by various experts on this increasingly important topic. Parts of the book focus on research and evaluation design, the applications of those designs to gifted education, and the uses of special evaluation instruments.

Daniel, N., & Cox J. (1988). *Flexible pacing for able learners.* Reston, VA: Council for Exceptional Children.
This book spells out the many different possibilities that exist for gifted students in schools wishing to move their students ahead on the basis of mastery of the curriculum. The term flexible pacing *incorporates such differentiated programming as early entrance to school, advanced level courses such as advanced placement, concurrent enrollment in high school and college, compacted courses, grade skipping, continuous progress, and credit by examination. Some specific examples of school systems engaged in flexible pacing are provided.*

Kulik, J. (1992). *An analysis of the research on ability grouping: Historical and contemporary perspec-* *tives.* Storrs, CT: The National Research Center on the Gifted and Talented.
This is one of the most authoritative reviews of the literature on ability grouping and its effects on students, with a particular emphasis on the effects on gifted students. Kulik discusses the various attempts to conduct meta-analyses on the wide range of studies that have addressed this interesting topic. He concludes that when a differentiated and accelerated curriculum is provided to gifted students, there appears to be substantial gains in favor of ability-grouped programs.

Silverman, L. (Ed.) (1993). *Counseling the gifted and talented.* Denver: Love Publishing.
This book is a compilation of chapters written by various experts in the field of counseling of gifted children. The book includes discussions of individual counseling, family counseling, group counseling, and the role of counseling in the schools. Many of the chapters feature the theory of Dabrowski on overexcitability (oversensitivity to stimulation) of gifted students as a way of understanding the special personal problems of gifted students and of directing the type of counseling approach that should be taken.

Southern, W., & Jones, E. (Eds.). (1991). *The academic acceleration of gifted children.* New York: Teachers College Press.
A selection of offerings help bring the reader up to date on the variety of evidence and opinion on the diversity of strategies that are included under the term *acceleration. Some insight can be gained as to why practitioners still have serious doubts about this educational strategy.*

References

Archambault, F. X., Jr., Westberg, K. L., Brown, S. W., Hallmark, B. W., Zhang, W., & Emmons, C. L. (1993). Classroom practices used with gifted third and fourth grade students. *Journal for the Education of the Gifted, 16* (2), 103–119.

Archbald, D. (1991). Authentic assessment: Principles, practices, and issues. *School Psychology Quarterly, 6* (4), 279–289.

Barbe, W. B. (1955). Characteristics of gifted children. *Education Administration and Supervision, 41,* 207–217.

Bartkovich, K. (1988). Motivating the most capable youths in mathmatics and science. In J. Dryden, S. Gallagher, G. Stanley, & R. Sawyer (Eds.), *Proceedings of the Talent Indentification Program/National Science Foundation Conference on Academic Talent.* Durham, NC: Talent Identification Program.

Barr, D. (1990). A solution in search of a problem: The role of technology in educational reform. *Journal for the Education of the Gifted, 14,* 79–95.

Brody, L. E., Assouline, S. C., & Stanley, J. C. (1990). Five years of early entrants: Predicting successful achievement in college. *Gifted Child Quarterly, 34* (1), 138–142.

California State Department of Education. (1971). *Principles, objectives, and curricula for programs in the education of mentally gifted minors.* Sacramento.

Callahan, C., & Caldwell, M. (1986). Defensible evaluations of programs for the gifted and talented. In C. Maker (Ed.), *Critical issues in gifted education Vol. 1: Defensible programs for the gifted.* Rockville, MD: Aspen.

Callahan, C., Covert, R., Aylesworth, M., & Vanco, P. (1981). Evaluating a local gifted effort: A cooperative effort. *Exceptional Children, 48,* 157–163.

Cronbach, L. J. (1982). *Designing evaluation of education and social programs.* San Francisco: Jossey-Bass.

Cross, J., & Dobbs, C. (1987). Goals of a teacher training program for teachers of the gifted. *Roeper Review, 9,* 170–171.

Daniel, N., & Cox, J. (1985, September). *NASSP Bulletin,* pp. 25–30.

Delisle, J., Reis, S., & Gibbins, E., (1981). The revolving door identification and programming model. *Exceptional Children, 48,* 152–156.

Eisenberg, A., & George, W. (1979). Early entrance to college: The Johns Hopkins experience. *College and University, 54* (2) 109–118.

Evans, E., & Marken, D. (1982). Multiple outcome assessment of special class placement for gifted students: A comparative study. *Gifted Child Quarterly, 6,* 126–132.

Feldhusen, J., & Wyman, A. (1980). Super Saturday: Design and implementation of Purdue's special program for gifted children. *Gifted Child Quarterly, 24,* 15–21.

Freeman, J. (1987). The International Baccalaureate. *The College Board Review, 143,* 4–6, 40.

Gallagher, J. (1991). Educational reform, values, and gifted students. *Gifted Child Quarterly, 35* (1), 12–19.

Gallagher, J., Coleman, M., & Staples, A. (1989). *North Carolina School of Science and Mathematics: The second decade study.* Chapel Hill, NC: Carolina Institute for Child and Family Policy, University of North Carolina at Chapel Hill.

Gallagher, J., Weiss, P., Oglesby, K., & Thomas, T. (1983). *Report on education of the gifted: Surveys and evidence of program effectiveness.* Los Angeles: National/State Leadership Training Institute on the Gifted and Talented.

George, P. (1988). Tracking and ability grouping: Which way for the middle school? *Middle School Journal, 20* (1), 21–28.

Gold, M. J. (1979). Teachers and mentors. In A. H. Passow (Ed.), *The gifted and the talented: Their education and development.* Seventy-eighth yearbook of the National Society for the Study of Education: Part I (pp. 272–288). Chicago: University of Chicago Press.

Hansen, J. (1992). Literacy portfolios: Helping students know themselves. *Educational Leadership 49* (8), 58–61.

Hebert, E. (1992). Portfolios invite reflection from students and staff. *Educational Leadership, 49* (8), 58–61.

International Association for the Evaluation of Educational Achievement. (1989). *Science achievement in seventeen countries: A preliminary report.* Oxford: Pergamon Press.

Kaplan, S. (1979). Language arts and the social studies curriculum in elementary schools. In A. Passow (Ed.), *The gifted and talented: Their education and development.* Seventy-eighth Yearbook of the National Society for the Study of Education: Part I (pp. 155–168). Chicago: University of Chicago Press.

Karnes, F., & Wharton, J. (1990). *America 2000.* Washington, DC: U.S. Department of Education.

Karnes, F., & Wharton, J. (1991). Teacher certification and endorsement in gifted education: Past, present, and future. *Gifted Child Quarterly, 35* (3), 148–150.

Kirst, M. (1982). How to improve schools without spending more money. *Phi Delta Kappa, 64* (1), 6–8.

Knight, P. (1992). How I use portfolios in mathematics. *Educational Leadership, 49* (8), 58–61.

Kulik, J., & Kulik, C. (1984). Synthesis of research on effects of accelerated instruction. *Educational Leadership, 42,* 84–89.

Maker, C. (1982). *Teaching models in education of the gifted.* Rockville, MD: Aspen.

Martinson, R. 1972. An analysis of problems and priorities: Advocate survey and statistics sources. *Education of the Gifted and Talented.* Report to the Congress of the United States by the U.S. Commissioner of Education, and background papers submitted to the U.S. Office of Education. Washington, DC: U.S. Government Printing Office.

Martinson, R. (1983). *Readings on gifted/talented education.* Downey, CA: Los Angeles County Superintendent of Schools.

Mitchell, P. (Ed.). (1981). *A policymaker's guide to issues in gifted and talented education.* Alexandria, VA: National Association of State Boards of Education.

Mitchell, R. (1991). *Performance assessment: What it is and what it looks like.* Washington, DC: Council for Basic Education.

National Commission on Excellence. (1983). *A nation at risk: The imperative for educational reform.* Washington, DC: U.S. Government Printing Office.

Oakes, J. (1992). Can tracking research inform practice? Technical, normative, and political considerations. *Educational Researcher, 21* (4), 12–21.

Olson, N. (1981). Youngsters speed through fast-paced summer programs. *Educational Leadership, 39,* 97–100.

Parke, B. (Ed.). (1989). *Standards for programs involving the gifted and talented.* Reston, VA: Council for Exceptional Children.

Renzulli, J. (1975). *A guidebook for evaluating programs for the gifted and talented.* National/State Leadership Training Institute. Ventura, CA: Office of the Ventura County Superintendent of Schools.

Renzulli, J., Reis, S., & Smith, L. (1981). The revolving door model: A new way of identifying the gifted. *Phi Delta Kappan, 62,* 648–649.

Resnick, L., & Johnson, A. (1988). Intelligent machines for intelligent people: Cognitive theory and the future of computer-assisted instruction. In R. Nickerson & P. Zodhiates (Eds.), *Technology in education: Look toward 2000.* Hillsdale, NJ: Erlbaum.

Robinson, A. (1992). *Cooperative learning and the academically talented student.* Storrs, CT: The National Research Center on the Gifted and Talented.

Ryder, V. (1972). A docent program in science for gifted elementary pupils. *Exceptional Children, 38,* 629–631.

Scriven, M. (1973). Goal free evaluation. In E. House (Ed.), *School evaluation.* Berkeley, CA: McCutchan.

Seeley, K., Jenkins, R., & Hultgren, H. (1979). Professional standards for training programs in gifted education. *Journal for the Education of the Gifted, 4,* 165–169.

Shavelson, R., & Baxter, G. (1992). What we've learned about assessing hands-on science. *Educational Leadership, 49* (8), 20–25.

Simmons, W., & Resnick, L. (1993). Assessment as the catalyst of school reform. *Educational Leadership,* February, 11–15.

Slavin, R. (1988). Ability grouping and student achievement in elementary schools: A best evidence synthesis. *Review of Educational Research, 57,* 293–336.

Slavin, R. (1990). *Cooperative learning: Theory, research, and practice.* Englewood Cliffs, NJ: Prentice Hall.

Slavin, R. (1990). Research on cooperative learning: Consensus and controversy. *Educational Leadership, 47* (4), 52–54.

Stevenson, H., Stigler, J., Lee, S., Lucker, G., Kitamura, S., & Hsu, C. (1985). Cognitive performance and academic achievement of Japanese, Chinese, & American children. *Child Development, 56,* 718–734.

Stigler, J., Lee, S., & Stevenson, H. (1990). *Mathematical knowledge of Japanese, Chinese, & American elementary school children.* Reston, VA: National Council of Teachers of Mathematics.

Terman, L., & Oden, M. (1947). *The gifted child grows up: Twenty-five years follow-up of a superior group* (Vol. V). Stanford, CA: Stanford University Press.

Townsend, F. (1980). *Beginning and administering & advanced placement program in a secondary school.* Evanston, IL: College Entrance Examination Board.

VanTassel-Baska, J. (1981). *Results of a Latin-based experimental program for the verbally precocious.* Available from Gifted Area Service Center, Matteson School District 162, 21244 Illinois St., Matteson, IL 60443.

Wiggens, G. (1989). A true test: Toward more authentic and equitable assesment. *Phi Delta Kappan,* May.

$C\ h\ a\ p\ t\ e\ r$ *12*

Special Populations

Key Questions

- What factors lead to gifted girls being singled out as a special population deserving of special attention?
- What are some suggestions for educational programming that would be particularly appropriate for gifted girls?
- How does one determine who is a gifted underachiever?
- What are some methods for remediating gifted underachievers?
- What are some strategies devised for identifying culturally different gifted students?
- What are some distinctions between the assimilationist and pluralist positions in designing curriculum?
- How does one discover gifted students with disabilities (learning disorders, visual disabilities, etc.)?
- What are some different coping strategies used by gifted students with learning disabilities?
- What type of differentiated curriculum can be provided for gifted students?

There has been a greater realization that there are many students who are gifted but whose talents, for a variety of reasons, go unrecognized. These students represent a vast loss of potential for themselves, their community, and ultimately the nation. One of the major objectives for educators of gifted students is to find and provide appropriate educational services for this group of students.

The reasons why giftedness may go unnoticed are numerous. These students may come from a culture different than that of middle-class America, so that their patterns of giftedness are not familiar to many of their teachers. They may have disabilities (e.g., deafness) that hide their special abilities. They may be underachieving in a traditional school to the point that no one believes that they have special abilities, or they may be so young that they receive little attention in educational circles. In each of these conditions, the challenge is to recognize, plan for, and implement an educational program appropriate to the special needs of the individuals in these groups.

In this chapter, five subgroups will be identified that are sufficiently different from the norm of gifted and talented children to cause significant differences in both their general characteristics and in the educational provisions that are designed for them. Although these five groups do not, in any sense, comprise the full range of possible subgroups, they are recognizable in most school settings.

1. The gifted *girl* may find her talents unappreciated and unrewarded, and lack motivation to pursue academic excellence.
2. The *underachieving* gifted child has special motivational problems that are frustrating to many educators.

3. The *culturally diverse* gifted student may come from different societal subgroups with different values and rewards for giftedness.

4. The gifted student with *disabilities* may have a special problem, such as deafness or blindness, that hides his or her intellectual gifts.

5. The *preschool* gifted child may be too young for traditional programs for gifted children.

Gifted Girls

One of the special populations that appear to need some special educational attention is that of gifted girls. It is clear that Zelda and Stephanie are going to have a harder road to travel to reach a productive career than is Cranshaw, since the acceptance of boys' giftedness comes more easily than that of the girls in our society. The national need to encourage girls to enter into professional careers has been presented in Chapters 4 and 5; this section will concentrate on more general concerns regarding helping girls realize their own potential. As usual, there is no one simple explanation. A combination of social, psychological, and educational factors will be discussed.

Historically, women have been underrepresented among high achievers and innovators in the sciences, the arts, and the humanities. This lack of prominence has been attributed largely to the fact that women lacked the opportunity to excel in cultures that undervalued their potential. Some of the first comprehensive comparisons of the accomplishments of a select sample of gifted individuals was in the famous Terman Study. Less than 40 percent of the gifted students identified in the original longitudinal study by Lewis Terman were girls (Terman & Oden, 1947) and the women that were identified in that study turned out to be less productive as adults than the men in their career fields. There are some obvious reasons for such limited productivity, including the dual responsibilities carried by many women of child rearing and career (Jacklin, 1989). Nevertheless, there have been many indicators that there are other inhibiting factors in the U.S. culture itself that limit the full development of gifted girls.

Have the times changed? The Women's Movement of the 1960s and 1970s attempted to change the status of women in our culture. In a recent study, Eccles (1985) found women to be underrepresented in almost all advanced educational programs and high-status occupations, so the problem has not ended with the Terman era. Reis and Callahan (1989) have presented a similar portrait of the absence of women in high-level occupations in government, education, and the arts and professions (see Figure 12–1).

Although the situation has improved somewhat in government since the piece was written in 1989, the basic message remains the same. If we are concerned at all with the full use of talent in our society and for equality of opportunity, then the limited participation of women in high-level occupations must represent unfinished business of major proportions for education and for society.

If it is true that the social attitudes toward women have changed over the past two decades, one might reasonably expect that the situation for gifted girls would improve, too. To determine the effect of social change on the attitudes and traits of gifted women, Walker, Reis, and Leonard (1992) surveyed women who had participated in gifted

FIGURE 12–1   The Slow Progress of Gifted Women

Government
Two women in Senate (6 as of 1993)
One woman on Supreme Court
Less than 5% of House of Representatives (Less than 10%, 1993)
One female cabinet member (4 as of 1993)

Education
36% of National Merit semifinalists
2% of all school superintendents
9% of college and university presidents
10% of full professors in U.S. universities

Arts & Professions
No top positions in top five U.S. orchestras
13% of lawyers
13% of doctors
7% of architects
5% of executive positions in U.S. corporations

Source: Adapted from Reis, S. & Callahan, C. (1989). Gifted females: They've come a long way—or have they? *Journal for the Education of the Gifted, 12* (2), 99–117. Reprinted by permission.

programs across several generations. Participants in the study graduated from high school at some point in the time span from the 1920s to 1980s. Women who participated in the study responded to a questionnaire that asked about their backgrounds, their characteristics, and their attitudes toward a variety of issues associated with their talents. The results of the study indicated that over two-thirds of the women from each decade worked outside the home, but the percentage increased substantively to 85 percent in the 1960s and 95 percent in the 1970s.

Attitudes and characteristics of the gifted women in the study from different generations did differ. Some of the differences are a little surprising: Women who graduated from high school in the 1970s reported more dependence than shown in the 1940s or 1950s! However, other data are more predictable; young women reported being more assertive and more ambitious than did older women. The data were also analyzed according to whether the women were career oriented or homemakers, with results suggesting that homemakers were significantly more worried about being able to cope with life's varied demands than were career women. Although generational differences separated the women in some ways, the authors concluded with the finding that made them similar across the years: "The common concerns include a vague and traditional school and societal expectations, lack of challenging curriculum, concerns about or denial of being labeled gifted.... The women...also cited lack of role models, little organized mentoring and few networking skills, and 'unhelpful, unchallenging, and perfunctory guidance counseling'" (Walker, Reis, & Leonard, 1992, pp. 205–206). Evidently it does not matter what generation she is born in or the adult role she wishes to adopt, a gifted woman wants to be trained to use her gifts to her fullest capacity!

Another part of the changing social climate is the recognition that educators and others have used constricted notions of "achievement" when measuring the accomplishments of gifted women. What does "reaching your full potential" or "high achievement" really mean? Any number of women could assert that homemaker and parent are full-time, challenging jobs that require both skillful reasoning and ingenuity, even though there is no Nobel prize for being a great parent!

In a study of gifted women's achievements, Hollinger and Fleming (1992) expanded their view of "achievement" to include both traditional and nontraditional views of achievement. Some 126 gifted women who had graduated from high school in the 1970s responded to a questionnaire that asked them about their accomplishments. Answers to the question, "What do you consider to be your three greatest achievements since you graduated from high school?" fell into three general categories: traditional career achievements, relationship achievements (spouse, children, friends, or religious), and personal achievements (health, political, or personal growth). Evidently, women perceived "achievement" to be much more than just excelling in a profession. Another interesting finding was that women did not think of having a profession or family as an "either/or" proposition but as a "both/and" situation that needs to be balanced. "Achievement" in the view of many women is achieving a successful balance in integrating professional, personal, and relationship goals into their lives. Hollinger and Fleming make the following conclusions based on their data:

> *First, diversity of life pathways needs to be recognized and valued. Second,... the need to emphasize the development of coping with multiple role demands is confirmed. Third, concepts such as "achievement" and "realization of potential" must be examined, clarified, and broadened.... For gifted women, and to an unknown degree gifted men as well, "achievement" is not limited to educational degrees and career status but includes personal and interpersonal or relational achievements as well. (p. 212)*

Conflicting Life Goals

Zelda, as has been previously noted, often feels lonely and isolated from her peers. Gifted girls and women often report feeling this way as students (Kerr, 1985). While it may be that this isolation provides gifted girls with the necessary time to reflect and develop their talents, the social cost is often higher than it is for boys, since girls are more often expected to be gregarious and outgoing. In some respects, however, this isolation may be self-imposed. Studies that focus on the characteristics of gifted women have consistently shown that they are likely to report traits that are more often associated with the traditional concept of masculinity, including independence, assertiveness, and risk taking (Callahan, 1979).

Girls who adopt the more traditional feminine sex role of being demure or conforming are not likely to break new intellectual or creative territory! On the other hand, girls who have characteristics associated with achievement orientation do not have much in common with their average-ability classmates. The inability for a gifted girl to be perceived as simultaneously intellectually strong and feminine is a continuing "Catch-22" in our society.

Despite the fact that gifted girls and boys share many of the same characteristics associated with achievement and leadership, girls are identified less frequently for special programs than their proportions in the population. Where could the imbalance begin? One obvious place to look is in the proportion of girls referred and initially enrolled in programs for the gifted. Officials who refer and select students for gifted programs may carry with them old stereotypes of sex roles for boys and girls and may, with or without knowing it, make biased selections in favor of boys. Or, as girls get older and begin to face social pressures to conform, they may become harder to find. To guard against this possibility, Silverman (1986) has suggested that a major effort be made to identify highly able girls in kindergarten and primary grades before the negative social effects can have an impact on the girls and reduce the likelihood of their identification.

Crombie, Bouffard-Bouchard, and Schneider (1992) conducted a study to investigate possible differences in both the rate of referral (the number of students who are suggested for the gifted program) and the rate of acceptance into the program (the number of qualified students who decide to enroll in the program) for boys and girls. These researchers wanted to determine whether differences in enrollment for boys and girls might be due to the biases of adults conducting the admissions process or because girls who are accepted might be hesitant to enroll and perhaps be perceived as "unfeminine." The results of this study, conducted across five different school systems, revealed no significant differences in the numbers of boys and girls referred for the gifted programs, although some variation was seen across districts. While optimistic about their initial findings, the authors tempered their conclusions with the observation that getting girls into a program is only half the battle; the girls must be encouraged to stay in the program despite the occasional censure they may receive for being "a geek" (a problem also faced by gifted boys).

Looking at who stays in and who leaves gifted programs may help explain why gifted girls, though initially well represented, eventually disappear from such groups (Silverman, 1986). One of the most significant sets of facts to recall as we try to understand this phenomenon is that girls substantially outperform boys in academic achievement until adolescence. Then, a subtle change seems to take place in their aspirations, expectations, and attitudes and they become ambivalent about the value of seeming to be scholarly or interested in high academic performance (Kerr, 1985). This would clearly indicate that the problem rests in the differential social pressures and rewards that are provided to boys and girls during the middle school and secondary school years.

Fox and Zimmerman (1985) reported a study by Fox that revealed that girls were less likely than boys to favor acceleration for themselves. One of the reasons commonly cited was the social rejection associated with academic achievement. The key to whether or not girls supported the idea of their own acceleration seemed to be self-esteem: Girls who had high self-esteem were more likely to want to be accelerated. Thus, when presented with the same option, Stephanie, who has complete assurance with herself, would be likely to take the opportunity to move ahead, while Zelda, who is equally capable, might choose to stay behind in the hope of gaining social approval.

The schools can also play a role in discouraging girls. Teachers appear to believe that boys are better at mathematics and at logical thinking skills than girls (Ernest, 1978; Cooley, Chauvin, & Karnes, 1984).

School counselors may also be reticent to encourage girls to take higher levels of mathematics and science in high school, despite the fact that high-level math and science are gateways to many mathematics, science, and engineering careers. For example, Casserly (1980) found that high school counselors often failed to encourage gifted girls to take courses in the Advanced Placement program. Colangelo (1988) reported other, more subtle practices, including asking girls, but not boys, whether or not a particular career path would interfere with raising a family. Perhaps this is an excellent question, but excellent for everyone—not just girls!

School Adaptations

Changes have been suggested in student counseling procedures and in the educational programming itself. The above information has led a number of investigators and educators to suggest that a major effort should be made in the career counseling of gifted girls (Colangelo, 1988; Garrison, Stronge, & Smith, 1986; Harding & Berger, 1979). Shore, Cornell, Robinson, and Ward (1991) sum up the situation as follows: "Talented women experience special problems. Early intervention and preventive efforts are defensible, in order to minimize the expected adverse effects of to recognize that talented women are likely to experience intrapersonal and interpersonal conflicts in career decision making, and that counseling may stimulate thinking and inquiry that bring potential and actual conflicts to the surface" (p. 244).

Teachers should be sensitive to the needs of girls in the classroom. Through workshops directed at the treatment of girls in the classroom (Sadker & Sadker, 1984), teachers can learn to call on girls as often as boys, to give girls good feedback (both praising and criticizing), and to resist overhelping girls.

Other classroom adaptations could focus on varying the format of classroom presentation. A growing body of research supports the idea that most women reason by making connections and seeing relationships, whereas most men reason through analysis and taking ideas apart (Belenky, Clinchy, Goldberger, & Tarule, 1986; Gilligan, 1988). Structuring classroom activities so that there is a balance between using *dissecting analysis* and *constructing relationships* could help girls feel more entitlement toward traditionally male-dominated fields.

Hollinger and Fleming (1988) believe that a key factor for girls such as Stephanie and Zelda is that they attain a high level of social self-esteem and that it is the role of the schools to create situations and environments that will allow them to do that. Social self-esteem appears to be made up of two major elements: *instrumentality* (the belief that one has the ability to act effectively) and *expressiveness* (a sense of responsiveness and caring). Armed with social self-esteem, these girls can do competitive academic battle with boys of equal ability.

It is the personal attitude that girls such as Zelda and Stephanie have that would seem to be a key to their feeling comfortable in the advanced academic environments. Kerr (1991) sums up this feeling: "Throughout their education, gifted girls need to be encouraged to take risks. This means taking the most challenging course work available, engaging in play activities that are physically challenging and occasionally competitive, and learning to speak out and defend their opinions in groups" (p. 411).

One of the suggestions made to improve the social self-esteem of gifted girls in the educational setting has been "single-sex" schooling. Although some women's colleges were originally formed because women were not allowed in male colleges, there has been evidence that women graduating from such schools as Vassar and Bryn Mawr have achieved more than those who have come from coeducational settings. The girls in such a single-sex setting are freed from the traditional dominance of males in the classroom or laboratory and from the necessity of playing a social role that may not be helpful to their intellectual or vocational development (Kerr, 1991).

A particular example of such a program is the Mary Baldwin College's Program for the Education of the Gifted, an all-female program that combines the last two years of high school with college over the course of six years. The program stresses a strong academic program, career guidance, and individual attention (Garrison & Rhodes, 1987).

Fox and Zimmerman (1985) presented five questions that teachers and administrators should ask to help guard against bias toward gifted girls and women:

1. *Are approximately equal numbers of boys and girls being identified? If not, why not? Are the selection procedures biased or the provision more attractive to one sex than the other?*
2. *Do girls and boys who participate in educational provisions for the gifted achieve equally well? If not, why not?*
3. *Are efforts made to use non-sexist instructional materials and language laid down in the program? If not, why not?*
4. *Are girls and boys encouraged to participate in intellectual risk-taking to the same degree? If not, why not?*
5. *Are the expectations, aspirations, and confidence levels of boys and girls in the classes about the same? If not, why not? (p. 237)*

U.S. society is in the process of redefining the roles of men and women, and this process of redefinition will continue to have a significant impact on gifted girls of which educators should be aware.

Underachieving Gifted Students

Underachieving gifted students, ably represented throughout this book by Joe, consistently show far less academic performance than measures of their intellectual aptitude would cause one to expect. In order to identify such youngsters, at least two measurements are needed: one indicating high intellectual aptitude (almost always an IQ score or academic aptitude test such as the Scholastic Aptitude Test) and some measure of actual achievement (either school grades or achievement test scores). If the achievement scores are substantially less than the high aptitude would predict (for example, a grade average of C or only grade-level performance on achievement tests), then that student may be called an underachiever.

Joe's past academic record is peppered with teachers' comments to the effect that they suspect this boy is bright, but he never seems to produce. His reaction to pressure and to stern disciplinary measures has been wholly unsatisfactory. What is Joe's problem? What is the basis for his seeming reluctance to use his ability? Is it that the poor school program is not stimulating? Is it the unfortunate values and attitudes of his peer group? Does the answer rest in his family relationships? Is it a part of Joe's own personality makeup? Naturally, these questions have to be answered on an individual basis. However, very interesting patterns have evolved from investigations on chronically underachieving youngsters.

Given the obvious loss of potential that this group of children represents (although definite prevalence figures are hard to come by, most observers would suggest that they comprise at least 10 to 15 percent of the intellectually superior group), one would think that there would be a major focus on this problem by professionals in the field. Nothing could be farther from the truth. The clearest indicator of the lack of interest in gifted underachievers during the last two decades is the almost total absence of substantive research or programming for such students.

One of the apparent reasons for this sudden lack of interest in what ordinarily would be considered a fascinating and troublesome problem may be the change in the criteria established in many states for eligibility into the programs for gifted students. As these eligibility requirements increasingly stress *production,* or *already demonstrated excellent achievement,* then students whose motivation or past performance has been mediocre will tend to be squeezed out of programs for the gifted. They will become "out of sight, out of mind." There is a definite need for a rebirth of interest and special attention to this topic.

Characteristics of Gifted Underachievers

Despite the variations in the procedures used to determine underachievement from one research study to another, there is a remarkable consistency in the literature concerning those characteristics that set gifted underachievers apart from gifted achievers. Not surprisingly, the earliest data on this topic, aside from individual reports, emerged from the Terman longitudinal study.

In their longitudinal study of gifted individuals, Terman and his associates (Terman & Oden, 1947) identified 150 men who seemed to have produced the lowest level of achievement (in the sample) and compared them with 150 markedly successful men. Terman also had a portion of each of these groups of men rated on personality characteristics by their wives, their parents, and themselves. The self-ratings of the individuals and the ratings of wives and parents agreed on four major characteristics that differentiated these underachieving individuals from effective achievers. These characteristics were:

A lack of self-confidence
The inability to persevere
A lack of integration to goals
The presence of inferiority feelings

A look at the earlier school records of these individuals found that teachers' ratings showed similar differences between these youngsters in the 1920s, even at the preadolescent level. The personality patterns that set these two groups apart as adults apparently were manifested early in the school program. The clear implication of these findings is that unless some major attempt is made to counteract these trends at an early age, these underachievers will turn out to be relatively nonproductive members of society, to the detriment of both society and themselves.

Family Relationships

The available research studies suggest that there are often significant problems in the family relationships of gifted underachievers. Whether these poor relationships are the cause or the result of the poor achievement, or some unfortunate combination of the two, is not immediately apparent.

Although teachers often search for reasons that explain a student's underachievement in the classroom and their own rocky relationship with the student, evidence is becoming increasingly clear that many of the problems of the chronically underachieving student lie in a complex relationship problem in the home. Rimm and Lowe (1988) studied in detail the family situation of 22 students who had been referred to a clinic because of poor school performance during the preceding 12 months. All of these students had a WISC intelligence score of 130 or above.

There were many similarities between the families of underachieving gifted and those families where gifted youngsters were characterized by later eminence and high performance. In both cases, the parents were generally older and more highly educated, and the child in question was more often the first child. In both cases, the family valued work and achievement and provided a nonauthoritarian family environment. But the differences between these family environments were also striking. The relationship between the underachievers and their parents were quite often negative. Few of the boy underachievers identified with their father, or girls with their mother.

Rimm and Lowe (1988) focused on the problem of the parents giving too much attention and making too much of the gifted youngster during the preschool years, with the result that their adjustment to coping with siblings and peer competition later can be difficult. One common pattern in these families of gifted underachievers was that there was a choosing of sides where some of the children allied themselves with the mother and others with the father. In the parents' attempts to be reasonable and flexible, the parents were more often viewed by their children as inconsistent, weak, and manipulative.

Another interesting difference was that, although these parents stressed the importance of achievement, many of them complained bitterly about their own work situation. The fathers would tend to complain about the conditions of their job and the mothers would often complain about the time the professional fathers spent away from the family and that their own career goals went unfulfilled.

The child, with few positive role models and many negative emotions, appeared to drift into a pattern of chronic underachievement in the schools. This does not mean, of course, that the school is helpless or that the school environment is irrelevant to the situation, but full recognition of the total pattern of coping problems that the child is revealing could be helpful in putting the problem in context. Parental counseling on these issues may be one reasonable strategy in the program for any of these gifted underachievers.

Joe was once asked, along with his classmates, to write a composition, using a picture for a stimulus. The picture showed a boy staring out a window. There was no obvious story from the picture itself, so the theme and the feelings in the story had to come from within the students themselves. Joe's story went like this:

> This boy is thinking about how lucky some people are and how unlucky he is. He is thinking about Pete who lives down the street from him. Pete has a nice family, a father that goes fishing with him instead of yelling at him all the time; his teachers like him so he gets good grades and he has money to buy his own "Go Kart" [miniature gas-powered racer]. This boy wishes he could trade places with Pete.

Contained in this story, and in others of a similar type, are some of the themes often found in reactions of the underachiever. Somehow Joe's troubles are the fault of someone else or fate. His feeling of not being understood in his family is not an uncommon theme. Also, note how Joe resolves the story. He does not "take arms against a sea of troubles, and, by opposing, end them," but instead "wishes he could trade places" with the lucky one, ignoring the possibility that he could, through actions of his own, improve his situation.

The belief in luck and fate, or rather bad luck and ill fate, is often adopted when the individual no longer believes in himself or herself. Building the confidence of a student who wishes to avoid the very experiences that would bring self-confidence is a task that may need a team of people with varied professional experiences and insights to plan an educational strategy for Joe.

Figure 12–2 summarizes some of the manifestations of the bruised self-image of the underachiever that should surely be familiar to many teachers. These patterns of escape, shifting of blame, and denial have the unfortunate effect of compounding the original problems.

Although most of the discussions of the personal patterns of underachievement focus on the patterns of learned behavior that have emerged out of the family context, Silverman noted a particular pattern in the test profiles of gifted underachievers, which is also suggestive of a possible neurological imbalance in some underachieving students.

> *We have found remarkable consistency in the test profiles of underachievers; high scores in vocabulary, abstract reasoning, spatial relations, and mathematical analysis coupled with low scores in tasks requiring sequencing.... This pattern is indicative of a spatial learning style and also may suggest auditory sequential processing deficits. (1990, p. 312)*

Such youngsters resemble children with learning disabilities; they might require some specific educational attention either to improve such deficits or focus on their areas of special strengths (a specialist in learning abilities might help). Whitmore summed up the literature that has been collected on the distinctive personality and behavioral traits

FIGURE 12–2   Protecting the Bruised Self-Image of the Chronic Underachiever

What He or She Says	*What He or She May Mean*
School is terrible. Teachers are against me, and they aren't any good anyhow.	If the system is bad, no real blame can come to me if I don't succeed in it.
I think I would like to be a jet pilot, a movie star, or a politician.	I want to do thrilling and glamorous things, but I cannot stand a position with a long period of training preceding it or where sustained hard work is needed (e.g., surgeon, electrical engineer, or president).
I am not gifted, and those tests are crazy anyhow.	The label *gifted* puts the pressure on me to succeed. One way to take the pressure off is to lose the label.
Some people are lucky and some aren't. I wish I could hit it lucky for once. I dream about breaking the bank at Las Vegas.	If life is a game of chance, I am less personally responsible for my ultimate success or failure.
My old man is a grouch. He is from nowhere.	My father and I do not understand each other and cannot communicate. I cannot model myself after him.
Future? What future? The bomb will take care of our future. If not, things will work out somehow.	To think of the future requires planning and effort. These are too painful because I have failed too often before. I prefer to ignore it and to trust luck, to make things come out all right.

that describe many underachievers: "A negative self-concept, low self-esteem, expectations of academic and social failure, a sense of inability to control or determine outcomes of his efforts, and behaviors that serve as mechanisms for coping with the tension produced by conflict for the child in school" (1980, p. 189).

The School's Role

The school may not be able to do much about the relationship between Joe and his father, but they can do something about inappropriate pressures or assignments to Joe within the framework of the educational program. It is often within that limited scope and environment that educators are forced to operate.

Although much of the previous literature has focused on the characteristics of the individual—the gifted underachiever—many observers feel that there are some school climates that also can be considered a high-risk environment, where youngsters who tend to be underachievers will certainly be hastened to those nonproductive patterns.

Rimm has pointed out two such climates:

1. *An anti-intellectual school atmosphere that sets high priorities for athletics or social status, but not for intellectual attainment or preparation for higher level education.*

2. *An anti-gifted atmosphere that considers gifted programming to be elitist and emphasizes the importance of all students being "well adjusted" and "fitting into a mold." (1991, p. 329)*

These unfavorable environments would be expected to compound the problems of underachieving students with low self-esteem, such as Joe. With such hostile surroundings, Joe would be able to confirm his rationalizations that school is an unfriendly or irrelevant place to be. He could bring home educational "horror stories" each day to justify his own lack of interest in schoolwork and could even subtly encourage hostility between his father and the school leadership, distracting both from paying attention to Joe's lack of performance.

Educational Programming for Underachievers

There are two major strategies that have been used to help students like Joe: counseling and special classroom adaptations. Either method, or both, must be applied intensively if significant gains are to be made.

One way to look at underachievers is that each of them is in the middle of a circle of barbed wire. All the elements of their environment have contributed to the building of this wire circle—their families, friends, schools, and, most importantly, themselves. Any movements that they attempt to try to get out of the barbed wire are going to be painful to them. Sometimes it is more comfortable to sit quietly and passively in the middle of the trap and bemoan their own fate than to risk getting scratched trying to get out.

What, then, needs to be done? Attempts can be made to clear away the barbed wire in a particular area and allow Joe a path out. Such a path can be taken through family counseling, by placing him in a special school environment, or by trying to involve him with peers who are better models than his own group. Consider the following exchange:

Mr. Jenkins: Well, Joe, you did have some good ideas in the paper. But I looked at your records and I think I have a right to expect more from you than what you have done for me on the first paper.

Joe: Well, that's what I get from all my teachers. Ever since I took that IQ test, teachers have been telling me, "I expect a good deal from you." I don't see that this is fair at all. Why should I be expected to do any more than any other kid in class? Those tests are a lot of hooey anyway.

And so it goes. Joe has introduced Mr. Jenkins into the fascinating and baffling world of the passive-resistant underachiever. Unless the teacher is extremely skillful or extremely perceptive, or both, this little scene, with minor variations, is likely to be replayed many times during the school year. The tragedy of such scenes is that each participant tends to go away reinforced in his own nonproductive beliefs. Joe will continue to maintain that his teachers are unfair and that their expectations of him are too high. As long as he holds on to this position, he will not be motivated to change his habits. Mr. Jenkins is impressed by the fact that this is a difficult student—one who is going to require a good deal of watching. This is the information he had received previously in that remarkable communication center known as the teachers' lounge.

The rationale for the two approaches, counseling and learning environment adaptations, rests on what is known about the nature of the problem. The counseling approach focuses on the poor emotional adjustment of underachievers and their low self-concepts. By helping them to explore their view of themselves and their world, counseling should enable them to reorganize their self-concepts and perceptions into more constructive channels, and this, in turn, will result in better school performance.

The alternative educational approach assumes that the basic problem of these students is their inability to adapt to the educational situation. Their recognition of their failures intensifies whatever feelings they have toward education and increases their unfavorable response. Therefore, a change in that environment would allow underachievers to become more effective and might change their behavior patterns directly, and those effective behavior patterns will enhance their self-concepts and improve emotional adjustment.

An oversimplified summary of these two approaches would be that counseling attempts to improve school performance by raising students' self-concepts, whereas the education approach attempts to enhance their self-concepts through better school performance. In actual practice, few programs are restricted to one approach; most programs are mixtures of the two strategies.

Counseling

There have been many variations on this theme, from individual, to group, to family counseling. The longer the counseling is applied, the more effective it seems to be (Baymur & Patterson, 1960).

Fine and Pitts described the problems that face those trying to plan for youngsters such as Joe. They pointed out that giving a great deal of freedom to a child who is immature, impulsive, and prone to avoiding responsibility does not make sense. They stated, "The challenge of therapeutic intervention is to initially develop the necessary structure needed to support the child in acquiring a more appropriate behavior pattern, and then to modify the structure in order for the child to assume progressively more responsibility for his/her behavior" (1980, p. 53).

Fine and Pitts (1980) proposed a collaborative working relationship between home and family, where, through group discussions, it is possible to develop a course of action that specifies expectations over who will do what, including record keeping and similar tasks. They feel that it is extremely important that the parents and the school reach general agreement on the plan in order to avoid the possibility that the youngster, who often has become manipulative of adults, will sabotage the effort.

For example, Joe has become extraordinarily adept at reporting to his parents the latest indignity piled on him by the school. Sometimes this is embellished by his comments to his parents about how poorly the school is doing in their efforts. By continuing this dispersed conversation, he can keep these potential allies apart and arguing with one another. The cooperative agreement that Fine and Pitts (1980) recommended provides for the child a posture of "we care, we are concerned, and we will do something." Despite the child's manifest struggles to avoid the responsibility placed on him by this agreement, maintaining that caring posture is reassuring to the youngster.

In counseling the gifted underachiever, Kerr (1991) recommended that one should first search for the appropriate academic placement as the simplest answer to these problems. A more complex program could be devised if the need is warranted. Kerr believes that the bored, restless, and resentful student might begin to achieve if he or she is placed in a more challenging setting, such as having junior high or middle school students taking secondary courses or even college courses. She stated that "adding challenge to the student's life may be more effective than any number of counseling interventions" (p. 66). Kerr has also recognized that there are underachieving students who have personality disorders or behavior disorders above and beyond the realm of boredom and lack of challenge; she emphasized that for such students, who may be facing depression, substance abuse, or other conflicts, personal counseling is needed.

How do the characteristics of the school program and the characteristics of the underachieving gifted child interact? Sometimes the school program seems to be without high motivation or excitement. As Whitmore (1986) pointed out, sometimes adults expect children to work diligently on a task even if it is unrewarding. If large numbers of students seem to be bored or uninterested, then something beyond the children is involved. In such a situation, some redesign of the school program, instead of "disciplining" the students, would seem to be needed.

Delisle (1990) reported on various strategies that can be used with gifted, underachieving students, as reported by Whitmore:

> *Supportive strategies.* These approaches allow students to feel a part of the "family," including class meetings and curriculum focused on student interests.
>
> *Intrinsic strategies.* This is based on the principle that positive attitudes are likely to encourage achievement. Teachers encourage attempts (not just successes), use student input for classroom rules, and so forth.
>
> *Remedial strategies.* Students are given chances to excel in their areas of strength while opportunities are provided to improve their learning deficiencies.

Such strategies are effective when they are applied consistently and as part of an overall educational plan for a particular student.

Another systematic program of intervention has been described by Butler-Por (1987). Using Glasser's theory of *reality therapy,* she created a program for underachieving gifted children (ages 9 to 12) in a remedial classroom.

1. The teacher was provided a diagnostic profile of each underachieving pupil to guide him or her in enabling the child to recognize the need for change.
2. A meeting was held between teacher and pupil to discuss the need for change and the joint responsibility for that change.
3. The pupil set the tasks he or she would try to accomplish for the coming week and chose the rewards that would serve as reinforcers. A contract was signed by both.
4. Weekly meetings were held between teacher and pupil to review the past week and to set new tasks and rewards.
5. Near the end of the school year, a final meeting was held to assess the success of their joint efforts and agree that progress could continue without further meetings.

One key to this approach is that the student must accept responsibility for the plans and progress. Teachers are encouraged to raise their expectations and to provide positive reinforcement and feedback to the students. Demonstrable progress was made in the group in both academic and personal adjustment, but the progress was uneven; the teacher cannot reasonably expect uninterrupted progress. The "dance" of the underachiever remains two steps forward, one step sideways, one step backward, pause.

Another effort to provide a substantially different environment for the gifted underachiever is presented by Supple (1990). A special adaptive class for children in grades 3 through 8 was established, with the intent of providing an individualized program in a very different environment than the student faced in the elementary or middle school. With a small number of students—eight or less at any one time—in a room created to be homelike (couches, individual work stations, etc.), a program jointly worked out by teacher and student included the following:

1. *No lectures.* Learning should take place through games, movies, computer work, plays, and field trips.
2. *Positive reinforcement.* Students should know what to expect. They should know at once when they have done something well, and they should have their friends know, too.
3. *Flexible time schedules.* Students should be able to really get involved with something they like (although all agreed that some routine would help them adjust to real life).
4. *Food and other interesting breaks.* Students should be involved in social activities and should have responsibilities, such as animals to watch after and for which to care.
5. *Learning centers.* Students should be able to pursue *their* interests, not the teachers' interests.

This classroom was self-contained for the first two 50-minute periods of the school day, every day of the year. This created a consistent and predictable environment where the student could find safety and encouragement.

Such a plan will not be easily accepted in many schools, since it seems that they are providing a "country club" atmosphere for students who have not been doing "the right thing," and thus rewarding misbehavior or poor motivation. However, the program did seem to be effective in turning around some students with clear underachievement.

One of the special elements to the plan has been the development of a student journal. Only the teacher and student read the journal, unless they both agreed to share it with someone else. The student must write a minimum of three sentences each day. Although the journals may be stilted at first, Supple said that, over time, "these journals encouraged a caring, special kind of communication between teacher and student.... The journals often marked the point at which each student started to take control and responsibility for his or her own life and well-being" (1990, p. 35).

Other parts of the curriculum, such as language arts, were focused around the interests of the child. When the students were asked which part of the adaptive class program was most important in helping them achieve, they noted the individualized learning plan and the choice and control they were allowed to exercise over their goals and objectives. Both academic and social goals improved substantially during the time the students were in the adaptive classroom.

The evidence available is that positive movement for the underachiever requires sustained attention and a consistent plan. It is unlikely that the majority of students like Joe around the country will be involved in such special programs. Instead, it is likely that their unusual and self-defeating behavior will confront one puzzled teacher after another. What can the classroom teacher, even one who has received some special training, do for Joe? Several general ideas could be kept in mind by the teacher.

1. *Causation probably lies outside the classroom.* When things go wrong in the classroom, conscientious teachers often search for reasons within themselves for the disaster. It is appropriate that teachers do consider themselves first, particularly if such consideration leads to a change in teacher strategy. In Joe's case, however, the teacher would do well to consider his past history and the history of children like him. It is likely that Joe is pursuing patterns of behavior constructed long before he had contact with his present teacher. Understanding that pattern—rather than futile soul searching or asking oneself What did I do that went wrong?—would seem to be the more profitable approach.

2. *Remediation is a difficult road.* There is a fantasy, shared by almost all teachers, that they, the pure in heart, can come onto the scene and, by means of love, warmth, affection, or superior knowledge, touch a child who has remained impervious to the best efforts of other teachers and thus magically cast away affliction. This could be called the "Merlin the Magician" method. In dealing with the underachiever, a better image to bear in mind is that of teaching the child with cerebral palsy or polio to walk. There are no instant successes and the road is hard and slow, but greatly rewarding—if one can be accepting of small successes and many setbacks.

3. *Underachievers fear failure.* Almost everything that underachievers do, or fail to do, seems colored by the fear of failure. This is why they cannot sustain interest in a lengthy or complex problem. The experience of failure overwhelms them before they get to the end, and they retreat, thus confirming their own feelings of failure (see Figure 12–1). The instructional strategy to combat this fear is to give short and intrinsically interesting assignments so that their frustrations will not overwhelm them and cause retreat. Term papers or long reports are almost always overwhelming to underachievers. It is when doing short assignments, where the material is immediately available, that underachievers stand the best chance for success. These assignments can be gradually lengthened as the students tend to tolerate their frustrations more. They must be weaned away gradually from the comforts of ignorance and anonymity!

4. *Underachievers fear success.* Most teachers are familiar with the fear of failure and what it causes children to do, but many do not consider the fear of success. An example of this in Joe's case was the time Mr. Jenkins noticed Joe working on a short composition. The teacher had already commented favorably on it, but Joe seemed to be more agitated about his work as it approached completion. Finally, he took an eraser and with great strength rubbed the eraser across the composition tearing the paper and ruining it. The impending success seemed to be too much for Joe and his "old shoe" comforts of mediocrity.

   Mr. Jenkins, knowing Joe well, did not fall into the trap of scolding Joe for his carelessness, but instead praised Joe for the quality of work that had been in the composition and helped him to mend it the best he could. He then wrote a note on the bottom of the composition. "Good work, Joe, this is a great improvement. I am encouraged, and I know that you are, too." Joe didn't say anything about it, but seemed to sit up straighter and work a little longer the next day. But Mr. Jenkins knows that the end is not yet in sight, nor will it be for a long time, because these ingrained unfavorable habits are sure to emerge again when Joe becomes anxious, threatened, or just bored with the way things are.

Culturally Diverse Gifted Students

For the past two decades, there has been increasing concern that equal educational opportunities be provided to all children, especially those from culturally diverse backgrounds. The vast majority of that concern, however, has focused on children in educational difficulty—through programs such as Head Start, Follow Through, and Upward Bound. Until recently, relatively little attention has been directed to children with *outstanding ability* from these backgrounds. The terminology historically used to describe these groups—*culturally disadvantaged, economically disadvantaged, culturally different,* and so on—typically implied a problem to be solved. *Culturally diverse* is a more neutral and accurate term, and that is the term that will be used here.

Increasing concern has been expressed for identifying and planning for the talented child from cultural backgrounds far removed from the American middle-class stereotype. This search for talent represents a recognition, in part, that the human resources of the United States are not unlimited, any more than are our physical resources. We have more than enough societal problems to solve that should provide all our high-ability youth full-time employment for some time to come.

Frasier (1991) reported on the commonalities shared by gifted students from whatever culture they might come:

1. The ability to meaningfully manipulate some symbol system held valuable in the subculture
2. The ability to think logically, given appropriate information
3. The ability to use stored knowledge to solve problems
4. The ability to reason by analogy
5. The ability to extend or extrapolate knowledge to new situations or unique applications

From one culture to another, the way in which these abilities might express themselves may differ (e.g., in one culture through language, through another in drawings and paintings) but the essence of their operation remains the same.

Sam's Refrain: Nobody Loves a Smart Boy

It is rare that educators have a full appreciation of the diverse pressures that can be placed on talented youngsters who persist in their deviations from accepted cultural norms. Sam had one such experience burned vividly into his memory; it was an experience that influenced his school behavior from that time forward.

During one class, Sam became enthusiastic about an assignment and the teacher was able to see past the rough exterior and grasp the diamond-like quality of Sam's intellect. For an electric moment their minds touched, and the teacher and Sam had an exhilarating conversation, almost forgetting the rest of the class in their mutual enthusiasm.

That evening as Sam trudged home from school, he turned a corner and suddenly was confronted by five of his male classmates, obviously waiting for him. He was sure that he could handle any one of them physically, but he was equally sure that he was helpless before the group. Cold chills ran up his spine as the largest of the group approached him.

"Hey, Sam, how come you're suckin'up to the teach? We don't like guys actin' too smart, do we?"

A rumble of assent came from the assembled group, and several highly distinctive suggestions were made as to what might happen to someone who continued such unacceptable behavior. Sam held his ground, but the next day he was very distant to the teacher and resisted all attempts to reinstitute that special relationship.

Sam had made his choice. If he kept his distance from the teacher and continued to excel athletically, his intellectual interests would be accepted, though not without some scorn. It is this type of compromise, in one form or another, that is forced on talented students coming from a cultural background that may be essentially suspicious of the institution of the school or the usefulness of the pursuit of the intellect.

A different problem would face Sam's sister. She might not be threatened in so openly a physical way as Sam, but her aspirations to seek a writing career beyond the home and family, if expressed openly, might result in just as thorough an ostracizing as Sam's. The predominant belief in many subcultures of U.S. society is still that women produce babies, not books. So what do these youngsters do with their high ability? With their peer group, they "cool it." They hide their interests and aspirations when they are with their friends, and they are very cautious in the classroom.

Educators need to do more than decry the values that cause these talented youngsters to disguise their talents. They need to find ways that are less conspicuous for such youngsters to show their talents. There is hardly any more public arena than the open classroom discussion. Everything said there is open to peer-group monitoring. The wise teacher, understanding these factors, probably would have waited for their discussion until she had Sam aside for some reason, so that he wouldn't have been socially endangered by his own intellect.

The Search for Talent

One concept that continues to plague the process of identifying gifted children from culturally diverse backgrounds can be referred to as the "light under the bushel basket" idea. This concept holds that intellectual giftedness is maintained within the individual regardless of environmental conditions, however unfavorable environments may place a symbolic "bushel basket" over the light, preventing it from shining in all its potential brilliance. The task as educators, if they believe this idea, is to find some magical technique that will lift up the basket and let the light shine forth. However, it is time to recognize that the concept that genetic capabilities are not influenced by environmental conditions is an outmoded idea.

The key assumption is that high ability, or the measurement of such ability, is not influenced by the differential environmental conditions in which these ethnic children have been raised. This is a totally unreasonable assumption—one that rests on the belief that genetic inheritance is untouched or unmarred by interactions with the society. One of the acknowledged characteristics of many Asian and Jewish families, whose children appear in disproportionate numbers in programs for gifted students, is that they stress intellectual performance, hard work, and motivation for learning, and have, within the family unit, a high respect for intellectual achievement. This has been viewed as the true reason for such differences—a strong positive interaction between native ability and environment.

It is quite disturbing to many educators when differential gender or ethnic results emerge from their talent searches. When more boys than girls get higher scores on mathematics aptitude tests, or when more white students than black are in classes for the gifted, something is immediately assumed to be wrong. When teachers rate students on Scales for Rating the Behavior Characteristics of Superior Students (Renzulli, Smith, White, Callahan, & Hartman 1976), one may find higher ratings for Anglo than Hispanic or African-American students. This has been sometimes interpreted as representing a form of teacher bias or discrimination. In truth, it may be. However, there is another, just as reasonable, conclusion: Teachers are faithfully reproducing what they observe, and what they observe is the result of differential stimulation and encouragement for school learning. At school age, such differential encouragement can result in clearly different behavior in the classroom.

In other words, the analogy of the lantern applies here. Instead of the always burning lantern, one might substitute the candle that is very sensitive to the amount of oxygen stimulation it receives. One can snuff out intellectual ability or disguise it to a point where it no longer functions or operates as it might have if it had been given early encouragement and stimulation (Maker, 1983).

Another important reason for these great discrepancies in the prevalence of gifted students from different ethnic groups might be the different cultural styles that are reflected in the students from various groups. Hilliard (1989) pointed out that various subgroups have different approaches toward problem solving and that, if a group's style differs considerably from the style of the dominant population, then the performance of the culturally different group could well seem to be depressed. This would be particularly true if the aptitude test items are constructed to reflect a majority culture style (e.g., requiring speed of response rather than associative thinking).

Further, once a student has established himself or herself as one of the nonperforming students, a number of things happen. Teachers have styles of their own, which often includes how they treat high-performing students versus low-performing students. Hilliard (1989) pointed out that when teachers' responses to high-performing students are compared with their responses to low-performing students, teachers tend to:

Wait less time for low-performing students to answer questions.

Criticize low-performing students more often than high-performing students for failure.

Praise low performers less frequently than high performers for success.

Pay less attention to low performers and interact with them less frequently.

Seat low performers farther away from the teacher than high performers.

Accept more low-quality or more incorrect responses from low performers.

Such a teaching style will make it less likely that the talents of the student from a culturally diverse background would be recognized or nurtured.

The Search for Hidden Talent

There have been a variety of efforts adopted to supplement, or even take the place of, standard measures of intellectual development. Some of these strategies are as follows (Borland & Wright, 1991):

Alternative instruments. A variety of instruments have been employed that would seem to measure intelligence in a different, less culturally biased, fashion.

Observation. Those adults who know the children best—teachers and parents—are asked to respond to rating scales covering characteristics of gifted children.

Peer ratings. One of the best observers of who is the most creative or imaginative student may well be the peer group, who might be asked to name those students who will be able to solve a variety of practical problems that might be posed on a rating scale.

Portfolios. A teacher may collect the products of the students over an extended period of time into a portfolio; that collection can be reviewed to find outstanding performance or rapid growth in skill.

Best practices. This approach looks for the most outstanding skills of the child and assumes that the other abilities would be the same, if equal opportunity had been provided to the student.

Talent development. A set of lessons designed to stimulate imaginative or creative response are provided to groups of students and note is taken as to which students perform well in these settings.

Abolishing standard tests of academic ability does not solve all of our problems; such tests often reflect what we know to be true. Such a reaction would be akin to breaking a thermometer when the weather is too cold for one's taste: the instrument for measuring the temperature is gone, but it is still cold. The educational weather will continue to be cold until families, society, and schools provide a social and educational environment so that youngsters born with innate abilities and talents can make full use of them.

The weight of the current evidence suggests that environments can be both constructive and destructive to the full use of intellectual abilities. An environment that does not reward high-level thought processes can substantially reduce the high talent and ability that might have been originally present in the child. The notion that potentially superior talent can actually be suppressed or destroyed should lend additional urgency to providing, *at an early age,* stimulating educational experiences for the potentially gifted from culturally diverse environments.

As stated in an earlier chapter, performance on an IQ test is determined, to some extent, by past opportunity and experience. How, then, can one use that information in evaluating the intellectual capabilities of the youngsters who come from manifestly different home and cultural backgrounds? One method, developed by Mercer (1979) and called SOMPA (the System of MultiCultural Pluralistic Assessment), is based on the assumption that, given equal opportunity, all cultural groups will form relatively equal distributions of intellectual ability. Mercer, therefore, uses a set of norms based on expected past experience and opportunity. The child is then compared not against all of the children on the standard test but against children from similar sociocultural back-grounds.

Mercer and Lewis (1981) described a child, Belle, who achieved a verbal IQ score of 111 on the Wechsler Intelligence Scale for Children under standard norms. When the pluralistic model is used, her estimated learning potential was a verbal IQ of 130, which placed her in the upper 1 percent of the children in her own sociocultural group. Using this approach, it is possible to identify Belle as a gifted child with manifestly greater learning potential than she now is able to show. In a similar fashion, one can identify children who have had different opportunities and adjust their test performance to their own group norm. Identifying such youngsters as gifted, of course, does not solve the problem of the different experiences they have had, and the program for Belle should reflect an attempt to compensate for these lost early experiences.

One common strategy for identifying giftedness in culturally diverse populations is to use tests of nonverbal abilities, which might more adequately identify such youngsters. Tests such as the nonverbal sections of the Torrance Tests of Creative Thinking or the Raven Progressive Matrices can be substituted for the usual verbal IQ tests.

A third strategy used by Wolf (1981) in her trial or audition-type program, is to create an enriched educational environment and then invite a large number of children to volunteer for participation. Some children will then demonstrate their special abilities by their actual performance in the enriched program. They will have identified themselves by their own responsiveness to educational stimulation, rather than by their test scores.

The often quoted statement that the United States is the great "melting pot" is an unfortunate portrait. It conjures up the picture of all of the participants losing their individuality and emerging in some form of homogeneous mass. An alternative concept is that of a societal "tossed salad." In this model, each of the cultural groups adds its own particular taste and spice to the total yet maintains its own distinctive character. The "salad" becomes uniquely our own without destroying the identity of the parts.

Shade (1978) reviewed the available literature on the characteristics of achieving African-American children. She found that the families of African-American achievers differed significantly from the families of African-American nonachievers primarily in characteristics that often have been related to middle-class membership. Parents of achievers tended to be warm, accepting, supportive, and, at the same time, demanded a better-than-average performance from their children. Yet another set of characteristics of these African-American achievers seems to fit their new, and not yet well-established, middle-class membership. These achieving students tended to be more cautious, con-stricted, and shrewd, while staying within the boundaries of conformity.

It is interesting to note that African-American girls have been identified in school as gifted at a 2 to 1 ratio over African-American boys, even though there are few differences obtained in measures of intellectual ability between the two sexes. There was a greater willingness on the part of teachers to accept African-American girls as high achievers, perhaps, due to their greater assumption of responsibility for their learning in school situations and conformity compared to the boys.

The establishment of close family ties, the maintenance of structure and order for the child, moderate amounts of discipline, expectations for achievement, and the availability of assistance when needed, all mark the African-American achieving families as coming closer to stable middle-class environment and membership.

Educational Adaptations for Culturally Diverse Students

There are two different approaches to the educational improvement of students who are both gifted and economically disadvantaged. The first of these is to attempt to improve the education of all children and, through such improvement, improve the lot of these students of high aptitude. This might be described as the "rising tide lifts all boats" approach.

The second approach, though supporting general improvement in education, insists that there must be some additional attention to the students who seem to possess unusual abilities. One illustration of this is the *accelerated school* approach by Levin (1987). This school is characterized by high expectations, deadlines for students to be performing at grade level, stimulating instructional programs, extended day programs, and comprehensive educational planning. Special attention is given to parent involvement; parents sign a written agreement that they understand the obligations of the school and parents to the education of the student. Parents also are encouraged to set high expectations for their child. In this way, the school can set high expectations, and students like Sam can perform in a setting more conducive to study and achievement without apologizing to peers.

Another illustration of this approach is to provide young students who have revealed special abilities with special opportunities to receive advanced learning, beyond that of the average students, even in an environment such as the accelerated school. The gifted students are encouraged to use language to solve problems and are given lessons at their appropriate level, which may well be beyond that of the average classmates.

It is a mistake to conclude that the special attention that is being requested for gifted students means that educators of gifted students are indifferent to the plight of other students, or that those interested in improving the history curriculum are indifferent to the science programs. In order to have an overall institution of excellence, it is important that each segment of education be improved to the maximum degree possible.

Two opposing philosophies drive the curriculum development and program organization for students with special gifts from culturally diverse backgrounds. The first of these philosophies can be referred to as the *assimilation approach.* Briefly stated, this approach believes that the best education for a gifted student from a culturally diverse home is to prepare him or her for a role in the mainstream U.S. culture. These students, according to the assimilation approach, should be able to compete on equal terms with students from the majority culture. They should be able to master advanced programs designed for students in the majority culture, with some additional help in meeting any deficiencies (e.g., language familiarity) that they might have.

The second philosophy is the *pluralist approach,* which focuses the educational program on the system and culture, with an emphasis on how to modify the majority society to take into account the needs and values of the various cultures within that society. The second approach, then, aims to impact on the educational system, the legal system, and the like, by reforming elements of the society to help ensure less inequities for culturally diverse students and citizens.

Table 12–1 provides a summary of the two approaches, as given by Kitano (1992). It is interesting to think about how literature courses and courses in political science might be taught differently with these two different philosophies at work. In using the first approach, the emphasis might well be on authors who have successfully assimilated in the society and are presented as models of how various groups have been incorporated into U.S. society (the "tossed salad"). In the pluralist approach, the focus might be on those authors who have placed their first concern on the maintenance of their minority culture and the preservation of those values, even when they are in conflict with the values of the majority society.

There are many opportunities for making some changes in existing curricula that could make the material more relevant and interesting to culturally diverse students. One of the key elements in such a program is a well-stocked library and classroom reference shelves that contain literature, history, anthropology, and so on relevant to the cultural

Table 12–1   Summary of Assismilationist and Pluralist Perspectives for Culturally Diverse Students

	Assimilationist	*Pluralist*
Source of underachievement	Within child based on culture and experience; need for intervention aimed at deficits	Within system or within interactions between system and child; need for empowerment of child
Purpose of schooling	Transmission of mainstream values toward maintenance of core culture	Understanding many cultural perspectives toward creation of a society that values diversity
Identification	Standardized assessment	Alternative assessment, nonbiased assessment, multiple measure assessment
Instructional processes	Focus on individual achievement; helping child fit the school	Focus on democratic structures; changing school to fit the child
Curriculum	Problem solving and critical thinking applies to mainstream culture and history	Problem solving and critical thinking applies to culture and history of many groups; building skills to transform society

Source: Kitano, M. (1992). A multicultural educational perspective on serving the culturally diverse gifted. *Journal for the Education of the Gifted, 15* (1). Reprinted by permission.

groups in that area. There should be opportunity to teach important ideas through a wide variety of examples.

The question of curriculum content in special programs for gifted students who come from culturally diverse families and settings is a substantial concern. Baldwin probably has represented the general consensus on this topic: "The curriculum content should include the inventions, explorations, drama, literature, music, and other contributions to civilization, of the student's culture"(1991, p. 423). Although there may be good reason to believe that the cultural background of the student will predispose him or her to certain styles of learning, the assimilative approach is to teach the student how to use alternative strategies when appropriate.

Sam has learned early that verbal facility is prized in his home and his neighborhood. He has become a very proficient talker and has impressed everyone with how quickly and easily he communicates orally. Yet it is the job of the teacher to also help Sam recognize that there are certain problems that do not easily yield to the approach of "talk first, think later." Some problems require study and thought before being attacked, and Sam is being taught to recognize those problems and adopt a different approach toward them.

The individualization of instruction and the full reference shelf found in gifted programs offer students from culturally diverse backgrounds choices as to what content they wish to explore. The history of Renaissance Italy or Elizabethan England may have less urgency and interest than the history of Africa or South America, yet the same basic generalizations of political science and economics should hold true in both places. Similarly, historical figures representing concepts of despotism or love for the people, leadership or mob rule, can be found in all lands and times. Still, the choice of setting may make more impact on those students if they can identify with the characters. The richness of literature the world over offers abundant opportunities to choose relevant materials.

Counseling

As noted earlier, students caught between competing cultures need special attention (Frasier, 1979). As upwardly mobile students, culturally diverse gifted children also can feel caught between the need to express their talents and the need to adhere to family patterns and values. Finally, they need to form their own self-identities and determine how those identities relate both to their own cultural group and to that of the majority culture.

In order to be effective in helping these students work their way through such problems, Colangelo and Lafrenz (1981) strongly suggested that the counselor become familiar with and immersed in the cultural backgrounds and values of the culturally diverse student population. They pointed out that counselors should spend less time learning the newest counseling techniques and more time understanding minority students and their lifestyles.

Most educational personnel who have grown up in middle- or upper middle-class families do not fully appreciate the emotional problems that youngsters like Sam have in breaking away from the established life patterns of their friends and neighbors in order to make full use of their levels of ability. Frasier (1979) pointed out some ways in which counseling can be helpful to such youngsters:

1. Help them deal with the problem of alienation from one subculture, which can become a frightening and lonely experience.
2. In the process of moving up the socioeconomic ladder (upward mobility), there is a price to be paid. There are few models from their own cultures to imitate, and in their immediate experiences they must leave behind the lifestyles to which they have become accustomed. One aspect of that lifestyle may be not asking questions, even though Sam and others like him have insatiable curiosities. Counseling can do much to encourage this questioning attitude, as can sympathetic and receptive teachers, so that students like Sam get rewards and encouragement for inquiry.
3. Finally, many gifted youngsters grow up in environments where the alternative paths available to them through further education and into a variety of possible careers are not known to them. Counseling can provide the awareness to alternative paths and potential occupations that fall outside their normal experiences.

Self-Image and Communication

One of the dimensions that many gifted children from culturally diverse backgrounds share with one another is a degree of discomfort with the use of verbal symbols. Therefore, specialized programmatic efforts need to be designed with that understanding in mind.

Wolf (1981) has presented a unique program of instruction in theater techniques for young children identified as gifted from culturally diverse backgrounds. The program has been carried out in New Haven, Connecticut, with African-American and Hispanic students. It has focuses on a four-step process of communication, people, and places, which allows the students to express themselves in theater and related arts areas of music and dance, minimizing the verbal requirements. The themes pursued in this program are Who am I? Who are the people in my world? and How do they interact? Wolf described the program as evolving in four stages:

1. *Introductory activities were aimed at creating a comfortable working atmosphere and enhancing the students' sense of values of their own individual contribution to the group.*
2. *Students recorded the events of their own lives from birth to present, keeping in mind the use of this material for joint dramatizations.*
3. *The students took surveys of their own neighborhood to provide historical demographic and geographic perspectives, which were then depicted through various artistically expressive modes.*
4. *Students examined literature for material that interprets urban and rural living in order to place these issues in a larger worldwide context. (1981, p. 114)*

Through this vehicle, students become more perceptive and expressive about themselves, their heritage, and their place in the world around them.

One interesting device to aid in the stimulation of young gifted students from economically disadvantaged circumstances has been reported by Wright and Borland (1991). They introduced a group of adolescent mentors who were engaged in a community service project in a secondary school from the same disadvantaged neighborhood. They were selected to be mentors if they enjoyed being with children, had younger siblings, and expressed a desire to act as role models.

These mentors were carefully prepared for their roles before they engaged their preschool students in games, offered tutoring, kept journals on their students, and went through regular debriefing with school staff. The mentors who came from the same economically disadvantaged environmental settings as the preschool students provided an invaluable and otherwise unattainable window into the lives of these young children. Mentor and student both seemed to enjoy the relationship and gain positive results from it, yet the value of the program requires careful and continued supervision to make it work.

Maker and Schiever summarized program suggestions from a wide variety of specialists concerned with Hispanic, African-American, Native-American, and Asian-American gifted children, as follows:

1. Identify students' strengths and plan a curriculum to develop these abilities.
2. Provide for the development of basic skills and other abilities students may lack.
3. Regard differences as positive rather than negative attributes.
4. Provide for involvement of parents, the community, and mentors or role models.
5. Create and maintain classrooms with a multicultural emphasis. (1989, p. 301)

The discovery and nurturing of talent from culturally diverse circumstances will likely be an emphasis in programs for gifted students for the foreseeable future.

Gifted Students with Disabilities

Recently, a new subcategory of gifted students has emerged. The students in this subgroup have, in addition to their outstanding mental abilities, identifiable disabilities. The focus of attention for such individuals has been on (1) discovery and (2) creating educational adaptations for them—mostly within the framework of the education they had been receiving as children with disabilities.

Upon reflection, one can probably think of many extraordinarily gifted individuals who carried with them substantial physical or emotional disabilities that they had to overcome. Ludwig van Beethoven, Thomas Edison, Albert Einstein, Woodrow Wilson, Helen Keller, Carl Steinmetz, and Franklin D. Roosevelt all had special characteristics that would meet the current federal definition of a disabling condition. Yet, clearly, these individuals also possessed outstanding intellectual and artistic gifts.

This dual condition creates a number of special challenges for educators. Many of the standard techniques and procedures discussed in previous chapters of this book will not work for gifted students with disabilities without substantial adaptation. For example, much of our measurement of creativity in students relies on their visual perception— obviously an inappropriate technique for children who are blind. Much of the innovative production that we ask of students as an indicator of creativity has a strong verbal component to it—which is not particularly appropriate for children who are deaf. A child with a learning disability may have an extraordinary storehouse of knowledge but an inability to express that knowledge easily.

Discovering Gifted Students with Disabilities

One of the special problems or issues related to the gifted disabled child is correctly identifying them. Often, the disabling condition itself may mask or disguise the child's outstanding talent. Whitmore provided an example of a child who not only went unrecognized as gifted but was actually considered mentally retarded.

Example: Kim

At seven years of age, this child with cerebral palsy had no speech and extremely limited motor control. In a public school for severely handicapped students, she was taught only self-help skills. Her parents, who were teachers, observed her use of her eyes to communicate and believed that there was unstimulated intellect trapped inside her severely handicapped body. Upon parent request, she was mainstreamed in her wheelchair into an open-space elementary school. After two months of stimulation, Kim began to develop rapidly. She learned the Morse code in less than two days and began communicating continuously, through the use of a mechanical communicator, with the teacher and peers. Within four months she was reading on grade level (second), and subsequent testing indicated she possessed superior mental abilities—an exceptional capacity to learn. (1981b, pp. 109–110)

It is not hard to imagine the unstimulating world in which Kim would have continued to live if she had not been given that opportunity to learn with the mechanical communicator.

Maker (1977) has suggested comparing the child with disabilities not against the norms of the nondisabled but against other children with similar disabilities (e.g., other children with learning disabilities or hearing impairments, and so forth). Those children who appear superior in such comparisons can then be given special study and additional opportunities to respond to more stimulating and challenging lessons. The first step is to alert those professionals working with children with disabilities to be sensitive to signs of talent hiding under the students' particular disabling condition.

There has been an increasing awareness of the presence of students with a variety of learning disabilities who also possess outstanding abilities. To some people, this would seem to be a contradiction in terms—to discuss "gifted students with disabilities." It is not difficult, however, if one remembers the models of seven intelligences by Gardner or the various components of Sternberg presented in Chapter 1. It is certainly possible for a variety of disabilities to impose a specific deficit in one of Gardner's seven intelligences but not to limit outstanding ability in other dimensions. Yet the presence of giftedness in children with disabilities is so often overlooked that this phenomenon surely represents a source of potential talent largely untapped by U.S. educators (Gallagher, 1988).

Much attention has been paid recently to gifted students with disabilities (Baum & Owen, 1988; Suter & Wolf, 1987). Whitmore and Maker commented that, "Intellectually gifted individuals with specific learning disabilities are the most misjudged and neglected segment of the student population" (1985, p. 204). If this is true, what can be done about it?

Coleman (1992) reported a study of 21 middle grade male students who met the state standards for learning disability and scored an IQ over 125 on WISC verbal or performance scales. The coping strategies employed by these students when facing frustrating academic situations were then compared with those coping strategies used by a group of similarly identified students with learning disabilities who scored in the average range of intellectual ability. Figure 12–3 indicates one of the scenarios presented to these students, who were then asked, "How would you respond?" There were *no differences* in the amount of responses given by the two groups of students, but *considerable difference* in the coping strategies reported by them. The gifted students with learning disabilities reported significantly more planful problem solving, such as:

> *When I was identified as LD, I had said to myself before the year began that, you know, I was going to get a separate notebook for each subject, keep them in my locker, in order. Now I even keep them in order of how I have the classes so I can just whip the books out.*

In contrast, the average students with learning disabilities developed a series of poor coping skills, such as *escape/avoidance:*

> *Go outside and probably play sports or something.*

Or *learned helplessness:*

> *It tells me that there's no difference than before. There is nothing I can do.*

Or *distancing:*

> *Well, you know, like you go to school, you're having fun, and if you get something bad, you like kind of just shrug it off if you're in a good mood, you know.*

Each of these strategies would seem to conspire to make the academic situation worse and to compound the future problems for these average-ability students with learning disabilities.

Although the gifted students with learning disabilities did show evidence that they had stumbled on some more useful coping strategies, that did not mean that they had

FIGURE 12–3   Sample Scenario

Joseph had a chapter test in math. He had studied for the test very hard, working problems and doing all the practice sections in the chapter. The day of the test, he felt pretty good. He knew that he could work the problems and he "understood the math."

When he got the test, he started working on it. But he couldn't remember how to do the first set of problems. Joseph became frustrated and nervous that he would not finish on time, so he rushed through the rest of the test.

As you might imagine, when he got his test back his grade was a 55 (He got an "F") and the teacher's comments on the top said: "Careless errors—You should be more careful. You can do better than this!!"

Source: Coleman, M. (1992). A comparison of how gifted/LD and average/LD boys cope with school frustration. *Journal for the Education of the Gifted, 17* (4). Reprinted by permission.

extensive command of good coping strategies to meet the variety of frustrations that the academic setting posed for them. Coleman proposed that coping strategies be directly taught to these students (gifted and average), plus a continuing counseling program with parental support and assistance to ensure that the students were responding well, given their various disabilities.

Another attempt to discover the nature of gifted children with learning disabilities was conducted by Baum and Owen (1988). They contrasted the performance of three groups—high-ability learning disability, average-ability learning disability, and high-ability students—on a variety of personal and academic measures and teacher ratings. They found major differences between the groups. The gifted learning disability group attributed their poor school performance to shyness, and were seen by their teachers as disruptive in class but possessing more creativity than the average learning disability group. There also was a strong lack of self-efficacy in the gifted/learning disability group.

The average-ability students saw success as a matter of luck, with a low self-image predominating in their responses. Baum and Owen (1988) stressed the importance of enrichment activities that would feature abstract and higher-level thinking processes, since success at lower-level tasks would not likely add to the sense of self-efficacy for gifted students with disabilities.

Educational Adaptations for Gifted Students with Disabilities

One of the difficulties in making practical plans for gifted children with disabilities is the geographic and psychological distance between the professionals who normally work with one or the other of the conditions. Whitmore presented three conditions she believes are necessary for better service for these children:

1. *The reintegration of special, regular, and gifted education with a significant amount of cooperation and collaboration occurring regularly.*
2. *Educators must more regularly and effectively use the expertise of professionals in community agencies, especially the medical and psychological professions.*
3. *The third important practice is that of early identification and intervention, preferably at the preschool age. (1981b, p. 112)*

A method called the *diagnostic prescriptive* approach features, as part of a case study, collecting comprehensive information about all aspects of personal and social development. This data collection is then followed by an individual education prescription. It has been tried and found successful for small numbers of gifted children with disabilities in special projects (Karnes & Bertschi, 1978; Blacher-Dixon & Turnbull, 1978; Leonard, 1977).

An example of curriculum adaptation within the framework of the program for the child with a specific disability was provided by Feinberg, who suggested how to encourage creative problem solving through listening to music.

1. *Before listening to the following music example (the opening section from Schubert's Symphony V in B flat), describe the different ways you think the main motif could be used in the music.*
2. *Three different themes will be played for you. After listening to them, pick out the two that you think were written by the same composer and explain how they are related.*
3. *I will play two themes for you. If you are asked to compose a bridge connecting these two themes, how would you organize such a passage? (1974, p. 55)*

Obviously, what is being presented to the student here is the opportunity to make transformations, understand systems, and draw implications using the same complex thinking modes as are required of gifted individuals who have no disabilities.

One of the fundamental problems faced by these youngsters of outstanding ability is that the educators who teach children who are blind, deaf, or learning disabled are not used to encountering youngsters of high aptitude. And, without realizing it, these educators have scaled down the level of intellectual and academic challenge they present so as to fit it more easily into the standard educational program for their other children with disabilities. Unless gifted children are recognized as such within this context, they often will have a thin soup of education upon which to dine.

Maker (1977) has presented a variety of programs in which outstanding stimulation is provided for gifted children with disabilities. In the area of learning disabilities, the students may have a very specific problem of decoding the written word or may have problems expressing themselves in certain channels; children with this kind of disability have been a particularly popular target for these stimulation programs. Maker reported some strategies that focus on not assuming that the students have mastered any one particular skill. The students must demonstrate their competence. This is because, even though gifted, they may have specific learning deficits that need careful developmental remediation. Curricula are often presented in short, small units to avoid students' wandering attention. As an additional aid to understanding the language, it is sometimes recommended that children learn the structure, the sound/symbol relationships of the language, as well as the content.

A particularly outstanding example of the development of unusual talent is the National Theater of the Deaf, which has performed often on television and has gone on many nationwide tours. The deaf actors use sign language while an interpreter narrates what is happening on the stage for the audience. The National Theater has presented to enthusiastic audiences an extraordinarily complex repertoire of plays. This group reveals how much talent is present in these children and causes one to reflect on how much more talent may be found if more such opportunities were made available (Maker, 1977).

One of the final questions that emerges in consideration of special programming for youngsters who have both intellectual superiority and a demonstrable disability is, What kinds of professional help should be delivered, and by specialists in which profession? There probably is not one easy answer to such a question. It is likely that someone well trained in either gifted education, learning disabilities, or emotional disturbance, with some additional training and information concerning the other specialty in which he or she is untrained, could provide effective educational programs for the youngsters in question.

The recent emphasis on team teaching and team planning would seem to be particularly useful for such students, as would the development of the Individual Education Program (IEP), which outlines specific objectives along with the educational strategies designed to reach those objectives.

Preschool Gifted Children

One of the areas of growing attention has been that of preschool gifted children. So far, this area has been beyond the range of specific action for the public schools. The importance of the preschool age range for the development of young children has been well accepted for a number of decades.

The attempts to provide some useful experiences for the very young gifted child have generally focused on three specific adaptations—parent counseling, skills training, and enriched curriculum in a variety of preschool settings. Delp (1980) has provided some useful information on how to live successfully with the gifted child—information that parents of the very young gifted often need for reassurance. Some of these guidelines were:

1. Gifted kids crave knowledge. *Gifted kids have a tremendous fund of information and have a need to file it away. At some point in their life, they may have a need to tell you everything they know.*
2. Gifted kids need to feel a sense of progress in what they are learning. *A gifted program needs to...provide ways for gifted kids to feel a sense of progress in what they're learning. They should know where they were when they started in the subject and where they are going.*
3. Gifted kids have an irresistible desire to devour a subject. *The irresistible desire to devour one subject to the exclusion of all others...a child who does that is seen to be persistent and stubborn.*
4. Gifted kids need to make observations, establish serial relationships, and comment on them. *A demand placed upon gifted children by their intelligence is the need to make observations and establish serial relationships between all kinds of things—important, significant things, or unimportant insignificant things.*
5. Gifted kids are sensitive to values. *They believe in honor, truth, and the other absolutes you and I have valued for a long time. They will respond to these values in literature; they will take strong stands about integrity, honesty, living up to expectations, and acting in accordance with certain values.*

The beginnings of these characteristics can be seen by parents; and if they are expecting them, they will not be as distressed or puzzled by them.

None of the behaviors of preschool gifted children are unique or extraordinary in their own right. The point is that these behaviors are not, themselves, particularly remarkable. The thing that makes them remarkable is that they have been mastered by children who are so very young.

Thus, the ability to read, to do simple mathematics, or to master spatial relations are all tasks that children of average ability can achieve. But these young gifted are mastering them at the ages of 4 or 5 instead of at 7 or 8, as would be normally expected. The magic is that the advanced concepts are mastered at a young age. The program goals for preschool programs for the gifted have been presented by a number of authors. Those stated by Roedell and Robinson are typical.

1. *Thinking skills, such as observing, predicting, classifying, analyzing, synthesizing, and evaluating.*
2. *Intellectual curiosity and persistence in developing creative approaches to problem solving.*
3. *Creative expression in a wide range of areas, including art materials, dramatics, movement and dance, and language.*
4. *Strong foundations and traditional academic skills with advanced work tailored to individual competencies.*
5. *Social perceptiveness, awareness of the needs of others, and social problem solving skills.*
6. *Large and small muscle coordination and dexterity. (1977, p. 9)*

Instructional Goals

The goals for a preschool curriculum for gifted students need to include *social* and *personal* goals, as well as *intellectual* ones, since it is at this time that constructive, or nonconstructive, patterns of behavior are being formed. Roedell listed several such goals:

> Self-understanding. *Children must come to accept and understand their strengths and weaknesses and develop a positive self-concept.*
>
> Independence. *Children must learn to make decisions and carry out plans.*
>
> Assertiveness. *Children must learn to stand up for themselves and express their needs in mature and effective ways.*
>
> Social sensitivity. *Children must learn to understand others' needs and feelings, and to help others; to share and cooperate with them.*
>
> Friendship-making skills. *Children must learn how to interact appropriately with peers and adults*
>
> Social problem-solving skills. *Children must learn to solve conflicts without resorting to violence. (1985)*

Students who are gifted may well come to a preschool setting with little understanding or tolerance for others who are not as quick to learn as they. Or they may have been the center of family attention and so are reluctant to leave the spotlight in favor of others. Through guided discovery, learning centers, or free exploration (Maker, 1986), the interaction of a Stephanie or a Cranshaw with other students can be noted and responded to by the observant teacher. The teacher can reward the constructive social behavior of young children and can create the opportunities for understanding and tolerance for others that are so important for adaptation in later school life.

Educational Planning for Preschool Gifted Children

One of the issues that has concerned educators of gifted students is how the program should be differentiated for very young gifted students in kindergarten or daycare programs. It is not often that gifted students are separated from students of average ability at such a young age; it is much more likely that they will be found in a heterogeneous classroom. So the fundamental question is, How can such a program be differentiated to their advantage while they remain in the setting?

Karnes and Johnson (1991) provided some strategies to use in such a circumstance. One such strategy is *teacher questioning* to help the bright students see the many facets to a particular problem or discussion point. *Specific projects* are also recommended as a way to focus on a particular product, such as building a dinosaur. Tasks of varying levels of ability can be given to students of differing developmental levels so that all children are performing effectively at their own levels. In this case, the gifted students may be asked to draw the dinosaur to scale or to do some research on why dinosaurs became extinct.

Such differentiated instruction can also be used in *curriculum units,* which are popular in the preschool classroom. Units on pets, or community helpers, or other similar topics are common in preschool. Using a unit on pets as an example, Karnes and Johnson (1991) suggested that the more able children could investigate unusual animals and birds, could make judgments on whether they would make good pets or not, and could determine what kind of special care they might require.

Another device would be to have gifted students do an *independent study*—for example, on a country that they and their families might be visiting or where they may have already taken a trip, so that the students could discover more about the country and its people. Another popular strategy is the development of a *science project,* such as the growing of plants under different lighting conditions. The availability of *microcomputers* allows for other opportunities for differentiation. Youngsters can create their own stories and pictures, do problem solving, or even invent their own problems using the computer. As their skills increase, they could use the computer to publish a class newspaper, for example.

As in other levels of development, gifted students can face a variety of problems within the preschool setting. For instance, gifted children may become frustrated when a discrepancy in growth interferes with their goals. It is not uncommon to have children wishing to write a story but be angered at their own inability to write. Their motor development proceeds much more slowly than their ability to create ideas. The availability of tape recorders allows such students to present their stories orally.

Boredom, which older gifted students often experience, is also not a stranger to bright students in the early grades, who may tire quickly of bead stringing and simple, repetitive lessons on topics with which the students are already familiar. Just because these students are in the regular classrooms, one should not fall into the trap of believing that they do not need special attention and a differentiated program that will prevent the development of bad study habits and lack of motivation and interest in school. Instead, one should capitalize on the curiosity and eagerness of these children to learn about the world around them.

As Karnes, Schwedel, and Linnemeyer pointed out, one of the problems of gifted children entering the first grade is that the teacher often underestimates their capabilities and will have them redoing simple exercises that they have long since mastered. These writers noted, "No gifted child should be forced to learn what he or she already knows, but too frequently this is precisely what happens" (1982, p. 198).

In Table 12–2, there are a number of opportunities in the content areas of science, art, social studies, and so on where teachers can utilize *divergent thinking* to help the young gifted student to extend or expand perception of things or events in his or her environment. To answer such commands as, Tell all the ways you can think of that we use water or Name all the people who keep us from being sick, gives the young child a task to draw associations from his or her environment that may have been perceived but never before brought together in a systematic fashion.

TABLE 12–2   Encouraging Divergent Thinking in Subject Areas

Subject Area	*Questions*
Science	• Tell all the ways you can think of that we use water. • Name as many things as you can that need electricity to run.
Language	• What might have happened if Goldilocks hadn't run away? • Describe the strangest space creature of which you can think.
Math	• Show all the ways a given set of objects can be classified and sorted (i.e., shape, color, size, edibility, indelibility, etc.). • What are the things you can think of that come in pairs?
Music	• Produce all the different sounds you can with a certain instrument. • List all the things a musical instrument could be saying.
Art	• Make the same object (e.g., a tree, a house) in different media. • Given a set of materials, make a home for an imaginary creature. • Create a new kind of bird with scrap materials.
Social Studies	• Name all the people who help us travel, keep us from getting sick, fix things, and build things for us. • Name different ways we could reuse empty egg cartons, paper bags, crayon stubs, pencil shavings.

Source: From Differentiating the curriculum by Karnes, Linnemeyer, & Denton-Ade, in M. Karnes (Ed.), *The underserved: Our young gifted children,* 1983. Copyright 1983 by The Council for Exceptional Children. Reprinted with permission.

Differing models can be established for a preschool program for the gifted. Karnes, Schwedel, and Linnemeyer described two such models within the same preschool setting. One of these is the *open-classroom approach,* which provides "an excellent environment for children to discover their own interests, pursue long-term special projects independently, use a variety of materials and resources, and solve real life problems" (1982, p. 208).

> *An example of using play as a vehicle for learning higher level thinking processes is seen when a gifted preschooler interacts with his teacher while playing with blocks. After Kevin had built a tall and shaky tower from wooden blocks, the teacher asked Kevin to define a problem related to the construction of the tower and to describe and validate from experiments with the tower how the problem could be solved. In this experience, play was used as a means of teaching problem solving and creative thinking skills. (Kaplan, 1980, p. 64)*

The second model is based on the *structure-of-intellect approach,* which provides a systematic basis for encouraging children to engage in divergent thinking, evaluative thinking, and higher intellectual processes (Meeker, 1969).

Another common model of intellectual performance used in the education of gifted students has been *Bloom's Taxonomy,* which presents a hierarchy of thinking operations whose highest levels are *analysis, synthesis* and *evaluation,* where even those processes can be utilized at the preschool level if enough concrete tasks and materials are used.

All of these models can provide the basis for exciting the child's intellectual processes during a time before the school will ordinarily play a significant role in his or her life but when the gifted child is ready to respond.

Chertoff (1979) illustrated how these various thinking operations can be brought into use in a unit on insects, as illustrated in Figure 12–4. Starting from the natural question of young children, "Where do insects go in the winter?" the teacher can invoke a number of activities for the students that can help them gain insight into the adaptation of living things to their environment. Although initial activities, such as reading stories, singing songs, making drawings, and so forth, are the staple of any preschool experience, the items under *synthesis* and *evaluation* are clearly pitched to the gifted student. The design of an insect that might be found on another planet tests not only the imagination of the gifted child but also the understanding of the necessity for adaptation. From these examples, it is clear that any number of topic areas and activities exist that can challenge the gifted child at a young age.

It has often been said that the business of young children is play. Through the vehicle of play, children learn to understand various relationships of objects and the physical properties of objects in their world; through fantasy and imagination, the youngsters can express and control the demands of the external world on them. If the teacher has a very clear goal in mind of stimulating thinking processes, then all of the everyday experiences of the children, from eating lunch to playground activities to clean-up activities, can be used to have them perceive more accurately the world around them and think about the relationships that are obtained in that world.

FIGURE 12–4   Insect Unit

Theme:
How do insects survive the winter? (Adaptation)

Problem:
Where did the ants go? (The children were curious about the disappearance of insects during the
    cold weather.)

Recall:
Located, identified, observed, and discovered the structure, function, life cycles, habitat, and
    environment of many insects.
Collected information from books and field trips.
Collected insects for the classroom, including an ant farm.
Joined "Ant Watcher's Society."
Interviewed resource people.
Viewed photographs and filmstrips.
Read many stories and poems about insects.
Sang songs about insects.

Application:
Collected insects.
Recorded what was discovered.
Made dioramas, paintings, and drawings.
Reported on research findings.
Constructed a schoolwide bulletin board to share information.
Taught and demonstrated at a schoolwide science fair as experts on ants.

Analysis:
Compared insects from many aspects.
Contrasted how insects and humans adapt to seasonal changes.
Graphed a variety of ways insects adapt to cold weather.

Synectics:
Thought of as many ways as possible to compare an ant with a truck.

Synthesis:
Combined information in order to create and design an insect (including habitat and environ-
    ment) that might be found on another planet in the future.
Hypothesized and predicted how this insect will adapt to its environment.
Discussed characteristics of this insect.
Created stories and poems about "Insects that Bug You." (We won a *New York Times* award for
    this publication.)
Combined two insects into one.

Evaluation:
Discussed and evaluated all original work done by the children with the children.
Held a panel discussion about whether the insects created had a chance to survive in their
    environment. Children had to substantiate their reasons.

Source: Beatrice Chertoff, Teacher of the gifted, Public School 221, District 26, Queens, NY. Reprinted by
permission.

Unresolved Issues

1. Can we devise and implement academic and counseling programs specifically designed to increase the self-image of gifted underachieving children? We appear to know how to do this, but few such systematic programs are in place.
2. How can we identify culturally diverse gifted youngsters early and initiate programs that encourage them to maintain their pride in their particular heritage, as well as in the language and patterns of the past, while allowing them to master the knowledge and skills of the dominant culture?
3. How can those educators working with gifted children who have disabilities be sensitized to the needs of gifted students in these special groups? Can this be done through preservice training, summer training programs, in-service training, or outside consultation?
4. Despite the fact that the majority of 4-year-olds are in some group situation for a part of the day, we have been unable to access these daycare or early childhood settings in order to provide a more stimulating environment for the young gifted children enrolled there.
5. How can we help families and society perceive the true potential of gifted girls?

Chapter Review

1. Gifted underachievers are those students with measured high aptitude but mediocre or poor school performance.
2. The current school emphasis on high academic *performance* as one indicator of giftedness, instead of *potential,* has reduced interest and special attention to the underachiever.
3. A consistent pattern of personality characteristics of male gifted underachievers reveals a lack of self-confidence, inability to persevere, uncertain goals, and inferiority feelings.
4. Several different forms of educational interventions are used to combat underachievement: acceleration, counseling, and a variety of school adaptations. In any of these strategies, intense and persistent efforts by professional staff appear necessary to produce meaningful changes in the students.
5. Classroom teachers need to understand that the behavior problems of underachieving gifted youngsters, including both the fear of failure and the fear of success, have their origins outside the school classroom, and that they, as teachers, are not the basic cause of these personal problems.
6. Gifted females may require special attention to help them overcome low cultural expectations.
7. Culturally diverse gifted students often must resist cultural norms in order to make full use of their abilities. This can result in feelings of alienation and conflict, which must be resolved.
8. Educational environments and tasks must be developed for students with special talents from culturally diverse environments in order to observe which students

respond best to that special stimulation.

9. The curriculum for culturally diverse gifted students is heavily influenced by two philosophies: *assimilation* (preparing the student to compete in mainstream culture) and *pluralist* (modifying the culture to fit the needs of diverse groups).

10. Recent interest in the subgroup of gifted children with disabilities has revealed that a variety of disabilities can often mask substantial untapped talent.

11. Professional teams, utilizing differing sets of skills, may be needed to encourage the early identification and the diagnostic-prescriptive approach to stimulating gifted children with disabilities.

12. Little attention has been paid to gifted youngsters in the preschool-age range, despite substantial parental eagerness for concrete help from the schools.

13. Preschool gifted students are developmentally advanced in areas such as reading. They perform many functions of the average 7- or 8-year-old, even prior to their entrance into school. A few exemplary programs exist, and those focus on the stimulation of productive thinking and imagination so that these youngsters maintain their excitement and enthusiasm for learning.

Readings of Special Interest

Delisle, J. (1992). *Guiding the social and emotional development of gifted youth.* New York: Longman.
This is a detailed review of information related to the emotional development of gifted children and youth and a discussion of the special problems of adaptation that such youth have in community and school. It is particularly helpful to counteract the many myths still abroad on the nature and personality of gifted youth. Many practical suggestions are made for educators.

Fox, L., Brody, L., & Tobin, D. (Eds.). (1983). *Learning disabled/Gifted children: Identification and programming.* Baltimore, MD: University Park Press.
This state-of-the-art volume is on a relatively new issue—the child who shows evidence of both giftedness and special learning problems. Much attention is given on how to find such youngsters in the first place. However, some discussions are provided on model or pilot programs for special services for the students. Much emphasis is placed on individual-diagnoses and clinical-treatment efforts.

Karnes, M. (Ed.). (1983). *The underserved: Our young gifted children.* Reston, VA: Council for Exceptional Children.
This much-needed volume assembles a variety of specialists to discuss the special issues of the preschool gifted child. In addition to the more standard issues of identification and affective development, there are detailed descriptions of how to differentiate the curriculum for the preschool gifted, the role the family can play in helping the child develop, and the link between creativity and play.

Kerr, B. (1991). *A handbook for counseling the gifted and talented.* Alexandria, VA: American Association for Counseling and Development.
This comprehensive volume addresses all elements of counseling for the gifted child, including career education, adapting to the social adjustment problems that follow from giftedness in this culture, special counseling needs of gifted underachievers, and so on. It provides general and practical guidelines.

Silverman, L. (Ed.). (1993). *Counseling the gifted and talented.* Denver: Love Publishing.
This book is a compilation of chapters written by various experts in the field of counseling of gifted children. The book includes discussions of individual counseling, family counseling, group counseling, and the role of counseling in the schools. Many of the chapters feature the theory

of Dabrowski on overexcitability (oversensitivity to stimulation) of gifted students as a way of understanding the special personal problems of gifted students and of directing the type of counseling approach that should be taken.

Supple, P. (1990). *Reaching the gifted underachiever.* New York: Teachers College Press.
This volume gives, in considerable detail, the work of a major program of intervention for

gifted underachievers. Stressing student participation in planning for programs, it provides a separate setting for the gifted underachiever who receives special attention from teachers who develop individual plans and provide considerable positive reinforcement and encouragement. The emphasis is on dealing with the affective side of the problem first, and then providing academic remediation.

References

Baymur, F., & Patterson, C. (1960). Three methods of assisting underachieving high school students. *Journal of Counseling Psychology, 1,* 83–90.

Bachtold, L. (1969). Personality differences among high ability underachievers. *Journal of Educational Research, 63,* 16–18.

Baldwin, A. (1987). Undiscovered diamonds. *Journal for the Education of the Gifted, 10* (4), 271–286.

Baum S., & Owen, S. (1988). High ability/Learning disabled students: How are they different? *Gifted Child Quarterly, 32* (3), 321–326.

Belenky, M. F., Clinchy, B. M., Goldberger, N. R., & Tarule, J. M. (1986). *Women's ways of knowing: The development of self, voice and mind.* New York: Basic Books.

Bernal, E. (1979). The education of the culturally different gifted. In A. Passow (Ed.), *The gifted and the talented: Their education and development. 78th Yearbook of the National Society for the Study of Education, Pt. 1.* Chicago: University of Chicago Press.

Blacher-Dixon, J., & Turnbull, A. (1978). A preschool program for gifted-handicapped children. *Journal for the Education of the Gifted, 1* (2), 15–22.

Bloom, B., Engelhart, M., Furst, E., Hill, W., & Krathwohl, D. (1956). *Taxonomy of educational objectives, Handbook 1: Cognitive domain.* New York: McKay.

Butler-Por, N. (1987). *Underachievers in school: Issues and intervention.* New York: Wiley.

Callahan, C. M. (1979). The gifted and talented woman. In A. Passow (Ed.), *The gifted and talented.* Chicago: The National Society for the Study of Education.

Casserly, P. L. (1980). Factors affecting female participation in Advanced Placement programs in mathematics, chemistry and physics. In L. H. Fox, L. Brody, & D. Tobin (Eds.), *Women and the mathematical mystique.* Baltimore, MD: Johns Hopkins University Press.

Chertoff, B. (1979). *Insect unit based on Bloom's Taxonomy.* Unpublished manuscript, Public School 221, District 26, Queens, NY.

Colangelo, N. (1988). Discussant reaction: Bright girls in math and engineering. In J. I. Dreyden, S. A. Gallagher, G. E. Stanley, & R. N. Sawyer (Eds.), *Developing talent in mathematics, science and technology: Talent Identification Program/National Science Foundation Conference on Academic Talent.* National Science Foundation Grant #MDR-8751410.

Colangelo, N., & Lafrenz, N. (1981). Counseling the culturally diverse gifted. *Gifted Child Quarterly, 25* (1), 27–30.

Coleman, M., & Gallagher, J. (1992). *Middle school survey report: Impact on gifted students.* Chapel Hill, NC: Gifted Education Policy Studies Program, University of North Carolina at Chapel Hill.

Coleman, M. (1992). A comparison of how gifted/LD and average/LD boys cope with school frustration. *Journal for the Education of the Gifted, 17* (4).

Cooley, D., Chauvin, J. C., & Karnes, F. A. (1984). Gifted females: A comparison of attitudes by male and female teachers. *Roeper Review, 6* (3), 164–167.

Crombie, G., Bouffard-Bouchard, T., & Schneider, B. H. (1992). Gifted programs: Gender differences in referral and enrollment. *Gifted Child Quarterly, 36* (4), 213–214.

Delisle, J. (1990). The gifted adolescent at-risk: Strategies and resources for suicide prevention among gifted youth. *Journal for the Education of the Gifted, 13* (4), 212-228.

Delp, J. (1980). How to live successfully with the gifted. In S. Kaplan (Ed.), *Educating the pre-school primary gifted and talented* (pp. 167–182). Los Angeles: National/State Leadership Training Institute on the Gifted and Talented.

Dowdall, C., & Colangelo, N. (1982). Underachieving gifted students: Review and implications. *Gifted Child Quarterly, 26* (4), 179–184.

Eccles, J. (1985). Why doesn't Jane run? Sex differences in educational and occupational patterns. In F. Horowitz & M. O'Brien (Eds.), *The gifted and talented: Developmental perspectives* (pp. 253–295). Washington, DC: American Psychological Association.

Ernest, J. (1978). Mathematics and sex. *The American Mathematical Monthly, 83,* 595–614.

Feinberg, S. (1974). Creative problem solving and the music listening experience. *Music Educators Journal, 61,* 53–60.

Fine, M., & Pitts, R. (1980). Intervention with underachieving gifted children: Rationale and strategies. *Gifted Child Quarterly, 24* (1), 51–55.

Fox, L., Brody, L., & Tobin, D. (Eds.). (1983). *Learning-disabled/Gifted children: Identification and programming.* Baltimore, MD: University Park Press.

Fox, L. H., & Zimmerman, W. Z. (1985). Gifted women. In J. Freeman (Ed.), *The psychology of gifted children.* New York: Wiley.

Frasier, M. (1979). Counseling the culturally diverse gifted. In N. Colangelo & R. Zaffrann (Eds.), *New voices in counseling the gifted* (pp. 304–311). Dubuque, IA: Kendall/Hunt.

Frasier, M. (1987). The identification of gifted black students: Developing a new perspective. *Journal for the Education of the Gifted, 10* (3), 155–180.

Frasier, M. (1991). Response to Kitano: The sharing of giftedness between culturally diverse and non-diverse gifted students. *Journal for the Education of the Gifted, 15* (1), 20–30.

Gallagher, J. (1988). National agenda for educating gifted students: Statement of priorities. *Exceptional Children, 55* (2), 107–114.

Garrison, C., & Rhodes, C. (1987). *Mary Baldwin College's program for educating the gifted.* Paper presented at the International Symposium on Girls, Women and Giftedness, Lethbridge, Alberta, Canada.

Garrison, V. S., Stronge, J. H., & Smith, C. R. (1986). Are gifted girls encouraged to achieve their occupational potential? *Roeper Review, 9,* 101–104.

Gilligan, C. (1982). *In a different voice: Psychological theory and women's development.* Cambridge, MA: Harvard University Press.

Gilligan, C. (1988). *Mapping the moral domain: A contribution of women's thinking to psychology.* Cambridge, MA: Harvard University Press.

Harding, P. B., & Berger, P. (1979). Future images: Career education for gifted students. In J. J. Gallagher (Ed.), *Gifted children: Reaching their potential* (pp. 134–145). New York: Trillium.

High, M., & Udall, A. (1983). Teacher ratings of students in relation to ethnicity of students and school ethnic balance. *Journal for the Education of the Gifted, 6* (3), 154–165.

Hilliard, A. (1989, January). Teachers and cultural styles in a pluralistic society. *NEA Journal,* pp. 65–69.

Hollinger, C., & Fleming, E. (1988). Gifted and talented young women: Antecedents and correlates of life satisfaction. *Gifted Child Quarterly, 32,* 254–259.

Hollinger, C., & Fleming, E. (1992). A longitudinal examination of life choices of gifted and talented young women. *Gifted Child Quarterly, 36* (4), 207–212.

Jacklin, C. (1989). Female and male: Issues of gender. *American Psychologist, 44,* 127–133.

Janos, P., & Robinson, N. (1985). Psychosocial development in intellectually gifted children. In F. Horowitz & M. O'Brien (Eds.), *The gifted and talented: Development perspectives* (pp. 149–295). Washington, DC: American Psychological Association.

Kaplan, S. (1980). The role of play in a differentiated curriculum for the young gifted child. *Roeper Review, 3* (2), 12–13.

Karnes, M., & Bertschi, J. (1978). Identifying and educating gifted/talented nonhandicapped and handicapped preschoolers. *Teaching Exceptional Children, 10,* 114–119.

Karnes, M., & Johnson, L. (1989, March). Training for staff, parents, and volunteers working with gifted young children, especially those with disabilities and from low income homes. *Young Children,* pp. 49–56.

Karnes, M., & Johnson, L. (1991). Differentiating instruction for preschool gifted children. In R. Milgram (Ed.), *Counseling gifted and talented children. A guide for teachers, counselors, and parents.* Norwood, NJ: Ablex.

Karnes, M., Schwedel, A., & Linnemeyer, S. (1982). The young gifted/talented child: Programs at the University of Illinois. *Elementary School Journal, 82* (3), 195–213.

Kerr, B. (1985). *Smart girls, gifted women.* Columbus, OH: Ohio Psychological Association.

Kerr, B. (1988). Career counseling for gifted girls and women. *Journal of Career Development, 14,* 259–268.

Kerr, B. (1991). Educating gifted girls. In N. Colangelo & G. Davis (Eds.), *Handbook of gifted education.* Boston: Allyn and Bacon.

Kitano, M. (1992). A multicultural educational perspective on serving the culturally diverse gifted. *Journal for the Education of the Gifted, 15* (1), 4–19.

Leonard, J. (Ed.). (1977). *Chapel Hill services to the gifted handicapped: A project summary.* Chapel Hill, NC: Chapel Hill Training Outreach Project.

Lynch, S., & Mills, C. (1990). The skills reinforcement project (SRP): An academic program for high potential minority youth. *Journal for the Education of the Gifted, 13* (4), 364–379.

Maker, C. (1983). Quality education for gifted minority students. *Journal for the Education of the Gifted, 6,* 140–153.

Maker, C. (1986). *Critical issues in gifted education: Defensible programs for the gifted.* Austin, TX: Pro-Ed.

Maker, C., & Schiever, S. (Eds.). (1989). *Critical issues in gifted education:. Defensible Programs for cultural and ethnic minorities* (Vol. 2). Austin, TX: Pro-Ed.

Maker, J. (1977). *Providing programs for the gifted handiapped.* Reston, VA: Council for Exceptional Children.

Meeker, M. (1969). *The structure of intellect: Its interpretation and uses.* Columbus, OH: Merrill.

Mercer, J. (1979). *System of multicultural pluralistic assessment technical manual.* New York: Psychological Corporation.

Mercer, J., & Lewis, J. (1981). Using the system of multicultural pluralistic assessment to identify the gifted minority child. In I. Sato (Ed.), *Balancing the scale for the disadvantaged gifted* (pp. 59–66). Los Angeles: National/State Leadership Training Institute on the Gifted and Talented.

Oakes, J. (1992). Can tracking research reform practice? Technical, normative, and political considerations. *Educational Researcher, 21* (4), 12–21.

Ortiz, V., & Volloff, W. (1987). Identification of gifted and accelerated Hispanic students. *Journal for the Education of the Gifted, 11* (1), 45–55.

Reis, S., & Callahan, C. (1989). Gifted females: They've come a long way—Or have they? *Journal for the Education of the Gifted, 12* (2), 99–117.

Renzulli, J. (1979). *What makes giftedness?* Los Angeles: National/State Leadership Training Institute on the Gifted and Talented.

Renzulli, J. S., Smith, L. H., White, A. J., Callahan, C. M., & Hartman, R. K. (1976). *Scales for rating the behavioral characteristics of superior students.* Wethersfield, CT: Creative Learning Press.

Rimm, S. (1991). Underachievement and super-achievement: Flip sides of the same psychological coin. In N. Colangelo & G. Davis (Eds.), *Handbook of gifted education* (pp. 328–344). Boston: Allyn and Bacon.

Rimm, S., & Lowe, B. (1988). Family environments of underachieving gifted students. *Gifted Child Quarterly 32,* 353–361.

Roedell, W. (1985). Developing social competence in gifted preschool children. *Remedial and Special Education, 6* (4), 6–11.

Roedell, W., & Robinson, H. (1977). *Programming for intellectually advanced preschool children.* ERIC Document Reproduction Service No. ED 151 094.

Sadker, D., & Sadker, M. (1984). *Final report—Promoting effectiveness in classroom instruction.* Washington, DC: National Institute of Education, #400-80-0033.

Shade B. (1978). Sociopsychological characteristics of achieving black children. In R. Clasen & B. Robinson (Eds.), *Simple gifts* (pp. 229–242). Madison: University of Wisconsin Extension.

Shore, B., Cornell, D., Robinson, A., & Ward, V. (1991). *Recommended practices in gifted education.* New York: Teachers College, Columbia University.

Silverman, L. (1986). What happens in the gifted girl? In C. Maker (Ed.), *Critical issues in gifted education: Defensible programs for the gifted.* (pp. 43–89). Rockville, MD: Aspen.

Silverman, L. (1990). Family counseling. In N. Colangelo & G. Davis (Eds.), *Handbook of gifted education* (pp. 307–320). Boston: Allyn and Bacon.

Sisk, D. (1989). Identifying and nurturing talent among the American Indians. In C. J. Maker & S. Schiever (Eds.), *Critical issues in gifted education: Defensible programs for cultural and ethnic minorities* (Vol. 2, pp. 128–132). Austin, TX: Pro-Ed.

Sparling, S. (1989). Gifted black students: Curriculum and teaching strategies. In C. J. Maker & S. Schiever (Eds.), *Critical issues in gifted education: Defensible programs for cultural and ethnic minorities* (Vol. 2, pp. 259–269). Austin, TX: Pro-Ed.

Suter, D., & Wolf, A. (1987). Issues in the identification and programming of gifted/learning disabled gifted. *Journal for the Education of the Gifted, 10* (3), 227–237.

Terman, L., & Oden, M. (1947). The gifted child grows up. *Genetic studies of genius.* (Vol. 4). Stanford, CA: Stanford University Press.

Udall, A. (1989). Curriculum for gifted Hispanic students. In C. J. Maker & S. Schiever (Eds.), *Critical issues in gifted education: Defensible programs for cultural and ethnic minorities* (Vol. 2, pp. 41–56). Austin, TX: Pro-Ed.

Van Tassel-Baska, J. (1989). The role of the family in the success of disadvantaged gifted learners. *Journal for the Education of the Gifted, 13* (1), 22-36.

Walker, B. A., Reis, S. M., & Leonard, J. S. (1992). A developmental investigation of the lives of gifted women. *Gifted Child Quarterly, 36* (4), 201–206.

Whitmore, J. (1980). *Giftedness, conflict, and underachievement.* Boston: Allyn and Bacon.

Whitmore, J. (1981a). The etiology of underachievement in highly gifted young children. *Journal for the Education of the Gifted, 3* (1), 38–51.

Whitmore, J. (1981b). Gifted children with handicapping conditions: A new frontier. *Exceptional Children, 48* (2), 106–114.

Whitmore, J. (1986). *Intellectual giftedness in young children: Recognition and development.* New York: Haworth.

Whitmore, J., & Maker, C. (1985). *Intellectual giftedness in disabled persons.* Rockville, MD: Aspen.

Wolf, M. (1981). Talent search and development in the visual and performing arts. In I. Sato (Ed.), *Balancing the scale for the disadvantaged gifted* (pp. 103–116). Los Angeles: National/State Leadership Training Institute on the Gifted and Talented.

Wright, L., & Borland, J. (1991). *A special friend: Adolescent mentors for young economically disadvantaged, potentially gifted students.* New York: Teachers College, Columbia University.

Zappia, I. (1989). Identification of gifted Hispanic students. In C. J. Maker & S. Schiever (Eds.), *Critical issues in gifted education: Defensible programs for cultural and ethnic minorities* (Vol. 2, pp. 19–26). Austin, TX: Pro-Ed.

1992 Listing of State Directors for Gifted and Talented Education

Alabama
Ms. Linda Evans
Education Specialist
Gifted and Talented
33466 Gordon Persons Bldg.
50 N. Ripley Street
Montgomery, AL 36130-3901

Alaska
Mr. Richard Smiley
Program Manager
Gifted and Talented ED
Department of Special Services
Post Office Box F
Juneau, AK 99811-9981

American Samoa
Mr. Lui Tuitele, Consultant
Gifted and Talented Education
American Samoa
Department of Education
Pago Pago, AS 96799

Arizona
Dr. Nancy Stahl
Gifted Dept. Program Specialist
Arizona Department of Education
1535 West Jefferson
Phoenix, AZ 85007

Arkansas
Ms. Martha Bass, Administrator
Programs for Gifted/Talented
4 Capitol Mall
Education Bldg., Rm. 105C
Little Rock, AR 72201

California
Dr. Cathy Barkett
Gifted/Talented Education
California Department of Education
560 J Street, Suite 570
Sacramento, CA 95814

Information from the Council of State Directors of Programs for the Gifted.

Colorado
Mr. Frank Rainey, Consultant
Gifted/Talented Education
Colorado Dept. of Education
201 East Colfax
Denver, CO 80203

Connecticut
Mr. Alan White
Gifted and Talented Program
Connecticut Dept. of Education
25 Industrial Park Road
Middletown, CT 06457

Delaware
Dr. Peggy Dee, State Supervisor
Gifted/Talented Programs
Delaware Dept. of Instruction
P. O. Box 1402, Townsend Bldg.
Dover, DE 19903

District of Columbia
Ms. Thirzia Neal
Gifted/Talented Educ. Program
Nalle Administrative Unit
50th & C Streets, SE
Washington, DC 20019

Florida
Dr. Mary F. Toll
Gifted Program Specialist
Bureau of Exceptional Children
Florida Dept. of Education
654 Florida Education Centre
Tallahassee, FL 32399-0400

Georgia
Mr. Christopher E. Nelson
Coordinator, Gifted Education
Division of General Instruction
1954 Twin Towers East
Atlanta, GA 30334-5040

Guam
Ms. Cheri Stock
Gifted and Talented Education
Guam Dept. of Education
Post Office Box DE
Agana, GU 96910

Hawaii
Ms. Betty Moneymaker
G/T Education Specialist
Office of Instructional Services
189 Lunalilo Home Road
Honolulu, HI 96825

Idaho
Mr. M. Jewel Hoopes
Idaho Dept. of Education
Len B. Jordan Office Bldg.
650 West State
Boise, ID 83720

Illinois
Ms. Susie Morrison
Education Consultant
Curriculum Improvement Sec. N-242
Illinois Board of Education
100 North First Street
Springfield, IL 62777

Indiana
Ms. Patricia B. Stafford
G/T Program Manager
Indiana Department of Education
229 State House
Indianapolis, IN 46204

Iowa
Mr. Leland Wolf
Gifted Education Consultant
Iowa Department of Education
Grimes State Office Building
Des Moines, IA 50319-0146

Kansas
Ms. Joan R. Miller
G/T Education Program Specialist
Kansas Dept. of Education
120 East 10th Street
Topeka, KS 66612

Kentucky
Mr. Charles E. Whaley
G/T Education Consultant
Kentucky Dept. of Education
500 Melo Street
1831 Capital Plaza Tower
Frankfort, KY 40601

Louisiana
Ms. Patricia Dial
State Supervisor
Gifted/Talented Programs
Louisiana Department of Education
Post Office Box 94064
Baton Rouge, LA 70804-9064

Maine
Ms. Valerie T. Seaberg
State Supervisor
Gifted/Talented Education
Maine Department of Education
    and Cultural Services
State House Station #23
Augusta, ME 04333

Maryland
Dr. Toni Favazza
Student Achievement Program Enrichment
    Branch
Maryland Department of Education
200 W. Baltimore St., Fifth Floor
Baltimore, MD 21201-2595

Massachusetts
Ms. Barbara Libby, Consultant
Gifted/Talented Programs

Bureau of Curriculum Service
Massachusetts Dept. of Education
1385 Hancock Street
Quincy, MA 02169

Michigan
Ms. Mary Bailey Hergesh
Gifted/Talented Coordinator
Michigan Department of Education
Post Office Box 30008
Lansing, MI 48909

Minnesota
Ms. Beth Aune
Gifted Consultant
Minnesota Dept. of Education
651-C Capitol Square Building
550 Cedar Street
St. Paul, MN 55101

Mississippi
Dr. Conrad Castle
Gifted/Talented Consultant
Mississippi Dept. of Education
Post Office Box 771
Jackson, MS 39205-0771

Missouri
Mr. David Welch
Gifted Education Director
Missouri Dept. of Elementary
    and Secondary Education
P. O. Box 480, 100 East Capitol
Jefferson, MO 65102

Montana
Mr. Michael Hall
Gifted/Talented Program Specialist
Office of G/T Education
State Capitol
Helena, MT 59620

Nebraska
Dr. Sheila Brown
G/T Program Supervisor
Nebraska Dept. of Education
300 Centennial Mall South
P. O. Box 94987
Lincoln, NE 68509

Nevada
Dr. Anne Keast
G/T Program Consultant
Special Education Branch
Nevada Department of Education
400 West King St., Capitol Complex
Carson City, NV 89710

New Hampshire
Ms. Rachel Hopkins
Gifted Education Administrator
New Hampshire Dept. of Education
101 Pleasant Street
Concord, NH 03301

New Jersey
Ms. Julia Stapleton
Bureau of Curriculum
    & Technology
Division of General Academic Education
New Jersey Dept. of Education
225 West State Street, CN 500
Trenton, NJ 08625-0500

New Mexico
Ms. Roberta Knox
G/T Special Education Director
Education Building
Santa Fe, NM 87501-2786

New York
Mr. David Irvine
Gifted Education Coordinator
New York Dept. of Education
Room 212 EB
Albany, NY 12234

North Carolina
Ms. Sylvia Lewis
Gifted Education Consultant
Division for Exceptional Children
NC Dept. of Public Instruction
116 W. Edenton Street
Education Building
Raleigh, NC 27605-1712

North Dakota
Ms. Ann Clapper
Gifted/Talented Education
North Dakota Department
    of Public Instruction
600 E. Blvd. Avenue
State Capitol Bldg., 10th Fl.
Bismarck, ND 58505-0440

Ohio
Ms. Nancy B. Hamant
Gifted Education Consultant
Ohio Div. of Special Education
933 High Street
Worthington, OH 43085

Oklahoma
Ms. Cindy Brown, Coordinator
Gifted/Talented Section
Oklahoma Dept. of Education
2500 N. Lincoln Blvd.
Oklahoma City, OK 73105

Oregon
Mr. Robert J. Siewert
Gifted/Talented Specialist
700 Pringle Parkway, SE
Salem, OR 997310-0290

Pennsylvania
Ms. T. Noretta Bingaman
Gifted/Talented Director
Bureau of Special Education
Pennsylvania Dept. of Education
333 Market Street
Harrisburg, PA 17126-0333

Puerto Rico
Primitive Medina Cross
Gifted Education Consultant
Puerto Rico Dept. of Education
Office of External Resources
Post Office Box 75
Hato Rey, PR 99024

Rhode Island
Dr. John J. Wilkinson, Consultant
Gifted & Talented Programs
Rhode Island Dept. of Elementary
   and Secondary Education
22 Hayes Street
Providence, RI 02908

South Carolina
Ms. Mary E. Ginn
Education Associate
Office of Programs
   for Exceptional Children
Rutledge Building, Room 511-E
1429 Senate Street
Columbia, SC 29201

South Dakota
Ms. Shirlie Moysis
Gifted Education Director
Division of Education
South Dakota Dept. of Education
700 Governor's Drive
Richard F. Kneip Bldg.
Pierre, SD 57501-2291

Tennessee
Ms. Janice Cobb
Gifted/Talented Programs
   & Services Consultant
Tennessee Dept. of Education
132-A Cordell Hull Building
Nashville, TN 37219

Texas
Ms. Evelyn L Hiatt, Director
Council of State Directors
   of Programs for the Gifted
Texas Education Agency
1701 N. Congress Avenue
Austin, TX 78701

Trust Territory
Mr. Harou Kuartei
Federal Programs Coordinator
Office Of Special Education
Trust Territory Office of Education
Office of the High Commissioner
Saipan, CM 96950

Utah
Ms. Linda Adler
G/T Education Specialist
Utah Dept. of Education
250 E. 500 South
Salt Lake City, UT 84111

Vermont
Ms. Donna D. Brinkmeyer
Gifted Education Consultant
Vermont Dept. of Education
Montpelier, VT 05602

Virgin Islands
Ms. Mary Harley
G/T Education Coordinator
St. Thomas/St. John School District
#44-46 Kongens Glade
St. Thomas, VI 00802

Virginia
Dr. Jane Craig
Gifted Programs Supervisor
Virginia Dept. of Education
Post Office Box 6Q
Richmond, VA 23216-2060

Washington
Ms. Gayle Pauley
Programs for the Gifted
Superintendent Of Public Instruction
Old Capitol Building
Post Office Box 47200
Olympia, WA 98504-7200

West Virginia
Dr. Virginia Simmons
Gifted Programs Coordinator
Office of Special Education
West Virginia Dept. of Education
Capitol Building #6, Rm. B-304
Charleston, WV 25305

Wisconsin
Ms. Welda Swed, Consultant
WI Dept. of Public Instruction
Post Office Box 7841
125 South Webster
Madison, WI 53707

Wyoming
Ms. Nancy Leinius
Language Arts
  & G/T Coordinator
Wyoming Dept. of Education
Hathaway Building
Cheyenne, WY 82002

Major Professional Associations and Advocacy Groups for Gifted Children

American Association for Gifted Children
(Talent Identification Program)
David Goldstein, Executive Director
Duke University
1121 W. Main Street, Suite 100
Durham, NC 27701
(919) 683-1400

> An advocacy organization that supports parents, children, and programs for the gifted. Promotes gifted awareness and supportive systems.

The Association for the Gifted (TAG)
Council for Exceptional Children
1920 Association Drive
Reston, VA 22091
(800) 336-3278

> A division of the Council for Exceptional Children, whose professional membership encourages program development and professional training in the education of the gifted. Plays a strong advocate role in legislation for the gifted.

Mensa, Gifted Children's Program
c/o Roxanne H. Cramer
5304 1st Place, N.
Arlington, VA 22203
(703) 527-4293

> Provides networking sources and advocacy allies. Membership is contingent on superior performance on an adult measure of intelligence, plus an interest in gifted children and adults.

National Association for Creative Children and Adults
8080 Springvalley Drive
Cincinnati, OH 45236
(513) 631-1777

> Dedicated to nurturing and appreciating creativity. Promotes projects, programs, and publications for fostering the same.

National Association for Gifted Children
Peter Rosenstein, Executive Director
1155 15th Street, N.W.
Suite 1002
Washington, DC 20005
(202) 785-4268

> Encourages membership of both parents and professionals. Affiliated chapters promote programs for gifted and talented children throughout the country. Provides important materials, guidance, and networking resources.

National Association of State Boards of Education
526 Hall of the States
444 North Capital Street, N.W.
Washington, DC 20001
(202) 624-5845

> Encourages studies and publications dealing with supervision, administration, and policymakers' guides to programs for gifted students.

The World Council for Gifted and Talented Children, Inc.

Promotes research for and about giftedness and creativity around the world. Provides an exchange of ideas and experiences from those interested in the gifted and talented, and gives worldwide recognition to advocacy for gifted and talented children through its publications and conferences.

Journals for Gifted Children

Advanced Development
Institute for the Study of Advanced Development
777 Pearl Street
Denver, CO 80302

> Each issue has a different theme and contains articles on a specific theorist, therapeutic applications, giftedness in women, and poetry. Published annually.

Challenge
Good Apple Publishers
Box 299
Carthage, IL 62321

> Contains reproducible activities, articles by leaders in gifted education, a calendar of events, and helpful ideas for parents. For preschool through eighth grade.

Creative Child and Adult Quarterly
8080 Springvalley Drive
Cincinnati, OH 45236
(513) 631-1777

> Emphasizes articles that focus on creative thought and creative children. Includes both theoretical work and practical applications of the construct of creativity for persons of all ages.

G/C/T
P. O. Box 637
100 Pine Avenue
Holmes, PA 19043-9937

Directed at parents, encouraging parental interaction and support for gifted and talented children. Articles often written by professionals but are directed at parents.

Gifted Child Quarterly
1155 15th Street, N.W., Suite 1002
Washington, DC 20005
(202) 785-9268

Provides a mix of research, program evaluations, and program descriptions for gifted and talented children. Journal of the National Association for Gifted Children.

Gifted Education International
c/o A. B. Academic Publishers
Post Office Box 42
Bicester, Oxon OX6 7NW
England

Features articles on gifted education from around the world. Descriptions of programs from other countries particularly emphasized. Few research papers.

Gifted Education Review
P.O. Box 2278
Evergreen, CO 80439-2278

Abstracts the latest articles from leading journals and magazines in gifted education. Published quarterly and provides an overview of the most recent information published.

Gifted International
College of Education
Lamar University
Beaumont, TX 77710
(409) 880-8046

Reports on worldwide issues related to the gifted and the talented, with an emphasis on program descriptions. Publication vehicle for the World Council for Gifted and Talented Children, Inc.

Journal of Creative Behavior
Creative Educational Foundation, Inc.
1050 Union Road
Buffalo, NY 14224

Devoted to research reports and program suggestions; designed to understand and enhance creative behavioral in children and adults, and is of substantial interest to those interested in gifted and talented children.

Journal for the Education of the Gifted
University of North Carolina Press
P. O. Box 2288
Chapel Hill, NC 27515-2288

> Reports on research, teacher training, and program suggestions for gifted and talented children. Publication vehicle for TAG (The Association for the Gifted).

Mensa Research Journal
19340 Dunbridge Way
Gaithersburg, MD 20879

> Produces a wide range of articles focusing primarily on the nature of the highly gifted child and adult and their interactions with society and societal institutions like the schools.

Roeper Review
Roeper City and County Schools
Post Office Box 329
Bloomfield Hills, MI 48303-0329
(313) 642-1500

> Focuses on practical suggestions for the gifted and talented. Occasionally has thematic issues in which all articles focus on a single topic such as counseling the gifted or social studies for the gifted.

Understanding Our Gifted
Open Space Communications, Inc.
P. O. Box 18268
Boulder, CO 80308-8268

> Short, scholarly articles on parenting, instructional strategies, the highly gifted and personalitites, creativity, current developments, reviews of children's books, and hidden gifted learners.

National Consortium for Secondary Schools Specializing in Mathematics, Science, and Technology

Academy for the Advancement of Science and Technology (1990)
200 Hackensack Avenue
Hackensack, NJ 07601

Academy of Science and Technology (1987)
27330 Oak Ridge School Road
Conroe, TX 77385

Alabama School of Mathematics and Science Program (1990)
700 North 18th Street
Birmingham, AL 35303

Alabama School of Mathematics
1255 Dauphin Street
Mobile, AL 36604

Baltimore Polytechnic Institute (1883)
1400 West Cold Spring Lane
Baltimore, MD 21209

Battle Creek Area Mathematics and Science Center (1990)
765 Upton Avenue
Battle Creek, MI 49015

Berrien County Mathematics & Science Center (1989)
711 St. Joseph Avenue
Berrien Springs, MI 49103

Blair Science, Mathematics, Computer Science Magnet (1985)
313 Wayne Avenue
Silver Spring, MD 20910

The Bronx High School of Science (1938)
75 West 205th St.
Bronx, NY 10468

Brooklyn Technical High School
Dekalb Avenue & S. Elliott Street
Brooklyn, NY 11217

Buffalo Academy of Science and Math (1987)
319 Suffolk Street
Buffalo, NY 14215

California Academy of Mathematics and Science (1990)
California State University
Dominguez Hills
Carson, CA 90747

Center for Advanced Technologies (1990)
Lakewood High School
1400 54th Avenue South
St. Petersburg, FL 33705

The Centers for Advanced Studies
The Eastern Center (1987)
415 Pecden Drive
Gibonville, NC 27249
and
The Southwest Center (1987)
4364 Barrow Road
High Point, NC 27265

Central Shennadoah Valley Regional Governor's School
Route 1
Box 252
Fisherville, VA 22939

Central Virginia Governor's School for Science & Technology (1985)
3020 Wards Ferry Road
Lynchburg, VA 24502

Eleanor Roosevelt High School Science & Technology Center (1976)
7601 Hanover Parkway
Greenbelt, MD 20770

High Technology High School (1991)
P. O. Box 119
Lincroft, NJ 07738

Illinois Mathematics and Science Academy (1985)
1500 W. Sullivan Rd.
Aurora, IL 60506-1039

The Indiana Academy for Science, Mathematics, & Humanities (1988)
Ball State University
Muncie, IN 47306

Kalamazoo Area Math & Science Center (1986)
600 West Vine Street, Suite 400
Kalamazoo, MI 49008

Lanier Academic Motivational Program (1984)
1756 S. Court Street
Montgomery, AL 36104

Louisiana School for Math, Science, and the Arts (1980)
715 College Avenue
Natchitoches, LA 71457

Macomb Mathematics Science Technology Center
275 Cosgrove
Warren, MI 48092

Manistee Intermediate School District
Chittenden Educational Center
1070 Nursery Road
Wellston, MI 49058

The Marine Academy of Science and Technology (1981)
Building 305
Sandy Hook, NJ 07732

The Mississippi School for Mathematics and Science (1987)
P.O. Box W-1627
Columbus, MS 39701

New Horizons Technical Center
The Governor's School for Science & Technology (1985)
520 Butler Farm Road
Hampton, VA 23666

The North Carolina School of Science and Mathematics (1980)
P.O. Box 2418
Durham, NC 27715

Oklahoma School of Science and Mathematics (1990)
1515 North Lincoln Boulevard
Oklahoma City, OK 73104

Roanoke Valley Governor's School for Science and Technology (1985)
2104 Grandin Road, SW
Roanoke, VA 24015

Science Academy of Austin @ L. B. Johnson High School (1985)
Austin Independent School District
7309 Lazy Creek
Austin, TX 78724

Science, Math, Technology Academy at Dudley (1991)
1200 Lincoln Street
Greensboro, NC 27401

Science, Mathematics, Computer Science Magnet (1985)
Montgomery County Public Schools
313 Wayne Avenue
Silver Spring, MD 20910

Science and Technology Center at Oxon Hill High School (1976)
6701 Leyte Drive
Oxon Hill, MD 20745

The South Carolina Governor's School for Science & Mathematics (1988)
306 East Home Avenue
Hartsville, SC 29550

Southwest Virginia Governor's School for Science, Mathematics, & Technology (1990)
Cougar Trail
P.O. Box 1739
Dublin, VA 24084

Stuyvesant High School (1904)
345 Chambers Street
New York, NY 10280

Texas Academy of Mathematics and Science (1987)
P.O. Box 5307
University of North Texas
Denton, TX 76203

Thomas Jefferson High School for Science & Technology (1985)
6560 Braddock Road
Alexandria, VA 22312

Javits Projects (Federal Programs for Gifted Education, 1992)

Dr. Dorothy Ann Sisk
Project Director
Project STEP-UP
Gifted Child Center
Lamar University
Post Office Box 10034
Beaumont, TX 77710
(409) 880-8046

Dr. W. R. Nash
Project Director
Identification of Creatively
   Gifted Children
Dept. of Educational Psychology
   Texas A & M University
College Station, TX 77843-4225
(409) 845-0559

Dr. James M. Patton
Project Director
Project Mandala
College of William & Mary
School of Education
522 Prince George Street

Williamsburg, VA 23187-8795
(804) 221-2362

Dr. Donna Rae Clasen
Project Director
Project STREAM
University of Wisconsin—Whitewater
6038 Winther Hall
Whitewater, WI 53190
 (414) 472-1960

Dr. Lillian Mein
Project Director
Jacob's Ladder
Yonkers Public Schools
Burroughs Jr. High School
Administrative Annex
150 Rockland Avenue, Rm. 4061
Yonkers, NY 10705
(914) 376-8213

Dr. Kay Haney
Project Director
Gifted & Talented/
   LD Training Project

University of North Carolina
Dept. of Teaching Specialities
Charlotte, NC 28223
(704) 547-2531

Dr. Sally L Flagler
Project Director
Project EXCEL
Wake County Public Schools
Post Office Box 28041
Raleigh, NC 27611
(919) 850-1925

Dr. Ann Clapper
Project Director
North Dakota Javits Project
Department of Public Instruction
600 E. Boulevard Ave., 10th Floor
Bismark, ND 58505-0440
(701) 224-2277

Dr. W. Thomas Southern
Project Director
Project SPRING
Bowling Green State University
451 Education Building
Bowling Green, OH 43403
(419) 372-7290

Dr. Beverly D. Shaklee
Project Director
Project EAEP
Kent State University
College of Education
404 White Hall
Kent, OH 44242
(216) 672-2580

Dr. Stuart A. Tonemah
Project Director
Project EIC
American Indian Research
   and Development, Inc.
2424 Springer Drive, Ste. 200
Norman, OK 73069
(405) 364-0656

Dr. Joyce VanTassel-Baska
Project Director
Science Curriculum K-8 for
   High Ability Learners
College of William & Mary
School of Education
Jones Hall, Room 304
Post Office Box 8795
Williamsburg, VA 23187-8795
(804) 221-2362

Dr. Robert Siewert
Project Director
Oregon Consortium Project
700 Pringle Parkway, SE
Salem, OR 97310
(503) 378-3598

Dr. Ellen Linky
Project Director
Jacob Javits Program
School District of Philadelphia
Administration Building, Rm. 705
21st Street South of the Parkway
Philadelphia, PA 19103-1099
(215) 299-2654

Dr. Evelyn L. Hiatt
Project Director
The Javits Project
Texas Education Agency
1701 North Congress
Austin, TX 78701-1494
(512) 463-9455

Dr. E. Susanne Richert
Project Director
Low Cost, High Quality Gifted
   Program: APOGEE
Educational Information &
   Resource Center, EIRC
606 Delsea Drive
Sewell, NJ 08080
(609) 582-7000

Dr. Elizabeth Nielsen
Project Director
Twice-Exceptional Child Project
Albuquerque Public Schools
Post Office Box 4395
Albuquerque, NM 87196
(505) 842-3741

Dr. Lila Edelkind
Project Director
Alternate Pathways
Community School District 22
2525 Haring Street
Brooklyn, NY 11235
(718) 368-8020

Dr. Joyce Rubin
Project Director
Javits 7+ G/T Program
Community School District 18
755 East 100th Street
Brooklyn, NY 11236
(718) 927-5246

Drs. Rena F. Subotnik
    and Anthony Miserandino
Project Directors
Discovery & Nurturance Project
Hunter College
695 Park Avenue
New York, NY 10021
(212) 772-4722

Dr. James H. Borland
Project Director
Project Synergy
Columbia University
Teachers College, Box 89
New York, NY 10027
(212) 678-4074

Dr. Barry Oreck
Project Director
Talent Beyond Words
Arts Connection

505 8th Avenue
New York, NY 10018
(212) 564-5099

Dr. Helen Stein
Project Director
Project STRENGTHS
Community School District 27
82-01 Rockaway Boulevard
Ozone Park, NY 11416
(718) 642-5724

Dr. Phyllis W. Aldrich
Project Director
Language Arts Curriculum (K-8)
    for High Ability Learners
Saratoga-Warren BOCES
Henning Road
Saratoga Springs, NY 12866
(518) 584-3239, Ext. 220

Dr. Sue Maxwell
Project Director
Javits Project
Chicago Public Schools
Division of Gifted & Talented
6 Center SW, 1819 W. Pershing Rd.
Chicago, IL 60609
(312) 535-8325

Dr. Marcia Dvorak
Project Director
High Success for the High Risk
Quincy School District, #172
1444 Main Street
Quincy, IL 62301
(217) 223-8700

Dr. Sharon Freden
Project Director
Comprehensive System of
    Program Development
120 Southeast 10th Avenue
Topeka, KS 66612-1182
(913) 296-3137

Dr. Julia L. Roberts
Project Director
Enhancing Educational Opportunities
Center for Gifted Studies
Western Kentucky University
Bowling Green, KY 42101
(502) 745-6323

Dr. Waveline T. Starnes
Project Director
Early Childhood Gifted
    Model Program
Montgomery Knolls Elementary
807 Daleview Drive
Silver Spring, MD 20901
(301) 279-3163

Dr. Joan Becker
Project Director
Urban Scholars Program
University of Massachusetts
100 Morrissey Blvd., M-3-008/009
Boston, MA 02125-3393
(617) 287-5830

Dr. Gary Compton
Project Director
New Horizons Intervention Project
Kalamazoo Public Schools
1220 Howard Street
Kalamazoo, MI 49008
(616) 384-0148

Dr. Patricia D. Hoelscher
Project Director
Future Problem Solving Program
Washington University
Campus Box 1183
One Brookings Drive
St. Louis, MO 63130
(314) 935-4864

Dr. Michael Hall
Project Director
Project EDGE

Montana Association of Gifted
    & Talented Education
Office of Public Instruction
State Capitol
Helena, MT 59620
(406) 444-4422

Dr. Norma S. Griffin
Project Director
The Nebraska Project
University of Nebraska—Lincoln
Teachers College
250 Barkley Center
Lincoln, NE 68583-0733
(402) 472-8449

Dr. Stephen D. Lapan
Project Director
Jacob Javits Getting Gifted Project
Center for Excellence in Education
Northern Arizona University, Box 5774
Flagstaff, AZ 86011-5774
602 523-7131

Dr. Ann Robinson
Project Director
Project Promise
University of Arkansas
2801 South University
Little Rock, AR 72204
(501) 564-3012

Drs. Kogee Thomas and
    Sharon C. McKinney
Project Directors
Native American Intertribal University
    Preparatory Summer Program
University of California
204 Administration Building
Irvine, CA 92717-5150
(714) 856-7818

Dr. Barbara Abbott
Project Director
Project Open GATE

Californian Dept. of Education
High School Education Office
Post Office Box 944272
Sacramento, CA 94244-2720
(916) 324-7240

Dr. Roberta M. Infelise
Project Director
Project VIA S.O.I.
Alisal Union School District
1205 East Market Street
Salinas, CA 93905

Dr. Dennis P. Saccuzzo
Project Director
Jacob Javits Gifted Project
San Diego State University Foundation
Joint Doctoral Program
  in Psychology
6363 Alvarado Court, # 103
San Diego, CA 92120-4913
(619) 594-2844

Dr. Joseph Renzulli
Project Director
NRC/GT Project
University of Connecticut
362 Fairfield Road, U-7
Storrs, CT 06269
(203) 486-4826

Dr. Thelma Mumford-Glover
Project Director
The Full Potential Program
Atlanta Public Schools
Instructional Services Center
2930 Forrest Hills Dr., SW
Atlanta, GA 30315
(404) 827-8185

Dr. Doris Ching
Project Director
Hawaii Summer Academy
Operation Manong
East-West Road 4, Rm. 2D
Honolulu, HI 96822
(808) 956-8442

Dr. Merle B. Karnes
Project Director
Project SPRING
University of Illinois
403 E. Healey Street
Champaign, IL 61820
(217) 333-4890